SOCIOLOGY

SOCIOLOGY

The Study of Society

Robert A. Stebbins
The University of Calgary

1817
HARPER & ROW, PUBLISHERS, New York
Cambridge, Philadelphia, San Francisco, Washington,
London, Mexico City, São Paulo, Singapore, Sydney

To Karin

PHOTO CREDITS

All photographs by Deborah Brown-Ridley and James G. Odell except as follows: pages 25 (*bottom*), 142, 167, 222, 292 (*top*), 319, 405, 407, 411, 430, 462, 463, 479 (*top*), 485, 486, and 490 courtesy of the Glenbow Museum, Calgary, Alberta; pages 130 and 188 courtesy of the *Calgary Herald;* pages 133 and 139 © Pacheco, EKM-Nepenthe; page 26 (*top*) Herwig, The Picture Cube; page 20 Maher, EKM-Nepenthe; page 26 (*bottom*) © Siteman, 1982, EKM-Nepenthe; page 457 courtesy of the Pharmacists Planning Service, Inc.

Sponsoring Editor: Alan McClare
Project Editor: David Nickol
Cover Design: Barbara Bert/ North 7 Atelier
Cover Illustration/Photo: John Fowler, Valan Photos
Text Art: RDL Artset Ltd.
Production Manager: Jeanie Berke
Production Assistant: Paula Roppolo
Compositor: ComCom Division of Haddon Craftsmen, Inc.
Printer and Binder: R. R. Donnelley & Sons Company

SOCIOLOGY: The Study of Society

Library of Congress Cataloging in Publication Data

Stebbins, Robert A., 1938–
Sociology: the study of society.

Includes bibliographies and index.
1. Sociology. I. Title.
HM51.S8967 1987 301 86–27012
ISBN 0–06–046493–3

86 87 88 89 9 8 7 6 5 4 3 2 1

CONTENTS

Part Four INSTITUTIONS

PREFACE

The purpose of this book is to introduce its readers to sociology by surveying the most prominent and best developed branches of the discipline. This is accomplished under the following plan: Part One gives the reader an overview of sociology, its nature, its theory, its history, and its research techniques. Part Two covers two basic processes found everywhere in social life: human interaction and socialization. These processes spawn several types of groups, which are discussed in Part Three. The two processes also give rise to certain cultural phenomena, the institutions considered in Part Four, the differentiation of people into roles considered in Part Five, and the dynamic social changes considered in Part Six. In other words, this book is organized along the lines of the general theory of society, which accounts for how societies are started, maintained, and changed. Society, as the subtitle of this book indicates, is the subject matter of sociology.

The use of comparisons is a good way to learn about sociology, or any other discipline for that matter. This book uses comparisons extensively, primarily between two countries: Canada and the United States. Where possible and desirable, all sociological concepts and theories presented in this book are illustrated with examples of research or everyday life from both countries. The comparative framework of this book, then, is North America, although it is North America as culturally defined, not as geographically defined (that is, it does not include Central America and Greenland).

Some readers (they are more likely to be Americans than Canadians) will ask: What is there to compare? Are not the two societies basically the same? Or the somewhat more perceptive among them might be inclined to assert that English Canada and the United States are basically the same. After all, a visit to the other country reveals many familiar sights: buildings, clothing, talk, gestures, shops, restaurants, city layout, motor vehicles, hair styles, and on and on. When my American friends and relatives visit me in Canada, they tend to forget they are in another country. They comment about the politics, sports, weather, and entertainment in "this country" as though they were at home. Perhaps some Canadians talk the same way when visiting in the United States.

This book demonstrates that those who believe that Canada and the United States are much the same socially are both right and wrong. Correctness on this issue depends on where one draws a comparison. For example, there is illegal drug use in both countries. But, while the proportion of users of marijuana is similar in Canada and the

United States, the proportion of users of cocaine and opiate drugs is significantly higher in the United States than in Canada. Consider ethnic pluralism, or the conscious promotion of ethnic identities. Canada is officially bilingual (French and English languages) and officially committed to a pluralistic existence for all its ethnic groups. Still, there is no evidence that pluralism is any less developed in the United States where there is no official policy of this sort.

Comparisons such as these form the context within which the readers of this book are introduced to sociology. Of course, I should point out that there are a number of places where comparisons are impossible. Sometimes a concept is considered at a level too abstract to make comparisons. Sometimes all available theories and facts indicate that the idea under consideration is a cross-cultural constant. People everywhere form selves and define, or give meaning to, situations, for example. What was especially frustrating while writing this book was the lack of data in some instances with which to make a comparison. For example, the two national governments do not always collect the same statistics about the same subjects in the same way. Nor do they collect those statistics in the same year.

Some instructors may find this book too long for the semester or quarter in which they teach their courses in introductory sociology. Others, whether or not they have time to cover all chapters, may prefer a different sequence of those chapters than what is given here. While the book was written and organized to impart a sense of continuity as the reader moves through the chapters, that sense is not seriously violated by arranging some of the chapters in a different sequence. In my view the first six chapters and Chapter 9 should not, however, be either omitted or rearranged. Much of the basic terminology is introduced in these chapters. Nonetheless, those who wish to underplay sociological methodology could omit Chapter 3 or place it elsewhere. From Chapter 7 onward instructors may "mix and match" and omit to their tastes. The Subject Index and the Glossary at the end of the book will help bridge any conceptual gaps that might emerge in the course of adapting this book to a particular style of teaching introductory sociology.

While I hold the ultimate responsibility for what is in this book, a small army of colleagues, editors, and secretaries were of inestimable help in making it possible. Colleagues at the University of Calgary and elsewhere contributed much by critically assessing the drafts of the various chapters. In this connection, I wish to thank professors Augustine Brannigan, R.S. Gandhi, Sheldon Goldenberg, Harry H. Hiller, Eugen Lupri, Marlene M. Mackie, Samuel Mitchell, J. Rick Ponting, Harvey Rich, Richard A. Wanner, and William L. Zwerman. The bulk of the burden of typing the manuscript fell to Gloria Hall, whose perseverance and understanding seemed to know no bounds. She is one of two unsung heroines of the project. The other is my wife, Karin, who typed most of the remainder of the manuscript and endured several years of playing second fiddle to "the book." My secretary, Myrtle Murray, was also unable to escape the typing of a few chapters. I am extremely grateful to Robert T. Hay for his editorial acumen, forbearance of sociological mysteries, high literary standards, and boundless patience. I shudder to think what this book would be like without his assistance.

The Department of Sociology at the University of Calgary gave generously of its word-processing, duplicating, and postage resources, all of which sped along the production and submission of the manuscript. Most of the photographic illustrations in this book were produced by Deborah Brown-Ridley and James G. Odell. Their ability to see sociological ideas through the camera has added another dimension of communication to this book. Last, but not least, I am indebted to Alan McClare, who has skillfully mediated, in a myriad of ways, the transformation of the manuscript into a book. Faith, wisdom, and insight were part of this alchemy.

Robert A. Stebbins

one

THE DISCIPLINE OF SOCIOLOGY

A study of sociology should appeal to you and to anyone else who is curious about the society in which we live. In your study of Part One, "The Discipline of Sociology," you will learn that sociology is the study of society. It starts with the study of *social action,* or of the events and activities which you experience in your daily life. Sociology is one of the social sciences. It is a science, and sociologists use the scientific method in their study of society—in making discoveries and in formulating theories, that is. Sociology is theoretical and methodical. It is a science and a craft, a means of understanding humankind in a world which never stands still. What does it all mean? This is the challenge on which you now are venturing.

chapter 1

The Study of Society

CHAPTER OUTLINE

INTRODUCTION

No one—neither you, a close friend, nor a stranger on the street—can avoid interactions with other people in his or her daily routine, whatever the routine might be. What is your routine? In what ways do you interact with others from day to day? How do you interact with fellow students and with your professors? What interactions come up when you drive a car or when you board a bus? Is there interaction when you wait for an elevator or stand in line at a supermarket? How do you interact with a stranger on the street?

Let us look at social life from another angle: that of large organizations, communities, and whole societies. In everyday life, we are often concerned with the power of, say, labor or business to do things that we oppose, but seem unable to stop. There are times when we feel overwhelmed with and frustrated by the vastness of government bureaucracy when forced to deal with it. And there are forces at work of which we have little awareness. For example, we shall see later that there are arrangements by which religion and government accommodate each other's interests, despite our belief in the separation of church and state. We also believe that Canada is a society in which there is equal opportunity for occupational advancement. Yet, on several pages of this book, there is evidence to the contrary.

Sociology is the study of society. As a study of society, it is by its very nature a concentrated effort to understand human interactions and human behavior in a social world. What is society? *Society* is a large group of people who interact with each other and who share the same territory and the same *culture,* or way of life. You live in a society. As a member of a society, you are not alone, for you share with others the environment in which you live. You share a common culture.

The people in a society—any society, be it your society or a third-world society—are social beings. That is, they interact with one another and seek to establish relations with one another. Individuals interact with one another in groups and organizations. Human beings are "joiners." To what groups and organizations do you belong? Whatever your routine or life-style, you hardly can remain apart from a group. Individuals who get together for lunch or who meet on a tennis court form a group. Have you ever joined a service club or worked for a large corporation? Corporations and service clubs are organizations.

Sociologists are much interested in groups and organizations and in how the groups and organizations function. In their study of society, they apply a *sociological perspective* to their experiments and observations. Their perspective, or viewpoint, is different from an ordinary view of the world and of the ongoing events in the world. It is an overview, with a scientific understanding of society's dynamics and underpinnings. Have you ever given a thought to society? What is your perspective?

PERSPECTIVE: WHERE TO LOOK

Albert Einstein once observed, "The whole of science is nothing more than a refinement of everyday thinking." In their research and investigations, sociologists agree with Einstein's thinking about science. Sociologists also find themselves at the same starting point from which poets, novelists, and journalists begin their work. All writers, when dealing with social life (or society), usually start with everyday thinking, or common sense. Like Einstein, writers and sociologists have a high regard for common sense.

Consider first an incident which the author and two friends observed while having dinner in a restaurant:

> We were enjoying an evening of dinner and conversation in a downtown restaurant, a place in which we could relax and be sociable. It was a festive occasion, for we were toasting our friend John, who was observing his fortieth birthday. As we were joking about this notable milestone, I happened to glance diagonally across the small dining room to another party of three, a man and two women. Suddenly, the middle-aged man at the nearby table dropped

---

SOCIOLOGY OR COMMON SENSE

What do you think?

Which of the following statements do you agree with? Which statements do you disagree with? Make a note of your answers. Check your answers when you have completed your study of this chapter. Are your answers to the statements the same as those a sociologist would give?

1. "Sociology." That's like psychology, isn't it?
2. The discipline of sociology is merely common sense clothed in fancy language.
3. A sociologist has little in common with an anthropologist or a political scientist.
4. A perspective is an optical illusion.
5. Sociology is really a form of socialism.

---

his head on his chest. Was he trying to make a conversational point?

No, he was not, for the man seemed to be in pain. The two women looked with alarm on their stricken companion, and one of them rushed from the dining room. Soon she returned with a busboy and a distinguished gentleman, a physician, I assumed. The physician examined the man, while the two women looked on anxiously. As we later learned, the gentleman had suffered a heart attack.

The busboy and the physician picked up the man in his chair. They made their way through the small dining room, stepping aside for tables and service stands. Meanwhile, the unconcerned waiters continued to serve dinners and take orders as if nothing had happened. The preoccupied diners in the room were scarcely aware of the goings-on. Once the physician and his patient were off the scene, a waiter went to the table and handed the two women a dinner check. The women paid their bill and left the room.

Within ten minutes after it all began, a busboy had reset the table at which the man had collapsed. Everyone in the room had settled once again into the muffled serenity of the restaurant, and the maitre d' had seated new patrons at the table. The newcomers, I am sure, had no idea of what had happened or of what they had missed. Our waiter began to serve our dinners. As he put the plates on the table, he smiled and said, "It's lucky a doctor was here."

An incident in a restaurant is only one of many events which come about in society. The same happenings often occur at the same time at different places, others overlap in time, and still others have a cause-and-effect relationship. Poets, novelists, journalists, and sociologists observe the incidents and occurrences. Each would have something different to say about the man's heart attack in a restaurant. Why? Their reactions and accounts would differ because writers see social life in different ways and have different thoughts about what they observe.

Sociologists strive to develop a scientific understanding of social events and situations. For example, they sometimes look for cause and effect. Novelists and poets, by writing artistic accounts, convey a humanistic appreciation of the event. They are concerned about feelings. With still another approach, journalists strive for objective reporting, whereby they hope to relate the facts without subjective opinions.

To develop a scientific understanding of the incident in the restaurant (i.e., to refine everyday thinking), a sociologist would look beyond the obvious details. He or she would see more than a stricken man and two alarmed women. The sociologist views more than what life initially appears to be as we go through it day by day. The result of the sociologist's perspective is a "transformation of consciousness," or the ability to see the world in an enlightened way (Berger, 1963: 21). Those who read sociology or do sociological research acquire a special outlook on the social world around them.

Sociology transforms our consciousness in at least two broad ways. First, it identifies meanings, processes, causes, and consequences hitherto unknown to those whose social world is under study. For example, Robert K. Merton (1968: 105) points out how certain arrangements in society have unintended consequences paralleling the intended consequences of the arrangements. We turn to psychiatric diagnostic practices for an illustration. In the psychiatrist's practice, labels such as "schizophrenic" and "paranoiac" are commonly used to diagnose and treat mental illness. But these labels remain with patients who have been discharged from hospitals as cured. The discharged patients are treated as if they were still sick (Scheff, 1984).

Second, sociology uncovers hidden meanings, processes, causes, and consequences that are known to those under study but kept secret or only reluctantly admitted. Revealing hidden meanings, known as "debunking" (Berger, 1963: 41–42), has a long history in sociology. Obviously, such exposés are less than welcome among at least some of those whose hidden ways have been revealed, although others may look on such notoriety as a harbinger for improving problematic situations.

For instance, Haas and Shaffir (1977: 74) studied a group of Canadian medical students whose professors were demanding and uncompromising. The students hardly could measure up to the professors' exaggerated and uncertain expectations. To cope with their anxiety, the would-be physicians donned, so to speak, a "cloak of competence." Their language and demeanor became the M.D.'s language and demeanor. They dressed in the physician's uniform, conservative suits for the men and plain dresses for the women. The students frequently hung around their necks a stethoscope, the physician's brassard.

PERSPECTIVE: WHAT TO LOOK FOR

What would sociologists look for in the incident at the restaurant? Broadly put, they would try to find some evidence of an existing society in the event which occurred. A society is ordinarily a large, relatively self-sufficient group of people who maintain direct or indirect contact with each other through a *culture,* or through shared language, beliefs, goals, norms, behavior patterns, and political systems. *Culture* is a society's way of life. Society is thus a social phenomenon, because each individual in a society shares much of his or her language, beliefs, goals, norms, and patterns with the other members of the society. All social acts or events occurring within the group are part of the society.

Any sociological investigation is a study of society. But few sociologists study the entire society. Rather, they concentrate on one or more of the analytic problems which must be dealt with in the study of any society. For example, what would sociologists look for in the incident at the restaurant? First, they would single out the *analytic problems* which arise in the scene at the restaurant.

Mennell (1980), a lecturer in sociology at the University of Exeter, has defined and explained five analytic problems. The problems to which Mennell calls attention are the problems of *action; knowledge; interaction and interdependence; power, order, and interest;* and *systems.* The remainder of this chapter is devoted to describing these five problems and some of the more important ways in which they relate to one another. The problems are of great concern to sociologists, for they are the central focus of sociological theory and research, the subjects of Chapter 2, "Sociological Theories," and Chapter 3, "Studying Social Life."

Action

One of the analytic problems in the social sciences, and one as old as sociology itself, is conveniently summarized by the saying "behavior versus action." For many scientists—both natural scientists and social scientists—behavior is an organism's reaction to a mental, physiological, or biological state without reference to conscious thought or interpretive reason. Left-handedness or right-handedness is an example

Action is social: Helping behavior is a common example of action in our society.

The Sociological Imagination

The practice of sociology, I argue in this book, demands invoking what C. Wright Mills has aptly called the 'sociological imagination' (C. Wright Mills, *The Sociological Imagination,* Harmondsworth, Penguin, 1970). The term has been so oft-quoted that it is in danger of being trivialised, and Mills himself used it in a rather vague sense. I mean by it several related forms of sensibility indispensable to sociological analysis as I conceive of it. An understanding of the social world initiated by the contemporary industrialised societies—present-day society as first formed in the West—can only be achieved by virtue of a threefold exercise of the imagination. These forms of the sociological imagination involve an *historical,* an *anthropological,* and a *critical* sensitivity. . . .

The first effort of sociological imagination that has to be exercised by the analyst of the industrialised societies today is that of recovering our own immediate past—the 'world we have lost'. Only by such an effort of the imagination, which of course involves an awareness of history, can we grasp just how differently those in the industrialised societies live today from the way people lived in the relatively recent past. . . .

The anthropological dimension of the sociological imagination is important because it allows us to appreciate the diversity of modes of human existence which have been followed on this earth. . . .

Combining this second sense with the first, the exercise of the sociological imagination makes it possible to break free from the straightjacket of thinking only in terms of the type of society we know in the here and now. Each is thus directly relevant to the third form of the sociological imagination that I want to point to. . . . In its third sense, the sociological imagination fuses with the task of sociology in contributing to *the critique of existing forms of society.*

SOURCE: Anthony Giddens. *Sociology: A brief but critical introduction,* pp. 15–17, 24, 26. New York: Harcourt Brace Jovanovich, 1982.

of behavior. The study of behavior centers primarily on the individual organism. The social factors potentially relevant to the explanation of behavior are secondary.

By contrast, *action* is inherently social. It is an act of will. Ways of thinking, feeling, and acting learned as a member of the community help a person to decide what act is all right in a given situation. Getting food at a supermarket is an example of action. The behaviorist view stresses the ways in which human beings and other animals are alike, whereas the actionist view stresses their differences.

Several early sociologists confronted the behavior-versus-action problem. They favored in some way an action frame of reference. They pictured sociology as a social science rather than as a behavioral science.

One school, *symbolic interactionism,* traces its intellectual roots to George Herbert Mead (1863–1921) and William I. Thomas (1863–1947), among others.[1] The two sociologists ar-

[1]The various schools of thought in sociology are only briefly introduced in this chapter. They are covered more fully in Chapter 2 and illustrated further throughout the book.

gued that people shape their own actions. They do so by defining or interpreting the various social situations in which they conduct their daily affairs. The resulting definitions are the meanings these situations have for the people acting within them. The definitions are based on linguistic and reflective skills acquired in the course of growing up in the community. Such definitions guide personal action in the immediate situation. A social situation could be observed in the restaurant in which the middle-aged man suffered a heart attack. At first, it appeared that his slumped head was a conversational gesture, a social action.

Emile Durkheim (1855–1917) approached the behavior-action problem somewhat differently from the symbolic interactionists (Durkheim, 1938: 13). His principal interest lay in what he called "social facts," or the ways of thinking, acting, and feeling that are general in a community or in an entire society. Social facts are identifiable as such when they exercise constraint over individual actions. Nevertheless, they exist independently of the individual.

Moreover, it takes other social facts to explain a single social fact. For example, to explain why the suicide rate is higher for Protestants than for Catholics and Jews, Durkheim compared Protestant, Catholic, and Jewish levels of social integration (see later). Protestantism endorses free religious inquiry, whereas Catholicism and Judaism do not. The Protestant orientation helps to foster a significantly lower level of solidarity among Protestants, which, in turn, encourages suicide (Durkheim, 1951: 158). Though less concerned with inner mental processes than Mead and Thomas, Durkheim did recognize their role; human actions are only partially determined by the social world in which they occur (Mennell, 1980: 27).

Max Weber (1864–1920), a German sociologist, also wrestled with the behavior-action problem. His ideas and those of Mead and Thomas have much in common. He declared sociology to be a science which attempts the interpretive understanding of social action in order thereby to arrive at a causal explanation of its course and effects (Weber, 1968: 3).

Human behavior may be classified as action if it has personal meaning for the individual actor, or person who carries out the action. Such action is either overt or covert; doing nothing is often as meaningful as doing something. A person's action becomes social when its personal meaning includes an understanding of what others in the setting are doing and the person's action is "thereby oriented in its course." In explaining action, the sociologist looks on the intended consequences as more important than the actual consequences. As with Mead and Thomas, Weber said the purpose or aim of the action must be considered.

Although Mead, Thomas, Durkheim, and Weber all embraced the action side of the behavior-action controversy, they differed among themselves as to how much action can be explained by the original, spontaneous interpretations of individuals and how much can be explained by the social facts of their communities. Clearly, Durkheim stressed social facts more than the others. Sociologists are still debating this complicated question.

Knowledge

Mennell (1980: 19–23, 131–41) takes us from the discussion of action to the question: "How is it possible to interpret the meanings, intentions, and purposes which lie behind people's actions?" The answer is found in the modes of thought and conceptions of reality held by members of the society in which the action occurs. This is by no means strictly a sociological problem. Yet sociology makes its own unique contribution along with anthropology, linguistics, and philosophy.

Common Sense Anthropologists have long recognized that language and grammar influence the ways people in a society think about their social life and physical world. Alfred Schutz (1899–1959), a philosopher, observed that people have unique personal stocks of knowledge derived from their experiences. This knowledge, however, is organized by means of socially learned categories and socially learned classifications known as *typifications.* Since typifications are a part of common sense, Schutz recommended the study of the commonsense views of life held by groups of people. Such views sometimes diverge sharply from those of science.

Sociologists Peter Berger and Thomas Luckmann (1966) helped disseminate Schutz's ideas among their colleagues by expanding his notion of commonsense knowledge. Schutz concentrated on individual stocks of knowledge. Berger and Luckmann theorized that these separate, personal systems coalesce into a reality shared by many members of a group, community, or society. Reality has both personal components and social components. Reality, they argued, is "socially constructed."

Ethnomethodology The study of the social construction of reality has gained considerable steam in the past fifteen to twenty years under the general, although sometimes obscure, title "ethnomethodology." *Ethnomethodology* is the study of how people share their definitions of reality. It is an analysis of the practical understanding which people acquire through interaction and everyday experiences. Early ethnomethodological studies concentrated on the "negotiation of social order," or how people entering a social situation (see earlier) come to agree on its meaning to them. Recently, emphasis has shifted to the study of "structuring," or giving meaning to situations by recognizing the shared but assumed background knowledge which members of a society bring to the situation (Frank, 1979: 175–183).

In Goffman's work (1974), for example, individuals are conceived of as vehicles for the expression in society of the previously learned and presently taken-for-granted beliefs and outlooks of the members of the society. Human beings are the "resources" who manifest the rules and categories that are part of our social background and that remain largely hidden from our conscious attention. It appeared, for example, that the two distressed women in the restaurant would have wept aloud had not the refined and public nature of the room prompted them (without their knowing it) to endure their anxiety in silence.

Interaction and Interdependence

Action and knowledge are two significant components of *interaction,* or the reciprocal effect of the social actions of individuals on each other. It is through human interaction that social and cultural structures eventually emerge and change. Interaction is the basis of all social life. Whenever at least two individuals are together, there is interaction. Individuals may act on each other intentionally or unintentionally.

Two other components, in addition to action and knowledge, are found in most interactions. The two additional components are *role* and *status.* There is disagreement on how to define these two ideas. In this chapter, we need only refer to definitions which are generally ac-

What sociological process do these men exemplify?

cepted. These two definitions bring out the relevance of roles and statuses to the analytic problem of interaction. *Status* is a position in a group. *Role* is a set of actions expected or required of those who have a particular status. Roles consist of rights and obligations. The physician in the restaurant was undoubtedly expected to take care of the stricken man and, if medically possible, to save his life. The waiter presumably felt the owner of the restaurant expected him to collect for the meal, regardless of the emotional state of the two women.

The busker has a difficult occupational role to play.

Interaction can also be observed in unstructured circumstances, outside any role-status expectation. A man who stops another man on a busy street to ask for a match is briefly interacting with the other man. But there is no role—no established set of expectations—for this sort of action, nor is there a status associated with it. Whether or not role and status are involved, much of sociological and social psychological research concerned with this level of social life has been on interaction with dyads and triads, that is, on two- and three-person interactive systems.

Nevertheless, the dyad-triad framework sharply limits the sociological analysis of interaction (Mennell, 1980: 44), for people are often linked together in what Merton (1957a) calls *role-sets,* or the relationships a person in one status has with those in all related statuses. Furthermore, these "role others" may make inconsistent demands on the individual in the central status. The result is *role conflict.* For example, a teenager and her grandmother, two important people in a mother's role-set, have been known to hold conflicting expectations of the mother's policy regarding dating.

Three particularly important characteristics of role behavior are that it is consistent, recognizable, and therefore predictable. Consistency, recognizability, and predictability enable people who are enacting different but related roles to coordinate their actions. Coordinated actions can lead, in turn, to interdependence. *Interdependence* means that each action combines with actions from related roles to make up a complete and meaningful sequence of actions leading to some end.

To return to our restaurant example, the role of the waiter is to take orders for meals, deliver the orders to the kitchen, and bring the prepared food to the diners. The role of the chef is to cook the food which the diners will be ordering. The role of the diner is to place an order for food and to eat (if it is palatable) what is brought by the waiter. These three roles are interdependent. A restaurant could not remain in business long if one of them were missing. Restaurant operations are at least temporarily halted when there are no diners, when the chef is home ill, or when the waiters are on strike.

Power, Order, Interest

Although, historically, the idea of power has had an uneven reception among sociologists, they have nevertheless given it sporadic attention since at least the late nineteenth century. Mennell (1980: 102) defines power in terms similar to the terms of Max Weber. Power is

> the process by which some actors in social relationships are able to carry out their will by changing the balance of advantage of alternative courses of action for others in the relationship.

One school of sociological thought with a major stake in the concept of power is *social exchange theory.*

The principal assumption of the social exchange theory is that "men enter into new social associations because they expect doing so to be rewarding" (Blau, 1968: 452). According to the theory, one who enters into an association hopes to gain something from the association; there is an exchange. With assumptions of this sort and with the observation made by Emerson (1976: 336) that social exchange theory can be simplistically described as the "economic analysis of noneconomic *social situations* [emphasis mine]," it is no wonder that research here has centered predominantly on social interaction and social relationships.

Power as an analytic problem emerges in this framework through the possibility that the rewards exchanged may lead to more than the establishing of friendly ties among peers. Such rewards may also engender differences of superiority and inferiority among the same people (Blau, 1968: 455).

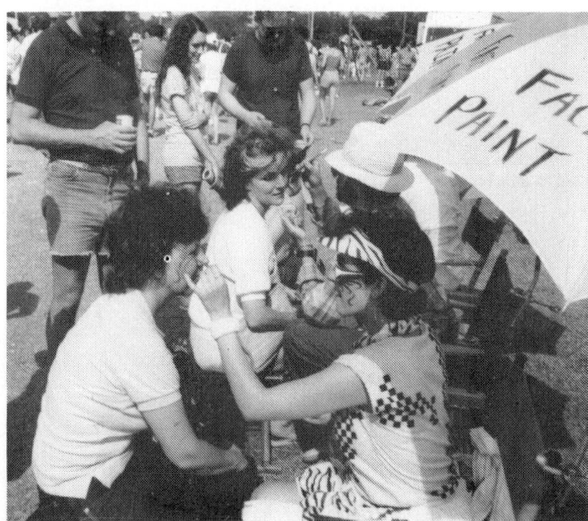

Social exchange is mutually beneficial social interaction.

A look at the list of potential power resources indicates that power, even within the exchange framework, extends well beyond the sphere of interpersonal interaction. Alongside the resources love and money we must also consider, as Weber has suggested, resources such as positions of authority and control in the larger community and in large-scale organizations. In fact, there are as many ways of acquiring and originating power as there are power resources (Mennell, 1980: 103).

As explained in Chapter 18, "Social Stratification," the sources of power are not available to everyone equally. Income, for example, is a source of power. Some individuals have more income than others. With their high incomes, the wealthy are more likely to obtain power than the poor. Knowledge and skills are sources of power. Different individuals in society differ in their knowledge and in the skills which they apply to earning a living.

Social Order Power, in Weberian terms, is personal and intentional. Someone is pursuing an advantage at the expense of someone else by means of a conscious strategy. But another set of forces constrains human action. These forces derive from the interdependence of the actions; one action is dependent on another action. An individual takes on roles that are enacted with reference to other roles. Hence, the individual must act in certain ways and refrain from acting in other ways (e.g., the chef is expected to prepare what the diners ordered, not what he or she thinks the diners should have ordered). In an individual's roles, he or she has specific privileges and responsibilities, but lacks other privileges and responsibilities. All roles constrain the behavior of those who enact them.

Power, interdependence, and role behavior contribute to the social order of a society. A *social order*

> is the outcome of complex forces of dependence and interdependence, of cooperation and conflict, of strength and weakness, of alliances and cleavages between people and groups. (Mennell, 1980: 94)

The social order at a particular time in a particular society is as much a product of the processes of conflict and the assertion of power as it is a product of the processes of cooperation and alliance.

Division of Labor A social order consists, in part, of the *division of labor* in society. Durkheim said the division of labor is best exemplified in industrialized nations by the specialized tasks which people voluntarily seek or to which they are assigned. A social order exists when the carrying out of the tasks is coordinated in such a fashion that group goals are reached with minimum conflict and with little inefficiency.

For example, the individual musicians in a symphony orchestra—the violinists, the bassoonists, the trombonists, the horn players, the tympani player—all have their own notes to play. When the goal of making music (i.e., playing the composition) is achieved, the coordination of the orchestra is accomplished. Coordination is achieved when each member of the orchestra plays his or her part accurately and with acceptable intonation.

Collective Action A social order also consists of *collective action.* In collective action, two or more interdependent people combine their efforts to reach a shared goal. To the extent that specialized tasks are carried out, collective action rests on a division of labor. But in some collective action many of the tasks may be more or less the same, as when four individuals push a car out of a snowdrift.

Social units from small groups to entire societies engage in collective action when their members share a commitment to or reach a consensus on at least some of the norms and values of the unit. *Norms* are the standards of action to which members of the group are expected to conform. They cluster around a particular role as its set of expectations. *Values* are a society's ideas of what is good and desirable; the good and the desirable satisfy a collective need or desire. Almost anything can be valued by members of a society. Among numerous values are religious doctrine, political ideology, popular music, natural scenery, beauty of person, styles of housing, and tastes for food.

Anomie and Alienation As previously noted, the study of any social order always entails a parallel examination of the nature and effects of the forces producing disorder. One of these forces is *anomie,* which is Durkheim's term for the normless state that occasionally upsets the established order. Anomie exists when a society's social norms are weak, if not defunct. During anomie,

> all regulation is lacking for a time. The limits are unknown between the possible and the impossible, [between] what is just and what is unjust, [and between] legitimate claims and hopes and those which are immoderate. Consequently, there is no restraint upon aspirations. (Durkheim, 1951: 253)

Another force producing disorder is alienation. *Alienation* is defined by Karl Marx (1818–1883) as the social circumstances in which workers, owing to overspecialization of their occupational tasks, become estranged from the fruits of their labor. In this situation, work is no longer an end in itself but a means to other ends. Workers on an automobile assembly line have experienced alienation. As one assembly-line worker put it, "I don't understand how come more guys don't flip, because you're nothing more than a machine when you hit this type of thing" (Terkel, 1974: 160).

Interest and Conflict Anomie and alienation may become the reason for overt conflict. Conflict can affect the social order in two broad ways. Sociologists from Georg Simmel (1858–1918) to the present have recognized conflict as producing potentially integrative forces, such as when cooperation and harmony increase dramatically in groups feeling an external threat. Even conflict within a group may generate more integration than disintegration. A family dispute may clarify a previously vague but contentious issue. The settlement of a labor dispute may satisfy everyone; management and the union are both willing to accept the terms. Notwithstanding commonsense bias against disagreement, conflict is not all bad.

But it should be recognized that groups and categories of people in modern societies sometimes have irreconcilable interests. Moreover, the resources of power are unevenly distributed, which is one of the bases of our social-class system. Group and class conflict is the result of uneven distribution; people with the greatest power (the most productive power resources) are able to realize their interests at the expense of the people with less power. Conflict theorists point out that the configuration of power in society shifts. As the social world changes, the control over resources waxes and wanes; alliances are made and broken, and power groups come to share their power with each other, or these groups may lose their power to groups that once were weak.

Marx wrote about conflicting economic interests, which he said were being polarized over the course of industrial history into two social classes: the workers, or *proletariat,* and the capitalists, or *bourgeoisie.* As a result of the increasing use of machinery to produce goods, workers become alienated from the fruits of their labor. In time, the exploited workers become paupers. The capitalists, in the meantime, reap huge profits from the toil of the workers. Marx proposed a course of action whereby workers would become conscious of their plight, revolt, and seize power from the capitalists. With a revolt, the proletariat would gain control of the means of production.

Systems

Systems are an analytic problem in sociology. A system—social, physical, or biological—is essentially a unit or whole consisting of interdependent parts; the interacting parts work together to perform specific functions. How is this functioning whole—the system, be it a small group, a large-scale organization, or a nation-state—established and maintained? The answer to this question is likewise an analytic problem.

Functionalism The *social system* is dealt with by sociology's functional school. *Functionalism* is a sociological perspective which seeks to explain social behavior on the basis of functions. Functionalists scrutinize the interrelated parts of a society. As they see it, social systems are individuals and groups which act together and perform a certain function. The individuals and groups in a social system have different but coordinated roles; they interact with each other in an established manner. Norms, goals, and shared values are adhered to by the separate role players in their routine activities. The *functions,* or consequences, of these activities help to maintain the group as an ongoing unit.

Consider the functional integration of a "crew" of professional card and dice hustlers. According to Prus and Sharper (1977: 32–36), the crew's goals are profit, safety, and competent play. Although sometimes larger, the crew usually consists of three or four members, some of whom assume multiple roles. There are three game roles: The "mechanic" manipulates the dice and cards to control the outcome of the game. The "shoot-up man" first establishes personal credibility and then tries to increase the size of bets among naive players in the game. A "muscle man" is optional. He provides protection for the crew when needed. Two nongame roles include the "contacts man," who locates places for hustling, and the "boss," who coordinates crew activities.

Functionalism has been around in one form or another since sociology's inception in the mid-nineteenth century. The early sociologists viewed society as analogous to (and, in extreme cases, as a version of) a living organism. This organismic model guided the work of Auguste Comte (1798–1857), Emile Durkheim (1858–1917), and Herbert Spencer (1820–1903), to mention but a few. These early sociologists sought to identify and describe the animal-like aspects of human societies such as life cycles and evolutionary patterns. Functionalism is fully explained in Chapter 2, "Sociological Theories."

The five analytic problems just presented are, in one way or another, evident in sociological theory and research. Brief mention was made throughout this chapter of their connection with the five major theoretical perspectives in sociology. We turn now to a more comprehensive review of those perspectives and the analytic problems associated with them. The perspectives form the backdrop for most research studies in sociology. The role of theory in research is considered in Chapter 3.

OUTLINE AND SUMMARY

You can review Chapter 1, "The Study of Society," by going over the following outline and summary:

I. Introduction
Sociology is the study of society.

II. Perspective: Where to Look
Sociology is a refinement of everyday thinking. Sociologists, poets, novelists, and journalists begin their work at the same starting point: everyday thinking, or common sense. A man suffers a heart attack in a restaurant. Sociologists would try to develop a scientific understanding of everything which entered into the incident.

III. Perspective: What to Look For
Few sociologists study an entire society. Rather, they concentrate on one or more analytical problems which must be dealt with in a study of society. Five such problems are the problems of *action; knowledge; interaction and interdependence; power, order, and interest;* and *systems.*

A. Action
Action is inherently social. It differs from behavior. Sociologists confront the behavior-versus-action problem.

B. Knowledge

1. Common Sense
Knowledge is organized by means of socially learned categories known as *typifications.* Typifications are a part of common sense.

2. Ethnomethodology
Ethnomethodology is the study of the social construction of reality. It seeks to explain how people entering a social situation agree on its meaning to them.

C. Interaction and Interdependence
Action and knowledge are components of interaction. Social and cultural structures emerge and change through human interaction. Whenever two individuals get together, there is interaction. Two additional components of interaction are *role* and *status.*

D. Power, Order, Interest
The *social exchange theory* helps to explain the concept of power.

1. Social Order
Power, interdependence, and role behavior contribute to the social order of a society.

2. Division of Labor
A social order consists, in part, of a division of labor.

3. Collective Action
A social order also consists of collective action. In collective action, two or more interdependent individuals combine their efforts to reach a shared goal.

4. Anomie and Alienation
Anomie and alienation produce disorder. *Anomie* is a state of normlessness in society. *Alienation* is the estrangement of workers from the fruits of their labor.

5. Interest and Conflict
   Conflict can affect the social order in two ways. It can lead to integration in groups. But groups of people in modern societies sometimes have irreconcilable interests. The resources of power are unevenly distributed.

E. Systems
   A *system* is a unit or whole consisting of interdependent parts. The interacting parts work together to perform a specific function. Systems are an analytical problem in sociology.
   1. Functionalism
      Functionalism is a sociological perspective which explains social behavior on the basis of functions.

FOR FURTHER READING AND STUDY

Bart, P. and Frankel, L. 1981. *The student sociologist's handbook,* 3rd ed. Glenview, IL: Scott, Foresman. A "survival kit" for students, which covers the theoretical perspectives of sociology, the sociology term paper, the mechanics of library research, and the definitions of statistical terms.

Berger, P. L. 1963. *Invitation to sociology: A humanistic perspective.* Garden City, NY: Doubleday. This is a lively, lucid book on the nature of sociology. The book concentrates on the larger implications and dimensions of the discipline.

Berger, P. L. and Kellner, H. 1981. *Sociology reinterpreted.* Garden City, NY: Doubleday. This book is a sequel to Berger's *Invitation to sociology. Sociology reinterpreted* is an essay about what it means to be a sociologist in modern times.

Berry, D. 1975. *Central ideas in sociology.* Itasca, IL: F. E. Peacock. A short, straightforward introduction to sociology's major concepts and theoretical perspectives.

Collins, R. 1982. *Sociological insight: An introduction to nonobvious sociology.* New York: Oxford University Press. This book is based on the assumption that sociology has more to offer than statements of the obvious. Collins highlights the unusual and unexpected conclusions reached over the years by sociologists.

Giddens, A. 1982. *Sociology: A brief but critical introduction.* New York: Harcourt Brace Jovanovich. This book is, at once, a historical, anthropological, and critical introduction to the discipline on a small scale. The author provides competing interpretations of society, class, change, family, gender, capitalism, the state, and the world system.

Henslin, J. M., ed. 1981. *Down to earth sociology: Introductory readings.* New York: Free Press. A collection of articles on a wide variety of topics typically studied by sociologists, including socialization, sex roles, groups, social structure, deviance, social control, inequality, institutions, and change.

Page, C. 1982. *Fifty years in the sociological enterprise: A lucky journal.* Amherst, MA: University of Massachusetts Press. A fifty-year excursion through American sociology, starting in the 1930s. An autobiographical, intellectual history of the development of sociology in the United States by a prominent scholar who has lived through much of it.

KEY WORDS

action An act of will.

alienation The social circumstances in which workers become estranged from the fruits of their labor.

anomie A state of normlessness in a society.

behavior An organism's reaction to a mental, physiological, or biological state without reference to conscious thought or interpretive reasoning.

common sense A prudent but sometimes unsophisticated judgment derived from everyday thinking.

culture Shared language, beliefs, goals, norms, family patterns, and political systems within a society; it is a society's way of life.

ethnomethodology The study of the social construction of reality.

functionalism A sociological perspective which explains social behavior on the basis of function;

the functions of the interrelated parts of a society are examined.

interaction The reciprocal effect of the social actions of individuals on each other.

perspective A perceived interrelation which provides an overall view of a subject and its parts; a sociological perspective is a view of society.

role A set of actions expected of an individual occupying a particular status.

society A large, self-sufficient aggregation of people who maintain contact with each other through culture.

sociology The study of society.

status A position in a group.

chapter 2

Sociological Theories

CHAPTER OUTLINE

INTRODUCTION

Professional persons (teachers and social workers, for example) have many significant attributes. Two of these attributes are the possession of a particular body of knowledge called theory and an adherence to cultural traditions which are unique to their calling. The two attributes help to distinguish one profession from another —teaching from social work, for example. They also bring out the differences between professional occupations and nonprofessional lines of work.

Sociology is a profession as well as a scientific discipline. Sociologists are professional workers. Many sociologists are teachers, or professors. Others have full-time jobs as researchers or as specialists in government, with associations, or with corporations. As professionals, the sociologists, too, are distinguished by the two significant attributes. The attributes help to define sociology and to set it apart from the other social sciences. With its own traditions and its own body of knowledge, sociology deals with society in a fashion which differs from the approach of economics or political science.

Accordingly, this chapter conveys the central tenets of sociology's principal theories. The tenets are summed up in five theories, or *theoretical perspectives.* The theoretical perspectives are *functionalism, ethnomethodology, conflict theory, symbolic interactionism,* and *social exchange theory.* Each theory stresses one or two of the analytic problems outlined in Chapter 1, "The Study of Society."

A *theory* is a set of *propositions*—facts, principles, and hypotheses—related to one or more analytic problems. In the most developed theories, those whose problems have been intensely studied for many years, the propositions are logically interrelated. The sociological theories are still developing this quality of logical interrelationship of propositions. For this reason, the theories are commonly referred to as *perspectives* or *frameworks.* The theories presented in this chapter are background for understanding the principles of sociology which are explained throughout the rest of this book.

SYMBOLIC INTERACTIONISM

To develop an understanding of *symbolic interactionism,* you first might consider the derivation of its name. The name is derived from the word "symbol." A *symbol* is something which stands for or suggests something else. Human beings not only react to the actions of others; they attach meaning to the actions and behavior of others in society. They interpret the interactions, and, with their interpretation, they recognize symbols which give meaning to the interactions. Among the commonly recognized symbols are language, gestures, sounds, body movements, and facial expressions. The symbols stand for reality and thus impart meaning to the social situation.

The symbolic interactionist perspective focuses on the analytic problems of action and interaction and interdependence. Thus it concentrates on process (action, behavior) and makes the individual the center of attention. As symbolic interactionists see it, the active human being tries to make sense of a social situation and give it meaning. Symbolic interactionists center their attention on the individual's interpretation of social interaction and on the symbols (language, gestures) which suggest the interpretation. With this approach to a study of society, sociologists gain an understanding of the social order and of society itself.

The symbolic interactionist theory rests on the assumption that, unlike other animals, human beings are capable of complex thoughts and acts based on their ability to use and interpret symbols. Human beings can reason. Arnold Rose (1962: 5) defines a symbol as

> a stimulus that has a learned meaning and values for people, and man's response to a symbol is in terms of its meaning and value rather than in terms of its physical stimulation of the sense organs.

The national anthem is a symbol. Upon hearing it played or sung, Canadians instinctively rise to their feet in response. Indeed, socialized Canadians need not be told to stand at attention. Experience and cultural transmission remind them that they should rise in respect when

---

SOCIOLOGY OR COMMON SENSE

What do you think?

Which of the following statements do you agree with? Which statements do you disagree with? Make a note of your answers. Check your answers when you have completed your study of this chapter. Are your answers to the statements the same as those a sociologist would give?

1. Karl Marx was a nineteenth century economist.
2. Sociology is an American invention.
3. Conflict theory seeks to explain the cause of war.
4. The parts of a social system always have functional consequences.
5. There is little difference between American and Canadian sociology.

---

it is announced that their national anthem is to be played. Nearly everyone knows the words and music to the national anthem.

The Individual and Society

The leading founders of symbolic interactionism—George H. Mead, W. I. Thomas, and Charles H. Cooley—had a hand in the early development of sociology at the University of Michigan and the University of Chicago. All three men viewed society and the individual as "twin born," or as inseparable units. Society and the individual are mutually interdependent. That is, people form the society in which they live; at the same time, the society which the people bring into existence partly determines their behavior.

Sheldon Stryker (1980: 53–85) sets forth a generalized outline of symbolic interactionism. Stryker's outline is based on the reciprocity between the individual and society. He points out that human beings act with reference to a classified physical and social world. Social and physical life is organized by human beings according to innumerable *categories,* or classes of objects and living things symbolized by language. Names are symbolic of the categories. As symbols, the names stand for diverse categories such as "house," "car," "skyscraper," "airplane," "river," "mountain," and "cable car." Names also symbolize living beings such as "dog," "cat," "landlord," "rapist," "woman," "baby," "rich people," "retiree," "senior citizen," and "nice guy." Schutz's typifications (discussed in Chapter 1, "The Study of Society") are one type of category.

Each category has expectations associated with it. Many of them are combined into roles, which, in turn, are associated with social statuses. That is, in identifying someone as a member of a particular category, we also bring to mind what to expect of him or her. We expect a rapist to be violent and lustful, a physician to be dignified and knowledgeable, a nice guy to be warm and friendly.

We also apply categorical names to ourselves. In our mind's eye, we are nice individuals, employed in a certain occupation, single or married, young or old, male or female, smart or dull, overweight or underweight, and so forth. These names, or symbols, become part of the *self.* The self contains internalized expectations for our behavior which are consistent with the symbols. The names and associated expectations are modified, however, through interaction with other people, particularly those whom we respect. What if we think we are warm, friendly individuals, but our closest friends say we are becoming distant and hostile? Under these circumstances we are likely to change our behavior, because we have altered our conception of ourselves (based on what our friends have said).

The categorical names that we apply to the physical and social world also become part of our definition of the many situations we pass through in our everyday lives. A *definition of the situation* is the meaning that a situation has for us, which certainly includes human beings and physical objects in the situation along with the expectations we have of them. Our definition of any situation helps us organize our behavior in the situation. For example, an individual who approaches a young mother who is caring for her child is unlikely to suggest that it is wrong to bring a child into a world which is struggling with overpopulation.

Nevertheless, categories and their associated expectations fail to determine human behavior. Put otherwise, human beings have the capacity to define situations as they and others have never defined them before. It is through this process, symbolic interactionists believe, that each individual contributes in his or her own small way to the shaping and reshaping of society. Of course, this contribution is made in an extremely complicated manner. It is one of the areas about which social scientists know the least. Some roles and situations allow for more creativity of this sort than others.

New roles typically encourage far more *role*

making (the making of new patterns of behavior) than old, established roles. An import from Sweden, the role of ombudsman is newer in North America than the role of the police officer. The ombudsman is a government appointee whose role is to receive and investigate complaints from citizens about abuses and capricious acts of government officials. Having been first tried in Alberta and New Brunswick in 1967 and in Hawaii in 1969, the role of ombudsman has not had nearly as much time to crystallize as a role (in North America) as police work has. Organized police work has been conducted in parts of North America since before the middle of the nineteenth century.

The Micro-Order

The interactionist perspective is concerned largely with the *micro-order,* or the numerous day-to-day activities in society. Many of the events may seem trivial and insignificant, yet they have much to do with the nature of society. The micro-order complements the *macro-order,* or the large-scale processes and structures in society. Many events and conditions in society take on a new meaning when the micro-order is applied to sociological analysis. The very nature of society is largely the product of human interaction on the micro-order level.

George H. Mead is generally regarded as the most influential early thinker in symbolic interactionism. His book *Mind, Self, and Society,* published in 1934, explains his ideas in detail. Mead's thinking still guides research in the interactionist approach to sociology and to an understanding of society. Mead was also instrumental in developing the discipline *social psychology,* one branch of which is symbolic interactionism.

ETHNOMETHODOLOGY

Ethnomethodology is the study of how the people in society make sense of their everyday world. It is an investigation of the methods which individuals use to interpret objects, events, and processes. Unlike symbolic interactionist research, which centers on conscious behavior, ethnomethodological research concentrates on discovering the assumptions people make as they encounter and react to other people, things, and events in their routine lives. That is, it is concerned with the analytic problem of knowledge.

Kenneth Leiter (1980: vi, Chapter 1) defines ethnomethodology as the study of commonsense knowledge. Three phenomena are encompassed by this definition: (1) Ethnomethodologists study the *stock of knowledge* that people have about the social and physical world around them. (2) With this stock of knowledge, people engage in *commonsense reasoning* about the events, processes, things, and characteristics experienced in everyday life. (3) When people reason together on a commonsense basis, their thoughts often combine to form a suprahuman reality, a *social reality.* The social reality transcends the thoughts of those in the situation who are doing the reasoning. Ethnomethodologists do not seek to confirm the validity of common sense. Rather, they note that, whether common sense is scientifically right or wrong, it is the way in which

One of our fondest socially constructed realities.

"we experience the social world as a factual object" (Leiter, 1980: 4).

Schutz's Phenomenology

Ethnomethodologists frequently trace the origin of their specialty to the work of Alfred Schutz, a Viennese lawyer, philosopher, and social scientist who emigrated to the United States just prior to World War II. Schultz learned his philosophy from Edmund Husserl, a leading German phenomenologist of the late nineteenth and early twentieth centuries. Phenomenologists hold, among other ideas, that we should concern ourselves only with that which is directly comprehended by the senses, or with things being as they appear to our consciousness. In other words, we should be concerned with phenomena and the sense data about the phenomena. It is from the phenomena and sense data that knowledge comes.

Schutz developed a sociological phenomenology. An explanation of his phenomenology was published in English in the early 1960s. The stock of knowledge is one of Schutz's many concepts. It consists of taken-for-granted recipes, rules of thumb, typifications, maxims, and definitions. Recipes are ways of doing things. We use a widely shared recipe when we write personal checks. We have learned what to put on the various lines of the blank check. In doing this, we are aided by maxims such as "don't stale-date the check," "don't strike over the writing on the check," and "allow no room for forged additions to the monetary value of the check." A major rule of thumb associated with check writing is that one should have enough money in the bank to cover the amount of the check.

Stocks of knowledge have several distinctive qualities. They are socially derived, in good part from friends, relatives, teachers, and other close associates. Furthermore, we play different roles, belong to different social classes, and espouse different religions. We therefore have different experiences and encounter different phenomena. This suggests that the stocks of knowledge vary among members of a society. This variation is also fostered by the availability of experts, or those individuals who possess technical stocks of knowledge which are of value to us.

Except for the technical knowledge of the expert, our stocks of knowledge are expressed in everyday language, which is often ambiguous or characterized by multiple meanings. Thus, the stocks of knowledge of people bear little resemblance to a good scientific theory. Not only is their knowledge frequently ambiguous; it is also unsystematic and illogical. The maxims, rules of thumb, recipes, definitions, and typifications are not logically intertwined. Thus, we may live in one instance by the maxim "fight fire with fire" and in the next by the maxim "discretion is the better part of valor."

Commonsense reasoning proceeds from the stock of knowledge. Consider this example: Some people believe that blood thickens when exposed for long periods of time to cold weather (how long is never specified) and thins when exposed for long periods of time to hot weather. Although these maxims have no basis in science, those who believe them reason that they will be more comfortable in the cold weather of winter and the hot weather of summer once their blood thickens or thins in adjustment to the new season.

To the extent that this belief about the thickening and thinning of blood is held by the participants of a given social circle, social group, or social class, it is a form of social reality. It has a consensual base to it; each participant knows that the others hold the same belief and that they know the participant holds it. Such a belief transcends individual participants. Early research in ethnomethodology studied the contrasts between scientific reasoning and commonsense reasoning (Garfinkle, 1967: 35–75). The "Sociology or Common Sense" feature that appears in each chapter of this book consists of questions asked from a commonsense standpoint. The answers to these questions show how common sense and science sometimes agree and sometimes disagree.

Goffman's Frame

More recent work in ethnomethodology is frequently guided by Goffman's (1974) concept of the *frame:* the hidden sets of rules and categories (of people, things, events) that are part of our cultural heritage. These sets of rules and categories are so deeply ingrained and so habitual in their application in our everyday lives that they go largely unrecognized. We are behaving according to hidden rules when we allow the person we are conversing with to finish his or her sentence before we begin to talk and when we take a certain physical distance in conversations with strangers (as compared with conversations with close friends). In Goffman's terms (1974: 21–27), human beings are the vehicles for the expression in interaction of previously and presently taken-for-granted or assumed cultural structures.

The analysis of frames has led still more recently to an interest in conversations, inasmuch as conversational routines are also based on hidden rules and categorizations (frames). Included here are certain educational sociologists with their interest in the structuring of classroom talk. We are indebted to them for the idea of "social competence" (Mehan, 1978). Successful classroom participants have learned how to interpret the speech and actions of other students and of the teacher in the classroom and to respond sensibly (as defined by the others) to the speech and actions of the others. In classrooms, this implies the integration of academic knowledge and interpersonal skills, some of which are unique to this setting. When interacting, socially competent teachers and students share meanings at a level high enough to accomplish normal schoolroom business.

SOCIAL EXCHANGE THEORY

The formal origin of social exchange theory is usually traced to a journal article written by George C. Homans (1958). Since then, several versions of this perspective have sprung up in economics, anthropology, psychology, and sociology. Sociologists have criticized the psychological version, an interpretation which includes Homans's ideas. The sociologists look with disfavor on the psychologists because, in the sociologists' view, the psychologists seem to believe that all social phenomena can be explained in psychological terms. For example, some exchange psychologists hold that learning theory accounts for social phenomena as diverse as the use of power in a two-person relationship and the formation and change of a social institution.

Benefits and Values

According to social exchange theory, individuals enter into associations with others because of the benefits they will receive from the associations. Richard Emerson (1981) identifies the common ground shared by all the social exchange propositions. All approaches to exchange take as their primary focus the benefits that individuals receive from and contribute to social interactions with others. Three assumptions, found in all approaches, have emerged from this focus. First, people find all sorts of objects, events, and behaviors to be beneficial, and they act in ways intended to produce these benefits. Depending on the circumstances, people define money, goods, and time as beneficial. They may also benefit from praise, attention, and gestures such as winks, smiles, nods, and clapping. This assumption includes the notion that people are rational. At least some of the time, people organize their lives in a way which makes it possible for them to obtain benefits.

Second, every class of benefits, or values, conforms with a principle of satiation. The more one receives of the benefit, the less it is valued;

in time, the benefit has less value than it had when it first came into being. A two-week holiday may be as satisfying to an overworked executive at the end of the two weeks as at the beginning. But the time will come when the value of the holiday begins to diminish, whether in three weeks or in three months.

Third, we gain benefits from interacting with other people when we exchange benefits with them. Others have given us benefits; in turn, we extend benefits to them: there is an exchange. To do this, both parties need *resources.* Consider the following example:

> In the typical department store, customers surveying high-priced goods like furniture and appliances will typically be approached immediately by a salesperson. Those in the process of selecting a handkerchief or pair of socks will not be so quickly attended and, when they finally are, will be dealt with more quickly. Likewise, clients who show interest in very expensive jewelry will be served at once and at length; those who are fascinated with costume jewelry will wait. (Schwartz, 1983: 273)

A customer with enough money to buy an expensive dining room set has a compelling financial resource with which to benefit a salesperson, who first benefits the customer by immediately and exclusively serving him. Customers whose purchases or potential purchases provide little financial benefit to the salesperson hardly encourage the clerk to provide them with the benefit of quick, personal service. The salesperson sees no significant exchange of benefit in the interaction.

Emerson (1981: 35–46) notes the crucial difference between the exchange theory of microeconomics and the social exchange theory of sociology; in the latter, long-term relationships are presumed to exist among those involved in the exchange, whereas this assumption is missing in the former. Microeconomists are concerned with independent, often fleeting, transactions in the marketplace; they would be interested in a customer's purchase of furniture or a handkerchief. Social exchange theorists study enduring social relationships. In such relationships, the exchange of benefits extends over a period of months or even years. Participants remember past exchanges and whether they felt rewarded or cheated. Questions of equity and justice sometimes arise, even among friends and spouses. A friend or a spouse may feel that the benefits have been one-sided or have been unduly delayed.

Power

Social exchange theorists have an interest in the study of power. Research indicates that the use of power in the *dyad,* or two-person relationship, results in dependence. As Emerson (1981: 45) puts it, "If one person is more powerful and uses that power advantage to gain benefits, he becomes more dependent and the advantage is lost." As the more powerful person presses his or her advantages, the more dependent he or she becomes on the other person for benefits. This dependence, of course, gives the other person power. Soon the balance of power in the dyad reaches "equity."

For instance, consider the shopkeeper who occasionally asks an employee to work overtime without pay. As an employer, the shopkeeper has the power to make this request. Since the requests are infrequent, the employee is willing to work overtime. Business gets better, and there are increased demands for unremunerated overtime. The employee feels exploited. With increased sales, there should be enough money to pay for the extra hours of work. By threatening to quit, the employee persuades the shopkeeper to pay for overtime work. The threat becomes the employee's power resource. The shopkeeper becomes dependent on the employee, who is an efficient worker and available on short notice for extra work. A power-dependence relationship is established. The balance of power in this dyad has become equal.

The study of power from the perspective of social exchange theory is still chiefly a study of power as exercised between individuals (a microtheory of power). The individuals are assumed to have the freedom to choose among a variety of resources to get what they want from other people (Emerson, 1981: 59–60). Even the relationships, to a significant degree, are voluntary. If they become unpleasant, participants in the relationships can withdraw from the associations.

Thus, from the standpoint of the study of power, the social exchange framework is limited. Those who are coerced have little choice but to accept the demands of the one who holds the power. The robber who points a gun at a victim during a holdup has coercive power. Governments have the coercive power to fine and incarcerate individuals who are thought to have violated the law. Big corporations have the coercive power to get laws passed that favor their interests, sometimes over the strenuous objections of less powerful interest groups. In the shopkeeper-employee example, the balance of power would not have achieved equity had the employee no alternative but to work, knowing that he or she could find no other job.

Coercive power is the focus of much of conflict theory. Conflict theory, although it has its microtheoretic aspects, offers a macrotheory of power. It does so in conceptual terms that are different from social exchange theory.

CONFLICT THEORY

Conflict theorists study social groups from a perspective that in some ways is dramatically different from the functionalist perspective. In other ways, the two perspectives are similar. Both the functionalists (see section which follows) and the conflict theorists are predominantly macrotheorists. Both, for example, approach the study of society *holistically,* or by emphasizing the functional relation among the parts of a whole. Both approaches can be compared with the microtheories of the symbolic interactionists and the social exchange theorists, who are inclined to examine society at the level of its elementary forms and processes. Between the macroperspective and the microperspective one finds ethnomethodology. Further, all functionalists and some conflict theorists share the presupposition that societies and other groups are somehow maintained as ongoing entities for long periods of time, although they differ in how this is accomplished.

Wallace and Wolf (1980: 76) list three assumptions underlying conflict theory. First, people have interests that often conflict with those of other people in the same society. Second, some people are able to gain more power than others; they use the power to pursue their own interests. Hence, there is always inequality. Third, special interests and the use of power to achieve the interests are justified with a loose system of ideas and values, or by an *ideology.* Thus, the main analytic problems for the conflict sociologists are power, order, and interest.

Martindale (1981: Chapters 8 and 10) divides conflict theory into two categories: *conflict ideologies* and *sociological conflict theories.* The first category roots primarily in the works of Karl Marx (1818–1883) and his collaborator Friedrich Engels (1820–1905). These two men and their twentieth century followers are among the conflict ideologists who reject the premise that societies are stable and unchanging. They argue instead that there is an ideal social order which can be established only through the use of force against those who have power.

A distinctive proposition in the Marx-Engels conflict thesis is that there is a fundamental relationship between society and nature (Bottomore, 1973: 38–40). Marx and Engels studied this relationship in historical perspective along with the concept of *human labor.* In their view, society and nature mutually influence each other by means of human labor and through humankind's attempts to exploit nature for survival and for economic gains.

There are many examples of this relationship. Steel mills in eastern Canada and the United States produce steel which is used to make cars, refrigerators, warships, skyscrapers, and other useful products. But the mills also spew sulfur and nitric oxide into the atmosphere. The pollution helps produce acid rain. Acid rain has killed fish in streams and lakes (a loss to those who fish), and it has contaminated the soil on farms (a loss to farmers).

Various processes of production and distribution intervene between the consumption of finished goods and the natural resources used to make the goods. Entrepreneurs also intervene; they arrange for the means of production, that is, for machinery, factories, and labor. Marx and Engels referred to the entrepreneurs as the *bourgeoisie,* or capitalists. They identified laborers as the *proletariat.* Marx and Engels believed that, over the course of industrial history, the bourgeoisie and the proletariat would become distinct social classes, with increasingly antagonistic attitudes toward each other. The bourgeoisie would seek to produce goods for profit, whereas the proletariat would object to their exploitation by the capitalists and to their alienation from the fruits of their labor. Marx and Engels predicted that there would eventually be a proletarian revolution. With the revolution, the workers would take over the means of production.

The sociological conflict theorists charge that the conflict ideologists are biased in their approach. The conflict ideologists are actually proposing programs of action which the sociological conflict theorists insist are inappropriate in science. Furthermore, in the eyes of the sociological theorists, Marx's tendency to define the economy as the dominant institution in society (and the one controlled by the power elite) is a simplification. Modern industrial societies are complicated. The sociological conflict theorists argue that many different groups clash in the course of pursuing their interests and that few of them achieve monopolistic power for long periods of time. The clashing, they say, is always evident in society. According to the sociological theorists, there is no ideal state such as that envisaged by Marxists; there is no state from which conflict and inequality are removed. Nonetheless, societies do survive the internal storms, though they may change a great deal as a result of them.

Which of Marx's concepts do you see in this picture?

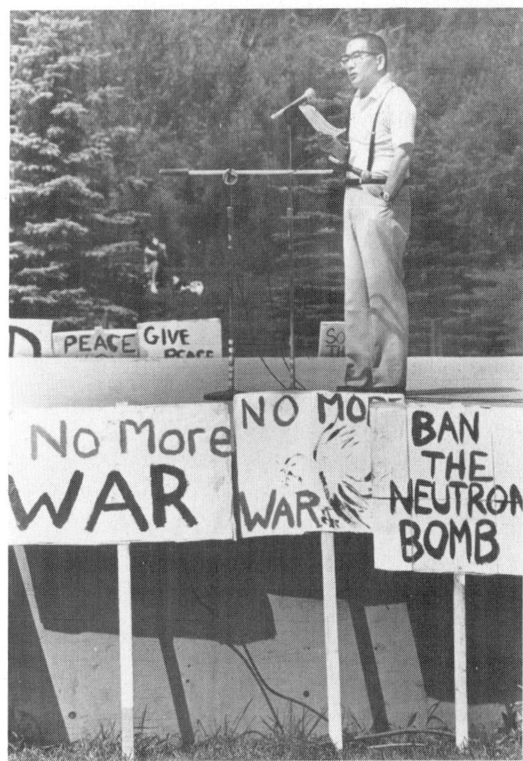

Conflicting interests are one of the foundations of modern industrial society.

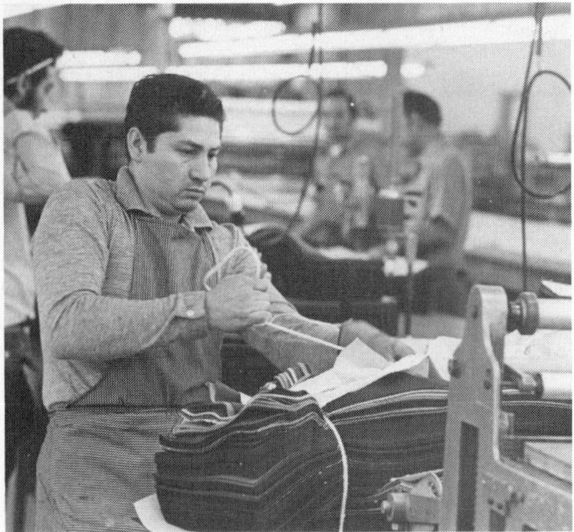

The proletariat work in manual labor occupations.

Several of today's sociological conflict theorists trace their ideas to the works of Max Weber. One of Weber's goals was to broaden the Marx-Engels thesis, which he thought was too narrow. As Weber pointed out, conflict is not confined to the economic sphere of life. Weber held that, wherever social classes form, conflict will arise over the scarcity of resources. Classes form around scarce resources such as prestige and power as well as around the Marx-Engels consideration of money and other forms of material wealth. For instance, not everyone can enjoy the prestige and power of a member of the Canadian parliament. There is hardly room in the House of Commons for everyone who would like to be an MP.

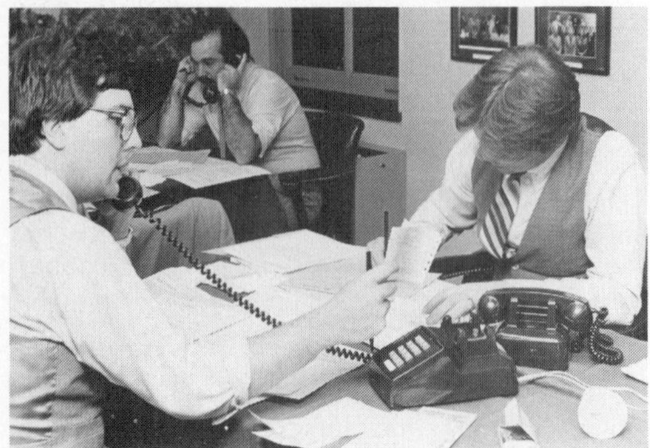

These office workers could be part of a capitalist enterprise.

Moreover, Weber observes that conflict also arises in organizations and bureaucracies. Leaders who manage the resources of a large industrial, governmental, religious, or military bureaucracy have a great deal of power; they can sometimes assert their will against the wills of other groups in the society and perhaps even outside the society (e.g., multinational corporations). Weber also studied the types of power. Bureaucratic leaders have power because those whom they lead are committed to carrying out their roles in the organization. Charismatic leaders (of, say, religious groups) have power because their followers fervently believe in the leaders' special abilities, wisdom, or visions. The followers are prepared to do what the leaders ask.

Conflict theory focuses on rivalries and struggles in society. With social conflict, according to the theorists, society is constantly in a state of change. This is one explanation of society and what it is like. Marx viewed the struggle as a conflict between classes, but sociologists of today often have a broader picture. They see conflict among many different groups and interests in society. For example, there are differences between the young and the old, between producers and consumers, and between urbanites and suburbanites. Conflict is not necessarily bad. With compromise and tolerance, it may come to benefit society.

FUNCTIONALISM

Functionalism departs from conflict theory, theoretically and in principle. Functionalists concentrate on the analytic problem of systems. They look on society as a system of interacting people and their institutions; everything is held together by a consensus on fundamental values and norms. With this theoretical outlook, functionalists study harmony, agreement, consistency, and balance in society. Their perspective contrasts with that of the conflict theorists, who are concerned with disharmony, disagreement, contradiction, and imbalance. Among many present-day sociologists the two theories are known as the *consensus model* and the *conflict model.*

Parts and Functions

The functionalist perspective is a view of the functions in a social system, that is, the functions of the system's individual parts. A *social system* is a unit consisting of interdependent parts. For example, in Canadian society, five parts of the social system are the family, the schools, the churches, the institutions of work and leisure, and the government (municipal, provincial, federal). Each part has special functions. The parts help to maintain the existence and viability of the larger entity, the system itself.

Functionalists identify and study the parts of a social system. They look for ways in which the parts help to maintain the system's structure and overall functions. Put otherwise, the parts are identified and studied in regard to the functions they fulfill, that is, with reference to their consequences; a function, it can be said, is a consequence, or the result of system operation. Sociologists are more interested in the actual consequences of a given element in a social system than in what its purposes are believed to be.

It could be assumed that one purpose of a family is to provide a home for its members. But the consequences of the family's actions are of more significance to the sociologist than the supposed purposes. For example, one consequence of family action is the children's acceptance and understanding of social values. The family imparts values to the children. The care of the young and the elderly is another function of the family. Still another function, or consequence, is sex regulation. By functioning as it does, a family helps to maintain the social system.

Equilibrium

When a system and its boundaries are maintained, it is hypothesized that the system will be consistent and stable. Talcott Parsons (1902–1979) of Harvard University was a preeminent source of functionalist ideas. He modeled his functional theory along the lines of the science of mechanics, referring to the parts of a social system as *mechanisms,* or mechanical operations. According to Parsons (1951), the operations give to the system its *equilibrium,* or balance. A system in equilibrium is stable, because there is a state of balance or adjustment among opposing forces. Functionalists believe that a society usually is in equilibrium. Equilibrium is the normal state.

Equilibrium presupposes a certain level of *integration,* or meshing of parts. Since people are the vehicles by which the parts (social roles, behavior patterns, etc.) are integrated, there must be a minimal *value consensus,* or agreement, among the individuals on the form integration should take. For instance, when faced with conflict between work and leisure, Canadians generally agree that work-role requirements must take precedence over leisure-role requirements.

Dysfunctions

Robert K. Merton was a student of Parsons. His (Merton, 1957b: 51) theory of functional analysis recognizes *dysfunctions* in social systems. Dysfunctions are disruptive and abnormal, resulting in impairment of a social system's equilibrium. A robber's holdup of a bank, for example, is dysfunctional for two systems: the bank and its customers, and society. The holdup threatens the safety and savings of individuals and contravenes society's moral code. As Merton points out, parts of the social system may be functional at times and dysfunctional at other times. For example, a power plant is a functional supplier of electricity, but its pollution of the atmosphere is dysfunctional for society.

Merton recognizes both manifest functions and latent functions. A *manifest function* is the intended function of a social element; it is the function which the institution or social arrangement obviously fulfills. For example, a manifest function of the Toronto Stock Exchange is to provide for the buying and selling of securities. A latent function of the exchange is to indicate how the nation's economy is faring. A *latent function* is a function which is unintended. For the most part, it is also an unrecognized function.

As we have noted, the holdup and robbery of a bank is dysfunctional. But Erikson (1981) points out that criminal acts are also functional. He explains how they reinforce the authority of the violated norms, thereby helping to locate the boundaries, or limits and restrictions, of the society. A glance at the headlines in a newspaper gives you an idea of the great interest which bank robberies and other crimes hold for many people. Erikson sees such acts as "entertaining." Finally, gun-wielding bank robbers remind us of the dangers lying outside institutionalized society and the forms these dangers can take. In sum, the functions and dysfunctions of the parts of a social system interact to produce an overall equilibrium.

All the parts of a social system have their functional and dysfunctional consequences. Additionally, some parts are *requisites:* they are the generalized conditions necessary for the development and maintenance of the social system (Levy, 1952: 62). A division of labor into roles is a necessary part of every social system. Further, every society needs a system of shared symbols of communication. Imagine for a moment what life would be like were there no language. Levy argued that, for a social system to take root and grow, emotional expression must also be regulated. In particular, certain negative emotions such as hate and anger must be discouraged, and certain positive emotions such as love must be encouraged.

The concepts of function, equilibrium, and system maintenance, which are central to functionalist theory, are based on two controversial assumptions: that of *self-regulation* and that of *goal-directedness* (Mennell, 1980: 64). Functionalists believe that social systems sustain themselves, even in the face of internal and external threats (e.g., crime, war). They also believe that the members of a social system and hence the abstract system itself strive to maintain the existence of the system. Conflict theorists contend that there are many occasions in social life where these assumptions are violated.

AN AMERICAN DISCIPLINE?

By now you may have the impression that sociology is chiefly an American discipline. Indeed, only four non-American theorists were cited in this chapter: Marx, Engels, Weber, and Schutz. And Schutz spent a significant part of his intellectual life in the United States. In one sense, the impression that sociology is especially American is correct; the United States is and always has been a world center of the discipline. Still, it should also be clear from reading this chapter and the preceding chapter that nearly all of the important nineteenth century sociologists were Europeans. In the main, the discipline got its start in France and Germany. Auguste Comte (1798–1857), a French social philosopher and social scientist, coined the word "sociology" in 1838. Had not two world wars devastated intellectual life in Europe, sociology might have developed there at the pace at which it developed in the United States from about 1890 to the present.

Since this book introduces sociology by comparing Canadian and American social life, a word is in order about sociology in general and about sociological theory in particular in Canada. Is it valid to conclude from the absence of any mention of Canadian theorists in this chapter that Canadian sociologists have been content to let others set theoretical paces for them? In general, the answer to this question is, "Yes." Sociology in Canada has been largely an application of the five theoretical perspectives to Ca-

"Binary Fission" in the History of Sociology

Seeded in Western Europe in the first half of the nineteenth century, sociology lay in a territory that did not know what to do with the new discipline. Sociology did not find its first supporting environment or first achieve successful institutionalization in Western Europe. Its most fertile ground was in time found elsewhere in the East and West. Sociology achieved successful embodiment in supporting establishments only after it underwent a kind of "binary fission," only after the two parts into which it became differentiated found different strata and different nations to sponsor it. One part of sociology, "Marxism," moved eastward and became at length, after World War I, the official social science of the then new Soviet Union. The other part, which I will call "Academic Sociology," moved westward and came to a different kind of fruition within American culture. Both are different sides of Western sociology.

The diffusion of sociology in each direction was carried by a different social stratum. Marxism was borne by unattached intelligentsia, by political groups and parties oriented to lower strata groups who were in rebellion against an emerging bourgeois society that excluded them. Academic Sociology was developed in the United States by university academicians who were oriented to the established middle class, and who sought pragmatically to reform rather than systematically to rebel against the status quo. Both, however, were early linked with social movements, in particular to what Anthony Wallace has called movements of "cultural revitalization." Each embodied a different conception of how the established order around it was failing and needed revision, and each had its own vision of a *new* social order.

After World War I, American sociology found itself becoming entrenched at the University of Chicago, in a metropolitan environment in which industrialism had burgeoned and was proliferating problems. It conceived of these as the problems of "urban communities." That is, they were viewed as due to the vast size and anonymity of urban communities, which were taken to be essentially alike, rather than as varying with the economy, the class system, or the property institutions of the particular city.

Marxism, on the other hand, took root in parts of Europe where industrialization had been slow and relatively retarded. When the Leninist version of Marxism seized power in Russia, its task was to accelerate and to consolidate industrialization. Marxism had defined European problems as essentially due to "capitalism," that is, to the perpetuation of an archaic class system and of property institutions that were seen as, at some point, impeding industrial development.

SOURCE: Alvin W. Gouldner. *The coming crisis of Western sociology,* pp. 20–21. New York, Avon Books, 1970.

dian social life. It is evident throughout this book that research in Canada has uncovered some striking differences and similarities when compared with similar research in the United States.

Nevertheless, it would be an unfortunate misrepresentation to allow the impression to stand that Canadians have contributed nothing to sociological theory. Consider the variant of conflict theory known as *political economy,* which is broadly defined as the study of the laws and relations of capitalist development, either critically from the Marxist perspective or traditionally from the liberal perspective (Chattopadhyay, 1974). As is the case with conflict theory in general, political economy has European roots. But it is the modern Canadian version that is receiving attention in the United States, demonstrating, in principle, that the flow of theoretical ideas between the two countries is not entirely one-sided. Since only the central tenets of the main sociological theories can be explained in this chapter, their application to specific areas of social life is undertaken in various sections of this book. Accordingly, political economy is explained in Chapter 13, "Economy."

OUTLINE AND SUMMARY

You can review Chapter 2, "Sociological Theories," by going over the following outline and summary:

I. Introduction
Five theoretical perspectives of sociology are *functionalism, ethnomethodology, conflict theory, symbolic interactionism,* and *social exchange theory.*

II. Symbolic Interactionism
The *symbolic interactionist perspective* focuses on human activities in society. Individuals interpret social interaction through an understanding of symbols (language, gestures, sounds). The interactionist approach enables sociologists to gain an understanding of the social order and of society itself.

A. The Individual and Society
There is a reciprocity between individuals and society. Human beings organize social and physical life according to enumerable *categories,* or classes of objects and living things symbolized by language. Many categories are combined with roles, which, in turn, are associated with social statuses.

B. The Micro-Order
The interactionist perspective is concerned largely with the *micro-order,* or the numerous day-to-day activities in society.

III. Ethnomethodology
Ethnomethodology is a study of how people gain an understanding of their everyday interactions with others. It is a study of the methods people use to interpret interactions and to understand the world in which they live. Ethnomethodological research seeks to discover the assumptions people make as they encounter and react with other people, things, and events in their routine lives. The perspective centers on the analytic problem of knowledge.

A. Schutz's Phenomenology
Phenomenologists hold, among other ideas, that we should concern ourselves only with that which is directly comprehended by the senses. Commonsense reasoning proceeds from a stock of knowledge.

B. Goffman's Frame
Goffman's *frame:* the hidden sets of rules and categories that are part of our cultural heritage. The rules and categories are deeply ingrained; they go largely unrecognized. We behave according to hidden rules.

IV. Social Exchange Theory
Several versions of the social exchange perspective have sprung up in economics, anthropology, psychology, and sociology.

A. Benefits and Values
According to social exchange theory, individuals enter into association with others because of the gains and benefits they will receive from the associ-

ation. Individuals in an association contribute benefits to each other. There is an exchange.

B. Power
The use of power in the dyad results in dependence. As the more powerful person exercises his or her advantages, the more dependent he or she becomes on the other person for benefits. Power is exercised between individuals.

V. Conflict Theory
Three assumptions underlie conflict theory: (1) people have interests that often conflict with the interests of others; (2) some people are able to gain more power than others; (3) special interests and the use of power to achieve them are justified through the use of ideologies.

VI. Functionalism
Functionalism is the theoretical opposition to conflict theory. The functionalist perspective is known as the *consensus model.* The conflict perspective is referred to as the *conflict model.*

A. Parts and Functions
The functionalist perspective is a view of a social system's individual parts. Functionalists identify and study the parts in regard to the functions they fulfill. They look for ways in which the parts help to maintain the system's structure and overall function.

B. Equilibrium
The parts and their functions give a social system equilibrium, or balance. There is a level of *integration,* or meshing of parts. Functionalists believe that a society usually is in equilibrium. Equilibrium is the normal state.

C. Dysfunctions
There are *dysfunctions,* or disruptions, in social equilibrium. Parts of the social system may be functional at times and dysfunctional at other times. There are *manifest functions* and *latent functions.*

VII. An American Discipline?
Nearly all of the important nineteenth century sociologists were Europeans. But the United States is and always has been a world center of the discipline. Canadians also have made contributions to social theory.

FOR FURTHER READING AND STUDY

Abrahamson, M. 1981. *Sociological theory: An introduction to concepts, issues, and research.* Englewood Cliffs, NJ: Prentice-Hall. Each chapter in this book is built around a major sociological concept, such as sex roles, deviance, and social change. Abrahamson presents a clear and interesting account of theory and research for each concept.

Collins, R. 1975. *Conflict sociology: Toward an explanatory science.* New York: Academic Press. Collins views society as made up of competing groups whose resources give them greater or lesser power in the struggle to realize their interests.

Collins, R. and Makowsky, M. 1978. *The discovery of society,* 2nd ed. New York: Random House. This book offers a history of the development of world sociological thought, starting with nineteenth century nationalism.

Georgopoulos, N., Fischer, N., and Patsouras, L., eds. 1982. *Continuity and change in Marxism.* Atlantic Highlands, NJ: Humanities Press. This anthology examines the connection between original Marxism and the twentieth century proponents of Marxist thought, including Marcuse, Habermas, Sartre, Lenin, and Gramsci.

Hiller, H. H. 1982. *Society and change: S. D. Clark and the development of Canadian sociology.* Toronto: University of Toronto Press. Chapter 1 contains a general history of the rise of sociology in Canada. The remainder of the book traces the role of Clark, a prominent sociologist, in developing the discipline of sociology in Canada.

Morris, M. B. 1977. *An excursion into creative sociology.* New York: Columbia University Press. A "demystified" introduction to the creative sociologies of ethnomethodology and symbolic interactionism and their phenomenological and existentialist backgrounds. Morris examines the familiar and the ordinary, which we take for granted and consider unproblematic.

Turner, J. H. and Maryanski, A. 1979. *Functionalism.* Menlo Park, CA: Benjamin/Cummings.

This book traces the history of the rise of functionalism out of organicism. After describing contemporary functionalist theory, the authors present a critique of it and speculate about its future in sociology.

KEY WORDS

attribute An inherent characteristic or quality.

conflict perspective A view of society which looks on conflict as an element of social life and as a cause of social change.

dysfunction A disruption in the social equilibrium; it lessens the adjustment of a system.

equilibrium A balance among the various elements in a social system; it is recognized by the functionalist theory.

ethnomethodology The study of how people define reality as they experience interactions from day to day.

exchange theory The idea that people control one another's behavior by exchanging rewards and punishments; with this exchange, they express approval or disapproval of another's behavior.

function A part of a social system that helps maintain the system.

functionalism A theoretical perspective which considers the relationships between the functions of a social system's various parts.

functionalist perspective A view of society which considers the relationships between the functions of a social system's various parts.

holistically With emphasis on the functional relation among parts and wholes.

ideology A loose system of ideas and values that are used to justify the use of power to achieve special interests.

integration A meshing of parts.

interactionist perspective A view of society which considers the interaction among people as they respond to symbols such as language, signs, and gestures.

latent function A function not necessarily intended.

macro-order The large-scale processes and structures in society.

manifest function The intended function of a social element.

mechanism The mechanical or machinelike operation of a part of a social system.

micro-order The numerous day-to-day activities in society.

social system A unit consisting of interdependent parts.

symbolic interactionism A theoretical perspective which considers the interaction among people as they respond to symbols such as language, signs, and gestures.

theoretical perspective A view of society and social behavior which provides for an assumption based on a theory.

theory A logically interrelated set of propositions.

value consensus An agreement among individuals on the form integration should take.

chapter 3

Studying Social Life

CHAPTER OUTLINE

INTRODUCTION

Sociologists, in their study of social life, have their own way of working and their own means of assessing data. Like other scientists, they make use of basic research *techniques,* or methods, but their procedures relate directly to a study of society, not to a particular event or condition in the environment. To some extent, the sociologist's methods set the discipline apart from the natural sciences and from the other social sciences. Sociology deals with analytic problems which are of no concern to a chemist or an economist.

In studying a group of people, sociologists must first gain an understanding of their social actions. Sociologists must have some understanding of the people's actions before they can gather data and draw conclusions about the consequences of the actions in the wider social world of groups, organizations, communities, and society. Acquiring an understanding of these actions is known as *exploration.* Some techniques in sociology are suited for this purpose and others are suited for *confirmation,* or testing hypotheses. The hypotheses are predictions about the social actions and the consequences of the actions of groups and communities that are derived from the preliminary understanding. There is a continuous progression from exploration to confirmation as sociologists come to know more about the social actions of those under study. In this fashion, sociologists accumulate a body of knowledge about the many consequences of social actions in the social world. In short, sociologists develop a science.

SCIENCE

Science is both a process (including the technique of data collection) and a product, which is to say that it is both a procedure for acquiring information and a body of knowledge gained from the use of this procedure. In broad terms, the scientific procedure, or *scientific method,* has five steps. The general direction of these steps is from exploration to confirmation.

(1) A research problem is identified. Some phenomenon, process, thing, or set of events is defined as needing systematic investigation. Questions are asked. (2) Careful exploratory observation of the object of study and related matters is then undertaken. Such observation is *empirical,* meaning that it relies on direct sense experience. (3) The data collected by means of observation enable the scientist to develop *hypotheses,* or tentative generalizations about the object of study. (4) These hypotheses are then tested in controlled studies; the studies are expressly designed for confirmatory purposes. (5)

Today empirical observation is often done with the aid of electronic equipment.

If the hypotheses are repeatedly confirmed in several such tests, they then become established generalizations. If they are not confirmed, the hypotheses may be discarded or modified, or new testing techniques may be tried.

SOCIOLOGY OR COMMON SENSE

What do you think?

Which of the following statements do you agree with? Which statements do you disagree with? Make a note of your answers. Check your answers when you have completed your study of this chapter. Are your answers to the statements the same as those a sociologist would give?

1. Since society cannot be studied scientifically, sociology is really not a science.
2. Scientists never make observations when they do experiments.
3. Science and technology are the same thing.
4. The sociologist's scale is a device for measuring weight.
5. The questionnaire survey is the sociologist's stock-in-trade.

Scientific laws are a product of the scientific process, or the scientific method. They are also part of the body of knowledge called *science.* Established generalizations, when combined with hypotheses to form a set of logically interrelated propositions or generalizations, constitute a theory. A theory explains a phenomenon or event. For example, the *theory of evolution* explains the development of living things over a period of many thousands of years. As we noted in the preceding chapter, a theory also relates to one or more analytic problems.

Technology

Technology is the application of scientific knowledge to the solution of practical problems (not research problems). It is applied science. It is a means of providing devices and advantages for human sustenance and convenience. An engineer who uses certain theories from physics to design a bridge is, strictly speaking, a technologist. As a technologist, he or she is an applied scientist rather than a pure scientist or research scientist. Although science and technology are not the same thing, they are closely related. Each serves as a source of new ideas for the other.

A scientific law: The meaning of objects is found in their use.

To some extent, technology is now looked upon as a social problem. Environmentalists feel that technology is largely responsible for the pollution of the atmosphere and the water in lakes and streams. For example, a coal-fired electric power plant releases sulfur dioxide into the atmosphere. Industries dump harmful wastes into lakes and streams. Many social scientists believe that society has become dependent on technology, with some loss in human dignity. As they see it, technology has replaced values which at one time added a great deal to society and to human life.

As an Institution

Science is a part of culture. It is one of the institutions in industrial society. *Institutions* are defined as sets of norms regulating human action in ways consistent with the means of achieving societal goals (see Chapter 9, "Society and Culture"). Ben-David (1984: 104–105) describes some of the science norms. One is the expectation that scientists are universalistic in their evaluation of scientific contributions. They must hold their own opinions in abeyance (i.e., be objective) when interpreting their own data and those of someone else. Another norm requires scientists to communicate their findings to the public for its use and criticism. Science is public property. A third states that there must be proper acknowledgment of the contributions of other scientists. Plagiarism is as unwelcome in science as it is elsewhere.

The science institution is made up of several organizational subdivisions. For example, the laboratories in industry, government, and universities are a part of science—a part of the institution, that is. Independent research institutes are contributing organizations. Associations, societies, and academic departments play a role along with the publishers of books and journals. Funding agencies cannot be overlooked. Together, the subdivisions make the institution of science what it is, an effort to learn about the world and to accumulate knowledge.

The work careers of individual scientists unfold within this organizational shell. Ben-David and Sullivan (1975: 211–212) note that "it is difficult to maintain organizations, or even careers, devoted to full-time research." Universities come close to the ideal objective (ideal from the standpoint of many scientists). But in universities teaching and administration demands take professors away from what many of them regard as their primary interest, which is research.

Like their associates in the other social sciences and in the physical sciences (physics, chemistry, biology, geology, astronomy), sociologists strive to uncover a reliable body of knowledge. They make discoveries and test their findings by means of the scientific method. All this is accomplished with exploration and confirmation.

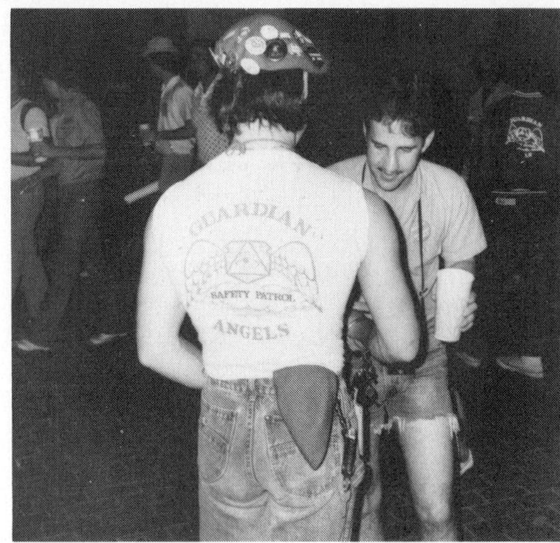

The Guardian Angels are a scientifically uncharted area of social life.

EXPLORATION AND CONFIRMATION

For some sociologists, the fascination with their profession lies in the uncharted areas of social life which call for new empirical generalizations, new hypotheses, and new theories. Despite the great volume of research done across an extremely wide range of topics, there remains a vast region of unexplored social phenomena beckoning the social scientist with a bent for pioneering. For example, there are established occupations that have received little or no sociological attention. Sociologists have yet to learn about some of the new religions, forms of leisure, recent immigrants, and popular social movements. What about popular culture and current fads and fashions?

Some of these interests and conditions are new. It is the nature of our social life to adopt or invent new traditions while sloughing off the old ones. But many old traditions persist. Sociologists have yet to explore occupations such as the work of the architect, the stockbroker, and the plumber. They have much to learn about the social aspects of trout fishing, stamp collecting, and amateur entomology. What could the sociologist discover from bumper stickers and the graffiti on a wall? What can be learned from sports magazines and radio talk shows?

Although contemporary research in sociology is largely confirmatory, exploration continues to be an important activity and one requiring its own peculiar approaches to data collection. Two of these approaches are explained by the terms "open-mindedness" and "flexibility." At the point of selecting an unexplored area of social life for study, the sociologist is said to have an *open mind.* Barney Glaser (1978: 2–3) explains:

> Enter the research setting with as few predetermined ideas as possible—especially logically deducted priori hypotheses. In this posture, the analyst is able to remain sensitive to the data by being able to record events and detect happenings without first having them filtered through and squared with preexisting hypotheses and biases. His mandate is to remain open to what is actually happening.

In fact, the sociologist may have neither an idea about the important questions in the unexplored area nor an answer to the questions.[1] This situation calls for *flexibility,* or for a flexible *research design* (the plan for collecting data), a design allowing for as many new facts and ideas as possible to come to the sociologist's attention. Generally, the researcher tries to learn about everything of significance in the lifestyle of the people whose social world is under scrutiny.

Grounded Theory

An exploratory study produces grounded theory. A *grounded theory* is an interrelated set of hypothetical propositions or generalizations constructed from systematically collected data (Glaser and Strauss, 1967). In other words, these propositions are not deduced from existing theory. Instead, the newly collected data provide the grounds for producing a theory. The propositions are generalizations developed from observations of social life, interviews with people, recorded life histories, and other efforts. In a section which follows, we shall refer to some of the more common methods used in exploratory studies to collect the data from which grounded theory emerges. At this point, it is important to remember that the formulation of a theory about an aspect of social life, whether elicited from one research project or several, is only the beginning of the *research process,* albeit a significant beginning.

Grounded theory is a mere beginning because it is untested and unconfirmed. Although it would be a helpful convenience, it is logically impossible to generate a theory and test the theory simultaneously. This is true because exploration demands an open mind and flexibility, whereas confirmation depends on two opposite approaches: *prediction* and *control.* Once a theory emerges, the sociologist begins to test some of the hypothetical propositions of the theory.[2] The hypotheses are tested on subjects (not the subjects studied earlier) participating in a segment of social life the same as or similar to the segment from which the theory originally emerged.

Confirmation

It is expected that these hypotheses will be verified. But meticulous testing of them, especially when done in an area of life adjacent to the one in which the hypotheses emerged, can lead to surprises. For example, one surprise may be the discovery of theoretical inconsistencies or of gaps in the data collected during exploration. There may be conceptual vagueness. These gaps, inconsistencies, and vaguenesses are most easily identified when the collection of research data is controlled, or when controls are used. A *control* is a procedure which allows for verification and comparison.

By means of controls, a group of subjects is studied along with two or three (perhaps even more) other groups. The groups are studied in parallel. The experiences and circumstances of the groups differ. By comparing the differences, sociologists can test hypotheses. In experimental research, the first group of subjects is referred to as the "experimental group" and the parallel groups as "control groups." All important differences between the experimental group and control groups are controlled except for the one being tested by the investigator. The methods used in confirmation are generally different from those used in exploration. Confirmation focuses the inquiry, whereas exploration diffuses the inquiry.

[1]Sociologists, though they lack scientific knowledge of the area of social life to be explored, may still have their own commonsense, even stereotyped, views of it. Because this personal stock of knowledge (see Chapter 1) is likely to be slanted, it is to be watched carefully for its influence on data collection and analysis.

[2]The most effective exploration and generation of grounded theory is done in one or more studies conducted separately from and prior to confirmation. Still, there are occasional attempts to combine these two stages of the scientific process as separate phases of the same project.

The testing with experimental groups and control groups goes on for many years. A theory is confirmed with precision and conceptual clarity. During this time, some researchers (usually newcomers to the investigation) may temporarily revert to exploration; they are dealing with changes in the social life under study or with deficiencies in the initial grounded theory. When this occurs, the investigators invoke again the open mind and flexibility approaches, which, as we have seen, come into play in exploratory data collection.

THE METHODS OF EXPLORATION

There are many methods available to a sociologist who wants to carry out an exploratory investigation. The four explained here are sometimes used in confirmation, but they are particularly well suited for exploration and for discovering new phenomena in the social world. These methods are *participant observation, unstructured interviewing, content analysis,* and *nonreactive measures.* The first two are perhaps the most widely used in exploration. They are a part of nearly all *fieldwork,* or field research. In fieldwork, groups of people are studied in their natural setting (without design controls), rather than in a contrived setting such as a laboratory (with design controls).

Participant Observation

Participant observation refers to the systematic, or carefully planned, watching of the social activities of a group or aggregate of individuals. At minimum, observers "participate" by being present in the everyday situations of their *subjects,* or those whom they are observing. Some participant observers develop an understanding of the group's life-style or the aggregate's activity by actually engaging in some part of the life-style or activity.

Sometimes the subjects are aware of the fieldworker's identity and research interests. In other instances, they are unaware of the observer's participation; the researcher does not identify himself or herself as a sociologist. In the latter situation, fieldworkers are accepted, purely and simply, as part of the group or aggregate they are observing. The aim of participant observation is to describe the routine social actions of the subjects and to use the description (called *ethnography*) as the foundation for formulating a grounded theory which explains one or more aspects of the life-style or activity.

One of the most celebrated participant observation studies in sociology is William Foote Whyte's fieldwork in a Boston slum, an Italian neighborhood. Whyte spent three and a half years in the community, boarding for a while with an Italian family. He learned the language. As a participant in the slum dwellers' daily activities, Whyte became familiar with their life-style and social attitudes. He was accepted as one of the group.

Whyte spent a great deal of time with the "corner boys" and the "college boys," two groups of young Italians. The young men in both groups hung out nightly on certain street corners, whiling away their time with little purpose or forethought. Through his close association with the youths, Whyte learned that each individual had his own group position. A youth's position remained unchanged for years. Moreover, the statuses were found to be interdependent, with the adjustments of one member forcing reciprocal adjustments by the others (see the discussion of systems, pages 26–28).

With each passing day, Whyte added to his field notes. The field notes told of the behavior and attitudes of the Italians with whom he lived, many of whom were immigrants from Italy. The notes provided information for Whyte's book, *Street Corner Society* (1981). Whyte's work (which was first published in 1943) became part of the theoretical foundation on which present-day small group research is based. Small group research now is conducted chiefly at the confirmatory stage.

The Scientific Method in Sociology and the Physical Sciences

Sociology is not a subject that comes neatly gift-wrapped, making no demands except that its contents be unpacked. Like all the social sciences—under which label one can also include, among other disciplines, anthropology, economics, and history—sociology is an inherently controversial endeavour. That is to say, it is characterised by continuing disputes about its very nature. But this is not a weakness, although it has seemed such to many of those who call themselves professional 'sociologists', and also to many others on the outside, who are distressed that there are numerous vying conceptions of how the subject-matter of sociology should be approached or analysed. Those who are upset by the persistent character of sociological debates, and a frequent lack of consensus about how to resolve them, usually feel that this is a sign of the immaturity of the subject. They want sociology to be like a natural science, and to generate a similar apparatus of universal laws to those which they see natural science as having discovered and validated. . . . It is a mistake to suppose that sociology should be modelled too closely on the natural sciences, or to imagine that a natural science of society is either feasible or desirable. To say this, I should emphasise, does not mean that the methods and objectives of the natural sciences are wholly irrelevant to the study of human social behaviour. Sociology deals with a factually observable subject-matter, depends upon empirical research, and involves attempts to formulate theories and generalisations that will make sense of facts. But human beings are not the same as material objects in nature; studying our own behaviour is necessarily entirely different in some very important ways from studying natural phenomena.

SOURCE: Anthony Giddens. *Sociology: A brief but critical introduction,* pp. 3–4. New York: Harcourt Brace Jovanovich, 1982.

Unstructured Interviewing

Unstructured interviewing often accompanies participant observation. This method is distinguished from the researcher's informal questioning of subjects. In unstructured interviewing, the sociologist uses an *interview guide,* from which he or she formally asks the subjects to comment on several topics. Subjects respond to the open-ended questions as they see fit. There is no restrictive set of prearranged answers. In other words, subject's responses are "unstructured." A section of the interview guide used by the author in a study of amateur magicians is reproduced in Figure 3.1.

Such a procedure is clearly flexible, allowing for the free expression of ideas by the subjects within the broad confines of the topical questions. Researchers usually have considerable experience with or knowledge about the social life of their subjects. Otherwise, it would be difficult to conduct an effective interview. A knowledge of the subjects' social life makes it possible to select topics which are pertinent and appropriate.

Whether unstructured interviewing is needed

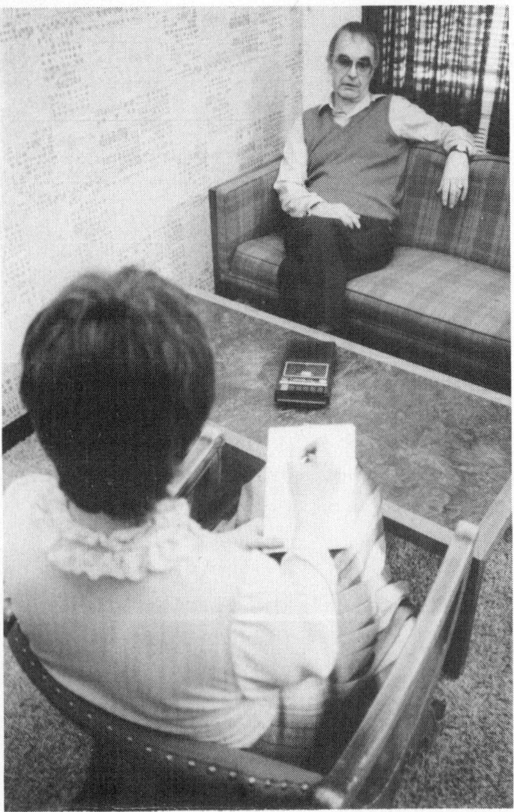

The unstructured interview is an important research method in sociology.

in a research project depends on the kind of information the sociologist seeks. Although research interests such as opinions, attitudes, values, beliefs, and interpretations can be inferred from actions to some extent, unstructured interviews can help identify, clarify, and amplify these feelings and impressions. Furthermore, biographies, case histories, and oral histories can be obtained only with the unstructured interview. This technique also is helpful in obtaining information about careers and in documenting accounts of unrecorded past events.

By using an unstructured interview guide supplemented by several structured questionnaire items (i.e., questions), Schlesinger (1976) carried out a study of remarriage as a solution to the family disorganization brought on by divorce. He sampled ninety-six remarried couples living in metropolitan Toronto. The husband and wife of each were interviewed separately by two interviewers. Schlesinger learned that earlier family disorganization is redressed by seeking personal qualities in the new partner unavailable in the first husband or wife.

All but two respondents, one male and one female, looked for the following qualities in their new husband or wife: higher intelligence, greater emotional maturity, greater sense of responsibility, deeper sense of affection and understanding, more similarity in values and interests, and more integrity and self-respect. Respondents said they were more cautious the second time around, hoping to make the new marriage a success.

Content Analysis

Sociologists often use content analysis to find out about the ideas and social attitudes which are prominent in society. *Content analysis* is an analysis of written, audio, or visual material —a newspaper, a journal, a motion picture, or a tape recording, for example. It is the identification and quantification of the underlying themes and symbols found in novels, speeches, films, songs, propaganda, paintings, photographs, magazine articles, newspaper stories, and papers in science journals. A content analysis is often used when the full meaning of whatever is being read (a novel, a monograph, a newspaper story) is not readily apparent. This technique can also be used on recorded communication (a tape or a record) to determine its meaning.

Mullins and Kopelman (1984) used content analysis to measure the increase in societal narcissism in the United States between 1950 and 1979. They analyzed the top ten best-selling books of each year during that period as indicators of narcissism. Societal narcissism is a preoccupation with personal life-style and with self-expression and self-fulfillment. Their analysis demonstrated that, as measured by the content

Figure 3.1 INTERVIEW GUIDE

Study of Amateur Magicians
II Career

A. Can you recall when you first became interested in magic? (If yes) Please describe the circumstances (your age, the place, with whom, etc.).
B. How did you continue your initial interest? (read books, watch live or televised performances, lectures, associate with magicians, join a club, etc.)
   1. Were any of your friends (neighborhood or school) or relatives in magic during your early years?
   2. Did anybody encourage you toward pursuing magic as a hobby or even an occupation?
   3. Did your parents encourage or discourage your magic interests?
C. When was your first public (paid or gratis) show? Where did it take place? For what function? How old were you? What was the fee if any?
   1. How did you get it?
   2. Was it a success or failure?
D. Would you say that you have had any thrills in magic (experiences that you defined at the time as exceptionally rewarding)?
E. Have you had any disappointments in magic (something more than the routine frustrations)?
F. Have you ever considered becoming a professional?
G. Has your involvement in magic ever been greater than currently?
   1. (If yes) Why did you reduce it?
   2. Have you ever quit magic temporarily?
H. Do you plan to continue at your present level of involvement or increase your involvement in the future?

of the books, it had increased steadily and markedly over the thirty years under consideration.

Nonreactive Measures

Nonreactive measures are defined by Webb et al. (1981) as those indicators of human behavior that the alert researcher can observe without disturbing the behaving persons. These measures are found in a great variety of places, some of which are also the domain of participant observation (when the observer's presence is unknown) and content analysis. For instance, people leave physical traces which tell us about their values, attitudes, sentiments, habits, and norms, as in the scrawling of graffiti. They also leave evidence of "erosion," as in estimating the rate of shoe wear to infer the level of children's activity. Archives are another nonreactive gold mine of sociological data. Within the archives are sources such as actuarial records, city budgets, and government vital statistics. Tombstones often reveal surprising facts. Nonreactive sources are ordinarily produced for practical reasons rather than for scholarly purposes.

Webb and his colleagues (1981: Chapter 8) note how modern technology, much of which is electronic, has aided the researcher in unobtrusively measuring social action. Researchers have found tape recorders and video recorders particularly helpful. For example, James F. Bryan used the tape recordings of his interviews with prostitutes not only to keep a record of their answers to his questions but also to monitor the number of phone calls they received during the interviews (reported in Webb et al., 1981: 243). This information provided a partial check on the amount of business activity claimed by each respondent.

Occasionally, nonreactive research takes on the characteristics of participant observation, although it is neither as representative nor as systematic in scope. John Howard Griffin (1977) offers a daring example. In late 1959, by means of ultraviolet rays and special medications, he transformed himself from a white man to a black man. For a month, Griffin passed as a black man in the American South. During this time, he gained direct experience with the malice of whites toward blacks. He observed the warm camaraderie of the blacks' social world, a fellowship which is the blacks' main refuge from white hostility.

METHODS USED IN CONFIRMATION

We turn now to three methods used in confirmation: *questionnaire surveys, structured interviewing,* and *controlled observation.* Although these techniques are also used in the "field"—that is, outside the laboratory—they are poorly designed for exploring the scientifically uncharted areas of social life. They are not usually classified as fieldwork techniques.

Questionnaire Surveys

Nearly all research sociologists regard the questionnaire survey as their stock-in-trade. For several decades, there has been a worldwide trend in sociology toward *quantitative research*—toward research, that is, which gathers data obtained by enumeration or measurement. The questionnaire survey effectively provides such data, making the survey the most common sociological method currently in use at the confirmatory stage of the scientific process. In harmony with this trend is the author's finding that nearly 59 percent (10 of 17) of all research articles published in 1984 in the *Canadian Review of Sociology and Anthropology* were based on evidence gathered by survey techniques.

The questionnaire survey as a means of collecting data is so common, both in sociology and in other disciplines, that few readers of this book are likely to escape completing at least one surveylike form in their lifetime (e.g., an opinion poll, an attitude survey). The typical survey instrument is composed of various questions or *items,* each of which is accompanied by a set of closed or structured responses. The overall survey resembles a multiple-choice examination, except that the number of structured responses to a given question may run from two to twenty or more. In sociology, the questionnaire is ordinarily used to gather data for confirming hypotheses, which are conceived (possibly as grounded theory) prior to the preparation of the questionnaire. The hypotheses serve as a guide for the contruction of the questionnaire. The use of hypotheses and questionnaires to test them demonstrates how the approaches of prediction and control are realized in this mode of sociological research.

The mailed survey and the telephone survey are possibly the most commonly used research techniques in sociology. For both, respondents are usually selectedly randomly. When samples of respondents are drawn randomly, each respondent has had an equal chance of being selected to participate in the study. Those in the mailed survey receive the form in the mail. They are asked to fill in the form and return it to a specified central location. The telephone survey has been evolving in recent years into a "yes" or "no" type of verbally administered questionnaire, thereby eliminating the necessity for conducting a structured interview (see next section) over the phone (Sudman, 1976: 112). Mail and telephone survey data may be obtained for one purpose and subsequently analyzed for another purpose by someone other than the original investigator. Survey data gathered by national census agencies, opinion research centers, government offices, and university research institutes are often reanalyzed sociologically.

Mary Maxwell and James Maxwell (1984) conducted a longitudinal survey of two private girls' schools in Canada. To determine how the students' occupational choices changed over the years, questionnaires were administered in 1966 and 1976 to girls in grades 9 and 12. The differences in occupational choices between 1966 and 1976 indicated that girls (at least the privileged ones in these schools) can plan to enter a significantly wider range of occupations in 1976 than they could in 1966. The girls surveyed in 1976 did not see themselves barred from their chosen work by sex segregation to the degree that their counterparts did ten years earlier.

Structured Interviewing

The structured interview puts interviewer and respondent in face-to-face contact. In the standard interview, the interviewer reads a question to the person being interviewed. The individual who is interviewed responds to the question, and the interviewer records the answer on the questionnaire form. In contrast to unstructured interviewing, there is a minimum of writing to be done by the interviewer (hence little need for audio recording). Typically, the interviewer fills in a form prepared beforehand. The form, which calls for fixed responses (often too complicated to be completed by the respondent), is known as an *interview schedule.* Being physically present, the interviewer can encourage the respondent's cooperation, clarify ambiguous questions and instructions, and "probe" vague replies for additional information; everything is recorded accurately. Respondents are usually interviewed by one person. In a large survey, that person may be working with a sizable team of interviewers.

Richmond's (1973) study of urban decline in Bristol, England, illustrates the use of the structured interview. A team of trained interviewers questioned more than 500 respondents from 260 households. Upon interpreting their findings, Richmond debunked some of the myths existing then about the Irish, West Indians, and Asian immigrants who had settled in the Bristol neighborhood under study. Bristolians believed the immigrants came mostly from rural backgrounds and therefore had had little experience with urban employment. The survey indicated, however, that more than half the immigrants had lived in towns and that the Irish workers were more likely to have been employed on farms than those from Asia and the West Indies. Moreover, it was assumed in Britain at the time that all immigrants were nonwhite, whereas Richmond's study verified the presence of Irish immigrants in the urban neighborhood said by Bristolians to be deteriorating because of the "coloured" people.

Controlled Observation

Controlled observation is a means of collecting data. It may be used in any confirmatory study, whatever the design or approach. But it is the experiment which makes maximum use of controlled observation.

The sociologist carries out two kinds of experiments: the *laboratory experiment* and the *field experiment,* or *natural experiment.* Whichever the form, experiment entails "carefully controlled observation carried out under conditions designed to separate the influence of several variables as well as to minimize errors of observation" (Caporaso, 1973: 8). A *variable* is a quantity that may assume any one of a set of specified values; it is something that is variable. For instance, we might study the simultaneous associations among the variables of age, sex, and

Some research using controlled observation takes place in specially constructed laboratories.

education. In the typical social science experiment, the experimenter manipulates one or more influences which are called *independent variables.* The independent variables have an effect on the subject's actions, which are known as *dependent variables.* Other factors possibly affecting these actions are "controlled" by various means, thereby enabling the experimenter to infer certain causal relationships between the independent variables and the dependent variables.

Control and manipulation are easier to achieve in the laboratory than in the field, which explains why most experiments in sociology are done in the laboratory. For example, Santee and Jackson (1982) designed a laboratory experiment to test the following hypothesis: females assess conformity as a more positive, self-defining form of behavior than do males. Santee and Jackson tested this hypothesis by comparing the reactions of two groups of undergraduate students to a simulated experiment in conformity, which the undergraduate observers watched through one-way glass.

The control group of observers was asked to judge how good or bad the experimental subjects were. This was done by asking each observer to respond to twenty-five adjectives that described the subjects. Each adjective was judged along a seven-point scale that ran from good to bad. The observers were also asked to state how honest, sincere, and secure each subject appeared to be. The experimental group of observers followed the same procedure. Additionally, they were told to judge the subjects in a way that left the experimenters with the best impression of them (the observers) as personalities. The experimenters were able to confirm the hypothesis: females are more likely than males to see conformity as an act that has positive implications. Others have a favorable impression of the one who conforms.

Field experiments in sociology are rarer than laboratory experiments, but the sociologist does go into the field from time to time. Stebbins (1976) investigated the hypothesis that people who feel they are expressing only modesty or pride when talking of their achievements are actually looked upon as conceited by those who are listening to them. With Stebbins as an observer, fifty-four university and high-school football players met in discussion groups. The players in the groups discussed their achievements in football. In half the groups, a professional football star moderated the discussions. The discussions, which were recorded, lasted for approximately twenty minutes. Afterwards, each member of a group used a special form to rate as modest, proud, or conceited all self-esteem statements made by himself and the others. Comparisons revealed support for the hypothesis; the hypothesis held true for both university players and high-school players. The pattern held regardless of whether the professional star moderated the discussion.

ARCHIVAL RESEARCH

Not all methods can be so neatly classified as exploratory or confirmatory as the ones which have been considered so far in this section. For example, archival research is an approach with its own techniques and interests. *Archival research* centers on audio recordings (tapes, phonograph records) and visual materials, (films, writings, photographs). The researcher finds the audio and visual materials in libraries, museums, government archives, business files, and private collections. In archival research, the sociologist has no direct contact with the people under study. Rather, he or she examines censuses, proceedings, official reports, and historical records for their human implications. Controls can be placed on this sort of data collection, depending on whether the researcher wishes to explore a subject or to test hypotheses.

ANALYSIS

The data which investigators collect must be analyzed. The ultimate goal of scientific analysis is to provide for the scientist an understanding, or explanation, of what is under study or to allow for a prediction, or to do both. Although there is overlap, the forms of data analysis are sufficiently different in exploratory research and confirmatory research to justify separate discussions of them here. The differences between the two types of research are also evident in the analysis phase of actual studies.

Exploratory Analysis

Perhaps the most significant characteristic of data analysis that differentiates exploration from confirmation is the time at which the analysis is undertaken. In exploration the analysis is conducted, for the most part, while the data are still being gathered, whereas in confirmation the data are usually collected first and then analyzed. There are exceptions to this procedure, some of which will be noted.

The underlying analytic process in exploration is *induction,* or inductive reasoning. *Induction* is reasoning from individual cases to an inclusive statement, or *generalization,* that is, from the particular to the general. For example, through inductive reasoning, Marlene Sway (1984) challenged the stereotype that Gypsies are nomadic because they love to wander or because they are too lazy to work at a regular job. Her repeated observations of Gypsy work habits led to the following generalization: "The primary motivation behind the Gypsies' frequent movement is the drive to exploit their skills and services in new markets after the others have been depleted" (Sway, 1984: 85). The Gypsies' skills and services include entertaining, carnival work, telling fortunes, picking crops, auto body work, and selling used cars. Sway's generalization was made while she was still in the field conducting her research.

Exploratory analysis also deals with the problem of constructing types (types of behavior, for example). Usually, types are constructed while the researcher is collecting data. Those who participate regularly in a particular social world conceive of the setting according to commonsense types of behavior, people, events, and situations. It is the fieldworker's job to discover the types, or to construct them.

Brettel (1980), for instance, identified several types of "ethnic entrepreneurs" among the Portuguese immigrants in Toronto. Ethnic entrepreneurs "employ ethnic symbols to establish themselves as mediators between those who share an identity and others in the society" (Brettel, 1980: 301). These mediators are necessary when many members of an ethnic group are unfamiliar with the culture of their community and are unable to speak its language.

One of the several types of entrepreneurs observed by Brettel was the travel agent. Located in an area of Toronto frequented by Portuguese immigrants, the travel agent—also a Portuguese—provides a variety of services in addition to arranging for travel. He is also a translator, legal advisor, expert on official forms, and a creditable witness for events such as weddings.

The final task in the analysis phase of exploratory research is to interrelate the generalizations and the types to form a grounded theory of the subject under study. An outline of the theory begins to take shape during the collection of data. In fact, the growing sense of how certain generalizations and types are interrelated often points to gaps in the researcher's knowledge of what is being studied. Thus, he or she is encouraged to observe, ask questions, and otherwise gather information to fill these gaps.

But, because theories are logical constructions of words and phrases, the finishing touches to the theory are made when the researcher writes his or her report of the fieldwork. At this time attention may be concentrated on finding the best words to explain the idea, the best sequence for outlining certain topics, and the most precise definitions of important concepts discovered in the study. It is in the writing part of the analysis that the researcher "can put it all together." This is where the researcher really learns what the study has led to.

Confirmatory Analysis

The analysis of confirmatory data is organized around the hypotheses that guided the collection of data. The objective is to analyze the collected data in a way that provides the best possible test of the hypotheses. Although exploratory analysis sometimes includes the quantification of data, it is the confirmatory stage of research in which the most sophisticated quantitative analyses are found. Because it is far more common to quantify data in confirmation than in exploration, many possible types of analysis are available to sociologists in confirmation.

Preliminary Analysis Some confirmatory studies require preliminary analyses. When methods such as participant observation and content analysis have been used, it is necessary to *code,* or place into categories, all observations or specimens that are not yet sorted. The categories are then given numerical values. Generalizations and types may also be formulated here, much as in exploration. The researcher is likely to quantify these as well, for they can then be manipulated statistically at a later stage of the analysis.

It is during the preliminary stage of the analysis that confirmatory researchers sometimes turn to scales. A *scale* is a graduated series of steps along a single dimension of a theoretical concept. The steps are intended as a measure of the concept. Scales in sociology come in several forms, only one of which is covered here. In the form explained here, a sequence of related questions or characteristics is arranged along a continuum to provide a countable measure of some quantifiable aspect of human action or mentality. When subjects answer the questions and fill in the scale, their attitudes can be measured, as can their beliefs, opinions, and sentiments.

The Bogardus Social Distance Scale measures attitudinal intensity toward seventy different ethnic, occupational, and religious groups. Subjects are given a list of these groups and asked to indicate on the following scale their feelings about each:

1. Would marry.
2. Would have as regular friends.
3. Would work beside in office.
4. Would have several families in my neighborhood.
5. Would have merely as speaking acquaintances.
6. Would have live outside my neighborhood.
7. Would have live outside my country.

Items 1 through 7 fall along a continuum reflecting a decreasing level of intimacy in social relations. It is assumed that each item is roughly equidistant in attitudinal intensity from its neighbor on the scale.

Researchers themselves sometimes fill in the scale. It is then referred to as a *rating scale.* A rating scale reflects the researcher's view of the object under study. Richmond (1973: 309) used this technique, among others, in his study of a decaying Bristol neighborhood. His scale dealt with the state of repair of the buildings in which his respondents lived. The scale is reproduced in Figure 3.2, "Example of a Rating Scale."

Multivariate Analysis Nearly all quantitative sociological research is analyzed by means of multivariate analysis. In this type of analysis, several variables are examined simultaneously. For instance, we might study the simultaneous associations among the variables of age, sex, and education. Following the sequence used by Babbie (1983: Chapter 14), we shall set the groundwork for the discussion of multivariate analysis by first considering univariate and bivariate analyses.

As the word "univariate" implies, *univariate analysis* centers on one variable only. Consider the variable of education. Although the types of analysis at this level are limited, there are still several ways of learning something new about, say, four hundred Canadians who told an interviewer how much education they had attained.

Figure 3.2. EXAMPLE OF A RATING SCALE

OBSERVATION PANEL

It will probably be best to complete this just *before* knocking on the main building door. Try out the Good-Fair-Bad assessments on a few buildings to ensure you can use the categories easily. When using this panel, just put a tick for the Repair of Building.

Repair of Building Paint-work	Good	Fair	Bad
(On doors, window-frames, gutters, eaves, but *not* on walls)	Gloss and colour intact. Film intact.	Lost gloss and is faded. Surface tends to chalk. No crazing, cracking or flaking.	Deep chalking or blistering, cracking, peeling, flaking.
Rendering	Must sound solid when tapped, no surface defects.	Sound solid but may have slight cracks or crazing.	Sounds hollow, breaking away from wall, cracked or crazed.
Brickwork	Bricks flush with each other. Smooth surface free from holes, chips, or decay.	Bricks flush with each other but slightly pitted or chipped at the edges.	Bricks loose, bulging or tilting, and decaying.
Painting	Cement is flush with walls or with itself if it has a recessed finish. No breaks or gaps, regular and even finish.	Cement slightly recessed here and there, finish pitted with tiny holes and is uneven.	Gaps and holes in the finish. Cement so recessed that edges of bricks stand out without support.
Windows	Glass intact. Frames square and complete.	Glass cracked. Woodwork badly cracked or bits missing.	Pieces of glass missing. Frames not square or sagging.
Garden	Cultivated within last few months.	Uncultivated. No rubbish.	Uncultivated. Rubbish in garden

Source: A. H. Richmond. (1973.) *Migration and race relations in an English city,* p. 309. London: Oxford University Press.

To analyze their responses, the researcher could, for example, classify the individuals by whether they had completed eight grades of school, up to twelve grades, up to one year of university, or up to four or more years of university. The grade completions could be further analyzed by converting them to percentages of the four hundred adults. Finally, the researcher could also determine the central tendency of the responses. A standard measure of central tendency is the arithmetic mean, or average. What is the mean number of years spent by the sample in getting a formal education?

Bivariate Analysis involves two variables, which can be compared. A major advantage of bivariate analysis over univariate analysis is the establishment of relationships by means of comparison. When we have established a relationship between two variables, we have developed an *explanation* of the variables. Univariate analysis is limited to the mere description of a single variable (e.g., numbers and percentages of people in each category, or central tendency).

Examine Table 3.1, "Example of Bivariate Analysis," in which sex and level of education are cross-classified. The data in this table, albeit fictitious, represent accurately, although broadly, certain educational trends in Canada. Table 3.1 indicates that women are somewhat more likely to complete high school than men, but that men are more likely to complete three

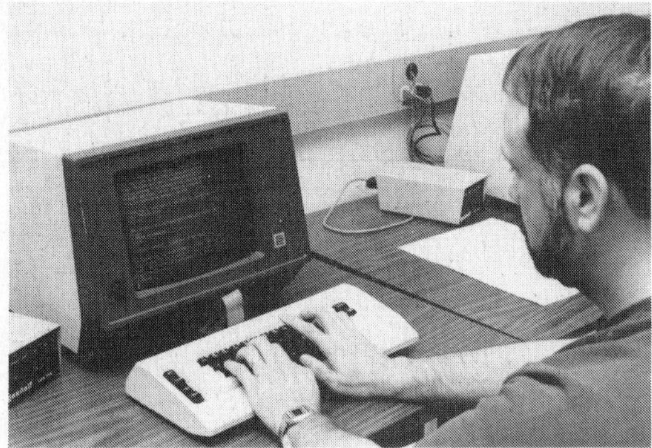

Today the computer is probably the most common implement in sociological research.

or more years of university than women. Had these two relationships between sex and education been hypothesized before the interviews were conducted, then the data in Table 3.1 would have constituted a confirmation of these predictions.

Multivariate analysis, as we have noted, centers on the relationships among three or more variables. In Table 3.2, "Example of Multivariate Analysis," the variable of age is added to the bivariate analysis. Had we hypothesized that younger men and women have attained more education than older men and women, we would have had our prediction confirmed by the data in Table 3.2.

Statistical Analysis is actually a part of multivariate analysis. It can commence, however, only after the raw data from the surveys, scales, and other sources have been arrayed along their underlying conceptual dimensions (e.g., age, sex, education). We have already encountered the simplest form of statistical analysis—descriptive statistics. As the term suggests, *descriptive statistics* describe a set of raw data (questionnaire responses, for example). Moreover, "descriptive statistics is a method for presenting quantitative descriptions in a manageable form" (Babbie, 1983: 408). The percentages and arithmetic means mentioned earlier are descriptive statistics.

The idea of descriptive statistics becomes clearer when contrasted with the idea of *inferential statistics.* When a sociologist draws a sam-

Table 3.1 EXAMPLE OF BIVARIATE ANALYSIS

	Education level			
	Elementary and secondary school		University	
Sex	0–8 years	9–12 years	1–3 years	4 years or more
Male	56	87	26	31
Female	57	99	23	21
Totals	113	186	49	52

Table 3.2 EXAMPLE OF MULTIVARIATE ANALYSIS

	Education level			
	Elementary and secondary school		University	
Sex and age	0–8 years	9–12 years	1–3 years	4 years or more
Male				
Under 30	18	46	15	21
Over 30	38	41	11	10
Female				
Under 30	17	55	14	14
Over 30	40	44	9	7
Totals	113	186	49	52

ple, he or she strives for a set of individuals, events, situations, or behaviors that are representative of the larger whole. That whole is called a *population.* The sample is studied with the assumption that, so far as the interests of the research project are concerned, the sample and the larger population are similar. Ultimately, sociologists want to make assertions about populations, not about samples. Inferential statistics help researchers decide that what they have learned about a sample can be safely generalized to the population from which the sample was drawn. A number of different techniques are available to help sociologists formulate the generalization.

The detailed procedures of sampling are beyond the scope of this book. Nevertheless, you should be aware that errors can mar the sampling process to the extent that generalizations made from the sample are invalidated. It was stated earlier that the generalizations made in this chapter about sex, age, and education are broadly representative of certain educational trends in Canada. Would you accept this claim if the four hundred men and women in the sample were all poor native people living in the Northwest Territories?

THE FINAL STEP

Completion of the data analysis is by no means the end of the research project for the sociologist or any other scientist. The findings must now be communicated. The norm of communality, described earlier in this chapter, is one of the important motives for writing a journal article or monograph (book-length research report) about the analyzed findings. Many sociologists are authors; their ability to write is one of their professional skills. Among those who read the articles and monographs are other sociologists and interested professionals from related disciplines and occupations. Laymen read the less technical reports. Simpler papers and journal articles are more common in exploratory research than in confirmatory research.

OUTLINE AND SUMMARY

You can review Chapter 3, "Studying Social Life," by going over the following outline and summary:

I. Introduction
Like all scientists, sociologists make use of basic research techniques. Their chief methods are *exploration* and *confirmation.* With these techniques, they seek an understanding of social action. They study society.

II. Science
Science is both a process and a product. That is, it is a way of finding out about things and also a body of knowledge. Scientists collect data and form hypotheses. They test their hypotheses by doing controlled research.

A. Technology
Technology is the appication of scientific knowledge to the solution of practical problems and to the invention of useful devices. To some extent, technology now is looked upon as a social problem. Many social scientists believe that society has become dependent on technology, with a loss in human dignity.

B. As an Institution
Science is a part of culture. It is one of the institutions in industrial societies.

III. Exploration and Confirmation
Contemporary research in sociology is largely confirmatory, but exploration continues to be an essential endeavor. The sociologist is primarily interested in exploring the uncharted areas of social life. At the beginning, the sociologist's mind is *open.* The situation calls for *flexibility,* or for a flexible research design.

A. Grounded Theory
An exploratory study produces

grounded theory. *Grounded theory* is an interrelated set of hypothetical propositions or generalizations constructed from systematically collected data. The theory is grounded in the data. Grounded theory is a beginning; it is untested and unconfirmed.

B. Confirmation

It is expected that hypotheses will be verified. To verify hypotheses, sociologists use controls in collecting data and in doing experiments. A group of subjects is compared with a control group. The differences are compared, making it possible to test hypotheses.

IV. The Methods of Exploration

A sociologist ordinarily employs four exploratory methods in carrying out an investigation. The four methods are *participant observation, unstructured interviewing, content analysis,* and *nonreactive measures.*

A. Participant Observation

In participant observation, observers participate in the everyday activities of their subjects. At times, the subjects are aware of the fieldworker's research interests. At other times, they are unaware of the observer's identity.

B. Unstructured Interviewing

Unstructured interviewing often accompanies participant observation. In unstructured interviewing, the sociologist uses an *interview guide.* The guide lists questions for the respondents who are being interviewed. The subject's responses are "unstructured." There is free expression of ideas.

C. Content Analysis

Content analysis is an analysis of written, audio, or visual material. Such an analysis is applied to media such as newspapers, journals, novels, motion pictures, and tape recordings. Sociologists use content analysis to find out about the ideas and social attitudes which are predominant in society.

D. Nonreactive Measures

Nonreactive measures are indicators of human behavior that can be observed without disturbing the persons under study. People leave physical traces which tell investigators about their values, attitudes, sentiments, habits, and norms. Archives also provide sociological data.

V. Methods Used in Confirmation

Three methods used in confirmation are *questionnaire surveys, structured interviewing,* and *controlled observation.*

A. Questionnaire Surveys

Research sociologists regard the questionnaire survey as their stock-in-trade. The questionnaire survey provides data obtained by enumeration or measurement. The mailed survey and the telephone survey are possibly the most commonly used research techniques in sociology. For both, respondents are usually selected randomly. The questionnaire is ordinarily used for verifying hypotheses.

B. Structured Interviewing

The structured interview puts the interviewer and respondent in face-to-face contact. In the standard interview, the interviewer reads a question to the person being interviewed. The individual who is being interviewed responds to the question, and the interviewer records the answer on the questionnaire form.

C. Controlled Observation

The experiment makes maximum use of controlled observation. In doing an experiment, sociologists and all other scientists use controls. By observing variables, sociologists and other scientists can test their hypotheses.

VI. Archival Research

Archival research is research into audio recordings (tapes, phonograph records) and visual materials (films, writings, photographs). The researcher finds the materials in libraries, museums, government archives, business files, and private collections. The researcher examines the records for their human implications.

VII. Analysis

The data which investigators collect must be analyzed. Although there is overlap, data analysis in exploratory research differs from data analysis in confirmatory research.

A. Exploratory Analysis

In exploration, the analysis is conducted, for the most part, while the data are still being collected. In confirmation, the data are usually collected first and then analyzed. The underlying analytic process in exploration is *inductive reasoning,* or reasoning from particulars to a generalization.

B. Confirmatory Analysis

The objective of confirmatory analysis is to test the hypothesis. Quantitative analyses enter into confirmatory analysis. It is more common to quantify data in confirmation than in exploration.

1. Preliminary Analysis

Some confirmatory studies require preliminary analyses. It is necessary to code all observations or specimens that are not yet sorted into categories. The codes are then given numerical values. Confirmatory researchers sometimes use scales.

2. Multivariate Analysis

Quantitative sociological research is analyzed by means of multivariate analysis. Several variables are examined simultaneously in multivariate analysis.

3. Bivariate Analysis

Bivariate analysis is an analysis of two variables. The variables can be compared. The comparison reveals relationships, providing for an explanation of the variables.

4. Statistical Analysis

Statistical analysis becomes possible after the raw data from the surveys, scales, and other sources have been interpreted. A simple example of statistical analysis is descriptive statistics.

VIII. The Final Step

As a final step, sociologists and scientists make their findings known to others. Many sociologists are authors. They write books, monographs, and journal articles. Communication is an important part of science.

FOR FURTHER READING AND STUDY

McCain, G. and Segal, E. M. 1981. *The game of science,* 4th ed. Monterey, CA: Brooks/Cole. An entertaining account of the way scientists do research and the philosophical assumptions underlying the research process.

Milgram, S. 1977. *The individual in a social world: Essays and experiments.* Reading, MA: Addison-Wesley. This book contains numerous examples of social science laboratory experiments. Milgram has done laboratory experiments on obedience and conformity and field experiments on the effects of television on antisocial behavior.

Mills, C. W. 1959. *The sociological imagination.* New York: Oxford University Press. This classic urges the sociologist when designing research and interpreting data to stand back and examine the larger historical context of individual behavior in terms of its meaning for the people being studied.

Prus, R. and Irini, S. 1980. *Hookers, rounders, and desk clerks: The social organization of the hotel community.* Toronto: Gage. An observational and interview study of the hookers, strippers, bartenders, waitresses, entertainers, patrons, rounders, and desk clerks who constitute the hotel community in an eastern Canadian city.

Reinharz, S. 1979. *On becoming a social scientist.* San Francisco, CA: Jossey-Bass. An autobiographical account of the attempts by a young woman sociologist to mesh her personality with the standard sociological research methods of participant observation and survey research. Over her career, she comes to recognize the strengths and weaknesses of both methods.

Shaffir, W. B., Stebbins, R. A., and Turowetz, A. eds. 1980. *Fieldwork experience.* New York: St. Martin's. A collection of twenty-one original papers on what it is like to do field research. The papers are grouped under the categories of getting into the research setting, learning the ropes, maintaining relations, and leaving the setting.

Watson, J. D. 1969. *The double helix: A personal account of the discovery of the structure of DNA.* New York: New American Library. For their work on DNA, Watson and his associates won the Nobel Prize. Watson's book points out the strengths and weaknesses of scientific research.

Yankelovich, D. 1981. *New rules: Searching for self-fulfillment in a world turned upside down.* New York: Random House. Using opinion surveys and interviews, Yankelovich reaches the conclusion that 80 percent of Americans are now committed in some degree to the search for self-fulfillment.

KEY WORDS

archival research Research into audio recordings and visual media found in libraries, museums, government archives, business files, and private collections.

bivariate analysis An analysis of two variables, which can be compared.

confirmation Demonstrating the validity of research findings by testing hypotheses.

content analysis An analysis of written, audio, or visual materials to find out about ideas and social attitudes which are dominant in society.

controlled observation An observation or an experiment which makes use of controls.

dependent variable A variable which can be changed by an independent variable.

exploration A means of acquiring an understanding of a phenomenon or event.

flexibility A flexible research design which brings about the discovery of new facts and ideas.

independent variable A variable which causes a change in another variable; a variable which can be manipulated by the experimenter.

inductive reasoning Reasoning from the particular to the general.

institution A set of norms regulating human action for the purpose of achieving society goals.

multivariate analysis An analysis in which several variables are examined simultaneously.

nonreactive measure An indicator of human behavior that the alert researcher can observe without disturbing the behaving persons.

open mind holding as few preconceived ideas as possible while being alert to new information.

participant observation A case-study method in which the sociologist takes part in a group's activities.

questionnaire survey A means of collecting data through the mail or by telephone with the use of a questionnaire.

science A *process* and a *product;* a way of finding out about things and also a body of knowledge.

statistical analysis An analysis that describes a sample or estimates how representative the sample is of a larger population.

structured interview An interview in which the interviewer records the respondents's answers to questions by filling in a form known as the *interview schedule.*

technology The application of scientific knowledge to the solution of practical problems; a means of providing devices and advantages for human sustenance and convenience.

theory A scientifically acceptable principle which explains a phenomenon or event.

unstructured interviewing The questioning of a subject with the use of an interview guide.

variable a quantity that may assume any one of a set of specified values.

two

SOCIAL PROCESSES

A *process* consists of a movement in some direction from one point to another. It is a series of actions or operations. A *social process* is the movement in some direction of a set of human actions, circumstances, or experiences. For example, human interaction (see Chapter 4, "Human Interaction") is a social process. Another social process is socialization (see Chapter 5, "Socialization"). *Socialization* is the process individuals go through in learning to become members of society and in learning how to be accepted by other members of society. As you work through the two chapters in Part Two, "Social Processes," you will be developing an understanding of the exchanges and interactions which make society what it is. As you will see, social processes are the substance and the underpinnings of society.

chapter 4

Human Interaction

CHAPTER OUTLINE

INTRODUCTION

As we observed in Chapter 1, "The Study of Society," action and knowledge are two important components of interaction. Action and knowledge are the root of all things social; the term "social" is defined as the sharing of language, beliefs, goals, and norms with other members of society. On a typical day, nearly everyone has a part in numerous interactions with others. Usually, these episodes are not nearly as dramatic as the following:

> Donald Downey, 27, a coach with Canada's national boxing team, was fined $250 in a Halifax court for punching a young woman in the

nose. Downey and the woman, Heather Doubleday, passed each other on the street. As they met, they gave each other "the finger." Downey then called Doubleday "useless white trash," and she responded with a slur. Downey, according to testimony in court, spit in Doubleday's face. In retaliation, she smeared Downey's face with her ice cream cone, rubbing in the ice cream with a vengeance.

Angrily, Downey slugged the young woman, hitting her in the nose and knocking her down. Doubleday had to have her jaw wired together for two months, and two of her front teeth were knocked loose. The crown prosecutor said she may lose the teeth. Downey, a professional boxer for five years, pleaded innocent. His lawyer said the punch was "simply a reflex action to the ice cream being rubbed in his face." (*The Citizen,* 1982: 55)

SOCIAL INTERACTION

Sociologists use the terms "social interaction," "social relations," and "interpersonal relations" interchangeably. Each term refers to the mutual effect of individuals on each other. Individuals in society guide their own behavior partly by taking account of the actions or possible actions of the other people in the immediate setting.

Action, knowledge, and social interaction are based on language. In broad terms, *language* is verbal and nonverbal communication. It is gesture—human gesture, that is. Mead (1934: 13, fn. 9) defines *gestures* as "the movements of the first organism which act as specific stimuli calling forth the (socially) appropriate responses of the second organism." Giving the finger, spitting on a person, slugging another person, and rubbing an ice cream cone in someone's face, as in the foregoing example, are as much a part of language as calling an adversary "useless white trash." Mead pointed out that the gesture is the foundation of all social life and, for human beings, the foundation of all society:

> The specialization of the human animal within this field of the gesture has been responsible, ultimately, for the origin and growth of present human society and knowledge. (Mead, 1934: 13 fn. 9)

In exchange theory, *interaction* is defined as "behavior in which the action of one man is a *stimulus* to, or *reward* for, the action of another" (Homans, 1974: 56).[1] Interaction often constitutes a direct exchange of benefits of some kind among those involved in the interaction. The list of possible benefits that might be exchanged is nearly endless; among the numerous rewards are love, money, favors, praise, gifts, admiration, privileges, and opportunities. Woods (1976: 183–184) observed in his study of an English middle school several teachers who permitted their pupils to laugh and joke during lessons. The laughing and joking were allowed in exchange for the pupils' cooperation and diligence in accomplishing their classroom work.

As noted in Chapter 1, "The Study of Society," social action and social interaction some-

SOCIOLOGY OR COMMON SENSE

What do you think?

Which of the following statements do you agree with? Which statements do you disagree with? Make a note of your answers. Check your answers when you have completed your study of this chapter. Are your answers to the statements the same as those a sociologist would give?

1. Human actions are determined by forces outside the individual and beyond his or her control.
2. The study of motivation is the province only of psychologists.
3. Individuals experience interaction only with other individuals.
4. In Canada, an individual lacks the ability to change society.
5. *Power* is a force in friendships and marriages, just as it is in organizations and international relations.

[1]Italics added.

times can be looked on as the same kind of activity. But there is a significant difference between the two. The difference is that social interaction is a special form of social action. As a special form, it involves at least two people engaging in a reciprocal or mutual exchange of influences. In this sense, the exchange between the boxer and the young woman exemplified social action and also social interaction.

Social action is not always an exchange between individuals. For instances, you sometimes are guided by what others might think about your behavior, but in such instances there is no direct exchange between you and others. You act alone. There is no reciprocation or exchange of influences. Still, your response to or action in the situation has a social component.

Role-Taking

An action common to both social action and social interaction is role-taking. In *role-taking,* individuals imaginatively put themselves in the roles of other individuals. People put themselves in the place of others with whom they are interacting. This is largely an unconscious act, the intention of which is to find out how one's actions will be interpreted by others. Taking a role prepares an individual for subsequently carrying out his or her own actions.

McGuire and Weisz (1982) studied role-taking in a sample of 293 youngsters in grades 5 and 6. The investigators measured role-taking by asking each child to play the "nickel-dime game." In this game, a child hides a nickel or a dime in one of two boxes. Another child tries to guess in which box the coin is hidden. The hider's job is to arrange the money in the boxes in a way which prompts the guesser to guess wrong. How well the hider does this is a measure of how well he or she can take the role of the guesser. McGuire and Weisz found that children with friends are more likely than those without friends to develop high levels of role-taking skill. Popularity was not a factor in this result.

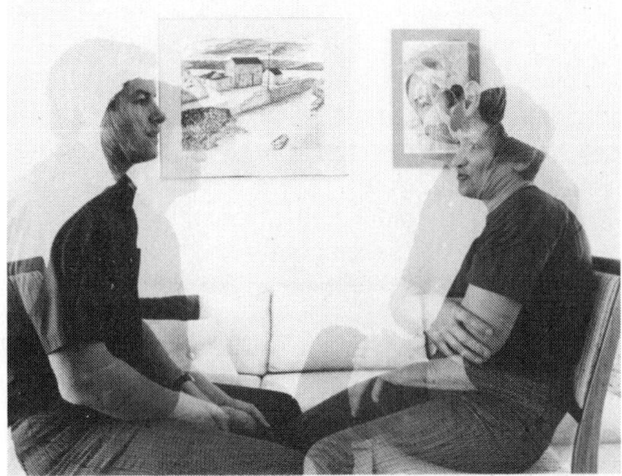

Role-taking is the imaginative placing of oneself in the role of another person.

Improvisation

The notion of role-taking draws attention to the fact that we do much more in social interaction than mechanically enact the expectations of a role. We also devise a performance on the basis of an "imputed other role" (Turner, 1962: 23). That is, interaction is always improvised to some extent; it is a performance of sorts. For example, professors fulfill a role when they deliver lectures to students; they are interacting with the students. The professors are also improvising part of their role performance when they make gestures and stride dramatically back and forth across the platform. Role expectations never tell us how to act in all circumstances.

Some social scientists draw a distinction between role-taking and empathy or sympathy. Role-taking, they say, is largely a cognitive or thinking process, whereas empathy or sympathy is one of feeling and emotion. Still, empathy does have its cognitive side, even though its dominant quality is emotional. Other social scientists, however, treat empathy and role-taking as synonymous.

INTERACTION AND INTERPRETATION

Although the term "interaction" suggests that it is chiefly a behavioral process, sociologists have concentrated more on its interpretive (i.e., social action) meaning than on its behavioral slant. With their emphasis on interpretation, the sociologists have given a great deal of thought to a social reality known as *definition of the situation.* They have also considered at length operations such as *motivation, cognitive processes,* and *expressive processes.*

Definition of the Situation

Generally speaking, a *definition of the situation* is the meaning people ascribe to the immediate settings in which they find themselves in the course of everyday living. To define a situation is to give it meaning; with meaning, it becomes a part of the social order. There is social order when people agree on the same definition of the situation.

A situation is defined in the following steps, or sequence:

1. Individuals enter a particular situation with particular intentions or goals to be realized.
2. Certain social and physical aspects of the situation related to these intentions, as perceived by the individual, activate dormant predispositions in the individual.
3. The perceived aspects of the situation, the intentions, and the activated predispositions, when considered together, lead to the selection or construction of a definition.
4. This definition directs subsequent action (or possibly inaction) in the situation until new information forces redefinition of it or until the individual definers have left the scene.

Predispositions (mentioned in item 2) introduce the consideration of past experience into the sequence. A *predisposition* is an enduring, acquired mental state; it is an attitude, a belief, or a personal value. Predispositions remain inactive or dormant until awakened by the perceived aspects of the immediate situation (Campbell, 1963: 87–112). At this point, the predispositions impinge on an individual's awareness, helping him or her to define the situation and to act appropriately within it according to the individual's reasons for being there.

It is stated in item 3 that definitions of the situation are either selected or constructed. Nearly all definitions of everyday life situations are selected, inasmuch as novelty in these situations is rare, perhaps even nonexistent. We have ready-made meanings and plans of action for dealing with the routine events in our lives. By way of illustration, people who frequently travel by commercial airline know how to use to their advantage facilities such as check-in counters, departure gates, waiting rooms, curbside porters, baggage conveyors, ground transportation, and very important person lounges. All these necessities are familiar to seasoned travelers, who make their way through airline terminals with little thought or advance planning.

But life has its novelties as well. Definitions of novel situations must be constructed. An unusual set of events demands a new meaning, or new interpretation. To construct this definition, people draw on personal experiences and cultural understandings. Emergencies tend to have unusual conditions, requiring us to construct partly or wholly a new definition of them. An episode on a Brooklyn street illustrates how personal construction built from past experiences can differ dramatically among individual participants, even when focused on the same objective circumstances:

> Maria Pellot, 24, left a house in Brooklyn one Sunday morning and found her car blocked by a double-parked automobile. She began pounding on the double-parked car with a lead pipe. James Gibson, a Housing Authority policeman wearing a civilian suit, came out of his house nearby and saw Miss Pellot hitting his car. When Gibson tried to take the pipe from the young woman, an unidentified man now sought by the police intervened, punching Gibson in the face. Gibson drew his service revolver, showed his badge, and ordered the man and Miss Pellot to lie on the pavement.
>
> An off-duty Correction Department officer, Robert Johnson, observed the goings-on from a passing bus. Johnson jumped off the bus, shouting, "I'm a police officer! Drop your gun!"

Hardly aware of Johnson's shout, Gibson apparently feared he was being criminally attacked. The first of nine shots rang out as the two men took cover behind parked cars.

Another off-duty police officer, City Detective John Britt, ended the stand-off. Britt rushed from his nearby home and persuaded Gibson and Johnson to surrender their guns. The officers then found Maria Pellot lying on the sidewalk with a bullet wound in her stomach. She died after surgery at Brookdale Hospital. (Dallas *Times-Herald,* 1974)

Interpretive Processes

Several processes, only some of which can be covered here, are put into operation in the third step of the situation-defining sequence. This is the step, remember, in which various factors lead to the selection or construction of a definition. McCall and Simmons (1978: 126–137) divide these processes into two categories: *cognitive* and *expressive.*

Cognitive Processes Role-taking is one of the cognitive processes. The process itself is a means of gaining knowledge. While trying to ascertain how others in the situation are interpreting our actions, we also learn about their roles and attitudes. Put otherwise, we begin to *impute roles* to them (Lauer and Boardman, 1971). Imputed roles serve as reference points to interpretation —to our interpretation of the various actions occurring in the situation, that is.

Knowing the roles of others also enables us to impute motives to the others. An understanding of their motives helps to explain their actions. How often have we encountered someone whose actions initially made no sense but which became sensible once we studied them and identified the role the person was enacting?

Of course, it occasionally happens that the role being enacted is foreign or unfamiliar, leaving us unable to make sense of the person's actions even after studying them. Thus, role-taking accuracy is affected by familiarity with the role in question. Familiarity leads to an understanding. We become familiar with a role by enacting it or by observing it being enacted by others.

Having determined to our satisfaction who the others are in the situation, we must now decide how we will pursue our interests. In other words, we must decide what role to adopt with reference to the others and how to play the role (McCall and Simmons, 1978: 132–133). In part, our role selection depends on the imputations we perceive the others to be making in relation to us. There could be disagreement, as the incident involving the two policemen indicates. To repeat, our own role in relation to the roles of the other people in the setting is often an improvised affair.

Expressive Processes Two *expressive processes* are operating when people define situations. The two processes are *altercasting* and the *presentation of self.* Goffman (1959) argues that the presentation of self, at least so far as city life is concerned, is fundamentally a performance. In such a performance, we engage in *impression management:* the "attempt by one person . . . to affect the perceptions of her or him by another person" (Schneider, 1981: 25). In presenting ourselves, we hope the target audience in the situation will impute the role to us we desire.

Goffman (1959) and Tedeschi (1981), among others, explore how imputations come about. The importance of language and nonverbal communication is undeniable here, for choice of words, pronunciation of the words, grammar, topics of conversation, dress, bearing, physical gestures, facial expressions, voice inflection, eye contact, and props can all potentially influence the impressions others have of us in response to our situated performances. As Goffman (1959: 2) notes, people "give off signs" which, along with the communications they are imparting, are interpreted by those who are on the scene. Expressions given off by people influence their definitions of the situation.

At the same time, we also engage in *altercasting,* or placing other people in particular identities and role types (Lauer and Handel, 1983:

Fritters as Accounts

A fritter is "a justification a student gives to himself for not doing student work in response to felt pressures to work. . . . [Fritters] may be divided into four classes (1) person-based, (2) social-relation based, (3) valuative-based, and (4) task-based. . . .

Valuative-Based Fritters

While the above-mentioned fritter techniques are common and successful, they do not have the guilt-binding power of valuative fritters. One way work can be avoided especially, but not exclusively, in the early college years is using time to discuss values. Political, moral, and aesthetic topics are common in these conversations. Finding out who you are, "getting your shit together," and so on are important tasks. Mundane work considerations do not look very important measured against this large activity. Valuative fritters based on already-held values place work and work avoidance within a larger framework of values and choices. It is here that considerations of nonstudent activities enter with greatest effect. Three primary types of valuative fritters may be described and ordered in terms of increasing generality and abstraction.

Higher Good

In the higher-good work-avoidance strategy, the student ranks being a student as less important to him in his scheme of values than other interests and aspects of his identity. Here friendship, love, cultural values (e.g., charity, service), political interests, physical fitness (the sound-mind-in-a-sound-body fritter), and much else can be justified as more worthy of attention for the moment than the study tasks at hand. These other values, of course, vary in strength and, therefore, in their guilt-free binding power in role management. For this reason, the strength of each of the alternative values is enhanced immeasurably if it can be asserted that the opportunity for acting on that value is soon to be gone. Stated another way, *rare events,* or at least infrequent events, have a special ability to bind time from studying, even if the value of the act would otherwise be questionable in relation to the pressure to study. Makes-Jack-a-dull-boy valuative fritters, involving, say, a movie, will be more potent the last day the picture is playing than the first day of an extended run, concerts involving great and infrequently heard performers are able to appease guilt from role violation, and eclipses of the moon draw crowds of guilt-free students as an audience.

Experience Broadens

The experience-broadens fritter is less specific in the sense of presenting a less clear-cut value conflict. It has, nonetheless, the attraction of serving as a ready back-up to the post-facto unjustified valuative fritter (say, the movie was lousy, the instruments out of tune, the friend crabby, the eclipse cloud-ridden, or what have you). In such an event, or generally in any event, it can be argued somehow that experience qua experience broadens the person, makes him more complete, or wiser, or what have you. This can bind successfully enormous amounts of time on a scale much larger than the mere work requirements for a specific course. Even career decisions (or decision evasions) can be justified under the experience-broadens rubric. The crucial difference from the higher-good fritter is that any experience will do.

Existential

The most general of valuative fritters is the existential, or the what-the-hell-sort-of-difference-will-it-make fritter. In this strategy, the decision to work or not work is cast as having no lasting practical or existential effect on the course of one's life (or sometimes, other's, as in the would-be author's no-one-will-be-reading-novels-in-ten-years-anyway fritter). Scholastic failures of prominently successful individuals may be remembered. Einstein's failure of a high-school math course can offer solace to the fritterer. If one's activities are ultimately of no consequence anyway, the immediate consequences of work avoidance are not even worthy of consideration. Extreme application of this principle can lead to failure in the student role, in which event one's very studenthood may be justified as an experience-broadens fritter from what one should really be doing.

SOURCE: Stan Bernstein. Schedules for students. *Urban Life* 1: 275–292, 1972.

305). Our performance expresses our image of the people with whom we are associating. For example, in Alan Lerner's *My Fair Lady,* Colonel Pickering always treats Eliza as a lady, and, to him, she is a lady.

> Colonel Pickering . . . always showed me that he felt and thought about me as if I were something better than a common flower girl. You see, Mrs. Higgins, apart from the things one can pick up (the dressing and proper way of speaking, and so on), the difference between a lady and a flower girl is not how she behaves, but how she is treated. I shall always be a flower girl to Professor Higgins, because he treats me as a flower girl and always will. But I know I shall always be a lady to Colonel Pickering, because he always treats me as a lady, and always will.

Motivation

Motivation is a state of mind that incites a person to action. The state of mind is a response to a need, an idea, an emotion, or an organic condition. The terms "motive" and "motivation" are often used interchangeably by psychologists and sociologists. The term "motivation" can be defined as a process. It is the process of inciting people to action—of motivating them to something, that is.

The common view is that motivation is the province of psychologists. To a degree, this is true, but sociologists have studied the problem of motivation for more than forty years (see Mills, 1940). According to Shibutani (1961: 181), the challenge for a sociological theory of motivation is "to account for the *patterning, timing,* and *direction of behavior,* especially for "persistent movement toward a goal." By contrast, the traditional conception of motivation in psychology has been causal; origin is stressed at least as much as patterning, timing, and direction of behavior. According to R. S. Peters (1958: 38–40), when mentalistic interpretations in psychology (e.g., wish) became unfashionable, the idea of "drive" as an internal state

Altercasting: The bad report card often leads to a specific role placement of the child by a parent.

gained acceptance as a more tough-minded notion of the causal conditions thought to initiate goal-directed behavior.

Psychologists have been preoccupied with the question of the origin of goal-directed behavior (deCharms and Muir, 1978: 92). With only a passing interest in origin, sociologists have centered their attention on the patterning, timing, and direction of goal-directed behavior. Processes such as patterning, timing, and direction invite sociological treatment, since it is human beings and their culture that provide the goals to be pursued and structure the patterning and timing of the pursuit.

Sociologists and sociologically oriented social psychologists have contributed to a sociological theory of motivation in several ways. Mills (1940), for example, suggested that motives are acceptable and anticipated verbal justifications (rationalizations, in psychoanalytic parlance) for past, present, and future actions. As Mills put it, we develop "vocabularies of motives." Such justifications may be imputed to others (as we have just seen) or avowed by individuals in defense of their own behavior. When we act, we anticipate the need to provide a creditable "vocabulary of motives" should the act be questioned.

Scott and Lyman (1968) carried this line of thought a step further in their essay on accounts. An account is similar to Mills's idea of vocabulary of motives. *Accounts* are verbal defenses of future behavior, and they come in two types: excuses and justifications. *Excuses* are socially approved mitigations which seek to relieve responsibility for questionable actions. *Justifications* cast a favorable light on an act in the face of someone's claim to the contrary. A justification is an assertion that an act is favorable. Justifications, like excuses, are socially acceptable.

INTERACTION AND SOCIETY

Early in this chapter and in Chapter 1, "The Study of Society," it was stated that social interaction is the basis for the social world, for society. In this section, we shall begin to exam-

What sociological concept do you think she is expressing?

ine why interaction has a bearing on society and the social world. Four processes are considered: *negotiation, shaping the working agreement, reality construction,* and *interpersonal attraction.* Part Six, "Societal Trends," in general, and Chapter 23, "Social Change," in particular, will pick up where this section leaves off.

Negotiation

Negotiations occur in a multitude of circumstances ranging from situational encounters to international relations. Here we shall be considering only the situational negotiation, a kind which is local in nature. It could be argued that situational negotiation and the opportunity (or necessity) to engage in it demonstrate the working of modern democracy at its best. This form of negotiation is possible only when those involved are willing to compromise their values and consider the values of others in the situation. Negotiation is possible only when no one has enough power to demand and to get his or her own way. Negotiation enforces the principle of fairness, although sometimes at a less than ideal level. In negotiation, all who are involved obtain a bit of what they want, although rarely everything they seek.

McCall and Simmons (1978: 137–138) define situational negotiation as "the process of bargaining or haggling over the terms of exchange of social rewards. . . . It takes the form of an argument or debate over who each person is." The authors use the term "reward" in much the same way as the term "benefit" was used earlier in this chapter in our reference to exchange theory. They go further, however, by grouping rewards (or benefits) into three types as utilized in situational negotiations: extrinsic gratification (e.g., money, labor, favors, goods), intrinsic satisfaction (e.g., expression of competency, enjoyment of learning), and social support (e.g., praise, encouragement, love).

Negotiation is an overreaching process composed of several subprocesses, including compromising, reaching tacit understanding, and making deals (Strauss, 1978: 1). So far as interaction is concerned, negotiation revolves around four issues: *social identities, interactive roles, agendas,* and *life courses* (McCall and Simmons, 1978).

Social Identity There are times when one or more people in the interaction feel they must negotiate an important *social identity.* When this occurs, those in the interaction reach either an agreement or a compromise about the social category, or status of each person who will be honored by the others. Robert Prus (1975), for instance, studied the negotiation of identities by isolating and describing four tactics deviants use to resist unfavorable labels: (1) challenge the designation, such as by questioning its application to oneself, (2) challenge the designation by asking, in effect, "Who are you to make this judgment?", (3) strike a compromise with the designator; the designated person must have something of value which he or she can exchange with the designator (e.g., money, privilege, services), and (4) reappeal to the agent, which is sometimes done by indicating that one will never behave this way again or that one has seen one's errant ways. In this fashion, a situa-

Children often play at enacting adult social identities.

tional "character" is negotiated for each person in the interaction (McCall and Simmons, 1978: 84).

Labor in childbirth offers a good illustration of identity negotiation. What is negotiated is whether the woman is truly in labor:

> The definition of the situation that participants arrive at through their negotiations becomes the reality with which they have to work. Let us take as an example a woman at term having painful contractions at ten-minute intervals, who has not yet begun to dilate. Whether she is or is not in labor will depend on whether she then begins to dilate or the contractions stop and begin again days or weeks later. Whether a woman is in labor or "false labor" at Time 1 depends on what will have happened by Time 2. If she presents herself to the hospital claiming that she is in labor, and by the use of tears, pleading, or personal status-based power she is admitted, the medical acknowledgement of her labor will have been established. If she does not begin to dilate for twenty-four hours, and then twelve hours after that—thirty-six hours after her admission—she delivers, that woman will have had a thirty-six-hour labor. On the other hand, if she is denied or delays admission and presents herself to the hospital twenty-four hours later for a twelve-hour in-hospital labor, she will have had a twelve-hour labor preceded by a day of discomfort. (Rothman, 1978: 127)

Interactive Roles When *interactive roles* are negotiated, the focus shifts to the behavior to be allowed in the setting. Martin (1976) observed schoolteachers in a Toronto open-plan system exert group pressure on their classes. The teachers compared their classes with other classes. They employed emotional tactics (e.g., sadness, ingratiation) to negotiate orderliness and satisfactory academic performance with their pupils. The pupils, in turn, were observed using tactics such as humor, friendliness, ingratiation, and flirtation with the teachers to achieve a better schoolroom environment for themselves.

Agendas An *agenda* is a schedule of activities to be carried out over a period of time such as a day, a week, or a month. An agenda is negotiated with others who share the individual's interest in his or her time (a day, a week, a month). Roth (1963: 48–54) describes how patients in several tuberculosis hospitals bargained, usually unsuccessfully, with their physicians for an early release from the hospital. They would solicit independent professional judgments of their cases, threaten to leave the hospital against medical advice, or refuse to take prescribed medication.

Life Courses Negotiations are constantly under way in the course of one's life. One's *life course* is subject to processes similar to the negotiation of interactive roles. Individuals are constantly bargaining, compromising, and making deals with those who make demands on their time. The negotiations are carried out as individuals try to coordinate and pursue effectively activities and goals in their different roles. The predicament of the adult amateur baseball player illustrates the nature of life-course negotiation associated with the roles of parent, spouse, and part-time athlete.

> Another strategy, used by some of the sample, is to yield to pressure to take one or more of the children to a practice or game, thereby giving their wives a break and enabling them to pursue their own leisure interests. This is definitely a compromise for the players. For example, one father arrived at a late Sunday afternoon practice with his two young boys: "My wife had to be away this afternoon," he commented. "She said you watch them or stay home." He had to leave the field several times during the workout to break up a fight between them or soothe a minor injury incurred while scampering around the bleachers or surrounding area (Stebbins, 1979: 220).

One might conclude from all this that life is one continual negotiation over something or other. As Maines points out (1977: 243), any complex set of activities has undergone negotiation at some time and to some extent, but a level of stability is eventually reached, eliminating the need for further negotiation. Moreover, there are constraints on this process. As we shall see shortly, negotiation, like other interactive processes, is conducted within a context of available alternatives, such as power differentials, exchangeable resources, and so on.

Working Agreements

Goffman (1959: 9–10) and McCall and Simmons (1978: 139–143) have identified and described the arrangement known as the *working agreement.* A working agreement can be defined as an understanding among a set of interacting people as to who each person is (social identity) and as to what he or she is to do (interactive role). It is depicted in Figure 4.1. Working agreements are immediate products of interaction and negotiation. Thus, they constitute an elementary form of society. Reaching a working agreement in unfamiliar situations occurs in two steps.

First, the social identities of the individuals on the scene must be negotiated. Second, interactive roles appropriate to these identities then are negotiated as the individuals try to shape the behavior of the others in ways agreeable to them. In both steps, negotiation is conducted, as mentioned earlier, by manipulating the costs and rewards others will experience. The others, of course, are attempting to do the same thing at the same time. In other than routine circumstances, goal-directed activity within the situation is mostly stymied until negotiation, first over identities and then over roles, is completed.

Working agreements are being accepted daily in countless ways by members of society. Often it is unnecessary to negotiate identities, since they are known from earlier interchanges. But the role associated with the identities may require negotiation from time to time with respect to new demands or the need to adjust to old ones. Examples include professor and students negotiating the deadline for a term paper, husbands and wives negotiating the division of labor for Saturday's chores, and workers in an office negotiating the responsibilities for the annual picnic. Working agreements related to interactive roles emerge in such circumstances. The process becomes more complicated and the outcome more uncertain when identities have to be negotiated as well. Fortunately for the ease of everyday living, the need to negotiate both identities and roles is infrequent.

Establishing a working agreement sometimes results in an exercise of power. As applied to the dyad (a group of two), Emerson (1981) defines *power* as the potential of person A to obtain more favorable rewards of some sort at person B's expense than B is able to obtain at A's ex-

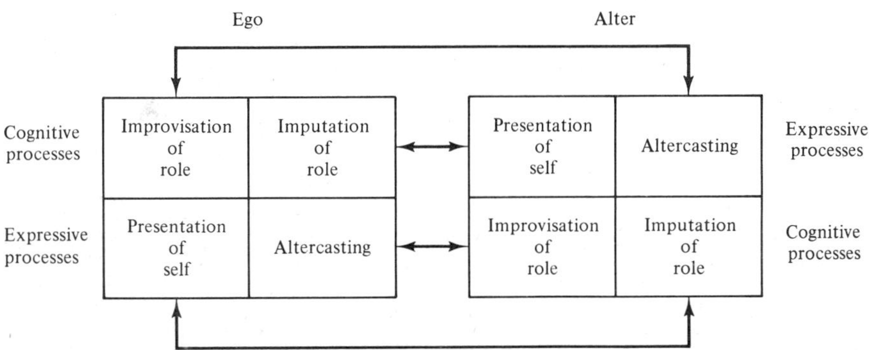

Figure 4.1 The Working Agreement. (*Source:* G. J. McCall and J. L. Simmons, 1978. *Identities and Interactions,* rev. ed. New York: Free Press, p. 193)

pense. In this exchange theory definition, A is the more powerful of the two individuals. Emerson argues, however, that A eventually becomes dependent on B because B is providing rewards valued by A. In time, a power equilibrium is reached; person A loses power while B gains it. The power resources to be exchanged in interaction are nearly infinite; they include money, honor, knowledge, strength, skill, authority, equipment, and sexual favors.

Given the power differentials that can potentially emerge in unfamiliar social situations, it is understandable that people may be reluctant to reward others (at least intentionally) until they receive some assurance that they will be rewarded in some way by the others. This is one reason why negotiation continues beyond the initial step of establishing a working agreement over identities to the second step of establishing the roles to be played by all concerned.

Once everyone has defined the situation, once goal-directed actions are possible (an agreement on identities and roles having been tentatively agreed upon), additional, more complex forms of society can begin to emerge. These forms are generated from the interaction of individuals by means of several more processes, two of which are considered here: *reality construction* and *interpersonal attraction.*

Reality Construction

Arthur W. Frank (1979: 167) defines *reality construction* as

> the generation and maintenance of some organization of affairs, whether a family or a factory, a friendship or an illness. For members of society, this "reality" is the unquestioned conceptualization of what they are doing and the context in which it is done.

Reality construction is concerned with how the definitions of the situation of interacting individuals coalesce in a collectively recognized understanding of what is going on (e.g., a working agreement). Collective definitions spawn new, complex social forms or social facts and modifications of existing ones. Berger and Luckmann (1966: 51) suggest that "habitualization" as a standard definition of a given situation is a necessary precondition for the emergence of any social form related to the situation.

Social forms, as seen by members of society, fall into five types (Stebbins, 1974a: 107–108): (1) *Moral order forms,* which pertain to what is considered good and desirable, are the values and norms that help direct much of human action. (2) *Usages* are the actual behavioral uniformities found among groups of people, as seen in their customs, folkways, and other conventions. Fashions, fads, and crazes are usages. The Grey Cup parade, banquet, and football game are familiar Canadian usages. (3) *Structural relationships* are the abstracted orientations linking a community's social identities, such as the generalized relationships between chiefs of police, detectives, and patrolmen or between physicians, nurses, and orderlies. (4) *Beliefs* are the shared truths or world view of members of a community, including rumor, gossip, and scientific facts. (5) *Meanings* are the interpretations of natural signs and symbols in a human being's environment.

Meaning: What does the music mean to this audience?

People define commonly perceived events and changes in their social and physical environment. Over time and through interaction within each definer's social circle, these collective definitions coalesce into a consensually held view of what has happened and perhaps will happen. Eventually, these collective definitions spread to other social circles in the community and society via the social network ties of the original definers of the event or change.

Ross and Mirowsky (1984) emphasize the taken-for-granted nature of many of our definitions of the situation in association with reality construction. Individuals move through many routine situations in the course of everyday living. They apply standard definitions, which, however, require continual validation as workable. This is accomplished in social interaction with others in the setting, especially significant others:

> Every society must define a reality within which its members live. These definitions are held in common by the members of the society and thus acquire an objective, taken-for-granted character. However, the socially constructed reality must be constantly validated in interactions with others who share the same views and assumptions. Validation is produced . . . by interaction and conversation that takes the existence of a common reality for granted. (Ross and Mirowsky, 1984: 283)

Usages and structural relationships spring from their own social interactional process. This process is known as *coordinated action.* Coordinated action is an intervening condition linking individual definitions of the situation and the emergence of usage and structural relationships. It consists of members of a group fitting together their individual lines of action to form an identifiable usage or structural relationship. This usage or structural relationship is different in its entirety from the mere suggestion or sum of the actions. Among numerous examples of usage and structural relationships are war, marriages, trading transactions, church services, and parliamentary debates.

Coordinated action is a common element in social interaction.

Interpersonal Attraction

Sociologists and social psychologists who study interpersonal attraction do so within the framework of interpersonal relationships. An *interpersonal relationship* (as opposed to a structural relationship) is the sustained orientation of one person toward another; the relationship is perceived by both as being reciprocal. Like all other social things, such ties between individuals are rooted in interaction. Among the relationships most familiar to us are those between kin,

Interpersonal relationships are enduring mutual orientations between two people.

friends, lovers, enemies, and employers and employees.[2] Relationships are believed to develop in four stages (Backman, 1981): (1) unilateral awareness, (2) sampling and estimation, (3) social penetration, and (4) maintenance and dissolution. Since concern in this chapter is with the emergence of socially constructed realities, attention here is restricted to the second and third stages.

Among the important contingencies in sampling and estimation is an individual's first impression of another individual. After reviewing several studies, Backman (1981: 241) concluded that, wherever possible, people tend to notice and distort the characteristics of others in the direction of their current motivational states. For example, a young man might observe that a young woman has an appealing personality. This observation causes him to look favorably on her other traits. He likes her smile, her hairdo, and her choice of clothing.

Two additional contingencies in the second stage are similarity and physical attractiveness. Turning to the first contingency, we note that it is well established empirically that similarity is related to interpersonal attraction. Individuals with similar thoughts and traits are attracted to one another. A set of experimental studies (Backman, 1981: 245–248) indicates that similarity in values, personality traits, leisure interests, and social background (e.g., religion, education, social class) is very likely to be a factor in the development of a friendship or in the beginning of a love affair.

Physical attraction has a master-status effect in sampling and estimation. Laboratory studies have shown that males with a friendly smile and females who are pretty and stylishly dressed are attractive. These qualities elicited positive feelings and high concern for these people. Less attractive males and females, such as those who are nervous and facially disfigured, brought out negative feelings in the observers. The observers did, however, feel some concern for them (Baron and Byrne, 1984: 221–222).

The social-penetration stage centers on two processes: the development of interdependence and the conduct of role negotiation in the dyad. One of the hallmarks of positive interpersonal relationships is the rising level of self-revelation practiced by the two individuals. Additionally, people are attracted to those whom they see as accepting them as they see themselves (Backman, 1981: 249). As noted earlier, each individual becomes increasingly dependent on rewards now being consistently provided by the other.

Holism

The common theme in this sketch of interaction within society is *holism:* the philosophical theory that entities in nature cannot be broken down to their component parts and cannot be analyzed as mere sums of the parts. Definitions of the situation and interactions within the situation are clearly the basis for the social facts of society, but the social facts emerging from these definitions and interactions have a quality of their own not wholly traceable to these processes. In short, negotiations, working agreements, constructed social realities, and emerging interpersonal relationships are more than the simple sums of their interactive and definitional parts.

Once a negotiation has been concluded or a working agreement established, something new has arisen that was missing in the interaction and definition leading up to the negotiation or agreement. It is for this reason, among others, that many sociologists contend that their discipline can never be reduced theoretically to the principles of psychology and biology; sociology can never be wholly explained by psychology or biology. In particular, the discipline cannot be explained by learning theory.

[2]While enemies have a social relationship (Stebbins, 1969), much of what is said throughout the remainder of this section is inapplicable to this kind of enduring interpersonal orientation.

THE CONTEXT OF INTERACTION

Another reason for this stance on the irreducibility of social phenomena to the psychological level is the fact that social interaction is greatly affected by the context in which it occurs. There are many different contexts of interaction, four of which are considered here: *resources and alternatives, territoriality, history,* and *frame.* In effect, each of these contexts constrains situated behavior in certain ways, circumscribing an individual's interaction with other people in the setting.

Resources and Alternatives

One constraint already touched upon is the power of the other person or persons in the interaction. Power is founded on available resources. Available resources may be unequally distributed to the advantage or disadvantage of individuals in the situation.

For those desiring the services of another person, there are four alternatives to accepting a power relationship in which the other person is ascendant (Blau, 1964: 118–119). (1) They can supply the other person with the services needed by him or her with the hope that the desired service is reciprocated. (2) They can seek the desired service elsewhere, provided it is available. (3) They can coerce the other person to give the service. This assumes they can establish a dominance over the person. (4) They can resign themselves to doing without the service. They then find a substitute service, which indicates a change in their values. If none of these four alternatives is acceptable or available, then the individuals have no choice but to accept the original service on the other person's terms.

Territoriality

Lyman and Scott (1970: 89) note that "all living organisms observe some sense of territoriality; that is, some sense—whether learned or instinctive to their species—in which control over space is deemed central for survival." These authors distinguish four types of territories, all of which are germane to human interaction. The four types are *public territories, home territories, interactional territories,* and *body territories.*

Public territories are those areas open to all who belong to the community and to the society. Among the public territories in a city or town are parks, streets, sidewalks, and public conveyances. Without public territories, the sense of community in municipalities would decline markedly. People must go through or meet in public territories to interact with each other. *Home territories,* unlike public territories, are areas where regular participants have relative freedom of behavior accompanied by a sense of intimacy and control over the surroundings. People's homes, homosexual bars, and private clubs exemplify this type.

More central to the subject of this chapter are the *interactional territories,* or the places where social gatherings occur. Ballparks and dance halls are interactional territories. There is an invisible boundary surrounding the gatherings in interactional territories; the boundary remains intact for the duration of the assembly. Who may enter and who may leave under agreed upon conditions is governed by the understood rules familiar to the habitués. The invisible boundaries of the interactional territory separate a family having a picnic in a public park from other picnickers. Three people dining together in a restaurant are separated by such boundaries from others who are having dinner in the restaurant.

Finally, there are *body territories.* The human body itself and the space it encompasses are body territories. For many people, the body is the most private and inviolate of all the territories individuals call their own. Even here, however, there are social rules about the use and touching of our bodies by ourselves and others. Among the rules are guidelines pertaining to masturbation, medical examination, public display of affection, and the use of cosmetics. There are also rules specifying the appropriate distance between the bodies of males and females and the bodies of friends and strangers.

It should be evident that territoriality sometimes guides and sometimes restricts interaction among individuals. Territoriality forms a context within which men and women associate with one another. It helps to explain their definitions of situations. Territoriality explains why individuals define situations in the way they do. Hence, territoriality helps explain why people act as they do.

History

In Chapter 1, "The Study of Society," we defined history as the record of significant events, the study of human experience through the years. Histories are kept not only of societies, provinces, and cities but also of collectivities, associations, groups, neighborhoods, firms, and clubs. To the extent that they are remembered and are relevant, histories influence everyday interaction. They put a constraint on interaction.

"Each interaction situation is not a brand new society, but is influenced by interaction that has gone on before" (Charon, 1985: 171). In other words, the histories of which we speak are broader than, but encompass, those recorded in some formal or official manner. They may be simply collectively remembered events of great importance, such as the exceptional Christmas party three years ago or the time when the building caught fire because someone carelessly left a solvent-soaked rag near the water heater.

Frame

As you may recall, there is a reference to frame in the section "Ethnomethodology" in Chapter 2, "Sociological Theories." Frame is the hidden set of social rules and categories (categories of people, things, events, conditions) that are a part of our cultural heritage. These rules are largely unrecognized because they are so deeply ingrained and so habitual in their application to our everyday lives. The concept of frame was exemplified in Chapter 2 by two rules of conversational etiquette: letting others finish their sentences before we commence talking and keeping the proper physical distance between ourselves and strangers.

Usually, we give little thought to the hidden rules. We instinctively keep our distance when we chat briefly with a stranger. Are we ever tempted to drive through a red light? Do we sometimes drive on the left side of the street? We simply follow the rules of driving; we enact them, so to speak. Frames precede a situation or come into a situation when individual participants become active in the situation. Human beings are the vehicles for the expression in interaction of the numerous frames.

THE SOCIAL CAUSATION CYCLE

Perhaps it has become evident by now that there is a causal relationship of sorts among the many phenomena discussed in this chapter. There is a *social causation,* to use Robert MacIver's (1964: 291–313) words, wherein a number of factors are brought into a single system; the system is referred to here as the definition of the situation.[3] This definition, in turn, becomes the basis, in interaction with other people and their definitions, for all aspects of society, only some of which have been covered in this chapter. In time, these aspects become the context within which future definitions are selected and constructed. Hence, we have the social causation cycle—a cycle which takes in the definition of the situation, interaction, social forms, and context.

The social causation cycle is depicted in rudimentary form in Figure 4.2. Depending on their research interests, sociologists break into the cycle at different points: interaction, reality con-

[3]MacIver used the term "dynamic assessment" to label what is referred to here as the definition of the situation.

struction, context, or definition of the situation. This chapter started with the definition of the situation and its subprocesses of role-taking, presentation of self, and so on. People define situations before engaging in goal-directed interaction. In general, before goal-directed interaction can occur, the individuals must negotiate a working agreement, if one is not already established. Some episodes of interaction are also a part of the process of reality construction, wherein new social forms and interpersonal relations are brought into being. Constructed reality, particularly the social forms, becomes part of the context in which social interaction is conducted and in which people define situations.

The broad themes explained in this book are culture, institutions, differentiations, social structure, social dynamics, and, above all, society. The themes complicate the simplified social-causation model. But the principle of the cycle of social causation remains valid, starting, as it does, with the definition of the situation and social interaction.

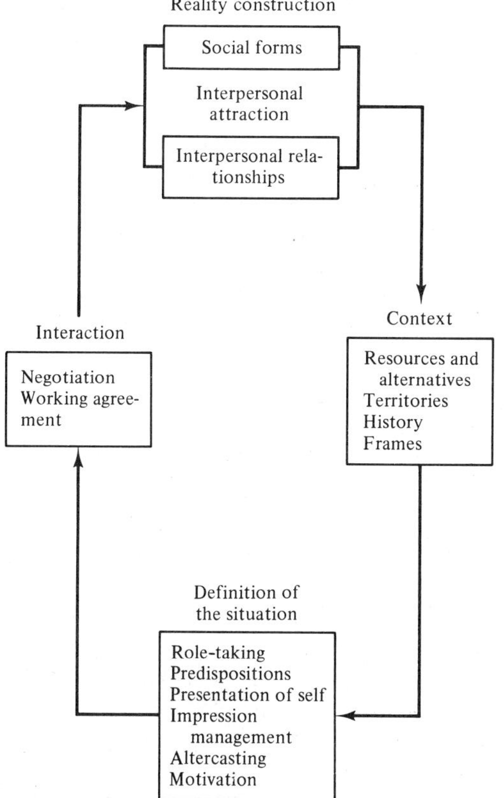

Figure 4.2 The Social Causation Cycle

OUTLINE AND SUMMARY

You can review Chapter 4, "Human Interaction," by going over the following outline and summary:

I. Introduction
Action and knowledge are the roots of all things social. The term "social" is defined as the sharing of language, beliefs, goals, and norms with other members of society. A boxer hitting someone who insulted him is an example of social interaction.

II. Social Interaction
Social interaction defined: The mutual effect of the actions of individuals on each other. Action, knowledge, and social interaction are based on *human gestures:* the words and movements of a person that act as specific stimuli calling forth the socially appropriate responses from another person. In exchange theory, interaction is defined as behavior in which the action of one person is a stimulus for or reward for the action of another.

A. Role-Taking
Role-taking is the process where individuals imaginatively put themselves in the roles of other individuals. This is a largely unconscious process.

B. Improvisation
After imputing a role to other people in the interaction, we improvise, in part, our own actions with reference to them.

III. Interaction and Interpretation
Sociologists have concentrated on the interpretive meaning of the term "interaction." They have given a great deal of thought to a social reality known as *definition of the situation.*

A. Definition of the Situation
Situations are defined in a four-step sequence: (1) entering a situation with a

goal, (2) perceiving aspects that activate predispositions, (3) arriving at a definition of the situation through perceptions, goals, and predispositions, and (4) direction of action in the situation by the definition of the situation.

B. Interpretive Processes
Several processes are put into operation in the third step of the situation-defining sequence. McCall and Simmons divide these processes into two categories: *cognitive* and *expressive.*

1. Cognitive Processes
Role-taking is one of the cognitive processes. The process itself is a means of gaining knowledge. Knowing the roles of others enables us to impute motives to others. An understanding of their motives helps to explain their actions. Our role selection depends on the imputations we perceive the others to be making in relation to us.

2. Expressive Processes
Two *expressive processes* are operating when people define situations. The two processes are *altercasting* and the *presentation of self.* Presentation of self is a performance. We engage in *impression management.* In presenting ourselves, we hope the target audience in the situation will impute the role to us we desire. *Altercasting* is the placing of other people in particular identities and role types. Our performance expresses our image of the people with whom we are associating.

C. Motivation
Motivation is a state of mind that incites a person to action. The state of mind is in response to a need, an idea, an emotion, or an organic condition. Motivation is the process of inciting people to action—of motivating them to something, that is. Sociologists have contributed to a sociological theory of motivation in several ways. Motive is conceived of as an end in view. A motive is a verbal justification for past, present, and future actions. *Accounts* are verbal defenses of future behavior; they are *excuses* and *justifications.* The sociological theory of motivation is also ethnomethodological.

IV. Interaction and Society
Social interaction is the basis for the social world, for society. Four processes enter into social interaction. The four processes are *negotiation, shaping the working agreement, reality construction,* and *interpersonal attraction.*

A. Negotiation
Negotiation defined: The process of bargaining over the terms of exchange of social rewards. Negotiations occur in a multitude of circumstances ranging from situational encounters to international relations. Negotiation is possible only when those involved are willing to compromise their values and consider the values of others in the situation. Negotiation revolves around four issues: (1) social identities, (2) interactive roles, (3) agendas, and (4) life courses.

1. Social Identity
There are times when one or more people in the interaction feel they must negotiate an important *social identity.* Labor in childbirth offers a good illustration of identity negotiation.

2. Interactive Roles
When *interactive roles* are negotiated, the focus shifts to the behavior to be allowed in the setting. A teacher's negotiation in a classroom is an example. The pupils also negotiate, using tactics such as humor, friendliness, ingratiation, and flirtation.

3. Agendas
Agendas are schedules of activities to be carried out over a period of time. They are negotiated with others who share an individual's interest in an allotment of time. An example is the efforts of hospital patients to obtain an early release.

4. Life Courses
Negotiations are constantly under way in the course of one's life. An individual is constantly bargaining, compromising, and making deals with those who can make demands on his or her time. The predicament of an amateur baseball player is an example of life-course negotiation.

B. Working Agreements
A *working agreement* is an understanding among interacting people as to who each person is (social identity) and as to what he or she is to do (interactive role). Working agreements are the immediate products of interaction and negotiation. There are two steps in reaching a working agreement. First, the social identities of the individuals on the scene must be negotiated. Second, interactive roles are negotiated.

C. Reality Construction
Reality construction is concerned with how the definitions of the situation coalesce into a collective understanding of what is going on. Complex definitions spawn complex social forms. People define commonly perceived events and changes in their social and physical environment. Collective definitions coalesce into a consensually held view of what has happened and perhaps of what will happen. Definitions of the situation have a taken-for-granted nature in association with reality construction. Individuals move through many routine situations in the course of everyday living. Usages and structural relationships spring from their own social interactional process.

D. Interpersonal Attraction
Sociologists study interpersonal attraction within the framework of interpersonal relationships. An *interpersonal relationship* is the sustained orientation of one person toward another. Among familiar relationships are those between kin, friends, lovers, enemies, and employers and employees. First impressions are important. Two additional contingencies are similarity and physical attractiveness. An important variable is the degree of commitment and attachment to the bond.

E. Holism
The study of interaction within society is holistic. *Holism* is the theory that entities in nature cannot be broken down to their component parts and cannot be analyzed as mere sums of the parts. Social facts emerging from interactions and from definitions of the situation have a quality of their own. Once a negotiation has been concluded or a working agreement accepted, something new has arisen.

V. The Context of Interaction
The context in which it occurs has a great influence on social interaction. Four contexts of interaction will be considered here: (1) *resources and alternatives,* (2) *territoriality,* (3) *history,* and (4) *frame*.

A. Resources and Alternatives
Power is founded on the available resources and alternatives of both the dominant person and the subordinate person. Available resources may be unequally distributed to the advantage or disadvantage of individuals in the situation. Those desiring the services of another person have four alternatives: (1) hoping for reciprocity, they can supply the other person with certain services, (2) they can seek the desired service elsewhere, (3) they can coerce the other person to give the service, and (4) they can resign themselves to doing without the service.

B. Territoriality
All living organisms observe some sense of territoriality. There are four types of territories: (1) *public territories,* (2) *home territories,* (3) *interactional territories,* and (4) *body territories.* An organism seeks to control its territory. Control over space is regarded as necessary for survival.

C. History
There are histories not only of societies and cities but also of collectivities. To

the extent that they are remembered and are relevant, these histories influence everyday interaction. Each interaction situation is influenced by interaction that has gone on before. History puts a constraint on interaction.

D. Frame

Frame consists of hidden sets of rules and categories that are a part of our cultural heritage. Frames are applied more or less unthinkingly in everyday affairs. The social rules are largely unrecognized because they are so deeply ingrained and so habitual in their application to our everyday lives. A primary framework is independent of any prior or original interpretation or definition of the situation. Nevertheless, primary frameworks help make events meaningful.

VI. The Social Causation Cycle

A complicated causal chain exists in the sequence of definition of the situation, interaction, reality construction, and context. The cycle brings a number of factors into a single system. The system is the definition of the situation. The cycle also takes in interaction, social forms, and context.

FOR FURTHER READING AND STUDY

Altman, I. and Taylor, D. A. 1973. *Social penetration: The development of interpersonal relationships.* New York: Holt, Rinehart & Winston. An excellent readable review of the theory and research bearing on the emergence of interpersonal relationships.

Birenbaum, A. and Sagarin, E., eds. 1973. *People in places: The sociology of the familiar.* New York: Praeger. A collection of famous articles on how ordinary people manage themselves and their affairs in ordinary situations, such as bars, subways, intimacies, errands, restaurants, and gift giving and receiving.

Derber, C. 1979. *The pursuit of attention: Power and individualism in everyday life.* Cambridge, MA: Schenkman. A study of how we compete with other people in social situations for their attention to ourselves.

Goffman, E. 1959. *The presentation of self in everyday life.* Garden City, NY: Doubleday. An intriguing account of how we present ourselves to other people in everyday situations based on the analogy of the theater. A modern classic.

Lofland, J., ed. 1978. *Interaction in everyday life: Social strategies.* Beverly Hills, CA: Sage. A miscellaneous set of exploratory studies on human interaction in the contexts of solitude, subordination, and superordination. The topics covered include the frittering away of time, the milkman and his customer, and the bearing of bad news.

Martin, W. B. W. 1976. *The negotiated order of the school.* Toronto: Macmillan of Canada. A study of the ways teachers negotiate interactive roles and social identities with other teachers (as in team teaching) and with students.

McCall, G. J. and Simmons, J. L. 1978. *Identities and interactions,* rev. ed. New York: Free Press. A conceptually clear and easy to follow treatment of the social psychology surrounding human interaction and the formation of interpersonal relationships.

Weigert, A. J. 1981. *Sociology of everyday life.* New York: Longmans. Weigert examines the construction of social reality, the use of time, the importance of identity, and the use of space in our daily interaction with others.

KEY WORDS

account Verbal defense of future behavior; two types are *excuses* and *justifications.*

agenda A schedule of activities to be carried out over a period of time.

altercasting The placing of other people in particular identities and role types.

body territory The human body itself and the space it encompasses.

definition of the situation The meaning people ascribe to the immediate setting in which they find themselves in the course of everyday living.

empathy Participation in the feelings and emotions of another.

excuse A socially approved mitigation which seeks

to relieve responsibility for questionable actions.

frame The hidden set of social rules and categories that are a part of our cultural heritage.

gesture The movement of an individual which acts as a stimulus calling for a response from another individual.

history The discipline that records and explains significant events of the past as they comprise a sequence of human activities.

holism The philosophical theory that entities in nature cannot be broken down to their component parts and cannot be analyzed as mere sums of the parts.

home territory An area where regular participants have relative freedom of behavior accompanied by a sense of intimacy and control over the surroundings; a home, a homosexual bar, or a private club.

impression management The attempt by an individual to influence another person's impression of him or her.

interaction Behavior in which the action of one individual is a stimulus to the action of another.

interactional territory A place where social gatherings occur; a ballpark, a dance hall, a supper club.

interpersonal relationship The sustained orientation of one person toward another; a reciprocal interaction between individuals.

justification A favorable light on an act in the face of someone's claim to the contrary.

language Verbal and nonverbal communication.

life course The experiences and changes which occur from day to day in an individual's life.

motivation A state of mind that incites a person to action; a process of inciting people to action.

negotiation A process of bargaining or haggling over the terms of an exchange of social rewards.

predisposition An enduring, acquired mental state; an attitude, a belief, or a personal value.

presentation of self An attempt to get someone else to impute to us the role we would like to play.

public territory An area open to all who belong to the community or society; a park, sidewalk, street, or public conveyance.

reality construction A conceptualization of what one is doing and the context in which the action is done.

role-taking Putting oneself into the role of another individual.

social Related to a sharing of language, beliefs, goals, and norms with other members of society.

social causation cycle A cycle which takes in the definition of the situation, interaction, social forms, and context.

social identity An agreement or a compromise about the status or social categories of each person who is honored by others.

social interaction The mutual effect of individuals on each other.

territoriality An organism's attachment and to and control over space which it deems central for survival.

working agreement An understanding among interacting individuals as to who each person is and as to what he or she is to do.

chapter 5

Socialization

CHAPTER OUTLINE

INTRODUCTION

The action, knowledge, and interaction trilogy explained in the preceding chapter is one of the foundations of modern society. The broad message of Chapter 4, "Human Interaction," is that without this trilogy there would be no society. But, paradoxically, without society there would be no action, knowledge, or interaction. People interact with each other and acquire a stock of knowledge as members of society. They live in a society.

The capacity to act and interact from a stock of knowledge is, to a substantial degree, *learned.* Early in life human beings begin to develop a stock of knowledge; they learn about society through their interaction with other people, or by means of socialization. *Socialization* is the broad process of learning to be a member of society and of developing a personality which is more or less acceptable to others in the society. An infant who fails to acquire this knowledge fails to become human. Or, to put it another way, the infant lacks socialization. The process is paramount in the early years of life, but it is also an ongoing experience which continues into old age.

Sociology's debt to psychology is possibly no more apparent than here, for learning is the essence of socialization. In general, learning is both a process and a product. It is the process of acquiring or modifying enduring responses (e.g., knowledge, skills, habits) through practice, experience, and exercise. It is also the *product,* or acquired behavioral change resulting from such practice, experience, and exercise.

The sociological approach to socialization is built on a psychological foundation. Sociologists have not ignored psychology. But sociology has its own approach. It is a discipline within itself. The sociological approach to socialization is based on functionalism and symbolic interactionism, two key perspectives.

THE SOCIOLOGICAL APPROACH

Writing on the sociological approach to socialization, Viktor Gecas (1981: 165–166) abstracts two distinct theoretical perspectives which have a bearing on the process of socialization. *The functionalist perspective* is the more prominent of the two. It centers on the individual's adaptation and conformity to role expectations, others' opinions, social norms, and societal values. The functionalists consider the outlook of the group (e.g., small group, large organization, society) and how it molds the thought and behavior patterns of its members, child and adult. This helps the group perpetuate itself. The essence of this perspective is the transmission of culture to new members of the group, particularly as it bears on the roles they play (Parsons, 1951: 205). This is the *passive* side of socialization.

The *symbolic interactionist perspective* is based on the outlook of the individual rather than that of the group. Emphasis is on the development of individuals as unique persons. The symbolic interactionist study of socialization, as we shall see shortly, deals with the rise of the self, the acquisition of attitudes and values, the formation of predispositions, and the habitualization of behavior patterns. The functionalist model treats individual *socializees,* or those who are being socialized, as passive recipients of transmitted culture. In contrast, the symbolic interactionist model deals with socializees as *active* personalities. These individuals define situations, improvise roles, and shape their own characters. Learning is considered a part of this process, too, but it is seen as leading to a different outcome.

The act of learning is common to both perspectives: For the group, socialization is a mechanism through which new members learn the values, norms, knowledge, beliefs, and interpersonal and other skills that facilitate role performance and further group goals. From the perspective of the individual, socialization is a process of learning to participate in social life (Mortimer and Simmons, 1978: 422). This learning accumulates gradually through experience as one goes through life. Both meanings are important to a full sociological understanding of the process of socialization.

These two perspectives focus scientific analysis in special ways. Some sociologists, however, prefer to analyze socialization from a third perspective in which one or both of the first two may be incorporated. The third perspective is known as the *context of socialization.* The context takes in organizations and institutions within which *agents of socialization,* or socializers, transmit culture. Socializees receive the transmitted culture and interpret it. There are five contexts: family, school, peer relations, occupational resocialization settings, and radical resocialization settings. The latter, which is considered in Chapter 16, "Social Control," includes prisons and mental hospitals and, under certain conditions, military establishments, rehabilitation groups, and religious and political organizations.

CHILDHOOD SOCIALIZATION

Sociologists have centered most of their attention on childhood socialization. Inkeles (1968: 76) summarized the nature of their interest in childhood:

> Despite a good deal of incidental variation, almost all of the current definitions of child socialization describe it as the process whereby a person acquires the attitudes, values, ways of thinking, need dispositions, and other personal, yet social, attributes which will characterize him in the next stage of development.

Socialization is an important part of child-rearing. Hence, there is concern among socializers of children, to the extent they are conscious of being socializers, that the children learn the proper attitudes, values, and norms. For this reason, children are mostly objects of primary socialization. *Primary socialization* is the first socialization by means of which they are trained to be satisfactory members of society.

The Socialization Process

Active socialization is rooted in the person. It springs from the individual's personality and self. *Personality* is a "stable set of characteristics and tendencies that determine those commonalities and differences in the psychological behavior . . . of people [and] that have continuity over time" (Maddi, 1981: 10). It includes one's conscious attitudes, values, skills, and knowledge. In normally functioning people, these behavioral regularities, attitudes, values, and the like coalesce into a stable organization of traits.

The *self* is the social and situational part of personality. It has two components (Wylie: 1974: 1): (1) the active, spontaneous, mostly unconscious self and (2) the self as a social idea known to the individual. The latter is known as the *self-concept.* The complicated interrelationship between these two components is still only partly understood. John Kinch (1963) has summarized the reflexive process underlying the development of our self-concept. Its general form is circular: (1) The individual's self-concept is shaped or further shaped by how he sees others in the situation responding to his actions there. (2) This self-concept helps direct subsequent actions of the individual. (3) Such actions influence the behavior of the others. (4) Their behavior is perceived by the individual as a reflection of his or her earlier actions.

By means of this process, we as individuals monitor our own behavior and conform (usually) to the expectations of others. In doing so, we take our own selves as objects, evaluating our selves as objects as we might evaluate any other object in the world. And, because we have learned (i.e., been socialized to) certain stan-

---

SOCIOLOGY OR COMMON SENSE

What do you think?

Which of the following statements do you agree with? Which statements do you disagree with? Make a note of your answers. Check your answers when you have completed your study of this chapter. Are your answers to the statements the same as those a sociologist would give?

1. Our personalities are more or less permanently formed by the time we reach adulthood. They change little after that.
2. *Adolescence* is a universal stage of life recognized in all societies.
3. There is considerable difference in our society between the values and behavior of teenagers and the values and behavior of adults.
4. Canadians and Americans are much alike in personality.
5. Learning is of primary interest to psychologists and of little interest to sociologists.

Self-concept development is one of the consequences of receiving an award.

dards by which to evaluate our behavior, we feel some sort of sentiment, such as pride or mortification, toward the self we see reflected back to us in the behavior of others, in the social "looking glass" (Cooley, 1922: 184). The *looking-glass self* is the reflection of one's self cast by the behavior of others in reaction to one's own behavior. Depending on the sentiment, we are motivated to continue or abandon the behavior associated with the reflection.

The standards by which we evaluate the actions of all members of society, including our own standards, are derived from our significant others. *Significant others* are individuals whose judgments of our behavior are most likely to be *internalized,* or incorporated within ourselves as personally guided principles. Significant others are parents, relatives, close friends, and public heroes. A high degree of intimacy is sometimes unnecessary with a significant other, as with the hockey star, a public hero who is a significant other for thousands of Canadian youngsters. What is necessary is that such heroes be well respected.

Another source of standards for evaluating behavior is the reference group. A *reference group* is a group of individuals who are admired and respected by an individual (Lauer and Handel, 1983: 117–120). Reference groups provide us with a perspective or frame of reference from which to view parts of the social and physical world and the human behavior therein. People aspire to gain membership in some of their reference groups. On the other hand, they have no interest in joining some of the groups. For example, many people whose tastes in clothing are influenced by the television and film elite have no desire to join the ranks of motion-picture stars and TV personalities or to mingle with them socially.

Significant others, reference groups, and the looking-glass self are chiefly external influences on the self-conception. An important internal influence is referred to by Mead (1934: 173–178) as the "me." The "me" is composed of the person's many role-identities. A *role-identity* is a person's "imaginative view of himself as he likes to think of himself being and acting as an occupant of a particular social position or status" (McCall and Simmons, 1978: 65).[1]

The concepts of role-identity and "me" illustrate the active dimension of human socialization. As socialization comes about, individuals devise patterns of behavior for themselves that are somehow, albeit only partly, different from the set of expectations commonly associated with a given role. Socialization has been accomplished when these improvisations are compatible with the individual's broader personality and the common set of expectations. These concepts show how both the functionalist perspective and the interactionist perspective are crucial to an adequate understanding of socialization. Many sociologists regard the acquisition of roles as a key part of the socialization process.

[1]See Chapter 6 for further discussion of role and status.

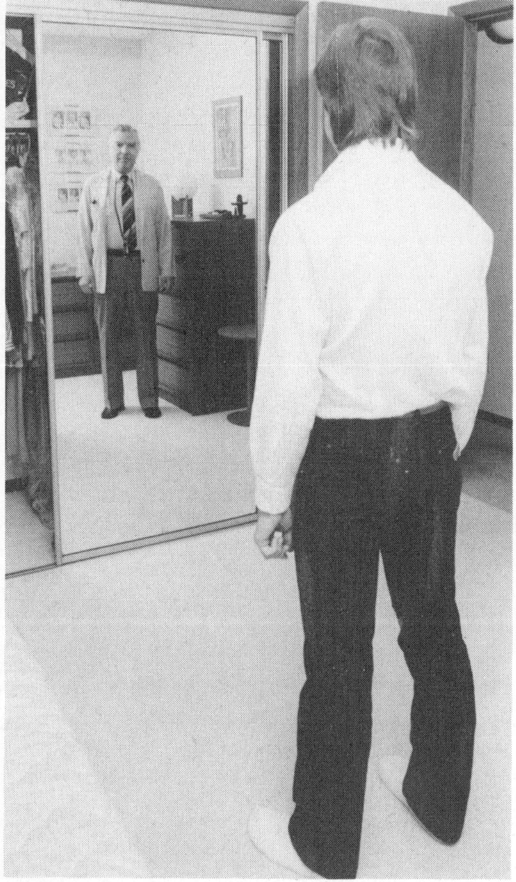

What is this young man's role identity?

The Rise of the Self

Thus far in this section we have been discussing the self, and particularly the self-concept, as more or less fully developed. But how does this very important personal meaning get established in the first place? Mead (1934: 152–164) saw the self as rising in two somewhat indistinct stages: that of *play* and that of the *game.* In play, children are still acquiring their linguistic foundation. They "play at roles" they see enacted in their everyday lives.[2] That is, they play at being mother, father, policeman, doctor, nurse, teacher, storekeeper, police officer, or fire fighter. From this activity they gain a sense of their own individuality, a sense of themselves as objects.

But only adult roles are played at, which suggests that children are also trying to learn these roles and not just trying to separate themselves from those around them. After observing young children playing house, Stone (1981: 253) noted how difficult it was for them to recruit one of their playmates to be the baby or child. A doll usually became their baby or child.

The play stage in self-development is unorganized. The roles played at are poorly interrelated in the child's mind, since he or she has only a vague notion of what is expected of those who actually enact the roles. In other words, one's self-concept is composed, in part, of the roles one plays in life. Thus, when many of the roles are vaguely understood, one's self-concept is fuzzy or indistinct.

In the *game stage* these deficiencies begin to be eliminated. Here children develop a substantially clearer understanding of what others ex-

[2]Playing at a role is different from *role playing* or *role performance:* the earnest enactment of a role-identity.

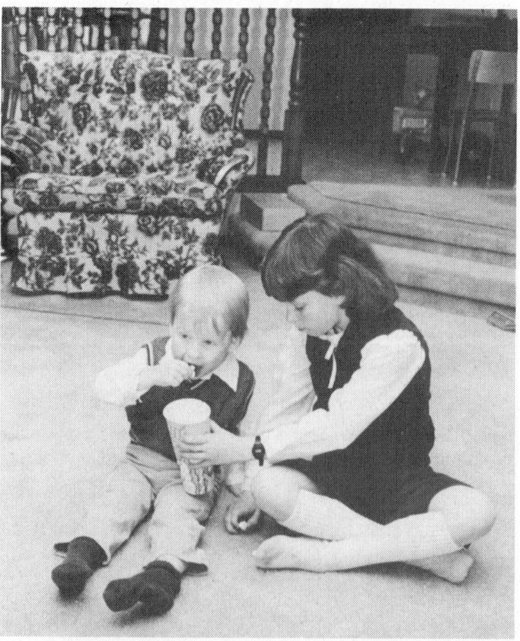

The principle of sharing is an important component of the generalized other.

pect of them in the roles they play in real life as children (e.g., son, daughter, pupil, friend). Mead called this understanding the *generalized other.* It is akin to the idea of conscience and, as noted later, similar to Freud's concept of the superego. The guiding principles internalized from significant others are part of this moral development. The child's initial sense of the generalized other comes from playing with other children in collective games guided by a common set of rules. Mead used the baseball game to illustrate how this sense develops. Novice players learn, for example, that batters are out after three strikes, runners must touch each base in the specific sequence, and foul balls cannot be counted as a third strike. Like social life in general, the baseball game is unplayable unless the participants follow the rules.

First through these games and then through everyday experience, the child learns that, depending on the role, other children and adults in the community (i.e., the generalized other) expect him or her to behave in certain ways. Once children are able to "take the role of the generalized other," as Mead phrased it, they start to see how their several roles are related and, as they learn more about community life, how their roles are related to the roles of others whom they know. Thus, the self moves toward a level and form of organization similar to the social organization of the society in which the child lives.

The Family Context

Much of the research on childhood socialization has centered on the variables of class, culture, and sex (Bush and Simmons, 1981: 160). The family is one of the main areas for this research, in part because socialization in the family is perhaps more pervasive and consequential for the young child than in any other context. Gecas (1981: 170) points out that a primary goal of parenting is to raise children to become competent, moral, self-sufficient adults.

Some of the socialization practices of middle-class families differ from the practices of blue-collar families. Such differences have been noted in both Canada and the United States. For example, middle-class families are more egalitarian than blue-collar families. The former place more stress on individual autonomy than on conformity. Middle-class families also use less punitive child-rearing practices than blue-collar families. Finally, middle-class families encourage more open and more flexible role playing than do blue-collar families (Kohn, 1959a; 1959b; Garigue, 1968; Seeley et al., 1956).

Crysdale (reported in Crysdale and Beattie, 1977: 133) found in the late 1960s that differences in aspirations among a sample of inner-city Toronto children could be explained by their father's level of education. These findings are paralleled by those of similar studies done in the United States (Zigler and Child, 1969: 487). Higher aspirations were recorded among children whose fathers had a high level of education (e.g., high school graduation, two years university) than among those whose father had a low level of education (e.g., grade eight or less).

Turning to gender-role socialization in the family, sociologists have noted that boys are treated differently from girls. Some of the differ-

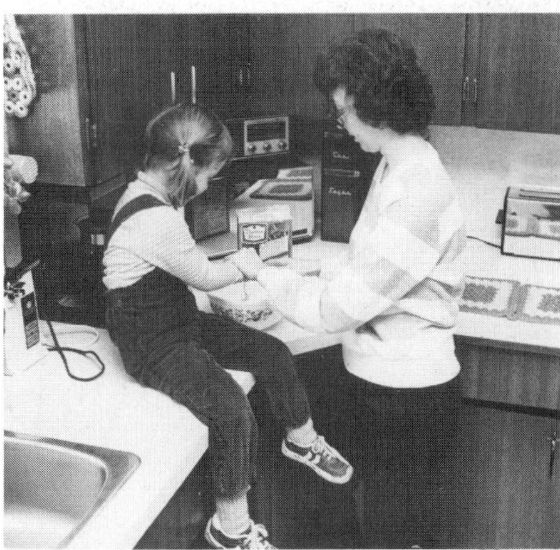

The family socialization context is the source of many important life skills.

ences are obvious, such as dress and hair style, whereas others are subtle. Indeed, it is here, in childhood, that many observers see the attitudes, outlooks, and values distinguishing adult men and women starting to develop. It is here in the contexts of family, school, and peer group that gender-role differentiation commences.

Children are encouraged to adopt or develop different personality traits. For instance, boys learn to be assertive and active. Girls learn to be passive and dependent. In the end, girls are socialized toward the adult roles of wife and mother, whereas boys are socialized toward the roles of husband and breadwinner (Weitz, 1977; Ambert, 1976). Working-class families, however, are more traditional in this respect than middle-class families (Gaskell, 1975; Mussen, 1969: 711). Parents are generally influential models, inasmuch as they are major sources of support for their children's needs and interests and inasmuch as they exert control over their children's behavior (Bronfenbrenner, 1970: 133). Girls and boys often encounter their first examples of femininity and masculinity at home while observing their parents.

The family is one of the main settings in which children are exposed to the mass media. They view television, listen to the radio, and read books, newspapers, and magazines. The advertising, news stories, fictional dramas, and variety shows all carry subtle, and sometimes not so subtle, messages about how people ought to act in our society. Some writers (e.g., Report of the Task Force on Sex-Role Stereotyping in the Broadcast Media, 1982: 4–5) are convinced that adult gender roles are significantly shaped in childhood by the mass media. Women, for example, are sometimes portrayed in the broadcast media as homemakers and mothers and other times as sexual lures or decorative objects. Still, White (1977: 105–106) warns against easy acceptance of the hypothesized links between such portrayals and personality development:

> Nevertheless, the relationship between mass media and society is far from being clear and consequently its effect as an agent of socialization upon adults and children remains problematic, and requires much greater work by sociologists.

We can glimpse the cultural variation in childhood socialization by looking at some of its subcultural manifestations in contemporary North American ethnic groups. Danziger (1974) describes how Italian immigrant families in Toronto try to preserve their old-country culture by shielding their girls from acculturation into Canadian society. By imposing a rigid feminine role socialization, allowing girls less autonomy than boys, and being far less permissive with their daughters than with their sons, they have had moderate success socializing the girls. The boys, their parents reason, have to bear the brunt of learning the new culture, since they must face commitments and competition in the larger society. The boys, it is assumed, will be of little help in keeping alive the old ways.

Rosen (1959) examines six ethnic groups in four Northeastern states for differences in their "achievement syndrome," which is a composite measure of achievement motivation, relevant value orientations, and aspiration levels. White Protestants, Jews, and Greeks ranked higher on each component of the syndrome than French Canadians and Italians. Blacks fell between the French Canadians and Italians. They ranked high, with Protestants and Jews, on indicators such as future planning and encouraging self-reliant behavior, and low, with Italians and French Canadians, on vocational aspirations.

The School Context

For most children, schools continue and reinforce the socialization started by the family (Berg and Boguslaw, 1985: 136–137).[3] Ward (1969) and Richer (1979), for instance, have observed how sex-role identities learned in

[3]This is not necessarily true for the children of some ethnic minorities (e.g., Bhatnagar, 1976) or those from poverty-stricken homes (e.g., Valentine, 1968).

What Happens When Children Are Not Socialized: The Case of Anna

By the time we arrived on the scene, February 7, Anna had been in her new abode, the county home, for only three days. But she was already beginning to change. When first brought to the county home she had been completely apathetic—had lain in a limp, supine position, immobile, expressionless, indifferent to everything. Her flaccid feet had fallen forward, making almost a straight line with the skeleton-like legs, indicating that the child had long lain on her back to the point of exhaustion and atrophy of her foot muscles. She was believed to be deaf and possibly blind. Her urine, according to the nurse, had been extremely concentrated and her stomach exceedingly bloated. It was thought that she had suffered at one time from rickets, though later medical opinion changed the diagnosis to simple malnutrition. Her blood count had been very low in haemoglobin. No sign of disease had been discovered. . . .

Anna was born March 6, 1932, in a private nurse's home. Shortly thereafter she was taken to a children's home. For a time she was boarded with a practical nurse. To those who saw and cared for her, she seemed an entirely normal baby—indeed, a beautiful child, as more than one witness has asserted. At the age of six to ten months she was taken back to her mother's home because no outside agency wished the financial responsibility of caring for her. In her mother's home she was perpetually confined in one room, and here she soon began to suffer from malnutrition, living solely on a diet of milk and getting no sunshine. She developed impetigo. The doctor, according to the mother, prescribed some external medicine which made the child "look like a nigger," and which the mother ceased to use for that reason. The mother, a large woman of twenty-seven, alleges that she tried to get the child welfare agency to take Anna, but that she was refused for financial reasons. The mother, resenting the trouble which Anna's presence caused her and wanting to get rid of the girl, paid little attention to her. She apparently did nothing but feed the child, not taking the trouble to bathe, train, supervise, or caress her. Though she denies tying the child at any time, it is perhaps true that the child was restrained in some way (by tying, confining in a crib, or otherwise) and gradually, as her physical condition became worse, due to confinement and poor diet, became so apathetic that she could be safely left unrestrained without danger of moving from her chair. Anna's brother, the first illegitimate child, seems to have ignored her except to mistreat her occasionally.

The bedroom in which Anna was confined was reported to have been extraordinarily dirty and contained a double bed on which the mother and son slept while Anna reclined in a broken chair. The mother carried up and fed to Anna huge quantities of milk. Toward Anna's fifth birthday the mother, apparently on advice, began feeding her thin oatmeal with a spoon, but Anna never learned to eat solid food.

Anna's social contacts with others were then at a minimum. What few she did have were of a perfunctory or openly antagonistic kind, allowing no opportunity for

Gemeinschaft to develop. She affords therefore an excellent subject for studying the effects of extreme social isolation.

SOURCE: Kingsley Davis. Extreme social isolation of a child. *American Journal of Sociology* 45: 554–565, 1939.

American and Canadian families during the preschool years are strengthened in the schools. The schools also promote the images of males as breadwinners and females as full-time homemakers and mothers. This is evident in the content of teaching, the reading material made available to pupils, and the counseling they receive on course selection (Leslie and Korman, 1985: 332). This situation may change during the 1980s, however, as more and more teachers and textbook authors strive to portray women in other than traditional roles.

Schools promote their own norms, especially those of independence, achievement, universalism, and specificity (Dreeben, 1968). *Universalism* is the requirement that we apply uniform standards to our treatment and evaluation of other people. By observing universalism, a person avoids discriminating against someone else or favoring a friend or a relative. People are differentiated strictly by the relevant uniform standards rather than by the private feelings (e.g., love, hate, fear, jealousy) of the person applying them. Dreeben says that relations characterized by *specificity* are segmented. They are temporary and narrow in scope, such as those between teacher and pupil, as compared with the enduring and pervasive relations of parent and child. Learning these norms fulfills one of the school's main goals, which is to prepare the child for effective functioning in adult life.

Yet some pupils fail to learn these standards, or, if they learn them, they refuse to accept them. This is another point at which socializees become active in the socialization process (Gecas, 1981: 182). They try to protect their self-esteem against the label of failure put on them by their teachers. Two patterns of achievement motivation develop: one oriented toward having success, the other toward avoiding failure (Covington and Berry, 1976). In the second strategy, students eschew participation where failure is imminent or, if forced to participate, they put in minimum effort or procrastinate, so as to be able to say that the performance is no indication of their actual abilities.

By placing children among a variety of students and confronting them with a succession of different teachers, schools teach the art of flexibility (Seeley et al., 1956: Chapter 5). Furthermore, they learn about the stratification of achievement and merit, as they come to identify themselves by their scholastic level and grade in school. Finally, by "teaching" the *hidden curriculum,* schools unwittingly promote the transition to adult life. For this curriculum consists of the demands found in all such institutions, which students must learn and heed if they are to survive within them (Snyder, 1971). For example, some students learn which methods for doing problems will earn them the highest marks and which assignments to neglect without fear of reprisal. They have found out about their school's hidden curriculum.

The Peer Context

Our *peers* are our equals. At the adult level, peers hold the same social or organizational rank. The salespeople in a department store are peers, as are professional football players, commissioned officers in the military, and men and women who work in the same profession (lawyers or sociologists, for example). The peers of adolescents and children are usually defined as those who are more or less the same age. Children in kindergarten are peers; freshmen in a college are peers. At this point, you will be directing your interest toward the childhood peer context. Peers have much to do with a child's socialization.

Gecas (1981: 185) writes that, although peer socialization is usually unintended as such, it nevertheless occurs in three broad areas: (1) development and validation of the self; (2) development of competence of self-presentation, using the processes of role-taking and impression management; and (3) learning about matters overlooked or avoided by parents. Friendships among child peers still tend to form chiefly between those of the same sex, although cross-sex relationships are more common than they used to be (Elkin and Handel, 1984: 172). As they make friends and mingle with others, children learn about adult life from their peers. This learning often contradicts, or counteracts, what they learned in school and at home.

After observing several children's groups, Gary Fine (1981) concluded that child peers teach those in the group sex practices, informal rules (e.g., how to exploit school and family), and pastimes, including vandalism, general mischief, and the use of drugs and alcohol. Indeed, sexual socialization comes largely from peers, starting in childhood and continuing through adolescence (Gagnon and Simon, 1973). Lever (1976) observed play in a schoolyard. She found that the conservative influence of the school on gender-role socialization continued on the playground. The boys played outdoor sports more than the girls did. John and his peers played team sports and "war," while Jane and her friends engaged in board games or played with dolls. Girls gained status by playing with the boys, but the boys seldom mingled with the girls. Playing with the girls hardly added to their status.

Vaz (1976: Chapter 5) describes how children learn deviance from their peers. The influential peers offer a perspective to would-be members of their group; the group becomes a reference group. Peers teach deviant behavior such as shoplifting and stealing hubcaps from a car. The peers give new members of their group a vocabulary of motives with which they can justify their deviant behavior to parents, teachers, and juvenile authorities. To steal may be wrong, but "ripping off" a candy bar from a grocery counter is only an innocent pastime.

ADOLESCENT SOCIALIZATION

Although the self begins to take shape in childhood, when moral issues are of major concern, it is during adolescence, or the period running approximately from ages twelve to twenty, that self-concept and personal identity assume overriding importance (Simmons et al., 1973). This is also the period during which adolescent values are decidedly idealistic when compared with the realistic values of adults, whose sobering life experiences have tempered their own earlier utopian outlooks.

In North America adolescence is recognized as a transitional status between childhood and adulthood. Campbell (1969: 821–827) treats it as a social role with its own rights and duties. At age sixteen, most Canadians have the right to drive a car. A person who is eighteen years old can leave home and live as an independent adult. On the other hand, adolescents are denied some rights. For example, there are age limits on voting and being served alcoholic beverages.

Adolescents, it is assumed, behave in more mature ways than children. They are expected to broaden their social contacts, thereby becoming less dependent on their parents and more dependent on their peers and adult acquaintances. Teenagers are supposed to enter into various lines of activity, gain new experiences, and strive to become singular individuals in society (i.e., a person with a recognizable status—the status of a musician, a football player, a drugstore clerk, for example). Last, but not least, they must learn to be adults, which entails learning social skills, conforming to moral standards, and taking an interest in work and a job.

Adolescence is also a period of widespread *anticipatory socialization,* or the process by which aspirants to a particular social role begin to discern what it will be like to function in that position. Through their interaction with actual role incumbents and by observing how the role is played in the media, adolescents begin internalizing the outlook, expectations, rights, and privileges of the roles.[4] Our symbolic capacity enables us to act vicariously. We can imagine what it would be like to carry out the roles to which we aspire (Stryker, 1980: 63).

Campbell (1969: 824–825) points out that adolescence now begins at an earlier age than in the past. It also lasts longer than formerly. Puberty starts earlier today, and so do activities such as dating and dancing. Girls use cosmetics at an earlier age than formerly. Meanwhile, the required amount of formal education calls for more years of schooling than in past years. There is a demand for a better-trained labor force. The trend toward further education has extended the years of a youth's dependence on the family and, in some cases, on the state. Many young people remain dependent in their mid-twenties or even in their late twenties.

As an adolescent grows older, he or she expresses a demand for independence. Many young people would like to find a steady job or get married, but their interests are frustrated by an effort to earn a university degree or complete trade-school training. The adolescent is called upon to make many decisions. It is no wonder that adolescence is a time of personal tension and anxiety.

Characteristics of Adolescence

Campbell (1969: 825–826) identifies eight emergent characteristics of adolescence bearing on the socialization of people at this stage of life. (1) Adolescence is the first time that one's self-image is so consciously manipulated by oneself. Here people experiment with different ways of presenting themselves. As mentioned earlier,

Manipulation of the self-image is a central part of adolescence.

personal identity is a dominating concern at this time. The adolescent asks, "Who am I?"

(2) Adolescents play a more active role in developing their personalities than they did as young children. They not only work to shape their identities, but also help to define their rights; they negotiate the kind of treatment they receive from others. (3) There is pressure at this time to make a decision about the occupational future. Correspondingly, there is intense interest in the opportunities and alternatives in the job world and in careers.

(4) In adolescence, socialization occasionally assumes a rather different character: individuals must *unlearn* some of the values and interests of childhood and replace them with (i.e., learn) adult values and interests. Perhaps the most obvious example of this replacement is the increasing attractiveness of the opposite sex and the drift toward mixed-sex peer relations.

(5) Adolescence is also a period of certain irrevocable choices that bear on important interests. On graduating from high school, adolescents must decide whether to get a job or to continue with their education, either in college or in trade school. A young man may decide on a military career in the Canadian Forces. Many young people also are thinking about getting married. They have a choice to make—a choice of a spouse.

(6) Adolescence is a time when personal

[4]Anticipatory socialization into occupational roles is covered in Chapter 11, "Education," and consequently omitted here.

identity is often in its greatest flux. Young people enter many new roles with which they have scant familiarity. Understandably, they experience considerable anxiety about how they will perform these roles. Gripped by uncertainty, adolescents may leave one role and try another. They may retreat temporarily to a role which is more familiar and manageable, a role which is less threatening than a prior role.

(7) Adolescents undergo rapid social growth. In the span of a few years, they learn a myriad of interpersonal skills and how to apply them in diverse settings. (8) Lastly, it bears repeating that this is the time when idealistic values take root and, it may now be added, these values clash on occasion with the sometimes more realistic values of adults.

James Coleman (1961: Chapter 1) holds that adolescence, as a distinct period in life, is a product of industrialization. He traces the distinctiveness of adolescence in the modern high school. Within the school and reinforcing the separateness of the students is the adolescent subculture, with its distinct tastes in music, dress, films, recreation, and food. In the modern high school, students are extensively educated in certain skills and bodies of knowledge. A family hardly can impart the skills and knowledge learned in today's high schools. When the adult occupational and social roles were less specialized, the family could socialize children in a comparatively short period of time. Unlike those of today, children of a bygone era were ready to enter the adult world of work and responsibility in their midteens.

Family and Peer Contexts

One of the puzzles for those who study adolescent social life is the question of continuity and discontinuity. How much continuity and discontinuity exist between childhood and adolescence? What about continuity and discontinuity between adolescence and adulthood? Is this transition smooth or rough? Is there *continuity,* or an uninterrupted progression? Or is there *discontinuity,* or a lack of a smooth transition?

The upheaval in values among the youth of the late 1960s and early 1970s gave the clear impression at the time that the transition was rough (i.e., the youth were alienated; they embraced social values). Davis (1971) and other writers supported this interpretation of the American adolescent's situation. But Kandel and Lesser (1972), among others, found evidence of continuity. Discontinuity occurs, they argued, only on superficial issues. Adolescents generally have the same values as adults. Moreover, parental influence is generally deep and lasting, when compared with that of peers, teachers, and mass media. Elkin and Handel (1984: 149) concluded after reviewing the literature in this area that the evidence for continuity outweighs that for discontinuity. In their view, "adolescent values and behavior have been more reflective of adult values and behavior" than earlier thinkers supposed.

What about this facet of socialization among Canadian adolescents? Results from a survey of university and high-school students in Toronto are congruent with those of Kandel and Lesser (Kallen and Kelner, 1976). The respondents had internalized the values of their parents, although they did reject certain aspects of their parents' moral code, including its rigidity.[5] For example, the students repudiated the exploitativeness and competitiveness of the work world, but accepted the goals of higher education and the professions.

Whatever the extent of "adolescent society" (Coleman, 1961), there is evidence from a sample of Minneapolis youth that peers can provide an alternative to the school as a source of self-esteem and can even repair damage done to the self-concept by the school (Gecas, 1972). Coleman's observation that influential students as members of the "leading crowd" determine aspirations rather than teachers or parents under-

[5]See Chapter 9, "Society and Culture," for additional discussion of moral changes in today's younger generations.

scores the important role played by peers at this stage of socialization. He found that it was more important for boys to succeed in athletics than in scholarly endeavors (see Chapter 11, "Education," for a further discussion of this point in regard to Canadian students).

But the degree of continuity (or discontinuity) is by no means uniform across the population of North American adolescents. The differences are traceable, in part, to the kinds of relationships prevailing between parents and their adolescent offspring. These relationships vary along several dimensions. For example, not all parents discipline their children in the same way. Some parents are strict, and others are permissive. There are differences in authority patterns. Parental support for youth interests varies among families. The orientation toward self-direction in young people is more apparent in some families than in others.

Melvin Kohn (1959a; 1963) theorized that class differences in parent-child relationships in general flow from differences in parental values, which, in turn, stem from variations in social-class life-styles. In other words, middle-class occupations frequently require a great deal of self-direction; hence, middle-class parents value this orientation and encourage their children to adopt it. By contrast, working-class occupations require employees to follow a supervisor's explicit directions. In response to this influence, working-class parents emphasize conformity to rules in disciplining their children.

Evidence that this theory holds for American society is available in several studies by Kohn and others (see Kohn, 1963: 472, f.n.3), while Tremblay (1966) has come to similar conclusions about parent-child relations in the French Canadian family. Pineo and Looker (1983), in their study of Hamilton parents, found that they valued self-direction in their children at least as much as the parents in Kohn's studies. Whether the presence of these values varies with the nature of the occupational level and working conditions of the parents, as Kohn found, remains to be determined.

The School Context

Even though its role is substantially shared with the peer group, the school continues to be an important socializing agent as the child enters and moves through his or her adolescent years. Schools channel pupils into different courses of instruction, thereby preparing them for different kinds of occupational careers. Moreover, the intellectual level and educational readiness of a youth's classmates either encourage or discourage his or her own intellectual growth (Campbell, 1969: 847).

But the school has stiff competition in socializing adolescents. As Campbell (1969: 850–851) notes, some of the effects of peer culture on individual teenagers get general parental and adult approval, not withstanding their occasional incompatibility with educational aims. Peers help each other develop social skills. They expand heterosexual contacts and promote hedonism. Peers also honor athletic achievements and, at the same time, in the United States, look with indifference on academic distinction. Campbell writes:

> The mother who complains that her daughter spends too much time on the telephone and receives too many requests for dates is not nearly so pained as the mother who complains that her daughter reads books endlessly and seldom goes outside the house.

The influence of parents, teachers, and peers, although considerable, is nonetheless passive. That it is actively mediated by the adolescents themselves is clear from research on the effect which the pupil's self-concept of ability has on school achievement. Pupils' perceived evaluations of their past academic performances by significant others (parents, teachers, peers) have a bearing, to some extent, on their grade-point averages. For instance, when parents tell their children they are stupid, the children, whatever their actual intellectual ability, perform poorly in school. Such self-appraisals have also been shown to affect, in similar ways, the educational and occupational aspirations of Canadian and American high-school students (e.g., Anisef, Okihiro, and James, 1982; Cohen and Manion, 1981: 73–74). The more favorable the students' self-concept, the higher are their aspirations. Put in the context of this chapter: variations in behavior are influenced by variations in socialization.

ADULT SOCIALIZATION

Adult socialization begins once general education is completed, whether that be after secondary school, trade school, or university (Mortimer and Simmons, 1978: 423–424). In some way, adult socialization synthesizes what has been learned during childhood and adolescence. For example, it includes the reduction of conflicting role expectations. The emotionally charged quality of socializer-socializee relationships present in childhood and adolescence is often diluted in adulthood, even though adults sometimes become students for brief periods. Adults are also less malleable as socializees than children and adolescents, in part because they initiate much of their own socialization, as in selecting a job, deciding to have children, and choosing friends. Thus, the adult socializee is a more active participant in the socialization process than are children and adolescents.

Adult socialization is sometimes called *secondary socialization:*

> The internalization of institutional or institution-based "subworlds." . . . the acquisition of role-specific knowledge, the roles being directly or indirectly rooted in the division of labor . . . (and) the acquisition of role-specific vocabularies. (Berger and Luckmann, 1966: 127)

Secondary socialization builds on the "core" or "basic" personality developed earlier. Consequently, changes in personality during adulthood are usually superficial when compared with the major psychic formations that occur up to this point. Furthermore, if the socialization process has been effective, the general norms of society have been learned by now. Norms learned in adulthood are added to this foundation of primary socialization in connection with the new group and new life-cycle positions of later years. In sum, while both change and stability are found throughout adult life, they come into play at different levels of personality.

Life-Course Perspective

Socialization at the adult level seems to have no limits. In this book, it will be considered in discussions of politics, education, work, leisure, deviance, and age and gender roles. What remains to be done in this chapter is to provide a general picture of the ways adults move through socially defined, age-linked roles that tie together these specific contexts of socialization. Sociologists have made a unique contribution to the study of this process.[6]

The life-course perspective, which actually encompasses the entire span of life, is particularly germane to the adult years, for it is concerned with age-graded norms, generation effects, role transitions, and historical contexts. Correspondingly, the life-course perspective pays little attention to the psychological and biological foundations of socialization.[7] The adult portion of the *life course* is charted over a terrain of varied but interlinked roles and transitions between roles. However, there is no single pathway of roles along which North Americans typically travel. Rather, in Atchley's words (1975: 261), there is "a crude road map with quite a few alternative routes for getting through life's various stages."

In considering age-graded norms, some scholars have noted that such norms provide a timetable for important role transitions (e.g.,

[6]The remainder of this section draws heavily on Bush and Simmons's (1981: 155–157) excellent review of the life-course perspective.

[7]Bush and Simmons (1981: 150–155) also review the biological and psychological perspectives on socialization over the lifetimes of people.

Neugarten and Hagestad, 1976). For many Americans and Canadians, reaching age thirty or forty is an important, if not "alarming," example of the recognition of an age-graded norm. Still, personal, historical, and structural reasons may force some people to deviate from the standard timetable. There are those who marry late and consequently have younger children than other couples their age. The worldwide recession in the early 1980s along with high interest rates forced many young people to postpone the purchase of a house. Thus, for them, owning a home before retirement is a North American dream they may not realize. Structurally speaking, a few fortunate individuals have no worries about their livelihood or occupational advancement. They inherit a business from a parent or from a close relative. The heirs start at the top.

The importance of historical circumstances in adult socialization should never be underestimated. Elder's (1974) study of American children who lived during the Great Depression confirms the soundness of this dictum. There is good reason to believe that much of what he found can be applied to Canada, since both nations experienced the Depression at the same level of intensity, at the same time, for approximately the same duration, and for many of the same reasons (Elder, 1974: 332–334). Elder discovered, for instance, that women from deprived homes, when compared with those from nondeprived homes, were much more inclined toward traditional roles. The deprived homes relied heavily on female children for domestic assistance. When the girls reached young adulthood, they were more likely to marry early; they expressed greater interest in being a homemaker than in pursuing a career. Fewer girls from deprived homes went to college than did girls from privileged homes.

National Character

Together, primary socialization and secondary socialization shape the *national character,* or *national identity,* of a society. Crysdale and Beattie (1977: 14) define national identity as "the sense which citizens have of belonging to a national society, distinguishing them from 'foreigners,' and binding them with other citizens in shared meanings, common institutions, social systems, and social strata." Studies of national character search for the significant differences in traits, patterns, or configurations of personality typical of national populations, rather than for unique characterological distinctions (DiRenzo, 1977: 298).

Anthropologists have studied how culture is transmitted via socialization to new members of the society, and how this process differs from one society to another. It was through their work that socialization was conceptualized as a mediating process by which conformity to cultural demands is effected. Additionally, many anthropologists hold that modal personality characteristics can be similarly traced through socialization to culture.

This area of the social sciences is fraught with methodological and conceptual problems, which give a tentativeness to most studies here. Within these limitations, however, sociologists have attempted to sketch the American and Canadian national characters and, in some instances, compare the two. The discussion here is restricted to the comparisons; no attempt is made to draw a complete picture of the two national characters. One caveat: what follows appears to hold best for English-speaking, native-born, white North Americans, and less for the first generation of ethnic groups on this continent. The place of French Canadians in this portrayal is considered separately.

Possibly the most extensive test of national character in North America has been carried out by Arnold and Tigert (1974), who surveyed 1838 white, middle-class American male and female householders and 2675 Canadians of similar status. Guided by the hypothesis that Americans are greater risk-takers and more individualistic than Canadians, these authors cast their results into two dimensions: active and liberal. At the time the data were gathered,

Americans were found to be significantly higher than Canadians on the *active* dimension. That is, Americans are more self-assured. They have greater leadership ability and more confidence than Canadians. When compared with Canadians, Americans are more likely to assert their independence. They are also more community-oriented and more willing to participate in community affairs. They are optimistic about their personal future. Canadians are financially conservative in matters such as borrowing money and buying on credit.

Canadians, however, are found to be significantly more *liberal* than Americans. They are more socialistic, inasmuch as they favor a strong central government. They are morally less conservative. For example, Canadian men and women are more permissive in the areas of sexual behavior, movie censorship, television violence, male-female roles, and discipline of both adults and children. Canadians are also more inclined to accept changes in traditional values, such as those values pertaining to moral issues and control by the state. Americans resist encroachment by government on individual rights and responsibilities.

How do French Canadians stack up in these comparisons? John Porter (1979: 89–102) believes English and French Canadians are more alike in their traditionalism, religiosity, authoritarianism, and financial conservatism than previous thinkers have suggested. But Porter's ideas, like those of others who have written in this area, still can be looked upon only as impressions. Research efforts, such as the work of Arnold and Tigert, do reveal differences in Canadian-American national character, but differences that are clearly conceptualized and hence amenable to empirical study.

THE OTHER DISCIPLINES

Up to this point in this chapter we have focused almost entirely on the contributions of sociologists to the study of socialization. The time has come now to branch out, to consider the theoretical advances achieved in other disciplines. Sociologists have had considerable intellectual help from biologists, psychologists, psychoanalysts, anthropologists, and others in their quest for an understanding of how human beings become social.

Nature vs. Nurture

The phrase "nature vs. nurture" refers to the following question: How much of human social action ultimately can be accounted for by natural forces such as heredity and reflex reactions (nature), and how much can be accounted for by the training and general learning acquired while growing up (nurture)? Nurture, in answer to the question, is really a synonym for socialization. The nature-nurture controversy stretches back at least to the 1920s, when psychologists were beginning to challenge the conventional wisdom of the day, namely that intelligence and achievement are innate and hence impossible to change through education and other environmental experiences. Studies conducted by psychologists at the University of Iowa revealed that the intelligence side of human nature is modified early by nurtural experiences with parents and by preschool activities (Skeels, 1940).

Our overall understanding of the relationships between nature and nurture has advanced little beyond the conclusions reached by psychologists roughly fifty years ago: human social actions are accounted for by both natural forces and nurtural forces. The explanation of socialization in this chapter indicates that, in general, sociologists think nurtural forces are the more important of the two forces. At least, very little has been said about natural forces. Still, there is an increasingly prominent branch of sociology that tries to counterbalance the tendency of sociologists to favor nurtural explanations. That branch is referred to here as the *genetic-constitutional approach* to socialization.

The genetic-constitutional approach stresses the biological characteristics of the individual as they bear on the socialization process. The link between biological processes and social behavior is too complicated and hypothetical to incorporate in this discussion. But the possibilities are tantalizing: Barchas (1976: 303), for example, holds that social processes may set in motion events influencing biochemical mechanisms. And biochemical mechanisms may profoundly alter the ability of people to respond to their environment. Age and sex are two crucial biological variables which often enter into our definitions of situations and hence into our interactions in social situations. Barchas (1976: 327) reminds us of the importance of a sociobiological approach to human action and socialization:

> As the individual behaves, physiology adjusts to his position in the environment. Through his behavior he may alter the environment for himself and others, producing a continuous flow of interrelationships between physiology, behavior, and social structure. Social life is inextricably bound to biologic life, each functioning and setting the stage for the other. We are just beginning to understand how to inquire into that interaction.

The Psychoanalytic Approach

Psychoanalysis pioneered the idea of long-term personality development, running from infancy through adulthood. Sigmund Freud (1856–1939) and his followers saw individual personalities forming over time through the interaction of three systems: the *id,* the *ego,* and the *superego.* The *id* is the instinctual, innate, unorganized, undisciplined, biological side of personality (i.e., the active self, page 77). Antisocial urges, chiefly those of a sexual and aggressive nature, originate here. The *ego* is the reactional, conscious part of personality, similar in ways to the "me" discussed earlier. Its energy comes from the id, while it is controlled by the moral directives of the *superego.* The superego operates like a conscience; it can be said that it is the conscience. The ego performs the reality-testing function of personality and is influenced by this process. As children mature, their superegos develop through interaction with their significant others and with socially acceptable ways of channeling the urges of the id. Erik H. Erikson (1963: Chapter 7), a neo-Freudian, writes that one's ego identity develops through the "eight ages of man." At each of these ages of development, the individual demonstrates that his or her ego is "strong enough to integrate the timetable of the organism with the structure of social institutions" (Erikson, 1963: 246). Thus, each age builds on the ages preceding it.

(1) The first age is one of *basic trust* vs. *basic mistrust.* Infants who trust have learned to rely on the sameness and continuity of the behavior of those who provide for them. One aspect of infant trust is the willingness to let the mother out of sight. (2) In the second age, infants develop *autonomy.* That is, they gain a sense of outer control over their environment through free choice. In making choices, they manipulate and discriminate objects. To manipulate and discriminate too much, however, leads to shame and doubt.

(3) As the infant grows into a child, he or she develops *initiative,* which is added to the already developed sense of autonomy. To free choice is added the quality of direction; with direction, the infant plans activity, undertakes activity, and is on the move. Erikson says the danger at this age is the feeling of guilt resulting from seeking the wrong goals or initiating the wrong acts. (4) During the *industry* vs. *inferiority* age, the child enters primary school. Here children learn to gain recognition by producing with the use of tools and acquired skills. Pleasure is derived from competently completing a project. A sense of inferiority develops from aborted attempts to be industrious.

(5) The advent of puberty ushers the child into adolescence. *Identity* is the primary concern in this age of man; adolescents worry about how they appear in the eyes of others. There is also an effort to connect the roles and skills

cultivated in the age of industry with nascent occupational interests. But doubt can set in with respect to one's developing identity and occupational interests, engendering role confusion.

(6) As the adolescent emerges into adulthood, the search for identity gives way to a search for *intimacy.* People of this age are ready to fuse their identities with certain others in concrete affiliations. The fear of ego loss in such relationships can lead to a profound sense of isolation. (7) *Generativity* vs. *stagnation* is the ego development dilemma of older adults. The idea of generativity includes creating things and producing them. It also includes guiding the next generation (i.e., creating and producing future adults). People can fail here as well. With failure, they sink into stagnation.

(8) The final age is one of *ego integrity* vs. *despair.* Integrity is reserved for those whose egos have developed according to the first seven ages:

> Only in him who in some way has taken care of things and people and has adapted himself to the triumphs and disappointments adherent to being, the originator of others or the generator of products and ideas—only in him may gradually ripen the fruits of these seven stages. (Erikson, 1963: 268)

For those who have failed to develop successfully through the seven ages, there is only despair in the eighth age.

The Developmental-Cognitive Approach

The *developmental-cognitive approach* to socialization has its origin in the theories of Jean Piaget (1896–), a French psychologist who sees the cognitive ability of children (i.e., thinking, reasoning) as developing in five stages.[8] The first is the *sensorimotor stage,* which runs from birth

[8]Piaget's theories are extremely complicated, making them difficult to summarize adequately in so little space. This summary is based on that of Donald Taylor (1963: 481–485).

Intimacy is needed to balance the impersonality of modern urban life.

to an age of eighteen months to two years. Here the infant operates without any linguistic facility. Hence, the child is unable to produce any representations of external events and is therefore unable to engage in any cognitive activity.

From ages two through four the child is in the *preconceptual stage.* At this point children begin to develop a capacity to respond to symbols and signs. But cognition is based only on what Piaget calls "preconcepts," something midway between a class concept and the individual members of the class. That is, children are unable to determine whether successive instances of an event belong to a specific class or a different class of events.

In the *intuitive stage* (ages 4 to 7), the aforementioned inability to discern individual members of a class is overcome. But children at this stage are still unable to see how classes abstractly relate to one another. For instance, a young girl at this stage could distinguish her own cat from cats as a class of animal, but still be unable to understand that cats as animals prey on birds and are often chased by dogs.

The stage of *concrete operations* occurs between ages seven or eight and eleven or twelve. The preoperation child can put two objects together and take them apart, but the boy or girl fails to realize that he or she has returned to the beginning of the operation. In the stage of concrete operations, operations become, cognitively speaking, truly "reversible," and two successive operations may be combined to yield a new operation. Moreover, the same outcome may now be reached through two or more different series of operations.

During ages eleven or twelve to fourteen or fifteen, individuals move into the stage of *formal operations.* Here they deal not only with objects, classes, and simple relations, but also with verbal statements about these phenomena. They now learn to handle propositions about the phenomena; they understand relations between the propositions. At this stage, the child begins to reason abstractly.

SOCIALIZATION AND CONFLICT

One should never conclude from the content of this chapter that everyone comes to accept the same values, goals, norms, beliefs, and behavior patterns. Socialization is a universal process; it occurs in every society. But some people in the society may be socialized to values, goals, norms, and beliefs that others in the society reject. Not all people march to the same drummer. Those who hear a different beat are also socialized, but they are socialized to their own special views and ways. At times, these views and ways are so strongly held that those who hold them are driven to take a stand against those people who reject their views and ways. The members of society who are socialized to march to a different drummer may even be a majority, albeit one with insufficient power to establish their views and ways as dominant. In other words, socialization helps explain why there is conflict between groups and social classes, just as it helps explain why there is also consensus among groups and classes.

OUTLINE AND SUMMARY

I. Introduction
Socialization is a core concept in sociological theory. It is the broad process of learning to be a member of society and of developing a personality that is more or less acceptable to others in the society. The learning acquired along with socialization is both extensive and varied.

II. The Sociological Approach
Two theoretical perspectives have a bearing on socialization. The two perspectives are the functionalist perspective and the symbolic interactionist perspective. The functionalist perspective centers on the individual's passive adaptation and conformity to role expectations, others' opinions, social norms, and societal values. The symbolic interactionist perspective emphasizes the development of individuals as unique persons through the rise of self, acquisition of attitudes and values, formation of predispositions, and habitualization of behavior patterns. Another perspective is the context of socialization. The five contexts are *family, school, peer relations, occupations,* and *radical resocialization settings.*

III. Childhood Socialization
Socialization is an important part of childrearing. Children are mostly objects of *primary socialization,* or the first socialization by means of which they are trained to be satisfactory members of society.

A. The Socialization Process
Active socialization is rooted in personality and self. The standards by which we evaluate our own behavior and the behavior of others are derived from *significant others* and *reference groups.* An internal influence is an individual's "me." The "me" is represented by a person's many role identities.

B. The Rise of the Self
The self arises in two stages: *play* and *game.* Children play at the roles they are enacting in their everyday lives. They play games. In the game stage, children develop an understanding of what others expect of them in the roles they play in real life as children.

C. The Family Context
Socialization practices of middle-class families differ from those of blue-collar families. Middle-class families are more egalitarian than blue-collar families. Boys are treated differently from girls.

D. The School Context
Schools reinforce the socialization started by the family. Sex-role identities are strengthened in the schools. Schools promote their own norms, especially those of · independence, achievement, universalism, and specificity.

E. The Peer Context
Peer socialization is usually unintended as such. It occurs in three broad areas: development and validation of the self, development of competence of self-presentation, and acquisition of knowledge of matters overlooked or avoided by parents.

IV. Adolescent Socialization
In adolescence, self-concept and personal identity assume overriding importance. Adolescence is a distinct social role in North America. It is a period of anticipatory socialization.

A. Characteristics of Adolescence
This is the first time that one's self-image is so consciously manipulated by oneself. This is a period of irrevocable choices. There is pressure to make occupational decisions. Personal identity is often in its greatest flux. Adolescents must unlearn some of the values and interests of childhood.

B. Family and Peer Contexts
Adolescents generally have been found to have the same values adults have. Parental influence is deep and lasting. Influential peers may have more to say about an adolescent's choice and aspirations than teachers or parents.

C. School Context
For most children, schools continue and reinforce the socialization started by the family. Schools also promote the norms of independence, achievement, universalism, and specificity. Furthermore, they teach the hidden curriculum: the demands students must learn and heed if they are to survive the schooling process.

V. Adult Socialization
Adult socialization is sometimes called *secondary socialization* because it builds on what has been learned in childhood and adolescence. It is more active than earlier socialization. Secondary socialization builds on the "core" or "basic" personality developed earlier.

A. Life-Course Perspective
Adult lives are influenced by age-graded norms, the generation's unique experiences, major role transitions, and important historical events. The perspective encompasses the entire span of life. The life course is charted over a terrain of varied but interlinked roles and transitions between roles.

B. National Character
Primary socialization and secondary socialization shape the national character. The *national character* is the relatively enduring personality characteristics and patterns that are modal among the adult members of a society. Many studies of national character have been impressionistic.

VI. The Other Disciplines

A. Nature vs. Nurture
How much of human social action can ultimately be accounted for by natural forces (heredity, for example) and how much by learning while growing up (nurture)? Sociologists tend to favor nurtural explanations of behavior. This bias is counterbalanced somewhat by the genetic-constitutional approach to socialization.

B. The Psychoanalytic Approach
According to Sigmund Freud, personality forms over time through the interaction of three systems: the *id,* the *ego,* and the *superego.* The psychoanalytic approach examines long-term personality development, running from infancy through adulthood. Erikson theorized that identity develops through eight ages in an individual's life: (1) basic trust vs. basic mistrust, (2) autonomy vs. shame and doubt, (3) initiative vs. guilt, (4) industry vs. inferiority, (5) identity vs. role confusion, (6) intimacy vs. isolation, (7) generativity vs. stagnation, and (8) ego identity vs. despair.

C. The Developmental-Cognitive Approach
The developmental-cognitive approach looks at the growth of thinking and reasoning ability in children and adolescents. According to Piaget, cognitive ability develops in five steps: (1) sensorimotor, (2) preconceptual, (3) intuitive, (4) concrete operations, and (5) formal operations.

FOR FURTHER READING AND STUDY

Barash, D. P. 1982. *Sociobiology and behavior,* 2nd ed. New York: Elsevier. This textbook on sociobiology is written by one of the leading scholars in this field.

Elkin, F. and Handel, G. 1984. *The child and society,* 4th ed. New York: Random House. A short introduction to and survey of the field of socialization.

Erikson, E. H. 1963. *Childhood and society,* 2nd ed. New York: Norton. Erikson presents his statement on the "eight ages of man" in this book along with many other insights bearing on socialization and personality development.

Gove, W. R. and Carpenter, G. R., eds. 1982. *The fundamental connection between nature and nurture.* Lexington, MA: Lexington Books. A compendium of research findings in the fields of psychiatry, genetics, psychology, sociology, economics, and biostatistics. The editors believe that human behavior should be understood in terms of the interaction of nature and nurture.

Haas, J. and Shaffir, W., eds. 1978. *Shaping identity in Canadian society.* Scarborough, Ont.: Prentice-Hall of Canada. This anthology examines the formation of personal identity from the perspectives of history, society, social psychology, and large-scale organizations.

Hollingshead, A. B. 1975. *Elmtown's youth and Elmtown's youth revisited.* New York: Wiley. This study was first conducted in the 1940s and centered on the impact of the local institutions of an American county-seat community on its adolescents. The subsequent study traces the life course of many of the original respondents over the intervening thirty years.

Lott, B. 1981. *Becoming a woman: The socialization of gender.* Springfield, IL: Thomas. A textbook, written in a lively manner, that traces the socialization of females through the life cycle. Lott synthesizes a great deal of the literature in this area.

Medrich, E., Roizen, J., Rubin, V., and Buckley, S. 1982. *The serious business of growing up: A study of children's lives outside school.* Berkeley, CA: University of California Press. A study of the ways children spend their time with parents, watching television, participating in organized activities, and doing chores and jobs.

Williams, F., LaRose, R., and Frost, F. 1981. *Children, television, and sex-role stereotyping.* New York: Praeger. This is a summary of research carried out by the authors to help develop the television series "Freestyle" for use in schoolrooms. The purpose of this series is to counteract sex-role stereotyping in nine- to twelve-year-olds.

KEY WORDS

adolescence A period in life from approximately age twelve to age twenty.

anticipatory socialization The process by which aspirants to a particular role begin to discern what it would be like to function in that role.

context of socialization A condition in which the agents of socialization of organizations and institutions—the socializers—transmit culture.

continuity An uninterrupted progression.

discontinuity Lack of a smooth transition.

ego The reactional, conscious part of personality.

id The instinctual, undisciplined side of personality.

looking-glass self The reflection of the self cast by the behavior of others in reaction to one's own behavior.

"me" An internal representation of an individual's many role identities.

national character The relatively enduring personality characteristics and patterns that are modal among the adult members of a society.

nature A natural force such as heredity.

nurture Training and general learning acquired while growing up; a synonym for socialization.

peer One who belongs to the same group in society to which others belong; the members of the group are similar in age and status.

primary socialization The first socialization by means of which children are trained to be satisfactory members of their society.

reference groups Groups that provide us with a perspective from which to view parts of the social and physical world and the human behavior enacted therein.

role-identity A person's imaginative view of himself or herself in a particular status.

secondary socialization The socialization which adults experience.

self The core of personality.

self-concept A social idea known to the individual.

significant others Those whose judgments of our behavior are most likely to be incorporated within ourselves as guiding principles; they are parents, relatives, and close friends.

socialization The broad process of learning to be a member of society and of developing a personality that is more or less acceptable to others in the society.

socializees Those who are being socialized.

superego The control of the ego; it is conscience.

universalism The requirement that we apply uniform standards to our treatment and evaluation of other people.

three

SOCIAL ORGANIZATION AND CULTURE

The terms "culture" and "social organization" slip easily off a sociologist's tongue, but this is not to imply that the usage of the terms is necessarily loose. Sociologists have a precise understanding of the terms culture and social organization. You will be developing your own understanding of the terms as you work through the chapters in Part Three. *Social organization* is a stable interrelationship of a society's groups and social institutions. Canadian society can be looked on as vast networks of groups, both large and small. Among the groups in society are communities, small groups, and large-scale organizations.

chapter 6

Small Groups

CHAPTER OUTLINE

INTRODUCTION

You might give some thought to your daily activities and to your interaction with others from hour to hour. What do you do as you go about the day's business? Are you alone from one hour to the next, or do you find yourself working and living with others? Do you interact with other men and women in your classroom and within your community? Or do you remove yourself from those around you, preferring to remain apart? Do you look to others for pleasure and necessities? Or are you wholly independent?

As a socialized human being, you are not alone. In fact, you are likely to spend much of your time living with other people and sharing your experiences with them. You belong to groups. A group is an assembly of individuals who interact with each other. As an active individual, you belong to several different groups; each has something to say about your status and role. A group can be an informal gathering or a formal organization such as a club or a baseball team.

Your family is a group. Your co-workers, your associates in a club, and the members of your class are united in groups. Everyone in each group interacts with everyone else. Each has something in common with the others. The members of a group can be close friends, or they can be strangers who know little about each other. The group can be large or small.

WHAT IS A GROUP?

A *group* is an assembly of two or more persons who interact with each other while sharing common interests. Those in a group have a sense of belonging to the group. They have an understanding of each other's behavior and a recognition of the statuses and roles of those in the group. Individuals in a group often strive for a common goal and have a desire for achievement and recognition. They work together or play together, or sometimes both.

How would you define this collection of people in sociological terms?

The groups to which individuals belong and within which they interact differ in size and makeup. Some groups are large and include many individuals. Other groups are small, consisting of only a few individuals. A man and a wife with no children make up a small group, a *dyad* (a group of two persons). A mother, a father, and one small child comprise another small group, a *triad* (a group of three persons). A corporation, such as General Motors, or a service club with many members in many countries, such as Rotary International, are large groups. Even communities and societies are groups.

Thus, groups are not aggregates. *Aggregates* are gatherings of people in temporary proximity who have no enduring ties or other marks of social organization. For example, people standing on a street corner waiting for a bus form an aggregate. Everyone pausing in a theater lobby during the intermission is in an aggregate. Nor is a group a category. A *category* is made up of people who have something in common, but their commonality fails to bring them together in a lasting relationship or intimate interaction. For example, all the mothers of the children in a kindergarten class make up a category. All

---

SOCIOLOGY OR COMMON SENSE

What do you think?

Which of the following statements do you agree with? Which statements do you disagree with? Make a note of your answers. Check your answers when you have completed your study of this chapter. Are your answers to the statements the same as those a sociologist would give?

1. Two individuals do not make up a group.
2. A society is a group.
3. Those who belong to groups abide by the norms of the group.
4. A small group has much in common with a *primary group*.
5. Human beings have a desire to form groups.

---

women wearing wigs, executives making $50,000 a year, and girls standing five feet tall are individuals within a category.

Distinguishing groups from aggregates, categories, and other grouplike assemblies turns on several criteria. Hare (1976: 4–5) lists five criteria:

1. There is interaction among members of a group.
2. The members of a group share one or more goals, which motivate group action.
3. The members of a group adhere to a set of norms, which guide goal-directed behavior and interpersonal relations.
4. If the group persists, a stable set of roles eventually emerges.
5. Over time, a pattern of interpersonal attractions also emerges, reflecting the likes and dislikes of those in the group toward each other.

THE SMALL GROUP

Sociology has been wedded to the study of small groups for more than half a century. In part, the tie between small groups and sociology has been a marriage of convenience, for social scientists discovered early that much could be inferred about entire communities and societies by studying the nearly innumerable small groups within them. Within small groups are many of the same structures, processes, and patterns found in communities and societies. The small group is a far more manageable object of research than a community or society.

Small groups also interest sociologists because they are central to human existence. They can be observed in nearly all spheres of life—the family, work, leisure, school, play, deviance, politics, religion, neighborhoods, organizations. The few cases of children reared in isolation indicate that infants are wholly dependent on their elders for their food, drink, warmth, and nurture (see the case of Anna, page 83). Therefore, throughout the world, the family is the first and, in some ways, the most important small group of which individuals are a part.[1] But it is clear from the preceding chapters alone that from birth there is a lifetime of interaction with many small groups, each with a different makeup and with different goals. The family is a small group; it is the group with which infants first become identified. Peers in a schoolyard and workers in an office or factory are small groups. Friends, neighbors, and playmates form into dyads and triads and also into somewhat larger groups. Activists who work together to achieve a political goal get together as a group. These collectivities are not only microcosms of society but also commanding agents of influence on the members of the society.

Although small groups share some important traits with communities and societies, they also exhibit some noteworthy differences. Because of these differences, sociologists long have given small groups special theoretical thought and empirical attention. One of the significant differences is the membership. A small group is made up of only a few members.

Specialists in group research classify as a small group any organized unit of two to twenty individuals. But this classification is arbitrary. Whatever its numerical size, however, a group becomes "large" when regular interaction is substantially limited and intimacy is no longer experienced; the group becomes large when the amount and quality of intermember communication are diluted. Under these conditions there is a tendency for subgroups to form and for the subgroups to become stratified along some dimension considered important by the collectivity as a whole. Even if nothing else happens, expanding small groups begin to lose their informal characteristics, a situation that requires more attention to control, coordination, administration, and rule-making. In some instances, a small group is made up of more than twenty members. Even with twenty or more members the group's small size is maintained when the individuals within it retain face-to-

[1]For exceptions to this rule see Chapter 9.

face contact and have a distinct impression of each other. This also occurs in small communities.

Table 6.1 shows how rapidly the number of potential relationships increases with the addition of one member at a time to a group. It is easy to see that even a group of five individuals creates a complicated social life, a situation requiring a great deal of individual effort and ability to handle affairs effectively. We shall return to the consequences of group size later in this chapter.

A consideration of various factors led Kurt Back (1981: 320) to define a small group

> as small enough for all members to interact simultaneously, to talk to each other or at least to be known to each other. Another requirement is a minimum conviction of belonging to the group, a distinction between "us," the members of the group, and "them," the nonmembers.

Informal and Primary Groups

Among the small groups are *informal collectivities,* or informal groups. An *informal group* is a group which may not necessarily have clearly defined roles and goals. Friends having lunch together are an informal group. Informal groups are held together by their members' recognition of the group's distinction of being a group of accepted individuals to the exclusion of others. Correspondingly, the members of an informal group often develop a strong loyalty to the group.

To many sociologists, the informal group and the primary group are identical. A *primary group* is a small number of people who interact with each other on a face-to-face basis over an extended period of time. A family is a primary group. Other examples are a street gang, a bowling team, and students who live together in a dormitory. Significant others in the primary group impart treasured values, attitudes, beliefs, and standards of behavior to those who are new members of the group. Peer groups and individuals in a family are both informal and primary.

A casual usage of the term "primary group" can occasionally raise a question, as when large collectivities—a rural community or a fraternal lodge, for instance—develop the characteristics of a primary group (intimacy, with an enduring relationship). Can a community or a lodge be considered a primary group? Small groups formed temporarily to accomplish a finite task often break up before primariness can take root (e.g., juries, ad hoc committees).

Formal and Secondary Groups

Among other groups in society are formal groups and secondary groups. *Formal groups* are groups with rules, roles, and goals that are

Table 6.1 RELATIONSHIPS WITHIN GROUPS

	Potential relationships with one person		Potential relationships with two or more people	
No. of members	**For one member**	**For all members**	**For one member**	**For all members**
2	1	1	1	1
3	2	3	3	6
4	3	6	7	22
5	4	10	15	65
6	5	15	31	171
7	6	21	63	420

Source: W. M. Kephart. Quantitative analysis of intragroup relationships. *American Journal of Sociology* 55: 544–549, 1950.

An informal group is an intimate, face-to-face collectivity.

A formal group has explicit rules, roles, and goals.

more or less explicit. They are often intentionally formed to attain an agreed-upon goal. Thus, formal groups may be legally chartered or, at the very least, have some sort of written or public recognition as a group. In this sense, all large-scale organizations are formal groups. Some small groups may also be formal groups. For example, a basketball team, a jazz quartet, and a corporation's legal department are formal groups.

Formal groups tend to be secondary groups. A *secondary group* is a group of individuals who have no emotional ties and who join together for a specific, workaday purpose. Governments, corporations, hospitals, labor unions, and educational institutions (colleges, universities, school systems) are secondary groups. When compared with primary groups, secondary groups are characterized by impersonal relations among members of the group; everyone in the group fills an individual, specialized role. The roles limit contact between members of the group. Roles also channel interaction toward role-related matters, hindering the gaining of broader personal knowledge about the role players.

The subject of this chapter is *small groups,* primary and otherwise. The larger collectivities —organizations, communities, societies—are covered in the next three chapters. This chapter concerns the formation, structure, processes, and culture of the small group. A review of small-group theory follows.

GROUP FORMATION

Groups come into existence either spontaneously or through an intentional effort on the part of those who organize the group. For example, a group arises spontaneously when youngsters on a playground team up for a game of touch football. A group is formed intentionally when politicians form a committee to work for the victory of their candidate in an election. Whatever their origin, groups satisfy a human being's desire to affiliate with others. The desire to affiliate and the subsequent progression referred to as *group development* are two important aspects of group formation, or the emergence of a collectivity.

The Desire to Affiliate

Interhuman affiliation satisfies personal motives, or needs, categorized by Crosbie (1975: 36–41) as *instrumental, expressive,* and *ascriptive. Instrumental motives* are satisfied by obtaining the group's goals. Many people who join groups for instrumental reasons have little interest in the interaction between the group's members except as it is related to the pursuit of the group's aims. Labor unions, activist cliques, interest groups, and political parties, although usually large, are typically made up mostly of instrumentally oriented individuals.

The Near-Group

The concept of the near-group may be of importance in the analysis of other collectivities which reflect and produce social problems. The analysis of other social structures may reveal similar distortions of their organization. To operate on an assumption that individuals in interaction with each other, around some function, with some shared mutual expectation, in a particular normative system as always being a group formation is to project a degree of distortion onto certain types of collectivities. Groups are social structures at one end of a continuum; mobs are social structures at another end; and at the center are near-groups which have some of the characteristics of both, and yet are characterized by factors not found fully in either.

In summary, these factors may include the following:

1. Individualized role definition to fit momentary needs.
2. Diffuse and differential definitions of membership.
3. Emotion-motivated behavior.
4. A decrease of cohesiveness as one moves from the center of the collectivity to the periphery.
5. Limited responsibility and sociability required for membership and belonging.
6. Self-appointed and disturbed leadership.
7. A limited consensus among participants of the collectivities' functions or goals.
8. A shifting and personalized stratification system.
9. Shifting membership.
10. The inclusion in size of phantasy membership.
11. Limited consensus of normative expectations.
12. Norms in conflict with the inclusive social system's prescriptions.

Although the gang was the primary type of near-group appraised in this analysis, there are perhaps other collectivities whose structure is distorted by autistic observers. Their organization might become clearer if subjected to this conceptual scheme. Specifically, in the area of criminal behavior, these might very well include adult gangs varyingly called the "Mafia," the "National Crime Syndicate," and so-called International Crime Cartels. There are indications that these social organizations are comparable in organization to the delinquent gang. They might fit the near-group category if closely analyzed in this context, rather than aggrandized and distorted by mass media and even Senate Committees.

Other more institutionalized collectivities might fit the near-group pattern. As a possible example, "the family in transition" may not be in transition at all. The family, as a social institution, may be suffering from near-groupism. Moreover, such standardized escape hatches of alcoholism, psychoses, and addictions may be too prosaic for the sophisticated intellectual to utilize in escape from himself. For him, the creation and perpetuation of near-groups requiring limited responsibility and personal commitment may be a more attractive contemporary form of expressing social and personal pathology. The measure of organization or disorganization of an inclusive social system may possibly be assessed by the prevalence of near-group collectivities in its midst. The delinquent gang may be only one type of near-group in American society.

SOURCE: Lewis Yablonsky. The delinquent gang as a near-group. *Social Problems* 7:108–117, 1959.

Some people join groups for *expressive purposes.* Their chief interest lies in interacting with other members, not in pursuing the group's goals. The group provides a sense of belonging; it serves as an outlet for feelings and wishes. As a rule, people join Greek-letter societies, singles clubs, ethnic associations, and informal groups of neighbors, co-workers, and friends for expressive reasons.

The *ascriptive motive* is, in one sense, no motive at all. Affiliation is forced on the person because of his or her birth or someone else's decision. Prisoners and some patients in mental hospitals are locked up against their will. Men who are drafted into the military are not in uniform voluntarily. A baby usually experiences one form of ascription, namely, birth into its family. Nearly everyone accepts the involuntary placement in a family. What other choice does a person have?

Many people join groups or form groups for instrumental and expressive reasons. These reasons may become motives for staying in an ascribed group after one has gained the freedom to leave it. For example, a soldier may decide to reenlist or a congressman may decide to run for reelection. In nearly all instances, one of the three motives—ascriptive, instrumental, expressive—tends to predominate, making it possible to understand and predict group behavior and member interaction (Crosbie, 1975: 40).

The decision to affiliate with an existing group or participate with others in forming a group (where formation is intentional rather than spontaneous) is, at bottom, part of one's definition of the situation (a certain situation). One defines the situation of group membership as desirable, as fulfilling certain interests and meeting certain needs. When a new group is formed, a new part of society (i.e., a set of interpersonal relationships) emerges from the interaction of those involved. Thus, the study of groups—small, medium, or large—begins where we ended our discussion of interaction in Chapter 4. The small group, seen through the sociologist's eyes, is one kind of building block with which society is constructed. Here lies still another incentive for its scientific examination.

Group Development

The formation of a group continues beyond the affiliation of its members, for it takes time to develop a social unit that at least approaches stability. This progression is called *group development.* In group development, the basic statuses, structures, and processes are the first conditions to be established, and this may occur in the initial hour or two of interaction among the members of the group which is being formed. According to Caple (1978), groups growing to maturity do so in five stages:

1. *Orientation stage:* There is considerable testing of values and attitudes among members and tolerance between members and the leader. Ambiguity predominates; hence, anxiety is high. Some members hesitate to commit themselves to the group.
2. *Conflict stage:* Polarization occurs between socioemotionally oriented members of the group and task-oriented individuals in the group. There is a tendency to stick to safe discussion topics. Roles are undefined and inconsistent. Anxiety remains high. Values are the cause of the conflict.
3. *Integration stage:* There is an evaluation of

the group's need and past performance. Cohesion develops as members realize they must contribute to the group's social attainment. The role of the leader is clarified at this point.
4. *Achievement stage:* The group has developed into a productive unit. Norms and roles are now well established. Problem solving is easier and more effective than before. The interpersonal relations among members of the group are known and understood.
5. *Order stage:* The group now strives to continue its success. Ways of doing things become institutionalized, thus limiting flexibility and efforts at renewal. Tradition may outrank group goals in importance.

Parsons (1961) proposed another model of group development, called AGIL. His model unfolds in four stages, corresponding to the four functions groups must perform to ensure their survival. In *adaptation* (A), the group organizes its resources to pursue its goals. *Goal attainment* (G) is the phase in which the group reaches its goals. *Integration* (I) refers to the adjustments made by the subsystem of the group to facilitate goal attainment. *Latent pattern maintenance* (L) refers to the need to maintain stable patterns of behavior through adherence to group norms. Students of small groups still disagree to some extent over which sequence these four phases should follow. Nonetheless, Hare (1976: 110) concludes, after reviewing the theory and research in this area, that most groups go through an L-A-I-G sequence.

Using the L-A-I-G sequence, let us consider how a committee formed for the purpose of organizing and holding a school dance develops into a group. Among the group patterns that must be maintained (L) are regular and punctual attendance at committee meetings and fulfillment of assignments given to each member. The committee adapts (A) by using its money to hire a band, drawing on free janitorial services available from the school, and borrowing art supplies with which to decorate the school gymnasium. There is evidence of integration (I) when the committee member who hires the musicians is given a check by the treasurer with which to pay the musicians, and when those who are responsible for serving the food coordinate its preparation with those who have planned the evening's skit. By carrying out first one task and then another, the committee reaches its goal (G) of holding a school dance.

GROUP STRUCTURE

A study of groups brings up one of sociology's most enduring and distinctive concepts, namely the concept of social structure. In the study of small groups and organizations, *social structure* is usually defined as a collectivity's stable pattern or arrangement of the abstract relationships discussed in Chapter 4. Just as a building such as a cottage or a skyscraper has a structure, society, too, has a structure. Society has a social structure, or a patterning and organization of the components which make up the social system.

Role and Status

Each person in a group has a *role* and a *status.* The roles and statuses are part of a group's social structure. For example, the structure of a baseball team, a group, is the interrelationship of the different positions (roles)—pitcher, catcher, infielder, outfielder. Each player has a role and a status. The social structure of the Canadian family is based on the ways in which the positions (roles and statuses) of the mother, father, and children are interrelated as a unit.

Nearly all group structures evince some sort of ordering along lines such as age, sex, race, knowledge, and prestige, or a combination of these. Sometimes a placement in these categories and dimensions is a matter of rank, of better or worse; sometimes it is only a matter of difference. A pitcher may have more prestige than a left fielder on a baseball team. A father's status in a family is different from the status of a son or daughter.

As noted off and on before, roles are associated with statuses within a group. Many of the norms applied to roles are enacted with reference to other status-role combinations which an individual experiences within a group. For example, a pitcher on a baseball team can throw a fast ball (a norm), but may not be a good hitter (the pitcher has the status of a pitcher but not that of a hitter). There is a tendency in sociology when studying a group's structure to consider the entire mosaic of interrelated statuses and roles.

Sociometry

Sociometric patterns are among several well-studied aspects of small group structure. The field of *sociometry* was inaugurated in the 1930s by Jacob Moreno, who defined it as a technique for describing socioemotional relations among members of a group. Sociometry deals with the study of relations.

To conduct a sociometric study, sociologists use questionnaires. When respondents fill in a questionnaire, they typically (not all questionnaires are the same) answer questions about whom they would be willing to work with, eat with, play with, sit next to, and so on. These responses are then displayed in a *sociogram,* or two-dimensional picture of everyone's socioemotional preferences. Sociograms depict cliques, isolates, lines of influence, and related aspects of small-group life. They offer some obvious practical benefits, such as determining the most effective use of personnel in a work force or suggesting the best seating arrangement in a classroom.

In a study of two traditional smallholders' cooperatives in Israel, known as Agur and Zakharya, Weintraub and Bernstein (1966) found that Zakharya was more developed than Agur, partly because Zakharya had greater success in freeing itself from the old patterns of interaction. Settlers were asked to name their two best friends. A sociogram constructed from their responses indicated that in Agur kinship and political affiliations influenced the responses, while in Zakharya they did not. The sociogram for Zakharya in Figure 6.2 shows seven groups of friends, all having nothing to do with kin and political groups. It bears little resemblance to Agur's sociogram in Figure 6.1. The "sociometric stars" mentioned in Figures 6.1 and 6.2 are those settlers who received a disproportionately large number of choices as best friends.

One of the criticisms of the sociometric approach to group structure is its stress on socioemotional relations (e.g., friends, enemies) to the exclusion of relations that are task-oriented (Olmsted and Hare, 1978: 98). Groups have within them both socioemotional relations and task-oriented relations, and the link among all the relations is especially important. Neglecting one relation biases our understanding of the nature of groups.

GROUP PROCESSES

The study of small groups has concentrated on four major processes of interaction. These processes weave the social structure of individual groups into a unique tapestry of associations among a set of human beings. The four processes are *leadership, power, coalition formation,* and *communication of information and commands.* How the four processes are manifested in a particular group depends on many factors, one of which is the size of the group. Whether a group is a dyad, a triad, or a unit consisting of four or more persons has a bearing on the way individuals interact within the group.

Leadership

Leadership is the capacity to make important decisions binding on all or nearly all members of a group. The leader's role is to make decisions, and the role of the rank and file is to abide by the leader's decisions. In nearly all groups, there is a tendency for one person to gain power and authority and thereby to gain recognition as the leader (Bjerstedt, 1965). But there are groups in which the leadership is formally or

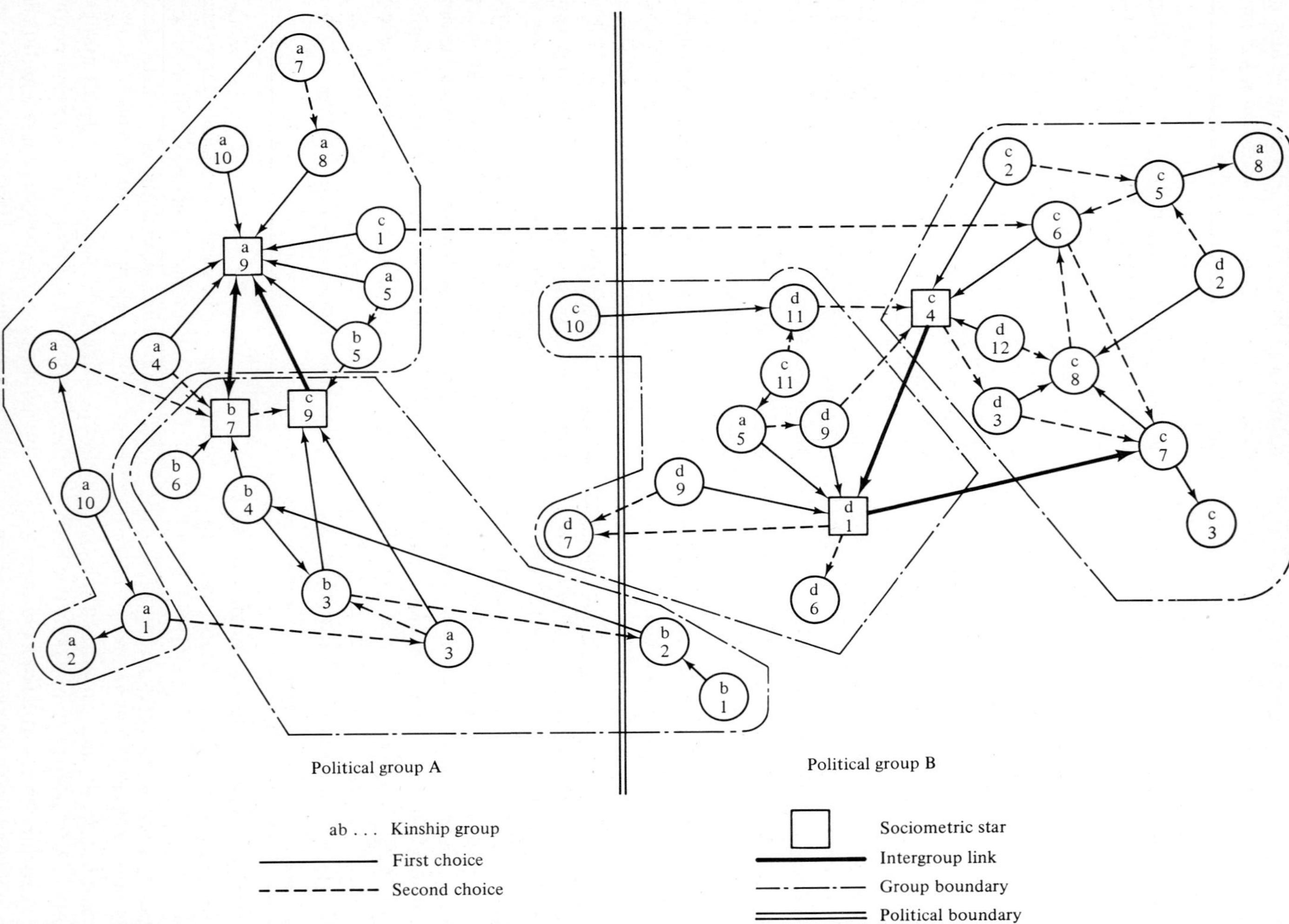

Figure 6.1 Sociogram of Friendship in Agur (first two choices). (*Source:* D. Weintraub and F. Bernstein, Social structure and modernization: A comparative study of two villages. *American Journal of Sociology* 71 (March 1966): 513.)

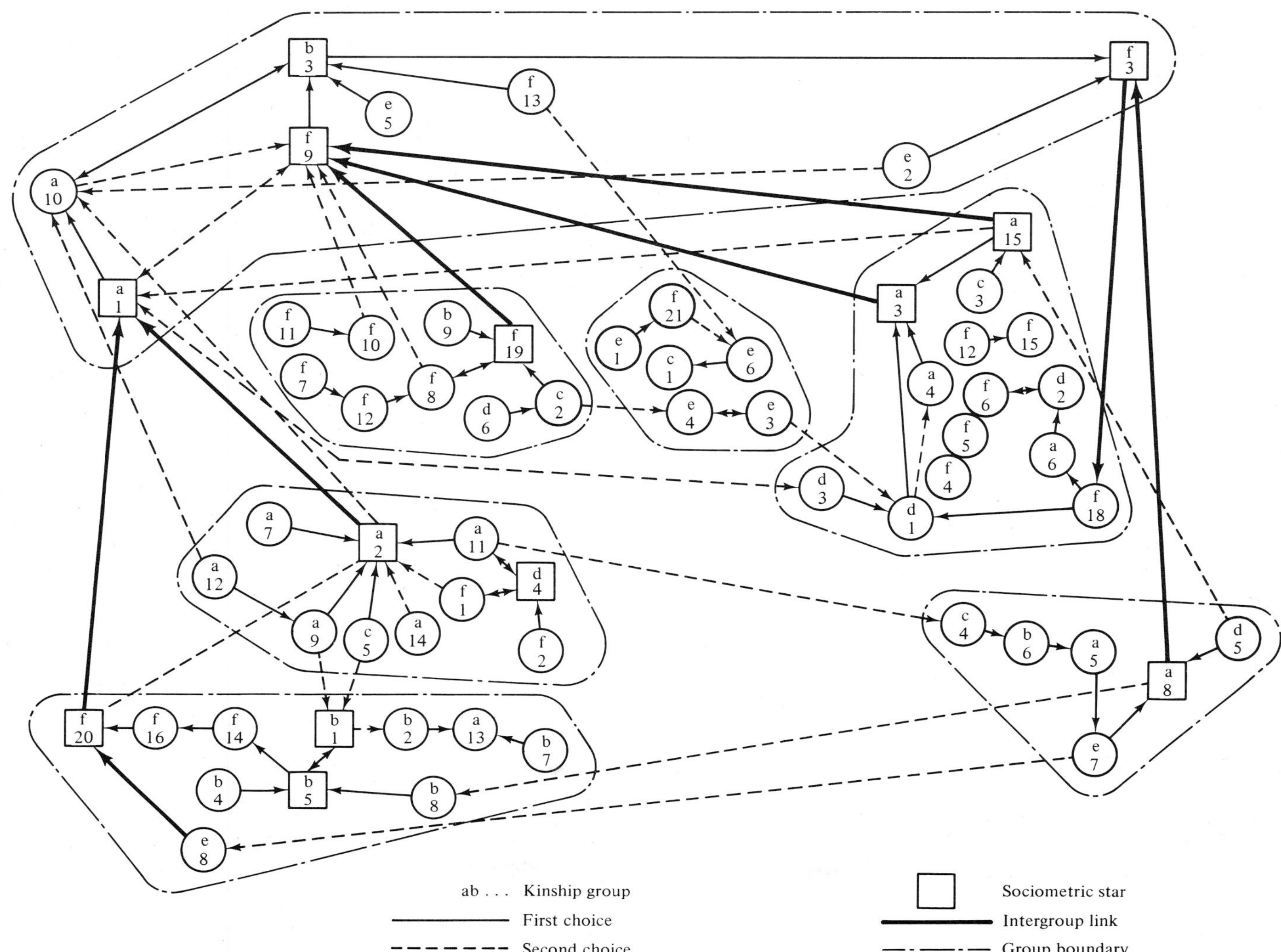

Figure 6.2 Sociogram of Friendship in Zakharya (first two choices). (*Source:* D. Weintraub and F. Bernstein, Social structure and modernization: A comparative study of two villages. *American Journal of Sociology* 71 (March 1966): 514.)

informally divided among two or more members. This often occurs along task-oriented and social-emotional lines. Research reveals that task leaders are apt to be authoritarian and less well liked than their social-emotional counterparts (Bales and Slater, 1955: 297–298).

After reviewing the extensive research undertaken in this area, Stogdill (1974: 30) concluded that leaders of small groups typically perform six functions:

1. Defining objectives and maintaining goal direction.
2. Providing means for goal attainment.
3. Providing and maintaining group structure.
4. Facilitating group action and interaction.
5. Maintaining group cohesiveness and member satisfaction.
6. Facilitating group task performance.

Schutz (1961) added a seventh function to this list in noting that leaders are usually "completers." They have the clearest notion of their group's purposes and reasons for existing. Moreover, leaders can apply their skills to solve the problems with which the group must deal.

A study by Chow and Billings (1972) of leadership styles in specially-assembled, laboratory groups of undergraduate females provides support for functions 5 and 6. Workers in these groups who received personal supervision from their leaders produced more than those who were shown no interest by their leaders. Leaders gave personal supervision by attending to the worker as a person and by giving some thought to the task she was carrying out.

Another issue in group process is the question of how much support a leader has. To what extent is he or she supported by the rank and file? Does a leader who is appointed from outside the group have more support than a leader who emerges spontaneously from within? Laboratory studies of appointed leaders suggest that they receive the same degree of support as do emergent leaders (e.g., Hollander and Julian, 1970). But both types of leaders were members of ad hoc groups. Natural groups may make their decisions collectively; with collective decision making, the groups may be leaderless, or members of the group may shift the leadership responsibilities from one person to another, depending on the situation at hand. When a clear leader does emerge, there is usually a task of some sort to perform.

In whatever way leaders gain their position, there tends to be less turnover at the leadership level than at other power levels in the group. Indeed, once the status structure of a group is set, it resists change (Wilson, *Informal Groups,* 1978: 152). As noted earlier, the small group, in some ways, is a microcosm of the larger society. In this respect, the resistance of group social structure to change is mirrored in the resistance to change observed in the various institutions of society.

Elkin, Halpern, and Cooper (1962) conducted a field experiment on mob leadership with a group of twenty fraternity pledges attending a Canadian university. The accomplices, or "stooges," of the experimenters incited the pledges to moblike action in two experimental situations—avenging the theft of trophies stolen by a rival fraternity and tearing down the goalposts after a football game. The data support the proposition that emergent leaders appear when there is a task to be carried out. The same leaders emerged in both experimental situations, indicating that such leadership is stable.

In considering the question of size, Hare (1976: 229) concludes that since dyads have no true leader, whereas groups of three or more do have leaders, the problem of deadlock is most acute in the dyad. And, while deadlocked, both individuals in the dyad are without support, which typically makes for high levels of tension. Yet overt disagreement must be avoided if the relationship is to survive. In addition, Ridgeway (1983: 298) concludes that groups with four to ten members are the best for most tasks.

Deadlock in the dyad is a more common aspect of everyday life than we would like.

Power

Power is the ability to control others and to dominate a situation; it is coercive. It is different from *influence,* which is the use of persuasion to affect change in other people and their behavior. Power is an element in social interaction. The motivation to use power is a subject of constant speculation among small-group specialists. Tedeschi et al. (1972: 323–327), for instance, argue that the use of power is stimulated by a conflict of interest. Individuals with power fear that someone in their group is about to act against their interests or is about to use power more effectively than they can.

A number of conditions nonetheless temper the use of power, even when conflicts of interest exist (Cartwright and Zander, 1968: 219). For example, the use of power depends on the net advantage gained by the person having the power. It also depends on the perceived positive and negative consequences that the wielding of power will have on the rank and file and on the subjective probability that powerful acts will succeed.

By way of illustration, imagine a professor who is pondering whether to request an extra term paper from the students. The professor has the power to make such a request. But it could be argued that the students will resent this assignment, because they see it as an unfair and unexpected infringement on their scarce time. Resentment could offset any learning they would gain from writing the paper. Moreover, the unfair and unexpected nature of the assignment could become grounds, justifiable in the eyes of the students, for plagiarizing the paper or having it ghostwritten by a friend or a freelance writer.

How do the seemingly identical concepts of power, authority, and leadership differ in their technical usage in sociology? In sociology, authority and leadership are often looked on as synonyms for legimate use of power; that is, the leader is given the right to use her or his power by those subject to it. Put otherwise, people gain power by assuming a legitimate leadership position; with the position, they have access to resources of power. Still, as Homans (1974: 92) points out, to acquire the authority to lead effectively, one may be forced to exercise illegitimate power:

> The difficulty is always to get him (the person to be led) to obey the first time, and for that purpose power over him may be necessary. If he can be induced or compelled to obey once, he may obey spontaneously thereafter.

Power has a bearing on the social structure of a group. For example, research shows that people pay more attention to those with a great

In legitimate power the leader is given the right to use his power.

deal of power than to those with only a little or with none at all (e.g., Rubin and Lewicki, 1973). Thomas et al. (1972) found that lower-power individuals do more role-taking than those with high power. Hence, the low-power individuals generally have a better understanding of other roles in the group than the high-power individuals. Crosbie (1975: 353) concludes, after reviewing a number of studies, that the distribution of power resources in a group places limits on the use of power of its leaders when they interact with rank-and-file members.

But, even when it is legitimate, power can be ephemeral in small groups. It seems that there is always someone who disagrees with the leader. The person who disagrees may have almost as much power as the actual leader. The person may be new to the group; he or she may be a disgruntled member who is poorly integrated into the group (Nixon, 1979: 220). We will see shortly that the formation and re-formation of coalitions also influence the power of a leader. All this brings us once again to the issue of group size.

Hare (1976: 226–227) writes that a "delicate balance of power exists" in the dyad and that this balance is rarer in larger groups. Even though there is a tendency for one of the two individuals to be more active than the other in initiating dyadic activities, the other has veto power. As long as both members of the dyad enjoy the relationship (no one is motivated by the principle of least interest), then the use of power is checked through exchanges of information and by mutual agreement (O'Dell, 1968).

Relations between husbands and wives illustrate well the forces of power in the dyad. Donald Wolfe (1959) interviewed more than seven hundred wives in the Detroit area. Among other things, he learned that in husband-dominant families the husband gains power through his high income, job success, and attendant family status. When the husband has low income and little power, the wife is ascendant. Wives in husband-dominant families are usually not gainfully employed and hence lack a countervailing source of income and authority. The dominant spouse tends to handle family fiscal matters, thereby strengthening his or her dominance in general. Wolfe's data also suggest that a wife's need for love gives her husband an additional source of power in husband-dominant families, but not in wife-dominant families.

Balances of power in groups larger than the dyad often have a different slant and modality, owing in good part to the possibility of coalition formation.

Coalitions

A *coalition* develops when two or more members of a group try to pool their power resources to gain certain advantages for themselves (Komorita and Chertkoff, 1973). Coalitions are thus temporary liaisons in which it is tacitly agreed that matters unrelated to the coalitional goals will be discreetly ignored for the time being. Coalitions, then, whether in informal triads or international relations, often bear out Charles Dudley Warner's dictum that "politics makes strange bedfellows."

According to Gamson (1961: 565–566), full-fledged coalitions develop when the following conditions are present:

1. There is a decision to be made and there are more than two social units attempting to maximize their share of the payoffs.
2. No single alternative will maximize the payoff to all participants.
3. No participant has dictatorial powers; i.e., no one has initial resources sufficient to control the decision by himself.
4. No participant has veto power; i.e., no member must be included in every winning coalition.

A "decision" is a selection among alternatives. "Winning coalitions" are those with sufficient resources to control the decision. A "social unit" is an individual or subgroup that embraces the coalition strategy while it is in force.

By way of illustration, let us suppose that a local social service agency has received a government grant for improving service to its clients. The seven-person board of directors must decide between two alternatives (Gamson's condition 1): (1) renovating the agency's deteriorating physical facilities or (2) commissioning a study of the need for and the effectiveness of its services. Since boards of directors are typically collegial bodies (i.e., the members have special expertise but equal authority), conditions 3 and 4 are met. Still, the board is sharply divided over which alternative to select, which meets condition 2. By meeting all four of Gamson's conditions, the board will decide on a coalition. The coalition will push the board as a whole toward selecting one of the alternatives.

Only part of Gamson's "minimum resources" theory of coalition formation has been presented here. It is the part specifying the conditions leading to coalition formation. His theory also predicts, for example, that the weakest member of a group is most often found in its winning coalitions. Moreover, that individual's share of the winnings (i.e., the goals of the coalition) is larger than his or her strength would warrant. This occurs because other members of the group see such individuals as powerless and hence as easily persuaded to join their coalition. Gamson's theory is one of several in social psychology.

The process of forming a winning coalition has been the subject of considerable empirical investigation and theoretical conjecture. Frequently, bargaining and negotiation are tried as coalitionists strive to form a winning combination. The strength of various dyadic ties within the larger group sometimes enters the picture (e.g., close friends who support each other through thick and thin). On the opposite dimension, an accepted value or ideological differences may prevent some people from joining a coalition with certain others (despite Warner's dictum). And, according to Bales and Borgatta (1965), forming a winning coalition is easier in odd-sized groups composed of three, five, or seven, and so on, than in even-sized groups composed of two, four, or six. Deadlocks are impossible in odd-sized groups.

Coalitions are especially sensitive matters in the three-person group. Hare (1976: 228) believes that its members may intentionally form new coalitions from one disagreement to the next to maintain solidarity and avoid the recurrent exclusion of one member. Otherwise, the very existence of the group as a three-person unit is threatened, since the continually excluded member has little to lose by abandoning it.

Communication Networks

Communication is fundamental to all human social life. In Chapter 4, the significance of communication was underscored by noting that the gesture, verbal or nonverbal, is the basis for action, knowledge, and social interaction. It follows that leadership, use of power, and the formation of coalitions in small groups also depend on communication among the members of the group. Indeed, the very formation and development of groups ultimately rest on interhuman communication.

The comcon communication network is a familiar arrangement in our society.

A number of factors have much to do with communications in small groups. Among these factors are the individual members' status, proximity, and degree of centrality. The socio-emotional relations among members of the group and their levels of participation also enter into communications. These factors and others vary with the type of communication network within the group. Social psychologists have identified and studied several different networks. Researchers have given the most attention to the networks shown in Figure 6.3. In the figure, dots represent positions, lines indicate communication channels, and arrows stand for one-way channels.

One individual often occupies a central position in a group or in a communication network. A *communication network* is a set of interconnected individuals within a group or between groups. Since others pay attention to this central individual, he or she can exert a great deal of influence on the group or network. As one might expect, occupying a central position greatly increases one's chances of becoming the leader (Shaw, 1981: 153). In laboratory groups at least, two or more positions of equal centrality (e.g., the "comcon" and the "circle") tend to hinder the emergence of any leader.

The type of communication network also has a bearing on the satisfaction of members in the group. Mills (1984: 76) concludes that decentralized networks, such as the "circle," engen-

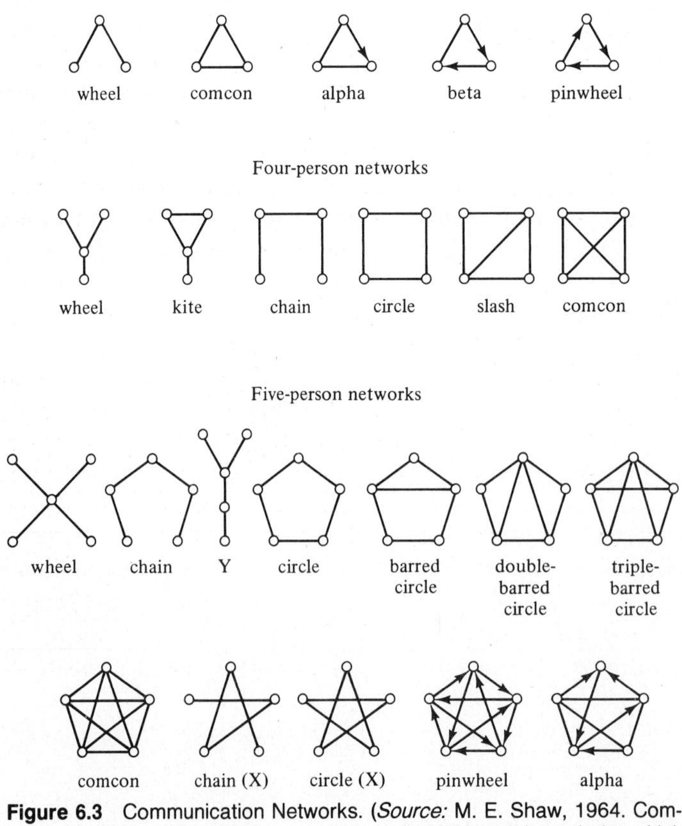

Figure 6.3 Communication Networks. (*Source:* M. E. Shaw, 1964. Communication Networks. In *Advances in experimental social psychology,* Vol. 1, ed. L. Berkowitz. New York: Academic Press, p. 113.)

der more satisfaction among members and hence higher group morale than centralized networks, such as the "wheel," in which most participants occupy peripheral positions. Their frustration is mixed with antagonism when the person in the central position is of lower status than they are (Johnson et al., 1972). Decentralized networks tend to be leaderless, however, which, under certain conditions, promotes inefficiency and disorganization. Mabry and Barnes's (1980: 137) review of the network effectiveness literature led them to conclude that centralized networks are more efficient for solving simple tasks, whereas decentralized networks are more efficient for solving tasks which are complex and difficult to carry out. It appears that a strong centralized leader can organize and control interaction well enough to complete simple tasks. But complex tasks require the help of every member of the group. Each member can do his or her part only when there is a network of communication among the members or when there is time to organize a more effective communication structure.

The use of power can also have an effect on a group's communication network. Bavelas et al. (1965) argued that a powerful member with no leadership role can still reshape the network. This individual becomes the center of the group's communications. Such a reshaping and transformation, however, is usually situational and temporary.

GROUP CULTURE

Culture is a key anthropological concept borrowed by sociologists with little modification. One classic definition of culture reads this way:

> Culture consists of patterns, explicit and implicit, of and for behavior acquired and transmitted by symbols, constituting the distinctive achievements of human groups, including their embodiments in artifacts; the essential core of culture consists of traditional (i.e., historically derived and selected) ideas and especially their attached values; cultural systems may, on the one hand, be considered as products of action, on the other, as conditioning elements of further action. (Kroeber and Kluckhohn, 1952: 181)

"Culture," as a social-science term, refers to all our collective representations; it is a reference to our collective stock of knowledge, art, ideas, customs, values, norms, beliefs, laws, goals, outlooks, technologies, patterns of behavior, and human-made things. The meaning of culture is much broader than the popular notion of the fine arts, or *high culture. Culture* is a society's way of life.

Culture is the ultimate construction of social reality in any group, since it encompasses all enduring smaller-scale constructions of the collectivity. The only important difference in the sociological vis-à-vis the anthropological usage of the term is sociology's tendency to neglect material components and concentrate on its nonmaterial or ideational components.[2] *Material culture* consists of the artifacts and things which human beings make (wheels, clothing, rockets, typewriters, books, skyscrapers, computers). *Nonmaterial culture* consists of abstract inventions such as customs, ideas, laws, novels, languages, job skills, family ways, and political parties.

Culture is found in every collectivity, be it a small group or a national society, that has endured long enough for collective representations to emerge. And, to continue the earlier analogy, culture at all levels of social organization serves as the *thread* with which the processes just covered weave the social structure of individual groups into a unique fabric of associations among a set of human beings.

Of course, culture is much simpler in small groups than in national societies. Nevertheless, small groups have their norms, values, outlooks, goals, and patterns of behavior. Social psycholo-

[2] An exception to this rule is found in the next chapter, where the relationship of technology and large-scale organization is discussed.

gists have been able to demonstrate the emergence of norms in the laboratory. Muzafer Sherif and Carolyn Sherif (1956) accomplished this by asking their subjects how far an actually stationary pinpoint of light seemed to move in a totally dark room, a perception called the "autokinetic effect." Because this stimulus was ambiguous and there was great uncertainty about the distance the light moved, subjects were particularly attuned to each other's judgments. Under these circumstances, eight of ten judgments were congruent with the emergent group norm, or with an agreed upon conclusion about the movement of the light.

Conformity and Nonconformity

The discovery of the existence of small-group norms soon led to an interest in conformity and nonconformity. Do individuals in a group conform to the norms or do they ignore the norms and do as they please? We typically conform to certain beliefs and values and to the expectations of behavior, or norms, of certain groups. Conformity in behavior is obviously easier for members of the group to monitor than conformity in ideas; hence, there is frequent pressure from the group for individuals to fall in line with the standards of the group. Perhaps the most celebrated laboratory experiment demonstrating humankind's tendency to conform was carried out by Solomon Asch (1958). In a visual discrimination test, Asch asked students to observe vertical lines on two cards. A single line, the standard, appeared on one card. Three lines showed up on the second card. One line on the second card was the same length as the standard, while the other two lines were noticeably shorter or longer (by ½ to 1¾ inches) than the standard.

Asch worked with groups of seven to nine students. Only one student in each group was actually a subject in the experiment. The others (at least six students in each group) were Asch's accomplices. One by one, the members of each group were asked to state which line on the second card was the same length as the standard. In making a choice, all the accomplices selected a line which was shorter than the standard. The accomplices chose an incorrect line. Yielding to the majority (the accomplices), the subject chose the same incorrect line in about one-third of the tests. The experiment demonstrated the power of a group to induce conformity.

A maverick's rejection of group norms has been shown to elicit characteristic reactions from members of a group. Interaction with the maverick intensifies as those in the group attempt to communicate and clarify the appropriate conduct. The interaction then drops off as conformity occurs or nonconformity continues and the individual is given up as a lost cause (Hare, 1976: 52). Meanwhile, conformity in thought and action by other members of the group is publicly lauded in a further attempt to emphasize the norm, or the correct behavior. In the end, those in the group will reject the maverick if they believe they can function without him or her. But, when the mavericks have high status within the group, they receive more lenient treatment for their nonconformity than lower-status members who act the same way (Gowan et al., 1984). This occurs because they accumulate "idiosyncracy credits" (Hollander, 1964), which help to insulate them against the charge of nonconformity. This situation may even precipitate a change in group norms.

Morale and Cohesiveness

Group culture includes group *morale,* which is often defined in somewhat concrete terms as *cohesiveness,* or sticking together. Cohesiveness is measured, among other ways, by determining how attractive the group is to its members and how motivated the members are to remain in the group.[3] Four factors promote cohesiveness:

[3]A few scholars do distinguish between morale and cohesiveness. For them cohesiveness refers to the wish to remain in the group, while morale refers to the inclination to work toward its goals.

high levels of (1) interdependence among the members, (2) interpersonal attraction, (3) attractiveness of group goals and activities, and (4) special norms and practices that build commitment to the group (Ridgeway, 1983: 107–118).

For example, a cohesive basketball team would be composed of members who want to win at a game they enjoy playing, while excelling as individuals both offensively and defensively. The members of a cohesive basketball team like each other and have respect for each other. When players tell one another that they are playing well, this recognition motivates those receiving such praise to do their best to help the team win games. A team that is cohesive in these ways would likely be a winning team. Winning games would raise still further the team's level of cohesiveness.

Cohesiveness is generally a desirable quality of group life. It is also a basic quality, for it is one of the preconditions of group development as seen in Parsons's *latent pattern maintenance* and Caple's *integration stage* (see earlier). Considerable absenteeism and labor turnover have been found among factory workers with little cohesiveness (Hare, 1976: 171–172). High cohesiveness increases the amount and quality of interaction among members of a group; with cohesiveness, the individuals enjoy greater satisfaction than they would otherwise. For instance, individuals in a cohesive group cooperate with each other and are receptive to the influence of the others. They are also more likely to conform to group norms. Finally, although some of the evidence is equivocal, cohesive groups are more likely to attain their goals than noncohesive groups (Shaw, 1981: 216–226).

Goals and Problem Solving

A group's goals or purposes constitute another part of its culture. Some social psychologists treat the terms "goal" and "task" as interchangeable. Others distinguish between them, defining *task* as a subgoal to be accomplished before the main goal of the group can be attained.

In the study of small groups, pursuing a goal is looked on as a form of problem solving. Hare (1976: 11–12) assumes that all human behavior is primarily directed toward solving a problem, particularly the one of survival. He identifies four main problems. Two of these concern the group: the "task problem," or that of reaching the group's goals, and the "socioemotional problem." The latter is the more nebulous of the two, inasmuch as it arises from shared anxieties generated in the course of routine group life. Socioemotional problems are called "personnel problems" in business and industry.

The remaining two problems are related to individual members of a group: task problems associated with publicly proclaimed individual goals and socioemotional problems of individuals as they attempt to interact with each other and achieve personal integration. From the standpoint of the individual, the second set of problems is the more important of the two. The second set must be solved in some minimally acceptable manner before the group's problems can be tackled (see Caple's second and third stages).

Since groups eventually must deal with all four problems, but seem capable of concentrating on only one at a time, the *equilibrium problem* (Mills, 1984: 32–34) frequently arises. That is, groups are inclined to swing from task problems to socioemotional problems and back again as they try to simultaneously keep their members satisfied, shore up cohesiveness, and work toward the ends that brought them together in the first place.

Many factors impinge on the group problem-solving process. There is evidence that the higher the level of satisfaction of each member the more likely the group is to accomplish its task (Hagen and Burch, 1985). Research has further demonstrated that, in general, cooperation among members of a group during their drive to reach collective goals makes for more effective problem solving than does competition (Shaw, 1981: 380–383). On the other hand, as the number of members increases, individual ideas are overlooked and participation in the group declines.

THEORETICAL APPROACHES

Throughout this chapter there has been considerable, albeit piecemeal, consideration of the major theoretical approaches to the study of small groups. All that remains now is to explain these frameworks in order to impart a sense of the conceptual background of those who do research in this branch of sociology. Four approaches are briefly examined: *exchange theory, field theory, systems theory,* and *interaction process analysis.*

Exchange Theory

We encountered the *exchange theory* earlier in this book. Consequently, we need spend little more time on this perspective at this point. According to exchange theory, individuals control one another's behavior by means of exchanges. They exchange rewards and punishments for approved behavior or for behavior which is unapproved. Exchange theorists focus on individual members of groups, whom they see as motivated to maximize their rewards and minimize their costs. For these thinkers, group behavior is a product of the adjustments individual members of a group make to one another as they seek the best personal bargain they can strike in social relations.

Field Theory

Field theory started with the imaginative writing of Kurt Lewin (1890–1947). Lewin probably did more than anyone else to promote the laboratory study of small groups, and since his work laboratory study has become a prominent research design in social science. To produce a theoretical framework, Lewin combined phenomenology (the study of the development of human consciousness) with topology (a nonquantitative geometry applied to the study of classification based on types). Usually, Lewin and his associates tested their hypotheses in the laboratory, but they occasionally validated their findings in the field. As a phenomenologist, Lewin believed it was important to consider the view of those under study. He referred to the subjects' views as "naive psychology" and contrasted them with the scientific view of reality (see, Alfred Schutz and ethnomethodology).

As a topologist, Lewin looked on groups and members of groups as "locomoting" toward collective goals within their subjectively defined environment, or "life space." Groups and the members of groups were said to be attracted to certain regions in this space ("positive valences") and repelled by other regions ("negative valences"). *Power fields* and *group forces* can change the *vector,* or direction, of groups and individual locomotion and sometimes even the goals of the groups. From this metaphor, Lewin developed the notion of group cohesiveness.

Do you recall the example of the cohesive basketball team? The players' love of basketball attracts them to this athletic region of their life

Positive valence: Students at a martial arts school strive for higher skill and rank.

space. Team cohesiveness, or group force, pushes the players toward (a vector) an intense desire to reach such group goals as winning games, tournaments, and playoffs. All told, Lewin created a bold new social scientific paradigm that led to the present-day concepts of group dynamics and to laboratory and field experiments.

Systems Theory

Homans's present exchange theoretic stance, which is rooted in behavioral psychology, marks a significant intellectual shift away from an earlier period in his career, when he expounded a systems theory of individual action and group behavior. Indeed, he has been credited with offering a clear statement of systems theory in his book *The Human Group* (Homans, 1950). In this book, Homans conjectured that group life constitutes three critical elements: *activity* (i.e., things people do), *sentiment* (emotions, feelings, drives), and *interaction.*

The interrelationship of Homans's elements can be observed in two systems, one *external* and the other *internal* (this is the systems theory). The external system is one of several possible solutions to the problem of group survival in the social and physical environment. It is considered external because it develops in response to the group's milieu. The closest Homans (1950: 107) comes to a definition of the *external system* is the following:

> If we must have a definition in words, we can say that the mutual dependence between the work (i.e., activity) done in a group and the motives (i.e., sentiment) for work, between the division of labor and the scheme of interaction, so far as these relationships meet the condition that the group survives in an environment—this we shall regularly speak of as the external system.

The internal system is not directly conditioned by this milieu. As Homans (1950: 110) phrases it: "We think . . . of the internal system as group behavior that is an expression of the sentiments toward one another developed by the members of the group in the course of their life together [i.e., activity, interaction]. . . ." Such hallmarks of group culture as norms, values, leadership, and social ranking develop through the interaction of group members and become part of the internal system. The internal and external systems "react" to each other, thereby forming the total system of the group. The work of Talcott Parsons, some of which has been referred to in this chapter, is another systems approach to small-group behavior.

Interaction Process Analysis

Robert Bales is the chief architect of the research technique known as *interaction process analysis.* As previously noted, he believed that all group activity is essentially problem solving, whether it is affective or expressive or more directly related to goal attainment. Bales (1950) started with interaction, which he viewed as a continuous stream of acts, words, symbols, gestures, and the like flowing between individuals over the life of their group. He devised a twelvefold taxonomy for categorizing different aspects of this process in laboratory groups and in natural groups. These aspects are presented in Figure 6.4. With such data, he began theorizing about group social structure and particularly about its relationship to status links, power resources, control over members, and solidarity. *Solidarity* he defined as the sum of the mutual loyalties and affections among members of the group. We have already come across one important distinction arising from Bales's research, namely the distinction between socioemotional leaders and task-oriented leaders.

GROUP PERSPECTIVES

Small-group researchers and theorists share the assumption that groups are "real" (Borgatta, 1981); they are distinct forms of social reality created, maintained, and changed by the people

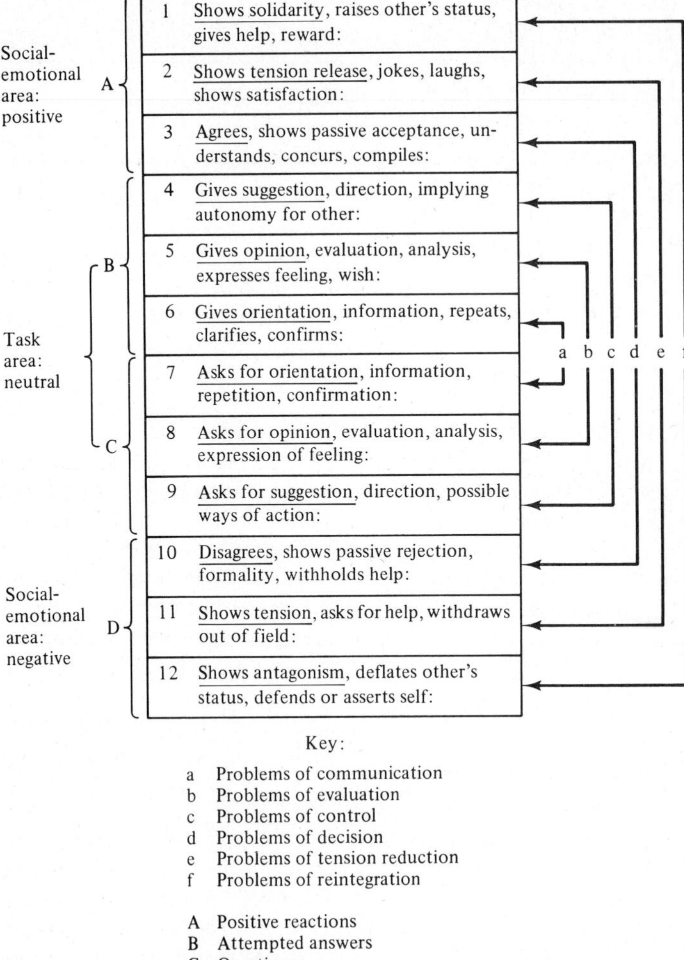

Figure 6.4 Interaction Process Analysis. (*Source:* R. F. Bales, 1950. *Interaction process analysis: A method for the study of small groups.* Reading, MA: Addison-Wesley, p. 9.)

who make them up. Thus, it should come as no surprise that one of the main interests of these sociologists is in the analytic problem of systems. Theoretically, the small group as a system has been studied from the functionalist perspective. The theories presented in this chapter developed by Homans, Lewin, and Bales are functionalist. Functionalist theory has guided research on group development, conformity and nonconformity, morals and cohesiveness, and goals and problem solving.

But the study of small groups is also a fruitful way in which to examine the analytic problem of interaction and interdependence and, on the micro level, the analytic problem of power, order, and interest. While continuing to share the assumption of the reality of groups, some small-group researchers have turned their attention to the desire to affiliate, the development and interconnection of statuses and roles, the nature of communications networks, and the formation of sociometric patterns. In this manner, they have examined the problem of interaction and interdependence. Concern with the problem of power, order, and interest has been manifested in the many studies of leadership, power, coalitions, and social exchange in groups.

The "small groups movement" (Borgatta, 1981), once a vibrant part of the social sciences, is presently "having a hiatus." As our earlier review of small-group theory demonstrates, one of the problems is the absence of new theory with which to integrate research in this area. Nevertheless, many other branches of sociology draw on small-group research and integrate it into their own theoretical perspectives. The study of large-scale organizations is one such area. In fact, the areas of small groups and large-scale organizations share many scholarly concerns.

OUTLINE AND SUMMARY

I. Introduction
   As a socialized human being, you are not alone. You belong to groups. Your family is a group.

II. What Is a Group?
   A *group* is a set of two or more persons who interact with each other while sharing common interests.

III. The Small Group
   A *small group* is an organized unit of two to twenty people, or, in some instances, a few more than twenty.
   A. Informal and Primary Groups
      An *informal group* is a group which may not necessarily have clearly defined roles and goals. A *primary group* is a small number of people who interact with each other on a face-to-face basis over an extended period of time. A family is a primary group.
   B. Formal and Secondary Groups.
      Formal groups have rules, roles, and goals that are more or less explicit. They are often intentionally formed to attain an agreed-upon goal. A *secondary group* is composed of people who have no emotional ties and who join together for a specific, workaday purpose.

IV. Group Formation
   Groups come into existence either spontaneously or by means of an intentional effort on the part of those who organize the group. Groups satisfy a human being's desire to affiliate with others.
   A. The Desire to Affiliate
      People join groups for *instrumental, expressive,* or *ascriptive* reasons and often for a combination of instrumental and expressive motives.
   B. Group Development
      Group development defined: the progression of stages or phases through which groups pass en route to an enduring state.

V. Group Structure
   Group structure defined: a collectivity's stable pattern of abstract relationships. Society has a social structure.
   A. Role and Status
      Each person in a group has a *role* and a *status.* The roles and statuses are part of a group's social structure.
   B. Sociometry
      Sociometry defined: a technique for describing socioemotional relations among the members of a group. A *sociogram* is a two-dimensional picture of all the members's socioemotional preferences. To conduct a sociometric study, sociologists use questionnaires.

VI. Group Processes
   Four processes of interaction within a group are *leadership, power, coalition formation,* and *communication of information and commands.* Size is one factor which has much to do with how the processes are applied in a group.
   A. Leadership
      Leadership defined: the capacity to make important decisions binding on all or nearly all the members of a group. The leader's role is to make decisions.

B. Power
Power is an element in social interaction. It has a bearing on the social structure of a group. A leader or others in the group have power. *Power* is the ability to control the behavior of others.

C. Coalitions
A *coalition* develops when two or more members of a group join forces by pooling their power resources to gain advantages for themselves.

D. Communication Networks
Communication is fundamental to all human social life. A *communications network* is a set of interconnected individuals within a group or between groups.

VII. Group Culture
Culture defined: the sum of all a group's patterned ways of thinking, feeling, and acting. Culture is a group's way of life.

A. Conformity and Noncomformity
The existence of small-group norms accounts for the sociologist's interest in conformity and nonconformity.

B. Morale and Cohesiveness
Morale is a part of group culture. The term "morale" is sometimes defined as *cohesiveness,* or sticking together.

C. Goals and Problem Solving
There are four main problems to be solved in groups: (1) group task problems, (2) group socioemotional problems, (3) individual task problems, and (4) individual socioemotional problems.

VIII. Theoretical Approaches
Four theoretical approaches to the study of small groups are *exchange theory, field theory, systems theory,* and *interaction process analysis.*

A. Exchange Theory
Exchange theory focuses on individual members of a group. According to this theory, individuals in a group exchange rewards and punishments for approved behavior or for behavior which is not approved.

B. Field Theory
Field theory, to some extent, is based on phenomenology and topology. Field theorists separate the naive view from the scientific view of reality.

C. Systems Theory
Homans's *systems approach* to small groups stresses the interrelation of *activity, sentiment,* and *interaction* in the internal and external systems of any collectivity (the systems theory).

D. Interaction Process Analysis
As a research technique, *interaction process analysis* rests on the assumption that all group activity is essentially problem solving.

IX. Group Perspectives
Small groups researchers and theorists share the assumption that small groups are "real." Many branches of sociology have drawn on research from this area of the discipline.

FOR FURTHER READING AND STUDY

Freud, S. 1949. *Group psychology and the analysis of the ego,* trans. J. Strachey. New York: Liveright. Freud argued that people form groups to deal with a common problem of an authority figure and the related problems of power and control.

Janis, I. L. and Mann, L. 1977. *Decision making.* New York: Free Press. A thorough study of why and how we make decisions and of the consequences of decisions made. The authors also review major research findings and consider ways of challenging outworn decisions and improving the quality of decision making.

Kanter, R.M. 1972. *Commitment and community: Communes and utopias in sociological perspective.* Cambridge, MA: Harvard University Press. A study of the strength of identification with communal and utopian life-styles in the nineteenth and twentieth centuries.

Lasch, C. 1979. *Haven in a heartless world: The family besieged.* New York: Basic Books. For Lasch, a historian, the haven in the heartless world of modern industrial society is the nuclear family, which strengthens its members to cope with the demands they face in the outside world.

McFeat, T. 1974. *Small-group cultures.* New York: Pergamon. An anthropologist examines the cultures of small groups in natural settings and in the laboratory. Among the issues addressed are how these cultures are organized and how they evolve.

Olmsted, M.S. and Hare, A.P. 1978. *The small group,* 2nd ed. New York: Random House. A short and very readable introduction to the field of small groups.

Smith, P. B. 1980. *Group processes and personal change.* London: Harper & Row. Smith examines the elements and effects of sensitivity training, the creation of the effective group, and the varieties of group experience in such programs as transactional analysis, structured encounters, and self-help groups. He also discusses the social context of group work.

Whyte, W.F. 1981. *Street corner society,* 3rd ed. Chicago: University of Chicago Press. A classic study of the daily lives of a small group of young men in a large eastern American city.

Zander, A. 1983. *Making groups effective.* San Francisco: Jossey-Bass. This book is about how to arrive at agreements about group-work procedures, strategies for resolving conflicts, flowing communication, realistic group goals, pride in group achievement, and group unity. Zander is an established scholar in the study of small groups.

KEY WORDS

aggregate A gathering of people in temporary proximity who have no enduring ties or other marks of social organization.

ascriptive motive An involuntary need to join a group; the joining is forced on one by circumstances or by someone else.

category A class of people who have something in common but who have no lasting relationship or intimate interaction.

coalition The joining of forces by individuals in a group; the individuals pool their resources of power to gain advantages for themselves.

cohesiveness The sticking together of individuals in a group.

culture A society's collective stock of knowledge, art, ideas, customs, values, norms, beliefs, laws, goals, outlooks, technologies, and patterns of behavior; society's way of life.

dyad A group of two persons.

expressive motive A need to join a group because of a desire to interact with members of the group.

formal group A group with rules, roles, and goals that are more or less explicit.

group An assembly of two or more persons who interact with each other while sharing common interests.

group development A progression which leads to the formation of a group; statuses, structures, and processes are established.

group formation The emergence of a collectivity.

informal group A group which may not necessarily have clearly defined roles and goals.

instrumental motive A need to join a group because of an interest in the group's goals.

leadership The capacity to make important decisions for all or nearly all members of a group.

material culture The artifacts and things which human beings make (wheels, clothing, rockets, typewriters, books, skyscrapers, computers).

power The ability to control the behavior of others and to dominate a situation.

primary group A small number of people who interact with each other on a face-to-face basis over an extended period of time.

social structure A collectivity's stable pattern of abstract relationships.

sociogram A two-dimension picture of an individual's socioemotional preferences.

sociometry A technique for describing socioemotional relations among members of a group.

triad A group of three persons.

chapter 7

Large-Scale Organizations

CHAPTER OUTLINE

INTRODUCTION

For many decades the trend in Canada and other industrialized nations has been toward greater individual involvement with impersonal, bureaucratic, large-scale organizations than with small groups. Few people can get away from the modern organization, which is big in size and big in influence; the large organization is the center of interest and activity for workers, managers, volunteers, customers, clients, and stockholders. People directly feel its practices and ethos. The large-scale organization touches the life of everyone.

A large-scale organization—a government, a university, a corporation, a labor union, a service club—is a massive social group formed for a specific purpose (to make money or to promote a cause, for example). The people who make up the group carry out specific tasks and routines. They are governed by rules, and everyone in the group has a particular role to play. The jobs and the people who hold the jobs are put into a hierarchy. A chart showing the chain of command and individual responsibilities can be drawn up for any large-scale organization (see Figure 7.1). Responsibilities within the organization are attached to a position or office, not to an individual.

Based on the presumption that small groups and large-scale organizations have something in common, the plan of this chapter resembles that of the preceding chapter. This chapter covers structure, processes, culture, and organizational formation. But, unlike their study of small groups, the sociologists' study of large-scale organizations includes a look at the environment in which the organizations operate; sociologists consider the problems which large-scale organizations engender. Environment and problems are taken up in the sections which follow. The chapter concludes with a review of three prominent theories of organization. We turn first, however, to a comparison of small groups with large groups.

LARGE AND SMALL GROUPS

There are ways in which large-scale organizations are akin to small groups. In this chapter we will see that the two evince similarities in formation, structure, process, and culture. Like small groups, large-scale organizations form around goals; the pursuit of the goals leads to status-role differentiation, authority structures,

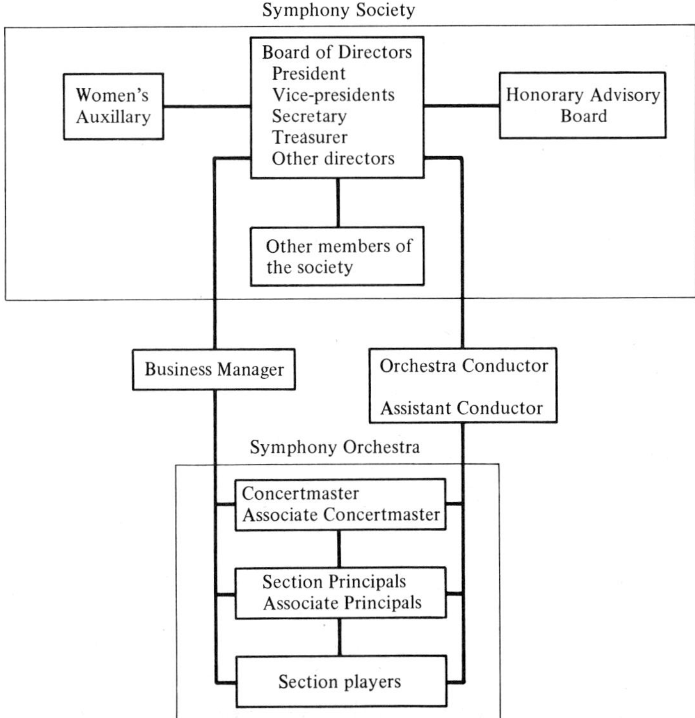

Figure 7.1 Organization of a Symphony Orchestra

and normative expectations. Communication is a more important process in large organizations than in small groups. Leaders in large organizations are as concerned as those in small groups with morale and cohesiveness and with conformity and nonconformity.

In view of these similarities, it is hardly surprising that sociologists turn to some of the same dimensions to define both the small group and the large-scale organization. One such dimension is size. Because of their size, large groups give significantly more attention than small groups to coordination and rule making. They also are more concerned with administration and control than are small groups. The attention which large organizations give to processes such as administration and rule making is one reason why they are described as *large-scale* or *complex.*

Secondary Groups

Another dimension is the degree of primariness or secondariness of groups. In the preceding chapter, we saw that nearly all small groups are primary. This is not so with large-scale organizations. In view of their size, large-scale organizations, with few if any exceptions, are secondary groups. Sociologists define secondary groups as collectivities characterized by comparatively cold, impersonal relations among members who fill specialized roles. These roles limit contact with other members of the group. They also channel interaction toward role-related matters, hindering the acquisition of broader personal knowledge about the role players.

The definition of secondary group presented in the preceding paragraph is an *ideal-typical* definition. It contrasts with the ideal type of the primary group presented in Chapter 6. As exemplified in these two definitions, an ideal type is an abstraction of theoretically significant aspects of empirical reality which, when interrelated, form a unified concept. Unlike a true theory or scientific concept, this type is not expected to correspond to this reality. Rather, the ideal type is a research tool used by social scientists to compare and test hypotheses bearing on reality (see Lopreato and Alston, 1970). In reality, organizations vary in their degree of secondariness (e.g., a small business vs. a large corporation). Moreover, secondariness as a composite measure of the aforementioned characteristics is even more pronounced in groups such as cities and societies.

Large-scale organizations, like small groups, are distinct entities; they are unique for many of the same reasons small groups are distinct. In addition, nearly all large-scale organizations in business and industry are legally established as companies; others are organized as associations, charities, schools, service clubs, or political entities (parties and governments) (Coleman, 1974). A legal charter is not, however, a necessary condition of organization, as attested by organized crime (e.g., the Mafia, drug pushers, numbers rings). Legal or illegal, organizations do develop "personalities" (McGuire, 1963: 160–163). As Presthus (1978: 87) puts it, a "complex peculiarity" characterizes the bureaucratic situation.

SOCIOLOGY OR COMMON SENSE

What do you think?

Which of the following statements do you agree with? Which statements do you disagree with? Make a note of your answers. Check your answers when you have completed your study of this chapter. Are your answers to the statements the same as those a sociologist would give?

1. Large-scale organizations are the main way of satisfying human needs in modern society.
2. Bureaucracy is essentially red tape, inefficient, and insensitive to human problems.
3. Increases in organizational size and complexity lead to increases in job alienation and job dissatisfaction.
4. Voluntary organizations are democratic organizations.
5. People can affect large organizations very little. Organizations do what they want.

But there are significant differences between small groups and large-scale organizations. These differences are evident in Hall's definition (1977: 22–23) of *large-scale organization:*

> An organization is a collectivity with a relatively identifiable boundary, a normative order, ranks of authority, communications systems, and membership-coordinating systems; this collectivity exists on a relatively continuous basis in an environment and engages in activities that are usually related to a goal or a set of goals.[1]

Communications, continuity, ranks of authority, and membership-coordinating systems distinguish large-scale organizations from small groups, although, more often than not, this is a matter of degree. Some small groups exist with considerable continuity, aided by slow membership turnover. Small groups may remain in existence for many years (e.g., community theaters and church choirs).

Types of Organizations

As Table 7.1 shows, large-scale organizations are found in nearly every corner of life in Canada. This diversity has been the focus of numerous classificatory schemes. W. Richard Scott (1981: 28–41) identifies five elements of organization used by sociologists to construct typologies. The five elements are *goals, social structure, technology, participant,* and *environment.* Examples are available in the works of Parsons and Weber.

Parsons (1960: 44–56) also used his AGIL framework (see Chapter 6) to classify organizations by their goals or functions. Adaptive organizations (A) engage in economic production (e.g., businesses). Goal-attainment organizations (G) are concerned with the generation and allocation of power (e.g., banks, government agencies). Integrative organizations (I) contribute primarily to efficiency through, for instance, the courts and political parties. Organizations dealing with latent pattern maintenance (L) emerge in the fields of religion and fine arts.

Table 7.1 ORGANIZATIONS IN CANADIAN SOCIETY

Area of social life	Illustrative organizations
Religion	Churches Synagogues
Politics	Parties Pressure groups
Health	Hospitals Professional associations
Education	Schools Parent-teacher organizations
Labor	Unions Employees' associations
Law enforcement	Prisons Police forces
Economics	Businesses Manufacturers' associations
Military	Armed forces Veterans' groups
Public service	Civil service bureaucracies Social service agencies
Arts	Symphony orchestras Theater companies
Philanthropy	United Way Red Cross
Leisure	Circuses Amateur and hobbyist clubs

Weber's Organizations

Let us consider Max Weber's (1947: 328) three ideal types of organizations. They are based on his three forms of legitimate authority: *rational-legal, traditional,* and *charismatic.* In the prerationalistic era of world history, organizations were either traditional or charismatic. Today, the rational-legal type predominates.

Rational-Legal Authority In an organization founded on rational-legal authority, the in-

[1]Hall actually defines "organizations" rather than large-scale organizations. Still, his conception of the former is consistent with the present treatment of the latter.

The Indian chief is one of the few remaining examples of traditional authority in Canada.

dividuals who are elevated to positions of authority are legitimated by a system of formal rules. Those in authority are given the right to use their power by those who are ruled. The rank and file are expected to obey their leaders, not because of the leaders as individuals (i.e., because of who they are) but because of the positions the leaders occupy in the organization. The jurisdiction of each position is limited to a particular responsibility. Rational-legal organizations are composed in part of a hierarchy; the leaders and their subordinates make up the hierarchy. Those who fill the leaders' roles are selected according to their technical qualifications (e.g., having a university degree, passing a civil service examination).

Of Weber's three types of organizations, the rational-legal organization is the most familiar today. Among examples of such organizations are corporations, hospitals, universities, and government agencies. When we think of large-scale organizations, we tend to think of the rational-legal organization. In modern society, the traditional organization and the charismatic organization contrast starkly with the rational-legal organization.

Traditional Authority A *traditional authority* organization rests on the long-established right of individuals in authoritative positions to rule other members of the group. The members of the group cannot remember when the leaders acquired their authority. In this type of organization, obedience is in response to the leader as a person, not to the position he or she occupies or to any of the position's associated rules. Traditional authority figures have a range of discretion available to them. A member of a ruling family or clan often holds the leadership position.

Although now relatively rare, examples of traditional authority do exist in Canada and other parts of the Western world. The monarchy in Britain is a form of traditional authority. At the other end of the scale of respectability lies the Mafia, which, of course, can never be legally organized. The Mafia, however, is an impure case, for it also operates within a moderately complicated quasirational-legal form of organization.

Charismatic Authority Organizations ruled by charismatic authority accord legitimacy to their leaders on the basis of their special gifts—heroics, exemplary character, mysterious power—which are widely respected by their followers. These leaders have *charisma,* or "supernatural, superhuman, or at least specifically exceptional powers or qualities. They are such as are not accessible to the ordinary person" (Weber, 1947: 358–359). It is the duty of this type of leader to recognize his or her charismatic mission and act accordingly. The adherence of the followers to the demands of a charismatic leader is based on an emotional attachment to that individual. Other positions in the organization, which are few, are filled by disciples.

Organizations based on charismatic leadership lie outside the realm of everyday routine. Religious cults and revolutionary groups coalesce around charismatic personalities. We shall see later, particularly in Chapter 15, that such people sometimes induce social change. Unlike the circumstances of rational-legal authority and traditional authority, there is little regard in charismatic groups for past or present circumstances.

For the most part, the power of an American president or Canadian prime minister rests on legal-rational authority. But the president and the prime minister also function with traditional authority. At one point in his career, Pierre Trudeau was recognized for his charismatic personality. It could be said that he attained legitimacy from charismatic authority as well as from traditional authority and legal-rational authority.

FORMATION OF ORGANIZATIONS

Large-scale organizations form in much the same way that small groups come about. Wright (1977: 38–44) presents some of the key conditions of organizational emergence. First, there must be a reason for organizing. That is, one or more individuals with a common need or needs believe that these needs can be more effectively met through organization than through any alternative. Meeting these needs becomes the initial goal of the fledgling organization. Once a direction is chosen, organizations, because they typically are made up of many people, require leaders to allocate resources and coordinate the use of resources in pursuit of collective aims. As in small groups, the leaders are often, although not always, legitimated. The members of the group grant authority to the leader and permit him or her to direct them in specified ways.

Division of Labor

An inescapable aspect of organizational life emerges soon after the collective pursuit of common goals emerges. That aspect is the *division of labor:* the development and integration of the group's specialized roles into an effectively functioning unit along the lines of the main goals. Some of these specialized roles are intentionally established, often by the leader (e.g., secretary, treasurer), whereas others emerge spontaneously out of the interaction of the members of the organization. These roles gain general recognition only after they have crystallized. This is the beginning of the organization's social structure. It is also the route along which goal-related tasks are delegated to the rank and file, allowing them to participate in goal attainment.

One of the difficulties created by the division of labor is that of *role conflict.* A person beset with role conflict faces inconsistent demands made by other people associated with one or more of his or her statuses. Such conflict may be seen by the person as existing within a single position or between two or more positions he or she fills. Nancy Goldman (1973) describes the conflict in role expectations among American women in the armed forces. Unmarried officers and unmarried enlisted women experience the most strain as they try to adjust to the traditions which were developed when the armed forces were staffed chiefly by married males. The women find it difficult to cope with the cult of masculinity (as expressed in heavy drinking, daring feats, and sexual aggressiveness).

Role conflict is stressful, which leads to attempts to escape its effects. Those who face this predicament develop one or more strategies for coping with it (Stebbins, 1971b). For example, some people solve interrole conflict by favoring a position associated with the group having highest priority for them. For others, the conflict, whether within or between roles, is reduced by striking the best possible balance between rewards and costs. In sum, it is evident, from the point of view of those who participate in them, that organizational structures mesh imperfectly.

Alternatives to Organization

It should be noted that organizations are only one of several sources of satisfaction of human needs when satisfaction depends on the cooperation of others. Scott (1981: 143–144) discusses three alternatives. Another source is the primary group, including kin networks. For example, families sometimes provide certain kinds of nursing care normally provided by hospitals. Still another alternative is the market, in which buyers and sellers negotiate an exchange of goods and services. The market, at least ideally,

The Large-Scale Organization of Sport

The bureaucratization of top-level sports implies a system of social roles like that existing in the world of work. Within a sports club, as in an industrial enterprise, every active person acquires a rank that fixes his area of activity. In a goal-oriented, social, behavioral apparatus, such a status is precisely defined. Depending on its goals, tasks, and responsibilities, every enterprise creates subordination and superordination by the structure of its roles. "Formal social organization is . . . a system of social roles related hierarchically and organized to make possible the fulfillment of the goals of the enterprise." Every social role is linked on the basis of objective determinations to expected behavior on the part of those who fill the role.

Top-level sports have copied this model of ordered status and roles in their elementary forms of social organization. Like the director of an economic enterprise the president of a sports club (or the chairman of its executive committee) incorporates the highest level of control and decision-making. He speaks authoritatively, utters the principles of club politics, and appears in public as representative of the club. When there are conflicts of interest with other institutions, he acts as the negotiating go-between. In his leadership role, one expects to find typical qualities in him—e.g., specialized information, rhetorical ability, identification with the tasks to be accomplished, and organizational tact. The president of a sports club can be seen as a general manager who exercises a high-level coordinating function within the club management. Alongside of him stand the experts whose spheres of activity are objectively determined: the vice-president (or second officer) who is responsible for administration and organization, the director of sports and play who coordinates the whole field of athletic activity, the press secretary, the treasurer, and such yet more specialized roles as legal advisor. These roles correspond to those of the directors of an industrial enterprise. Every division of a sports club has its chief whose functions match those of the superintendent or divisional manager of a business firm. He carries out the directions of his superiors in the management and acts independently to accomplish the tasks delegated to him. The margin of independence for the divisional leader of a sports club is, however, greater than that in an economic enterprise because, in most cases, the former is an unpaid volunteer within an athletic organization whose existence is not primarily goal-oriented nor dependent on successful decisions. There is no strictly formal set of regulations. On the other hand, the role of the athletic trainer is like that of the top-level athlete himself—clearly determined by goal-oriented norms which define their status and the characteristics of their position—the characteristics, that is, of specialized knowledge, practical mastery of the specific athletic discipline, leadership characteristics such as empathy with the psychic situation of an athlete, ability to assume group leadership, capacity to make objective decisions. In short, the trainer must have personal and objective prerequisites enabling him to direct training at the optimal level of achievement in order to accomplish the central goal of the specialist. In the United States there are team sports (baseball, American football, basketball) with trainers solely responsible for the physical conditioning of the team while the head coach and his assistants teach strategy and prepare the players for the contest itself.

The role of the top-level athlete himself, like that of the worker and the employee, is based on his promise of specific achievement. One expects achievement-oriented behavior from him: training (work), industry, punctuality, fulfillment of the training tasks (work quotient), etc. All these expectations are normally written up in the form of a formal pledge or a professional contract, which fixes the role and is binding on the signatories.

Team sports offer the most typical example of the division-of-labor role system in sport. In the descriptions of the individual playing positions, one can see quite explicitly the definitions of the roles: "middle stormer," "right runner," "left defender," "goalies," etc. These names determine a spatial bounding of the field upon which the game takes place (e.g., the goalie), a prescribed function for each player (e.g., defenseman), or a specific role-expectation (a forward). Every description of the position contains a catalogue of characteristics which imply a prescribed pattern of behavior for the individual player. Differentiated roles appear, but not in isolation one from another; they appear within the team as part of a system of roles. Teamwork is the guiding principle. Nowadays, socially and politically progressive industrial firms look upon the sociological concept of teamwork as a model of effective work organization.

SOURCE: Bero Rigauer. *Sport and work,* trans. Allen Guttman, pp. 48–51. New York: Columbia University Press, 1981.

is free of direct human interference. There is no coordination from a central authority or leader, as there is in organizations. The institution of work, particularly the professions, constitutes a third alternative. Professionals tend to perform their work roles according to an internalized set of standards as framed in a code of ethics. Their work is self-regulated. These three alternatives —primary group, market, work—demonstrate that complex goals can be pursued without recourse to a large-scale organization.

Nonetheless, the alternatives to organization are frequently less appealing (perhaps we should say *usually* less appealing) than organization. Like other Western nations, Canada and the United States are extensively organized. Indeed, Scott and Hart (1979: 1–2) go so far as to maintain that the modern large-scale organization is an American invention:

> The primary instrument of our successes in this century has been neither our military prowess nor our wealth, but our most successful social invention: the modern organization. Americans have moved into this last quarter of the twentieth century with only the slightest awareness that the modern organization, with its accouterments of power and control, has become the dominant force in our lives, shaping and changing American

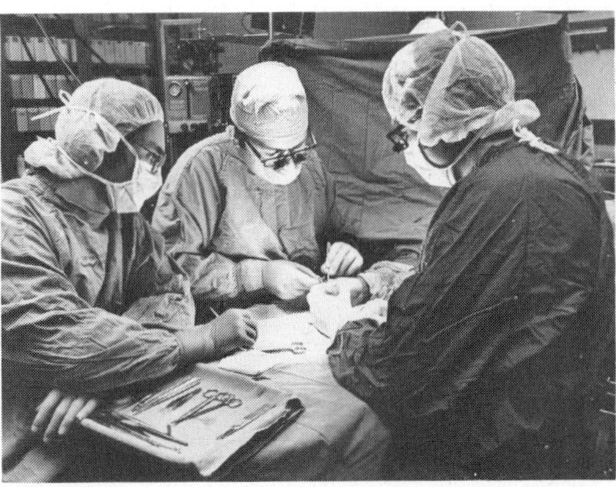

What aspect of organizational life do you see here?

> values and the American people to suit its requirements.

Still, Scott and Hart's conception of organization may be too narrow, for such groups as armies, churches, voluntary associations, professional associations, and social movements (at the administrative level) exist and have existed historically in Europe and non-Western countries (Van Doorn, 1979: 61).

ORGANIZATIONAL STRUCTURE

Like small groups, large-scale organizations have a social structure, or stable pattern of interrelated statuses. A social structure becomes evident once the group's labor has been divided in a workable way (i.e., the process of the division of labor in organizational development). Understandably, organizational structures are ordinarily more complicated than small-group structures (see Figures 7.2 and 7.3). Organizations diverge from small groups by developing formal and informal sides to the structures, or patterns.

Formal Structure

All organizations are *formal* (note the use of the term "formal" in Chapter 6), inasmuch as they are legally chartered or, at the very least, have some sort of written or public recognition as groups. In the study of organizations, the idea of *formal structure,* while not excluding this matter of tangible identity, recognizes the explicit or definitive nature of organizational positions and their interrelationships. The positions are interrelated in two ways. One way is along the lines of a hierarchy; that is, different ranks are interrelated. The other way is according to the function each position performs in helping the organization achieve its goals. Formal role expectations are manifested as rules and regulations, which are often written as "job descriptions" or otherwise clearly understood by all concerned as "the way things are done around here." Figures 7.2 and 7.3 show the formal sides of the Canadian and American federal governments (minus their rules and regulations).

Bureaucracy

One of the principal objects of research in the matter of formal organization is the set of structures and processes called *bureaucracy.* The term "bureaucracy" has been bandied about in everyday discourse to the point where it has lost much of the precision needed for effective scientific communication and understanding. Lay usage suggests the notions that bureaucracy is essentially troublesome, inefficient, insensitive to human problems, and synonymous with large-scale organization; in line with these notions, it is the bureaucrat who perpetrates horrors such as red tape and computer readouts on a defenseless public. Blau and Meyer's (1971: 4) definition of *bureaucracy* suggests that these perceptions may be more fiction than fact. As they put it, *bureaucracy* is a

> type of organization designed to accomplish large-scale administrative tasks by systematically coordinating the work of many individuals. . . . This concept then applies to organizing principles that are intended to improve administrative efficiency and that generally do so, although bureaucratization quite often has the opposite effect of producing inefficiency.

Bureaucracies are staffed by individuals at the middle level of organization—the *managerial level,* in Thompson's (1967: 10–11) terminology. The manager's job is to mediate between the organization's technical level and its clients (customers, pupils, inmates, patients). The functions of the organization are carried out on the technical level by, say, nurses, teachers, prison guards, and assembly-line workers. The managers serve these personnel, as seen in the roles of foreman, assistant principal, deputy warden, and head nurse. Meanwhile, at the institutional level, high-ranking officials make

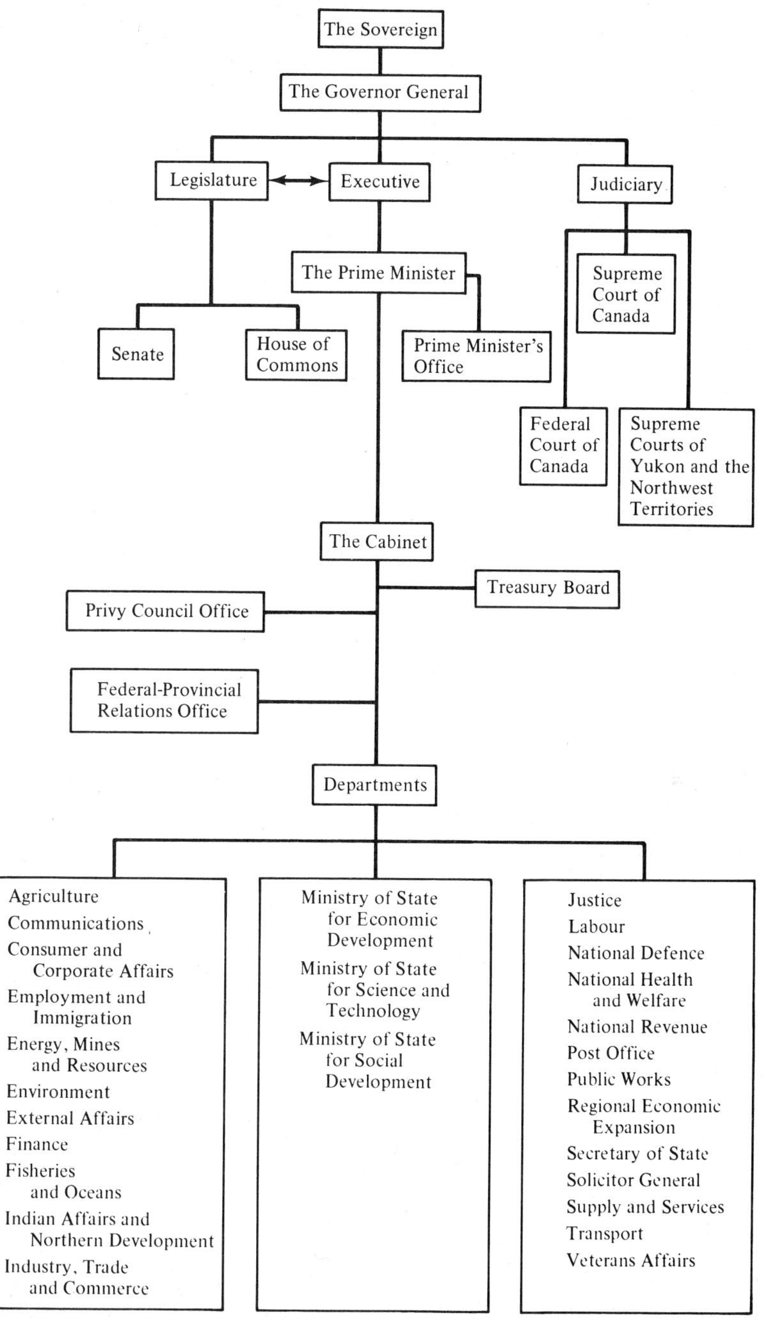

Figure 7.2 Government of Canada, June 1980. (*Source:* Canada Yearbook, 1980–1981. Ottawa: Statistics Canada, 1981, p. 84.)

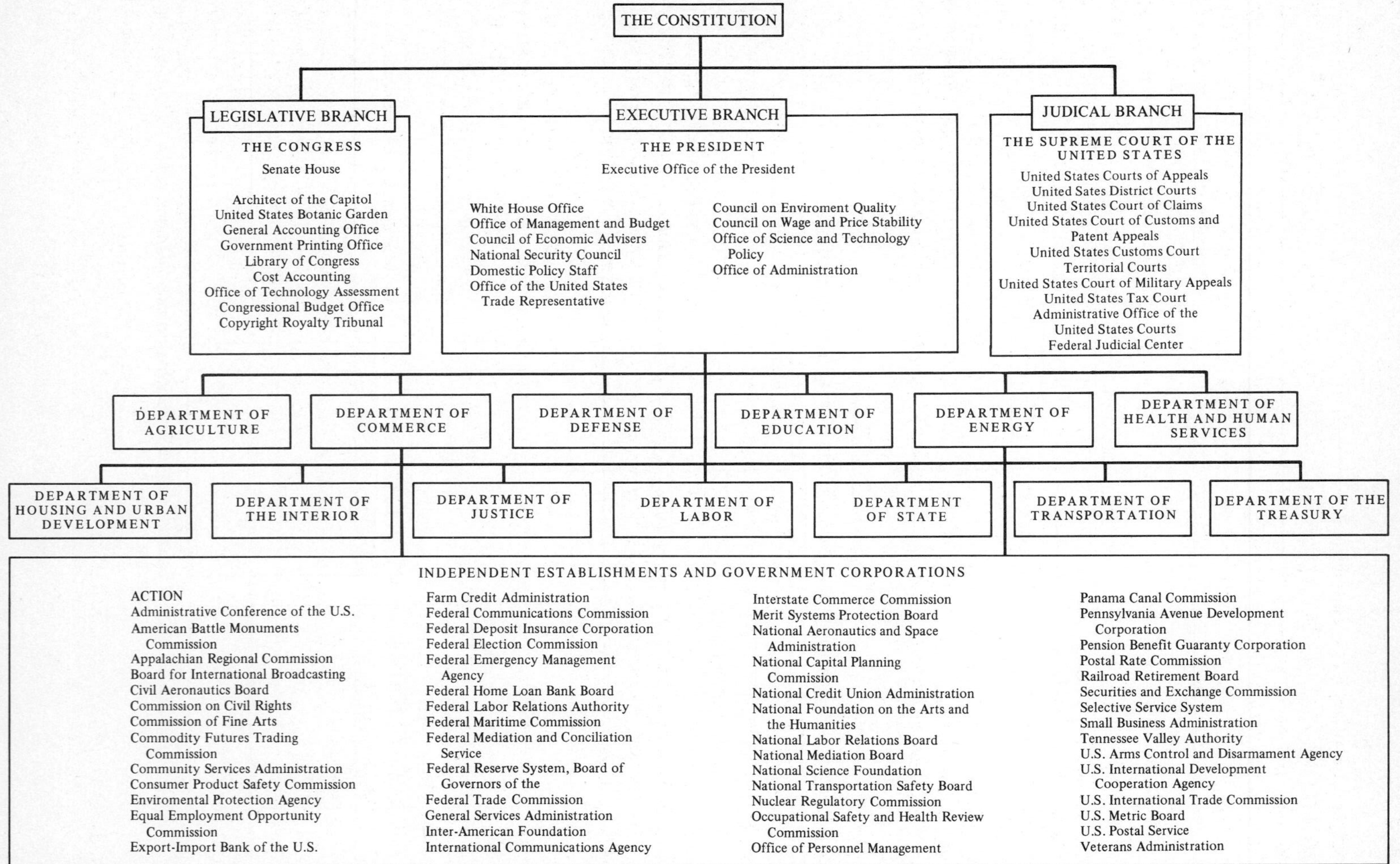

Figure 7.3 Government of the United States, 1980. (*Source: Statistical Abstracts of the United States* (101st ed.). Washington, D.C.: U.S. Bureau of the Census, 1980, p. 254.)

sure the organization has a role in community affairs and in the affairs of the society of which the organization is a part. Among such leaders are the company president, school principal, prison warden, and hospital administrator.

Informal Structure

Sociologists see a contrast between an organization's formal structure and its informal structure. The *informal structure* is a pattern of relationships and behaviors; the relationships and behaviors are neither codified nor obvious. There are subtleties in such relationships. There is, within the informal structure, significant interaction among the individuals who play roles and hold positions in the formal structure; there are relationships, for example, among the workers on an assembly line and among the sales clerks in a department store. Compared with the formal interaction, informal interaction may be warm, friendly, hostile, cooperative, indifferent, or competitive. Indifference or cooperation among workers can have a striking impact on an organization's chances of reaching its goals. The following illustrates the articulation of an organization's formal structure and informal structure:

> This is Perkins, Potter, Parker, and Potts. Good morning!
>
> Is Mr. Potter there?
>
> May I ask who is calling?
>
> This is Mr. Sullivan's office, of Sullivan, Chadwick, Bicknell, and Jones.
>
> Just a moment, I'll connect you.
>
> Mr. Potter's office? Mr. Potter, please. Mr. Sullivan would like to talk to him.
>
> Will you put Mr. Sullivan on the line, please?
>
> Mr. Sullivan? Ready with Mr. Potter.
>
> Hello, Pete. This is Joe. Okay for lunch? Good! See you.

Research into the formal structure of organizations has proceeded along several lines, including that of the *role set.* Robert Merton (1957a: 100), who coined the term "role set," defines it as "that complement of role relationships in which persons are involved by virtue of occupying a particular social status." Merton illustrated his concept with the status of a medical student, a status linked with professors, fellow students, nurses, social workers, medical technicians, and others who, together, constitute the role set for the social category of medical student. Pfeffer and Salancik (1975) studied first-level supervisors in the housing division of a large midwestern American university. They found that the conduct of supervisory activities was influenced, in part, by the perceived expectations of the other individuals in the role set.

Size

The structural variable of size, so prominent in small groups, is no less so in the realm of large-scale organizations. Size is typically defined in this field as the number of members in the organization. Despite the stereotype of the large and impersonal organization, the majority of organizations in the modern world are small. Perhaps fewer than 25 percent have more than four paid employees (Carroll, 1984: 76).

We consider two possible correlates of size—complexity and centrality of decision making. Each must be considered in organizational research, for a large-scale organization is both complex and centralized. We turn first to size and complexity.

Contrary to common sense, neither size nor complexity seems to have much effect on alienation and job satisfaction. John Gartrell and Terrence White, in separate studies of Canadian work organizations, examined these variables for possible correlations, but they found few of them. They concluded that factors other than size and complexity play a much greater role in promoting alienation and job satisfaction. (Royal Commission on Corporate Concentration, 1978: 365–367).

As for size and centrality, it may come as a

surprise to learn that organizational size fails to vary with the degree of centrality of decision making. Research in the United States and England have consistently verified this apparent anomaly (e.g., Blau and Schoenherr, 1971; Pugh et al., 1969). But there are many crucial problems in the study of organizational size and social structure (Kimberley, 1976). One problem is how to measure size, since the number of members in an organization is sometimes vague, inaccurately counted, or fluctuating. This is particularly true in collectivities such as churches, prisons, political parties, labor unions, and voluntary associations. The relationships among size, complexity, centrality of decision making, and other variables, such as technology and environment, are extremely intricate and still only partly understood. Blau and Schoenherr (1971: 57) argue that "size is the most important condition affecting the structure of organizations," while Scott (1975: 14–15) argues that this sweeping generalization is unfounded. As if to complicate matters, investigators have found cross-national differences in the relationships between size and centralization. Hickson et al. (1979: 38–39) discovered that large organizations in Britain, Germany, and the United States tend to decentralize (delegate decision making to lower levels), while those in Canada, Sweden, and Japan do not. This finding is yet to be explained.

ORGANIZATIONAL PROCESSES

As in small groups, three processes have much to do with the interaction and social exchanges within the large group. These processes are the exercise of leadership, the use of power, and the communication of information and orders. A large-scale organization soon would collapse without leadership, power, and communication. The top administrators exercise leadership and exert power. They depend on communication for their success in directing the fortunes of the organization.

Leadership

The leaders in a large-scale organization, just as in small groups, are task leaders and socioemotional leaders. At the organizational level, nearly all research (Filley et al., 1976: 219–229) corroborates the hypothesis that, under certain conditions, supportive socioemotional leadership is more likely to produce favorable, goal-oriented attitudes and hence greater output than authoritarian task leadership. Nevertheless, a few studies report no differences between task leadership and socioemotional leadership. According to these studies, authoritarian leaders encourage the same levels of attitude and output as socioemotional (Dubin, 1965).

Filley and his associates, in an exhaustive review of the literature, concluded that two types of leadership, supportive and participative, are the most effective, although only under certain conditions. Supportive leaders encourage subordinates in their group-related efforts, a practice especially likely to bring favorable results when the subordinates are denied some kind of satisfaction or are frustrated and tense. Participative leaders solicit subordinates' opinions, ideas, and knowledge. Such leadership is most effective when tasks are ambiguous to both leader and followers, when followers are knowledgeable about the task, and when the followers want independence. Conversely, leadership in stable, clear-cut circumstances safe from external threat is more likely to be successful if it is autocratic (Fiedler, 1972).

A "conceptual overview" (Wright, 1977: 177–178) enables the leader to obtain a comprehensive grasp of the organization and its environment. With this understanding, the leader can deal with the organization in all its complexity and can solve the aforementioned problems. Having a conceptual overview is an indispensable asset for successful leaders.

There are a number of consequences of "component thinking," or having too narrow an outlook. One is the tendency to see particular segments of the organization in isolation when, in fact, the segments are integrated. This leads to impractical decisions and ineffective or nonexistent delegation of authority and functions. Such leadership flaws thwart the purpose of the organization, since its parts are now inadequately coordinated. The problem is worsened by the leader's inability to guide authority. Leaders may not know how to do their subordinates' work, but they should know how the subordinates' functions fit in the overall operation.

Consider the problems that could develop were the contractor responsible for coordinating the building of a high-rise office tower lacking a conceptual overview of the construction process. For example, when internal wall construction has reached a certain stage, the plumbers and electricians must be called in to lay pipes and lines before the walls are covered with plasterboard. Since it is expensive on large projects to have workers sitting around waiting to do their jobs or have the project stand idle because the plumbers, for instance, were scheduled too late, precise timing of the performance of each activity is critical. The contractor must be able to anticipate when certain types of workers are needed and see to it that they are on the site.

Power and Authority

The study of power and authority in large-scale organizations is guided by several classifications of these two processes. We have already encountered Weber's tripartite distinction of rational-legal, traditional, and charismatic authority. Originally written in German, his papers were translated and published in English in 1947.

The next classification was developed by French and Raven (1959). They identified five types of power that subordinates see their superiors using. *Reward power* evolves from the resources (e.g., promotion, pay increase, praise) the superior uses to reward subordinates for satisfactory service. *Coercive power* entails actual or threatened use of verbal or physical abuse—insult, incarceration, bodily harm—to gain the subordinate's compliance. Leaders with *expert power* achieve ascendancy by means of their superior knowledge or skill or both. The power which the authors refer to as *referent power* succeeds when superior and subordinate are friends and the subordinate wishes to please the superior. *Legitimate power* is identical to Weber's rational-legal authority.

The lawyer achieves ascendancy by means of expert power.

In large-scale organizations, the expression of power is channeled downward through the hierarchical structure of the organization. This expression varies because hierarchical structures vary. Wamsley (1970: 53) portrays organizations as falling along a continuum consisting of highly bureaucratized groups (many administrative offices) at one end and slightly bureaucratized groups (few administrative offices) at the other. The expression of power varies along this dimension:

> At the bureaucratic end power or authority would tend to be hierarchic; each level would have just the amount of power necessary to carry out its responsibilities; ascendant levels in the hierarchy would have increasing power based on broader knowledge about the organization and/or greater task expertise; the apex of the pyramidal structure would use its broader knowledge to reconcile distinct tasks in accomplishing over-all goals and would thus have final power over operations and behavior of lower echelons. (Wamsley, 1970: 33)[2]

[2] Wamsley uses power and authority interchangeably.

Near the high bureaucratic pole we find the military and the federal government. At the opposite pole lie bureaucracies such as universities and Protestant denominations.

Organizations, no matter how bureaucratized, distribute power throughout their hierarchies. But only repetitive decisions and decisions that can be anticipated in advance are delegated to lower levels (Galbraith, 1977: 43–44). There is relatively little delegation of discretionary authority, which, by definition, is exercised only in unusual circumstances.

It should also be recognized that power relationships form horizontally. Hall (1977: 215–222) addresses the contradiction inherent in the phrase "horizontal power relationships." We have become accustomed to using the term "power" to refer to unequal relations among people. But power can become a crucial condition when individuals or units in a formal, lateral relationship compete over matters such as budgetary allocations, output quotas, hiring priorities, and personnel changes. The most influential individual or unit gains a temporary power advantage over the others, even though they all are formally equal on the organizational chart.

Oligarchy

One troublesome expression of power in organizations was noted years ago (1915) by Robert Michels: oligarchic tendencies inhere in them. He concluded that there is an "Iron Law of Oligarchy," which has subsequently been translated (Michels, 1959) into the now famous maxim: "Who says organization, says oligarchy." In other words, there is a tendency in large-scale organizations for power to drift into the hands of a few individuals. This is an ineluctable trend, since the rank and file are inclined to leave decision making to their leaders.

Michels's thesis applies mainly to voluntary, ostensibly democratic organizations such as labor unions, political parties (which Michels studied), voluntary associations, and professional associations, and not to intentionally oligarchic collectivities (e.g., businesses, prisons, hospitals, police forces). Nearly all writers, including Presthus (1978: 31–32) and Scott and Hart (1979: 24), agree that Michels's law is basically correct. Still, there are deviant cases, such as the New York local of the International Typographical Union (Lipset et al., 1956) and the Toronto local of the Amalgamated Clothing Workers of America (Shepard, 1949), suggesting that democracy can prevail in voluntary organizations despite opposing tendencies. The as yet unanswered question for sociologists is, What are the conditions promoting democracy here?

Communication

Power and leadership in organizations would not exist were it not for organized systems of communications; with communication systems, leaders and other powerful individuals can pass their demands down the line. Davis and Scott (1969: 255) believe that:

> without communication, there can be no organization and, hence, no group productivity, because communication is the only process by which people are tied together in a work group. If there is no communication, there can be no group. Communication is the bridge over which all technical knowledge and human relationships must travel.

Communication is not the cause of everything occurring in organizations, as Chester Barnard once proclaimed, but it clearly plays a key role in organizational theory.

In any large-scale organization, communication travels along both informal and formal structures. There are advantages and disadvantages to both kinds of channels (Champion, 1975: 175–190). The formal organization helps organizational leaders coordinate goal-related activities and learn whether the group is reaching its goals. If the goals are not being reached, the leaders know they must eliminate waste and inefficiency. Meanwhile, the continued use of the network serves to reinforce the existing social structure, especially its hierarchy of power.

Nonetheless, formal communication nets are generally slow at conveying critical information. Furthermore, the hierarchical nature of organizations fosters the notion that information only flows down from the top, although there are times when lower-echelon workers pass along important messages to their supervisors. Third, conflict and competition among units in an organization lessen the effectiveness of its formal communication system.

Informal communication nets within organizations partly offset these disadvantages. Overcoming the disadvantages is accomplished by providing alternative channels along which information travels. For example, news of an important administrative decision might pass from the manager's secretary to the manager's cronies in the organization. Often the informal exchange of information via "the grapevine" is quicker than formal communication. Moreover, since informal nets are more flexible than formal nets, they more easily surmount the barriers of conflict and competition. At least for organizational leaders, these informal nets have the disadvantages, however, of allowing inaccurate and wholly fallacious information to circulate (e.g., rumor, gossip). Informal systems may also undermine official pronouncements, norms, and authority.

At least two points concerning formal and informal communications in large-scale organizations are clear: first, both systems are inevitable. It is impossible to eliminate either one and still have an organization. Second, many organizations operate quite effectively through some complex intermingling of the two, which suggests that they may, in general, be more complementary than antagonistic.

ORGANIZATIONAL CULTURE

The cultures of organizations and small groups have much in common. Both are made up of standard behavior patterns, norms, and rules. Both the small group and the large-scale organization have dominant values, beliefs, and goals. In organizations, the collective image of the group is called *organizational climate.* One aspect of organizational culture not found in small-group culture is the technology of particular organizations. From a cultural standpoint, large-scale organizations resemble small-scale societies. In this section we look briefly at goals, organizational climate, and technology.

Goals

The organizational goal is a core concept in the study of organizations. Given the stress placed on this notion in this chapter and in preceding chapters, there can be little doubt about the truth of this claim. Yet, Scott (1981: 261) sounds an important warning: "The concept of organizational goals is among the most slippery and treacherous of all those employed by organizational analysts." He cautiously defines goals as "*conceptions of desired ends*—conditions that participants attempt to effect through their performance of task activities" (p. 16).[3] To be clear about this definition, these goals are related to the organization. They are usually shared by some or all of its members.

There are, however, occasional and sometimes significant discrepancies between participants' personal goals and those of the organization as a whole (Gross and Etzioni, 1985: 13).

By running, these people will help the Canadian Cancer Society reach its goals.

[3]Italics in the original.

The organization's goals may be only the goals of its leaders or of a couple of dominant units within it, while others in the group have different aims. Apart from the question of whose goals they are is the fact that they may be put to various uses. The goals may be simultaneously used to motivate participants to work for the organization, to direct the participants, to justify the organization's existence in the community, and even to evaluate the organization (Scott, 1981: 261–262). At times, these uses are incompatible. Notwithstanding all the confusion, sociologists have found it impossible to study organizations without some conception of goals.

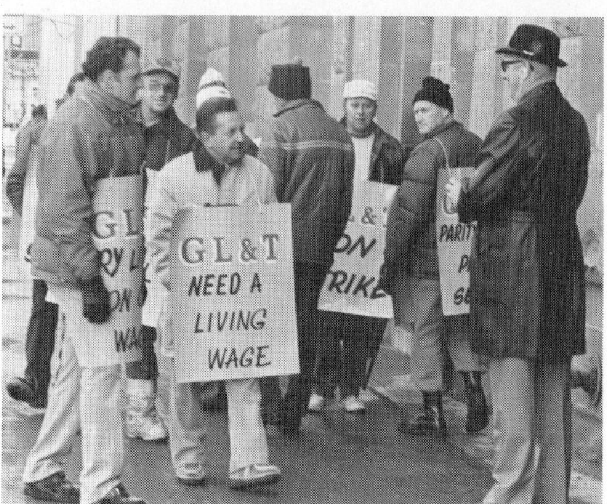

What is the organizational climate for these employees?

Organizational Climate

An organization's climate is the collective perception or image of the organization which its members have (Davis, 1977: 91–93). Its climate makes the organization unique. For example, the Boy Scouts of Canada is a unique collectivity. The Boy Scout troops are both social groups and training cadres for youth. The Boy Scouts have their own climate, making them different from such organizations as the Red Cross and the Salvation Army. Organizational climate is the group equivalent of individual personality.

Wright (1977: 129–130) points out that organizations develop their own conventional modes of thinking, acting, and interacting. They also relate in special ways to the outside world. Solutions to the problems of internal nonconformity and motivating and rewarding contributions of the members are also likely to have a flavor peculiar to the organization. The concept of organizational climate also encompasses the idea of group morale (see Chapter 6).

The climate in an organization can have a bearing on its goal attainment. Kuty (1979) studied four artificial kidney care units, two in Belgium and two in France. Two of the units (one in each country) had an "affective milieu." Doctors frequented the care setting, relations with patients were personal and intense, and patients interacted a great deal with one another. Consequently, the patients were well informed about their state of health. The "bureaucratic milieu" of the other two was characterized by distant relations among patients and the staff. Nurses always referred up the hierarchy to the physicians for routine decisions. Patients in the first milieu had the support of the general staff and their fellow patients during their tribulations. This was conspicuously absent in the second milieu.

Alienation

Part of the climate of some work organizations is the feeling of alienation at some levels of the company. "Alienation" has been defined in several different ways. A definition first stated by Karl Marx (he had several definitions of *alienation*) identifies alienated people as individuals estranged from the products of their work.[4] As Marx saw it, entrepreneurs employ workers, and the workers' creative energy goes into making a product for the entrepreneurs. The entrepreneurs then sell the product, giving the workers a wage for their labor. This ex-

[4] Marx is credited with introducing the idea of alienation into social science.

change of labor for wages estranges workers from that which they created and gave value to. The intrinsic value of the product to the workers is lost when they surrender it to the entrepreneur. It is replaced by an extrinsic value; that is, the product becomes a means to an end (i.e., wages, livelihood).

According to Seeman (1975: 93), most empirical research into alienation is social psychological (the concern of social psychologists). Earlier, Seeman (1972) identified six kinds of alienation, which give an overview of the scope of research in this area. The six kinds are (1) alienation as *powerlessness,* or the sense of little control versus the mastery of events; (2) alienation as *meaninglessness,* or the sense of incomprehensibility versus understanding the events of one's life; (3) alienation as *normlessness,* or high commitment to unconventional means versus high commitment to conventional means of achieving goals; (4) *cultural estrangement,* or individual rejection of commonly held values in the society versus commitment to existing group standards; (5) *self-estrangement,* or individual engagement in activities that are intrinsically unrewarding versus intrinsic involvement in a task or activity; and (6) *social isolation,* or the sense of exclusion or rejection versus acceptance.

While nearly countless studies of all six dimensions have been undertaken (Seeman, 1975), those searching for American-Canadian differences and similarities are rare. A study by Robert Blauner (1964) of several industries in the United States was replicated in Canada by Fullan (1970). Both men studied workers who use one of four technologies: assembly lines, machine tending, continuous process, and craft work. They found that the senses of powerlessness, meaninglessness, self-estrangement, and social isolation are most acute among assembly-line workers. Such feelings diminish as workers gain more control, knowledge, and responsibility. These qualities of work increase as they move from machine tending through continuous process to craft work.

Technology

Charles Perrow (1979: 160–162) notes that theorists have only recently begun to classify organizations by their technology. *Technology* is defined as the technique, or method, used by organizations to reach their goals. The concept of technology covers more than the machinery of production or even the electronic devices now commonly used in modern offices.

Hickson et al. (1969) identify three types of technology: the *physical materials* worked on, the *operations* (techniques) used on the materials to transform them into products which the organization wants, and the *knowledge* needed to acquire the materials, carry out the operations, and effectively handle the finished product (physical or nonphysical). Based on the assumption that organizations transform inputs into outputs, Scott (1975: 5–8) has cross-classified these three types with three processing stages: the *input stage,* the *throughput,* or *transformation, stage,* and the *output stage.* Table 7.2 lists some of the technology of an automobile plant when viewed from the intersection of these six variables.

Perrow (1970: 176) has said of the study of organizational technology:

> Organizational structure varies with the type of work done. A fundamental fact about organizations is that they do work; they transform raw materials into acceptable outputs. The characteristics of this work process will tell us more about the structure and function of the organization than the psychological nature of the organization's members, their wants, motives, and drives.

Accordingly, on studying forty-three industrial organizations in the United States, Harvey (1968) learned that as technical specialty increases, certain organizational characteristics expand. These include the number of specialized subunits and levels of authority, ratio of managers and supervisors to personnel, and extent of programs directing organizational activi-

Table 7.2 TECHNOLOGY IN AN AUTOMOBILE PLANT

Processing stages	Technology		
	Materials	**Operations**	**Knowledge**
Input	Glass Metal Rubber Plastic	Purchasing glass, metal, rubber, plastic	Purchasing experts
Transformation	Auto design Assembly Painting	Work scheduling Schedule coordination Personnel management	Auto designers Plant managers Personnel officers
Output	Meeting and maintaining demand	Sales Advertising Marketing	Sales, advertising marketing experts

ties. After reviewing the research in this area, Hall (1977: 246) concluded that technology sets limits on the amount and kind of circumstances and conditions introduced into organizations. Technology limits what leaders can do.

An Organization's Environment

While it is possible that the environment is as important a factor in the life of small groups as it is in that of large-scale organizations, far more attention has been devoted to environment in the study of large organizations than in the study of small groups. An organization's *environment* is the set of virtually all influences impinging on it from outside its boundaries. Every institution in society can potentially affect the functioning of a given organization; the institutions having the greatest influence are education, religion, politics, family, leisure, business and the economy, government and law, and science and technology. In addition, the physical environment figures heavily in the fortunes of some organizations (e.g., the weather for airline companies). All organizations have a public (citizens, customers, clients).

We can point to many examples of environmental influences. The discovery of synthetic fibers (nylon, Dacron) has meant a great deal to the chemistry industry and the individual companies within the industry. The transistor has revolutionized the electronics industry. Changing attitudes toward increased leisure have brought changes in business practices and corporate policies. To comply with government regulations, automobile manufacturers have installed safety devices on cars and trucks. In recent years the public has become more hostile toward large-scale organizations. The growing importance of family life is significant.

Consider the effect of rumor on business organizations, for example:

> In the fall of 1978, for instance, a story circulated throughout the American South that

For businesses, their organizational environment includes shoplifting.

McDonald's was mixing earthworms into its hamburger meat as a protein additive. Over a subsequent nine-week period, sales at McDonald's 50 Atlanta-area outlets dropped by as much as 30 percent, and didn't rebound until the company held a press conference, displaying a letter from the U.S. Department of Agriculture certifying that the company's regularly inspected meat met its standards and that it is 100-percent pure beef.

Exactly how damaging that incident was to McDonald's 1978 profits, the company won't say. However, even if a dollar estimate was available, the figure wouldn't reflect the total price it paid. As George Cohon, president of McDonald's Restaurants of Canada, Ltd. says, any company's time spent fighting hearsay is time diverted from developing new products and creating new jobs.

In tight economic times, losing the faith of customers is a frightening prospect. "Today, people who are involved in the consumer-products industry recognize that anything that happens out there that further reduces the consumer's confidence in you is extremely damaging to business," says David Gee, president of Toronto's C & C Yachts Ltd. And he knows what he's talking about. Last summer, his company, which is North America's largest yacht builder and exporter with 1982 sales of $34.5 million, was the victim of an unverified report that it was on the verge of bankruptcy. Though Gee maintains that a newspaper article on C&C Yachts' healthy financial standing killed the story before it affected sales, he admits that he was very concerned about the effect it could have had in the yachting community. "I tend not to take a cavalier attitude about rumors," says Gee. "They may start out to be harmless, but they can end quite the opposite."

Trécie Fennell, assistant manager of corporate communications for General Foods' head office in White Plains, N.Y., has been through the rumor mill, too. She knows that they "can devastate both a company's reputation and its product sales." In 1979, Fennell worked virtually "full-time" tracking down and defusing stories that Pop Rocks, the company's then-new and extremely popular, carbonated candy, exploded in kids' stomachs. Until that point, Pop Rocks had been selling so well in test markets that a retailer's two-month supply "would be bought up in a week," she says. But late in 1978, sales of the candy in the northeastern United States suddenly dropped off so sharply that General Foods will only describe its losses as "substantial." To combat the rumor, the company spent a reported $500,000 for full-page ads in 45 major newspapers to reassure parents that Pop Rocks were perfectly safe. Sales rebounded almost instantly.

General Foods' use of the media was not without precedent. In 1977, New York-based Life Savers Inc., manufacturer of Bubble Yum bubble gum, invested $100,000 in a series of full-page newspaper ads. Headlined "Someone Is Telling Your Kids Very Bad Lies About A Very Good Gum," the ads ran in 30 New York City-area papers to rebut a local rumor that Bubble Yum contained spiders' eggs. Company figures prior to this, on Bubble Yum's performance in northeastern U.S. test markets, showed it had outstripped the leading favorite, Bazooka, in its first six months on the shelf. While Life Savers will not discuss how deeply the spiders' eggs story cut into corporate profits, a spokesman for the company says, "It was worth $100,000 to prevent the risk of further deterioration in sales." Today, he adds, Bubble Yum is the number-one seller in the field. (Matthews, 1983: 27)

A main conduit of environmental influence on an organization is its members. Those who belong to organizations are also members of families, churches, political parties, and voluntary associations. They bring perspectives, habits, and needs from these groups that, on balance, both help and hinder the organization in reaching its goals. For example, the employees of a corporation, which is a large-scale organization, desire salaries which will enable them to support a family. Perrow (1970: 112) observed that "the environment is always both a threat and a resource."

Robert Perry (1971: 49–52) provides an example from interviews conducted in Galt, Ontario (now Cambridge), where 60 percent of the industry is American-owned. Certain environmental advantages accrue to the parent companies in the United States from branch plants such as those in Galt. For instance, with their geographic separation, the parent companies escape the brunt of unfavorable local opinion. Parent companies have been known to force their subsidiaries in Galt to buy materials from American suppliers, in either ignorance of or indifference to the fact that Canadian firms could fill their needs as efficiently or even more so.

THEORIES AND MODELS

James Thompson (1967: 4–7) classifies the plethora of theoretical approaches and models pertaining to large-scale organizations in two categories: *closed systems* and *open systems.* The closed system provides for an insider's view of organizations. Some of these theories rest on rational social action, or the pursuit of goals through the use of means such as technology, communications, and improved organizational effectiveness. Other theories rest on nonrational social interaction such as sentiments, morale, or values. The open system concentrates on the organization's environment and the environmental pressures to which it must respond. Three models exemplifying the rational closed system, the nonrational closed system, and the open system are explained here.

The Rational Closed System

Weber's (1946: 196–198) *bureaucratic model* is possibly the most celebrated of the rational closed-system models. He believed the ideal-type bureaucracy has the following characteristics:

1. There is the principle of fixed and official jurisdictional areas, which are generally ordered by rules, or by laws or administrative regulations.
   a. The regular activities required for the purpose of the bureaucratically governed structure are distributed in a fixed way as official duties.
   b. The authority to give the commands required for the discharge of these duties is distributed in a stable way and is strictly delimited by rules concerning the coercive means . . . at the disposal of officials.
   c. Methodical provision is made for the regular and continuous fulfillment of these duties and for the execution of the corresponding rights; only persons who have the . . . qualifications are employed.
2. The principles of office hierarchy and of levels of graded authority mean a firmly ordered system of supervision and subordination in which there is supervision of the lower offices by the higher offices.
3. The management . . . usually presupposes thorough and expert training.
4. When the office is fully developed, official activity demands the full working capacity of the official. . . . Formerly, official business was discharged as a secondary activity.
5. The management of the office follows general rules, which are more or less stable and more or less exhaustive, and which can be learned.

This ideal type is seldom, if ever, seen in actuality. Yet it is useful for showing how actual bureaucracies approximate it and how rational-legal authority is manifested in organizations.

The Nonrational Closed System

By concentrating on the personal interests of the participants in an organization, the *human relations approach* offsets, to some extent, the excessive rationalism of the bureaucratic model. The human relations approach started in the 1920s with the research of Elton Mayo, who rejected the rational model. He held that workers' sentiments have a considerable impact on morale and on levels of productivity. In other words, workers' sentiments affect organizational climate and goals. Keith Davis (1977: 6–7) lists six facets of the human relations approach as it has evolved to the present.[5]

1. Human relations concentrates on people.
2. These people carry out their activities in organizations, not outside them.
3. A key activity in the organization is to motivate its members.
4. These members should be motivated toward teamwork involving coordination of their work and cooperation with each other as they pursue common goals.
5. Attempts should be made to fulfill both employees' needs and the organization's goals.
6. Employees and the organization should seek results with minimum costs in relation to rewards.

The Open System

The open-system approach has given birth to a new generation of models, one of which is *contingency theory.* Lawrence and Lorsch (1967) coined this term in their study of industrial organizations. They learned that different firms encounter different problems with their environments. For instance, some organizations operate in an environment of much uncertainty and change.

Galbraith (1977: 35–39) describes what happens in these circumstances. Let us say that a plant, in response to community pressure for cleaner air, is required to reduce the pollutants that its smokestacks pour into the atmosphere. This task is technically complicated and uncertain, since the organization has no clear idea of how to reduce the pollution or what level of reduction will satisfy the community. Contingency theory predicts that, under conditions of task complexity and information uncertainty, the managers of the plant will continue to seek new information and hence to make and remake decisions as the task is being carried out.

[5]Davis now refers to this approach as "organizational behavior." The label "human relations" was used in earlier editions of his book. Both labels have been applied to the same set of six ideas.

But organizations have a limited capacity for processing information and dealing with uncertainty. Within these limitations they adopt different organizing modes (structures and processes) to come to grips with the problem. According to contingency theory, organizations can develop internal processes and structures that enable them to adapt well to their external environments.

THE RADICAL CRITIQUE

One of the aims of this chapter has been to note the similarities and differences in the study of small groups and the study of large-scale organizations. Because large-scale organizations are composed of numerous small groups, it has been possible to explore at the organizational level the same analytic problems that are explored at the small-group level. The examination of large collectivities, however, brings with it the opportunity to concentrate on fresh analytic problems. Two of these are the problem of systems and the problem of power and interest.

The large-scale organization is a much more complicated social system than the small group. Its culture, social structure, division of labor, and flow of communication and authority are far more involved than their counterparts in small groups. Still, an organization is a far more manageable system to study than a society, which helps explain why functionalists have been so interested in this area of sociology. But, as pointed out in Chapter 2, theories are perspectives; they provide us with one point of view while denying us other points of view.

One process that the functionalist analysis of organizations has blinded us to is conflict, the analytic problem of power and interest. In recent years, various theorists have begun to expand our understanding of organizations by engaging in a "radical structuralist critique" of the functionalist position. Burrell and Morgan (1979: Chapter 11) note that the critique is not in itself a theory. Nonetheless, it is possible to identify several common themes in the diverse theoretical and ideological traditions that comprise the radical critique of organizational analysis.

To gain a sense of what is being overlooked in mainstream organizational analysis, let us consider six of the themes identified by Burrell and Morgan. First, the radical critique points to the fact that organization theory revolves around problems defined as such by management. Certainly, the less powerful, subordinate majority who work in organizations have unique problems, too. Indeed, at least some of these problems are caused by management. Second, radical thinkers charge that mainstream theorists consciously or unconsciously contribute to humankind's degradation and alienation in the workplace. All theorists should become aware of how their theorizing contributes to degradation and, through their theories and research, stress practices that avoid it or eliminate it.

Third, mainstream organizational analyses are seen by the radical structuralists as neglecting class relations. How much of what goes on inside organizations and between organizations and the wider community can be traced to class differences? Those who run many of our largest organizations are upper-middle-class and upper-class people. At least some of the employees of these organizations and some of the members of the wider community have interests that are different from and at times opposed to the interests of the organizations' leaders. These employees and community members are in the middle and lower classes.

Fourth, the radical critics say that functionalists have ignored the role played by the state, and fifth, also have ignored the importance of other macro-level factors that bear on organizations. For example, journalists have long recognized the existence of intimate links between big business and government. Why have social scientists been so slow to study these links? Sixth, organizational analysis traditionally has been static; it has concentrated on equilibrium, consensus, and unity. But there are contradictory forces in society, some of which change organizations. Perhaps the concept of organizational environment will prove to be a useful theoretical tool for sharpening our understanding of how the outside world affects organizations and vice versa.

One important facet of the environment of any organization is the community in which it is located. Here organizational interests merge with the clash and interplay of a multitude of other interests—economic, political, religious, moral, and recreational. In the community people who are members of large organizations and small groups interact with one another in the course of conducting their daily affairs. It is to an examination of communities that we now turn.

OUTLINE AND SUMMARY

I. Introduction
   Much of human experience today is acquired in impersonal, bureaucratic, large-scale organizations.

II. Large and Small Groups
   Large-scale organizations and small groups are similar in formation, structure, process, and culture, but there are differences between the two.
   A. Secondary Groups
      A *secondary group* is a collectivity characterized by comparatively cold, impersonal relations among members who fill specialized roles.
   B. Types of Organizations
      One type of organization follows Parsons's AGIL classification.
   C. Weber's Organizations
      Weber classified organizations according to three kinds of authority: *Rational-legal* authority is legitimated by a system of formal rules. *Traditional* authority is the established right of people in certain positions to rule other members of the group. *Charismatic* authority is

granted on the basis of the leader's special and widely-respected gifts.

III. Formation of Organizations
Small groups and large-scale organizations form in much the same way. First, there must be a reason for organizing.
   A. Division of Labor
   A division of labor emerges as the organization is developed. Role conflict may occur.
   B. Alternatives to Organization
   Among the alternatives to organization are the primary group, the market, and the institution of work.

IV. Organizational Structure
Like small groups, large-scale organizations have a social structure, or stable pattern of interrelated statuses.
   A. Formal Structure
   All large-scale organizations are formal, inasmuch as they are legally chartered or, at the very least, have some sort of written or public recognition as groups.
   B. Bureaucracy
   A *bureaucracy* is a type of organization designed to accomplish large-scale administrative tasks by coordinating the work of many individuals.
   C. Informal Structure
   The *informal structure* includes the patterns of relationships and behavior that are neither codified nor obvious.
   D. Size
   Size is the number of members in the organization.

V. Organizational Processes
As in small groups, three processes in the large group have much to do with the interaction and social exchanges within the group: *leadership, power, oligarchy,* and *communication.*
   A. Leadership
   Supportive socioemotional leadership is more likely to produce favorable, goal-oriented attitudes and hence greater output than authoritarian task leadership.
   B. Power and Authority
   Weber's three types of authority are *rational-legal, traditional,* and *charismatic.* French and Raven's types of power are *reward power, coercive power, expert power, referent power,* and *legitimate power.* Power is distributed down and across organizational hierarchies.
   C. Oligarchy
   Oligarchic tendencies inhere in large-scale organizations; there is an "Iron Law of Oligarchy."
   D. Communication
   Communications travel through formal and informal channels.

VI. Organizational Culture
The cultures of small groups and large-scale organizations have much in common; both are made up of standard behavior patterns, norms, and rules. Both have dominant values, beliefs, and goals.
   A. Goals
   Goals are desired ends.
   B. Organizational Climate
   Organizational climate consists of the members' collective perceptions of the organization. Climate bears on goal attainment.
   C. Alienation
   In the view of Karl Marx, alienated people are individuals estranged from the products of their work.
   D. Technology
   Technology is the technique, or method, used by organizations to reach their goal.
   E. An Organization's Environment
   An organization's *environment* is the set of virtually all influences impinging on it from outside its boundaries.

VII. Theories and Models
Models pertaining to large-scale organizations are the *closed-system* and *open-system* models.
   A. The Rational Closed System
   The rational closed system is exemplified by Weber's ideal type of bureaucracy.
   B. The Nonrational Closed System

The nonrational closed system is exemplified by the human relations approach.

VIII. The Radical Critique
The functionalist analysis of organizations overlooks conflict. Theorists have expressed a "radical structuralist critique" of the functionalist position. Radical structuralists contend that mainstream organizational analyses have neglected class relations.

FOR FURTHER READING AND STUDY

Blau, P. M. and Meyer, M. M. 1971. *Bureaucracy in modern society,* 2nd ed. New York: Random House. This book offers a readable, succinct discussion of bureaucracy. It is based on Weber's ideal type of bureaucracy.

Blauner, R. 1964. *Alienation and freedom.* Chicago: University of Chicago Press. A well-known study of the alienating potential of work when it is characterized by little control, knowledge, and responsibility. In other words, worker alienation was found to vary with the technology of the workplace.

Boren, J. H. 1982. *Fuzzify! Borenwords and strategies for bureaucratic success.* McLean, VA: EPM Publications. A humorous account of the ridiculous side of organizational life and how to survive in it.

Perrow, C. 1979. *Complex organizations: A critical essay,* 2nd ed. Glenview, Ill.: Scott, Foresman. Written from the point of view that an organization is a powerful tool for those who run it and for certain groups outside the organization who are linked to it through other organizations.

Pfeffer, J. 1981. *Power in organizations.* Marshfield, Mass.: Pitman Publishing. This book presents and compares four models of organizational decision making. It also contains the author's own model of organizational change. The book contains an extensive synthesis of the relevant literature.

Presthus, R. 1978. *The organizational society,* rev. ed. New York: St. Martin's. Presthus defends the "hierarchical institutions," despite their weaknesses. He holds that we should strive to improve the existing structures and eliminate obvious inequities.

Scott, W. R. 1981. *Organizations.* Englewood Cliffs, N.J.: Prentice-Hall. A textbook surveying the field of organizational studies. Scott is one of the leading contributors of theory and research to this branch of sociology.

Woodward, J. 1981. *Industrial organization,* 2nd ed. Oxford: Oxford University Press. A pioneering study of several manufacturing firms. Woodward found technology to be the chief determinant of the structure of these companies.

KEY WORDS

bureaucracy A hierarchical authority structure designed to accomplish large-scale administrative tasks by systematically coordinating the work of many individuals.

division of labor The specialization of individuals' tasks in a group; the development and integration of the group's specialized roles into an effectively functioning unit.

large-scale organization A massive social group formed for a specific purpose.

role conflict Any situation in which a role player within a group perceives that he or she is confronted with incompatible expectations.

secondary group An organization of people who have little intimate contact but who work together for a specific purpose.

size The number of members in an organization.

technology The technique, or method, used by organizations to reach their goals.

chapter 8

Communities

CHAPTER OUTLINE

INTRODUCTION

Communities have a place in Canada; they are the focal point of much interaction and social exchange within society. The community is one of sociology's oldest and most enduring objects of study and research, dating to Durkheim and Weber, who defined and shaped the concept of community scientifically. But, as is true of other topics taken up in this book, an exact definition of community as a working scientific concept has been gradually blunted by casual lay usage and emotional overtones. Marcia Effrat (1974: 2) explains the problem:

> The term "community" is frequently invoked in tones of profundity by ideologues (social scientists as well as "lay persons") from the far left to the far right. Like motherhood and apple pie, it is considered synonymous with virtue and desirability.

For many people the term "community" suggests belongingness, togetherness, camaraderie, and similar states of idyllic social relations. From a sociological standpoint, a *community* is a social group with a common territorial base. Those in the group share interests and have a sense of belonging to the group.

For the most part, this chapter is concerned with the general notion of community and with differentiating the rural community and the urban community. Sections follow on community development and shifting community boundaries. The environment of cities and the nature of urban life are then considered. The chapter closes with references to selected issues in community studies. Before turning to this sequence of topics, however, a brief look at the traditions of community research is in order.

SOCIOLOGY OF THE COMMUNITY

The interests of sociologists in the community fall into four traditions (Effrat, 1974: 4–21). These are the traditions of the *complete community,* the community of *limited liability,* the community as *society,* and the *personal community.* In the *complete community* tradition, collectivities ranging in size from villages to metropolises are studied *holistically.* That is, the sociologist observes the functional relations between the parts of the community and the community as a whole. This tradition is similar, in its philosophical roots, to the holistic interaction-as-society approach covered in Chapter 4. *Holism* is the theory that entities in nature cannot be broken down to their component parts and cannot be analyzed as mere sums of the parts. The entity can be analyzed only as a whole with its own distinctive properties.

The tradition of the community of *limited liability* concentrates on neighborhoods and similar areas of larger communities; it considers the sentiments and motivations which enter into neighboring. Research in this tradition recognizes the tendency for human beings to form communities within communities. It seems that such needs as familiarity, intimacy, and friendship go unfulfilled when populations reach a certain size and density. Hence, there is a development of smaller communal groups within the larger unit.

The tradition of the community as *society* centers on the various groups for whom prestige or moral worth or both are in some way important (e.g., ethnic minorities, deviants, members of a profession, participants in a life-style). The prominence of the dimension of prestige has led some sociologists to analyze these communities as status communities (e.g., Stub, 1972). Status groups often provide the familiarity, intimacy, and friendships found in communities of limited liability, but they do so independently of a geographic location.

In the *personal* community tradition, attention is directed to communes and to certain organizations which have a sense of community (e.g., fraternal orders, service clubs, amateur

---

SOCIOLOGY OR COMMON SENSE

What do you think?

Which of the following statements do you agree with? Which statements do you disagree with? Make a note of your answers. Check your answers when you have completed your study of this chapter. Are your answers to the statements the same as those a sociologist would give?

1. Communities have a geographic basis.
2. A community is apart from society.
3. Cities are anonymous, impersonal places where relationships are formally prescribed.
4. The mass media, which are often national in scope, are destroying communities (both rural and urban) as distinct groups.
5. A subculture is isolated from the society as a whole.

---

and hobbyist groups). A geographic location is more apparent in the personal community than in the community as society. The basis of a personal community is one of shared personal interests in which prestige or moral worth, if an issue at all, is of minor importance.

This chapter is chiefly concerned with the complete community, although we will review certain aspects of the community of limited liability in a consideration of cities. The communal quality of North America's many status groups is touched on at various points in this book. In this chapter, the topic is covered in the section on subcultures. The personal community in organizations and small groups has already been examined in the sections on group morale and organizational climate.

WHAT IS A COMMUNITY?

The accumulation of ideas and data about communities has been hampered by the difficulty sociologists have had in agreeing on a definition.

George Hillery (1955: 119) brought this difficulty to light in his review of ninety-four definitions of the term "community." He pointed out in his review that "beyond the concept that people are involved in community, there is no complete agreement as to the nature of community." Still, some definitions are more commonly accepted than others. Sjoberg (1964: 114) came up with a generally accepted definition: "A *community* is a collectivity of actors sharing a limited territorial area as the base for carrying out the greatest share of their daily activities."[1]

Community as a Group

Sjoberg's definition is consistent with the view that communities are a type of group (Hiller, 1941)—a group that is larger than any we have dealt with so far in this book. As groups, communities meet Bales's five distinguishing criteria (the criteria listed in Chapter 6). (1) There is interaction among members of a community, although in large communities each member seldom, if ever, communicates with all the other members. (2) The members of a community share one or more goals, which focus group action (e.g., a new sports arena, an improvement in airline services, a reduction in the crime rate). (3) The members develop, and most of them adhere to, a set of norms, which guide goal-directed behavior and interpersonal relations (e.g., traffic regulations, juvenile curfews).

(4) In time, should the group remain a community, a stable set of roles eventually emerges; among the roles are those of the mayor, city manager, police officers, fire fighters, and parks and recreation functionaries. (5) Over time, a pattern of interpersonal attractions also emerges, reflecting the likes and dislikes of members of the community. Examples are hostilities between ethnic groups or neighbors, patterns of tolerance such as that expressed in San Francisco toward gays, and regard for local entertainers and sports personalities.

Like small groups and large-scale organizations, communities have social structures, although they are likely to be more complex than the social structures of small groups and large-scale organizations. This complexity is manifested as the community's division of labor, which develops along the lines of local social institutions (e.g., family, education, religion, government, health care, law enforcement). Little more is said here about these institutions, since they are the subject of Part Four. Group pro-

A typical mountain rural community in Western Canada.

[1]Italics added.

cesses are also evident at the community level. The distribution of power and the enactment of leadership roles in the community help produce a system of stratification (see Chapter 19). Communities have cultures, too, as explained in the next chapter.

Rural Communities

Sanders and Lewis (1976: 35) identify rural communities by the following criteria. (1) They are relatively small in size. (2) They are nonmetropolitan; that is, they lie outside the compass of a metropolitan area. (3) They are patently rural in character. In other words, they "exist in the midst of an agricultural area, an area characterized as a 'primary economy,' or one marked by other obvious nonurban cultural, social, and ecological characteristics" (Sanders and Lewis, 1976: 35).

By these criteria, many different groups can be looked on as rural communities. Besides farming communities or agricultural service centers, there are many primary economy towns (and cities) in Canada that are primarily concerned with extracting or harvesting natural resources such as ore, wood, fish, oil, and natural gas. Some rural communities are one-industry towns, defined by Lucas (1971: 16) as places with a single industry run by one firm employing at least 75 percent of the population.[2] The workers in the towns that Lucas studied were employed by mines, mills, and railways. Some tourist resorts and miscellaneous service centers also meet the Sanders and Lewis criteria.

We have seen that size is one dimension of a group. Nevertheless, size, although still significant, is probably the least important of the three Sanders and Lewis criteria and is certainly not one treated with any precision by sociological students of the community. Since their interests lie in such matters as life-style, social structure, and culture, they gain little to go on from precise census definitions of "rural" and "urban." Furthermore, the census definitions are precise because they refer to areas rather than true communities (an area is not necessarily a community). In the United States areas of population less than 2500 are classified as rural, while in Canada those of population under 1000 are classified as rural. But, sociologically speaking, not all rural and urban areas are communities. Yet, by these definitions, we know that at the beginning of the 1980s between 75.7 and 76.9 percent of the people in Canada and in the United States, respectively, lived in places of population 1000 or more.

The difference between rural and urban communities, as opposed to rural and urban areas, is clarified by Sanders' fourfold typology (1975: 62–69). The *isolated, relatively self-sufficient rural community* is small. Such communities are becoming rare in Canada. They still exist, however, among the Amish, the Hutterites, the Inuit, and the northern Indians.[3] Such a community meets most, if not all, of its needs. Its members grow their food, make their clothing, and build their shelters from materials at hand. They provide an education for their children, express a faith in their own religion, and exercise social control. They may even practice a practical medicine.[4] Some communities in the roadless areas of Newfoundland and northwestern Ontario and off the beaten path of the Ozarks and the Appalachians in the United States are of this type.

Town-country communities are more common than isolated rural communities. The town itself may be a small city with many services and shops patronized by people from its rural hinterland. Sanders (1975: 63) believes the people living in a rural hinterland (e.g., farmers, acreage residents) are most accurately seen as an

[2]Some single-industry communities are small cities.

[3]*Inuit* is the North American Eskimos' name for themselves, meaning "the people." It distinguishes them from outsiders and from the Eskimos of Asia and the Aleutian Islands. The Inuit's dislike for the label "Eskimo" is explained in Chapter 20.

[4]Health specialists and the police may occasionally administer outside assistance, thus diluting the pure self-sufficiency of these groups.

exurban neighborhood, a part of the town-country community.

Urban Communities

An *urban community* is still more inclusive than a rural community. At its center lies a medium-sized or large-sized city, with which those in nearby town-country communities identify. In other words, people outside the central city identify with two locales. They may work in the city and live nearby in the country or a small town, a suburb. Or they may work outside the city. Either way, they use the professional, commercial, and recreational services of the urban center. The geographic limits of the urban community fall at the point at which it is no longer convenient to travel, by any means, to the central city to work or obtain services.

But in the giant urban communities of today, where millions of people are jammed into a small area, the sense of community is weakened. The center is no longer able to integrate its many components, a circumstance which leads to increased congestion, conflict, and expansion (Mumford, 1968: 448). Under these conditions, metropolitan communities begin to form. *Metropolitan communities* are massive urban communities composed of a large central city and numerous surrounding satellite town-country communities. Sanders sees these as recent developments, in which people become loyal to an urbanized area and are willing to join with others there to reach common goals. Residents identify in an abstract fashion with the central city, but they see their satellite town-country communities as more desirable than the city and as the locale for their daily round.

The definitions of rural community and urban community in this section are general and lengthy. Nearly all adult Canadians know when they are in a city or in a rural town. Yet the critical differences between these two types of community are difficult to understand and put into a few sentences. Mumford (1968: 447–448) distinguishes cities from rural communities and also explains why defining these two types is a questionable undertaking quietly shunned by nearly all sociologists:

> An adequate description of the city must not deal merely with structure, process, stage, and purpose, but also with certain identifying characteristics reflected in layout and architectural forms in space and a tissue of associations, corporate enterprises, and institutions that occupy this collective structure and have interacted with it in the course of time. The size and complexity of the city bears a direct relation to that of the culture it assembles and passes on. Hence the inadequacy of attempts to define the city by purely quantitative measures—area, density of occupation, range of communication —while passing over at least equally significant qualitative indications.

Common Elements

The foregoing discussion of different types of communities provides a basis for considering the common elements in the sociological definitions of the community. Hillery (1955: 118) found three elements common to most of the definitions: *geographic area, social interaction,* and *shared ties.* Among sociologists the first is the most controversial.

Geographic Area Many sociologists, including Sjoberg, whose definition was stated earlier, believe that all complete communities have some sort of geographic or territorial basis (see Effrat's conceptualization of the complete community earlier in this chapter). As Poplin (1979: 9) notes, the relationship between the members of a territory and the members of a community is a two-way street. "Territorial factors help to account for the location, universality, and persistence of communities and . . . community members constantly modify the territorial milieu in which they live."

There are many reasons for the location of communities in the places in which they are found. On the urban side, three theories have

What process of community origin does this picture suggest?

been advanced to account for location: *break-of-bulk, central place,* and *industrial location.* Each brings into play a different form of economic activity.

Cooley (1894) was the first sociologist to propose that cities grow at *breaks in transportation.* Among such breaks, as Cooley explained, are a good harbor, a navigable waterway, or the intersection of two rail lines. At these points facilities and services spring up in connection with transshipment of goods, a supportive enterprise. Among the flourishing businesses are banks, warehouses, accounting firms, insurance companies, customs brokers, and rail lines. Goods are exchanged and shipped in cities such as Chicago, Vancouver, Thunder Bay, Quebec City, New York, and New Orleans.

Central place is exemplified by these elevators, which store grain from nearby farms for later shipment.

Another sociologist, Walter Christaller (1933), systematically developed the *central place theory.* He and others before and after him (including Cooley) recognized that some cities begin as collection points for the shipping of local produce, both agricultural and manufactured (e.g., the small Great Plains cities that store grain). Because they are collection points, these cities become *central places.* Such communities also function as service centers for the same hinterland for which they collect and ship goods.

Among the factors helping to account for the location of *industrial cities* are a helpful labor force, the availability of raw materials, the proximity of profitable markets, minimal costs (e.g., taxes, shipping), and the accessibility of related governmental and industrial support services. It is no accident that the oil refinery cities of Houston and Edmonton are located near major petroleum reserves or that Pittsburgh is close to a supply of coal for operating its steel mills.

Smith and Weller (1977: 103) list other factors behind the emergence, if not the actual location, of communities. Sometimes religious reasons influence the decision to establish a community, as in the case of San Francisco. Some sites originally had strategic police or military significance, as did Calgary, Winnipeg, and Fort Worth. Or there may have been political reasons, as evidenced in the selection of the sites for Ottawa and Washington, D.C. as national capitals. Some communities also developed around leisure attractions (e.g., Atlantic City, Las Vegas, and Aspen, Colorado).

Social Interaction Discussions of social interaction in the city seldom continue for long without a reference to Louis Wirth's (1938) article entitled "Urbanism as a way of life." In this famous essay, Wirth sketches many of the unique qualities of city living and, by contrast, the unique qualities of rural living. According to Dewey (1960: 64–65), there is evidence supporting Wirth's hypothesis that substantial increases in size and density of a community's

How Urban Pedestrians Monitor Their Environment

Any study of how people relate to each other on the sidewalk requires that some consideration be given to their performance of the taken-for-granted task of "monitoring" the environment. Pedestrians monitor the environment not only for the purpose of avoiding culturally proscribed intrusions but also to evaluate the potential behavior of others. As noted earlier, pedestrians normally adhere to certain position patterns; people who deviate from these patterns in various ways may be reported, avoided, or held suspect. For example, a person who walks directly behind another pedestrian at a close distance for more than a short period when the head-over-the-shoulder pattern could be sustained or a person who walks in parallel (side-by-side) at a close distance for more than a short period without making an effort to move out of this pattern is just as suspect as the person who enters an empty bus, subway car, or luncheonette and sits down beside you. Because he could have done otherwise, and because people normally do, he is suspect.

In addition to scanning frontward and to the sides, pedestrians engage in several other monitoring behaviors. First, although window-shopping, "appreciation," and curiosity viewing are common pedestrian behaviors, individuals regularly* turn their heads at least one quarter-turn off the perpendicular (straight ahead). This movement allows them to glance quickly and inconspicuously out of the corner of their eyes and monitor whatever is behind them without appearing to be concerned, irritated, interested, or the like. Second, pedestrians scan the faces of pedestrians coming toward them. If the oncoming pedestrians appear to be fixating in the same direction and, more importantly, are expressing surprise, fear, or general excitement, this is taken to be a cue to make a full head-turn, stop for a full check-out, or both. In this sense, pedestrians use other pedestrians as a "rear-view mirror" much as animals in herds are warned of danger by the movements of other herd members. In spite of the cultural proscriptions against ambush, attack from behind, and so forth, apparently we have developed the habit of performing several operations that enable us to "watch our back" while moving through open spaces.

These operations are more difficult to perform at night on dark streets with few other pedestrians nearby. This may explain in part why surprise attacks are historically more common at night despite increased vigilance.

*How regularly is an interesting empirical question.

SOURCE: Michael Wolf. Notes on the behavior of pedestrians. In *People in places: The sociology of the familiar,* eds. Arnold Birenbaum and Edward Sagarin, pp. 35–48. New York: Praeger, 1973.

population result in the accentuation of five qualities: (1) anonymity; (2) division of labor; (3) heterogeneity, induced and sustained by (1) and (2); (4) impersonal and formally prescribed relationships; and (5) symbols of status which are independent of personal acquaintance. We shall see later that, at the neighborhood level of city life, 1 and 4 do not hold.

Cities are characterized by impersonal and formal relationships.

Interaction in urban communities, compared with rural communities, is characterized by greater anonymity and a more complex division of labor. There are more kinds of people in the city than in the country. In the city, people differ greatly in occupation, leisure interests, ethnic background, and deviant ways. City people have a higher regard for recognized status symbols (e.g., diamonds, Cadillacs, mink coats, swimming pools) than country people.

Shared Ties Just as we differentiated small groups and large-scale organizations by their primariness and secondariness, respectively, we can also differentiate rural communities and urban communities. Lucas (1971: 170) says of communities which have a single industry that their citizens

> are used to living within a web of primary relationships, where walking down the street is an experience of personally greeting individuals they meet—knowing the person, his family, parents, loves, failures, and peculiarities. Each purchase or transaction is a relationship with a neighbor. To walk in the street of any urban centre with no one stopping to say "hello" or ever thinking or caring for the other is a bewildering experience for one who passes his life in a small community.

Contrast this primariness with the secondariness of the city described by Lyn Lofland (1973: 3):

> The city, because of its size, is the locus of a peculiar social situation: the people to be found within its boundaries at any given moment know nothing personally about the vast *majority* of others with whom they share their space. . . . The city then, among all the other things that it may be, is also a world of *strangers.*[5]

One way of measuring the extent of shared ties among rural and urban people is to find out how many of them belong to voluntary associations. According to one study (Curtis, 1971), the memberships are nearly identical. Excluding the membership in labor unions, roughly 50 percent of all Canadians and Americans join voluntary associations.

But the evidence is contradictory. Smith and Baldwin (1974: 281) concluded, after reviewing the literature, that a somewhat larger proportion of people who live in communities of population 10,000 or less join voluntary associations than do people in larger communities; persons who live in small towns, it seems, are more likely to participate in voluntary organizations than persons who live in cities. In both the United States and Canada, the inclination to join voluntary associations is directly related to socioeconomic status and not, as some have predicted for Canada, to linguistic, ethnic, religious, or regional differences (Frizell and Zureik, 1974: 273).

Tönnies's Ideal Types

Ferdinand Tönnies's two ideal types of community —*Gemeinschaft* and *Gesellschaft*— offer a perspective on the issue of rural-urban differences and the extent of shared ties. The Gemeinschaft community is a rural community characterized by close interpersonal relationships

[5]Italics added.

among kin and friends. Tradition is important in such places, as are consensus, informality, cooperation, family background, and the sharing of group goals.

In the Gesellschaft community, interpersonal relationships are more formal, specialized, and impersonal than in the Gemeinschaft setting. The Gesellschaft relationships tend to develop for particular purposes, as means to ends, rather than as ends in themselves, which is typical of social ties in Gemeinschaft communities. Gesellschaft relationships are likely to be segmented or specific; that is, they are purposeful and objective. Moreover, competition and even conflict are pervasive, with little cooperation between individuals.

Clearly, the Gemeinschaft-Gesellschaft typology has much in common with the primary-secondary dichotomy and with the five concrete qualities identified by Wirth and Dewey to distinguish urban from rural. It should be remembered that all three are ideal types. The actual dichotomy of rural and urban is blurred by degrees of differences and overlapping traits. For example, Fischer (1984: 126) notes that combined with the sense of anonymity and impersonality in city life is a sense of strong attachment to key intimate groups (e.g., the family).

URBAN ECOLOGY

Urban ecology is the study of the geographic and temporal distribution of individuals, groups, and services in a city. The early urban sociologists began their work in the 1920s. They were known as the "Chicago school" because they conducted research at the University of Chicago and many of their ideas were based on observations made in the city of Chicago. They discovered that, as soon as a community begins to grow, various functions within the community begin to compete for space. This competitive process quickly begets other processes, all of which help to shape the town in its early years. Among the processes and influences are concentration and centralization. Dispersion, segregation, invasion, and succession also enter the picture (McKenzie, 1968: 23–31).

Ecological Processes

Concentration is the gathering of people in densely populated areas. Once this occurs, certain important enterprises (notably banks, food suppliers, department stores, medical services, law offices) *centralize,* or collect, in the central business district (CBD), where they are more or less equally accessible to all residents. Somewhat later *dispersion* begins to occur, as people, facilities, and functions are lured from the center by attractions on the periphery (e.g., less congestion, lower taxes).

Dispersion is also a response to the clash of incompatible functions, for example, residences versus factories or railway switchyards versus hospitals. These conflicts are eventually resolved by the emergence of *segregated* areas of

Concentration is a fact of life in the core of a large city.

more or less homogeneous functions. Thus, the factories gravitate (or are confined) to certain parts of the city, leaving other parts to the residences.

But, in a way, communities are living, dynamic entities. A segregated area may be *invaded* by functions and facilities from adjacent areas. Expansion of the downtown core—the spread of "downtown" into adjacent neighborhoods—is a common form of invasion. Encroachment of entertainment strips and outlying business districts on residential areas is another form. Where invasion eventuates in displacement, *succession* is said to have occurred. There is now a new population or type of land use, or both.

Patterns of Growth

The classical urban ecologists were interested in how these six ecological processes produced certain spatial patterns of urban growth. While recognizing that law and edict and, today, urban planning can arbitrarily alter land-use patterns, the founders of the classical school chose to concentrate on the natural processes of the market. The patterns, they argued, form from "similar demands on the environment and similar ability to pay for them" (Bernard, 1973, 36). Three sociological theories, each calling for a certain pattern of growth, have received a great deal of thought and attention. The three theories are the *concentric zone theory,* the *sector theory,* and the *multiple nuclei theory* (see Figure 8.1).

Concentric Zone Theory Ernest Burgess (1925) first proposed the *concentric zone theory.* He pictured growth in American cities as an accretion of increasingly larger rings, each of which is the center of different functions. Natural barriers, such as hills, rivers, and lakes, distort the ideal pattern, but, according to the predictions, urban communities approximate the concentric zone pattern in significant degree. Burgess regarded the city of Chicago as the classic example.

According to the theory, the modern city consists of several concentric zones. The zones, one by one, spread out from the central city, and there is a difference in the land use in the different zones. The *central business district,* with its stores and offices, is the first zone. The second zone is the *zone of transition.* Here business and industry are encroaching on residential neighborhoods, causing housing in these neighborhoods to deteriorate. A third zone is a *zone for working people.* A fourth zone is a *residential zone* for middle-income people. Finally, beyond the city limits, lies the *commuters' zone.* The commuters' zone consists of small towns, or suburbs. People travel from the suburbs to the city to work and hold jobs. They commute.

Sector Theory Homer Hoyt (1939) studied 142 cities in the United States prior to constructing his *sector theory.* According to Hoyt and his data, a city grows from its center in sectors, not in concentric zones. The sectors are formed along principal transportation routes (rail, water, road). There are, more or less, homogeneous functions in the sectors; there are different functions for different land uses. Following the course of a transportation route, as they do, the sectors tend to be wedge-shaped.

High-income residential neighborhoods develop initially near the central business district. In time, as the area ages, these areas move farther out in the sector. Keeping its character, the area in which the neighborhood originated is not wholly abandoned. Upper-class neighborhoods show up on the outer edge of high-rent sectors. Factories and other businesses also settle into wedge-shaped sectors, not into concentric zones. The arrangement of sectors varies from one city to another.

Multiple Nuclei Theory C. D. Harris and Edward Ullman (1945) viewed urban growth from still another angle. As they saw it, a city is a composite of centers and subcenters called *nuclei.* There are many kinds of nuclei. Among the different kinds are residential nuclei, financial nuclei, wholesale nuclei, manufacturing nuclei,

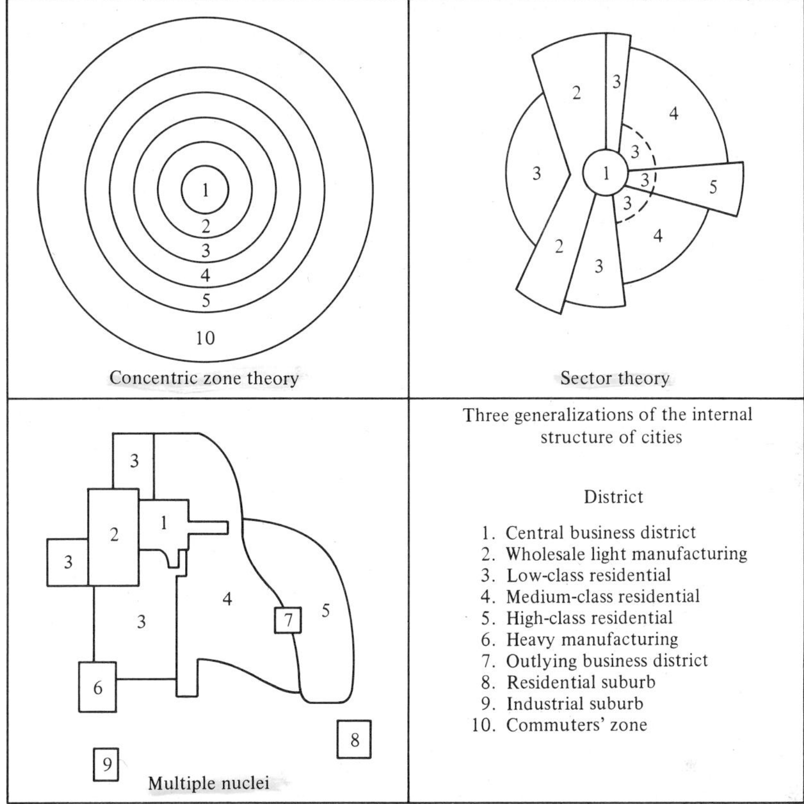

Figure 8.1 Three Theories of the Internal Structure of Cities. (*Source:* C. D. Harris and E. L. Ullman, 1945. The nature of cities. *Annals of the American Academy of Political and Social Science* 242: 13.)

recreational nuclei, and business nuclei (in the core and also in outlying areas). Each city develops a unique constellation of nuclei. The circumstances of a city's location and history make a difference.

How well do these theories fit the facts in North America? Schnore and Jones (1969) and Blumenfeld (1949) found that the older and larger industrial cities in the United States, especially Chicago and others in the Midwest and Northeast, approximate the concentric zone pattern rather well. Research by Guest (1969) and Balakrishnan and Jarvis (1979), however, indicates that Canadian cities, as they become older, tend to diverge from this pattern to the extent that residential socioeconomic status is involved. According to their findings, the pattern of Canadian cities tends to be sectorial, with some of the wealthiest residential districts occupying concentric zone 2 next to the CBD.

COMMUNITY DEVELOPMENT

Community development, or community action, as it is sometimes called, is a planned change in a local setting. Planned local change is undertaken when a sufficient number of people in the group perceive a collective problem demanding an active response. Sanders (1975: 458) describes community development as progressing by stages from an initially undesirable condition of the community's social and physical environment to a changed and desired condition. He points out that the amount of citizen decision making in community development varies. Decisions may be made by one or two individuals, by an elite, or by the entire population. Likewise, participation in the development project may involve only a few individuals, many individuals, or everyone in the community. The expertise needed to complete the development may come wholly or only partly from the community.

What are communities likely to strive for when they undertake community development? In general, communities seek to develop anything—an improvement or an addition—which the members of the community have singled out as important. An example can be seen in St. Pascal, a small industrialized town in eastern Quebec (Gold, 1975: 167–168):

> The Centre Social is an organization of prominent young businessmen whose initial mission was to provide leisure facilities and activities for St. Pascal. Among their early achievements were a skating cabin and a major winter carnival and regular dances and children's recreation. In 1968, the Centre redefined its objectives to include the expansion of leisure opportunities in the community. They wanted to retain its emigrating youth and satisfy the local desire to have something more than factories in their town. To this end, they hired an outsider to act as a full-time recreation director. They sought funding for a tennis court, golf clinic, and lighted baseball field and for gym equipment. Later they organized a local sports league and equipped the town's baseball and hockey teams for competition with neighboring communities.

Sometimes the members of a community are too disorganized or demoralized to work collectively for their own interests. Or they may be ignorant of the ways to bring about a desired change. Furthermore, there are often individuals or groups in the community, and possibly outside the community, who like things the way they are, even if some members find the existing conditions harmful.

The Alinsky Approach

Saul Alinsky's (1971) "radical" approach to community development came into play some years ago. A team of developers, usually Alinsky and associates, came to the community, identified local leaders, helped them organize their fellows, and taught them how to fight for desired changes against those who control their fate. One of Alinsky's latest campaigns was the Citizens Action Program (CAP), which began in 1969 in Chicago (reported in Lancourt, 1979: 26–29):

> CAP began as a campaign against air pollution in Chicago, after a local newspaper antipollution editorial generated hundreds of letters from citizens supporting the editor's position. Considerable public outrage had developed earlier on this issue when a weather inversion smothered the city in dense pollution for a week. The editor gave the letters to Alinsky who arranged for the formation of a group of concerned citizens. They, in turn, went to a public hearing on a rate increase being proposed by Commonwealth Edison, an electric utility, and one of the major polluters. They were denied admission. This rejection led to the formation of CAP, which is composed of white and blue-collar workers, environmentalists, scientists, and a handful of young radicals. Its first published goals were to persuade Commonwealth to use low sulphur fuel, to persuade the state regulatory commission to reduce the requested rate increase, and to encourage the city council to pass an antipollution ordinance.
>
> Alinsky workers helped CAP organize neighborhood chapters throughout the city, each with a representative steering committee. Then, armed with Commonwealth stock proxies gathered from local investors, hundreds of members descended on the company's next shareholders' meeting. Meanwhile, several local chapters were conferring with their aldermen and trying to arrange an audience with Mayor Daley. One was finally scheduled, but he refused to see anybody when one thousand people turned up at his office. Nevertheless, three months after the publication of CAP's

goals Commonwealth had switched to low sulphur fuel. The next month saw friendly aldermen help pass a strict antipollution ordinance. And three months later the state commission reduced the company's requested rate increase.

By the mid-1970s CAP had become a strong local citizens' organization with an enviable success record for advocating changes in the public interest.[6]

Urban Planning

Urban planning is a special type of community development. Today the job or vocation of urban planning is a vigorous profession, with roots extending at least as far back as ancient Rome. The goals of urban planning have been summarized by Gold (1976: 846):

> Economic: efficiency of land use and circulation patterns; preservation or enhancement of the economic base. Social: adequate provision for human needs; work, home, play; maximum choice of living environment; congenial social contacts, educational and cultural opportunities within easy reach. Physical and sound land use planning (types, quantities, and relationships); proper distribution and density of population (present and projected); efficient circulation and services; preservation of scenic and historic areas and other amenities.

The scope of urban planning is broad. In many instances, plans call for a change in zoning, a renewal of blighted areas, and New Town planning. Planning may center on the social and economic revitalization of CBDs or the location of streets and highways. Planners give thought to the location of institutions such as schools and hospitals, police jurisdictions, and homes for the aging.

Since the 1940s (Michelson, 1977: 576–579), North American cities have been modified, sometimes dramatically, by the schemes of professional planners. Much of what has been accomplished is *replanning,* or *urban renewal.* Blighted neighborhoods are restored. An objective has been to establish stable communities within the larger city.

Michelson has explained how urban renewal in the United States differs from urban renewal in Canada. American renewal has been financed almost entirely by government, chiefly at the federal level. It is believed that urban renewal is too costly for private enterprise. Furthermore, the private sector, it is believed, hardly can cope with the problem of land use. The planning itself, however, is usually a local undertaking, not a federal responsibility.

Canadian renewal has been carried out primarily by private interests. The private sector in Canada has operated on a smaller scale than has the government in the United States. In part, the renewal costs in Canada are comparatively modest because Canadians consider it fashionable to live in districts near the center of town. (It was mentioned earlier that the concentric zone theory lacks support in Canada.[7]) As a result of all this, there are fewer blighted neighborhoods in Canadian cities than in cities of the United States. But Canadians pay a price for their fashionable inner-city homes. Property values are likely to be high in their unblighted neighborhoods near the CBDs.

The Canadian situation, it could be said, is a mixed blessing. Cities in Canada may soon face the problem now being experienced in Third World cities: the rich acquire much of the land around the CBD, forcing the poor to move beyond this and other established areas to the outskirts of town, where property values are lower (Michelson, 1977: 579). Here many of the advantages of central city living are unavailable. In the United States, the affluent, who are

[6]Lancourt (1977: Chapter 1) presents several cases of community development carried out by Alinsky methods.

[7]Michelson (1977: 578) says the United States is about the only country in which the concentric zone theory holds. This may help explain why government money is needed for renewal, since ingrained preferences for the periphery preclude the voluntary establishment of stable moderate- to high-income subcommunities near the core.

mostly at the periphery, can at least afford to go into the city when they want to.

SHIFTING COMMUNITY BOUNDARIES

One problem facing community sociologists and the communities themselves is how to identify their social and economic boundaries, as opposed to their corporate town limits. At issue is the question of membership in the community. Who is in the group? Who is outside it? The issue is never fully settled in many North American communities. The questions remain unanswered because perceived community boundaries are constantly shifting in response to growth on the periphery, improved and extended transportation, and changes in the availability of basic services.

The days have mostly passed when communities literally die, as in the demise of an American town following the switch from coal- to diesel-powered railroad locomotives (Cottrell, 1951). The ghost towns dotting the Canadian and American West usually died from afflictions of this sort, of some vital change in their economic base (e.g., depletion of a total natural resource, bankruptcy of their only industrial firm). Such changes still occur, but inhabitants, in the spirit of community development and often with the aid of government, attract new industry—i.e., shift their economic base—to survive and possibly even prosper.

According to Stein (1972: 296), the three forces of industrialization, bureaucratization, and urbanization cause community boundaries to shift. *Industrialization* is the mass production of goods in a factory by means of power-driven machines and other implements. Industry replaces many of the craftlike enterprises operating in homes and small shops. *Bureaucratization,* in this context, is the extension of decision making and ownership from a central office to its branches. It is also the development of intercity linkages, which now exist among a wide range of political, social, and economic organizations (Wilson, 1984: 287–288). These linkages give the impression that many local interests are controlled from another community (e.g., a head-office decision to move the firm's headquarters from one city to another). *Urbanization* is the migration of large numbers of heterogeneous people from the countryside to cities. Their presence affects in many ways the services, institutions, and culture of the cities. In time, the migrants adopt urban habits, life-styles, and responsibilities.

To understand how industrialization changes community boundaries, you need only contemplate the remarkable development of the automobile in North America. The automobile industry has produced efficient, high-speed, widely available personal transportation for a vast majority of North Americans. That development has been followed by improved highways, expanded parking facilities, and convenient service. All this has made it possible for people to travel afar for goods and services. Thus smaller communities have moved within the orbit of larger cities. Likewise, remote bureaucracies can now transfer people into and out of branch-plant towns with ease, forcing those people to adjust frequently to new sets of friends and life-styles.

Urbanization is possibly the most dramatic of the three causes of a change in community boundaries. The impact of urbanization is evident when viewed from the standpoint of the small community. Many small communities have experienced the departure of numerous residents, many of whom are young. Historically, the scope of urbanization in North America is staggering. The total population of the cities in Canada and the United States reflects the impact of urbanization. Michalos (1980a: 35–36) writes that, on the one hand, Canadians are increasingly living in towns of population 2500 to 3000 as well as in cities of population 100,000 to 500,000. Fewer Americans are living in communities of these sizes. On the other hand, Canadians these days are less likely to live in cities of a half-million people or more when compared with Americans, who are increasingly likely to live in large cities.

Americans are clearly more likely than

Canadians to live amidst great agglomerations of people. It is doubtful whether any Canadian metropolitan area will ever reach the population of the New York and Los Angeles metropolitan areas (17,539,000 and 11,498,000, respectively, in 1980). In 1981, Toronto was Canada's largest metropolitan area, with 2,998,947 people (Montreal was slightly smaller with a population of 2,828,349). Toronto ranked tenth in size among North American metropolitan areas.[8]

According to Simmons and Simmons (1969: 14), this discrepancy in the size of the largest cities in Canada and the United States is explained to some extent by Canada's slower recovery from the Great Depression, when compared with the United States. With less money to invest, Canadians, during the early postwar period, improved basic services and facilities such as housing, roads, schools, and parks. The sharp increase in automobile ownership and low-density housing came later in Canada than in America, and so did the aftereffects of suburban shopping centers and expressways.

THE NATURE OF CITIES

One characteristic of cities which sets them apart from rural towns is their internal structure. The internal structure of a city is relatively more complicated than the structure of a rural town. A hint of this has already been given in connection with the preceding discussion of ecological processes and growth patterns. This section elaborates on structure and growth patterns by considering the development of suburbs, natural areas, and subcultures.

Suburbanization

As just explained, the great suburban expansion of North American cities began earlier in the United States than in Canada. Commuters have been riding the trains and buses in New York and Chicago for many years. But, in both countries, the massive move to the suburbs followed World War II (see Edmonston 1975; Yeates, 1975). New suburbs with their ranch houses and split levels sprang up (Don Mills near Toronto and Park Forest near Chicago, for example).

Geographers and sociologists have plotted *density curves* to map the redistribution of people in metropolitan areas. Density curves depict the levels of concentration of population in various parts of a community. These curves show in general that population concentrations are relatively high in the CBD, are even higher in the zone immediately surrounding it, and then decrease as distance from the CBD increases.

At least two facts distinguish Canadian cities from American cities in this respect: (1) Canadian density curves show a significantly smaller decrease in density from city center to periphery than American curves (see Figure 8.2), and (2) suburban development is noticeably less in Canada than in the United States. It is said that Canadian curves are "flatter" than American curves. What accounts for these differences in density curves?

The differences in the urban density curves between Canada and the United States have their roots in urbanization (Yeates and Garner, 1980: 235; Simmons and Simmons, 1969: 12–

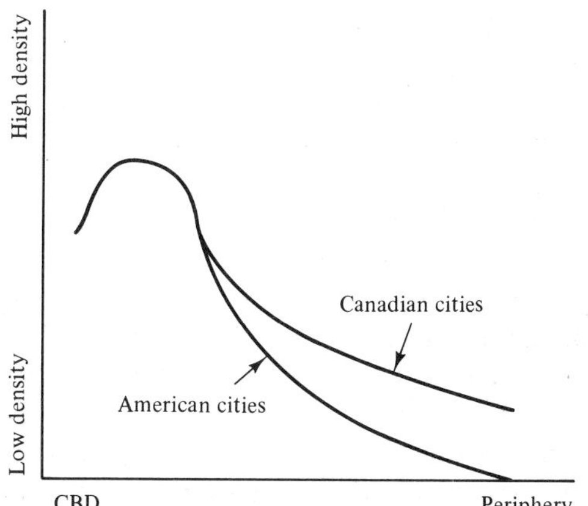

Figure 8.2 Typical Density Curves for American and Canadian Cities

[8]These population figures are not entirely comparable, since the U.S. census definition of its "consolidated Metropolitan Statistical Area" (CMSL) differs from the Canadian census definition of its "Census Metropolitan Area" (CMA). These differences, however, are not large enough to affect the broad comparison being made here.

14). One of the conditions leading to suburbanization or deconcentration in American cities has been racial. Whites who could afford to do so moved out of neighborhoods being invaded (as this term is used in urban ecology) by blacks. The whites moved farther from the city core. Many of them moved to the suburbs.

Although racial prejudice exists in Canada, too (see Chapter 20), there are comparatively few blacks anywhere in Canadian cities. Blacks, at least, are not in numbers great enough to provoke the widespread flight of whites from neighborhoods being invaded. In addition, since 1951 Canada has had a greater influx of immigrants than the United States. Many of the immigrants are middle-class whites or success-oriented individuals of varied ethnic and socioeconomic backgrounds. Some of the immigrants have blended into the outlying areas of the cities, while others have mixed with middle- and upper-class native-born Canadians near downtown.

The consequences of the late recovery in Canada from the Great Depression also help account for the difference in density curves. In addition, there is more government control of urban expansion in Canada than in the United States. One consequence of such control is the tendency for the central city to annex communities springing up on its perimeter; such annexation is legally permitted. The desire for community autonomy in the United States has prevented such annexation and has contributed to growing tiers of suburbs around U.S. cities.

Finally, as S. D. Clark (1966: 145–151) has observed, many Canadians have repudiated the suburban life-style. Thousands flocked to the suburbs in the postwar period, lured by the propaganda of the housing industry. That industry claimed that such places were better than city neighborhoods for rearing children and that it was better to own your own home than to rent. But there were undisclosed costs, among them large mortgages, long drives to work, and, at one time, inadequate shopping facilities. But, then, Canadians, unlike many Americans, had a central city to which they felt they could return; they had a genuine alternative to the suburbs.

Still, some changes may be in the offing. Census data comparing central city growth rates for 1976 and 1981 show eastern Canadian cities losing population from the urban core, while gaining population outside the core and in the rural-urban fringe. Western cities, by contrast, are gaining population in all three locations (Statistics Canada, 1984c). On the whole, American cities have growth rate patterns like the eastern Canadian cities, except that the entire central city is losing population to the suburbs and the fringe (U.S. Bureau of the Census, 1985: 17, Table 20). Indeed, as Heaton and Fuguitt (1980) point out, there is a substantial countermovement of Americans from urban to rural areas beyond the metropolitan fringe. A similar trend has been noted among Canadians (Statistics Canada, 1984c).

Natural Areas: The Neighborhood

Sociologists of the Chicago School in the 1920s, particularly Robert Park and Ernest Burgess, saw cities as composed of *natural areas,* or geographic sectors identifiable by some sort of common characteristic. Central business districts are natural areas. So are skid rows and slums, which exist in Canadian cities as well as in the United States (Nader, 1975: 90–91; Jackson, 1973: 123). There are also industrial, recreational, entertainment, and commercial areas. But it is mostly people who occupy cities, which brings us to the *neighborhood,* a residential natural area.

Suttles (1972: 55–64, 82–107) identifies five types of neighborhoods: the *face-block neighborhood,* the *defended neighborhood,* the *community of limited liability,* the *expanded community of liability,* and the *contrived neighborhood.* The types differ from one another in several ways. You can find an example of each of the five types in the city in which you live.

The *face-block,* so familiar to many North Americans, consists of families and individuals who live in one or more buildings with a common entry and who share certain important facilities. Or it may consist of families and individuals living in single-family dwellings on the same city block face. The front and back doors of apartment buildings, courtyards serving several buildings, common play areas for children, and the like demarcate these neighborhoods. Here, on the basis of propinquity and homogeneity (of social class, family life cycle stage, etc.), people develop at least acquaintances, if not friendships. The city street faced by all houses in the block forms the basis for a face-block neighborhood.

In the *defended neighborhood,* intercourse with the outside world is obstructed in some crucial way. Some obstructions are intended (e.g., gates, walls, shrubbery, security guards), but others are unintended (e.g., rivers, cliffs, expressways, railyards). Residents have a sense of belonging to the neighborhood, for they share many aims, concerns, and beliefs. They often organize associations and pressure groups. Many of the ethnically segregated areas in North American cities are defended neighborhoods. Among such neighborhoods are Chinatowns, Jewish ghettos, black communities, Indian slums, Polish enclaves, and Italian districts.

Defended neighborhoods create an urban mosaic in many North American cities.

The boundaries of the *community of limited liability* are more indistinct than those of the face-block neighborhood and the defended neighborhood. The community of limited liability may be a street community (the people on a certain city block or street) or a district community (a district within the city). Sometimes the neighborhood's boundaries are imposed by an external agency which performs a specific function or service for an area of the city. For example, the community might form around the area served by a fire house, a grade school, a high school, an electoral riding, a police jurisdiction, or a church parish. These services and functions partially overlap one another. They touch the lives of those living in the neighborhood in specific ways, but they relate only to a small part of an individual's life and existence.

The *expanded community of limited liability* is established over a large part of a city, with several different neighborhoods in the section. A basis, or reason, for the neighborhoods may be the same as for a community of limited liability. For example, an expanded community of limited liability is formed when residents of adjoining neighborhoods join to resist a city council proposal to run an expressway through their part of town. Such an effort normally brings together several neighborhoods, which previously had little to do with each other.

Suttles refers to residential areas designed and built by developers and planners as *contrived neighborhoods.* Whether at the city's edge or in a redeveloped inner zone, these communities within a community often have a street plan and clear-cut boundaries. The neighborhoods have restrictive architectural codes and eye-catching names (e.g., Sunrise Acres, Appleyard Mews, Seaside Heights). Inhabitants are likely to be of similar socioeconomic status. A sense of community eventually emerges as the neighborhood becomes locally recognized and its residents share with each other their complaints about the developer, builders, and municipal authorities.

Subcultures

Crosscutting the urban and suburban natural areas of North American cities are numerous subcultures. Many of the subcultures have a national scope and some even an international scope, although we are usually most aware of their local manifestations. A *subculture* is a distinctive configuration of values, norms, beliefs, artifacts, and patterns of behavior which, together, constitute a special way of life for its members (see Effrat's *community as society,* mentioned earlier). Habitual gamblers form a subculture. Among other examples are Jews, jazz musicians, serious tennis players, and old-car collectors.

The members of a subculture also share the values, norms, and practices of the larger culture; all this suggests that the subculture is often an addendum to the larger formation. This is especially true of occupational, ethnic, adolescent, and leisure subcultures. Deviant subcultures, while adding certain elements, also reject others; for example, a thief may cast aside the value of honesty or homosexuals may cast aside the value of heterosexuality. City dwellers may belong to more than one subculture, each of which is foreign to those outside it.

A subculture is a distinctive configuration of values, norms, beliefs, artifacts, and patterns of behavior.

Like neighborhoods and kin groups, subcultures help reduce the anonymity, loneliness, and impersonality of big cities. Thanks to subcultures, "urbanites at least as much as ruralites are integrated into viable social worlds" (Fischer, 1984: 38). The fact that subcultures flourish in cities and not in the countryside is one of the differences between urban communities and rural communities.

A TRUE URBAN COMMUNITY?

Just how important is the geographic basis for a community? This question has provoked lengthy debate from the very inception of community sociology. Bertrand (1972: 149–150) takes the negative, arguing that some sociological reasoning in this area suffers from the "geographic fallacy" or

> the tendency to think of a community as an area with rather easily identifiable geographic bounds. It is true that any social unit must occupy physical space simply because of the biologic nature of man. However, a community as a sociological concept must be seen primarily as occupying social rather than physical space. In other words, a community is not an area but a social system. It is delineated in terms of role relationships. . . .

As cities grow into metropolises and metropolises blend into a megalopolis, the physical base of these communities fades in importance.[9] The physical setting is replaced, if at all, by a vague awareness of community, a feeling that "people around here" (a reference to a vaguely bounded area) belong together as a group.[10]

[9]Megalopolis is Jean Gottman's (1961) term for a string of metropolitan areas so close in proximity that they appear to be one more or less continuous city. The prime example in North America is the "Bos-Wash" megalopolis running from southern New Hampshire to northern Virginia and from the Atlantic Coast inland approximately one hundred miles.

[10]Some sociologists would like to discard the concept of community. They see it as an idea that has outlived its usefulness. The fall issue of *Daedalus,* vol. 97 (1968), contains several statements arguing that the concept of community is antiquated.

But within the sense of community there is a frail *sense of locale* (as in the parenthetical phrase in the preceding paragraph) which resists total elimination. This resistance succeeds, despite the destructive effects on it of the mass media, long-distance telephoning, and air travel (see Bernard, 1973: 181–186). Entertainment on television, the stories in newspapers, the articles in magazines, and the information in books are anything but local. A network broadcast on radio is national in character, not local. Even the advertising, though often intended to generate local sales, is beamed to a national audience. Were the mass media and air travel as destructive of community life as some thinkers claim (e.g., Marshall McLuhan), then the only real communities left in modern North America would be the Canadian and American societies and their cultures (the subject of the next chapter).

But many of our daily activities are conducted away from and without reference to the mass media. We are active in schools, in churches, in synagogues, at town halls, at neighborhood picnics, and at community festivals. Those of us with jobs are at work in offices, in shops, and in factories. Our daily activities occur in *places* within a geographic area. The boundaries of these places, although sometimes vague, constitute an essential part of the inhabitants' sense of community.

OUTLINE AND SUMMARY

I. Introduction
   A *community* is a social group with a common territorial base; those in the group share interests and have a sense of belonging to the group.

II. Sociology of the Community
   Community research falls into four traditions: (1) *complete community,* (2) *limited liability,* (3) *society,* (4) *personal community.*

III. What Is a Community?
   A *community* is a set of actors sharing a limited territorial area as the base for carrying out the greatest share of their daily activities.
   A. Community as a Group
      A community is a group; there is interaction among the members of a community.
   B. Rural Communities
      Rural communities are relatively small in size, clearly nonmetropolitan, and patently rural in character.
   C. Urban Communities
      Urban communities are distinguished from their rural counterparts by their layouts, architectural forms, tissue of associations, corporate enterprises, and typically urban practices and lifestyles.
   D. Common Elements
      1. Geographic Area
      2. Social Interaction
      3. Shared Ties
   E. Tönnies Ideal Types
      Ferdinand Tönnies's two ideal types of community are *Gemeinschaft* and *Gesellschaft.*

IV. Urban Ecology
   Urban ecology is the study of the geographic and temporal distribution of individuals, groups, and services in a city.
   A. Ecological Processes
      As a community begins to grow, various functions begin to compete for space within it. These functions are *concentration, centralization, dispersion, segregation, invasion,* and *succession.*
   B. Patterns of Growth
      Three different theories explain the patterns of growth of the cities in Canada and the United States: Some American cities have developed according to the *concentric zone* pattern. Canadian cities along with other cities in the United States tend to present *sectorial* and *multiple nuclei* growth configurations.

V. Community Development
   Community development is planned local change.
   A. The Alinsky Approach
      Saul Alinsky taught community lead-

ers how to fight for desired changes against those who control their fate; he encouraged community action with his approach.

B. Urban Planning

Urban planning is a special type of community development.

VI. Shifting Community Boundaries

Three developments cause changes in community boundaries: (1) *industrialization,* (2) *bureaucratization,* (3) *urbanization.*

VII. The Nature of Cities

One characteristic of cities which sets them apart from rural towns is their internal structure.

A. Suburbanization

The massive moves to the suburbs followed World War II.

B. Natural Areas: The Neighborhood

The natural area of the neighborhood has been classified into five types: (1) the *face-block,* (2) *defended neighborhood,* (3) *community of limited liability,* (4) *expanded community of limited liability,* (5) *contrived neighborhood.*

C. Subcultures

A *subculture* is a distinctive configuration of values, norms, beliefs, artifacts, and patterns of behavior, which together constitute a special way of life for its members; it is a group which shares in the general culture of a society but has its own norms and beliefs.

VIII. A True Urban Community?

The question of just how important is the geographic basis for a community has provoked lengthy debate from the very inception of community sociology. Today's megalopolis tends to obscure its own physical boundaries. Within it, however, is a frail sense of locale that resists total elimination.

FOR FURTHER READING AND STUDY

Blackwell, J. E. and Hart, P. 1982. *Cities, suburbs, and blacks.* Bayside, N.Y.: General Hall. This is one of a very few studies of the attitudes of urban and suburban American blacks which takes up some of the vexing issues of city life. Measures are made of the blacks' attitudes toward health information, access to health care, social participation, alienation, distrust of power, and future orientation.

Clairmont, D. H. and Magill, D. W. 1974. *Africville: The life and death of a Canadian black community.* Toronto: McClelland & Stewart. Africville is a Halifax slum which, before it was relocated to its present site, was a pleasant middle-class urban subcommunity. The authors examine the relocation program and how it was carried out.

Gans, J. J. 1967. *The Levittowners: Ways of life and politics in a suburban community.* New York: Pantheon Books. A classical sociological study of a new American suburb centering on its origin, its quality of life, its effect on the behavior of its members, and its politics and decision making.

Gold, G. L. 1975. *St. Pascal.* Toronto: Holt, Rinehart & Winston of Canada. This study documents the changing economic leadership of a small town in rural Quebec. The town changed from a local agricultural and forestry service center to an extralocal industrial community.

Karp, D. A., Stone, G. P., and Yoels, W. C. 1977. *Being urban: A social psychological view of city life.* Lexington, Mass.: D. C. Heath. The authors examine the social organization of everyday city life, the diversity of urban life-styles, tolerance in the city, and stratification and power in cities. They also review some of the classical theories of city life.

Lofland, L. H. 1973. *A world of strangers.* New York: Basic Books. A study of the ways strangers interact in the public spaces of the modern metropolis. Strangers in a city create their own social and psychological order.

Stein, M. R. 1972. *The eclipse of community,* expanded ed. Princeton, N.J.: Princeton University Press. This book interprets the problems and prospects of American community life, with references to sociological field studies conducted since the 1920s.

Warren, D. I. 1981. *Helping networks: How people cope with problems in the urban community.* Notre Dame, 2nd.: University of Notre Dame Press. A study of when and how social networks of friends, family, and other relatives give help and thereby reduce the impersonality and uncaring atmosphere of the city.

KEY WORDS

community A social group with a common territorial base; those in the group share interests and have a sense of belonging to the group.

concentric-zone theory A theory that a city is an accretion of large rings, or zones, which radiate out from the downtown center; there is a different type of land use in each zone.

Gemeinschaft A rural community characterized by close interpersonal relationships among kin and friends.

Gesellschaft A community in which interpersonal relationships are more formal, specialized, and impersonal than in the Gemeinschaft community.

multiple nuclei theory A theory that a city is a composite of centers and subcenters called *nuclei.*

sector theory A theory that a city grows from its center in sectors, not in concentric zones.

subculture A distinctive configuration of values, norms, beliefs, artifacts, and patterns of behavior which, together, constitute a special way of life for its members.

chapter 9

Society and Culture

CHAPTER OUTLINE

INTRODUCTION

In Chapter 1 we defined society as a relatively self-sufficient, usually large, group of people who maintain direct or indirect contact with each other through a culture. We defined *culture* as the shared language, beliefs, goals, artifacts, and experiences that coalesce into a unique pattern. Or in summary, *culture* is a society's way of life.[1] A detailed definition of culture was set forth in

[1]World-system theory and its parent, modernization theory, which it has rejected, are global rather than societal frameworks (Chirot and Hall, 1982). Despite a growing interest in the world system, North American sociology is still overwhelmingly societal in its organization. World-system theory is considered in Chapter 23.

Chapter 6. Part Three, of which this chapter is a part, makes it clear that small groups, large-scale organizations, communities, and societies all have cultural components.

A primary aim of this chapter is to flesh out the shorthand definition of society given in the preceding paragraph. Another objective is to interrelate the concepts of *culture* and *institution,* two major components of society. Unlike anthropologists, sociologists rarely study culture per se (Peterson, 1979: 158–159). Rather, sociologists study certain parts and subsystems of culture, notably the institutions and social structures of a society and its internal communities. They study these institutions and structures as they are created and changed and as they influence the human interaction taking place in groups ranging in size from dyads to the society itself.

Moreover, culture is essentially a static concept; it centers on the products of human interaction rather than on the processes leading to these products. By contrast, we have seen that sociologists, when studying society, also examine processes such as human interaction, socialization, group formation, community development, and urbanization. Later in this book we will look at still other processes, namely those of control (Chapter 16), social differentiation (Part Five), and societal trends (Part Six). Society is both a static and a dynamic entity.

For sociologists, the concept of culture serves as a handy theoretical summary of the totality of a society's institutions. Culture also serves as an empirical backdrop against which sociologists can compare the cultural subsystems that have caught their fancy. These include ethnic subcultures, youth culture, popular and elite cultures, occupational subcultures, and deviant subcultures. But we are getting ahead of ourselves. Before we consider the place of culture in society and the discipline of sociology, we must understand what society is. In this chapter, we examine the concept of society, the four most common perspectives from which sociologists study society, and the most frequently discussed types of societies. The final section looks at culture and its nature and relationship to the concept of social institution. By way of example, it discusses the contemporary subsystems of folk culture, popular culture, and high culture.

THE CONCEPT OF SOCIETY

An extended definition of society can be derived from Leon Mayhew's (1968: 577) statement concerning the common elements found in the standard definitions: "Analytical definitions usually treat a society as a relatively independent or self-sufficient population characterized by internal organization, territoriality, cultural distinctiveness, and sexual recruitment." The different definitions put varying stresses on these elements, depending on the theoretical frameworks within which they are embedded. We shall see later how this is done when the major frameworks for the study of society are reviewed.

The notion of self-sufficiency no longer implies economic independence, as it did when sociologists occasionally and anthropologists usually studied preindustrial societies. *Self-sufficiency* now is looked on as a condition made possible by social institutions; the institutions are necessary for the existence of the group. *Institutions* are relatively stable sets of abstract relationships, patterns of behavior, roles, mores, and values that emerge as solutions to the problems of collective living (a subsection on institutions follows). The resources (e.g., capital, food, consumer goods, military equipment, raw materials for production) required by these institutions may come from both inside and outside the society. Except in remote corners of the world, economically self-sufficient (i.e., nontrading) societies have vanished.

Defining Society

The concept of society figured prominently in the rise of sociology as a separate social science in the late nineteenth century. Comte and Spen-

National communities are demarcated by distinct political boundaries.

cer and especially Durkheim sought to establish the idea of society as an entity in a class of its own. In other words, these early sociologists examined society holistically, or as a whole—a whole which is more than the sum of its parts. Society is more than the actions, thoughts, values, and wishes of its members; it is more than the groups to which members of the society belong. Although complex and abstract, society is as much a part of reality as individual behavior, and, according to many of sociology's founding fathers, its study is what demarcates the discipline of sociology from psychology and economics. Like social facts, which interested Durkheim (see Chapter 1) and which are part of the larger society, society itself is known through or manifested in the constraints it imposes on its members. A society's norms, customs, outlooks, and values act, in their special ways, to constrain personal behavior and thought. Perhaps the most dramatic example is found in the action of military suicide squads.

Today, the term "society" often refers to the same group of people as the terms "nation," "nation-state," and "country." The idea of a nation, a nation-state, or a country, however, is a narrower concept than the concept of society. A nation suggests only the political boundaries and political institutions identified with a group of people constituting society. It should be recognized that small, culturally and geographically isolated groups within nations (e.g., the Australian aborigines, the Lapps of Scandinavia and Finland) are also societies. Quebec, particularly since its interest in "sovereignty association" with the rest of Canada, is a society within a nation. These smaller societies are sometimes referred to by sociologists as *communities.* The idea of society and the idea of community are similar in many ways.

Popular usage of the term "society" diverges, at times broadly, from its scientific usage. For sociologists as scientists, society never denotes a special social circle such as "high society," "artistic society," "polite society," or "leisure society." Nor does it signify a voluntary association, as in the name "Royal Astronomical Society of Canada." Sociologists may loosely use the term "society," however, to refer to a civilization (for instance, "Western civilization" or "Western society").

Institutions

The concept of *institution* is as indispensable to the sociologist's work and understanding of society as any other idea or interpretation. The concept is widely used by sociologists of all per-

---

SOCIOLOGY OR COMMON SENSE

What do you think?

Which of the following statements do you agree with? Which statements do you disagree with? Make a note of your answers. Check your answers when you have completed your study of this chapter. Are your answers to the statements the same as those a sociologist would give?

1. A society is too large to be conceived of as a group.
2. Americans are more strongly identified with the United States than Canadians are with Canada.
3. Conflict in society is not inevitable; it can be eliminated.
4. The culture of sociology students differs from the culture of other students.
5. Folk culture no longer exists in Canada.

---

suasions. Six defining criteria of *institution* are set forth here for the purpose of anchoring the sociological meaning of this term and establishing prerequisites for the study of Part Four.

(1) Institutions form around the major *problems of collective living.* Martindale (1962: 31–48) has classified these problems in three groups: (a) those concerning the mastery of nature (e.g., food, shelter, clothing), (b) socialization, and (c) social control of undesirable actions. If people are to live together (or live at all, in the case of mastering nature), these problems must be identified and solved in some minimally effective manner.

(2) Institutions consist of *patterns of behavior,* ranging from distinctive *routinized* forms of social interaction to complex *standardized* organizational and communal procedures. Examples include shaking hands, dressing formally for dinner, driving the speed limit, making out tax forms, going through marriage ceremonies, and registering for university courses.

(3) Institutions also consist of *abstract relationships* linking individuals who occupy certain positions and linking groups that carry out certain functions. That is, institutions have a social structure. The manifestations of the social structure at the group level have already been referred to. By way of illustration, the abstract teacher-pupil relationship in any educational institution is manifested in actual teacher-pupil interaction in thousands of schoolrooms across North America. As bridging entities, institutions also interrelate the many groups associated with them. In education there are abstract links between schools, between schools and the school boards, and between schools and parent-teacher organizations.

(4) Institutions are composed of *roles,* the sets of expectations directed at individuals and at groups occupying the abstract positions. As in the case of institutional relationships, abstract norms are applied to countless concrete situations in the daily routines of associated groups. Socially approved norms (deviants are sometimes guided by antisocial norms) are known as *folkways.* The rules of etiquette are familiar folkways. Norms with great moral and emotional significance are referred to as *mores* (e.g., rules against incest and fraud). A *custom* is a folkway so long established that it has become traditional (e.g., standing when the national anthem is played).

(5) Institutions also have values. A *value* is a worth which satisfies a collective need or desire; it is the target of a collective attitude. It is simultaneously a collective goal to be pursued (see Chapter 1). In North America, the belief that able-bodied adults should perform work roles is both a requisite and an institutionalized economic value.

Theater rehearsals are one of many patterns of behavior in everyday life.

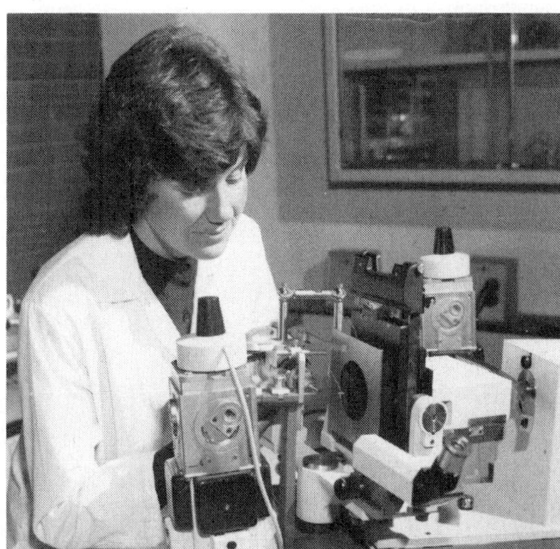
Scientist: An institutionalized role in modern industrial society.

A distinction is commonly drawn between institutional or societal values, on the one hand, and personal values, on the other. The latter are often little more than an individual's internalization of the former. Deviants, however, develop, or internalize from outcast groups, values that are out of step with certain institutions.

(6) Because the society of which they are a part endures over time, institutions are said to have a *history*. That is, they have both an extensive past and an extensive future. In fact, they easily outlive the groups and patterns of behavior that are associated with them over a given era. For instance, our institution of leisure started long before the advent of television or the amusement park. It could happen that, in the future, new leisure attractions will emerge; the new leisures, in all probability, will be as appealing as television and roller coasters. Some institutions are literally as old as the society itself and will disappear only when the society passes out of existence.

As they mastered nature, socialized new members (children and immigrants), and controlled unwanted behavior, modern industrial societies evolved their own peculiar set of institutions. Institutions have been classified in five spheres (see Eisenstadt, 1968: 410).[2] The five spheres, or kinds, are (1) family and kinship, (2) education, (3) economy, (4) polity, and (5) cultural institutions. Each is a part of the modern industrial society.

Family and *kinship institutions* form around the procreative and biological relations between people and also regulate the socialization of the young. *Education* extends the socialization started in the family and also undertakes a general cultural transmission. The *economy* centers on the production, distribution, and consumption of goods and services. Its domain is work and, to some extent, leisure. The *polity* organizes the distribution of power, control of force, and internal and external maintenance of the society's boundaries. The *cultural institutions* of a society emerge in connection with the creation and conservation of human-made objects and ideas; they provide for the distribution of objects and ideas within the society. The fields of science, religion, art, and some aspects of leisure fall under the heading "cultural institution."

Dubin (1976: 10–11) concludes that, for industrial societies, there is no basis to the claim that one of these institutions or institutional spheres has a greater impact on behavior than the others. No single institution is "focal," or dominant. The institutions must therefore be considered "multiequal." Multiequal institutions are largely independent of one another. That is, they are poorly coordinated, since effective coordination is impossible in societies as complex and heterogeneous as the modern industrial state. The result is that contemporary institutions compete against one another for the allegiance of the individual. For example, the family encourages its breadwinner to spend time at domestic activities, while the economic sphere demands some time at work. The harried breadwinner is left to find a *modus vivendi* by which he or she can satisfy the two antagonists.

SOCIETY AS A GROUP

Starting with dyads, triads, and other small groups, we have worked our way upward in size of collectivity through large-scale organizations to rural and urban communities to societies. As groups grow larger, they tend to become more *comprehensive*. Society is the most populous and comprehensive group of all. Comprehensiveness has been a quality of all except the smallest groups considered in this book. Even the larger small groups break down into subdivisions, normally a clique or two. Thus we may say that, among other things, all groups (excluding the tiniest) are assemblages of smaller groups. A society, however, is the only collectivity spanning rural and urban communities and, hence, all their constituent groups.

The ways in which the different-sized groups

[2]Eisenstadt lists stratification as a sixth institutional sphere. In this text stratification is treated as a process of differentiation, whereby societal members are arrayed along the dimensions of wealth, prestige, and power in all the institutional spheres of their society (see Chapter 18).

are connected within the overarching societal group (society) is unique for each society. This complex pattern is an important part of a society's *social organization,* defined here as the stable interrelationship of the society's groups, institutions, and networks of social relationships. This is a static rather than a dynamic conception. Social organization is the stability of an existing mosaic of group interrelationships, not the set of processes leading to the formation of the mosaic and to a change in the mosaic. Anthropologists are much in agreement.[3]

It is perhaps difficult to conceive of Canadian society as a group. An assemblage as large as these two collectivities is dramatically different from an adolescent peer group or even a city and its populace. But, true to the sociological perspective, it is possible to observe similarities between a society and a small group. Notwithstanding its massiveness, a modern industrial society still meets the five criteria for distinguishing groups listed in Chapter 6.

(1) There is certainly interaction among the individuals belonging to a society. The interaction can be observed in groups—small groups, large-scale organizations, communities. Yet there are times when societal members interact as part of an aggregate outside the smaller groups but still within the society. The conversation between strangers who find themselves seated next to each other on an airplane is one example. Another example is the frustration and interchange among those coping with a malfunctioning vending machine. In both instances, the verbal and nonverbal gestures made by the individuals involved are part of a common set of communication symbols that members of the society are presumed to have. The set of symbols is not shared exclusively within one or a few subgroups in the society.

(2) There is no doubt about the existence of goals shared by nearly everyone in the society. The goals motivate the members of the society to individual action; they cannot be ignored or cast aside. For example, Canadians desire peace, prosperity, and security. They also support, in general, the goal of protecting their political system. Still, there is often a disgruntled or rebellious minority who reject certain societal goals altogether; for example, members of the Communist party are not wholly in accord with the goal of preserving the existing political system in Canada. Indeed, as noted in a section which follows, there can be conflict in and between groups and social classes over goals or how to achieve them or both. But, in spite of conflict and disagreement, the shared goals help keep the society from disintegrating and disbanding.

(3) Society is a comprehensive group whose members adhere to the same norms observed by many of its constituent groups. For instance, Canadians are expected to eat meat with a knife and fork, whether at home, in the company cafeteria, or in a downtown restaurant. As we have noted, there will be a few who violate this rule of etiquette, perhaps by feeding themselves with their fingers. There are also norms that are exclusively societal norms; they have no locus in any particular subgroup of the society. For example, the income tax laws and the laws against treason are societal laws.

(4) There are stable sets of roles at the subgroup level of a society and, spanning the subgroups, at the societal level. The subgroup roles of father and mother and teacher and pupil have been referred to in earlier chapters. The social structure of the federal governments of Canada and the United States (see Figures 7.1 and 7.2) exemplify societywide roles.[4]

(5) The criterion of patterned likes and dislikes of groups is possibly most evident at the societal level, if for no other reason than that it is so visible here. Regional antipathies exem-

[3]When sociologists speak of one or more social organizations as *groups* rather than social organization as a *characteristic* of groups, the term is synonymous with large-scale organization.

[4]In Chapter 7, the two federal governments were treated as large-scale organizations. As such they are unique, for their missions are also to develop goals, norms, and organizational structures to serve their entire societies and not only or particularly the formally elected, appointed, and hired members of them as organizations.

plify the patterns of dislikes, as in North versus South in the United States and eastern and western provinces versus Ontario and Quebec in Canada. Congenial and respectful relations also exist at the societal level. For instance, people look with admiration on personages such as national sports heroes, venerated political leaders, and beloved stars of film and television.

THEORETICAL PERSPECTIVES

The nature of particular societies (their goals, norms, behaviors) has been a leading concern in sociology since its inception around the middle of the nineteenth century. Sociologists who specialize in the study of the nature of society approach its culture and social organization from different perspectives and, in so doing, arrive at different conclusions about its social life. Given the duration of the interest in examining whole societies, it is hardly surprising that the four main perspectives for its study have served as guidelines for many years. The perspectives seek to interpret society from the standpoints of social system, economic struggle, general conflict, and symbolic interaction.

The Social System

The early study of society as an entity in itself, with its own constraining qualities, subsequently lost its appeal, albeit only temporarily. In its place arose the concept of society as a social system (Mayhew, 1968: 583), an orientation that began its bloom roughly forty-five years ago. This intellectual shift redirected attention to the identification of the internal units, such as organizations and institutions, and maintenance mechanisms, such as roles and behavior patterns. Sociologists also began to give some thought to the boundaries of society. As mentioned in Chapter 1, many similarities exist between the organismic models of Comte and Durkheim and the modern functionalist or social systems analyses of Parsons, Merton, Levy, Homans (in the 1950s), and others. Nevertheless, these differences in focus were sufficient to set sociology on a fruitful new course of investigation.

Levy's (1952: 113) definition of society is typical of those found in the social systems literature:

> A society is a system of action in operation that (1) involves a plurality of interacting individuals . . . whose actions are primarily oriented to the system concerned and who are recruited at least in part by the sexual reproduction of members of the plurality involved, (2) is at least in theory self-sufficient for the actions of this plurality, and (3) is capable of existing longer than the life span of an individual involved.

This definition and its attendant theory are applied to all human societies.

In studying Levy's definition, we learn that individuals whose actions are oriented primarily toward the system concerned contribute to the system's survival. The individuals act as they do within the system's rules and, therefore, deviate only in minor ways, if at all. In other words, the functionalist perspective treats people as more or less integrated in their society. In addition, one of the distinguishing characteristics of societies, when compared with the social systems considered previously (communities, etc.), is their need for new members; there can be no society without the individuals who are part of the society. The society is perpetuated, for people are added to it by means of sexual reproduction; human beings, the members of society, reproduce. Modern industrial societies, of course, also grow by immigration and by means of conquest.

Functional Requisites Another distinctive characteristic of societal social systems is their self-sufficiency. We touched on this subject in a general way at the beginning of the chapter. In the systems framework, self-sufficiency is established when the functional requisites of society are met. A *functional requisite* is "a generalized condition necessary for the maintenance of the unit (i.e., society) with which it is associated" (Levy, 1952: 62). Put otherwise, one identifies the functional requisites of a society by discovering how it is maintained in its physical and social settings at the minimum level of operation. Levy (1952: 151–197) discussed the requisites:

1. *Provision for an adequate physiological relationship to the setting* and *provision for sexual recruitment.* The society must maintain sufficient numbers and types of individuals for adequate functioning.
2. *Role differentiation* and *role assignment.* In any society, there are extensive and varied activities that must be regularly performed if the society is to persist. The roles are allocated to individuals trained and motivated to carry them out.
3. *Communication.* Every society needs a system of shared symbols of communication with which to maintain a common set of values.
4. *Shared cognitive orientations.* These are items of knowledge and belief about situations and things in the everyday lives of societal members. They constitute an orientation that helps the members to adapt to and predict these situations and things and to account for the situations over which they lack control.
5. *A shared, articulated set of goals.* The goals (i.e., values) must be sufficiently clear to ensure the performance of activities necessary for the society's survival.
6. *Regulation of the choice of means.* Some means for reaching the goals are more appropriate than others and must therefore be clearly specified.
7. *The regulation of affective expression.* If the society is to persist, some emotions must be discouraged (e.g., hate, anger), while others mustbeencouraged(e.g.,love,respect).
8. *Adequate socialization.* Members must learn enough about their society and their position within it to enable effective performance of their roles.
9. *Effective control of disruptive forms of behavior.* Paradoxically, the preceding requisites tend both to prevent disruptive behavior and to foster it. Hence, there is a need to control disruptive behavior, especially the prominent forms of disruptive behavior—force and fraud.
10. *Adequate institutionalization.* Levy (1952: 102) defines *institution* as a particular set of norms regulating human action in ways consistent with the means for reaching societal goals. People in the society generally live by these rules and expect others to do the same. (This is a narrower conceptualization of institution than the one presented earlier in this chapter.)

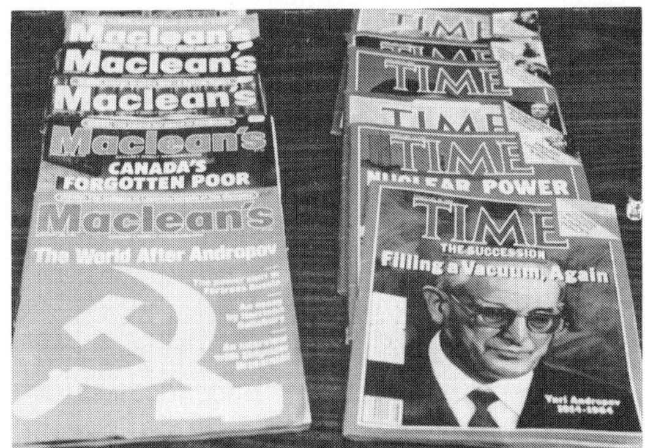

A society needs a system of shared symbols of communication.

Functional requisites are an important class of *functions,* defined in Chapter 1 as the consequences of human actions helping to maintain a group (or society, in the present instance) as an ongoing entity. Disruptive behavior is said, in the language of social systems analysis, to be *dysfunctional;* that is, its consequences weaken the group's adaptation to its setting and hence its chances of survival. But there are sociologists who disagree with the idea that dysfunctional behavior necessarily weakens society. As they see it, deviance (often looked on as dysfunctional) can be functional (e.g., Erikson, 1981: Davis, 1976: 248–249). Davis notes, for example, that prostitution serves as a safety valve, allowing for the satisfaction of sexual urges unfulfilled elsewhere.

Canadian and American Systems A truly informative comparison of the American and Canadian social systems would be a holistic undertaking of enormous proportions; it would require a thorough examination of all the parts of each society, along with a study of the interrelationships and system-maintenance properties. Although no comparison of this sort exists, separate analyses have been made for Canada (e.g., Rossides, 1968; Vallee and Whyte, 1968) and the United States (Parsons, 1960; Hertzler, 1961). Two brief comparisons, as illustrative of the social systems framework in use, are all that can be referred to here. We will compare the recruitment of technical and professional personnel in the United States with the recruitment in Canada. In addition, we will look at national identity in the two countries.

One dwindling difference between the American social system and the Canadian social system lies in the way the two countries recruit technical and professional personnel to fill key work roles and organize capital for the development of industry. Together, these methods of recruitment help to meet certain national goals (requisites 1, 2, and 5). In Canada, personnel and capital once came mostly from outside the country, while in the United States, the money and professional workers have been found internally for the most part (Porter, 1965: 43, 54–56; Rossides, 1968: 189–190).

Colleges and universities are a major source of technical and professional personnel. In the United States in 1981 the colleges and universities graduated slightly more than one-third as many as those in Canada in the same year (U.S. Bureau of the Census, 1984, 169, Table 276; Statistics Canada, 1982c: 66). The difference in size of the populations of Canada and the United States does not account for this gap. The gap, however, is now considerably smaller than in the past (Michalos, 1981: 153, Table 20). Lipset (1964: 175) holds that elitist values in Canadian society, which were inherited from Great Britain, historically discouraged mass enrollments in institutions of higher education, while equalitarian and achievement values in the United States encouraged enrollments.

An important shared cognitive orientation (requisite 4) in modern industrial societies is national identity: the awareness of an emotional attachment to the status of a citizen of a particular country. In comparing two representative descriptions of national character in the United States and Canada by Martindale (1963: 323–325) and Porter (1979), respectively, it becomes clear that Americans, at one time, were more self-consciously or strongly identified with their social system than Canadians were with theirs.

But this discrepancy appears to be less today, owing to the substantial dramatic rise in Canadian nationalism in recent years. Canada now has its own constitution. Since 1965 it has had its own flag and national anthem. For years Canadians have been reminded that they are different from Americans and citizens of other countries by familiar organizations and practices, among them the Canadian Broadcasting Corporation, the National Film Board, the official policy of bilingualism, and the national holidays of Canada Day and Victoria Day. There is reason to believe that the typical Canadian of today identifies more with his or her country than ever before.

The Economic Perspective

Wallace and Wolf (1980: 72), among others, charge the functionalists in sociology with political conservatism. Certainly, concepts such as systems maintenance, equilibrium, functional requisite, and unit boundary tend to steer analysts away from considerations of change toward considerations of stability. Indeed their interest lies in the study of the cooperation and alliance side of *social order* rather than its conflict and power side (see Chapter 1). What disharmony there is is thought not to be disruptive (see Parsons, 1951: 30). Functionalists attempted to meet the charge of conservatism by incorporating into their theories ideas such as "dynamic equilibrium" and "dysfunction" (see

Chapter 2 for definitions of these terms). Nevertheless, the debate is far from over.

Among the adversaries in this debate are those who work within the economic framework, the origins of which are traced to Karl Marx. In Marx's intellectual background are the ideas of philosophy, particularly the *dialectic* of thesis, antithesis, and synthesis (explained in the section which follows). Marx studied society from a holistic standpoint, as do modern functionalists. But Marx was interested in dynamic processes, such as the dialectic, rather than in steady states. Moreover, he saw change in society as continuous, and occasionally radical, change caused by economic forces.

Marx and Capitalism The economic theme in Marx's thought is set out in *The Communist Manifesto,* written with Friedrich Engels (and published in 1848). This book is possibly both the most celebrated and, at least in the United States, the most controversial of either man's writing. The Marx-Engels economic theme rests on the assumption that the most basic human needs are material (e.g., food, shelter, clothing) and that society is essentially the outcome of struggles between its social classes for satisfaction of these needs. In Marx and Engels' view, contradiction in general, but economic or material contradiction in particular, is the central dialectical process causing continuous change at the societal level.

Economic conflict is depicted as occurring between two emerging social classes, the *capitalists,* or entrepreneurs, and the *proletariat,* or workers. According to Marx and Engels' theory, the capitalists, who are the bourgeoisie, gradually acquire the means of production, with which they exploit their proletariat laborers (thesis). This alienates the laborers, engendering a consciousness of their own kind and a unity founded on bitterness toward the capitalists (antithesis). Revolution follows. The prediction is that intellectuals, who are also exploited by the capitalists, will join the proletariat, thereby providing some of the leadership the proletariat needs to succeed. The dialectical synthesis is a radically changed society. It rests on communist principles. It seeks to abolish private ownership of the means of production. It anticipates the evolution of a classless state, a classless society.

Radical Sociology Capitalists still are entrenched in late twentieth century North America, but Karl Marx and his theories have been influential. The success of capitalism fails to weaken the analytic power of Marx's dialectical materialism. A new, and frequently provocative, kind of sociology known as *radical sociology* has come into its own in recent years. Radical sociology is primarily an application of the earlier works of Marx and Engels (Flacks and Turkel, 1978: 193–196).

Examples of research from this perspective exist in both the United States and Canada. Harry Braverman's (1975) study of work and its degradation in the United States argues that industrialists seek to cheapen the labor they buy from their employees. Industrialists hope to accomplish this by weakening the laborers' capacity to organize their own work and by simplifying the skill and knowledge base of each work role to the point where those who fill the role are easily replaceable by other workers. Similar forces are said to be operating in the white-collar occupations.

Mahon (1984) calls attention to a different side of radical sociology in her analysis of the semi-independent Canadian Textile and Clothing Board, established in 1970 by the federal government to help implement its national textile policy. Such bodies are called on to keep the target industry operating in the national interest. The Textile and Clothing Board is supposed to bring about an adjustment to the competitive demands of the international textile market. But Mahon reveals that the board became sensitive to a compelling need of the industry: a need to be protected from the competition of imported goods. This sensitivity developed through confidential discussions between the agency and representatives of the industry and through committees made up of industry representatives. The committees were established to review agency recommendations. In these situations, there were opportunities to negotiate compromises. The compromises often favored the industry and, at the same time, ignored agency recommendations calculated to serve the national interest.

No doubt nearly all sociologists working within the social systems perspective would define the compromises as dysfunctional, should they come to their attention. But perspectives are just that, perspectives; they focus attention on certain aspects of society and away from other aspects. Given their interest in system maintenance mechanisms, functionalists are inclined to overlook the disruptive consequences of these mechanisms as long as their long-range impact is one of promoting equilibrium. Hence, the economic and social systems perspectives complement each other to the extent that adherents of the former are quite unlikely to study the economic functions helping to sustain capitalist societies.[5] That is, social theorists often label the functionalists as conservative, or oriented to the status quo. They look on those who work within the economic framework as radical, or oriented to significant historical change.

The Conflict Perspective

The economic perspective is part of the more inclusive social science framework known as *conflict theory.* In Chapter 2 we divided conflict theory into the categories of conflict ideologies and sociological conflict theories. The economic framework tends to be ideological. This section concentrates on the conflict theories. We expand here on the paradox that antagonistic forces of conflict can be the basis of social order, a situation touched on in Chapter 1, "The Study of Society."

The first conflict sociologists were introduced to their subject through the earlier writing of philosophers and biologists. In the seventeenth century, Hobbes explored the question of how to prevent "a war of all against all." He concluded that this could be accomplished by means of the "Leviathan," a society wide government so strong that no individual or group could successfully oppose it. By the nineteenth century, Darwin had observed for animals what Hobbes had observed more than two hundred years earlier for human beings: *competition for valuable but scarce resources is inevitable and pervasive.*

In spite of the seemingly destructive competition in human societies, societies still form and survive. Conflict theorists offer the following explanation: In any complex society, no matter how long established, there are numerous groups competing for an endless list of values. In our society, these struggles center on issues such as wages, hours, and working conditions (labor vs. management) and the use of the environment (environmentalists vs. industrialists). The location of a new airport (citizens groups vs. each other and citizens groups vs. the municipality) may result in conflict. Another example exists in the question of legalizing the use of marijuana (proponents vs. nonproponents). Conflict has arisen over the establishment of new government social welfare programs (pressure groups vs. pressure groups).

Conflict eventually stabilizes at a level which permits the group to persist. The settlement of conflict may be peaceful (this may be merely competition), while at times it is not (true conflict). In either case, members of modern societies, with their diverse interests and roles, are inevitably thrown into conflict with others on occasion, but, in other instances, the people who were in conflict may find it advantageous to cooperate. Thus, each person has an interest in the survival of his or her groups. Moreover, a group competing with or struggling against an-

[5]Further readings on the radical sociology of American and Canadian societies are available in collections edited by Reynolds and Henslin (1973) and Grayson (1980), respectively.

other group often demonstrates a high degree of cohesion, while "the unity of the group is often lost when it has no longer any opponent" (Simmel, 1955: 97).

Dahrendorf (1959: Chapters 5 and 6) says that conflict may become institutionalized. The conflicting parties continue to go at each other's throats for many years. But even under these conditions, those who rule cannot count on holding their positions permanently. Dahrendorf notes that governments are like a medium through which decisions made by other groups pass rather than being the source of the decisions. Some pressure groups manage, usually when their political party is in power, to have their interests recognized, while others must await a change in government to realize their aims.

A degree of social order or equilibrium also develops when, after successive trials of strength, two contending groups tacitly settle on a particular accommodation, even though it compromises their ideal goals (Coser, 1956: 133–137). The standoff in Canadian cities between those advocating different legal approaches to the control of prostitution—the police, the citizens, and the women themselves—is a current example.

The Interactionist Perspective

The essentials of the interactionist perspective as they bear on society were explained in the "Interaction as Society" section of Chapter 4. There it was stated that social interaction is the basis of society; society roots in the human interchanges that go into negotiating, constructing reality, shaping working agreements, and developing interpersonal relationships. Little more will be said here about this perspective, except to note that it is presumed by the preceding three perspectives.

This becomes clear from an examination of Parsons' (1937) early works, Simmel's (1955) essay on conflict, Durkheim's writings (Stone and Farberman, 1967), and Marx and Engels' collaboration (Batiuk and Sacks, 1981). Although these thinkers, and others associated with the first three perspectives, espoused a microsociological approach to the study of society, they all, including Durkheim, who was intent on distinguishing sociology from psychology, recognized that society originates, develops, and changes through the social interaction of its members.

TYPES OF SOCIETIES

Through the years, four typologies of societies have come to the forefront. The four types are Durkheim's societies based on mechanical and organic solidarity, Tönnies' *Gemeinschaft* and *Gesellschaft,* Becker's sacred and secular societies, and anthropology's three preindustrial types (hunting and gathering, horticultural, and agricultural). All are ideal types. Tönnies' Gemeinschaft and Gesellschaft were explained in Chapter 8. The remaining three are covered in this section.

Mechanical and Organic

Mechanical solidarity develops when the average members of a society share similar states of consciousness (Durkheim, 1933: 129–132). The shared states of consciousness in question are beliefs and sentiments, referred to collectively by Durkheim as the *collective conscience.* In mechanical solidarity societies, individual members tend to resemble each other psychologically. Durkheim saw this form of solidarity as analogous to the physicist's mechanics: universal forces act on bodies that are essentially alike and that, together, comprise a mass. People in mechanical solidarity societies resemble these bodies to the extent that they respond as a mass to universal social forces. Durkheim demonstrated how the social force of criminal or "repressive" law operates, when violated, to offend the collective conscience and spawn a popular emotional reaction in the form of punishment or some other negative sanction.

A society characterized by *organic solidarity* has a complex division of labor. Its component roles and their interrelationships are analogous to the organs and their interrelationships in the body of animals; the analogy explains the term "organic solidarity." Because members enact different roles in such societies, they develop individual personalities. Individuality is also fostered by the relative absence of a dominating collective conscience, which gives people room to improvise their everyday behavior. Legal forms such as the contract, commercial law, constitutional law, and administrative law are supreme in organic societies, although repressive law is by no means absent. Canadian society is welded together by organic solidarity, while nearly all Inuit bands are unified by mechanical solidarity.

Sacred symbols are indispensable to the unity of the nation-state.

Sacred and Secular

Howard P. Becker (1957) developed Durkheim's ideal typical concepts of *sacred* and *secular.* He defined as "sacred" those objects, practices, places, ideas, communities, and societies that are traditional, venerable, and inviolate. He used the term "sacred" in the broadest sense to refer to things religious and also nonreligious. Becker contrasted the sacred with "secular" objects, practices, and places. The secular objects and practices have the opposite qualities of being nontraditional, new, corruptible, and destructive. They, too, may be religious or nonreligious.

Becker's conceptualization of the *sacred society* stresses the traditional and venerable qualities of the values, beliefs, and sentiments comprising its collective conscience. These elements, along with the abstract structural relationships of the society, are held to be unchangeable, absolute, and natural. In some societies, they may be regarded as God-given. Sacred symbols, practices, beliefs, relationships, and so forth, because they appear as part of the natural order, are seldom, if ever, questioned. Though not national societies, nearly all small, isolated rural communities in North America are sacred. Clearly, many mechanically solidary societies are also sacred societies and vice versa.

Similarly, many secular societies are also organically solidary societies. Change and innovation are commonplace, with a corresponding lack of respect for tradition. Rational action (pursuing ends by the most efficient means) prevails here, while traditional action (action habituated by long practice) is dominant in sacred societies (Weber, 1947: 115). The United States and Canada are secular societies.

Preindustrial Types

There are several types of preindustrial societies. They are referred to here as hunting and gathering societies, horticultural and pastoral societies, and agricultural societies. Together

Modern society contains many secular places and practices.

these societies constitute the first three stages of a four-stage sequence of societal evolution. The sequence culminates in the modern industrial society, exemplified in this book by Canada and the United States. Societies in the first three stages can be characterized as sacred, *Gemeinschaft,* and mechanically solidary.

Hunting and Gathering Societies Overall, the social and institutional structures of hunting and gathering groups are the simplest of human societies. These groups are chiefly subsistence units, small in size, generally nomadic, and devoid of formal control institutions such as police, courts, and legislatures. They have comparatively little differentiation of wealth and prestige. What differentiation there is occurs along sex and kin lines. Hunting and gathering peoples are forced to move, usually seasonally, because the animals they hunt have migrated or the local edible plants they gather have been consumed.

Horticultural and Pastoral Societies Drought encouraged humankind to experiment with the controlled breeding of animals and with the harvesting of plants. With breeding and harvesting, societies had food; the individuals could rely on themselves to breed animals and harvest food. Horticultural societies came into being along with the harvesting of food. With their hoes and cultivation, the societies sustained a sedentary, agrarian way of life. Subsistence farmers formed the smallest and most simply structured horticultural societies. Surplus horticulturists developed larger, more densely populated collectives, requiring more sophisticated political structures. The surplus horticulturists were also oriented to internal and sometimes external markets and to the exchange of goods and services.

The pastoral societies are centered on the domestication and breeding of animals such as sheep, goats, cattle, reindeer, and horses. As the term "pastoral" implies, pastures on which the cattle and other animals can graze must be found. The scarcity of good pastureland forces some pastoral societies to become nomadic; animals must be moved from pasture to pasture at times during a year. Other pastoral societies, whose main economic activity is horticultural, send their herds to distant pastures for the summer; herders manage the livestock at these distant places. There are also sedentary pastoralists who settle in a more or less permanent village. Here, too, the breeding and rearing of animals is the principal economic undertaking.

Agricultural Societies Agricultural groups fall still further along the scale of societal evolution. The important differences between them and horticultural societies are found in the spheres of technology and social structure. The agriculturalists developed the plow and elaborate irrigation systems. Concurrently, men returned to the fields and to monogamous families. Multiple wives were now an economic liability, since they were no longer needed to work the crops. In general, the size of the family shrank. Agricultural production had become efficient enough by this time to supply nearby towns and cities and even foreign markets. The advent of agricultural societies spelled the dawn of civilization.

CULTURE AND INSTITUTION

We may now turn to a second goal of this chapter, namely to interrelate the concepts of *culture* and *institution.* We noted earlier that a sociologist's interest in a culture is focused on certain parts and subsystems of that culture, notably social institutions and their social structures. In this vein, we have been discussing culture in piecemeal fashion, beginning with Chapter 4;

Nonverbal Communication in Our Culture

Bob leaves his apartment at 8:15 A.M. and stops at the corner drugstore for breakfast. Before he can speak; the counterman says, "The usual?" Bob nods yes. While he savors his Danish, a fat man pushes onto the adjoining stool and overflows into his space. Bob scowls, and the man pulls himself in as much as he can. Bob has sent two messages without speaking a syllable.

Henry has an appointment to meet Arthur at 11:00 A.M.; he arrives at 11:30. Their conversation is friendly, but Arthur retains a lingering hostility. Henry has unconsciously communicated that he doesn't think the appointment is very important or that Arthur is a person who needs to be treated with respect.

George is talking to Charley's wife at a party. Their conversation is entirely trivial, yet Charley glares at them suspiciously. Their physical proximity and the movements of their eyes reveal that they are powerfully attracted to each other.

José Ybarra and Sir Edmund Jones are at the same party, and it is important for them to establish a cordial relationship for business reasons. Each is trying to be warm and friendly, yet they will part with mutual distrust, and their business transaction will probably fall through. José, in Latin fashion, moves closer and closer to Sir Edmund as they speak, and this movement is being miscommunicated as pushiness to Sir Edmund, who keeps backing away from this intimacy, which in turn is being miscommunicated to José as coldness. The silent languages of Latin and English cultures are more difficult to learn than their spoken languages.

In each of these cases, we see the subtle power of nonverbal communication. The only language used throughout most of the history of humanity (in evolutionary terms, vocal communication is relatively recent), it is the first form of communication you learn. You use this preverbal language, consciously and unconsciously, every day to tell other people how you feel about yourself and them. This language includes your posture, gestures, facial expressions, costume, the way you walk, even your treatment of time and space and material things. All people communicate on several different levels at the same time but are usually aware of only the verbal dialogue and don't realize that they respond to nonverbal messages. But when a person says one thing and really believes something else, the discrepancy between the two can usually be sensed. Nonverbal communication systems are much less subject to the conscious deception that often occurs in verbal systems. When we find ourselves thinking, "I don't know what it is about him, but he doesn't seem sincere" it's usually this lack of congruity between a person's words and his behavior that makes us anxious and uncomfortable.

SOURCE: Edward T. Hall and Mildred R. Hall. *Playboy,* pp. 139–140, 204, 206, June 1971.

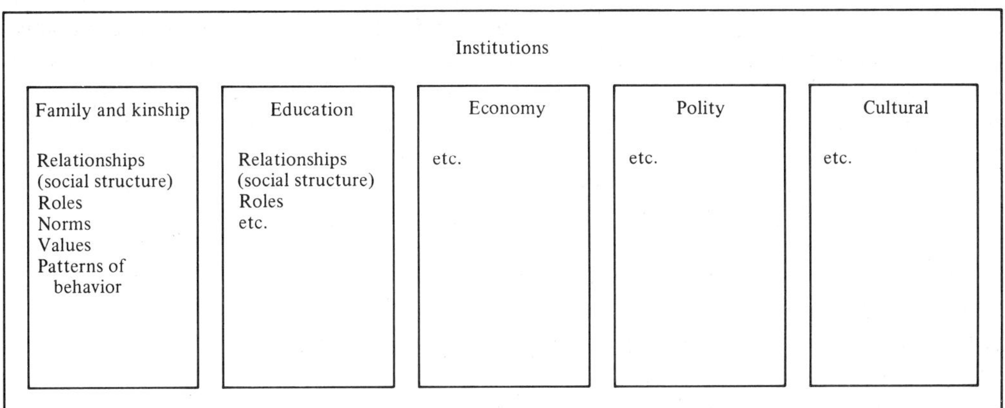

Figure 9.1 The Relationship of Culture and Institution in Sociology

there will be numerous references to culture in chapters and sections which follow. We have already examined attributes of American and Canadian culture such as language, norms, patterns of behavior, goals, roles, relationships, and outlooks. With the partial exception of language, this list falls within the scope of one or more institutions in a society.

How, then, are culture and institution related? A social institution, which is composed of abstract relationships (i.e., social structure), patterns of behavior, roles, norms, and values, is a more inclusive idea than that of social structure. Still, a social institution is only a segment of a society's overall culture, because that culture is made up of all the society's institutions. In sociological usage of the term "culture," there are but a few referents made to phenomena falling outside the scope of the concept of social institution. One such referent is the exchanges among strangers in noninstitutionalized interstices of life (e.g., asking directions, asking for a match). These exchanges are based on language.

Figure 9.1 portrays the theoretical relationship of culture and institutions. Cultural institutions—art, science, religion, leisure—are but segments of a society's total culture. The ideas of folk culture, popular culture, and high culture are derived from an industrial society's institutions of art and leisure. In short, institutions are *subsystems* of the main cultural system. Institutions are discussed in detail in Part Four.

But institutions are not the only cultural subsystems studied by sociologists. There are systems of this sort that span certain social institutions while still constituting only part of the total culture. These include subcultures (see Chapter 8) and the spheres of leisure and art known as *folk culture, popular culture,* and *high culture.* We now turn to those last three to illustrate how certain cultural subsystems can span two or more institutions.

Folk Culture

Folk culture is a traditional cultural subsystem. It is shared and experienced directly through the senses (sight, sound); it is also transmitted through one or more of the senses (a fiddler plays, a painter paints).[6] Folk culture is simple in form, when contrasted with popular culture and high culture. This becomes evident by comparing a folk song with an operatic aria. In general, the creator of an item of folk culture is unknown, which also contrasts with the known and often highly publicized creators of nearly all

[6] The characteristics of folk, popular, and high cultures presented in this section are taken from Lewis (1978: 16–17), Truzzi (1978: 283–284), and Stebbins (1984: 136–137).

Folk culture is still a vibrant part of Canadian and American societies.

popular culture and high culture. Moreover, no one owns the items of folk culture, which means they are available at no cost to consumers. Change in folk culture is similar to change in any tradition; it is a slow, informal process of diffusion of the new cultural item (a song, dance, symbol) through the folk society. To the extent that the items of folk culture are part of the everyday life of the folk society, a folk culture can be said to span all the institutions of that society.

Folk culture shows up in preindustrial societies of the sort just described and also in isolated enclaves of societies such as our own. The totem poles of the Northwest Coast Indians are folk culture. Another example of folk culture which still can be seen in North America is the indigenous instrumental and vocal music of the Appalachian region. Step dancing in Newfoundland outports is another example. The commercial production of these folk arts is best classified as a kind of popular culture.

Folk leisure patterns are nowhere to be found in the mainstream of North American life. Rather, one must turn to certain marginal groups such as the Hutterites for examples:

> Commercial amusements such as movies, shows, concerts, and sporting events are *verboten* in all of the *Laut* (the three main Hutterite groups). Even within the *Bruderhof* (Hutterite colony) entertainment—as the term is commonly used—has a limited connotation. Parties, games for young people, musical instruments, radios, record players, home films, television—such things are considered too worldly. Hutterites read to a fair extent, but their reading is confined largely to daily newspapers, farm journals, religious works, and German Mennonite literature.
>
> The chief form of recreation for Hutterites everywhere is visiting, and in this respect they are like the Amish. Within the *Bruderhof,* visiting is more or less continual, members thinking nothing of dropping in at all hours. Hutterites are ready conversationalists, and there is usually a good deal of joking, teasing, and banter. Visiting also takes the form of journeying to other colonies, and since some of the trips are overnight, they represent highlights in the Hutterian social calendar. (Kephart, 1976: 255)

Popular Culture

Turning to the mainstream of American and Canadian art and leisure, we mostly see and hear *popular culture.* Popular culture is called *mass culture* when transmitted via the mass media.[7] Popular culture has wide appeal, although its attraction is largely confined to a particular social class or other grouping in the society. It is defined as a cultural subsystem of products shared by a large number of people (a

[7]Lewis (1978: 15) notes that "mass" is a pejorative reference to the tastes of the masses. Sociologists prefer the term "popular culture" because of its neutrality.

What form of culture do you see in this scene?

mass) who are in the same social class or other group or category.[8]

In addition to what has already been said about popular culture, it is important to note that the creators of popular culture believe their works should be patented or in some way restricted in ownership. The same may be said of the creators of high culture. Popular culture contrasts with elite culture inasmuch as the former is consumer-oriented whereas the latter is creator-oriented. For example, the producers of a rock tune are primarily concerned about whether the tune will become a hit (sell well). The author of a literary novel, however, is primarily concerned about writing a novel with artistic merit, a quality of the work that may discourage sales.

Popular culture differs from high culture in two other ways. Popular culture can be made widely available at moderate cost; high culture is scarce (by comparison) and expensive. Compare the availability and cost of television films at home versus the availability and cost of downtown live-theater productions (if you live in the suburbs). Popular culture and high culture are found in our institutions of art, leisure, family, and economy.

Examples of popular culture in North America are legion. Dance, song, and instrumental music are enjoyed by almost everyone. Novels, short stories, comics, and drama (live, televised, filmed) are much a part of the culture. Amusements (e.g., magic, comedy, ventriloquism, juggling, clowning) and the visual arts (paintings, posters, street signs) also have a wide appeal. Alberoni (1966) notes that the United States is the international epicenter of popular culture. Many countries are consumers of this American export; the music and literature of America are popular in Canada, Great Britain, and West Germany. Other nations are only moderate consumers—for instance, Spain and Italy—and others such as the Soviet Union are nonconsumers.

The dearth of indigenous culture in Canada's arts and leisure institutions is seen as a major problem. The following indicates some of what the United States has and Canada lacks in the way of their own popular cultures:

> There is, for example, no national cinematic industry producing for popular consumption. Even such a Canadian-controlled medium as the Canadian Broadcasting Corporation . . . has not produced from Canadian history fictionalized or actual folk heroes who have caught the public imagination. Canadian poetry and fiction are neither widely known nor widely read in Canada, probably because they are produced by and for a relatively small group of university-associated writers. (Porter, 1979: 95)

Peers (1970) writes that 75 percent of all magazine sales in Canada are issues printed in the United States. Figure 9.2 shows the current

[8]This definition is abstracted from the definitions of Gans (1974: 10), Lewis (1978: 18), and Kando (1980: 14).

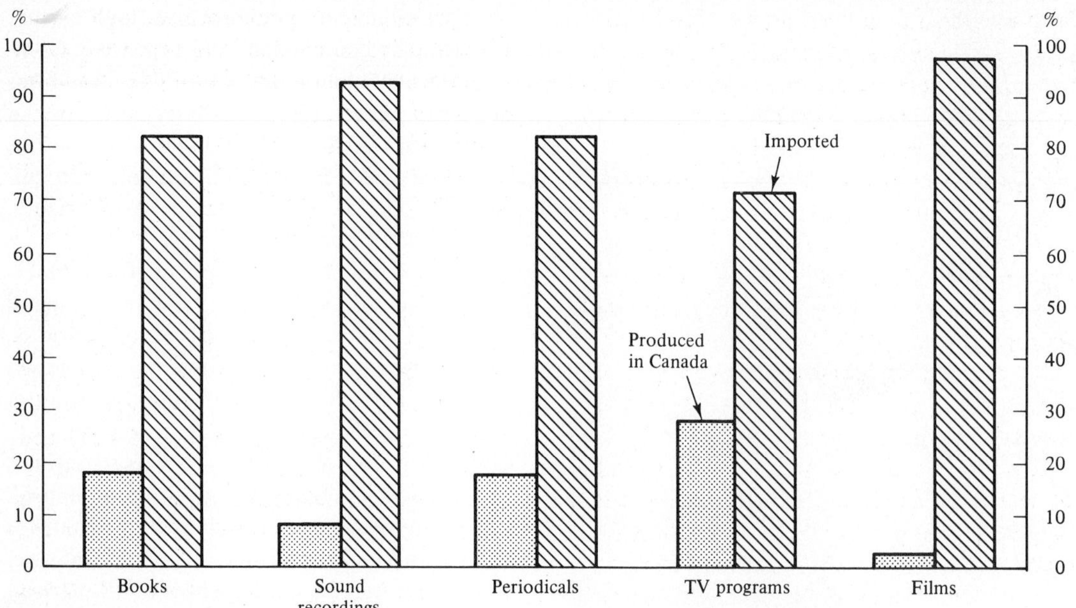

Figure 9.2 Cultural Goods in Canada. (*Source: Canadian Statistical Review* 55 (October 1980): X, Cat. No. 11003E. Ottawa: Statistics Canada.)

heavy reliance in Canada on imported sources of popular culture from all countries.[9] Book imports in the United States provide an illustrative contrast: in 1979, the United States imported 5,458 books (excluding translations), while in the same year it printed 45,182 new books or new editions of old books (U.S. Bureau of the Census, 1980: 595–596).

High Culture

Gans (1974: 75–76) defines *high culture* as a collection of those products consumed by a special public, or category of consumers; a public that is dominated by creators and critics. The creators and critics set the standards for the users, or consumers. High culture is the taxonomic home of "serious" writers, painters, composers, musicians, dramatists, and thespians. These professionals create as much for each other (who therefore constitute part of the consumer group) as they do for a sophisticated public.

The differences in rates of consumption in Canada of Canadian high culture and imported high culture are unknown. Some small proportion of the books, films, and sound recordings mentioned in Figure 9.2 are undoubtedly high culture rather than popular culture. It is Porter's (1979: 98) impression that "Canadians are overwhelmingly and enthusiastically consumers of United States culture, both popular and high." Nor does there appear to be any information on how reliant the United States is on imported high culture. One suspects that it imports more high culture than popular culture, given the historical dominance of Europe in this realm.

CONFLICT AND CONSENSUS

It has been stated at various points in Part Three that social organization and culture are static, not processes. Social organization and culture, at the macro level, give you a picture of society at any moment in history. You can see

[9]Data gathered two years later show that, at least for books and periodicals, the ratio of imported to domestic culture remains more or less the same (Statistics Canada, 1984a; 1984b).

how social life is at any particular time. In sociology and other social sciences, a picture of society frozen in time has spawned two major perspectives which stand in partial opposition to each other—the conflict perspective and the functionalist perspective. Once the culture and social organization of a society have been recognized and understood, the next logical scientific step is to determine what parts of culture and social organization *change* and why and what parts *persist* and why.

Questions about persistence of culture and social organization have been most frequently considered by sociologists who work with the consensus model of functionalism. Sociologists who study conflict have raised questions about changes in culture and social organization. (Symbolic interactionists study change, too, but chiefly at the micro level.) Both the functionalists and the conflict theorists have been accused of having political motives, to preserve the status quo in the case of the functionalists and to induce radical change in the status quo in the case of the conflict ideologists (though not the sociological conflict theorists; see Chapter 2). Neither set is anarchist, however; both look on society as a social order. Functionalists contend that social order is the outcome of cooperation, alliance, and consensus within a self-maintaining system (i.e., society). Conflict theorists contend that social order comes about when changes that redistribute power occur (perhaps only temporarily) and give expression to other legitimate interests in society.

In several of the remaining chapters in this book, you will have the opportunity, as you did in this chapter, to view the macro level of society from both the consensus perspective and the conflict perspective.

OUTLINE AND SUMMARY

I. Introduction
The concept of society is one of sociology's broadest and most abstract concepts. Sociologists' interest in culture stems from their interest in certain parts and subsystems of culture, notably the institutions and social structures of a society and its internal communities.

II. The Concept of Society
Society defined: a relatively independent or self-sufficient population characterized by internal organization, territoriality, cultural distinctiveness, and sexual recruitment.
   A. Study and Understanding
   The concept of society figured prominently in the rise of sociology as a separate social science in the late nineteenth century. Its study is what demarcates the discipline of sociology from psychology and economics. Society itself is known through or manifested in the constraints it imposes on its members.
   B. Institutions
   Six defining criteria of institution are: (1) problems of collective living, (2) patterns of behavior, (3) abstract relationships, (4) roles, (5) values, (6) history.

III. Society as a Group
A society is the largest and most comprehensive of all its constituent groups. Despite its size, a society meets the five criteria for distinguishing groups: interaction, goals, norms, roles, and likes and dislikes. In regard to the criteria, societies are different from smaller groups.

IV. Theoretical Perspectives
Four theoretical perspectives for the study of society have served as guidelines for many years. These are *social system, economic struggle, general conflict,* and *symbolic interaction.*
   A. The Social System
   The concept of society as a social system replaced the early study of society as an entity in itself. Levy defined society as a system of action in operation. He listed ten functional requisites.
      1. Functional Requisites
      A *functional requisite* is a generalized condition necessary for the maintenance of society.
      2. Canadian and American Systems
      A comparison of Canadian and

American social systems is a holistic undertaking. One difference between the American social system and the Canadian social system lies in the way the two countries recruit technical and professional personnel to fill key work roles and organize capital. Americans are more strongly identified with their social system than Canadians.

B. The Economic Perspective
The functionalists have been charged with political conservatism and an overwhelming interest in the consensus side of social order. Functionalists have attempted to meet this charge by incorporating into their theories notions such as dynamic equilibrium. Among the adversaries in this debate are those who work within the economic perspective, the origins of which are traced to Karl Marx and Friedrich Engels.

1. Marx and Capitalism
Marx's thought rests on the assumption that the most basic human needs are material and that society is essentially the outcome of struggles between the component groups for the satisfaction of these needs. Economic conflict occurs between two emerging social classes, the capitalists and the proletariat. According to Karl Marx, the proletariat will come out on top.

2. Radical Sociology
Radical sociology is primarily an application of the earlier works of Marx and Engels. Radical sociology is concerned with economic conflict. In spite of conflict, societies will form and survive.

C. The Conflict Perspective
The economic perspective is part of the more inclusive social science perspective known as *conflict theory.* In any complex society, there are groups competing for an endless list of values. But their conflict eventually stabilizes at a level permitting the society to persist.

D. The Interactionist Perspective
The *interactionist perspective* is based on the thinking and viewpoints of the symbolic interactionists. Social interaction as the basis for society is presumed by the social system perspective, the economic perspective, and the conflict perspective. Society develops and changes through the social interaction of its members.

V. Types of Societies
Four types of societies are Durkheim's societies based on mechanical and organic solidarity. Tönnies' *Gemeinschaft* and *Gesellschaft,* Becker's sacred and secular societies, and anthropology's three preindustrial types (hunting and gathering, horticultural and pastoral, agricultural).

A. Mechanical and Organic
Mechanical solidarity develops when the average members of a society share similar states of consciousness. Organic solidarity emerges from a complex division of labor.

B. Sacred and Secular
A *sacred society* stresses the traditional venerable and inviolable qualities of the values, beliefs, and sentiments comprising its collective conscience. In secular societies, changes and innovation are commonplace, with a corresponding lack of respect for tradition.

C. Preindustrial Types
Hunting and gathering societies are the simplest of human societies, small in size and generally nomadic. The *horticultural and pastoral* societies center on either the cultivation of crops or the management of domesticated animals. *Agricultural* societies are founded on a more complex technology and social structure than the first two types.

VI. Culture and Institutions
The sociologist's interest in a culture is focused on parts and subsystems of that culture, notably social institutions and their social structures.

A. Folk Culture
Folk culture is a traditional cultural subsystem shared through the senses (sight, sound, hearing) and directly transmitted through one or more of the senses. It is found in preindustrial soci-

eties and in isolated enclaves of industrial societies.

B. Popular Culture
Popular culture is a cultural subsystem of products shared by a large number of people (masses) who are in the same social class or other category or group. The products appeal to a particular class or other grouping in society.

C. High Culture
High culture is a collection of those products consumed by a special public, a public that is dominated by creators and critics.

FOR FURTHER READING AND STUDY

Auletta, I. 1982. *The underclass.* New York: Random House. Auletta, a journalist, talked for two and a half years with American long-term welfare recipients, drug addicts, high school dropouts, and street criminals. He concluded that the conservative and liberal-radical approaches alike are too abstract to deal with the day-to-day problems of these people.

Gans, J. M., Glazer, N., Gusfield, J. R., and Jencks, C., eds. 1979. *On the making of Americans: Essays in honor of David Reisman.* Philadelphia: University of Pennsylvania Press. A collection of original essays on what is American about Americans and on the nature of present-day American institutions and subcultures.

Grayson, J. P., ed. 1980. *Class, state, ideology, and change: Marxist perspectives in Canada.* Toronto: Holt, Rinehart & Winston of Canada. A collection of journal articles and original papers on the state and social classes and on ideology and social change written from the radical perspective.

Hiller, H. H. 1976. *Canadian society.* Scarborough, Ontario: Prentice-Hall of Canada. An examination of Canadian society from several perspectives: the organismic model, stratification and internal power model, external power and domination model, ethnic group conflict model, comparative model, and identity model.

Martorella, R. 1982. *The sociology of opera.* New York: Praeger. This study, the first of its kind, centers on the performers (singers, composers, conductors) in the opera of today. The study also goes into the organization of the performing opera and into the market for its performances. A fine example of the sociology of high culture.

KEY WORDS

agricultural society A society which grows and harvests plants with the use of plow and irrigation systems.

capitalist An entrepreneur who owns the means of production; one of the bourgeoisie.

culture A society's shared language, beliefs, goals, and experiences that coalesce into a unique pattern; a society's way of life.

folk culture A cultural subsystem experienced directly through the senses (sight, hearing).

functional requisite A generalized condition necessary for the maintenance of the unit.

high culture The products consumed by a special public dominated by creators and critics; it is the culture of writers, painters, composers, musicians, dramatists, and thespians.

horticultural society A preindustrial society which subsists on its members' harvesting of plants and breeding of animals.

hunting and gathering society A preindustrial society which subsists on the food its members hunt and gather.

institution A relatively stable set of abstract relationships (social structure), patterns of behavior, roles, mores, and values that emerge as solutions to the problems of collective living.

mechanical solidarity Social cohesion in a society made up of members who share similar states of consciousness; the states of consciousness are beliefs and sentiments.

pastoral society A society centered on the domestication and breeding of animals such as sheep, goats, cattle, reindeer, and horses.

popular culture Mass culture transmitted indirectly by media and technology; it constitutes a culture of a social class or other large category.

proletariat Workers; those who labor for capitalists.

radical sociology A new and provocative kind of sociology; an application of the earlier works of Marx and Engels.

social organization The stable interrelationships of the society's groups, institutions, and networks of social relationships.

four

INSTITUTIONS

Institutions are inherently conservative. This conservativeness gives them a stable and static quality, which is also the quality that makes them the foundation for societies the world over. But despite the indispensability of institutions to society, they are subject to attack. Some people realize that they can ignore or even strive to change certain institutionalized ways. They realize that the values, norms, beliefs, and patterns of behavior constituting an institution are arbitrary; objectively, the institution could be made up of different values, norms, beliefs, and patterns. Indeed, the institution in other societies *is* different to some extent.

An attack on an institution may occur through clandestine, even deviant, actions. Or it may take the form of an open campaign against the status quo. When large numbers of people engage in clandestine actions or join a campaign against a particular institution, then a liberal attack can be said to have been mounted against it.

The struggle between liberal and conservative forces at the institutional level is characteristic of modern societies. Given the variety in human interest, temperament, and experience, it is safe to predict that this struggle will always exist. Each chapter in Part Four conveys some sense of this opposition. Our family, work, leisure, education, economic, political, and religious institutions are all under fire for their deficiencies. Needless to say, these institutions also have their defenders who stand firm in the fray and even counterattack.

chapter 10

Family

CHAPTER OUTLINE

INTRODUCTION

The cultural, historical, and even zoological universality of the family is beyond dispute:

> The family is certainly just as old as human culture. One could even, with some certainty, maintain that family and marriage are older than human culture, because it seems definitely to be the case that man has inherited family and marriage from several higher animal species. (König, 1974: 20)

König goes on to point out that some nonhuman species live together as opposite-sex couples, whereas others live together in families. Among the latter are parental families, as when both parents participate in rearing the offspring (the gibbon is an example). Other animal families are either maternal or paternal. In such families, the mother (e.g., bears) or the father (e.g., certain species of fish) does the rearing.

A valid definition of the universal family—a definition of the "family" as this term is used in every society on earth—is still unavailable. Why? Because sociologists and anthropologists still disagree over the essential nature of the family. We do know, however, that every family is composed of individuals related to each other by blood, marriage, or adoption. We know that these people constitute a small group, as this concept is defined in Chapter 6. As members of a group, the individuals in a family interact with one another through special roles, such as mother, brother, aunt, grandfather, and cousin. Like other small groups, families create and maintain a common culture that is at least partly centered on child rearing. It is unclear whether these attributes of the human family are essential attributes and, if they are, whether they, possibly along with other attributes, should be included in a definition of *family*.

Moreover, families across the world may be conceived of as both institutions and groups. The chief emphasis in this chapter is on the family as an institution. Nonetheless, we should never lose sight of the fact that all institutions guide the behavior of the individuals and groups of individuals embodying them. The mores, values, and beliefs comprised by the institution of the family are manifested in the patterned actions and interactions of individual members of the family as they go about their daily, family-related routines.

We take up the family institution in a subsequent section. As background for this inquiry, we turn next to the most common form of Canadian family: *the nuclear family*. This leads to the section on institutions and from there to a consideration of the *careers*, or pursuits, that Canadians have in the family segment of their lives. Then the career turning points of divorce, remarriage, and widowhood are examined. This section is followed by a discussion of certain alternatives to the family institution as we know it today. Three theoretical frameworks are then summarized. The chapter concludes with a brief look into the future of the family in North America.

THE NUCLEAR FAMILY

Let us return to König's comparison of animal families with human families. Sociological definitions of the family suggest that significant differences exist between the animal family and the human family. What is being referred to here is the "nuclear family," labeled as such because sociologists believe it is irreducible in size and is the building block for all larger or extended family units (Nimkoff, 1965: 5). It is a *nucleus*, or the center from which the extended family arises. In commonsense terms, the nuclear family is a group consisting of one or both parents and dependent offspring. A sociological definition of the *nuclear family* suggests that it is a far more complex group than common sense would have us believe:

> The family is a group of persons united by ties of marriage, blood, or adoption; constituting a

---

SOCIOLOGY OR COMMON SENSE

What do you think?

Which of the following statements do you agree with? Which statements do you disagree with? Make a note of your answers. Check your answers when you have completed your study of this chapter. Are your answers to the statements the same as those a sociologist would give?

1. Some animals live together as opposite-sex couples; others live together as families.
2. North American adults strongly oppose premarital sexual intercourse.
3. The marriage rate in North America is declining.
4. The divorce rate in North America is declining.
5. Remarriages are harmful to the children in reconstituted families.

The family organizes economic survival in ways such as by supplying food.

> single household; interacting and communicating with each other in their respective social roles of husband and wife, mother and father, son and daughter, brother and sister; and creating and maintaining a common culture. (Burgess et al., 1971: 7)

One of the main functions of the nuclear family is primary socialization.

Missing from animal families are certain social processes and structures that are found in all human families (König, 1974: 21). For example, the definition of nuclear family just set forth implies there are levels of kin relationships surrounding it like concentric rings. Human beings also forbid choice of a mate in certain parts of this extended kin structure, although the parts restricted vary from culture to culture. (Some nonhuman animals restrict intrafamilial mating, too.) Finally, only *Homo sapiens* develops an extensive culture, which is learned through socialization and which helps the individual to develop a socially acceptable personality.

In view of the universality of the family, it should be stressed that our definition of the nuclear family holds best for families of advanced industrial nations—Canada, for example. Coresidence or living in a single household, for instance, is absent in the Nayar family, the Israeli kibbutz, and the mother-centered family of Jamaica. Some scholars also question whether the nuclear family is always the basic building block for more complex familial structures (Smith, 1968: 303). They contend that the present state of family theory allows us to say only that some form of child-rearing, kinship-based group is universal.

THE FAMILY INSTITUTION

There is no disagreement, however, on the proposition that the family is one of society's fundamental institutions. Application of the defining criteria set out in the preceding chapter is proof enough of this assertion. The six criteria are that (1) institutions form around major problems of collective living, (2) institutions consist of patterns of behavior and (3) abstract relationships, (4) institutions are composed of roles and their associated norms, (5) institutions are made up of values, and (6) institutions have a distinctive history.

First, the family, like other institutions, forms around complex, socially significant problems. Solving the problems is critical to collective living. George Murdock (1949: 4–11) lists four essential functions served by the nuclear family; the functions serve as solutions to four major problems of society. He says the nuclear family, usually in conjunction with other institutions, (1) regulates sexual relations, (2) accounts for economic survival, (3) controls reproduction, and (4) socializes children. Of the four, some thinkers regard socialization as the most central and the most distinctive function of the family (e.g., König, 1974: 47; Reiss, 1965: 449). In other words, the family helps solve the problem of regulating sexual expression, surviving economically, reproducing new members of the society, and socializing the new members.

Second, there are distinctive patterns of behavior characteristic of the family institution. In Canada, for example, many families go to church on Sunday, rise and retire together at fixed times in keeping with school and work schedules, and engage in recurrent forms of recreation such as watching television during the evening and going on camping trips on weekends.

Third, the family interacts along the lines of a set of unique relationships. For example, there is a special relationship between a husband and a wife and between a brother and a sister. There is a parent-child relationship, which begins with the child's infancy and continues through his or her adolescence. There are also parent-teacher, parent-pediatrician, and parent-neighbor relationships. Individuals have numerous relationships with many others in the society.

Fourth, key family roles exist, each with its own set of norms. Although there is considerable change in the matter of gender roles at present (see Chapter 19), traditionally husbands served as breadwinners while wives managed the household. Traditionally, the husband-father engaged in task, or instrumental, activities, while the wife-mother concerned herself with socioemotional, or expressive, matters (Parsons and Bales, 1955).

Fifth, the family institution has its own values, which, these days, are often in conflict with society at large. Kirkpatrick (1963: 90–95) discerned ten major value dilemmas in the American family:

1. Freedom in family experience versus order and efficiency.
2. Work achievement versus the love-reproduction function.
3. Personal self-expression versus devoted child-rearing.
4. Flexible, general training versus rigid, specific training.
5. High aspiration level for children versus realistic expectations.
6. Family loyalty versus community loyalty.
7. Extensive, casual association versus restricted, intensive association.
8. Love experience versus love safety.
9. Free sex expression versus sex restraint.
10. Early marriage versus mature, discriminating mate selection.

Are these same value dilemmas found in the Canadian family? The answer to this question is that presently we have no idea. Research is still lacking on the subject. Ishwaran (1976: 4–7) warns against assuming an affirmative answer. Larson (1976: 24–25) takes the opposite position, arguing that value similarity between Americans and Canadians is far greater than value difference.

Sixth, there have been some important historical changes in the North American and Western European family. Over the years, for instance, American, Canadian, and European families have come to share some of their central functions, including socialization, with entities such as the school, the peer group, and, to a lesser extent, the church. Family size, as measured by fertility rates, has been declining steadily for several decades (see Chapter 22), and more and more women, many of whom are also mothers, are joining the paid labor force (see Chapter 12). The number of mothers who are strictly homemakers continues to dwindle.[1]

THE FAMILY CAREER

Robert Rapoport and Rhona Rapoport (1975), in their influential study of family, work, and leisure in an English industrial town, note that a career exists in each of these spheres. A full discussion of the idea of career must wait until Chapter 12. There career is defined as the history of stages, turning points, and contingencies one passes through during one's continuous and enduring enactment of a role. In sociological terms, one can have careers in areas of life outside work. The Rapoports' analysis, like the one here, is based on the *family life cycle,* which is described as unfolding in four imprecisely bounded phases: (1) adolescence, (2) young adulthood, (3) establishment, and (4) later years

[1]For a detailed presentation of the histories and demographic profiles of American, Canadian, and western European families, see works by Adams (1980: Chapter 4), Nett (1976), and Leslie and Korman (1985: Chapter 6).

(Rapoport and Rapoport, 1975: Chapters 2–5).[2] In other words, we have careers in our familial roles. The stages of these careers are the phases of the family life cycle.

Adolescent Phase

The adolescent phase of the family career runs from birth to somewhere between ages sixteen and eighteen. (Primary socialization is a central process throughout this period [see Chapter 5]). Toward the end of this phase North American teenagers, at least initially, usually come to grips with the stressful practice of dating and the accompanying sentiment of romantic love. A *date* is an occasion of social activity arranged in advance with a member of the opposite sex.

Dating performs five functions: (1) recreation, (2) socialization into heterosexual relations, (3) provision of age needs (e.g., feeling important, sexuality), (4) placement in the local status system, and (5) selection of a marital partner (Adams, 1980: 207–208). Dating begins serving these functions when teenagers begin dating. Evidence in the United States indicates that the age at which most respondents start dating has dropped slightly from between fourteen and fifteen in the 1950s to between thirteen and fourteen in the 1970s (Lowrie, 1956; Dickinson, 1975). In Canada, regular dating commences around age fourteen to fifteen (Mann, 1968; Wakil, 1973), with the first date likely to be earlier and hence in accord with American practice.

Courtship grows from steady dating. With day-to-day dating, one or both of the partners may become serious about the other and wish to deepen the emergent relationship (Waller, 1937). *Courtship* is an intimate relationship between a male and a female, which may become serious enough to lead to engagement and subsequent marriage.

A number of factors affect the beginning of this sequence. One is the *incest taboo.* This taboo, which, depending on the society, is embedded in law or custom or both, prohibits sexual intercourse between closely related individuals in a kinship group. Another is *residential propinquity,* or the geographic closeness of the partner. The probability of initiating a relationship with someone of the opposite sex, whether or not the outcome is marriage, is closely associated with the probability of the pair meeting for the first time. For this to happen, they must be in close proximity (Katz and Hill, 1958). Still another factor is summed up in the term "homogamy." *Homogamy* is the tendency to date people of the same race, religion, and social class (Kerckhoff and Davis, 1962; Moon, 1980: 30). Dating in North America these days always carries with it the possibility of *premarital sexual* activity. American family sociologist Ira L. Reiss (1976: 164–165) has proposed a theory of premarital sexual permissiveness, which Charles Hobart (1980: 41) believes holds for the Canadian scene as well. Reiss says there are two major causes of sexual permissiveness. First, a youth's independence from adult institutions encourages such permissiveness. A young person gains independence, for example, by falling in love, interacting with peers, and adopting a liberal philosophy toward independence. Second, adults now express only moder-

Homogamy characterizes both dating and marital relationships in Canada.

[2]Space limitations prevent discussion of the several subdivisions of these phases identified by the Rapoports.

ate opposition to sexual activity among the young. Reiss (1976: 165) concludes:

> Together these factors seem to add up to support for the general proposition that by freeing oneself from adult institutions and by living in a community where adult institutions are not strongly against sexual permissiveness young people become more involved in the higher permissive subculture of youth.

But, as young people progress into courtship and marriage, they move into the somewhat less permissive adult world. This world tends to be more conservative toward adolescent sexuality.

Leslie and Korman (1985: 352) have identified 1965 as the most accurate cutting point between traditional and liberal sex norms in the United States. Prior to 1965, gradual increases in premarital sexual intercourse had been recorded, but they were largely confined to courting relationships, chiefly those leading to marriage. This is still true, although many more young couples are now sexually active. Zelnick et al. (1981) in a nationwide American study report that 18 percent of unmarried fifteen-year-old females are sexually experienced, a figure that rises to more than 55 percent by age nineteen. In an earlier study by two of the same authors (Kantner and Zelnick, 1972), about half the sample said they had intercourse only with the man they intended to marry. Teenagers, it appears, are not especially promiscuous. Since 1965, several opinion polls have revealed a growing liberalization of adult attitudes toward teenage sexual activities, including the increasingly common belief that youth should have access to birth control (Leslie and Korman, 1985: 353). Still, the responsibility for saying "no" and setting the limits on how far the couple may go is largely that of the female. Little has changed here (Herold, 1984: 16).

Young Adulthood

The young adulthood phase of the family career starts around age sixteen to eighteen and runs approximately to age twenty-five. During this phase, the individual begins to identify with the major social institutions of his or her society. Unlike the preceding phase, in which the concern was with personal identity (as established, in part, through dating), young adulthood is a period of social identification. This is the time during which most North Americans extend their dating to the courtship level, get married, and begin adjusting to life with a spouse.

In the matter of premarital intercourse, the circumstances for university students are the same as for teenagers, only more pronounced. Freedman and Lozoff (1972) concluded that the extensive increase since 1965 in premarital sexual intercourse among students in American colleges has occurred predominantly in serious, intimate relationships, albeit not alliances necessarily destined to become marriages. Hobart (1980: 56) has summarized the Canadian research on premarital sexual behavior among university students. Data from the late 1960s indicate that American students then were more permissive than Canadian students. Today, however, the permissiveness levels are similar. Women in both countries have also shown a tendency to be as permissive today as the more liberal men. A national Canadian survey (Bibby, 1982) found that three of four adults now approve of premarital sexual intercourse.

Homogamy, propinquity, and the incest taboo have much to do with mate selection, just as they have a bearing on the choice of a date. But, as steady dating shades into courtship, the personal characteristics of one's partner gain importance. At present, research evidence is inconclusive on the question of whether, in courtship, people look for characteristics in their partners that match or complement their own. Winch et al. (1954: 242) hypothesized that "the need pattern of B, the second person or the one to whom the first is attracted, will be *complementary* rather than *similar* to the need pattern of A, the first person." While Winch's research supports this proposition, as does to some extent that of Kerchkoff and Davis (1962), most studies provide evidence only of homogamy or matching of personality characteristics among married couples (e.g., Murstein, 1970; Levenger et al., 1970).

Another factor in mate selection is the set of preferred traits which are looked for in a spouse. Data from the United States and Canada show that six traits are consistently seen as desirable; partners should (1) be dependable and honest, (2) faithful in marriage, (3) considerate and understanding, (4) pleasant and easygoing, (5) emotionally mature, and (6) have a good sense of humor (Wakil, 1973; Hill, 1955; McGinnis, 1958). For the vast majority of North Americans, these traits are sought in someone with whom they are "in love." *Romantic love,* as opposed to brotherly love, is a "strong emotional attachment . . . between adolescents or adults of opposing sexes, with at least the components of sex desire and tenderness" (Goode, 1959: 41–42). Love is also a mutual perception and expression of affect requiring time to develop to a satisfactory level (Larson, 1976: 138). Hastily arranged marriages frequently lack this dimension, which helps to explain their shakier existence compared with those based on a long period of courtship.

Quantitative data on marriage and divorce reveal that Canadians and Americans evaluate marriage more or less equally. Such data are frequently presented as "crude" rates of marriage or divorce. These rates are calculated as the number of marriages (or divorces) per one thousand population in a given twelve-month period. This kind of rate is "crude" because it is based on a general population instead of a more pertinent category of people within the population (e.g., women aged 15 to 44). We shall consider crude population rates again in Chapter 22.

Figure 10.1 shows a somewhat lower crude marriage rate for Canadians than for Americans, which Michalos (1980b: 295) traces, in part, to higher remarriage rates among the Americans (discussed later in this chapter). The higher remarriage rates are influenced, to some extent, by the higher divorce rates in the United States (see Table 10.5). The proportion of married persons in the population has been falling slowly since 1961 in Canada, where it was 66.6 percent (Kalbach and McVey, 1979: 312) and since 1965 in the United States, where it was 73.2 percent (U.S. Bureau of the Census, 1980: 41). Table 10.2 contains figures on the proportion of married persons relative to the total population of persons 18 years old and older in each country in 1980 and 1981.

Current data on marriage patterns in North America support Horowitz's (1973: 340) conclusion that "the differences between Canada and the United States, at the level of values, are better framed in terms of cultural lag than in terms of polarized . . . value differences." As a further illustration of this proposition, consider the converging trends in median age of first marriage (Table 10.3). Comparing the years 1950 and 1951 with 1980 and 1981, we see that Canadian men and women are now much closer

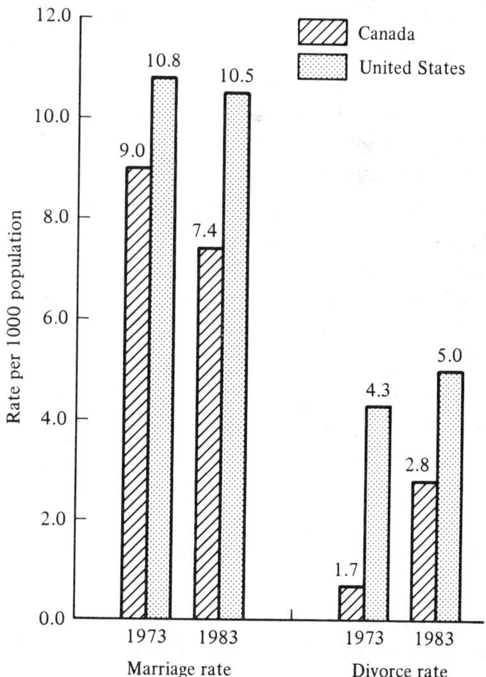

Figure 10.1 Crude Marriage and Divorce Rates in Canada and the United States, 1973–1983. (*Sources:* Statistics Canada, *Vital Statistics: Marriages and Divorces,* Cat. 84-205, Ottawa, 1973–1983; U.S. Bureau of the Census, *Statistical Abstract of the United States,* 1985, 105th ed. Washington, D.C., 1985, p. 57.)

Table 10.1 MARRIAGE RATES PER 1000 POPULATION, 1950–1981

Year	United States	Canada
1950	11.1	
1951		9.2
1960	8.5	
1961		7.0
1970	10.6	
1971		8.9
1975	10.1	
1976		8.4
1980	10.6	
1981		7.8

Sources: U.S. Bureau of the Census, *Statistical abstract of the United States, 1984,* 104th ed., p. 84, Washington, D.C., 1984; Statistics Canada, *Vital statistics,* vol. II, Cat. No. 84-205, Ottawa, 1975 and 1981.

Table 10.2 PERCENTAGE OF MARRIED PERSONS, 1980–1981[a]

Sex	Canada (1981)	United States (1980)
Female	66.9	63.4
Male	69.6	68.6

Sources: Statistics Canada, *1981 Census of Canada,* Cat. No. 92-901, Table 4, Ottawa, 1981; U.S. Bureau of the Census, *Statistical abstract of the United States, 1984,* 104th ed., p. 84, Washington, D.C., 1984.

[a]The Canadian figures are lower, in part, because they include 15- to 17-year-olds, almost all of whom are unmarried. The U.S. data include only those 18 and over.

Table 10.3 MEDIAN AGE AT FIRST MARRIAGE AMONG NORTH AMERICANS

	United States		Canada	
Year	Males	Females	Males	Females
1950	22.8	20.3		
1951			24.8	22.0
1955	22.6	20.2		
1956			24.6	21.7
1960	22.8	20.3		
1961			24.0	21.2
1965	22.5	20.4		
1966			23.8	21.3
1970	22.5	20.6		
1971			23.5	21.4
1975	22.7	20.8		
1976			23.8	21.7
1980	23.6	21.8		
1981			24.5	22.5

Sources: U.S. Bureau of the Census, *Statistical abstract of the United States, 1984,* 104th ed., p. 84, Washington, D.C., 1984; Statistics Canada, *Vital statistics,* Vol. II, *Marriages and divorces,* Cat. No. 84-205, p. x, Chart 3, Ottawa, 1981.

in median age of first marriage to American men and women than they were nearly twenty years ago. It is also clear from Table 10.3 that, at least during the 1970s in North America, members of both sexes were marrying for the first time at an increasingly later median age. Women, especially those in the United States, began delaying their marriages before men delayed theirs.

Establishment Phase

The establishment phase of the family career starts at approximately age twenty-five and runs to age fifty-five or so. It is the period during which one shapes one's occupational, familial, and community life-style. Individuals are preoccupied with succeeding at work, raising children, and maintaining an acceptable family existence.

The establishment phase is a period of intense familism for many North Americans. *Familism* is the value elevating the family's interests and welfare over those of the individual members. Those who emphasize familism have a strong sense of family identification, loyalty, and concern with the perpetuation of the family group. A man is expressing familism when he refuses to take a job that requires him to work on Saturday, the day he reserves for family activities.

Among the forces promoting families in North America is the tendency for each nuclear family to be *neolocal.* That is, the married couple is directed by custom to establish a household which is apart from the homes in which they were raised. This separateness helps to distinguish the *family of procreation,* or the newly established family, from the *family of orientation,* or the husband's or wife's parental family.

Despite its neolocality, the North American nuclear family is by no means left to drift alone

Which type of family do you see in this picture?

For many North Americans, the extended family is small.

in the vast impersonal sea of American and Canadian mass society. Kinship ties through husband and wife to their separate extended families are often seen as important and are frequently sustained across thousands of miles (e.g., father and mother live in the East, and a son or daughter is on the West Coast). In the *extended family,* kinship is traced consanguineously from the husband *or* wife of the nuclear family to their parents and grandparents, to their brothers and sisters, to the children of their brothers and sisters, and to the children of the husband and wife. This constitutes at least a three-generational unit. Extended family members are blood relations, in contrast to the husband and wife of the nuclear or conjugal family, so named because the couple is related by marriage. All societies recognize an extended family of some kind, although its composition varies widely from society to society.

The members of extended families visit each other frequently. Axelrod (1956) found that 49 percent of family members sampled in Detroit visited relatives weekly, while another 25 percent visited monthly. Much the same pattern was found in Los Angeles (Greer, 1956); visiting in Boston, on the other hand, occurs less frequently (Reiss, 1965). According to Young and Wilmott (1957), Adams (1968), and Garigue (1956), mother-daughter visiting is especially common in London, Montreal, Quebec, and Greensboro, North Carolina. Irving (1972) and Pineo (1976) found an equal rate of mother-daughter and father-son visiting in samples taken in Toronto and Hamilton, Ontario. Geographic distance seems to have little effect on the visiting of relatives, which no doubt has something to do with the efficiency (though perhaps not the cost) of modern transportation (Litwak, 1960; Osterreich, 1965; Piddington, 1973).

Kin contact involves more than visiting. It includes frequent exchanges of service, gifts, money, and goods. For example, a study done in the United States showed that 82 percent of the respondents said they both gave and received some form of help from their spouse and 62 percent from a relative (Warren, 1981: 32) Similar patterns have been recorded among Canadians (e.g., Osterreich, 1965; Irving, 1972). Specifically, this mutual aid includes furnishings, babysitting, yard work, house repairs, emergency services, low-interest loans, interest-free loans, and the use of facilities such as a boat or a summer cottage.

Performing one's family roles is an activity in the establishment phase. Ivan Nye (1974) has identified eight of the roles, five of which are traditional: the roles of child care, child socialization, provision of money, keeping house, and

New family role: facilitator of recreation.

maintaining contact with kin. Historically, the husband has filled the role of financial provider, although we will see later in this section and in Chapter 19 that many wives are beginning to claim this responsibility, too. The role of housekeeper is dwindling in the face of modern conveniences and the woman's pursuit of work and leisure outside the home. Maintaining contact with relatives is perhaps less important today than it once was.

In the meantime, three new roles are emerging in the American family. One of these is recreational. This emerging role contains "a set of responsibilities incumbent on occupants of (this) position to facilitate the recreational activities available to others" (Nye, 1974: 240). The second is therapeutic. One family member offers assistance to another member, thereby helping solve a practical or emotional problem he or she may have. The third emerging role pertains only to males (since the female counterpart has long been in existence). It is a sexual role. The husband is called upon to meet the sexual needs of his wife. It now is assumed that women, too, are entitled to the pleasures of sex.

There is no equivalent analysis of Canadian family roles. Still, Nett (1980) reviews a number of studies which, together, indicate or suggest that families in Canada also carry out Nye's eight roles.

One role has changed dramatically during the past twenty years. This is the provider role. Data from the U.S. Bureau of Labor Statistics indicate that women's participation in the labor force in the United States jumped from 15 percent in 1940 to 51.6 percent in 1980. Census data in Canada reveal a similar trend: women's labor force participation rose from just over 11 percent in 1951 to 52.0 percent in 1981. As Table 10.4 reveals, mothers with children under eighteen years of age are currently contributing to this trend more than mothers who have children age eighteen or over or who are childless.

Just what effect does the employment of the wife and mother have on others in the family? Research to date into this matter is mostly inconclusive. So far, it has been impossible to determine whether marital dissatisfaction results from a married woman's participation in the labor force or whether her participation adds to marital satisfaction. Emily Nett (1980: 73), in summarizing several pertinent Canadian and American studies, concluded that, in general, husbands do suffer a significant degree of tension as a result of their wives' gainful employment.[3]

The effects on children are less clear: Research contradicts the idea of significant differences between the children of working and nonworking mothers. Maternal employment operates in interaction with too many other variables to be studied alone. Scattered research indicates that there may be some relationship with juvenile delinquency at middle-class levels, that part-time maternal employment has a favorable effect upon adolescent children, and that the effects upon younger children may vary by sex. Any general conclusions that maternal

[3]But there are data contradicting this general conclusion. See Booth's (1977) and Lupri and Frideres' (1981: 294) studies of working wives and their husbands in Toronto and Calgary, respectively.

Table 10.4 LABOR FORCE PARTICIPATION BY MOTHERS WITH CHILDREN (HUSBAND PRESENT)[a]

Children	Mothers to married women in the population (percent) in years					
	1960	1970	1971	1975	1976	1979
Canada						
None under age 18			35.1		44.5	
Ages 6 to 17			27.4		48.5	
Under age 6			21.4		36.5	
United States						
None under age 18	34.7	42.2		43.9		46.7
Ages 6 to 17	39.0	49.2		52.3		59.1
Under age 6	18.6	30.3		36.6		43.2

Sources: Statistics Canada, *Census of Canada, 1971 and 1976,* Cat. Nos. 94-774 and 94-836, Ottawa; U.S. Bureau of the Census, *Statistical abstract of the United States, 1980,* 101st ed., p. 403, Table 671, Washington, D.C., 1980.

[a]No equivalent Canadian data are available prior to 1971.

employment is undesirable appear unwarranted (Leslie and Korman, 1985: 498).

Later Years[4]

At age fifty-five or so, parents (and childless couples) move into the later years of the family career. These years are a time for consolidation of life's past involvements, a time to achieve a sense of social and personal integration in the careers of family, work, and leisure. Role specialization, started early in the family career, continues and reaches its peak here. It seems as if husbands and wives become locked into roles they began playing at the beginning of their marriages, which, in some cases, are traditional, stereotyped sex roles (e.g., housekeeping for the wife, working at a job for the husband). The later years find the couple drifting farther apart as they strive to integrate their lives around their separate careers (Axelson, 1960: Orthner, 1975). Thus, the attempts at social and personal integration to which we have referred may end in partial or total failure, which engenders a sense of futility and despair.

One question to emerge from this situation is whether love and marital satisfaction swing upward after the child-bearing and child-rearing years. Research results are contradictory. Gilford and Bengston (1979) review several studies which show a linear decline in marital satisfaction with advancing age. They also review several other studies which suggest that satisfaction begins to increase in the later stages of the family life cycle. The second set of studies depicts marital satisfaction as having a U-shaped history, or a cycle from much satisfaction to less satisfaction to renewed satisfaction. The only Canadian study of this question disclosed a U-shaped pattern (Lupri and Frideres, 1981). Whether there is an upswing in marital satisfaction in the later years depends partly on how estranged the couple becomes during the financially and psychologically turbulent child-rearing years.

Marital dissatisfaction in the establishment and later years phases as a correlate of ethnicity is perhaps more prevalent in Canada than in the United States; there is a greater proportion of foreign-born people in Canada than in the United States (see Chapter 20). Families who immigrated to North America from Third World countries or who led an isolated, traditional life-style until they were suddenly uprooted by political or economic forces in their homeland face special adjustment problems in

[4]The Rapoports refer to the later-years phase of the family career as "retirement." Their terminology has been avoided because of the confusion it causes with occupational retirement.

postindustrial Canada. Marital instability is often a by-product of these problems (Nett, 1980: 74–75).

TURNING POINTS

Although there are others, three family career turning points stand out in the experience of many North Americans. These junctures are *divorce, remarriage,* and *widowhood.* Table 10.5 indicates that divorce is increasing in the United States and Canada. In both countries, a more accepting attitude toward divorced persons, greater willingness to dissolve a troublesome union, and, perhaps, a higher level of stress in everyday life help account for this trend. This long-term upward trend, however, masks the tendency for divorce rates to drop during economic depression and war and rise significantly, but briefly, just after hard times and warfare.

Divorce

Why the divorce rate is higher in the United States than in Canada is still only partly understood. To some extent, this difference has been artificial, for Canadian rates moved closer to American rates following the introduction of Canada's federal Divorce Act in 1968. Canadians can now divorce on either fault-related (e.g., physical cruelty, adultery, homosexuality) grounds or simply on the grounds of a marital breakdown. Adultery had been the only ground prior to 1968. Moreover, lower Canadian divorce rates, whether calculated before or after 1968, cannot be taken as evidence of greater family harmony in Canada than in the United States. Canadians may simply be less willing to deal with disharmony through the courts. Perhaps fundamental value differences lie behind these discrepant rates. Larson (1976: 30) concludes:

> In general, these statistical differences are indicative of more traditional marriage patterns in Canada than in the U.S.: fewer divorces, fewer remarriages, and fewer young marriages. . . . The use of the term "traditional" is of course interpretable in many ways. It may mean that the family system is more stable, more rational, and more familistic. Or, in contrast, traditionalism might be thought of as less flexible, more conservative, and more backward.

Table 10.5 DIVORCE RATE PER 1000 POPULATION, 1950–1981

Year	United States	Canada
1950	2.6	
1951		0.4
1960	2.2	
1961		0.3
1970	3.5	
1971		1.4
1975	4.9	
1976		2.4
1980	5.2	
1981		2.8

Sources: U.S. Bureau of the Census, *Statistical abstract of the United States, 1984,* 104th ed., p. 84, Washington, D.C., 1984; Dominion Bureau of Statistics, *Census of Canada,* 1951, 1961, Ottawa; Statistics Canada, *Vital statistics: Marriages and divorces,* Cat. No. 84-205, Ottawa, 1981.

Remarriage

The growing divorce rate (helped somewhat by a slowly declining widowhood rate) has contributed significantly to the recent increase in a variant of the nuclear family known as the *single-parent family.* In 1981, 10.6 percent of the heads of families in Canada were lone females and 2.2 percent were lone males (Statistics Canada, 1984d: Table 3). The proportions were very similar in the United States for the same year: there 11.0 percent of the heads of families were lone females and 2.3 percent were lone males (U.S. Bureau of the Census, 1982–83: 46). A serious problem for the single parent is "task overload" (Beal, 1980: 256). Low income is often a problem for the mother-only family. All single parents face the staggering demand of having to fill both the parental role and the householder role. A single parent is a mother, a father, a breadwinner, and a housekeeper.

Single-parent families have become common in recent years in our society.

Divorce commonly leads to remarriage. Nearly all divorced persons remarry within three to four years after the divorce, although men and young people do so more quickly than women and older people (Norton and Glick, 1976; Schlesinger, 1980: 159; Kuzel and Krishnan, 1973: 220). With divorce rates climbing throughout North America, it is hardly surprising that remarriage rates are likewise increasing (U.S. Bureau of the Census, 1980: 83; Statistics Canada, 1980a: 31; 1980b: 6).

Remarriage ceremonies are usually brief and without ritual, unless it is a remarriage only for the groom and the first marriage for the bride. Nye and Berardo (1973: 528) observe that remarriages, especially when it is a remarriage for both partners, are often as practical and businesslike as they are romantic. The man and woman who enter into a remarriage usually have pressing needs. In all likelihood, they are concerned with responsibilities such as alimony, child support, child-rearing, and domestic assistance. All this enters into the selection of a mate.

With children becoming increasingly involved in reconstituted families, people have begun to wonder about how the children react to their stepparents. After studying this situation, Bernard (1956) concluded that most remarriages produce little harm to children. Three factors are at work here: (1) the children's favorable attitude toward the new parental union, (2) the new parent being seen as a salvaging influence, and (3) the resilience of nearly all human beings.

Widowhood

Although the absolute number of widowed individuals has been growing in the United States and Canada for many decades, their proportion to the population has been dropping somewhat. There is no doubt that the loss of a mate imposes severe strains on the survivor. Are these strains greater for the surviving widow or for the surviving widower? Some argue that the widower is left more socially isolated and domestically incapacitated than the widow. Still, others have noted that marriage is socially more important to the widow than to the widower. The widow, like other women, is expected to be less aggressive than a man in seeking companionship with the opposite sex. Widows find it difficult to find a new partner because they are large in numbers; men seem to have a choice. Indeed, being without a spouse is, for the most part, a woman's problem, for 85 percent of wives outlive their husbands today.

Among the problems faced by many widows is the social and economic burden they impose on their children. At this point in time, the children are usually married and struggling with

Widowhood: There are few men anymore in the lives of these women.

limited financial resources; they have the responsibility of raising their own children and maintaining family stability. In all too many instances, widows have only the alternative of spending their final years in loneliness and poverty (Gates, 1977: 216–217), a fate that many widows endure with remarkable courage and forbearance.

ALTERNATIVES TO MARRIAGE

The falling proportion of married people in the overall North American population and the rising rates of divorce are, themselves, evidence of the increasing popularity of chosen alternatives to the institution of marriage and its traditional norms. Further evidence comes from the gap between dissolution of the first marriage and commencement of the second. Glick (1975) estimates that three-quarters of all divorced persons remarry within five years of the termination of their earlier union. It is clear that some individuals have found other solutions to the problems of collective living conventionally solved by our family institution. For example, the once-married see certain advantages in cohabitation, as do some of those who are yet to marry.

Cohabitation

Cohabitation occurs when a man and a woman live together over an extended period of time without being legally married. In line with Margaret Mead's (1966) notion of a two-step marriage in which the first step is a trial for the second, scholars have conceived of cohabitation as an exploratory phase of courtship. Cohabitation gives those concerned an opportunity to see if their interpersonal relationship can withstand the stresses of everyday living and, at the same time, continue to be satisfying (Clatworthy, 1975). Yet, marriage is not inevitable, since the trial may prove the union to be unworkable. Research by Clayton and Voss (1977) and Hobart (1975: 426) suggests that many younger people define their cohabitation as a prelude to marriage. Clayton and Voss found that men whose marriage had dissolved turn to cohabitation either as an interim arrangement or as a long-term substitute for marriage.

In general, the research on cohabitation has been centered on university students. Robert R. Bell (1979: 99) points out that there is an emotional commitment between cohabitating partners. Nonetheless, these young lovers look on their association with one another as something other than husband and wife. Their living together is no traditional marital relationship, although cohabitation, to some degree, follows the traditional roles of conjugal life. Cohabitation lasts only as long as both members see its rewards as outweighing its costs (Cole, 1977). Are the assumed benefits of cohabitation real benefits or merely wishful thinking? This question is yet to be answered. The benefits, if any, are untested (Davids, 1975: 441).

Communes

Our first thought about the notion of "commune" was a fleeting reference in Chapter 8 to the fact that communes are objects of study in the personal community research tradition. Since communes frequently form around families and cohabiting couples, we will now undertake a further consideration of the commune. The diversity of communes rules out at this time all but the simplest definition of the commune: "a type of community characterized by collective ownership and use of property by members" (*Encyclopedia Britannica,* 1982: 44). Ramey (1972: 647) adds to this definition the criterion that, for a commune to form, there must be a degree of personal commitment among a group of people:

> When individuals agree to make life commitments as members of one particular group, rather than through many different groups, they may constitute a commune. The number of

common commitments will vary from commune to commune, the critical number having been reached at the point at which the group sees itself as a commune, rather than at some absolute number.

Rural communes are typically organized along religious principles, and they are put into practice with the shared labor and material resources of their members. The rural commune constitutes a type of agrarian economy. The Hutterites exemplify well this form of communalism. The larger Hutterite community has, since its inception in 1535, been at odds with the family for control of labor, property, production of goods, and consumption of goods. It also plays a part in child socialization and in mate selection (Peter, 1976). Hutterite religious ideology emphasizes communalism in these practices and responsibilities, but family attachments prevent its full realization.

In the Israeli kibbutz, where the visibility of the nuclear family was once even fuzzier than today, families are now permitted to eat separately instead of collectively in the community center. They are also permitted to live in their own dwellings rather than in the barrackslike quarters of the past. Communal child-rearing is still practiced, however (Clayton, 1979: 189–191).

Urban communes are more diverse than those in rural areas. Some are little more than housing cooperatives, wherein families share common living quarters on the assumption that it is cheaper to live together than separately. Others form on the basis of some common interest, such as drug use, sexual satisfaction, or personal growth through intimacy and communication. Although these common interest experiences are usually short-lived, they are organized by people dissatisfied with life and with what they perceive as an unfriendly, competitive, insincere world. They wish to establish on a larger scale a form of collective living having the warmth and safety of the nuclear family.

Swinging

Some kinds of communal living are little more than prolonged *swinging,* or mate swapping, defined by Walshok (1971: 488) as "the agreement between husband and wife to have sexual relations with other people, but in contexts in which they both engage in such behavior at the same time and usually in the same place." Leslie and Korman (1985: 453) point out that swinging, as far as the United States is concerned, is neither new nor particularly unusual. Temporary liaisons for sexual leisure known as "wife swapping" occurred in the 1940s and 1950s, often through clandestine "key clubs." In this arrangement, several wives would place the keys to their homes in a hat. Each wife would then spend the night with the husband (not her own) who drew her key from the hat.

Gilbert Bartell (1971: 57–58), in a participant observer study of swinging, hypothesized that this practice fulfills the sexual fantasies of the American males; the men first experienced their fantasies during adolescence. For wives, swinging is a way of maintaining a satisfactory relationship with their husbands, who seek to realize their fantasies. Some wives reason, apparently, that if swinging is necessary to keep their husbands' love, then they should do it. By swinging, the couple indicates that their marital relationship is considerably less than ideal, but that they hope to find an adequate level of satisfaction and thus sustain their marriage.

A study of Toronto swingers reveals that the interest in swinging and the decision to try it are usually the husband's (Henshel, 1973). Indeed, nearly half the wives interviewed said that, for them, the discomfort of swinging outweighs the pleasure. Denfield (1974) writes that some swingers' wives fear losing their husbands, some husbands and wives find their marriages threatened by such activity, and some husbands become jealous of their wives' popularity or sexual performance with other men.

Because swinging is commonly regarded as a form of noncriminal deviance (see Chapter 17),

Ambivalence toward Love

Cynicism, joking, and sentimentality alike bespeak a fundamental ambivalence toward love. Cynicism is the attitude of a person who is afraid that he will become the victim of illusions—illusions which he believes exist, entrap others, and are dangerous to himself. He hungers and thirsts for beliefs he can trust, but he never finds any that he can trust. Joking is the classical symptom by which the field ethnologist identifies status relationships that evoke conflicting emotions. And sentimentality is of course the lavish counterfeiting of genuine emotion that occurs when genuine emotion is deemed appropriate in a particular social situation but is not forthcoming spontaneously.

Freud believed that ambivalence was characteristic of all human love, and he also appeared to believe that the characteristic complement of love was hate. There is much truth to what he says, but at the present time some refinement and qualifications are required. In general, the appearance of ambivalence in love relationships is probably peculiar to our own highly competitive society and may not be characteristic of other times and places. To suggest that it may happily be made to disappear in our own time is the only preachment I would proffer in this paper.

To understand how ambivalence toward love may diminish and disappear requires more precise analysis than is implied by the simple concept of ambivalence as the concurrence of love and hate. In a competitive society as Bacon long ago pointed out, "he that hath wife and children hath given hostages to fortune." One who entrusts himself fully to another may find his credulity and kindness exploited. His love may be rejected or betrayed. To expose oneself to another is to run the risk of getting hurt. It may take only foolhardiness, among specialists in human development, to talk about love, but it does take courage to love in a society like our own. Many dare not try; they fear involvement. In short, fear rather than hate appears to be the original rival of love in the ambivalent situation that one encounters daily.

To be sure, when the fear seems justified by some act of the other, then the sense of betrayal is keen, and hostility is at once engendered. Several years ago I formed a habit of collecting clippings about domestic crimes in which wives, husbands, and children burned, poisoned, shot, and butchered each other. These clippings mounted so fast that I soon had a manila folder full of them. . . . was very glad to terminate the habit by donating the whole batch to Robert Hess of the Committee on Human Development, who has been doing a study of aggression in families for the United States Public Health Service. Aggression against the other is always potential in love relationships, but it forms a secondary and conditional phase, the fear of being hurt oneself is primary and continuous. Yet, to the extent that one is withheld from entering into love relationships by fear of being hurt, he is deprived of love and may crave it all the more.

This unrequited craving for love, in a society which demands the seal of love upon most interpersonal relations, leads not only to the characteristic expressions of cynicism, joking, and sentimentality, but also to a kind of self-renewing vicious circle. The signs of love are demanded, disbelieved, and demanded again. The oftener they are required, the oftener they are simulated; the more often they are distrusted, the more often further reassurance is demanded—until it is a wonder that any sound currency for conducting valid exchanges remains in use at all.

SOURCE: Nelson N. Foote, "Love." Copyright by The William Alanson White Psychiatric Foundation, Inc., 1953. Nelson N. Foote, "Love," *Psychiatry,* XVI (1953), pp. 245–251. Reprinted by special permission of The William Alanson White Psychiatric Foundation, Inc., copyright owners.

it is indulged in secretively, which makes estimating its frequency difficult. Four percent of a random sample of American women drawn in 1974 reported engaging in some swapping (Bell, 1979: 430). After reviewing various attempts to estimate the proportion of American male and female swingers, Paul J. Reiss (1976: 294) put the figure at no more than 1 percent of all married couples. Generalizing for the United States and Canada, Larson (1976: 212) says there is evidence that mate swapping is increasing, albeit slowly.

THEORIES OF THE FAMILY

Family sociology is rich in theory. Numerous hypotheses and theories have been offered as explanations of the family and of the ideas discussed so far in this chapter. Sociologists have had much to say about the family as an institution. Four of the broad perspectives commonly encountered in the family literature are covered here. These are the *functionalist, conflict, developmental,* and *symbolic interactionist* perspectives.

Functionalist Perspective

The functionalist perspective combines the ideas of structure and function in a wide-ranging explanation of family life. We turn first to *structure.* The main structures are the nuclear family, the extended family, and the relationships among the members of the family. Researchers using the functional approach study the linkage of family structures with the structures of the school, the church, and the social service agencies. They seek to determine how the school, the church, and the social service agencies have a bearing on the family structure. Parsons and Bales (1955: 23), for instance, argue that the American occupational system places responsibility for the family's financial care on the father, the adult male in the family.

Functionalists also examine the family's functions, or the ways the family helps to maintain the larger social system. For example, one function of the family is to provide the primary socialization of the society's young. McIntyre (1966) discusses another kind of functional analysis of the family, namely that of the functional prerequisites it fills. Functional prerequisites are the conditions that must be met if the social system is to continue to exist. One of these is replacing members of society who die or leave, which the family carries out by means of the reproductive function.

Conflict Perspective

Marx and Engels saw the family as they did other institutions in society and society itself: these collectivities are filled with inherent contradictions and episodes of conflict. They held that the family contains the first division of labor—man and wife in breeding children—and the first antagonism between classes, which takes the form of exploitation of women by men. This exploitation is especially prominent in the monogamous marriage, a relationship which appeals to the vast majority of Canadians. The family also provides labor for the capitalist system of production. At the proletarian level, entire families are absorbed into this mode of production in one way or another. Marx and Engels felt that this absorption eventually eroded the family authority patterns as the family became subservient to the demands of capitalist employers.

The dominance of the functionalist perspective in family sociology has left its mark. Eugen Lupri (in press) notes that, until recently, sociologists ignored the presence of conflict in the family and the place of the family in social class conflict and in the economic system. Until recently, family sociologists were chiefly oriented by the consensus mode. Lupri reviews several studies that examine the use of physical force, coercion, and other forms of domination to settle domestic disputes. Child abuse and wife beating are examples of family violence.

One of the conditions promoting exploitation and violence noted by Lupri and others is that the family group is not entirely voluntary. Although divorce, suicide, running away, and the murder of a spouse are possible ways out of an intolerable situation, such acts are unappealing enough to make them alternatives of the last resort. Entrapment in an unpleasant family situation is a possibility for all who are members of a family and an actuality for some individuals. The exploitation of wives by husbands and by society as a whole has received considerable attention from radical feminists. We shall consider this form of family conflict in detail in Chapter 19.

Developmental Perspective

The *developmental perspective* is strong where the functionalist perspective is weak. That is, the developmentalists introduce a *temporal,* or time, dimension to the sociological analysis of the family, whereas the functionalists tend to ignore this dimension. The family career section in this chapter is developmental. The number of divisions in the span of time running from birth to death referred to here is fewer than found in other developmental theories of the family. Joan Aldous (1978: 86–87), for instance, lists seven stages of the family life cycle:

Stage 1: Newly established couple.
Stage 2: Childbearing.
Stage 3: Families with schoolchildren.
Stage 4: Families with secondary school children.
Stage 5: Families with adult children.
Stage 6: Families in the middle years (children have left home).
Stage 7: Aging families.

Whatever the number of stages, the family performs different functions at each stage. The roles of the husband and wife and the father and mother also change stage by stage. The presence and absence of children, as well as their ages when they are on the family scene, have much to do with family activities and life-style. As they advance from one stage to another, the members of the family react to the new activities and requirements thrust on them. We saw earlier, for example, how marital satisfaction varies by the stage of the family life cycle.

Symbolic Interactionist Perspective

The developmental perspective shares with the functionalist perspective an interest in the functions of family roles. Developmentalists share with symbolic interactionists an interest in social processes and change. The stagewise development of families and of individuals within them is extended by the interactionists; they concentrate on the roles family members play, the meanings of these roles for other members, and the development of the meanings in interaction with the others. Children, for instance, modify their child role to fit their personalities as well as conform (at least some of the time) to general community expectations held for them. In North America, children are expected to be respectful of adults. When an adult denies them a want, they are expected to suffer this denial without becoming impudent toward the adult. A bright youngster, however, may come to be known and get what he wants (modify his own role) through an exceptional ability to reason with adults.

The sociologists also look into definitions or interpretations of different family situations. Symbolic interactionists are usually more concerned with the improvised interactions emerging spontaneously among the members of the family than with the fixed patterns of interaction constituting part of the institution of the family. Sheldon Stryker (1962: 50), for example, found that role taking is more accurate when the persons whose roles are taken are blood relatives than when they are in-laws.

The self is a major symbolic interactionist concept. Since socialization and self-identity development are dominant family processes, symbolic interactionists have made many contributions to the family studies literature in reference to the self. Thus, the family is seen as an auspicious arena for the development of the child's sense of his or her uniqueness as a person. And, in this same setting, children learn to evaluate themselves and their actions as good or bad.

This family is promoting the self-actualization of its members.

THE FAMILY'S FUTURE

The volume of predictions and comments concerning the family's future is too large and space too limited to allow more than a partial sampling. Ira L. Reiss (1976: 431–434) raises two crucial questions concerning the family of tomorrow. First, how important will the dyad or married couple be in the American family? Reiss believes the dyad will retain its centrality, despite the interest of some people in cohabitation, swinging, group marriage, and communal living. Whitehurst (1975: 433) apparently agrees with this forecast when he notes that there are no convincing indicators that more than a very small minority of Canadians are seriously interested in the alternatives to traditional marriage.

Reiss's second question concerns intimacy and exclusivity. Does exclusivity have a bearing on intimacy? The traditional view is that intimacy demands exclusivity; that is, the more one is emotionally attached to another person, the more one should confine one's intimate behavior and revelations to that person. The emerging view is somewhat different: intimacy can be shared beyond the dyad, thus expanding exclusivity. In this view, the marital dyad is still preserved when, for example, the couple swings with other couples or one partner talks about his or her sexual problems with a friend. Having said that most Canadians are uninterested in the existing set of alternatives, Whitehurst notes "there are indicators that the content of changes in some of the expectations, norms, and ideals of marriage may make for different kinds of marriage."

Clayton (1979: 615–616) is in accord with much of this. The nuclear family, he says, will continue to exist, although differences in family relationships will appear. He believes a more egalitarian family is imminent, accompanied by more flexible roles and a sharing of duties between husbands and wives. He also sees the grandparent role gaining in importance. Since there will be greater opportunities to experience family responsibilities prior to assuming them in marriage, in Clayton's view, divorce is unlikely to increase much beyond present rates. Clayton goes on to say:

> All in all, the family of the future will be a healthy unit promoting strength and self-actualization anchored in a familial context that emphasizes manhood, womanhood, childhood, and personhood as ultimate goals. (Clayton, 1979: 616)

OUTLINE AND SUMMARY

I. Introduction
Although family structures exist among nonhuman species, only human beings form nuclear families, establish circles of kin relationships, adhere to rules about the choice of a mate, and develop a culture which is transmitted partly through the family system.

II. The Nuclear Family
A *nuclear family* is a group of persons who are united by ties of marriage, blood, or adoption and who constitute a single household.

III. The Family Institution
The family is one of society's fundamental institutions. It meets the six defining criteria of an institution.

IV. The Family Career
A. Adolescent Phase
Dating, courting, and shaping one's personality are of paramount importance during the adolescent phase.
B. Young Adulthood
In the young adulthood phase, the individual begins to identify with the major social institutions in society; courtship leads him or her into marriage.
C. Establishment Phase
The adult couple shares occupational, familial, and community lifestyles during the establishment phase.
D. Later Years
This is a time for consolidation of life's past involvements.

V. Turning Points
Three family career turning points of significance are *divorce, remarriage,* and *widowhood.*
A. Divorce
A more accepting attitude toward divorced persons, a greater willingness to dissolve a troublesome union, and, perhaps, a higher level of stress in everyday life help to account for an increase in the divorce rate in the United States and Canada.
B. Remarriage
A remarriage is motivated by practical needs as well as romantic interests; remarriage apparently does little harm to the children.
C. Widowhood
Whether widowhood is more stressful for the surviving man or the surviving woman is still an open question; widowed individuals, most of whom are women, tend to impose a social and economic burden on their adult children.

VI. Alternatives to Marriage
A. Cohabitation
Cohabitation is sometimes considered a trial marriage; those who cohabit have a strong emotional commitment to one another, although they look on their relationship as something other than husband and wife.
B. Communes
A *commune* is a type of community characterized by the members' collective ownership and use of property. Rural communes are typically organized along religious lines based on

some sort of agrarian enterprise. Urban communes may be little more than housing cooperatives or groups sharing a common interest.

C. Swinging

Swinging is an agreement between husband and wife to have sexual relations with other people, but in contexts in which they both engage in such behavior at the same time and usually in the same place.

VII. Theories of the Family

Theories of the family are based on four perspectives: *functionalist, conflict, developmental,* and *symbolic interactionist.*

A. Functionalist Perspective

The functionalist perspective examines the links between the family and the school, the church, and the social service agencies; it also examines the functions of the family in the larger society.

B. Conflict Perspective

The conflict perspective examines exploitation and violence within the family and the place of the family in the capitalist system of economic production.

C. Developmental Perspective

The developmental perspective examines the temporal dimension of family life; the phases of the family life cycle are of central concern.

D. Symbolic Interactionist Perspective

The symbolic interactionist perspective examines the roles played by members of the family, the meanings of these roles, and the development of these meanings through interaction with the members of the family.

VIII. The Family's Future

A. The marital dyad appears to be assured of its continued existence.

1. New values point to less exclusive sharing of intimacies, more egalitarian, more flexible roles, and more emphasis on personal development.
2. The various family alternatives seem unlikely to be accepted by most North Americans.

FOR FURTHER READING AND STUDY

Bartell, C. D. 1971. *Group sex.* New York: Peter H. Wyden. Bartell, an anthropologist, and his wife work as a team of participant observers to study the social interaction at swingers' parties.

Hyman, H. H. 1983. *Of time and widowhood.* Durham, N.C.: Duke University Press. A secondary analysis of nationwide American surveys on the pain and experiences of widowhood. Younger and older widows alike show surprisingly good adjustment to their new family status.

Leslie, G. E., and Korman, S. K.1985. *The family in social context,* 6th ed. New York: Oxford University Press. An established textbook in family sociology oriented primarily to the family in the United States.

McAdoo, H. P., ed. 1981. *Black families.* Beverly Hills, Calif.: Sage. This collection brings together a range of articles published over a period of twenty years on various aspects of the black family in the United States and elsewhere.

Ramu, G. N., ed. 1980. *Courtship, marriage, and the family.* Toronto: Gage. A collection of articles on family-related topics pertaining to the Canadian scene.

Veevers, J. E. 1982. *Childless by choice.* Toronto: Butterworth. This exploratory study examines the attitudes of Canadian couples who have chosen to remain childless. Many of Veevers' respondents expressed a strong commitment to a "childfree" life-style, which they often have to defend against friends and relatives.

KEY WORDS

cohabitation An association in which a man and a woman live together over an extended period of time without being legally married.

commune A type of community characterized by collective ownership and use of property by the members of the community.

courtship An intimate relationship between a male and a female which may become serious enough to lead to engagement and subsequent marriage.

extended family A three-generational unit which includes a nuclear family, grandparents, aunts, uncles, and cousins.

family A set of individuals related to each other by blood, marriage, or adoption, or, in rare instances, by another form of social ascription to a family.

nuclear family A group consisting of one or both parents and dependent offspring.

romantic love A strong emotional attachment between adolescents or adults of opposite sexes, with at least the components of sex desire and tenderness.

chapter 11

Education

CHAPTER OUTLINE

INTRODUCTION

Education is an important institution in society but, as far as we know, no one has ever tried to show that it is the most central institution in modern societies, as Karl Marx did for the economy and Thomas Hobbes did for the polity. In fact, nearly all contemporary social scientists hold that there is no central institution; instead, there are several *core institutions* (education, work, religion, economy, polity, family). Each is vitally important. Education and the other institutions make unique contributions to the functioning of society.

One potentially significant contribution made by the educational institution in both Canada and the United States is the following:

> Education is universally the factor most directly affecting occupational attainment; in every country studied its effects transcend the direct effects of occupational inheritance. (However, education is itself greatly affected by class background.) (Ramirez and Meyer, 1980: 388)

> Nation-wide studies of intergenerational occupational mobility in Canada and elsewhere . . . all conclude that education is a most important facilitator for those who move up. . . . Recently, however, there have appeared trenchant criticisms of the model of upgrading and opportunity. (Porter, 1979: 263–264)

The proposition that education is *the* key or at least *a* key to occupational attainment has been the target of considerable debate in recent years. The question is taken up in this chapter and also in Chapter 18. In both chapters the conflict model stands as a rejection of this proposition. The proposition is a part of the consensus model.

But occupational attainment is only one function of education. We saw in Chapter 5 that schools help transmit culture, thereby assisting in childhood socialization. Schools also promote loyalty to society by advocating respect for the existing order (Mifflen and Mifflen, 1982: 228; Parelius and Parelius, 1978: 24). Conflict theorists argue, however, that the existing order includes many undesirable inequalities. As some conflict theorists see it, the existing order, instead of being respected and upheld, should be overthrown and replaced (e.g., Bowles, 1971). In short, schools have much to do with the functioning of society. Whether their influence is truly functional and contributory is a subject of much controversy.

EDUCATION AS AN INSTITUTION

Education is the act or process by which we educate others. *To educate* means

> to develop (as a person) by fostering in varying degrees the growth or expansion of knowledge, wisdom, desirable qualities of mind or character, physical health, or general competence especially by a course of formal study or instruction; provide or assist in providing with knowledge or wisdom, moral balance, or good physical condition especially by means of a formal education. (*Webster's Third International Dictionary of the English Language.* Springfield, Mass.: G & C Merriam Co.)

This definition implies that education need not be confined to schools. It can occur at home or on the job. The distinguishing criteria are that instruction, wherever it is received, must be formal and provided as a course of study. The sociology of education has been chiefly concerned with school-based instruction and its origins and consequences and with the vast social,

---

SOCIOLOGY OR COMMON SENSE

What do you think?

Which of the following statements do you agree with? Which statements do you disagree with? Make a note of your answers. Check your answers when you have completed your study of this chapter. Are your answers to the statements the same as those a sociologist would give?

1. Men and women who become teachers usually make teaching their lifework.
2. Teachers find their work satisfying because there are many opportunities for promotion and advancement.
3. Parent-teacher organizations generally have little influence on the school and on the activities and policies of the school board.
4. High schools, colleges, and universities allocate adult work roles.
5. The peer group is an alternative school.

---

political, and economic system within which it operates. That is, it is concerned with *schooling.* Schooling and school-based instruction are the interests of this chapter as well.

Although there are some engrossing historical and contemporary differences between Canadian schools and American schools, the overall impression gained from a study of the two is how similar they are today. This should not be surprising, for Canada has been moving in the direction of the American comprehensive high school since World War II (Blyth, 1972: 305).

The Defining Criteria

Does education conform to the six defining criteria of institutions set out in Chapter 9? We turn to the first of the criteria: institutions solve one or more of the major problems of collective living. One such problem which the institution of education helps to solve is socialization of the young (primary socialization) and, through higher education, socialization of adults (secondary socialization). Both the elementary and secondary levels of formal education transmit the culture of society to individuals within the society. Schools at the secondary and tertiary levels allocate adult roles by conferring success on some students and failure on others (Meyer, 1977).

There are many familiar educational *patterns of behavior* in our society. Children walking to school each day, playing at recess on the school grounds, getting report cards, advancing (usually) from grade to grade, and engaging in team athletics are among the examples. Different patterns hold true for teachers and administrators, even though they are less visible to the public; these include annual salary settlements for teachers, annual budget decisions by the school board, and occasional evaluation programs which are undertaken by the school board.

Likewise, there are many recognizable *abstract relationships* in education. An obvious one is the teacher-pupil relationship. The teacher-parent relationship is familiar to parents from direct experience. Behind the scenes, so to speak, are additional ties of significance in educational affairs, namely those between teacher and principal, principal and superintendent, and teacher and counselor along with the sundry associations between school boards and government. Each relationship, as indicated earlier, forges a link between two different roles (the role of teacher and the role of principal, for example). The roles of the pupils, teacher, principal, and superintendent are taken up in later sections of this chapter.

Educational Values

As they discharge their socialization function, schools transmit many of the society's values. Among the values are the individual's conforming to rules, being honest, being diligent, and cooperating with others. There are also values peculiar to the educational institution itself. In fact, education itself is of value to all who are willing and able to acquire it. Behind this observation lies the conflict still raging in many countries over the merits of mass secondary education versus elite secondary education.

Another value of education is that it prepares students for their adult occupational roles. Education is further valued for the understanding of the social and physical environment it imparts. Still, the fact that educators try to impart such values is no indication that everyone who goes to school learns and accepts these values. Were the educators and other socializers always successful, there would be no deviance and no social conflict.

To some extent, as noted in Chapter 9, Canada's approach to education and its values differs moderately from the approach of the United States. Canada is heading toward full implementation of mass elementary and secondary education and, through higher education, toward the student's preparation for his or her life work. Yet in the late 1970s it still lagged somewhat behind the United States in regard to the extent of mass education and vocational education. Nevertheless, Canada is part of the nearly universal trend toward mass education that has been under way around the world since the late 1940s (Meyer et al., 1977).

History of Education

Like other institutions, the institution of education has a history. An example of a differentiating historical development in North American education is found in the open-space, or open-plan, school. One of the earliest of these schools in North America opened in 1957 in Carson City, Michigan, whence it spread to California and Canada (Stebbins, 1974b: 62–63). The open-space school is now common in both Canada and the United States, replacing, to some some extent, the self-contained classroom boxes that constitute the "egg-crate school" and that once dominated formal education the world over.

A typical open-plan school is composed of several areas of unbroken space, each of which may contain between three and five regular-sized classes. Within this setting, which is designed to encourage interaction among pupils and teachers, the teachers sometimes form teams (team teaching) to improve the process of education and further facilitate interaction among themselves. In some open-plan schools, pupils are allowed to advance at their own pace in individual subjects (called "continuous progress") rather than wait until the end of the school year for formal promotion to the next grade. The open-plan concept is apparently no flash in the pan (Boocock, 1978: 19; Martin and Macdonell, 1982: 202), partly because it seems to be more harmonious with today's child-rearing practices than the self-contained classroom was. Still, its superiority over the traditional type remains generally unproved (Bennett, 1976).

The institution of education has a distinct history.

THE CLASSROOM

School-based education (as opposed to education in the home and elsewhere) is a complex system. It is a system of people, roles, relationships, groups, organizations, and processes, all contributing in their unique ways to the establishment and maintenance of the classroom as the principal instructional setting. The acquisition of knowledge, wisdom, and desirable qualities of mind and character may occasionally be accomplished in other settings. Students, for example, can acquire knowledge on field trips or in school assemblies, but the classroom (open or self-contained) is where many educators believe nearly all teaching and educating is done.

The classroom is where the outcomes of the struggles over government funding and teachers's salaries have their payoff. Curriculum content, class timetables, selection of books and equipment, and administrative policies all come together in the classroom. Although principals, superintendents, librarians, counselors, legislators, members of the school board, and other functionaries have roles to play, they are fundamentally support personnel. To the extent that they have no teaching responsibilities, they are behind-the-scenes workers in the theater of the classroom.

The events of the classroom are, in certain ways, analogous to the episodes of a dramatic production. Both the theater and the classroom

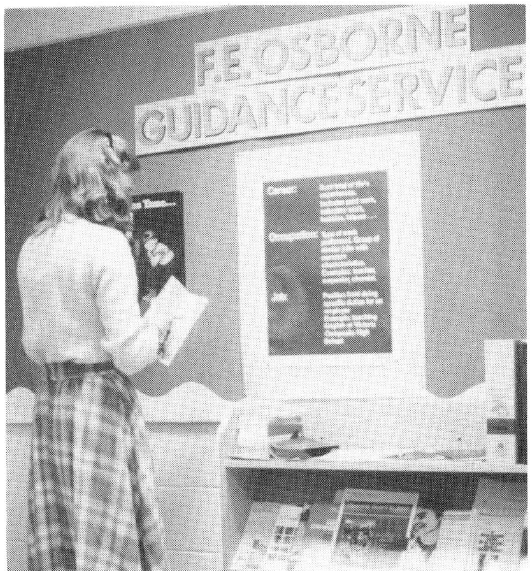

One nonteaching function of the school is student counselling.

have their props, scenery, and action. Each functions in a physical and temporal space (Stebbins, 1974b: 22–28, 47–58).

For example, pupils and teachers enter and exit this setting according to the daily class schedule. Structure is evident in each class period, whether the period lasts forty minutes or two hours. First, there are the preliminaries of taking the attendance, collecting money for class projects, and saying prayers (in religious schools). The preliminaries are followed by the three-phase sequence of classroom teaching—the lesson, the seatwork, and the recapitulation.

The physical space of the classroom is more than a floor, a ceiling, and four walls.

The sequence begins with the teaching of the lesson. Seatwork is next. In assigning seatwork, teachers deal with a number of problems, some of which are discussed later. In the recapitulation phase, the teacher again takes charge of the class as a unit, summarizing the lesson, clarifying misunderstandings, and perhaps illustrating certain points with exemplary student work. There are, of course, occasional temporary diversions from this sequence, depending on the ability of the pupils, special events, and imminent holidays and vacations.

The Pupils

After reviewing the scant evidence on pupils' views of schooling, Meighan (1977) concluded that, on the whole, elementary school students appear to be more satisfied with their educational experiences than high school students. He also found that, when dissatisfaction is expressed, it is as likely to come from successful students as from unsuccessful students. The studies reviewed were conducted in Britain and the United States. Research in Ontario suggests a similar outlook among high school students there (Ad Hoc Committee Respecting Student Matters, 1972).

But pupils vary socially and psychologically. In addition, these variations are related in complicated ways to their views of schooling and to the ways their teachers and other school personnel treat them. For instance, many classrooms are *heterogeneous,* with pupils coming from a range of socioeconomic backgrounds. It has generally been found that teachers, being middle-class individuals, identify best with middle-class pupils and also with upper-class pupils.

Often lower-class pupils receive less academic attention, more sanctions for misconduct, and fewer privileges (Martin, 1970). This depends, however, on the teacher's orientation to the job: is the teacher teacher-centered or student-centered? Richer (1974) observed in a study of three Ottawa elementary schools that lower-class pupils receive more than their fair share of attention from student-centered teachers.

Ecological segregation and socioeconomic status in North American cities are closely allied (see Chapter 8). In view of all this, it is not surprising that many neighborhood schools serve pupils with similar social-class backgrounds. Havighurst and Levine (1979: 154) point out that schools with enrollments of mostly lower-class pupils must deal with more severe teaching problems than those with enrollments of mostly middle- and upper-class pupils. Lower-class pupils have more often failed to master basic academic skills. Hence, they require a great deal of help from their teachers if they are to overcome their difficulties. Havighurst and Levine also note that the lower-class child's world is chaotic; financial problems and social uncertainties impede the child's learning at school. Teachers must somehow generate enough structure in the classroom for these underprivileged children to acquire an education—to develop a willingness and an ability to learn what they are taught.

Low income and ethnicity are frequently associated. Adult blacks and Hispanics in the United States are found in disproportionate numbers at the poverty level, which means that their children are more likely to be in disadvantaged positions at school than the children of white families (U.S. Bureau of the Census, 1980: 466, Table 774). As noted in Chapter 20, many Canadian Indian, Métis, Inuit, and black families face the same problems for the same reasons (Statistics Canada, 1980a: 174–175).[1]

From the standpoint of education, the correlation between low income and ethnicity is significant. In general, pupils with ethnic backgrounds come from low-income families, if not impoverished families. Moreover, there is a further correlation between social class and ethnicity, on the one hand, and levels of academic performance and orderliness, on the other. To illustrate, a lower-class Indian child is more likely to be a disorderly, low-achieving pupil than a middle-class white child.

Pupils in Great Britain and North America are further categorized by their teachers and eventually by themselves according to their behavior and academic performance. For example, some pupils are identified as troublemakers and low achievers. Others are looked upon as well-behaved and high achievers. In the eyes of the teacher, a child is either a good student or a bad student.

Do teacher categorizations of pupils as low achievers or high achievers lead to *self-fulfilling prophecies?* Or, to put it another way, do pupils achieve at the levels at which their teachers mentally classify them? Do they fulfill the teacher's expectations? The data on these questions are equivocal. Delamont (1976: Chapter 3) and Rist (1973: 164–195), for example, have found that the prediction, or prophecy, holds for both high achievers and low achievers. Other researchers, including McPherson (1972: 99–100) and Bird (1980), have found that teachers see their pupils as changing intellectually from time to time. McPherson and Bird found that teachers are prepared to recategorize pupils when a change occurs and to treat them according to their new labels.

Some pupils are intellectually or physically *exceptional.* That is, they are gifted or handicapped (Martin and Macdonell, 1982: 78–87; Dunn, 1973). The handicapped, if blind, deaf, crippled, or retarded, may be sent to special schools. The gifted may be enrolled in special programs of instruction at their neighborhood school or elsewhere. The general practice in North America, however, is *mainstreaming* (Sarason and Doris, 1979: 17), that is, integrat-

[1]The Métis are mostly the progeny of Indian women and Scots or French fur traders and settlers (see Chapter 16).

ing the exceptional child with the normal children wherever possible. The exceptional child then experiences ordinary social contact with others in the classroom.

The Teachers

Fuller and Brown (1975: 27) have compiled the following profile of today's teacher in the United States:

> At first glance teachers seem homogeneous, fitting a traditional image: hard working, kindly, and altruistic but less bright, more conforming, less competitive, and even less intellectually active than other professional persons. However, teachers are changing. The new teacher is younger and less experienced, but better qualified. Still typically a female, more and more of her colleagues are males. She has higher economic status, and is now more likely to come from a professional family background and to have an advanced degree. . . . She is geographically more mobile and is less likely to identify with her community or to live within the boundaries of the school system. This broad characteristic, however, covers a multitude of group and individual differences.

Some American teachers still come from lower-class families, however, which may encourage them to identify with pupils whose backgrounds are similar to theirs (Goodwin, 1977).

No informative, up-to-date profile is available for Canadian teachers. Nevertheless, examination of secondary sources produces a picture similar to Fuller and Brown's. It is clear from Statistics Canada data (1972–73: 44–45; 1983–84: 44–45) that qualifications have risen; the proportion of teachers with bachelor's or graduate degrees increased more than 31 percent between 1972 and 1983–84 to nearly 84 percent of all teachers. In 1983–84, 10.1 percent of Canadian teachers held master's or doctoral degrees. Still, four to five times as many teachers held these graduate degrees in the United States in 1980 as held them in Canada in 1983–84 (U.S. Bureau of the Census, 1981: 151).

There is no information on whether Canadian teachers are entering their profession earlier than previously and, therefore, with less experience. The sources cited in the preceding paragraph indicate that the average amount of teaching experience is increasing in both Canada and the United States. This is probably, in good part, the result of the restricted labor market of the early 1980s, in which fewer teachers were being hired and fewer were able to find alternative jobs (Statistics Canada, 1982–83: 12–13). Finally, there are no data pertaining to the geographic mobility of Canadian teachers or their inclination to identify with the local community and the local school district.

One thing about teaching as an occupation is the way it is looked on as a career. There is evidence in both Canada and the United States, some of which may not be too convincing, that the value commitment to the profession of teaching (value commitment is discussed in Chapter 15) is generally weak (Martin and Macdonell, 1982: 111–113; Lortie, 1975: Chapter 4). Few teachers believe they will retire in their profession. In fact, many men and some women leave the classroom for jobs in administration or for jobs in industry or government. Many women give up teaching for marriage and child-rearing. The teachers who take jobs in industry or government are likely to do so only if they can find a position with roughly equivalent prestige and remuneration.

The low level of value commitment can be traced, in part, to the "unbureaucratic" nature of the career of the elementary and secondary school teacher. With the occupation of teaching, there is no set of positions to advance through; promotion is not a part of teaching as is the career of a person in business. The opportunities for advancement lie in other jobs in education such as principal, vice-principal, department head, or student counselor. Moreover, teaching in some areas of North America pays poorly. Lortie (1975: 99) has this to say about the teacher's interest in advancement:

> The main opportunity for making major status gains rests in leaving classroom work for full-time administration. The primary benefits earned by persistence in teaching (annual increases in pay) are the outcome of seniority and course-taking; the incentive system is not organized to respond to variations in efforts and talent among classroom teachers.

In one study reported by Lortie (1975: 95), nearly every male teacher over forty years of age had a strong avocational interest outside teaching or a second source of income. These men appeared to be using their nonwork time to compensate for their uninteresting, low-paying work role.

Teachers and Pupils

So far we have referred to teachers and pupils as if they were separate categories of humanity whose paths never cross. Symbolic interactionist research reveals that nothing could be further from the truth:

> The teacher represents the established social order in the school, and his interest is in maintaining that order, whereas pupils have only a negative interest in that feudal superstructure. Teacher and pupil confront each other with attitudes from which the underlying hostility can never be altogether removed. Pupils are the material in which teachers are supposed to produce results. Pupils are human beings striving to realize their own results in their own way. Each of these hostile parties stands in the way of the other; in so far as the aims of either are realized, it is at the sacrifice of the aims of the other.
>
> The fundamental problem of school discipline may be stated as the struggle of students and teachers to establish their own definitions of situations in the life of the school. (Waller, 1932: 196, 297)

It was pointed out in Chapter 4 that people enter into situations with certain intentions or goals in mind. The intentions or goals help individuals define what is happening. Teachers working in the classroom initially define the disorderly conduct and academic performance situations they encounter with reference to two main goals: giving *intellectual training* (and sometimes moral and social training) and *maintaining order* (Stebbins, 1975: 45). If these two are not met, a third goal emerges, namely survival (Pollard, 1980). Research in the United States (McPherson, 1972: 106–107; Metz, 1978: 121–122), Canada (Martin, 1976), and Great Britain (Woods, 1976: 178) suggests that pupil goals include *maintaining order, receiving equitable treatment from the teacher, engaging in classroom activities,* and *avoiding boredom.*

Teacher Strategies Both teachers and pupils have strategies for reaching their classroom goals. The strategies and goals are evidence that North American classrooms are characterized by both conflict and consensus. *Strategies* are "specific and repeatable acts chosen and maintained in local relationships with one another to serve [these goals]" (Paisey, 1975: 14). Stebbins (1981: 248–249), in a review of North American and British research on definitions of classroom situations, lists eight teacher strategies. First among the eight strategies is domination. *Domi-*

Pupil Goal: Maintaining order is important for pupils too.

nation is a common strategy, particularly among teachers of low-ability pupils. It hinges on physical force, vocal superiority, establishing rules, and continuous surveillance. *Negotiation* is another widely used strategy. It rests on the exchange of valued possessions, privileges, opportunities, and relationships. Flattery and ingratiation are often part of the exchange in teacher-pupil negotiations (Metz, 1978: 115; Martin, 1976: 60–67). Some teachers attempt to win control of their pupils by *fraternizing* with them, by sharing their interests, styles of speech, fashions in clothing, and so forth.

Physically or psychologically, *removing* oneself from the classroom is how some teachers evade problems. In modified form, this strategy includes ignoring minor infractions of schoolroom rules. *Routines* serve as a means of control, since they help pace the activities of the classroom. *Occupational therapy* (Woods, 1979: 164) also restricts attention, such as by requiring students to draw maps or pictures. *Controlling talk* through questioning, lecturing, and limiting spontaneous pupil commentary is still another strategy. Finally, teachers maintain order by *not provoking* troublemakers.

Pupil Strategies Research on pupils' views of classroom life is less detailed than that on teachers' views. Nevertheless, six pupil strategies have been identified through ethnographic studies in Britain and North America (Stebbins, 1981: 250–251). They are "counterstrategies" in Martin Denscomb's (1980: 56) words. A seventh benign strategy has also been observed.

First, there are the forbidden acts of *talking* and *eating* in the classroom, justified as ways of making schoolwork tolerable. Next is the *noise* strategy; noisy children seek to disturb the flow of lessons and to annoy the teacher. Noise is most effective in self-contained classrooms. A third counterstrategy is to engage in *humor,* thereby gaining a respite from the tedium of a lesson or an unpleasant seatwork task. Fourth is *negotiation.* In this instance, negotiation is initiated by pupils rather than by their teacher. Fifth is the *exploitation* strategy. Pupils take advantage of the teacher's fraternization strategy or avoidance of provocation strategy, using them as a means of shirking their assignments or of gaining a respite from the work. Still another counterstrategy is *rebellion,* which commonly occurs when the pupils decide the teacher is incompetent. The *cooperative* strategy is evident when pupils try to determine what their teachers want in the way of academic performance and attempt to measure up.

THE CLASSROOM ENVIRONMENT

With a pinch of intellectual license, it is possible to apply the notion of organizational environment (Chapter 7) to elementary and secondary schoolrooms. The teachers and pupils who strut and fret their hours upon the classroom stage do so within a broad set of influences impinging on them from beyond its walls. These influences can be grouped in these categories: school, school district, and society. They have an impact despite the fact that the classroom is relatively sheltered from intervention by parents and others in the community and from systematic observation by administrators (Warren, 1973).

The School

The school is the immediate environment surrounding the classroom. Its social components include adolescent peer groups, administrative personnel, the teaching staff, and ancillary specialists (e.g., counselors, librarians). These individuals conduct their activities within the school but largely, if not entirely, outside the classroom of any given pupil.[2] The peer group and administrative personnel are considered here.

Peer Group Some peer-group activities are closely associated with the classroom effort.

[2]Peer groups also exist in the upper primary grades, but little is known about their impact on classroom processes.

Peer-group activities are an important part of the classroom environment.

Athletics is an example. The members of the basketball team and the football team must maintain an acceptable grade average to be eligible for the team. The consequences of peer-group activity in Canada differ from those in the United States.

A benchmark study in this area in both countries was James Coleman's (1961) research on American adolescents, wherein he concluded that norms different from the adult world guide their behavior. Academic ability was found to be neither honored nor despised. A strong interest in sports was, however, associated with peer popularity for boys, while a lack of interest in sports and an intense interest in bookish matters were stigmatizing. Girls wanted to be popular; in their view, being liked and admired was more desirable than academic success. Studies on males and females by Eitzen (1976) and Feltz (1979) suggest that such conclusions by Coleman and others are still applicable.

The ranking of these adolescent interests is strikingly different in Canada and the United States. Alexander and Farrell (1975) found, for example, that peers in Canada have considerable influence on the courses students take and on whether they abide by the school dress code, but only minor influence on how they evaluate teachers or conform to the school smoking rules. Friesen's (1968) data negated his own hypothesis, derived from Coleman's study, that Canadian students valued athletics, popularity, and academic achievement in that order. In the Alexander and Farrell study, both boys and girls ranked academic achievement first. Girls ranked popularity second and athletics third, while boys reversed these two. Jerome and Phillips (1971: 20) sum up the Canadian-American differences as follows:

> It is clear that, in the American secondary school, high recognition and accompanying status are achieved directly through athletic activities. Athletes are more likely to be members of the leading crowds than are scholars. . . . This does not appear to be the case in the Canadian school. The athlete is visible, but not to the same degree, and his acceptance into the leading crowd appears to be dependent to a greater degree on his scholastic aptitude.

Administration In large schools, the administration typically consists of a principal, one or more vice-principals or assistant principals, and several department heads. We know more about the principal than about the assistants and department heads. Martin and Macdonell (1982: 102–106, 126–131) and Lortie (1975: 192, 196–200) have reviewed the research on principals. Their reviews show that the role of the principal in Canada is much the same as the role in the United States: he or she is the school's educational leader and manager. Principals recommend in-service training for their teachers. They also assign students to teachers and teachers to classes. On the managerial side, they keep the school's records, allocate equipment, designate space, and construct course timetables. The larger the school, the greater is the number of assistants to whom the principal can delegate responsibilities. But the principal still holds the ultimate responsibility for all administrative functions.

Principals are also the final court of appeal in student discipline cases. A teacher may seek the principal's help with the difficult boy or girl; the principal is called on to work whatever magic he or she can to persuade the pupil's parents to help deal with the child's recalcitrance. As Lortie points out, however, this may put the teacher in the position of someday having to grant the principal a favor he or she may be reluctant to give.

The position of principal is a stressful one. It is foremanlike, with conflicting demands made on the principal by teachers, parents, and the superintendent (the principal's immediate superior). For example, teachers sometimes want more say in developing the course timetable and in making course assignments than principals are willing to allow. Parents sometimes complain about a teacher's disciplinary action, but the principal supports the teacher, believing he or she is justified under the circumstances. Some school systems require periodic evaluations of teaching, which may be resented. In these and in other conflicts, the principal is caught in the middle.

One delicate situation in which the principal is frequently the arbiter is the conflict between parents, on the one hand, and teachers and counselors, on the other, over the *tracking* and *streaming* of pupils. Brookover and Erickson (1975: 331) define tracking and streaming as:

> the arrangements in which students are placed in different curricula with somewhat different long-term goals for their learning. These are illustrated by what is commonly called college-bound and noncollege-bound curricula in American secondary schools. . . . The decision concerning the choice of tracks is commonly based upon some prior measure of achievement or presumed differences in aptitude.

Streaming (in Canada and Great Britain) or tracking (in the United States) bears directly on the proposition stated at the beginning of this chapter, to wit, that education is the key to occupational attainment (see also Chapter 18). Furthermore, it serves the related institutional value mentioned earlier of allocating people to various occupational roles in adult life. The functionalists hold that, by means of this process, the more capable students are identified and tracked into higher levels of academic training, while the less capable students are streamed into lower levels. The less able students often are encouraged to enroll in trade schools or community colleges.[3] In fact, these students come disproportionately from the lower class.

Many factors influence the decision to place a pupil in one stream or another. Schafer and Olexa (1971) and Rehberg and Hotchkiss (1972), among others, have found that intelligence test scores, socioeconomic status of the pupil's family, encouragement from parents, and educational aspirations of the pupil are frequently part of the streaming formula. Another factor is the advice of teachers and counselors and their reasons for a categorization of pupils. The categorizations were said earlier to carry the possibility of a self-fulfilling prophecy. And, whatever the plans of school authorities for streaming pupils, it appears that high school girls, when compared with boys, tend to avoid technical and advanced courses, selecting instead those that are commercial (Sudermann, 1979).

Writing from the conflict perspective, Samuel Bowles (1971) contends that, by placing students in different streams, schools engage in unequal education and perpetuate the existing division of labor. It is noted later in this chapter that intelligence is far more equally distributed among the social classes than the small number of university students and graduates would have us believe. Yet schools cannot be held solely responsible for this outcome, Bowles says, since it is embedded in the larger culture and social structure of the society. For instance, factors such as family socioeconomic status in a school's decision to stream a pupil are often unrecognized parts of the cultural frame within which the educational decision makers unwittingly operate. In other words, North American

[3]Streaming (tracking) is different from ability grouping. In the latter pupils are placed in classes with others of similar intellectual ability within a particular stream.

schools and especially their practice of streaming are contributing to the notorious inequality of educational opportunity noted in the United States by Rosenbaum (1976) and in Canada by Porter et al. (1982).

Streaming policies, the pupils' social-class background, the principal's leadership style, and the teachers' attitudes combine to create a school climate, or school subculture. The *school climate* is the constellation of attitudes, beliefs, values, norms, and behavior patterns of pupils, teachers, and school administrators. A school in a lower-class neighborhood run by an authoritarian principal would have a noticeably different climate from one in an upper-middle-class suburb run by a democratic principal.

The School District

There is an institutional chain of command in North American education. It starts in (1) the state, provincial, or territorial (Northwest Territories) government and runs through (2) each local school district and its board, (3) the superintendent of schools, (4) the assistant superintendents, (5) school principals, (6) assistant principals or vice-principals, (7) department heads (where they exist), to (8) the teachers. A variety of professional, clerical, and maintenance personnel fill out this basic structure.

Although North American public elementary and secondary education is largely guided by state, provincial, or territorial authorities, it is partly funded through local property taxes and administered in local school districts by their boards of education (Michalos, 1981: 97). Consequently, the school district (i.e., town, city, or rural area) in which a school is located can have a significant impact on the school. Sociologists say that influences on schools arise from four sources: the school boards, school superintendents, parents' associations, and religious organizations.

In Canada, school boards generally have two functions: (1) to provide facilities, equipment, and supplies for education and (2) to hire staff (Gue, 1977: 140). They also set municipal school taxes. Matters such as training and certifying teachers, establishing curricula, setting the number of days in the academic year, and selecting textbooks are the prerogatives of the provincial and territorial governments. The division of functions in the United States between its state governments and local boards of education is similar (Goldman, 1971: 25). The states, provinces, and territories also establish procedures for electing board members, or "trustees," as they are called in Canada.[4] School boards tend to be agents of the government, state or provincial and municipal.

School Superintendents Ann Parelius and Robert Parelius (1978: 125) describe the ideal and actual roles of the district school superintendent:

> Educational policy is supposed to be formulated by local school boards and carried out by the chief administrator—the school superintendent—hired by these boards. The superintendent is an employee who serves at the pleasure of the board and who may, therefore, be dismissed when the board members decide his or her performance is unsatisfactory. Ideally, there exists a clear and mutually understood division of labor between the school board and the superintendent. In reality, however, the situation is considerably more complex. The distinction between policy initiation and implementation breaks down in the daily operation of the schools. Superintendents can both initiate and sabotage policy through manipulating administrative procedures.

Superintendents are full-time professionals who can master the complicated procedures and regulations of local education. In assuming their responsibilities, they often submerge the part-time, volunteer members of the school board in details too abstruse for them to assess. Thus,

[4]Some provinces have provisions for appointed trustees (Gue, 1977: 140).

under certain conditions, superintendents may be more powerful than the boards who hire and evaluate them. Indeed, American school boards act mainly to legitimate decisions made in the superintendent's office (Scimecca, 1980: 121).

But superintendents have problems, too. Gross et al. (1958: Chapter 16), whose study of the role conflicts of a sample of American superintendents is still considered a landmark in the sociology of education, identified three sources of strain. (1) Most superintendents feel obliged to discharge their responsibility (delegated by the board) of hiring and firing principals and teachers on the basis of merit. Yet influential individuals and groups in the community may want other criteria used (e.g., religious, political, moral). (2) Because superintendents are highly visible in the community, they face incompatible expectations of how they should allocate their time. For example, they are often asked by local trade and professional associations to attend their meetings and otherwise participate in their affairs, while their families and school boards want them to use their work and after-work time for their benefit. (3) It is the duty of the superintendents to draw up budget recommendations for their districts. There are many individuals and groups who expect them to give higher priority to the community's limited financial resources than to its educational needs. In fact, this situation was defined as incompatible by the largest proportion of the sample (90 percent). There is no evidence of these tensions subsiding in recent years for the American superintendent (Travers, 1978). Nor does the superintendent's lot appear to be any better in Canada (Jepson, 1976), although no Canadian research exists to confirm this impression.

Parent-Teacher Groups The school environment is further composed of groups of parents, organized in North America into state chapters of the National Congress of Parents and Teachers (PTA) and provincial chapters of the Canadian Home and School and Parent-Teacher Federation. Brookover and Erickson (1975: 314) hold that such organizations have little influence on school affairs and school board decisions. Indeed, parent-teacher groups are often shaped and carefully controlled by school administrators. Teachers and other local educational functionaries resent any sort of community intrusion into their professional affairs.

Two studies of Home and School Associations in Edmonton suggest that they are more effective in marshaling community support for their schools than attacking the policies of those schools (McKendry and Wright, 1965). They were found to have a concern for the education of pupils, but they seldom tried to change school, school board, or provincial educational policy. In other words, these associations had about the same small degree of influence on school and school board activities as their American counterparts.

The effect of religion on the operations of the North American classroom is felt indirectly through two major channels: (1) legal control and (2) interest-group tactics. We turn first to the subject of *legal control.* In both the United States and Canada there are religious bodies with their own school boards. These organizations, however, are subject to certain government controls.

The processes of funding and control and the effect of religion are heavily intertwined in Canada. Some provinces and territories have only a public system, others only a religious system, and still others a public system and informal recognition of denominational schools. Indeed, five patterns of funding and control are evident in the provincial and territorial public and separate school systems (see Martin and Macdonell, 1982: 159 for a summary). The separate systems allow the teaching of religious doctrine, whereas this is forbidden in the public systems. In contrast with American practice, Canadian separate schools are funded with public monies.

The use of interest-group tactics is a strategy religious groups share with organizations which have a political, ethnic, or commercial concern with the school or with its funding and administration. Religious groups may pressure school boards and governments to consider favorably their special interests such as saying prayers in the classroom, abolishing references to biological evolution, or teaching courses in religion. As might be expected, other groups often apply countervailing pressures in an attempt to prevent the religious interests from succeeding. Teachers and pupils feel the outcome of these struggles in the classrooms. There may be new routines, new courses of study, or other changes in the classroom.

The Society

In both the United States and Canada, the historical tendency has been for the federal government to follow a hands-off policy with respect to elementary and secondary education. Historically, the grade school and the high school have been seen as primarily a local responsibility. In the United States, however, this policy is now undergoing some modification. Another societywide influence in the classroom comes from the national teachers organizations. We turn first to the effects of the federal government on local education. The federal government has assumed a fiscal responsibility and, in the United States, a legislative responsibility.

Schools and the Government Fiscal support from the federal governments in Canada and the United States, although not insignificant, is minor when compared with that of the state, provincial, and municipal agovernments. The federal governments of the United States and Canada contributed 8.5 percent (1980) and 3.0 percent (1977–1978), respectively, of the total cost of elementary and secondary education in their countries (U.S. Bureau of the Census, 1980: 140, Table 221; Statistics Canada, 1981e: 213).

The *legislative* effects are much more profound in the United States than in Canada. Chesler and Cave (1981: 58–60) summarize some of these. Since 1958, when the Soviet satellite Sputnik threatened American technological superiority, the U.S. Congress has enacted several measures related to education, the long-range effect of which has been to bring federal influence into the classroom. For example, in 1965 Congress passed the Elementary and Secondary Education Act in an attempt to improve the schooling of minorities and the poor. In 1979 Congress established the Department of Education, with a secretary of education in the president's cabinet. Supreme Court decisions from 1954 onward have barred, with some success, racial discrimination in public schools. The controversial busing program has the Supreme Court's approval.

By contrast, the federal legislative impact on Canadian classrooms is indirect and felt mostly through funding policies. There is no government department, separate or combined, with an administrative mandate in education. The lack of the federal government's interest and involvement in Canadian schools is explained by Fullan (1982: 240):

> The best introduction to the federal role in education is by way of money and policy. The federal government provides some of the former and extremely little of the latter, being explicitly discouraged from doing so by the provinces and by its own reluctance. The British North American Act (1867) states that provinces "may exclusively make laws in education" (Section 93).

Teachers Organizations Indirectly influential are the four teachers organizations. The two oldest came into being as purely professional groups, and they are known today as the National Education Association (founded in 1857 in the United States) and the Canadian Education Association (founded in 1867).[5] For many years, both organizations were primarily concerned with advancing the standards of teaching and teacher training, improving teacher ethics, and promoting the profession in the

[5]Both associations began under other names.

community. The founding of the Canadian Teachers' Federation in 1919 and the American Federation of Teachers in 1916 eventually forced changes in the goals of the two older associations.

As unionlike considerations of salaries, hours, and working conditions began to gain importance among teachers, the federations and their state, provincial, and territorial affiliates attracted many new members. The federations were willing to fight for salaries and working conditions, while the associations were calling such action "unprofessional." But, to counteract their recent losses in membership, the associations have had to take a greater interest in matters such as salaries and working conditions.

The welfare of pupils and the quality of classroom teaching are of prime concern to all four organizations. Nonetheless, the federations see the strategies of organized labor (e.g., strikes, collective bargaining) as the way to implement these concerns. Such strategies, they argue, are no longer unprofessional (since they are used by nurses, airplane pilots, police officers, university professors, and, in modified form, physicians). For example, the number of pupils in a classroom affects the quality of education that can be provided. The number of pupils per classroom can be negotiated as part of the collective agreement between a local teachers union and the school board.

Unions and teachers' associations are influential nationwide organizations which, through their members, bring extralocal policies and organizational power to bear on classroom events. Principals and superintendents are also organized on a national scale, but the policies of their associations are only indirectly felt at the classroom level.

ALTERNATIVES

Some sociologists defend all or much of the existing education system, as do some parents, teachers, and administrators. But others reject significant aspects of it. They propose numerous alternatives. Among the alternatives are free schools, alternative schools, no schools (deschooling), lifelong learning, and adult education. Other alternatives which have been suggested are voucher plans, return to basics, and home-based learning. Free schools, alternative schools, and deschooling are taken up in the sections which follow.

Free Schools

According to Graubard (1972), there are four kinds of free schools in the United States. Together, the free schools constitute the free-school movement. They have in common the principle of free choice and action for pupils. The *classical free school* resembles its prototype in Summerhill, England, founded in 1921. The Summerhill school is a boarding school; its aim is to create a warm, sensitive community of equals among the pupils. It offers a full program of elementary and secondary classes. Attendance is optional. Personality development and self-actualization are regarded as more important than intellectual achievement.

The *parent-teacher cooperative elementary school* is closely related to the classical free school. It is mainly distinguished by the fact that parents work closely with committed, though usually poorly paid, teachers. Since parents are routinely involved in the educational effort, these schools tend to be located in or near the communities in which the parents live. They are not boarding schools.

The *free high schools,* the third type, offer different approaches. Some offer a radical political education to white, middle-class youth. Others are more vocationally oriented, usually catering to lower-class pupils. The street academies are designed to educate disadvantaged minority students. The fourth type, the *community elementary school,* is the work of citizens who believe they should control the schools. They are inclined to stress ethnic consciousness and the acquisition of basic educational skills. In contrast to other types of free schools, community elementary schools are often strict and straitlaced.

From Mark Novak's (1975: 36–37) description of free schools in Canada, it is evident that all four of Graubard's types are represented in Canada as well. He mentions an Ontario communal farm program, several free schools in inner-city Toronto, and various suburban free schools, all of which embrace the principle of minimal system control over the lives of their pupils. The school studied by Novak, however, is best classified as an *alternative school.*

Alternative Schools

Some scholars treat alternative schools and free schools as synonymous. Others distinguish the two by noting that the free schools have gained acceptance by the school boards of North America, while the alternative schools have not. Vernon Smith (1974) describes some of the American alternative schools. There are those, he says, that are "schools without walls," educating their pupils through zoos, museums, factories, and newspapers. Others are learning centers, which draw pupils from the entire community instead of a single neighborhood. Educational parks, career-education centers, and specialized vocational and science schools are also alternative schools. Some alternative

This alternative school stresses ethnic culture and identity.

schools approach the Summerhill model. Nonetheless, being publicly funded and operated, the more radical programs of the free schools—e.g., those which stress ethnic pride, left-wing politics, or priority of pupil enjoyment—are apt to be shunned.

The alternative school in suburban Toronto studied by Novak (1975: 41) was established by the community's board of trustees. It is run on the following principles:

1. The school will be governed by a council consisting of 50 percent staff and administration. (Prior to establishment, the council will consist of 50 percent parents and 50 percent staff and administration.)
2. The total operational budget, including salaries, shall be allocated to the school council as one unit; the budget is to be divided by members of the council as they see fit.
3. The child shall have total personal freedom; the only limitations are that the child does not infringe upon the rights of others or endanger his or her health and safety.
4. The school will be concerned with the development of basic skills, although not necessarily in the traditional order.
5. At the inception of the school, classes will be provided for junior kindergarten level to the equivalent of the sixth level.
6. Enrollment in the school will be voluntary; parents who enroll their children must be in agreement with the basic principles of the school. Since enrollment is voluntary, parents shall be permitted to send their children to the school regardless of boundaries.

Several alternative schools have been established in Canada, nurtured in part by the educational reform movement in the United States (Carlton et al., 1977: 462–463). On both sides of the border, however, there is considerable skepticism about the success and contributions of the alternative schools.

Deschooling Society

The title of this section is also the title of a book written by one of deschooling's main proponents, Ivan Illich (1971). He, John Holt (*How Children Fail,* Dell Publishing Co.), Paul Goodman (*Compulsory Miseducation,* Horizon Press), Everett Reimer (*School Is Dead,* Doubleday and Co.), and others have led the deschooling attack on the educational status quo. Meighan (1981: Chapter 30) provides an excellent review of their ideas, to which we now turn.

The deschoolers are conflict theorists. They say the aim of schools should be to prepare students to make a better society and to live in it successfully. In other words, schools should be future-oriented, not past-oriented as they are now. To acquire this outlook, students must be taught learning skills, instead of subjects such as mathematics and English. Deschoolers see the child-learner as an explorer rather than a trainee or student. The model to follow is that of the self-taught person. Exploring learners are not ones who regurgitate what they have been taught by a teacher but ones who synthesize knowledge from available resources, possibly even generating insights and new knowledge.

The teacher's role in all this is one of consultant and facilitator. In the deschooling perspective, teachers respond to the initiatives of their collegial learners. Mass education, because it confines teachers to an instructional role, makes poor use of the teacher's abilities, which are likely to be underdeveloped anyway if they have been trained in the standard "professional programs."

Consistent with what has just been said is the position of the deschoolers that the best learning resources are first-hand experiences and a wide variety of secondary resources. Since these experiences and resources are found everywhere, learning can occur everywhere, even *in schools.* Thus, the "deschooling" slogan is somewhat inappropriate. Certainly, the walled, egg-crate structured edifice of modern mass education is hardly what the deschoolers have in mind. But some of them speak of "little schools" and "minischools," which amount to small learning cooperatives of parents, teachers, and pupils funded by government. As mentioned, learning can also occur in libraries, museums, streets, homes, factories, shops, concert halls, and resource centers, to mention a few nonschool locations.

According to the deschoolers, assessments of learning should be conducted by other learners or by someone designated by the individual learner. Deschooling proponents recommend the use of achievement profiles, rather than tests and certificates. The traditional examination system, they argue, is primarily an instrument of the powerful groups in society who seek to maintain the status quo and to protect their privileged position within society.

The overall aim of the deschooling program is to develop the pupil's ability to deal critically and effectively with the world in which he or she lives. Pupils must learn how to transform their world to make it better for themselves, although certainly not at the expense of others in society.

The deschooling proposals are not wanting for critics. Parelius and Parelius (1978: 381) have pointed to some of the critics' objections to Illich's ideas in particular. The critics ask, How are children to know what is important if their learning is never directed by someone who knows which experiences to avoid (e.g., delinquency, drug use) and which to seek? It is also argued that a laissez-faire approach to education will only continue the current of inequality, since the rich are better at training themselves than are the poor. Illich has also been criticized for throwing out certification. This could open the door to quacks and self-styled, but fundamentally inadequate, teachers, a problem Illich does acknowledge. Finally, the functionalists see as basic to every society a set of shared values, which, in industrial nations, the schools help transmit. They believe that, if Illich's proposals were adopted, society would eventually collapse in anarchy, since the common foundation of values would crumble.

HIGHER EDUCATION

We began this chapter by mentioning some of the contributions made by education to the functioning of society. One of these is the role played by education in fostering occupational attainment. Since the part played by higher education in the attainment process is obvious, little more need be said about it here. Rather, this section concentrates on two other functions of education: the allocation of adult work roles and cultural production.

Allocation

Allocation begins in the junior high schools with the practice of streaming, which, as we have seen, is itself the outcome of numerous factors. Functionalists argue that it is to a society's advantage to place its most capable members in its most difficult and essential roles. These scholars hold that the secondary educational system selects such individuals, steers them to university-bound streams, and encourages them to seek further instruction beyond high school. Four-year colleges and universities, according to the functionalist model, are elite systems of education reserved for students too talented to be wasted by filling work roles easily taken on by individuals of more modest ability.

When we return to the subject of allocation in Chapter 18, we shall see that there are theoretical problems with the functionalist stance. For the present, however, let us consider the critique made of it by the conflict theorists. Bowles and Gintis (1976) note that high intelligence is not as rare as the small number of university students and university graduates would have us believe. Moreover, many weaknesses inhere in the process by which students are placed in one stream or another in high school. Some of the factors referred to in the preceding paragraph attest to that. As a result, a significant number of objectively well-qualified students are shunted by the educational system into unchallenging jobs and discouraged from entering a four-year college or university.

Some of the less able students drop out of high school. Others, convinced that they are innately capable of doing university work, enroll in a community college; they hope to upgrade their qualifications and eventually work toward a university degree. Research in both the United States and Canada (Cohen and Brawer, 1982; Pincus, 1978) indicates, however, that these students are often counseled by their advisors to terminate their education in the community college.

Cultural Production

One of the major functions of the university in Canada and other Western nations is the making of culture, particularly new humanistic and scientific knowledge and new artistic works and expressions. An important part of the university professor's job is to do research or to contribute to the arts. This facet of academic life frequently goes unnoticed by the general public. Those who have never attended a university or who terminate their advanced education with a bachelor's degree usually see only the teaching side of the professorial occupation. It is hardly surprising, then, that such individuals are inclined to cast professors into the work role of the elementary and secondary schoolteacher—as preparers of lessons, givers of lectures, correctors of examinations, and beneficiaries of long summer vacations.

Graduate students know better. They are trained by those who practice what they preach in how to come up with new scientific or humanistic ideas or in how to create and express the arts. In many instances, the graduate students themselves will someday be professors. For them, the cultural production side of the professor's job is of direct benefit. Undergraduates are occasionally informed, usually through lectures, of the results of faculty research. But only the graduate students and a handful of undergraduate honors students actually have an opportunity to participate in the production of art, humanities, and science.

The Aesthetics of Food

Most vocational students have not previously excelled in school, as trade school represents a career option that does not require finely-honed academic skills. Although all students in these three classes had completed high school (or had received a high school equivalency diploma), most had no college training, and only two had completed college. The majority of students hope that trade school will provide an experience significantly different from their previous education, particularly in that it involves hands-on training.

Most students enter the chef training program largely unaware of what is involved in the occupation—even though all of them have cooked food previously (in some cases "professionally" for modest establishments). In their ignorance they are little different from medical students and other aspiring professionals, except their expectations are much lower and their images dimmer. With few exceptions students do not have a clear idea of the aesthetics of professional cooking, and may not even know that there is an aesthetic, although from cooking at home (and eating elsewhere), students are implicitly aware of various folk aesthetics. Thus chef instructors face formidable tasks in training their charges to be professionals and in teaching them the dimensions of the aesthetics of professional cooking. This training is an eye-opening experience for most of the students.

As in most occupational training programs, students are not taught about the grand philosophy of the occupation (if such exists); rather, they are taught particular skills and techniques that contain within them the aesthetic rules that students must generalize to related tasks. Although students are exhorted to make their food look appetizing, because "people eat with their eyes," this bon mot tells students little about how to achieve this goal.

The aesthetic rules for cooking are potentially more intricate than those of many other productive activities in that cooking appeals to at least four of our five senses: sight, taste, texture, and smell. Even sound is a component of eating—as in the enjoyment of the sound of a crisp item. However, the visual component has first priority in the aesthetic canons of food preparation.

Most of the aesthetic training in trade schools consists of learning the practical details of cooking. Students are taught during their first week in school when learning to make French bread that they should cut four slits in the top of their unbaked French bread dough: "they serve as decoration more than anything. You can throw [poppy or sesame] seeds on if you want to" (field notes, City TVI). Students take this advice to heart as they make slits and add seeds; some students even top their loaves with both types of seeds in order to make them look doubly nice. After the bread has been baked students comment on how impressed they are with how the loaves look. As one student remarks to a fellow student: "We did pretty good for rookies."

Such instruction was recurrent in learning to work with a variety of foodstuffs and techniques of cooking and baking. To bring out the red color in a cherry pie, for example, students are told to add red food coloring; cherries must be made to look like cherries. Although similar in some ways to home training in cooking, students are here taught "trade secrets" and are constantly reminded that they are cooking for paying customers, customers of whose taste they are unaware. As a result, students are taught that their standards must involve compromise—an attempt to hit the midpoint of taste. For example, one instructor tells his class that they must decide how much sugar to add to their whipped cream in that some enjoy the richness of the cream whereas others prefer the sweetness of the sugar: "Now sugar is a matter of personal taste. So we try to hit something in-between" (field notes, City TVI). The point is that cooks are constrained, however they might personally feel, to strive for the lowest common denominator—that level of food taste that will appeal to all of their customers. This assumes implicit knowledge of the tastes of their audience—tastes that will differ in different establishments.

As mentioned, cooking depends on four of the five senses: looks, taste, texture, and smell. Because there is more consensus on what looks nice than on what tastes good, much of the aesthetics of cooking is directed to visual appeal. And although smell is important in food appreciation, it is not often discussed separately from taste, and may not even be appreciated separately; "taste" is thus the generic term for both smell and taste.

SOURCE: Gary Alan Fine. Occupational aesthetics: Trade school students learn to cook. *Urban Life* 14: 11–13, 1985.

THE NECESSITY OF EDUCATION

Only one thing seems certain in all the debate about the quality of education, about its consequences for the community and the individual, and about the inequality of opportunity it spreads across the society: the institution of education is here to stay. We may change it to solve this problem or that—and no institution in modern society undergoes more change than education—but we are unlikely to eliminate it altogether. Even the deschooling proposals are proposals for education. Although experience outside the realm of education is also a great teacher, mass society requires a minimum level of education of its members, for their sake and for the sake of the society. Why?

> Perhaps the most valuable result of all education is the ability to make yourself do the thing you have to do, when it ought to be done, whether you like it or not; it is the first lesson that ought to be learned; and however early a man's training begins, it is probably the last lesson that he learns thoroughly.—Thomas Huxley, *Technical Education* (1877)

OUTLINE AND SUMMARY

I. Introduction
A major function of education: education is the key to occupational attainment.

II. Education as an Institution
Education is the process of educating others. *To educate* means to foster an expansion of knowledge, wisdom, and desirable qualities of mind and character.

A. The Defining Criteria
Education conforms to the six defining criteria of institutions. It is an institution.

B. Educational Values
Schools transmit many of the society's values. One value of education is that it prepares students for their adult occupational roles.

C. History of Education

The institution of education has a history. A historical development is the open-space, or open-plan, school.

III. The Classroom
The classroom is the focal point of the vast system of education. The events of the classroom are, in certain ways, analogous to the episodes of a dramatic production. Both the theater and the classroom have their props, scenery, and action.
  A. The Pupils
  Elementary school pupils are more satisfied with their educational experiences than secondary students. Variations in the ethnic and socioeconomic backgrounds of pupils lead to their differential treatment by teachers. Lower-class pupils generally receive less favorable treatment.
  B. The Teachers
  Teacher qualifications have been improving. But this has done little to alter the teacher's weak commitment to teaching as a calling. One of the problems is the unbureaucratic nature of a teaching career. Teachers have little opportunity for promotion.
  C. Teachers and Pupils
  To some extent, teachers and pupils have incompatible definitions of classroom situations.
    1. Teacher Strategies
    Teachers use various strategies to achieve their goals.
    2. Pupil Strategies
    Pupils have strategies, too.

IV. The Classroom Environment
The notion of organizational environment can be applied to elementary and secondary classrooms.
  A. The School
  The school is the immediate environment surrounding the classroom.
    1. Peer Group
    In the United States, boys generally rank athletics over popularity and popularity over academic success. Girls rank popularity as most important. In Canada, both boys and girls rank academic success first.
    2. Administration
    The principal is the school's educational leader and manager.
  B. The School District
  School boards provide facilities, equipment, and supplies for education; they are responsible for hiring the staff and for setting school taxes.
    1. School Superintendent
    The school superintendent implements the policies of the school board.
    2. Parent-Teacher Groups
    Parents and teachers are members of local and national associations such as the Canadian Home and School and Parent-Teacher Federation.
  C. The Society
  Among the societywide influences on the classroom are the fiscal and legislative policies of the federal government and the teacher's organizations.
    1. Schools and the Government
    The federal government's fiscal support of the schools is minor compared with that of the states and provinces.
    2. Teachers Organizations
    Four teachers organizations have an indirect influence on the schools.

V. Alternatives
Some sociologists reject significant aspects of the existing education system.
  A. Free Schools
  There are four kinds of free schools in North America: the classical free school, the parent-teacher cooperative elementary school, the free high school, and the community free school.
  B. Alternative Schools
  Alternative schools are sometimes distinguished from free schools by their formal connection with a school board.
  C. Deschooling Society
  The aim of schools, say the deschoolers, should be to teach students how to

make a better society and how to live in the society successfully.

VI. Higher Education
Higher education has two functions: (1) the allocation of adult work roles and (2) cultural production.

A. Allocation
Functionalists argue that it is to a society's advantage to place its most capable members in its most difficult and essential roles. Conflict theorists say this arrangement maintains upper- and middle-class advantages and overlooks lower-class talent.

B. Cultural Production
The university, besides being a teaching institution, is a center for the cultural production of new scientific and humanistic knowledge and new artistic creations and expression.

VII. The Necessity of Education
Education is here to stay.

FOR FURTHER READING AND STUDY

Chesler, M. A., and Cave, W. H. 1981. *A sociology of education.* New York: Macmillan. A textbook in the sociology of education. The book is concerned primarily with schools in the United States.

Coleman, J. A. 1961. *Adolescent society.* New York: Free Press. This classic surveys the world of American adolescents with reference to the school and nonschool experiences in their lives. The author is particularly concerned with the impact of adolescent values and activities on education.

Illich, I. 1971. *Deschooling society.* New York: Harper & Row. The aim of schools, says Illich, should be to prepare students to make a better society and to live in the society successfully. As he sees it, this can be accomplished, in good part, by getting educated outside the walls of the formal school.

Levine A. 1980. *When dreams and heroes died: A portrait of today's college student.* San Francisco: Jossey-Bass. A survey and description of American student attitudes (e.g., residential choices and political participation patterns). Levine found, for instance, that there is now a greater emphasis on one's own interests and future vocation than earlier.

Martin, W. B. W. and Macdonell, A. J. 1982. *Canadian education,* 2nd ed. Scarborough, Ontario: Prentice-Hall of Canada. A textbook in the sociology of education. The book concentrates chiefly on Canada.

KEY WORDS

allocation: The process by which schools distribute pupils into different curricula, which lead to different types of post high school education and work.

alternative schools: Free schools that have gained acceptance by a school board.

classroom environment: The surroundings of the school, peer group, and school administration within which classrooms operate.

community elementary schools: Schools controlled by community members.

cultural production: The process by which universities create new artistic, scientific, and humanistic knowledge and products.

deschooling: A program to develop the pupil's ability to deal critically and effectively with the world in which he or she lives.

education: The process of educating others by fostering an expansion of knowledge, wisdom, and desirable qualities of mind and character.

free schools: Schools that allow free choice and action for their pupils.

chapter 12

Work and Leisure

CHAPTER OUTLINE

INTRODUCTION

The following lines by nineteenth century poet James Russell Lowell convey the meaning of work for nearly every adult human being who has lived on this planet:

> No man is born into the world whose work
> Is not born with him; there is always work.
> And tools to work withal, for those who will;
> And blessed are the horny hands of toil.[1]

[1]From *A Glance behind the Curtain.*

These thoughts still apply. But whether they will be applicable at the turn of the century remains to be seen.

North Americans, for the most part, have always valued work. *Work* is a goal-oriented activity leading to a personally desired accomplishment. Work is a disciplined activity; it is carried out by means of persistent effort with the idea of achieving the intended goal. For workers in modern industrial societies who are alienated from the fruits of their labor, that goal is the wage they receive, the fringe benefits of the job, the security of employment, or all three. Nor, to qualify as work, need the disciplined activity be respectable. Making a living by forging checks, bootlegging whisky, betting on horses, or engaging in prostitution conforms to our definition of work, just as much as repairing cars or practicing law (Letkemann, 1973; Miller, 1978).

Today, we often include a second criterion in the definition of work, namely that a wage, salary, or profit is received by the worker for reaching the goal. In Canada, for example, most work (housework is a much publicized exception) is done for money. Thus, work is an occupation or job (including the "second job"). It constitutes all or part of one's livelihood. Correspondingly, the sociology of work is concerned with the social aspects of choosing, preparing for, entering into, and carrying out an occupation. It also gets into the question of why individuals sometimes give up an occupation.

It may seem a bit odd, at first blush, to find work and leisure juxtaposed in the same chapter. After all, many people regard work and leisure as antithetical. Yet it is precisely this antithesis that justifies discussing them side by side. Leisure is commonly defined by directly or indirectly comparing it with work. Consider this definition: *Leisure* is an activity or that part of an activity that is lacking in major obligation and responsibility and that is freely chosen for its own sake. As we shall see, this is an oversimplified definition. Surprising as it may seem, defining leisure is no easy task. In any event, we can develop an understanding of leisure only by developing an understanding of work and what it is.

WORK AS AN INSTITUTION

Work is considered here as part of the institution of the economy. The economic institution is defined in Chapter 13 as "the relatively stable set of relationships, patterns of behavior, norms, and values that emerge around the production, distribution, and consumption of goods and services." In general, work falls within the ambit of this production, distribution, and consumption. Even though work is only part of a larger institution, it still meets the six criteria for defining a social institution set out in Chapter 9.

First, what collective problems are solved by work? One problem it solves is providing a living for those who engage in it. In Canada and other modern societies, this is accomplished by means of an occupation. Second, there are many distinctive patterns of behavior in the sphere of work. Among these patterns are the established hours of employment (nine to five), the annual Christmas party, and the routine coffee break and lunch hour. The repetitive tasks performed by assembly-line workers and the standard legal procedures for establishing a small business are well-established patterns of behavior.

Third, many well-known abstract relationships are found in the workplace. For instance, there is an ongoing relationship between the employer and the employee. The employer directs the work of the employee and establishes the rules to be observed. Employees interact with each other while on the job. If the employee has a complaint about the working conditions, he or

SOCIOLOGY OR COMMON SENSE

What do you think?

Which of the following statements do you agree with? Which statements do you disagree with? Make a note of your answers. Check your answers when you have completed your study of this chapter. Are your answers to the statements the same as those a sociologist would give?

1. There are no such people as professional dry cleaners and professional auto mechanics.
2. At no time does leisure have anything to do with one's work.
3. Canada is a free country; any citizen can work at whatever job he or she prefers.
4. In the 1980s, work and other obligatory activities are more important to North Americans than leisure (nonobligated activities).
5. A serious interest in bowling can lead to divorce.

she may go to the union steward for help. Professionals have relationships with their clients. A partner and a copartner work together, agreeing on a plan to achieve their established goals.

Fourth, numerous expectations are associated with the roles of the employer, the employee, and the professional. For example, employees are expected to arrive at work on time or to have some reason for being late. Professionals are expected to apply their specialized knowledge to the case of each client regardless of their personal feelings for the client.

Fifth, the institution of work is held together by several compelling values, including the traditional outlook that work is spiritually beneficial. Some people value work for its self-realization potential. Nearly everyone values it for its remuneration (Fein, 1976: 494–501). Sixth, there is an engrossing history of work in North America. For instance, one of the most significant trends in this part of the economy has been the gradual weakening of the *Protestant ethic,* or the doctrine that conscientious, diligent work is a sure sign of one's ultimate religious salvation.

Whether viewed as a blessing or a curse, work has attracted no small amount of scientific attention. Sociologists have contributed to this scholarly effort by describing the nature and types of occupations and professions. On this foundation they have built theories explaining occupational choice and occupational socialization into the subculture of the chosen line of work. Movement into, through, and out of one or more occupations—that is, work career—is another enduring interest of specialists in this area.

OCCUPATIONS AND PROFESSIONS

Sociologists often use the words "work" and "occupation" interchangeably. When they differentiate the two words, "work" refers to the activity engaged in at the moment ("I am working"). An *occupation* is then defined as an activity associated with a work role. A profession is a special kind of occupation. We turn first to occupations in general.

Occupational Titles

Since we are in an age of specialization, it should come as no surprise that many different occupations enter into the economy in industrialized societies. The American *Dictionary of Occupational Titles* contains around twenty thousand entries. The *Canadian Classification and Dictionary of Occupations* is no less voluminous. The following scheme organizes the many different jobs under nine major categories, which convey a sense of the complexity of occupations in technologically advanced societies.

Occupational category	Illustrative occupations
Professional, technical, and managerial	Biologist, physician, chemist, lawyer, administrator, theologian, writer
Clerical and sales	Stenographer, stock clerk, computer programmer, telex operator
Service	Cook, barber, dry cleaner, hotelier, security guard
Agricultural, fishery, forestry, and related activities	Hunter, trapper, forester, farmer, fisherman, rancher
Processing	Workers in chemicals, coal, stone, paper, food, tobacco
Machine trades	Workers in textiles, printing, metal, wood, glass
Benchwork	Workers in making and repairing metal, plastic, wood, scientific, electrical, rubber, metal products
Structural work	Welders, electricians, painters, plasterers, tractor operators
Miscellaneous	Workers in motor freight, mineral extraction, amusements, packaging, graphic arts

What Is Workaholism?

While workaholics do work hard, not all hard workers are workaholics. I will use the word workaholic to describe those whose desire to work long and hard is intrinsic and whose work habits almost always exceed the prescriptions of the job they do and the expectations of the people with whom or for whom they work. But the first characteristic is the real determinant. What truly distinguishes workaholics from other hard workers is that the others work only to please a boss, earn a promotion or meet a deadline. Moonlighters, for example, may work sixteen hours a day merely to make ends meet, but most of them stop working multiple shifts as soon as their financial circumstances permit. Accountants, too, may sometimes seem to work non-stop, but most slow down markedly after April 15th. For workaholics, on the other hand, the workload seldom lightens, for they don't *want* to work less. As Senator William Proxmire has found, "The less I work, the less I enjoy it."

Time spent working would be an appealing index of workaholism, but it would also be a misleading measure. Although workaholics may work from 5 A.M. to 9 P.M. instead of the more usual 9 A.M. to 5 P.M., the hours they work are not the *sine qua non* of workaholism. It is in fact preferable to view workaholism as an approach or an attitude toward working than as an amount of time at work. Workaholics will continue to think about work when they're not working—even at moments that are, well, inappropriate. One energy specialist recalls dreaming about Con Ed and seeing barrels of oil in her sleep. One research and development director mentally designs new studies while making love to his wife.

But numbers and totals do count: Workaholics are given to counting their work hours and especially their achievements. . . .

Although I interviewed far more white collar than blue collar workers, I found that workaholics exist in every occupation, from managers and doctors to secretaries and assembly line workers. One man had a combined M.D.-Ph.D.; another had only a high school diploma. A friend once described her apartment building's janitor as a workaholic. "I feel very fortunate," she said, "to have a super who's a compulsive worker. He won't even stop and talk. Occasionally, he'll have a conversation with someone while he's sweeping the sidewalk."

Nor is workaholism restricted to just one sex. While women have been almost completely overlooked in the little that has been written about workaholism, there have always been women workaholics. If housework, for instance, were rightfully regarded as work, generations of compulsive cleaners could be considered workaholics. And so would the tireless organizers of charity events. Today, women's workaholism is merely more apparent, since more and more women work outside their homes.

From: Marilyn Machlowitz. *Workaholics: Living with Them, Working with Them.* Reading, MA: Addison-Wesley, 1980, pp. 10–15.

Some of today's occupations are anything but familiar. How often does one run into a clam sorter, a fish cake maker, a fountain pen turner, a lamp shade sewer, or an experimental rocket-sled mechanic?

Professionals are often discussed by sociologists in ideal-typical terms, with reference to attributes that professional women and men in a particular time in history have in significantly greater degree than people in other occupations. Nine of these attributes have been isolated through research on contemporary professionals (taken with modification from Stebbins, 1984: 34–35):[2]

> (1) They turned out an unstandardized product. (2) They are well versed in an exclusive body of theoretical or abstract knowledge underlying their specialized technique. (3) They have a sense of identity with their colleagues, with whom they constitute a select in-group. (4) They have mastered a generalized cultural tradition associated with their profession. (5) They use institutionalized means of validating the adequacy of a lengthy period of training and the competence of trained individuals. (6) Their work constitutes a "calling" in which they emphasize the consistent application standards and service as framed in a code of ethics rather than emphasizing material rewards. (7) They are recognized by their clients as members of a profession with an expert authority based on knowledge of and technique in their speciality. (8) Their work provides an avenue for frequent, reliable attainment or realization of important social values of the society. (9) Their work is self-regulated or autonomous.

There are also "marginal professions." These occupations manifest the attributes of a profession more than other occupations but less than the true professions. Among the marginal professions are photography, pharmacy, occupational therapy, and police work. Whether marginal or true, professionals are more than mere experts. In spite of the advertising claims, dry cleaning and automobile repair are not professions in the sociological sense.

[2]Roth (1974) discusses the risk in listing attributes of the professional in this fashion.

Although an old and established occupation, pharmacy is still a marginal profession.

Changing Occupations

Some significant changes have occurred in the North American occupational structure over the years. For example, occupations have disappeared, while others have emerged. The ice truck driver and the bowling alley pin boy are no longer on the scene. But we now have the computer programmer and the drug counselor. Certain occupations have been declining for several decades. For example, there are fewer farmers, loggers, fishermen, and hunters and trappers than in the past. The ranks of the fee-taking professional and the small businessman are also shrinking.

Related to the decline in some occupations is the continuous growth in the number of wage-earning employees compared with the concurrent decline in the number of independent entrepreneurs, commercial and professional. Accordingly, the white-collar ranks have swelled, particularly in the sales, clerical, and professional areas. The same can be said of blue-collar work. There now is a greater demand for

Although their numbers are shrinking, small businesses still play an important role in our society.

Table 12.1 CIVILIAN LABOR FORCE PARTICIPATION IN THE UNITED STATES AND CANADA

Year	Labor force to total working age population (percent)		
	Males	Females	Both sexes
	United States		
1965	80.7	39.3	58.9
1975	77.9	46.3	61.2
1982	76.6	52.6	64.0
	Canada		
1966	79.8	35.4	57.3
1975	78.4	44.4	61.1
1982	76.9	51.6	64.0

Sources: U.S. Bureau of the Census, *Statistical Abstract of the United States, 1984,* 104th ed., p. 407, Washington, D.C., 1984; Statistics Canada, *Historical Labour Force Statistics,* Cat. No. 71-201, Ottawa, 1982.

laborers, craftsmen, and service workers.

Moore (1966) and Gibbs and Browning (1966) have identified several worldwide concomitants of the process of industrialization. *Industrialization* is defined here as *the use of technology by profit-making enterprises to manufacture goods and services.* This is a broader definition than was stated in Chapter 8. One of these concomitants is the rising labor market participation, which is paralleled by a decline in unpaid family labor. The rate at which new occupational specialties come into being also accelerates. Paydarfar (1967) found that all advanced industrial societies have decreasing ratios of dependent children along with increasing ratios of female participation in the labor force (women holding full-time jobs, that is). Table 12.1 shows selected rates of labor force participation in the United States and Canada. As in other industrialized countries, the overall rates in Canada and the United States are rising over time. The increase is accounted for chiefly by women in the labor force.

OCCUPATIONAL CHOICE

Given the bewildering variety of occupations to choose from, how do people single out one and become attached to an occupation? As Van Maanen (1976: 82) points out, most sociological theories in this field center on how people weigh the many environmental factors and alternatives influencing their potential choices. This process culminates in a series of conscious decisions about the directions their work career should take.

Ginsberg and his colleagues (1951: Chapter 7) developed a three-phase theory of occupational choice. The first phase occurs roughly between ages six and eleven, during which children make *fantasy* choices. In the second phase, which unfolds from early to late adolescence, their choices become *tentative.* Their experiences up to this point, along with the continuous weighing of factors and alternatives, bring them in early adulthood to the third phase. Here they exercise *realistic* occupational choice.

Donald Super (1957) stresses the self-conception that emerges during the formative years. Ginzberg's theory helps to explain the self-conception. As self-conception crystallizes, the person tests it against the social world in which he or she lives. Kuvlesky and Beals (1972) found, by means of a longitudinal study, that occupational interest not only tends to narrow but also tends to get lower. For example, a young man who has recently graduated from a university takes a job with a large business as an accountant. He hopes at the time to rise within the company to a managerial position. As he becomes acquainted with the firm, he narrows his aspirations to becoming manager of one of its regional offices. Several years later he realizes that being chief accountant in one of those offices is the highest he can expect to climb. More than 75 percent of Kuvlesky's respondents failed to reach the occupational status level to which they had aspired ten years earlier.

But these are voluntaristic theories of occupational choice, and therefore they have their limitations. For one, they encourage the assumption that we are wholly in control of our work destiny. This is an oversimplification. Miller and Form (1980: 236–238) argue that such factors as sex, race, social class, nationality, place of residence, family background, native ability, historical circumstance, and personality set limits on the lines of work open to various groups and individuals in society. Even now, South Asians and women, for example, are often excluded from the boardrooms of Canadian corporations, notwithstanding the impressive occupational qualifications these individuals may possess. Or, being raised in the heart of cities such as Winnipeg, Edmonton, or Minneapolis gives one little contact with, and hence few aspirations for, occupations such as merchant seaman or tugboat pilot.

As noted in the preceding chapter, one of the most effective and subtle constraints on free occupational choice is role allocation within the education system. There is evidence, for example, that highly differentiated occupational systems, such as those in Canada and the United States, produce a wide range of attitudes and sentiments toward work across the population, but limited sets of opportunities in the labor market for each individual (e.g., Meyer et al., 1979; Treiman and Terrell, 1975). Opportunities are limited because, as we saw in the preceding chapter, students are often channeled into an academic or a nonacademic track in high school. They may also be sent to a private school instead of a public school or advised to enter a community college instead of a university. Graduates from these different routes are qualified for some lines of work and disqualified from others.

OCCUPATIONAL SOCIALIZATION

The process of occupational socialization has two components: (1) *formal* technical training and cultural indoctrination into a line of work and (2) *informal* learning about the skills and culture of the occupation before and after entering it. Formal training, as we have just seen, often begins in high school and sometimes even earlier (e.g., art, entertainment, sport). By way of illustration, we might consider those students who have been channeled into the nonacademic track in high school. They are taught not only subjects relevant to their predicted occupational future but also values and aspirations befitting individuals entering the particular trade or job. Trade schools and other postsecondary educational institutions continue this process in and around curricula designed to prepare students for particular jobs.

Part of the informal learning process is known as *anticipatory socialization.* Aspirants to a particular occupation begin to discern what it will be like to work in that capacity even before they acquire a job. Through interaction with actual practitioners and exposure to the mass-media portrayal of the occupation, they begin to internalize the privileges and expectations of the occupation. They also internalize its outlook. This process operates prior to the additional, realistic socialization occurring once the individual is on the job. Since anticipatory socialization often occurs even before the start of formal training for the occupation, it is possible that the socialization will engender misconceptions of the attitudes and suppositions of one's future co-workers. Pavalko (1971: 86) points out that:

> in general, the longer a person has been considering the occupation, the greater the opportunity he has had to imagine what work in the

occupation would be like, explore nuances of the role, etc.

Nevertheless, anticipatory socialization may aid or hinder formal training. And, to the extent that the anticipation is inaccurate, the neophyte is in for an abrupt confrontation with reality once he or she begins work.

In formal training, be it in a trade school, technical college, graduate school, or professional school, students begin acquiring necessary skills and knowledge. In graduate schools and professional schools especially, they also learn the norms, values, and ideologies of their chosen vocation. Here, too, is where they begin to develop a commitment to that vocation and, often, to an occupational specialty, which they may have encountered for the first time in the classroom. A high level of commitment among those in a work role is one of the ingredients in "occupational consciousness" (Krause, 1971: 86), which exists today among certain professional and labor groups (e.g., schoolteachers, air traffic controllers, organized truck drivers). Indeed, occupational socialization often produces changes in worker personalities (Kohn and Schooler, 1982).

Formal occupational socialization is the main way we learn a job today.

The clash of formal socialization with anticipatory socialization may be agonizing. Becker and Geer (1958) noted the disillusionment experienced by medical students at the University of Kansas. In their first year of professional training, these students are overwhelmed by the vast amount of medical knowledge they must learn and by the seeming irrelevance of their courses. They question the medical researcher's interest in solving medical or scientific problems rather than in directly helping suffering patients.

Occupational socialization never really ends. There are always new situations to meet and new technical advances to study. It constantly becomes necessary to adjust to new colleagues and to maintain a working relationship with others. Frequently, it becomes necessary to learn new organizational procedures. Even experienced workers are faced with the problem of how to continue to succeed in their occupation. Experience reduces the amount of learning to be done, but it never eliminates the requirement for learning and the need to add to one's knowledge.

OCCUPATIONAL CAREER

The word "career" is hardly new to you. Perhaps you define a career as a calling and a field of pursuit in professional or business life, with achievement and advancement as one gains experience. But, to the sociologist, the term has a broader meaning than this definition implies; sociologically, *career* is a scientific concept. The concept cannot be ignored in the study of work. We have already run across the idea of career in Chapter 10, "Family," and we shall encounter it again in Chapter 20, "Deviance." Accordingly, the concept of career is discussed here in terms broad enough to apply to the studies of family, work, and deviance.

Since the early sixteenth century, the term "career" has served as the English translation of French and Italian words meaning "race course," "gallop," and "carriage road." Originally, the term expressed one person's derogatory evaluation of another's rapid, unrestrained, and often questionable activity (Williams, 1976: 44). It took three hundred years of change and derivation before the word career became a synonym for "occupation" or for progress within an occupation. Contemporary sociological definitions of the term career have diverged substantially from this commonsense heritage. Sociologically speaking, an *occupational career* is

> the typical course or passage of people through the various stages that carry them into and through an occupational role, as well as their adjustments to and interpretations of the contingencies and turning points encountered while in each stage.

The term "career pattern" is used by sociologists to refer to those careers, whether of individuals or groups, that are composed of several occupations. For example, a worker might be employed in a factory as a machinist. The worker might subsequently accept the position of shop steward for the local union. Ultimately, he might be elected to full-time membership on the union's executive committee.

A career may be centered on one occupation or on several, but whatever the circumstances, the *continuity* over time of the experiences associated with a career give it meaning. We are accustomed to thinking of this continuity as the accumulation of rewards and prestige—as moving up from a starting point to a significantly higher level. As an example, consider the following successful career in advertising.

On graduation from the university, a young woman takes a job as a junior copywriter in an advertising agency. In time, she is promoted to the position of copy chief. The copy chief soon gains a new responsibility as an assistant to an account executive. Eventually, the woman becomes an account executive, a promotion that pays off in both money and prestige. Still later, she becomes a vice president of the agency. Then, some twenty years after starting out as a junior copywriter, this experienced employee is named president of the agency by the board of trustees.

But temporal continuity within a career is not always a success story. Continuity can also lead to retrogression. People employed by corporations are sometimes demoted. In the arts, sports, and entertainment fields, performance peaks are reached. Prestige and rewards then diminish as the limelight shifts to other, usually younger and more talented, performers or players. Those in art, sport, and entertainment see the following sequence as far too typical:

> First stage: Who is X? (e.g., Vladimir Horowitz, Pablo Picasso, Billie Jean King).
>
> Second stage: I want X.
>
> Third stage: I want somebody like X, but I don't want X because I've already seen him enough.
>
> Fourth stage: What ever happened to X?

Continuity in the work histories of people may occur largely within, between, or outside organizations. Careers in organizations such as the military, the government, and the corporation commonly unfold as individual workers move up through a hierarchy of positions or ranks, each of which offers the incumbent more attractive rewards and prestige. Downward mobility, though rarer, may also occur. House (1981) describes the career pattern of Calgary oilmen as they move up within large companies from low-level technical, engineering, and geological positions to high-level technical or managerial positions. As their careers peak, some oilmen, whether in technical or managerial positions, decide to leave the organization to work as independent consultants in the petroleum industry.

Athletes, artists, physicians, lawyers, freelance tradesmen, and small business entrepreneurs experience career continuity independently of a large-scale organization. For them, continuity comes from a growing reputation as skilled and knowledgeable practitioners in their vocations. With this image, they move into increasingly better situations with increased opportunities within their community and within their trade, business, or professional circles. Although some of these independent professionals become members of work organizations, their careers are largely independent of them. The frequent movement of professional athletes from one team to another exemplifies this independence.

Continuity in careers is seen from two angles. One perspective is *career history:* the chronological, descriptive, objective view of career as it unfolds over the work years of the typical worker in an occupation. The other is *subjective career,* which looks at a career from the eyes of those pursuing it. Their interpretation of what has happened, is happening, and will happen to them at various times during their work life forms the core of this perspective (Stebbins, 1970a). The study of career histories centers on, among other things, their various *contingencies,* which may be defined as unintended events, processes, or situations that occur by chance. That is, they lie beyond the control of the people pursuing the career. Career histories also have "stages" such as "preparatory" (home and school experiences), "initial" (first job), "trial" (trying out jobs), "stable" (sticking with one job), and "retirement." Subjective career analysis includes the study of the *turning points* the typical incumbent meets during his or her occupational lifetime.

UNEMPLOYMENT

Unemployment is both a major negative turning point (subjective career) and a major contingency (career history) in the occupational career. The recession of the early 1980s proved that being unemployed can threaten virtually everyone: the young, the old, the low-paid, the high-paid, the unskilled, and the highly skilled. In the early 1980s, unemployment became a problem for many persons at the beginning of their careers; initial, full-time jobs were denied to a range of people, from those with a high school diploma to those with a Ph.D. Others, as a result of diminished needs for their services, lost jobs, either temporarily or permanently, at the midpoint of their occupational careers. Finally, older workers, again including some with high-paying and high-status jobs, were forced to "retire" early, which, in their eyes, was tantamount to becoming unemployed.

There are causes of unemployment besides a deteriorating economy. Unemployment is also fostered by technological change. Today that change is emanating predominantly from microelectronics in general and computers in particular. The use of electronic mail and word processors, for instance, is reducing the need for the office stenographer. In addition, restructuring the flow of work, the lines of authority, and the relationship of internal units within a work organization may lead to layoffs in some areas (and perhaps hiring in others).

Whatever the cause of unemployment, its impact on a nation's workers is far from uniform. Miller and Form (1980: 87) explain:

> In a free economy, whatever the causes of unemployment, the consequences seem to be everywhere the same. Those who are economically most insecure—the youngest workers, the least educated, and those who are socially and economically marginal—are unemployed first and for the longest period. . . . Professionals, proprietors, managers, and technical and skilled workers experience the least amount of unemployment, whereas the semiskilled and unskilled workers endure the greatest amount.

LEISURE

In a society where work is dignified, it should come as no surprise that Canadians often define leisure by comparing it with work as the benchmark activity. This orientation is evident in the shorthand definition of leisure given earlier: *Leisure* is an activity or that part of an activity that is lacking in major obligation and responsibility and that is freely chosen for its own sake. Still,

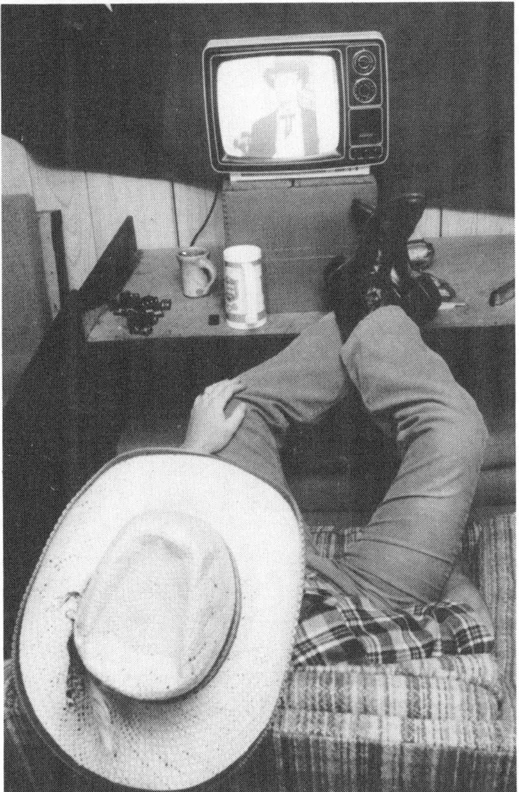

Can you think of a more common pattern of leisure than this one?

this definition omits several important conditions that help identify the essence of leisure. Max Kaplan (1960: 22) lists seven "essential characteristics" that should be incorporated in a complete definition of leisure:

> (a) an antithesis to "work" as an economic function; (b) a pleasant expectation and recollection; (c) a minimum of involuntary social-role obligations; (d) a psychological perception of freedom; (e) a close relation to values of the culture; (f) the inclusion of an entire range from inconsequence and insignificance to weightiness and importance; and (g) often, but not necessarily, an activity characterized by the element of play.

Among other things, leisure time is free time. It is time, that is, which is free from the obligations of work, family, religion, and politics (Dumazedier, 1974: 68–71).

Leisure as an Institution

Many sociologists consider leisure as an institution of the modern industrial society (Kaplan, 1975: 28–31), although there is disagreement about how important it is compared with, say, the institutions of work and family. The *collective problem* around which leisure has institutionalized is that of how to use our free time most effectively. Countless *patterns of leisure behavior* exist within various segments of the population; among these are stamp collecting, playing chess, watching television, going to the movies, and attending cocktail parties. Baseball games, electronic games, the amateur theater, the racetrack, the ski slopes—all are a part of leisure. There are many *abstract relationships* within leisure; an example is the relationship between amateur actors and the director of a theater group. At the group level, there are interrelationships among clubs, associations, centers, and the like.

Leisure roles are in evidence everywhere in Canada (in theaters, at hockey arenas, on trout streams, on ski slopes, over chessboards, in front of television sets). Among those who enjoy leisure are the camper and the backpacker. The skier, the concertgoer, the stamp collector, the amateur astronomer, the sports fan, the racketball player, and the volunteer teacher's aide have their moments of relaxation and escape. Roberts (1978: 167–168) lists three major leisure *values* associated with the institution of leisure in Western countries. The three values are (1) *hedonism,* or the desire for pleasure; (2) *humanism,* or the desire for variety in the experiences from which pleasure is derived; and (3) *liberalism,* or the desire to choose one's leisure. Choice is one of the pleasures of leisure.[3]

The institution of leisure has a *history.* It has

[3]There is evidence that leisure values in non-Western countries are similar to these values in Europe and North America; for example, Russia (Rogers, 1974).

Hedonism is a principal leisure value in North America.

changed considerably and will continue to change through the years (see final section of this chapter). In the eighteenth and nineteenth centuries, leisure was to be enjoyed only between stints of work. It was to be used for the recuperation or regeneration of workers, not for sheer pleasure or for experiencing an escape from the workaday routine:

> Sport was accepted if it served a rational purpose, that of recreation necessary for physical efficiency. But as a means for the spontaneous expression of undisciplined impulses, it was under suspicion; and in so far as it became purely a means of enjoyment, or awakened pride, raw instincts or the irrational gambling instinct, it was of course strictly condemned. (Weber, 1958: 167)

For those in a Calvinist society, any more leisure than Weber described was regarded as deviant (Shivers, 1981: 109–110). It was during this time that Isaac Watts penned his famous line: "For Satan finds some mischief still for idle hands to do." Bosserman and Gagan (1972: 113) explain how this has changed:

> Now that the work week is forty hours or less with sometimes a three-day weekend, and a year of less than 225 work days, leisure is no longer simply a time to recuperate or recover from work. *Leisure has become a means of personal expression and self-fulfillment* [italics in the original].

Adequate comparative data on the institutionalized patterns of leisure behavior of Canadians and Americans are unavailable. It is clear, however, that watching television heads the list of favorite nonobligatory activities in both countries. Television is followed in some order by listening to the radio, reading newspapers and magazines, and socializing with friends and relatives (Statistics Canada, 1978b: 68; Robinson and Godbey, 1978).[4] Contrary to the exaggerated claims made by the television rating services, Americans and Canadians watch television only two and one-half to three hours a day, respectively (Robinson and Godbey, 1978; Statistics Canada, 1978b). Our favorite leisure activities are obviously home-centered or family-centered (or both). They are also passive. Sports, hobbies, spectator events, and amateur pursuits, to the extent that they require more physical or mental effort and are conducted away from home, are engaged in less than home and family pastimes.

Sociologists have been particularly interested in the relationship of leisure to other institutions, especially work and family. Everyone has an interest in work and family throughout most of life. Are not leisure and the family life cycle also of great interest? As we have seen, leisure is closely associated with work. Many leisure activities (watching television, for example) are centered within the family circle.

Leisure and Work

As we have noted, one relationship between leisure and work has long been recognized. In the eighteenth and nineteenth centuries, leisure was considered appropriate only as a means of regenerating the worker for further productiv-

[4]Socializing with friends and relatives may no longer rank in the top four for Americans (Robinson and Godbey, 1978).

ity. The German philosopher Moritz Lazarus argued that play, instead of burning excess energy, either conserves energy or restores the energy lost earlier (Kando, 1980: 29). Dumazedier (1967: 13–17) found, by means of interviews with more than eight hundred salaried and wage-earning workers in France, that the workers conceive of their leisure in three ways: as *relaxation, entertainment,* and *personal development.* Idleness and aimless pastimes help the respondents recover from the pace of work, the trip to and from the job, and the arduous demands work makes on them.

The *spillover-compensation* hypotheses are related to the regeneration thesis. In their attempts to clarify the meanings of the concepts of "spillover" and "compensation," Kando and Summers (1971: 83–86) theorized that work affects leisure in two ways. In one way, the skills, knowledge, and life-style of the job are so attractive that workers, even when off the job, seek opportunities to experience the skills and knowledge. We say, here, that work *spills over* into leisure. In the other way, work may leave people feeling deprived of an important value, such as an opportunity for self-expression or self-actualization, for which they try to *compensate* by means of leisure. To test these hypotheses, Martin Meissner (1971) interviewed roughly two hundred industrial workers in a small city on Vancouver Island. He found a certain amount of support for the spillover idea:

> Experience with work of little discretionary potential carries over into reduced participation in formally organized activities. Similarly, the experience of social interaction opportunities on the job carries over into greater participation in voluntary associations. (Meissner, 1971: 253)

Kelly's (1974) distinction between *coordinated leisure* and *unconditional leisure* is an extension of the spillover proposition. *Coordinated leisure* is leisure that is related to one's job in form or content, but unrequired by the job. *Unconditional leisure* is an activity chosen without a reference to one's work. In a study of amateur archeologists in Texas, Stebbins found that nearly 50 percent of those in the sample who were employed viewed their jobs as related to and hence capable of facilitating their archeology, a scientific leisure pursuit (Stebbins, 1979: 156). Professional engineers, for instance, said their knowledge of construction principles helps them understand the dwellings they occasionally unearth as amateur archeologists. Theirs is coordinated leisure. Examples of unconditional leisure include the milk truck driver who collects handguns and the hardware store proprietor who spends a month each summer touring the country in a camper.

Elsewhere, Kelly (1982: 129–130) brings up another work-leisure issue. In our culture, time is scarce for many individuals and therefore valuable. The shortage of time begets the "time-income tradeoff" problem. Those few individuals who have all the income they need reach the following turning point: Should they cut back on their money-making pursuits in order to have more time for leisure? This implies, of course, that their work has lost some of its obligatory aspects. Most North Americans, however, fall short of the blissful state of income saturation. Individuals may crave more leisure and less work, but they are always confronted with the unsolvable question of how to afford the former when reducing the latter.

Leisure and Family

Joseph Levy (1980) organizes research on leisure and the family around the antecedents (preceding events and causes) and consequences of family leisure. The antecedents are the political, economic, and sociocultural variables that potentially explain leisure behavior and also provide some understanding of the attitudes and problems in the family. Although this side of the sociology of leisure is long on ideas and short on confirmatory research, key antecedents have received a modicum of empirical attention. One of these concerns the working mother and how her leisure has changed; the role of the working mother is especially controversial. Pat Armstrong and Hugh Armstrong (1984) point out that working wives hold two jobs: the paying job outside the home and housework in the home. Luxton (1981) found that when their wives started paid work, the working-class husbands helped them (on weekends) an average of a half-hour more than formerly, whereas middle-class husbands actually reduced their domestic work. In the meantime, the wives' time for their families vanished altogether.

Another antecedent explaining leisure behavior and attitudes in the family is the extensive job specialization of modern life. Haavio-Mannila (1971) studied workers in Helsinki, Finland, using the concept of *central life interest* as her theoretical starting point. Robert Dubin (1979: 419) defines the central life interest as that segment of an individual's life in which a substantial emotional investment is made. Although more than one segment of our lives may become a central life interest, limitations on time and money preclude us from developing many such interests. Haavio-Mannila found that upper-stratum workers in Helsinki (e.g., professionals, managers) are significantly more likely to have a central life interest in their job than those in the lower strata (e.g., semiskilled industrial workers). For those in the lower strata, family and leisure are central.

Although leisure sometimes gives rise to conflict, it also engenders a common outlook and a satisfying geniality among the members of a family. Leisure "becomes a cause, a clue, and an index of sources of respect, love, interdependence, and knowledge about the other," says Max Kaplan (1960: 59). Still, one of the problems in family leisure, as Lyle Larson (1971: 185) has noted, is that, for the most part, leisure is individual or couple-oriented, not group-oriented.

Orthner (1975) identifies three types of marital leisure activities: *individual* activities engaged in alone; *joint* activities requiring interaction (e.g., a card game); and *parallel* activities requiring little interaction but done together (e.g., watching a hockey game). Children in the family may make a difference. But it is unclear from Orthner's data whether, with children, individual activities threaten marital satisfaction or whether joint activities foster it. Colette Carisse (1975) argues, however, that married couples may drift beyond the range of the partner's tolerance of a certain leisure life-style, leading to family malfunctioning, discomfort, and even pathogenic actions. Carisse's observation is reminiscent of the cartoon in which two books were shown side by side in a trash can. The titles of the books were *Golfing Year Round* and *Divorce Made Easy.*

Joint leisure in marriage is an important unifying aspect of the relationship.

Intolerance of a spouse's leisure life-style may be eased if the couple can participate with each other in their leisure activities. For instance, there is conflict in families over the husband's or wife's intense interest in amateur baseball or amateur theater. In contrast, amateur archeologists and amateur astronomers often pursue their interests with little family conflict (Stebbins, 1979; 1980a).[5] Although they may object to the time-consuming involvement and enthusiasm of the baseball player or theatrical performer, others in the family are usually unable to participate in the baseball games or theat-

[5]This is the first published report of the responses of the families of amateur astronomers' to their avocation. Methodological details of the study are available elsewhere (Stebbins, 1980b:37).

rical performances. On the other hand, family members can become involved in archeology and astronomy. The following poetic exchange between the wives of two amateur astronomers illustrates both the conflict and the consensus that can emerge from serious amateur leisure[6]:

An Amateur Astronomer's Wife

I wake up with a start in the dead of the night,
I know something is wrong, and I turn on the light.
The place on the pillow beside me is bare,
My husband is missing, he's gone. Who knows where?
Perhaps he's recounting his variable stars,
Or seeing invisible markings on Mars.
When the moon is up high, and the earth's lights are dim,
Is he perched upon Plato's precipitous rim?
Oh, what is this thing that's come into our life?

There once was a time when my husband was mine,
Now he's way out in space where the galaxies shine,
And he spends all his time with his old telescope,
While I lie here alone, and I shiver and mope.
By the dawn he'll be back; as he grabs a few winks
He'll be dreaming of Venus, and Lepus, and Lynx.
And when he's awakened by coffee's sharp smell,
His eyelids will droop; he'll be grouchy, as well.
Oh, pity poor me, an astronomer's wife!
Mrs. Hedi E. Lattey

One Astronomer's Wife

I awake a few hours preceding the dawn
And find my astronomer-husband gone.
I bound out of bed—I cannot have this!
He's doubtless found something that I must not miss.
The moon, stars, and planets, the great nebulae,
Are worlds that my husband has opened for me.
Orion and Saturn are friends of us both,
Our telescope brings us a new means for growth.
What a wonderful thing has come into our life!

My husband, I note, is increasingly mine,
As together we go where the galaxies shine.
When he's perched upon Plato's precipitous rim
He's not there alone—I accompany him.
At predawn and midnight, in front of our house,
I gaze into far distant space with my spouse;
And while at breakfast we both may be tired,
I'm elated in sharing new knowledge acquired.
Behold lucky me, an astronomer's wife!
Mrs. Lorena M. Cole

[6]*Sky and Telescope* 18 (1958):87; 18 (1959):137.

Leisure and the Life Cycle

An impressive study of leisure and the life cycle is Rhona and Robert Rapoport's (1975) work with selected families and individuals in an industrial town in southeast England. They discovered that variation in leisure patterns according to life-cycle stage is greatest among those who are married, especially married couples with children. Consequently, in this chapter, the discussion is confined to leisure and the family life cycle.

The Rapoports (1975: 19–28) open with the observation that many people in Western society live out their lives in three areas: work, family, and leisure. As we have noted, a "career" exists in each of these three areas. The career in one area intersects with the careers in the other two areas, making it necessary for individuals to try to integrate their various experiences with each career. Most people who go through life in modern industrial countries find that their preoccupations, interests, and activities in the three areas change as their careers in these areas intersect. With resourcefulness, individuals adapt to these changes in different ways, depending on their position in the family life cycle.

This cycle, which was introduced in Chapter 10, is composed of four phases with fluid boundaries: adolescence, young adulthood, establishment, and later years (Rapoport and Rapoport, 1975: Chapters 2–5).[7] Adolescents are concerned with personal identity formation, which is accomplished by trying out new roles and activities for their compatibility. Since adolescents are blocked from entering most roles, their leisure roles are, by default, essential as sources of new experiences (Kelly, 1982: 142). Courtship is one of the major roles in which adolescents try out adultlike activities.

Young adulthood is said by the Rapoports to commence somewhere between ages sixteen and eighteen. It lasts for approximately ten years. It is the phase during which identification with key social institutions begins. This is *social identification,* not the adolescent preoccupation with personal identification. Young adults become committed to an occupation, they seek partners of the opposite sex (in or out of wedlock), and they may marry and start a family. These social identifications bring about changes in the leisure habits which the young adults established in adolescence. Working and parenting tend to cut deeply into the time formerly reserved for the couple's leisure activities. Orthner (1975), for example, reports that joint leisure activities of married partners correlate with marital satisfaction only in the early years of the marriage.

The establishment phase runs roughly from age twenty-five to age fifty-five. Here the primary preoccupation is finding acceptable life investments in one's job, family, and community. Early in this phase, there is typically concern with productivity; there is concern with producing and raising children and with success at work. In many instances, the lack of time and money for pleasure and enjoyment pushes leisure to the sidelines, as family- and work-related goals predominate.

In the midestablishment phase, the main preoccupation is with success in the family, work, and community roles to which the parents are now more or less firmly attached. These are the days of intense familism. Much of leisure is domestic and scheduled around the activities of increasingly more active children. Still, leisure remains a lower priority than work, family, and obligatory community involvements.

As their children leave school, parents gradually find more time to ponder their careers in all three areas. At this point they enter a period of evaluation in which they reassess the meaning of those careers and what the future holds for them. Life may degenerate into an existence of boredom, depression, and feelings of entrapment. Yet it is also a time for exploring new leisure roles, either together or individually. Now it is possible to pursue more active leisure outside the home.

The later years, the final phase, start at approximately age fifty-five. The preoccupation now is with achieving a sense of social and personal integration. People take stock of their lives. If somehow dissatisfied with the way things have gone, they may try to redress this imbalance through satisfying leisure activities. Others, whose work, leisure, and community involvements have been rewarding, ordinarily look forward to retirement in anticipation of continuing an appealing life-style. Old age is a time for consolidation of the three careers, a process increasingly determined by the "significant trilogy of education, income, and health" (Rapoport and Rapoport, 1975: 274). The level of leisure activity remains high as long as these variables are adequately realized.

THE FUTURE OF WORK AND LEISURE

John Wilson (1980: 22–24), in a partial review of American research in the sociology of leisure,

[7]We shall follow the procedure used in Chapter 10 and substitute the phrase "later years" for the Rapoports' "retirement."

poses two crucial, interrelated, but as yet unanswered questions: Do people want more free time? And, is the amount of leisure time increasing? Let us turn to the first question.

Evidence pertaining to the desire for more free time is inconsistent. Early research indicated that, to the extent increased free time results in lower wages, Americans will reject a shortened workweek. More recent research, however, suggests that, as long as the economy is stable, American jobholders are now more willing to trade a portion of their wages for more leisure.

But the issue is complicated. A study in the United States (Best, 1973: 33) and a review of research in Canada (Meltzer, 1974: 37) show that workers in both countries currently prefer the forty-hour workweek and prefer to find their additional leisure in occasional long weekends, paid holidays, extended vacations, and, in some cases, early retirement. In the United States, but apparently not in Canada, compressed workweeks (forty hours worked in three or four days) and reduced workweeks simply enable moonlighting, or the holding of a second, part-time job (Poor and Steele, 1973: 75–76; Tandan, 1974: 59–61).

Job sharing (two workers working part-time at the same job) might allow additional time for leisure. A certain number of Canadians are apparently interested in this alternative (Task Force on Employment Opportunities for the 80s, 1982). But one American study of job sharing found that the time gained from this occupational arrangement is devoted chiefly to domestic obligations. Only 18 percent of those interviewed use the free time for leisure (Meier, 1979: 45). As has been explained in this chapter, work in contemporary North America dominates over leisure, perhaps because individuals like work, identify with it, need the money, and hardly know how to use additional leisure time, or because they are influenced by some combination of these factors and other considerations.

Yet, turning to the second question, we note that many crystal-gazing scholars see increased leisure along with a reduced workweek in the future (not just one that is compressed). They are predicting that people will eventually cease moonlighting and will reject many other obligatory activities that presently eat up nonwork time. This change is occurring gradually; the average weekly hours of work for all workers in June 1984 were 35.3 in the United States and 37.9 in Canada (U.S. Bureau of the Census, 1985: 410; Statistics Canada, 1984e: 57). The average weekly hours of work are still near 40 in manufacturing and mining, however.[8]

Nonetheless, writers in the United States, Canada, and England (e.g., Kreps and Spengler, 1973: 89–90; Bryan, 1973: 8–9; Hameed, 1974: 18–20; Ross, 1971: 33; Jenkins and Sherman, 1979) envision a sweeping reduction in the amount of time the average person will work. At the root of this trend is the technological revolution being fostered by the microprocessor. Its ultimate effects are held to be shorter workweeks and fewer available jobs. Jenkins and Sherman (1979) recommend four-day workweeks, three-week work months, extra vacation periods, sabbatical leaves, and job sharing as possible ways of optimizing work and leisure in our own interests. Lefkowitz's (1979) interviews with a sample of Americans indicate that some of them are already informally expanding their leisure involvements by voluntarily accepting early retirement or unemployment.

Lefkowitz's (1979) suggestive findings signal a change in attitude toward gainful employment which, if this is a genuine sign of what is to come, will help many people along the route to greater leisure in an age when there will be less

[8]This pattern holds despite time budget data that Americans increased their leisure by about 10 percent between 1965 and 1975 (Robinson and Godbey, 1978). It is possible that this gain has been made largely by salaried workers whose hours of employment are not reflected in hourly rated wage earner averages. Or it may be a product of reduced nonwork obligations.

gainful employment for them. His interviewees want to do things that fulfill their human potential and that develop them as persons. Increasingly, they are searching for this opportunity in their leisure. Only one in five of this "new breed," as Yankelovich (1979: 11–13) refers to them, said their work means more to them than their leisure.

There will always be people who work. Some of them will do so because they find fulfillment in their jobs. The professionals of today and tomorrow fall in this category; the lines separating their work and leisure have always been imprecise. Many people will work then as they do now, except for shorter periods on the job, because to them work is satisfying and interesting, even if it lacks the emotional investment of a professional calling. But, assuming that the high unemployment of the mid-1980s abates, the central life interest of many North Americans is likely to shift to the leisure segment of life, encouraging men and women to work only long enough to make the money needed to enjoy their free time. For them, as for Aristotle, "The end of labor is to gain leisure."

OUTLINE AND SUMMARY

I. Introduction
Work is a goal-oriented activity leading to a socially desired accomplishment; work is an occupation or job for which the worker receives a wage, a salary, or a profit.

II. Work as an Institution
Work is part of the institution of the economy; it is a part of economic production, distribution, and consumption.

III. Occupations and Professions
Sociologists often use the terms "work" and "occupation" interchangeably. When differentiated, *work* is the activity engaged in and *occupation* is all the activities associated with a work role.

A. Occupational Titles
There are many occupational titles. Professions are a special kind of occupation. The professions are identified by nine ideal-typical attributes.

B. Changing Occupations
Significant changes have occurred in the occupational structure over the years. Some occupations have disappeared, and others have emerged.

IV. Occupational Choice
Many sociological theories of occupational choice are voluntaristic, centering on how people weigh the many environmental factors and alternatives affecting their choice.

V. Occupational Socialization
The process of occupational socialization has two components: (1) formal technical training and (2) informal learning.

VI. Occupational Career
Career is a series of an individual's adjustments to the institutions, large-scale organizations, and informal social relationships involved in the occupations which make up the work history of the individual or of a group.

VII. Unemployment
Unemployment is both a major negative turning point and a major contingency in the occupational career. Economic crisis, technological change, and organizational restructuring are causes of unemployment.

VIII. Leisure
Leisure is commonly compared with work; it is an activity or that part of an activity that is lacking in major obligations and responsibility. It is the antithesis of "work" as an economic function.

A. Leisure as an Institution
Leisure is an institution of modern industrial societies, forming around the collective problem of effective and acceptable use of free time.

B. Leisure and Work
Leisure can regenerate workers, making it possible for them to continue their work. Leisure may be a spillover from work or a compensation for work's deprivations. *Coordinated lei-*

sure is related to one's job. *Unconditional leisure* is an activity chosen without reference to one's job.

C. Leisure and Family
Research on leisure and the family is organized around the antecedents and consequences of family leisure. One antecedent is the effect of working mothers on the family. A possible consequence is the development and maintenance of a common outlook and geniality among the members of a family.

D. Leisure and the Life Cycle
People in Western society live out their lives in three major areas: work, family, and leisure. The life cycle consists of four phases: adolescence, young adulthood, establishment, and later years.

IX. The Future of Work and Leisure
Today, work is dominant; it dominates leisure. But social scientists predict a reduced workweek in the future. Men and women will seek leisure to fulfill their human potential, something which work often fails to do.

FOR FURTHER READING AND STUDY

Jenkins, C. and Sherman, B. 1979. *The collapse of work.* London: Eyre Methuen. These two British scientists argue that microprocessor technology will form the basis for the "third industrial revolution," which will dramatically alter the employment prospects in all sectors of the economy.

———. 1981. *The leisure shock.* London: Eyre Methuen. This is a sequel to *The collapse of work.* In *The leisure shock,* the authors hold that the millions left permanently unemployed by microprocessor technology will have to learn how to enjoy the free time forced on them.

Kahn-Hut, R., Daniels, A. K., and Colvard, R., eds. 1982. *Women and work.* New York: Oxford University Press. A collection of papers on the problems faced by working women and on the prospects of ameliorating these problems in the future.

Kando, T. M. 1980. *Leisure and popular culture in transition,* 2nd ed. St. Louis: Mosby. A textbook surveying the leisure and popular culture branches of sociology.

Kelly, J. R. 1983. *Leisure identities and interactions.* Winchester, Mass.: Allen & Unwin. Kelly analyzes leisure in the context of role changes through the life course and as a social context in which we work out the social identities that express who we want to be.

Miller, C. 1978. *Odd jobs.* Englewood Cliffs, N.J.: Prentice-Hall. This book is about unconventional occupations such as those of fences, strippers, prostitutes, bookmakers, confidence men, fortune tellers, and medical quacks.

Lowe, G. S. and Krahn, H. J., eds. 1984. *Working Canadians: Reading in the sociology of work and industry.* Toronto: Methuen. A set of previously published articles and book passages, most of which are written from a critical or political economy perspective.

Schön, D. A. 1982. *The reflective practitioner: How professionals think in action.* New York: Basic Books. This study of American professionals reveals that they engage in "reflection of action," or informal improvising that is seen as the essence of the application of professional knowledge.

Stebbins, R. A. 1984. *The magician: Career, culture, and social psychology in a variety art.* Toronto: Clarke Irwin. A comparative study of serious leisure among amateur magicians and serious work among professional magicians in Canada.

KEY WORDS

career A calling and a field of pursuit in professional or business life.

career pattern The different careers of an individual who has several occupations.

central life interest That segment of an individual's life in which a substantial emotional investment is made.

coordinated leisure Leisure that is related to one's job in form or content but unrequired by the job.

economic institution The relatively stable set of relationships, patterns of behavior, norms, and values that emerge around the production, distribution, and consumption of goods and services.

leisure An activity or that part of an activity that is lacking in major obligation and responsibility and that is freely chosen for its own sake.

occupation An activity associated with a work role.

social identification A phase of young adulthood during which identification with key social institutions begins.

unconditional leisure An activity chosen without reference to one's work.

work A goal-oriented activity leading to a personally desired accomplishment.

chapter 13

Economy

CHAPTER OUTLINE

INTRODUCTION

Why is sociology concerned with the economy? *Economics* is a discipline within itself; it need not look to sociology for answers to questions and solutions to problems. But the sociologist cannot turn away from the economy and economic affairs. The economy is a *social institution,* and this is why it is of interest to sociologists. As a discipline, economics does not undertake an analysis of economic output from an institutional standpoint. Analysis of the economy as an institution falls within the discipline of sociology.

Nearly all economists are concerned rather strictly with the production, distribution, and consumption of goods and services. Members of society utilize scarce resources to produce and distribute goods; they consume many desirables which satisfy their material needs and wants. From the sociological perspective, however, the production, distribution, and consumption of goods enters into many everyday situations and interactions within society. The economy affects and is affected by the income, work career, and level of education of society's members. Among other pertinent factors are religion, family, role conflict, leisure preferences, and job relations. Until recently, the science of economics had shown little interest in such sociological variables. *Economic sociology* has moved in to fill the intellectual gap and to answer numerous questions.

Economic sociology is rather narrowly specialized at times. Stinchcombe (1983: 1) points out that "the main use of economic sociology in current sociology is as a basis for explaining stratification and class conflict, or for explaining the long-term developments of a society's politics." The indebtedness of this branch of sociology to Karl Marx is clear. Nevertheless, the functionalists have also studied the economic institution of modern society. This chapter is chiefly about the contrasts between functionalist thought and conflict thought on the institution of the economy. Before turning to the functionalist and conflict models, we must first look at the institutional nature of our economy.

THE ECONOMY AS AN INSTITUTION

The economy is a basic institution in any society, whatever its size. *Economy* is the structure of economic life in a society; it is the way the economic life is organized. Down through history, several broad types of economy have flourished; these types are *hunting and gathering, horticultural and pastoral, socialist, Communist,* and *capitalist.* Specifically, the *economic institution* is the relatively stable set of abstract relationships, patterns of behavior, norms, and values that develop around the production, distribution, and consumption of goods and services. It is considered here with reference to the six defining criteria.

Collective Living

The first criterion is the existence of a solution to a major *problem of collective living.* The problem, in this instance, is economic; those who live together as a society must all attain shelter, sustenance, and protection. That is, they must somehow master nature. In North America, these general goals take the more specific and familiar forms of striving for:

> full employment; price stability; rapid growth in productivity and per capita income; a viable balance of payments with foreign countries; equitable distribution of income, wealth, tax burdens and benefits; a reduced public debt; elimination of poverty; an adequate supply of monetary reserves; efficient use of natural resources; and an expanding range of choice in labor and consumer markets. (Michalos, 1982: 2).

A group of people has obviously mastered nature to the extent that their society remains

---

SOCIOLOGY OR COMMON SENSE

What do you think?

Which of the following statements do you agree with? Which statements do you disagree with? Make a note of your answers. Check your answers when you have completed your study of this chapter. Are your answers to the statements the same as those a sociologist would give?

1. Economists and sociologists have no common interests.
2. The disciplines of economics and economic sociology are really the same thing.
3. The economy is an important institution only in an industrial society.
4. For the average city dweller, the advantages of urban population growth are outweighed by its disadvantages.
5. Canada has a free economy in which there are no constraints on consumer spending except financial resources.

---

intact. Still, in Canada, for example, we never truly have reached some of the aforementioned goals. Or, on reaching them, we have them with us for only short periods of time. Goals can be attained and then lost. One reason for a loss is that our economy is dependent on other societies. Goals are pursued in industrial societies from a predominantly external orientation; that is, emphasis is on mastering the physical environment and acquiring staples and goods through trade with other societies (Parsons, 1964: 133–138).

Behavior and Relationships

The next three defining criteria of institutions are their constituent *patterns of behavior, abstract relationships,* or social structure, and *roles.* There are literally thousands of these patterns, relationships, and roles in every sector of our economy (service, manufacturing, retail sales, etc.). For a relatively uncomplicated example, let us consider the production, distribution, and consumption of processed milk.

A dairy farmer (role) and his employees (relationship) milk their cows daily (patterned behavior). Each day the raw milk is sent to a dairy for pasteurizing, homogenizing, and packaging by another set of employees. On certain days, freshly processed milk is delivered to homes and supermarkets by the dairy's drivers. In the supermarkets, employees put the milk on refrigerated shelves. Shoppers pick up one or more cartons of the milk and pay for them at the checkout counter. At home, the milk is consumed at meals and along with snacks.

A pattern of economic behavior: the flea market.

Values and History

Value is another defining criterion. Work itself is valued in North America, but, say Yankelovich and Immerwahr (1984), it is valued today only under certain conditions. The *work ethic* is a norm associated with the value of doing good work for its own sake. Yankelovich and Immerwahr found that Americans still have a regard for the work ethic; that is, they are eager to work as long as the work leads to self-development. Such work is interesting, permits discretion, develops skills, and shows the worker the end results of his or her efforts. Moreover, work is valued to the extent that one is paid for the labor. Across-the-board raises, which are usually the outcome of a power struggle between labor and management, often have little to do with individual contributions.

The broad history of our present-day economic institution, which is fundamentally capitalistic, is contained in the dialectical analysis of Marx and Engels. The dominant economic system in medieval Europe was feudalism. The principal beneficiaries of this system were the nobility, who eventually engendered their own antithesis, or competitors, in the form of the *bourgeoisie.* The ultimate synthesis, or outcome, of this economic contradiction was the rise of capitalism and the entrenchment of the bourgeoisie. This situation, we noted in Chapter 2, soon led to the exploitation of workers and the rise of the proletariat (another synthesis). As Figure 13.1 indicates, Marx and Engels predicted that the synthesis of this economic contradiction will be the rise of communism or socialism and the entrenchment of the proletariat.

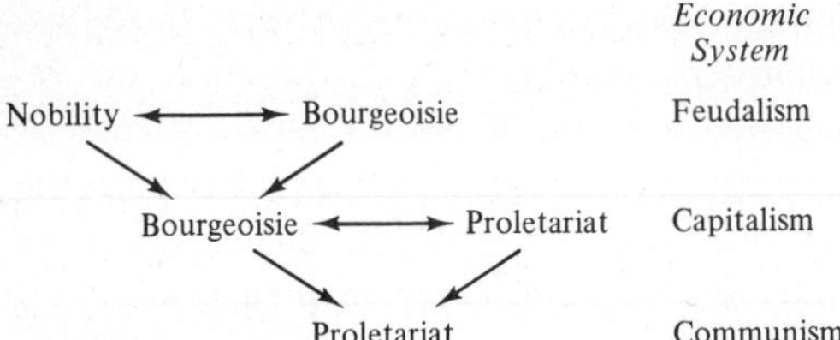

Figure 13.1 Historical Stages of the Western Economic Systems. (*Source:* J. T. Duke, *Conflict and Power in Social Life.* Provo UT: Brigham Young University Press, 1976, p. 22.)

ECONOMIC FUNCTIONS

Turning now to the functionalist perspective on the economy, we may ask: What are the main system-maintaining functions of this institution? According to J. O. Hertzler (1961: 266–276), the economic institution in an industrial society has two major sets of functions. He refers to the functions as *extractive-transformative* and *exchange-distribution.* On the concrete level, the functions are *jobs,* or occupations. A job is a specialized economic role in the society's division of labor.

Extractive-Transformative

The purpose of extractive-transformative functions is to obtain raw materials from the physical environment. The materials are used in making products which fulfill human needs. Some of these functions are *primary,* others are *secondary,* and still others are *tertiary.* As the designations suggest, the three functions follow one another sequentially. This sequence is evident in two ways: in the production of goods and services and in the evolution of societies.

Primary Functions We first learned about primary functions in Chapter 8. For example, the chief economic activity in some towns is the gathering of natural resources. Among the occupations in such towns are hunting, fishing, farming, lumbering, and mining. Functions such as mining and farming produce the raw materials for the production of goods and services in industrial societies. At the evolutionary stage of the preindustrial society, the primary functions (chiefly agriculture, hunting, and fishing) are the only economic functions.

Secondary Functions Workers performing secondary extractive-transformative functions transform raw materials into usable products. Here we find the manufacturing, construction, food-processing, and handicraft occupations. Energy-conveying industries fall into this group as well (e.g., hydroelectric power plants). Secondary functions are rare at the preindustrial stage of societal evolution. The secondary functions that are found in preindustrial societies are usually in the handicraft field. As preindustrial societies modernize, however, the secondary sector of the economy expands dramatically, with a concomitant decline in the primary sector.

Tertiary Functions. The tertiary functions provide various services. Repairing and maintaining equipment is a service occupation, and some of the equipment is used in the primary and secondary spheres. Barbering, dentistry, medicine, and tailoring are personal services. Accounting, banking, legal representation, and secretarial work are support services. Leisure services are provided by sports teams and motion picture studios. Secondary occupations which provide goods engender the need for the various tertiary occupations; secondary occupations and the consumers of products must be serviced.

On the evolutionary scale, the farther an industrial society advances, the more the tertiary sector of its economy expands. This is typically accompanied by a decline in the society's secondary sector and primary sector. Societies in the earlier stages of industrialization have a smaller tertiary sector than societies in the later stages of industrialization.

Exchange-Distribution

The *exchange-distribution* functions encompass, in part, those occupations concerned with getting the wanted products from producer to consumer. Among such functions are warehousing, shipment, advertising, and retail sales. To the extent that they advertise, printing and television are also exchange-distribution functions. Some of these functions are also classifiable as secondary transformative, since they convert raw materials into finished products. The publication of newspapers is an example.

The marketing system is an indispensable part of the economic institution of modern industrial societies. Many of the exchange-distribution functions contribute to marketing and how it is accomplished. Marketing specialists must deal with numerous problems:

> (1) Determining what the consumers want in the way of goods and services and how much, when, where they want them; (2) determining whether total costs can be met, plus a profit, by the prices purchasers will find it possible to pay; (3) informing the consumers of what is being produced and when and where it can be obtained; (4) getting the goods to intermediate producers and final consumers. (Hertzler, 1961: 270–271)

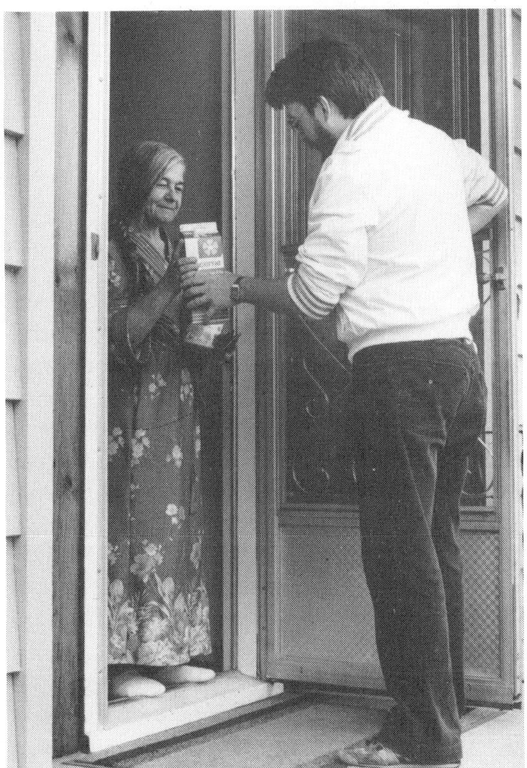

This milkman is carrying out an exchange-distribution function.

Business people have institutionalized ways of dealing with marketing problems. For example, they have the technology of communications (typewriters, computers, telephones); orders can be placed, and records can be kept. Standard weights and measures (metric in many parts of the world) are applied to the measurement of goods. The bookkeepers have systems of computation and accounting; they keep track of monetary transactions. Trucks, railroads, and airlines move the goods in a vast transportation network.

CONSUMPTION

The aforementioned economic functions are conducted only if there is an adequate consumer market for the products which the functions produce. People must purchase the goods and services. As noted, some—possibly many—of the consumers live in foreign countries. Whether the items consumed are imported or produced internally, consumption patterns are determined by several variables. Among the variables are age, sex, and race. Socioeconomic status, the size of the family, and the stage of the life cycle are also factors affecting consumption patterns. In addition, consumption varies by religion, home ownership, degree of urbanization, the compulsiveness of buyers, and future expectations. Finally, consumption is related to a society's standard of living. In 1984 Canada and the United States recorded the highest standards of living in the world, with Canada's being slightly below that of the United States (Harris, 1985: 10).

Roseborough (1960) has injected some order into this hodgepodge by identifying seven levels of social structure at which consumers make decisions on whether to obtain and use goods and services. The decisions made are broadly understood as stemming from consciously and unconsciously motivated acts of consumption. Roseborough's levels form a *funnel of consumption,* running from the most general and abstract to the most specific and concrete.

On the *first* and most general level people must decide whether to accept generalized purchasing power; that is, they must decide whether to live in a money economy. One could decide, as an alternative, to become a self-sufficient hermit or to join a small rural commune in which everyday needs are satisfied without recourse to goods and services vended by outsiders. Those who make the decision to accept generalized purchasing power move to the *second* level. At the second level, in spending their money, they must accept or reject the life-style of their society. The members of some ethnic groups in Canada (e.g., first-generation Chinese and East Indians) sometimes choose to retain a number of material ways of the old country, such as eating traditional foods or wearing traditional clothing.

At the *third* level, people who have accepted the life-style of their society must still decide for or against its overall standard of living. For example, some North American Indians would prefer the prevailing life-style of white Canadians, but find that they are unable to achieve it. Having also rejected their own native life-style, they sometimes wind up on skid row as participants in still another life-style.

The *fourth* level of decision making concerns the standards of consumption. Having accepted their society's standard of living, individual members are then faced with whether to accept

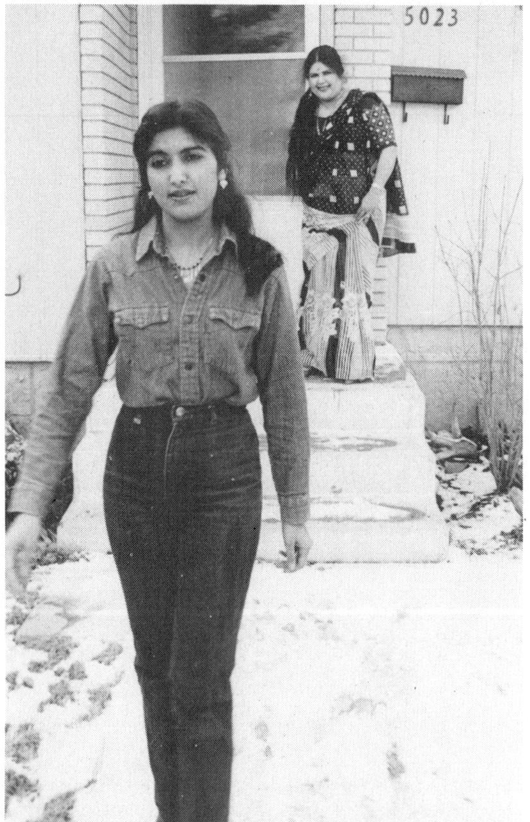

Which level of consumption do you see in this picture?

its standards of consumption. Thus, Canadians generally select food for its nutrition or tastiness, rather than because it is traditional fare (Thanksgiving and Easter being exceptions). The *fifth level* narrows the consumer's choice to the standards of the groups to which he or she belongs. A Coke and french fries constitute an acceptable snack for hungry teenagers, while a salad and a glass of wine are the choice of upper-middle-class professionals.

At the *sixth level,* we find the consumption standards associated with various roles. Elderly women generally dress according to the standards expected of elderly women rather than as young women in their early twenties. The *seventh level* is that of personal consumption standards. Some men smoke Marlboros because they identify with the advertising imagery; others smoke nothing at all because they value their health.

There can be no doubt that consumption is as much a sociological matter as an economic matter.

POLITICAL ECONOMY

Sociologists also have an interest in political economy. *Political economy* is broadly defined as the study of capitalism and the capitalist state, either critically from the Marxist perspective or traditionally from the liberal perspective. The liberal perspective affirms the legitimacy of the capitalist social system (Chattopadhyay, 1974). Like functionalism, political economy is a holistic and interdisciplinary study of society. There the similarity ends.

American Political Economy

In the United States, the branches of political sociology and economic sociology, for the most part, developed independently of each other (Kourvetaris and Dobratz, 1980: 13). The theoretical dominance of the inherently conservative, functionalist model from roughly 1950 to 1965 was broken in the response of sociology to the social unrest of the late 1960s and early 1970s. The political economy framework began to emerge during the latter period. In the study of urban politics, for instance, it comes up in the Marxian theme of domination by an elite who exploit the less powerful classes. This has aroused interest in the origins and focus of urban social policy and in popular reactions to the policy. One reaction is the collective action carried out through the complex social structure of cities (Walton, 1976: 301). We will return to a discussion of American urban political economy near the end of this chapter.

Canadian Political Economy

Canadian sociologists inherited the political economy framework from Europe.[1] In the 1930s, Harold Innis, W. A. Mackintosh, and others, writing in a liberal rather than a radical vein, developed the staple theory of economic growth. The central tenet of this framework is that, in Canada, unlike the United States and Europe, economic growth is predominantly tied to the export of staples or raw materials (fur, fish, lumber, wheat, minerals, oil, and gas) which other countries need and can use. Theory and research along these lines continued into the 1930s, when it became fashionable to study theoretical questions instead of societal questions. During most of the 1950s and 1960s, functionalists held sway in Canada, as they did in the United States; functionalists took an interest in bureaucracy, elites, management, technology, and other processes and activities from a systems-maintenance perspective. Such an orientation, as we have seen, concentrates on the economic and political status quo.

What Drache (1978: 32) calls the "new political economy" started forming in Canada in the late 1960s and early 1970s. It is an interdisciplinary product that grew out of Marxism and historical analysis (as well as other intellectual traditions) and is exemplified in the writing of scholars such as R. T. Naylor and Stanley Ryerson.[2] The empirical focus is on social-class relationships, economic elites, political elites, and national dependency. *National dependency* is the reliance of some nations on other nations for essential goods and services.

Dependent societies or regions are *peripheral.* They specialize in supplying inexpensive raw materials or selected manufactures to a dominant core nation or region, while being forced, as a result of their thin economic base, to satisfy most of their everyday needs with expensive products imported from the core nation or region. Thus, Canadian political economy

[1]This paragraph and the next one draw heavily on Drache's (1978) article on the development of Canadian political economy.

[2]The founders of Canadian political economy also reassessed history in constructing the staple theory and similar frameworks.

delves into the topics of foreign ownership of local industry, dependence on technological developments made in the core, and international business elites. In the section which follows, the economy is examined from the change- and conflict-oriented political economy framework. Some of the most dramatic differences distinguishing the American and Canadian societies are referred to here. We will examine this dependency theme further in Chapter 23.

THE NORTH AMERICAN ECONOMIES

There are many ways in which the American economy can be compared with the Canadian economy. Economists perhaps are more likely to make such comparisons than are sociologists.[3] Still, sociologists have expressed a great deal of interest in comparing Canada's corporate concentration and foreign direct investment with the U.S. corporate concentration and foreign direct investment. These comparisons are made in this section as vehicles for presenting the critical, political economy perspective. Note that the focus is on the business enterprise, which, as Stinchcombe (1983: 2–6) points out, is central to Marx's sociology. Economic forces affect the enterprise and, in turn, the entrepreneurial forces of production affect the workers employed there.

Corporate Concentration

Corporate concentration is the ownership of industrial and financial organizations by a few individuals and the organizations they control. With corporate concentration, the control of a firm is funneled into the hands of a small number of owners and their managerial staff. There has been a global trend toward corporate concentration. The trend grew after World War II, spawning, among other things, the enterprise known as the *multinational corporation* (MNC):

> In resources, manufacturing, transportation, communications, and financial sectors, fewer but larger companies each year dominated the respective markets; simultaneously, fewer but larger companies controlled the largest subsidiaries in several fields. Corporate complexes emerged consisting of a single parent corporation holding controlling shares in numerous other companies throughout the world in every phase of industrial and financial activity. (Marchak, 1979: 36)

Corporate concentration is a fact of economic life in both the United States and Canada. The evidence, while sometimes difficult to collect, suggests that concentration is greater in Canadian manufacturing than in American manufacturing (Information Canada, 1971: 5–6); the reverse shows up in banking (Marchak, 1979: 47). Nonetheless, corporate concentration is present in all sectors of the North American economy.

Clement (1977: 10–11) has put forward the economic and social case against corporate concentration. With an actual or near monopoly, as Clement notes, these business monoliths easily control to their advantage prices of their products and employee wages (despite trade unions). They establish job conditions and also have much to say about the occupational careers of the individuals who work for them. They can conceivably mold individuals into certain personality types consistent with the organization's needs. Through advertising, MNCs also promote "mindless consumption" of their products.

Foreign Direct Investment

Corporate concentration on an international scale promotes foreign direct investment. *Foreign direct investment* (FDI) is an individual's investment of capital in assets or in ownership of a foreign enterprise. For example, American investors have put their money in European, Canadian, and Japanese firms. Europeans have invested in American corporations; Canadians

[3] See Michalos (1982: Chapter 12) for a set of more purely economic comparisons along the lines of inflation, gross national product, taxes, and other variables.

A Deviant Solution to the Problem of the Mastery of Nature

My aim here is to suggest how one elite, namely automobile manufacturers, create a "criminogenic market structure" by imposing upon their new car dealers a pricing policy which requires high volume and low per unit profit. While this strategy gives the *manufacturer* increased total net aggregate profit (by achieving economies of scale and by minimizing direct competition among oligopolist "rivals"), it places the new car dealer in a financial squeeze by forcing him to constantly free-up and continuously re-cycle capital into fixed margin new car inventory. This squeeze sets in motion a downward spiral of illegal activities which (1) inclines the new car dealer to engage in compensatory profit taking through fraudulent service operations, (2) under certain conditions, generates a "kickback" system which enables used car managers of new car dealerships to exact graft from independent used car wholesalers, and (3) forces the independent used car wholesaler into illegal "short-sales" in order to generate unrecorded cash for kickback payments. I shall present the evidence which provides the grounding for this model as I came upon it in the research process. What follows, then, is a natural history which reconstructs the stages of my investigation. . . .

I managed to arrange interviews with three different dealers. The following quoted interview lasted five hours, was granted on the basis of a personal tie, and therefore is most reliable and valid. In addition, the elicited material is highly representative of the other interviews. The general thrust of my questioning was first to ask the dealer to talk about issues which are problematic in the running of his own business, and then to comment on the "kickback" phenomenon at the urban agencies. I was interested mainly in knowing if the pressure to turn over capital and avoid interest payments would encourage a dealer to "look-the-other-way" on "kickbacks" or even split them.

Q: How long have you been a dealer?

A: A dealer? About 20 years. About five or six years after [I finished] college, my dad and I went in as partners. It's mine now.

Q: Have you enjoyed it?

A: Well, it's been good to me for a goodly number of years, but frankly, during these past three to four years the business has changed markedly. It's a tougher, tighter business. I'm more tied down to it now than ever before. I can't be as active in the community as I would like. You know, that's important to me.

Q: Why is that the case? Is the business expanding?

A: Not really, well it depends on how you measure it. I work harder, have a larger sales and service staff than ever, I've expanded the facilities twice and refurbished the fixtures and touched up several times, and yes, I'm selling more new cars than before, but is the business expanding? Well, I suppose, yes, but not the way I'd like it to.

Q: Could you elaborate on that?

A: Well, the point is—and I know this will sound anomalous, well, maybe not to you—but I wish I could ease off on the number of new cars and pick up somewhere else, maybe on used cars.

Q: Why is that?

A: It boils down to investment—return ratios. The factory [manufacturer] has us on a very narrow per unit profit margin [on new car sales]. But if I had the money and the cars, I could use my capital more effectively in used cars.

Q: In other words, G.M. establishes how much profit you can make on each new car you sell?

A: Just about. And more than that, they more or less determine how much [new car] inventory I have to carry, and the composition of that inventory.

Q: So, you have to take what they give you—even if you don't want or need it. How do you pay for the inventory?

A: I borrow money at prevailing interest rates to finance the inventory. And, sometimes it gets tight. Believe me, if I am unable to sell off that inventory relatively quickly, I'm pressed. I have got to keep that money turning or that interest begins to pinch.

Q: Is it fair to say that you compensate for narrow margins on new cars by making wider margins on used cars?

A: Not really, not in practice, at least not out here [in the suburbs]. Used cars, good used cars, are hard to come by. I imagine the city dealers have an easier time getting trade-ins. We get a lot of repeat customers, but I don't believe they trade up. They just buy new cars. Actually, we tend to pick up additional revenue from our service repair operation. I'm not particularly proud about it, but there is a lot of skimping going on. It's quite complicated. The factory has a terrible attitude toward service repair generally, and the [mechanics] union is overly demanding and inflexible. It's rather demoralizing and, frankly, I'm looking out for myself, too.

Q: Could you expand on that?

A: I prefer you not press me on that.

Q: If you had a choice, how would you prefer to set up your operation?

A: Well, if I had a choice—which I don't—I would rather have a low volume, high margin operation. I could get by with smaller facilities, a smaller staff, put less time into the business, and not constantly face the money squeeze.

Q: Do you think the really large city dealers would prefer the same kind of alternative?

A: I guess so, but it's hard to say. Their situation is somewhat different from mine.

Q: In what way?

A: Well, first of all, some of them, especially if they're located in [megalopolis] have even less control over their operation than I do. Some of them really run factory stores. That is, G.M. directly owns or controls the agency. Those outfits are really high-volume houses. I don't see how they can make a go of it. The factory really absorbs the costs.

Q: You did say that they probably had strong used car operations or, at least, had a lot of trade-ins. Do you think that helps?

A: Possibly.

Q: Do you think a really sharp used car man could do well in that kind of operation?

A: Well, he would do well in any operation in which he had used cars to work with.

Q: He could both retail and wholesale?

A: Oh, yes, if he had the cars to work with.
Q: Is it likely, in the wholesale end, he could demand and receive "kickbacks" from wholesalers?
A: Well, it's been known to happen. You know, those wholesalers, they're always willing to accommodate a friend. But it would only pay them to do that in relatively large operations where they could anticipate a fairly steady flow of cars.
Q: So, it would certainly make sense for them to accommodate friends in large, high volume, urban G.M. agencies?
A: Sure.
Q: Do you suppose the used car managers split kickbacks with their bosses?
A: Well, it's possible, but more than likely, the boss is more interested in moving those cars out quickly any way he can, so he can turn over that money and place it back into new car inventory.

SOURCE: Harvey A. Farberman. A criminogenic market structure: The automobile industry. *Sociological Quarterly* 16: 438–457, 1975.

have invested chiefly in Caribbean and American companies. Foreign direct investment is conventionally compared with portfolio investment, wherein the investor purchases securities, thus making his or her ownership indirect. Kresl (1981: 143) observes that countries with large numbers of MNC home offices have liberal FDI policies:

> An open international environment is of benefit to owners of capital who are then able to choose from among the greatest possible numbers of alternative investment projects, and to move their funds from one location to another with minimum cost and inconvenience. . . . The last thing wanted . . . is an . . . effective set of capital controls by the home government, since this might prove to be an inspiration to the governments of host economies.

Kresl goes on to note that Canada is a deviant case in this respect. Until 1975, Canada had a liberal investment policy but a small number of MNCs. Although this policy has since shifted to the conservative direction (in response to rising Canadian nationalism), 80 percent of FDI in Canada in 1975 came from the United States (another 10 percent came from Great Britain).[4] Going the other way, however, Canadian FDI in the United States in recent years accounted for only 20 percent of all such investment there (Kresl, 1961: 138–139). Since the totality of foreign ownership of corporations is smaller in the United States than in Canada, it has stirred less concern in the United States, but the same practice in Canada is presently a major public issue. In Canada, attention is focused particularly on American owners, both individual and corporate. Accordingly, there has been a modest increase since 1975 in domestic ownership of Canadian corporations.

Political economists argue that the large proportion of FDI in Canada has relegated the country to the position of a dependent peripheral society. The trade imbalance between Canada and the United States (a core society) supports this hypothesis. The United States exports to and imports from a variety of countries. Canada and Europe account for more than half the exports to the United States and 40 percent of the imports; European and Canadian exports and imports to and from the United States are

[4]American investors show a preference for the manufacturing, petroleum, and mining sectors of the Canadian economy. Canadian ownership in 1975 was less than 50 percent in each of these and in the second and third less than that of Americans. Banking and transportation are controlled wholly by Canadians.

about equal (Kresl: 1981: 138–141). By contrast, about 70 percent of Canadian import and export trade is strictly with the United States. Consonant with dependency theory predictions, Canada is a net importer of finished goods.

Political Economy Perspective

When seen from the political economy perspective, foreign direct investment and corporate concentration in MNCs have far-reaching sociological consequences. Clement (1977: 17–18) holds that Canadian dependency is fostered, in significant part, by sympathetic capitalists from inside the country. They have welcomed foreign capital, chiefly American, as a substitute for industrial development they might have carried out themselves. (Note how this is consistent with the passive quality of Canadian national character mentioned in Chapter 5.) A rather clandestine partnership has evolved between these two parties to the point where Canadian capitalists vigorously defend the actions of their cohorts across the border as being good for the Canadian economy. This, Clement says, has resulted in an international financial class, based on a system of mutual support of class interests in countries where its members reside. We shall return to this discussion in Chapter 18. "Stratification."

Marchak (1979: 100–101) points out that in Canada the power of this international class is concentrated in the country's metropolitan areas, particularly Ontario and Quebec. From here they collaborate with regional industrialists to exploit the raw materials available in the Atlantic, Prairie, and West Coast regions. This arrangement forces the hinterlands into dependency on the metropolises (notably Toronto and Montreal) and foreign sources for finished products, since there is no encouragement for them to develop secondary industries and become centers in their own right. And, sometimes, the raw materials of the hinterland are exploited by the hinterland itself. The 1985 energy pricing arrangement between the federal government and the governments of the three westernmost provinces is regarded, at least by federal opposition parties, as harmful to Ontario and beneficial to the West (*Globe and Mail,* 1985: 1–2).

In the United States, of course, the political economy perspective has been applied quite differently. The United States is a core nation. Moreover, its regional disparities (the core regions' dominance over hinterlands) are disappearing (Narr, 1974). Thus, as in Canada, political economy is used as a foil to the functionalist approach to the economy, except that one of its most fruitful applications lies in the study of urban economic power. Consider, for example, Molotch's (1976) theory of the city as a growth machine. He theorizes that a city's business elite, including its lawyers and realtors, join hands to promote population growth, which they claim increases property values, expands markets, and results in other material advantages. Their efforts are institutionalized by such "boosterism" techniques as establishing a chamber of commerce, publicizing the community through advertisements in business journals and travel magazines, promoting it with parade floats, and acquiring professional sports teams bearing the city's name. The local newspaper also helps foster a positive local image, for it, too, has something to gain from increased population; that is, it gains additional subscribers and readers. All this is justified on the grounds that the citizenry benefits.

The model of the growth machine predicts

The concept of the city as a growth machine emphasizes the problems of urban living that spring from growth.

otherwise. The burdens rise during the growth period, while the forecast increase in employment fails to materialize. The promised general increase in the quality of life usually ends up as an actual decrease in the quality of life (e.g., increased environmental pollution, greater traffic congestion, and overuse of parks). Lyon et al. (1981), in a study of forty-eight American cities, were able to substantiate a number of the propositions in Molotch's theory.

SURVIVING SOCIETIES

From the political economist's standpoint, the failure of the functionalist theory is, in part, one of neglect of certain crucial processes unfolding in the economy. That is, functionalism's concern with system maintenance and the functions by which this is effected has blinkered it to the power struggles and patterns of exploitation occurring among various groups in Canada and the United States. Yet, notwithstanding these tensions, the societies of both the United States and Canada are surviving—i.e., being maintained—as societies, although there was once doubt whether Canada would do so over the long haul (e.g., Grant, 1965).[5] Clearly, then, both perspectives are necessary for understanding the economic institution.

OUTLINE AND SUMMARY

I. Introduction
Economics is narrowly concerned with the production, distribution, and consumption of goods and services.

II. The Economy as an Institution
The economy as an institution is the relatively stable set of abstract relationships, patterns of behavior, norms, and values that develop around the production, distribution, and consumption of goods and services.

A. Collective Living
In general, the economy as an institution solves the collective problems of the mastery of nature; those who live together as a society must all attain shelter, sustenance, and protection.

B. Behavior and Relationships
There are literally thousands of patterns of behavior, abstract relationships, and roles in every sector of our economy. The production, distribution, and consumption of milk are an example.

C. Values and History
One of the main economic values is that of doing good work for its own sake. This value is still held under certain conditions. The history of our economic institution is seen in the rise and fall of feudalism and the rise and possible fall of capitalism.

III. Economic Functions
There are two major sets of economic functions: extractive-transformative and exchange-distribution.

A. Extractive-Transformative
The purpose of the extractive-transformative function is to obtain raw materials from the physical environment.

1. Primary Functions
The gathering of natural resources is a primary function. It is the chief economic activity in some towns.

2. Secondary Functions
Raw materials are transformed into usable products by means of secondary extractive-transformative functions. Such functions enter into handicraft, manufacturing, construction, and food processing.

3. Tertiary Functions
The tertiary functions provide various services. Among the services are medicine, dentistry, barbering, accounting, banking, secretarial work, and the repair of equipment. A professional football team is a leisure service.

[5]A Poll conducted in November 1982 (Gallup Poll of Canada, 1982) estimated that 67 percent of Canadians believed that Canada would not break up and 20 percent believed the country would. Thirteen percent of those polled did not know how to answer the question asked by the interviewer.

B. Exchange-Distribution
Exchange-distribution functions encompass, in part, those occupations concerned with getting the desired products from producer to consumer; a truck driver performs an exchange-distribution function.

IV. Consumption
The economic functions are conducted only if there is an adequate consumer market for the products which the functions produce. If there is a market, products are purchased according to the funnel of consumption: (a) deciding whether to accept generalized purchasing power, (b) deciding whether to accept the life-style of the society, (c) deciding for or against the society's overall standard of living, (d) deciding whether to accept the society's standards of consumption, (e) deciding whether to accept the standards of the groups to which one belongs, (f) deciding whether to accept the standards associated with various roles, (g) deciding on personal standards.

V. Political Economy
Political economy is the study of the laws and relations of capitalist development, either critically from the Marxist perspective or more traditionally from the liberal view that affirms the legitimacy of capitalism.

A. American Political Economy
Political economy in America has been applied to urban social policy.

B. Canadian Political Economy
In Canada, economic growth is predominantly tied to the export of staples or raw materials. Canada is dependent.

VI. The North American Economies
Corporate concentration is greater in Canadian manufacturing than in American manufacturing; the reverse is true in banking.

A. Corporate Concentration
Corporate concentration is the ownership of industrial and financial businesses by a few individuals and the organizations they control. The control of a firm is funneled into the hands of a small number of owners and their managers. The *multinational corporation* (MNC) is an example of corporate concentration.

B. Foreign Direct Investment
Foreign direct investment (FDI) is an individual's investment of capital in assets or in ownership of a foreign enterprise; there is little FDI in the United States but a great deal of it in Canada. Much Canadian FDI is in America.

C. Political Economy Perspective
When seen from the political economy perspective, foreign direct investment and corporate concentration in MNCs have far-reaching sociological consequences. In Canada, capitalists have welcomed foreign capital (chiefly American) as a substitute for their own industrial development. In the United States, the perspective has been applied to a study of urban economic power. According to Molotch's theory, the city is a growth machine.

VII. Surviving Societies
Despite tensions from within and without, Canada and the United States are surviving as societies.

FOR FURTHER READING AND STUDY

Clement, W. 1977. *Continental corporate power.* Toronto: McClelland & Stewart. A study of the degree of control and range of influence of the multinational corporations in Canada, many of which have their home offices in the United States.

Gaventa, J. 1980. *Power and powerlessness: Quiescence and rebellion in an Appalachian valley.* Urbana, Ill.: University of Illinois Press. This is a study of the institutionalization of "colonial" control by multinational mining corporations of the Appalachian region and of the failure of many attempts to break that control. Gaventa writes that the miners in the region have found it impossible to gain power at any level.

Gilder, G. 1981. *Wealth and poverty.* New York: Basic Books. Gilder represents the conservative viewpoint on wealth and poverty by arguing, for example, that economic inequality is justified because it generates growth, which leads eventually to a higher standard of living. Those at the bottom of the income ladder are said to benefit eventually from the new prosperity.

House, J. D. 1980. *The last of the free enterprisers: The oilmen of Calgary.* Toronto: Macmillan of Canada. This is a study of the social organization of the Canadian oil industry and of the values, beliefs, careers, and job satisfactions of the oilmen of Calgary.

Stinchcombe, A. L. 1983. *Economic sociology.* New York: Academic Press. This is a theoretical synthesis designed to develop an economic sociology that will complete and unify the works of Marx and his present-day followers. The theory is illustrated by a comparative examination of a primitive herding tribe in Uganda, the feudal agricultural state of eighteenth century France, and the contemporary United States.

Wallerstein, I. 1980. *The modern world-system II: Mercantilism and the consolidation of the European world-economy, 1600–1750.* New York: Academic Press. Wallerstein, a sociologist, presents a fascinating Marxian account of the seventeenth and eighteenth century antecedents of the contemporary world capitalist system.

KEY WORDS

capitalist: Entrepreneur who owns the means of production; one of the bourgeoisie.

corporate concentration: Ownership of industrial and financial businesses by a few individuals.

economic institution: Relatively stable set of relationships, patterns of behavior, norms, and values that emerge around the production, distribution, and consumption of goods and services.

economics: Social science whose central concern is the production, distribution, and consumption of goods and services.

economy: Social institution that develops around the production, distribution, and consumption of goods and services.

exchange-distributive function: Economic process in a society by which its members distribute products from producer to consumer.

extractive-transformative function: Economic processes in a society by which its members obtain raw materials from the environment and transform them into usable products.

foreign direct investment: An individual's investment of capital in assets or in ownership of a foreign enterprise.

gross national product: Total value of goods and services produced in a nation during a specified period, normally twelve months.

political economy: Study of the laws and relations of capitalist development, either critically from the Marxist perspective or more traditionally from the liberal view that affirms the legitimacy of capitalism.

chapter 14

Polity

CHAPTER OUTLINE

Introduction
The Polity as an Institution
- The Political System
- Values
- History

Political Culture
- Political Socialization

Political Parties
- *Third Parties*
- *Populism*

Political Participation
- *Sociodemographic Basis*
- *Voter Turnout*

A Politicized Society

INTRODUCTION

In Chapter 13 we asked, "Why is sociology concerned with economy?" In this chapter we have a similar question: "What does sociology have in common with political science?" Political science is a study of social life apart from sociology and a discipline in itself. A central focus of political science is the polity. The *polity* is a specified form of political organization; it is a politically organized unit such as the federal government or a local government. The polity is a social institution. As an institution, it is also within the domain of sociology. The domain is *political sociology.*

The polity (the federal government, a local government) has a powerful influence over the lives of Canadians. Everyone must obey the laws and must pay taxes; governments hardly can be ignored by those who are governed. In view of all this, political science is not wholly removed from sociology. Each discipline has something to offer to the other as a means of dealing with political studies. But sociology provides answers which are of peripheral concern to political science. Sociology deals with society and with the individuals in society.

The polity is the structure of political life in a society; it is the way political life is organized. Industrial societies organize political life by means of civil government, the task of which is to order and adjust relations between individuals and the state and between groups and the state. Some scholars draw a firm distinction between the *government* and the *state*. The government is a group; within the group are political parties and civil servants. The government's actions embody the apparatus of the state. The *state* is a cultural system; the system is perceived as legitimate by nearly everyone in society. The state and its structure defines and guides the actions of the government. Governments are voted in and out of office, while the state survives each such turnover. As an enduring entity, the state is within the political institution of a society.

THE POLITY AS AN INSTITUTION

The *political institution* is defined as the relatively stable set of abstract relationships, patterns of behavior, norms, and values that develop around the collective problems of distributing political power, managing violence, and maintaining societal boundaries. Marx observed that the distribution of political power and the management of violence are collective problems because people want to acquire power and use it for their own ends. In using power to get what they want, they often exploit other members of the society.

An institutional solution to the collective problem of managing violence.

The Political System

The defining criteria of *roles, patterned behavior,* and *abstract relationships* combine to form what sociologists call a *political* system. The social structure of this system is based on the distribution of power and authority.

> The unit analysis for these power relationships is usually "role. . . ." Political roles are concerned with the making of decisions in the name of society and the performance of actions which achieve or implement these decisions and allocate scarce values and costs. The set of these roles and the behavior which stems from them make up the political system. (Mitchell, 1968: 474)

Hertzler (1961: 395–396) notes that the polity is the largest and most inclusive of the social institutions, in the sense that its range and scope are wider than those of any other. For example, members of Parliament cannot overlook the needs and interests of family, school, and church as they try to establish and maintain public order. They maintain that order by using six types of coercive power: (1) police power to protect the safety, health, morale, and possessions of citizens (although citizens are not all equally protected); (2) right of eminent domain, which is the power to expropriate property for the public good; (3) taxing power as a means of raising money for government functions; (4) judicial power of the courts to interpret the law, settle disputes, and penalize violators; (5) penal power to correct and punish violators of the law; and (6) military power to establish, maintain, and use armed might against internal and external threats to the society.

Values

The polity, like other institutions, also rests on certain key *values.* The value structures and national characters of Americans and Canadians were referred to in Chapter 5 and need no further explanation here, except to note that some of the values in question are political. Among the political values are democracy, equality, civil liberties, and honesty in political action. The polity also pays heed to the more specific values of particular groups which seek to gain control of the political apparatus in order to implement their values. Schwartz (1981) describes several Canadian-American differences of this sort. For instance, she points to a greater tendency for people in the United States than people in Canada to organize over moral issues and for these issues to enter the realm of politics. The reasons for this difference are varied and complex, and they are beyond the scope of this chapter.

History

The *history* of the polity is evident in the many legal and structural changes brought about annually by government. Dramatic changes are, understandably, rather uncommon, although over the past twenty years or so, Canadians may have experienced more of them than Americans. In their efforts to achieve economic sovereignty and a national identity, Canadians have made significant changes in (or additions to) their political symbols (e.g., new flag and national anthem) and legitimating structures (e.g., the constitution of 1982). Changes of this magnitude in the polity are unknown to many Americans alive today, although lowering the voting age to eighteen in 1971 and abolishing the military draft in 1973 were hardly unnoticed changes in the political culture of the United States.

POLITICAL CULTURE

The six defining criteria, along with other considerations, have attracted considerable attention as forms of *political culture.* Other forms, in addition to the six criteria, are political socialization, political parties, political participation, community power, and protest movements. Sections of this chapter which follow discuss political socialization, political parties, and political participation. Community power and protest movements are covered in Chapters 18 and 21.

Political Socialization

Political socialization is, simply, the political learning of children and adults. This is a common definition. Political socialization begins in early childhood (Niemi and Sobieszek, 1977:

SOCIOLOGY OR COMMON SENSE

What do you think?

Which of the following statements do you agree with? Which statements do you disagree with? Make a note of your answers. Check your answers when you have completed your study of this chapter. Are your answers to the statements the same as those a sociologist would give?

1. By the age of ten or so, children in industrialized nations know the names of the president or prime minister of the country in which they live.
2. The modern political party is an American invention.
3. The polity touches our lives in more ways than any other social institution.
4. The United States is the cradle of democracy; voter turnout is high there in comparison with the turnout in other industrialized countries.
5. In Canada and the United States, politicians are respected members of society.

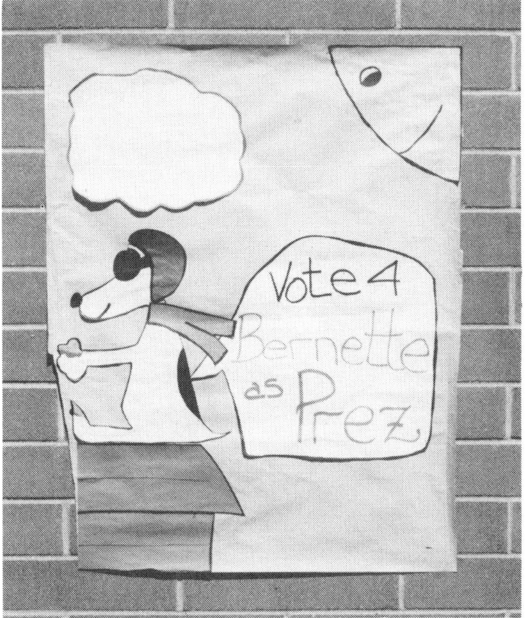

Political socialization: The school election teaches democracy.

209). The results of this special form of socialization have been summarized by Easton and Dennis (1969: 391–393) in four propositions. The first proposition is *politicization,* meaning that children soon learn of the existence of authority figures beyond those in their everyday lives at home and in school. By age seven to eight, they have developed a vague idea of this level of authority and its demands of obedience and respect. Research has established that in some parts of North America (Kentucky, Newfoundland, British Columbia) and among some ethnic groups (Chicanos, American blacks) this attitude in regard to obedience is sometimes withheld. The children have been found to have a "malevolent" view of authority (see Niemi and Sobieszek, 1977: 212–13; Zureik, 1975: 11).

Second is personalization. *Personalization* is the tendency of individuals to develop an image of political authority. For example, children and adults picture the police and national leaders as authority figures. This proposition holds for American children, but early studies of Australian and Canadian children (Connell, 1971; Pammett, 1971, respectively) showed that they were more likely to know the president of the United States than their own prime ministers. Higgins's (1976) more recent studies, however, indicate that this confusion is now rarer in Canada, although there are many more American children who can name their president by the time they are in grade 5 than Canadian children who can name their prime minister (Higgins, 1976; Landes, 1979: 376). Japanese children gave no indication of any leader. Leaders of other countries, although known by the children in those countries, were evaluated as other than kindly, powerful, and world famous—the American children's image of the president (Niemi and Sobieszek, 1977: 214).

This brings us to the third proposition, namely *idealization* of political authority as trustworthy, benevolent, and helpful. The initial studies in the United States support this proposition. But Watergate spoiled the American children's image of President Nixon, in particular, and the turmoil of the late 1960s and early 1970s (e.g., race riots, Vietnam War) tarnished their benevolent image of authority figures in general. Still, the facts are not all in. Niemi and Sobieszek (1977: 215–216) conclude from their review of the literature that many contradictions exist in the findings bearing on personalization and idealization of authority within and between countries.

Eventually, children's political socialization reaches a point of *institutionalization,* when they learn about impersonal structures such as Congress, Parliament, the Supreme Court, and "the government." Easton and Dennis's (1969) study of American children, which forms the basis for the institutionalization proposition, was replicated in British Columbia by Zureik (1971) with similar results. Canadian findings in this area, however, have been inconsistent (see Zureik, 1975: 15).

Knowledge of the impersonal political entities in an industrial society is acquired from various agents of socialization. Three of these

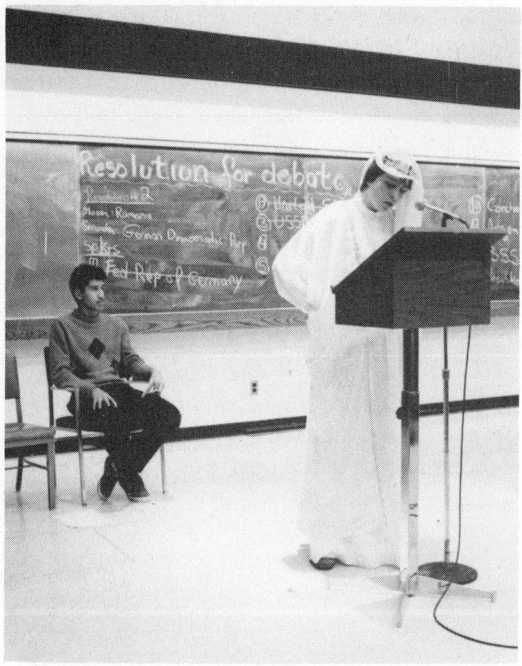

Institutionalization in political socialization: a model UN.

have been studied to a greater or lesser extent: the family, schools, and mass media. Niemi and Sobieszek (1977: 224) paint the following picture of research findings on political socialization agents in the United States:

> Clearly, the family does not by itself dictate how young people will emerge as political actors. Nor does the school seem to have an overwhelming effect. Rather, it is more amorphous factors, such as peers, the media, and events, that have gained prominence. Among other things, this increases the potential for change in political attitudes from one generation to the next. . . . Agents such as families and schools do not fully determine that the next generation will be reared in the image of the previous one. Rather, there is considerable room for development that is independent of or counter to the teachings of the older generation.

In comparison with the family and the mass media, the school is the least influential. The school's main contribution is idealization. Idealization in the school eventually lessens as the more realistic institutionalization sets in along with the child's growing ability to understand abstractions.

A promising finding in the study of the agents of political socialization of the young is the link between the young and events which are reported in the mass media. Watergate is an example. In Canada, there is evidence that all three agents (family, school, and mass media) have an influence on the young (see Zureik, 1975), but that political socialization comes about at an older age, which elevates the importance of the peer group as one of the agents of political socialization (Pammett and Whittington, 1976: 21–28).

Political socialization continues beyond adolescence into the adult years. Research in the United States shows that political attitudes change considerably as one grows older; there are changes even among older adults (Niemi and Sobieszek, 1977: 225–228).[1] Some of these changes are linked to the life-cycle stage of the individual (e.g., young adult, middle age, and old age). Others are part of the outlook of a generation; among the examples are the flower children of the 1960s, the "depression generation," and the children of the affluent fifties.

Furthermore, major events to which everyone is exposed leave indelible impressions on individuals. An example is the imposition of military rule in Quebec in October 1970 to end the disorder fomented by the Front de Liberation du Québec. Another is the decline of political trust in the United States and possibly in Canada in the late 1960s and early 1970s.[2]

From the functionalist viewpoint, political socialization helps account for the persistence of a society as a social system by accounting for the legitimacy of the state (Easton and Dennis, 1969). This is a theoretical claim. Research defies this interpretation, for it shows that adults not only change their political orienta-

[1] There appears to be no Canadian research on this subject.

[2] An unpublished study by Harvey Rich of political attitudes among a sample of Albertans suggests that decline of political trust may also have occurred in Canada.

tion but also fail to socialize their children completely in this regard.

Political Parties

There are other meanings of *political party,* but for our purposes we will use Schlesinger's (1968: 420) "office-seeking" definition: A *political party* is a "political organization which actively and effectively engages in the competition for elective office." North American political parties are motivated by many goals, but winning an elective office is paramount. People join a political party for many different reasons. For some, the party's social life has an appeal. Others are ambitious; they would like to be elected to an office. Many persons who join a party hope to receive political patronage (a job, public assistance) from the officeholders. Many also join political parties simply because they have a desire to shape public policy.

It should be recognized that political parties, as defined here, work within the existing polity and for the opportunities it provides them (Schlesinger, 1968: 429–430). The parties can seek only the public offices available in their political system. Moreover, the seeking of office must be undertaken according to the rules governing the election to an office; there is a regard for public opinion and for the will of the voters. Revolutionary groups whose aims are to change the polity dramatically hardly can be looked on as political parties. Pressure groups and debating societies are not political parties. Their goal is to highlight issues and influence official action, rather than to hold office. Political parties also deal with issues, but only as one of their many electoral strategies.

Orum (1983) holds that the modern political party came into being in the United States just before the presidential election of 1800. Its full development, as measured by public involvement, was reached in the 1820s and 1830s. Parties are one of the foundations of democracy; they allow for the expression of citizen concerns and for the attainment of legitimate power (Orum, 1983). Political parties in Canada arose in the midnineteenth century, although the disciplined, loyal member of today appeared only late in the 1800s (McMenemy, 1976: 10).

Third Parties In both Canada and the United States, only the two principal parties (Democrats and Republicans in the United States; Liberals and Progressive Conservatives in Canada) have ever held power in the federal governments. This is also true in the United States at the state level, but not so in Canada at the provincial level. This brings us to the role of third parties and their somewhat greater success in Canada than in the United States. The reasons for this may be found in the Constitution of the United States. In effect, the Constitution enforces a two-party system. This happens because of the principle of the separation of powers, for only a well-organized group (i.e., a political party) with an elected majority can gain control of one or more of the three branches of government. And then they have control only as long as their party remains in power. Political minorities who are unable or unwilling to align themselves with one of the two main parties lack this collective strength. The alternative—gaining political control of a state legislature—is futile, since successive Supreme Court interpretations have reduced the power of the state governments. (The opposite has been occurring in Canada.) While it has happened that individual maverick politicians (e.g., socialists) have been elected to Congress, they have been unable single-handedly to gain control of any of the three branches of government (Lipset, 1976: 36–52).

In Canada, elections, instead of being held at relatively short intervals, are held when the incumbent party decides to call one or loses a nonconfidence motion in the legislature, which forces one.[3] Both countries, so to speak, "inherited" the two-party concept from Britain.

Third parties have a somewhat better record of success in Canada than in the United States

[3]Incumbent parties are also obligated to call an election if five years have passed without one.

because of the relatively greater independence of provincial legislatures compared with the state legislatures in the United States and because of the different election system. It has also been possible for third parties to gain power in Canadian provincial legislatures (Schlesinger, 1968: 431) in part by capitalizing on certain ethnic allegiances in the legislature (Lipset, 1979: 301–302) and powerful regional sentiments. For example, a revealing contrast between Canada and the United States shows up in the populist and socialist movements which have occurred in the two countries from time to time.

Populism Conway (1978: 118) defines populism as "the political expression of a critique of capitalism and a proposed developmental alternative from the point of view of the agrarian petite bourgeoisie." In the 1890s, the Populist party stood for social reform in the interest of farmers and workers, the common people. Scholarly interpretations of the nature of North American populism (as opposed to that of Europe and Russia) are contradictory; some thinkers see it as progressive and reformist, and others define it as backward, racist, and confused (Conway, 1978: 99–101). Populism first became a political force in North America in the last half of the nineteenth century in various agricultural areas, principally in the Midwest and the plains.

The Populist party succeeded in seriously challenging the dominant parties in the American federal election of 1896. It emerged as an influential third party. But it went the route of all popular third parties in the United States; that is, the Populists' moderate principles were adopted by one of the principal parties—in this case, the Democratic party. Like other third parties, the Populist party was left with only its core of radical ideas, which turned out to be too extreme and hence were a major factor in its demise.

In Canada, populism gained its most notable successes in the West. The Cooperative Commonwealth Federation (CCF), a liberal, socialist amalgam of farmers, laborers, and intellectuals, gained power in Saskatchewan in 1944 and remained in office for twenty years.[4] In Alberta, the more typically conservative populist Social Credit Party won the provincial election of 1935, retaining office until 1970. It also dominated politics in British Columbia during roughly the same period. In 1961, the CCF was reorganized into the New Democratic Party (NDP), which has recently formed governments in British Columbia, Manitoba, and Saskatchewan and which in 1982 held nearly all the seats in Parliament not filled by Liberals or Conservatives.

Political Participation

According to Alford and Friedland (1975: 438), *political participation* refers to

> those present or past activities by private citizens and private or public organizations and groups that are more or less directly aimed at influencing the selection of governmental structures and personnel, and the actions they take or do not take.

There are many forms of political participation. Individuals are participating when they vote and when they work for electoral candidates. Joining a political party and running for office are forms of political participation. A person is politically active when he or she talks to a public official about a special interest. Two forms of political participation—voting and joining a political party—are considered here.

Sociodemographic Basis Although the principal political parties in Canada and the United States have as members individuals from a wide range of religious, social-class, ethnic, regional, and linguistic backgrounds, they draw unequally from these sources. French Canadians

[4]The Minnesota Farmer-Labor Party of the 1920s and 1930s was cut from the same agrarian cloth. It produced two U.S. senators and a state governor. In 1944 it amalgamated with the Minnesota Democratic Party to become the present Democratic Farmer Labor Party, which was once led by former Vice-President Hubert Humphrey.

have traditionally looked to the Liberals for representation (although not in the 1984 election), leaving the Conservatives to speak for the Anglophones. Overlapping this pattern has been the tendency for Quebec and Ontario, the metropolitan and industrial heartland of Canada, to support the Liberals, while the economic hinterlands in the East and West have tended to favor the Conservatives. However, tradition was violated in 1984 when the Conservatives won numerous seats in Ontario and Quebec. Several studies (see McMenemy and Winn, 1976) indicate that the most active members (i.e., candidates, convention delegates, elected officials) of Canada's three federal parties are of relatively high social status. When women are candidates, there is evidence that they lose more often than men, but chiefly because they contest seats that their party believes it has little chance of winning (Hunter and Denton, 1984).

The sociodemographic basis of American political parties has changed a great deal since the late 1960s. There is a prospect of a greater polarization than existed in the 1950s. Nie et al. (1979: 241–242) observed that the Democratic party in the United States is becoming more black (now about 20 percent), less southern, and more wealthy and aristocratic, while the Republican party is growing more southern, less black, less Catholic, less Protestant, and less wealthy and aristocratic. Democratic dominance in the South and Republican dominance in certain New England states have been substantially weakened. James (1974: 255) says the increasing attraction of the Republican party for business people and the Democratic party for laborers suggests that future political contests will increasingly offer voters right-of-center Republican and left-of-center Democratic candidates.[5] But even this alignment could change.

[5]This predicted alignment of left and right in the Democratic and Republican parties is not inconsistent with the earlier statement about the Democrats becoming more and the Republicans less wealthy and aristocratic. For example, American laborers are wealthier now than ever before. Some well-to-do professionals also support the Democratic party.

At a time when the two American parties are differentiating themselves along the liberal-conservative dimension, these differences in the two main Canadian parties are becoming blurred. The Conservatives have chafed under their image as the party of the business world, even though they failed, until 1984, to gain electoral support from the elite of that group (a result of regional factors, no doubt). In the late 1950s, the Conservatives were trying to project a populist impression, while the Liberals were trying to appear as the party of the economic elite (McMenemy, 1976: 22).

Voter Turnout One frequently used measure of voter participation is the proportion of eligible voters who actually show up at the polls and vote. Voter response in federal elections in the United States is proportionately among the lowest in modern democracies. In the 1980 presidential election in the United States, the voter turnout was 59.2 percent, compared with 75.7 percent in the Canadian federal election in 1984. Voter proportions have been dropping over the past two decades in both Canada and the United States. European countries, including Italy, Belgium, West Germany, and Great Britain, typically poll between 80 and 90 percent of their eligible voters. Michalos (1980c: 154) indicates that in other ways of participating (party membership and contributing money to a party or a candidate, for example) Americans excel over Canadians.

Another significant finding of voting behavior research is that the upper classes and the wealthy are more likely to cast ballots than individuals who have less education, low income, and working-class jobs. As Alford and Friedland (1975: 432) put it, "Social class remains the strongest correlate of political participation." This generalization holds for several countries around the world, including India, Japan, Great Britain, and the United States. The situation in Canada is yet to be studied. The implications of this form of voter participation are far-reaching.

Correlates of Voter Turnout

Some descriptive differences in voting turnout which have been located in a multitude of studies are listed in Table I. The specific explanations for these differences may be summarized under four very general explanatory propositions. A group will have a higher rate of voting if (1) its interests are strongly affected by government policies; (2) it has access to information about the relevance of political decisions to its interests; (3) it is exposed to social pressures demanding voting; (4) it is not pressed to vote for different political parties. A further classification of these factors found in concrete social groups is presented in Table II.

Table I SOCIAL CHARACTERISTICS CORRELATED WITH VOTING TURNOUT

Higher Turnout	Lower Turnout
High income	Low income
High education	Low education
Occupational groups:	Occupational groups:
Businessmen	Unskilled workers
White-collar employees	Servants
Government employees	Service workers
Commercial-crop farmers	Peasants, subsistence farmers
Miners	
Whites	Negroes
Men	Women
Middle-aged people (35–55)	Young people (under 35)
Older people (over 55)	
Old residents in community	Newcomers in community
Workers in western Europe	Workers in United States
Crisis situations	Normal situations
Married people	Single
Members of organizations	Isolated individuals

Table II SOCIAL FACTORS AFFECTING RATES OF VOTING TURNOUT

1. The relevance of government policies to the individual:
   a. Dependence on government as one's employer
   b. Exposure to economic pressures requiring government action
   c. Exposure to government economic restrictions
   d. Possession of moral or religious values affected by government policies
   e. Availability of relevant policy alternatives
   f. General crisis situations
2. Access to information:
   a. Direct visibility of effects of government policies
   b. Occupational training and experience making for general insight
   c. Contact and communication
   d. Amount of leisure

Table II (*Continued*)

3. Group pressure to vote:
   a. Underprivilege and alienation
   b. Strength of class political organization
   c. Extent of social contacts
   d. Group norms opposing voting
4. Cross-pressures:
   a. Conflicting interests
   b. Conflicting information
   c. Conflicting group pressures

Source: Seymour Martin Lipset. *Political man: The social bases of politics,* expanded ed., pp. 189–191. Baltimore: Johns Hopkins University Press, 1981.

> The poor, the less educated, and those in working-class occupations are those who are most affected by state policies (they pay higher proportions of their income in taxes, are likely to be on welfare or in prison, are subject to sanctions by various agencies, and pay most for the education of their children); they also are most dependent on the state (for unemployment insurance, health insurance, public transportation, home loans at reasonable rates, and so forth). They should be the most active in attempts to influence public policy and the structure of government, but in fact are the least active. (Alford and Friedland, 1975: 439)

We have been examining the voting and nonvoting proportion of each social class. Other possible differences lie in the distribution of votes by social class among those who do cast ballots. But Myles and Forcese (1981), after a reexamination of data collected somewhat earlier, conclude that differences in this respect between Canada and the United States are negligible and that the number of people who vote on the basis of social-class issues is low in both countries. What tendencies there are in this direction are expressed as preferences for the Democrats or Republicans in the United States and for a third party in Canada, which, these days, is the NDP (see Chi, 1976: 100–102). Still, as Ogmundson and Ng (1982) point out, there are problems of measurement in this area. Using different indicators of class position than Alford (1963) used in his benchmark study, they found Canada to be much like Great Britain, a country where class issues often influence politics.

A POLITICIZED SOCIETY

You may be wondering at this point why something as important as politics and the polity has been covered in so few pages. Has sociology nothing more to say on this subject? Have sociologists given so much more attention to other social institutions than they have to the polity? These questions can be answered by pointing out that sociologists have devoted considerable attention to the study of the polity. The fact of the matter is that the polity—our broadest, most pervasive social institution—is boundless. As one political sociologist sees it:

> One can legitimately ask . . . where politics and political sociology end. Clearly society has become consciously and legally more politicized. . . . One general example is studying the politics of interaction and power in interpersonal relationships and small groups and demonstrating that power is a pervasive phenomenon, not simply a manifestation of the political arena. More significant and interesting to me is the interplay of the political with other institutions. Just as one can examine conflicts that divide political institutions, e.g., equal rights for women . . . so too one can study conflict within families, organizations, and communities, and also how separate areas reciprocally affect one another. I personally find it hard to separate

political from general sociology and politics from society. (Hall, 1981: 19)

In other words, we have been studying the polity all along. For example, a central concept in political sociology is power. Recall how frequently you have seen it to this point in this book and in connection with which groups and institutions. Nor does this chapter spell the end of discussions of things political. Although references to them will sometimes be indirect, politics, power, and the polity are considered in all remaining chapters.

OUTLINE AND SUMMARY

I. Introduction
The *polity* is a specified form of political organization; it is a politically organized unit such as the federal government or a local government. The polity consists of the government and the state.

II. The Polity as an Institution
The *political institution* is defined as the relatively stable set of abstract relationships, patterns of behavior, norms, and values that develop around the collective problem of distributing political power, managing violence, and maintaining societal boundaries.

   A. The Political System
   A political system meets the defining criteria of *roles, patterned behavior,* and *abstract relationships.*

   B. Values
   The polity, like other institutions, rests on certain key *values.* Among the political values are democracy, equality, civil liberties, and honesty in political action.

   C. History
   The *history* of the polity is evident in legal and structural changes brought about periodically by the government.

III. Political Culture
The six defining criteria have attracted attention as examples of *political culture.*

   A. Political Socialization
   Political socialization is the political learning of children and adults.

   B. Political Parties
   A *political party* is a political organization that puts up candidates for elective office.

      1. Third Parties
      Third parties seldom take the place of the dominant political parties in America, but they have been more successful in Canada (at the provincial level) than in the United States.

      2. Populism
      In the 1890s, the Populist party in the United States—a third party—stood for social reform in the interests of farmers and workers, the common people, but it gave way to the Democratic party. Populism was more successful in Canada. It spawned the CCF in the 1940s, which eventually reorganized itself as the present-day NDP.

   C. Political Participation
   Political participation is the activity of individuals and groups in an effort to elect government officials and to have something to say about government structures and policies.

      1. Sociodemographic Basis
      Political parties have as members individuals from a wide range of ethnic, regional, religious, linguistic, and social-class backgrounds.

      2. Voter Turnout
      The percentage of eligible voters who cast ballots is lower in the United States than in other countries.

IV. A Politicized Society
The polity is our broadest, most pervasive social institution. One of its central processes is power, which pervades all groups and institutions.

FOR FURTHER READING AND STUDY

Clarke, H. D., Jenson, J., Leduc, L., and Pammett, J. H. 1979. *Political choice in Canada.* Toronto:

McGraw-Hill Ryerson. A statistically sophisticated survey of the social cleavages, party images, party leaders, issues, campaigns, and voters' choices in the 1974 federal election in Canada.

Fyre, H. T. 1980. *Black parties and political power: A case study.* Boston: G. K. Hall. The National Democratic Party of Alabama, a black independent party, is studied through a combination of field research and library research.

James, J. L. 1974. *American political parties in transition.* New York: Harper & Row. James describes and analyzes the activities, internal processes, and electoral consequences of American political parties. He also considers the functions of political parties in the governing process.

Kornberg, A., Smith, J., and Clarke, H. D. *Citizen politicians—Canada: Party officials in a democratic society.* Durham, N.C.: Carolina Academic Press. A survey study of activists in four Canadian political parties in Vancouver and Winnipeg. The authors examined social structural and political socialization issues.

Lipset, S. M. 1981. *Political man: The social bases of politics,* expanded ed. Baltimore: Johns Hopkins University Press. This is a revised edition of the 1960 classic by one of the world's most famous political sociologists. Among the topics covered are conditions of the democratic order, voting in Western democracies, political behavior in the United States, and the politics of trade unions.

Nie, N. H., Verba, S., and Petrocik, J. R. 1979. *The changing American voter.* Cambridge, Mass.: Harvard University Press. This book summarizes more than fifteen surveys of the political activities, beliefs, and behavior of American voters between 1939 and 1976.

Orum, A. M. 1983. *Introduction to political sociology,* 2nd ed. Englewood Cliffs, N.J.: Prentice-Hall. A text survey in the field of political sociology.

Pammett, J. F. and Whittington, M. S., eds. 1976. *Foundations of political culture: Political socialization in Canada.* Toronto: Macmillan of Canada. A collection of papers on political socialization in Canada.

KEY WORDS

government A group made up of political parties and civil servants; its task is to order and adjust relations between individuals and the state and between groups and the state.

personalization The tendency of individuals to develop an image of political authority.

political institution The relatively stable set of abstract relationships and patterns of behavior that develop around the collective problem of distributing political power and maintaining societal boundaries.

political participation Activities by private citizens that are more or less directly aimed at influencing the selection of governmental structures and personnel.

political party A political organization which actively and effectively engages in the competition for elective office.

political socialization The political learning of children and adults.

political sociology A cross-fertilization of sociology and political science.

polity A specified form of political organization; it is a politically organized unit such as the federal government or a local government. It consists of the government and the state.

populism The political expression of a critique of capitalism calling for social reform in the interests of farmers and workers, the common people.

state A cultural system which defines and guides the actions of the government.

chapter 15

Religion

CHAPTER OUTLINE

INTRODUCTION

With typical irreverence, George Bernard Shaw once observed, "There is only one religion, though there are a hundred versions of it." This aphorism probably explains as well as any other statement the longstanding preoccupation of sociology with religious social action. The institution of religion would be nonexistent if people the world over had the same religious beliefs, similar practices, and only one way of organizing the religious group. Were religion merely an invariant component of human nature, there would be nothing unique about any society's solution to the problems around which it forms and is expressed.

But variation is rampant. Old and new versions of religion in industrial societies have kept social scientists hard at work examining the factors influencing people to switch faiths, develop new ones, and modify old ones. Variation is also seen in the disparate manifestations of religion on the basis of region, nationality, ethnic group, and social class. Nor would the movement toward ecumenism exist, since there is nothing to unite when everyone is the same.

Shaw's observation about the diversity of religion holds true in North America (although one might question his reference to "one religion"). In Canada and the United States, the study of religion has become an established branch of sociology. That branch, say Demerath and Roof (1976: 9) in a review of American research, has enjoyed an "accelerating revival" since the mid-1950s. Crysdale (1976: 144) has noted a similar, albeit later, renaissance in Canadian research, starting around 1965. Some years ago there seemed to be a decline in sociologists' interest in religion. In the 1950s, sociological research into religion hardly measured up to the pioneering work of Durkheim and Weber. But it should not be assumed that religion is now insignificant in a secular world dominated by science. In fact, there recently has been renewed popular and scientific interest in religion in society. Demerath and Roof note that the present scientific revival stems from an interest in some of the very questions which Durkheim, Marx, and Weber were asking.

DURKHEIM, MARX, WEBER

Religious diversity was only one of the questions that attracted Durkheim, Marx, and Weber, the founding fathers of the sociology of religion. Durkheim (1954) conceived of religion as one of society's significant collective representations; such social constructions, he recognized, had constraining effects on the behavior of individuals in society. The power of the sacred or the holy is really the influence of society itself on the actions of people. Religion is a component of the collective conscience, which, particularly in mechanically solidary societies, is the inner voice that unites those in the group. In the religious sphere, the beliefs and sentiments shared by the faithful pertain to the supernatural and its perceived relevance to daily life.

How does the collective conscience influence the actions of people in everyday life? What constraining effects does religion have on people's lives? Marx wrote that religion constrains behavior by being an ideology. An *ideology* is a somewhat loosely integrated set of beliefs, theories, values, and goals constituting a sociopolitical program for change or maintenance of the status quo. As Marx saw it, religion maintains the social, economic, and political order of the society (we shall see later that deviant religions do not have this consequence). Religion accomplishes social stability by distracting people from their everyday difficulties in the present and by giving them hope of a better life in the future. Many religious faiths offer the promise of a better life after death. Indeed, religious doctrine may even encourage suffering in this world as a way of increasing one's rewards in the next one. It is in this connection that Marx wrote his own aphorism: "Religion is the opium of the people," particularly the lower classes.

Max Weber (1958) extended Marx's analysis to the middle-class business entrepreneurs who were influenced by Calvinism. This sixteenth and seventeenth century Protestant religion contained the doctrine of predestination: only certain people in the community were chosen by God for salvation from eternal damnation (i.e., they are predestined). Since one never knew whether one was chosen, it was obligatory to make the assumption that one was chosen and act as if that were true. Performing good works in this world was accepted as evidence of being chosen for salvation. One main form of evidence was devotion to one's occupation (or calling from God). Devotion was manifested by occupational success, by accumulation of capital and financial resources. These resources, however, only served as a sign of salvation if the life-style of the entrepreneur were frugal and the hard-earned resources used to build his enterprise. They were not to be used for hedonistic pleasures. This, the Protestant ethic, was said by Weber to be a prominent factor in the rise of modern capitalism.

RELIGION AS AN INSTITUTION

The institution of religion has, through the years, helped to solve certain *problems of collective living.* These problems are hinted at in Milton Yinger's (1970: 7) definition of religion: "A system of beliefs and practices by means of which a group of people struggles with . . . [the] ultimate problems of human life." Ultimate problems are beyond everyday affairs. Depending on the society, they are problems such as death, starvation, natural disasters, and unexplained diseases. Only religion can explain the ultimate problems.

In solving such problems, religion offers a special, sometimes supernatural, explanation of their underlying causes. It specifies what must be done by members of the group to prevent a recurrence of the problems; objectively, however, it must be recognized that the members frequently can do little to overcome the difficulties. In societies having scientific explanations of phenomena such as epidemic diseases and natural disasters (earthquakes, tornadoes), religion does not serve this purpose for most people. Since they have no science, preindustrial societies turn to religion for explanations and help with the frightening experiences in life.

If one takes the phrase "the ultimate problems of human life" in Yinger's definition to refer also to concerns less extreme than death and disaster, then religion can also be seen as solving problems in everyday life—the problem of earning a living, for example. This is one of Weber's legacies. As Peter Berger (1967: 100) notes, religion helps the believers interpret the significant events in their lives in a framework broader than common sense.

Some people believe their religion puts them in touch, so to speak, with a supernatural power, or being. As they see it, this being has control over matters of concern to them on earth and also in the hereafter. But this supernatural power, whatever it is called—God, Tao, Brahma, Allah—requires something in return from those who benefit from its intervention in the problematic events of this world. These requirements are institutionalized as *roles, relationships,* and *patterns of behavior* (i.e., the constraints discussed by Durkheim). Other religions, however, have no creed or concept of the supernatural (e.g., Unitarianism, Scientology). Yet they may be regarded as belief systems about either extreme concerns or everyday concerns or both (Yinger, 1970: 13–14). Accordingly, they also have roles, relationships, and patterned behavior. Prescribed roles help

---

SOCIOLOGY OR COMMON SENSE

What do you think?

Which of the following statements do you agree with? Which statements do you disagree with? Make a note of your answers. Check your answers when you have completed your study of this chapter. Are your answers to the statements the same as those a sociologist would give?

1. Religion is an ideology.
2. The significance of religion in Canada and the United States is declining in the face of worldly concerns.
3. Religion and government in North America interfere little in each other's affairs.
4. In North America, established religion unwittingly spawns the establishment of religious groups opposed to the doctrine and practices of the established religion.
5. Today's deviant sect may be tomorrow's respected denomination.

---

implement individuals' beliefs as they live from day to day.

Patterns of Behavior

In Canada, as in other countries, there are countless patterns of religious behavior. Among them are the religious *rituals;* these are practices which are regularly carried out in a prescribed and precise manner, practices that help to satisfy one's sense of doing what is demanded by one's religion. *Rituals* are symbolic gestures of faith and conformity. Among many examples of rituals are the act of taking communion, the Roman Catholic confessional, the Protestant singing of the doxology, and the Jewish commensal practices during Passover. Baptism is a religious ritual. Religious funerals and religious wedding ceremonies have their ritualistic touches. There are also nonritualistic patterns. Among such patterns is the religious opposition to pornographic bookstores and to commercial dealings on Sunday. A charity's fund-raising drive in behalf of the hungry is a nonritualistic pattern of behavior.

Religious Roles

As a member of a religious group, an individual has a role to play. Part of this role is the practice of rituals, with an expression of faith and belief. Religious roles vary, as do rituals; there are differences in the roles of Lutherans, Methodists, Presbyterians, Baptists, Roman Catholics, Jews, Moslems, and the members of sects. There are also role expectations beyond those associated with the rituals; among these are the Catholics' opposition to abortion, the Moslems' abstinence from alcoholic drink, and the Jehovah's Witnesses' refusal to undergo blood transfusion. The roles of clergyman, Presbyterian elder, Jewish schocket, Mormon deacon, and Roman Catholic nun are specialized sets of expectations.

A familiar Christmas-time pattern of religious behavior.

Relationships

Roles are undertaken and carried out in a complicated structure of religious relationships. One essential link is between clergy and laity, a link, that is, between the legitimate religious leader and his or her followers. But others exist, too, as indicated by the many diverse roles. There are more role relationships in the formalized, organized religions of Anglicanism, Lutheranism, and Roman Catholicism than in other denominations. For example, there is the complicated structure of Roman Catholic priests, bishops, archbishops, cardinals, nuns, brothers, and sisters. The institution of religion in Canada also includes relationships that go unnoticed by the laity. An example is the tie between professors of religion and divinity students. To some extent, the laity is unaware of the relationship between politicians and religious leaders (see the section on civil religion) and between religious educators and publishers of religious literature.

Religious Values

Turning to the defining criterion of values, we should note that, although they vary considerably among religions, the values can be reduced to certain common themes. Hertzler (1961: 470) describes some of these.

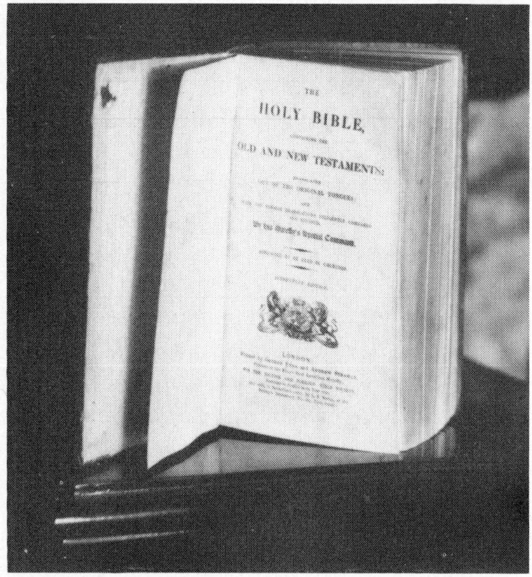

A major religious value in Canada and the United States.

> Most religions place values on man with respect to his place and function in the universe and in relation to the supernatural entities; he is insignificant in some, and of infinite worth in others. Most religions have values regarding the supernatural entities themselves; regarding the kind of quality of individual and group behavior that conforms to the will of the god or gods; regarding life and death; regarding here and now as against the hereafter and eternity.

By way of illustration, some Protestant sects and denominations value eternal salvation. For Roman Catholics, membership in the church is valued as proof of their religious commitment. Following prescribed rituals can lead to the attainment of certain religious values. Male circumcision is a Jewish value, ritually performed in the ceremony of the brith on the eighth day of a boy's life. The rituals constituting baptism enable the baptized person to attain the value of membership in a Christian church.

History

Any number of examples could be selected to illustrate the institutional defining criterion of history. The two selected here are the growth of secularism and the rise of individual religions. We turn first to the growth of secularism, which is a process known as *secularization.* It is felt in some quarters that secularization is increasing, an event defined as the declining significance of religion accompanied by increasing worldly concerns. Those who make this claim point to indicators such as increasing looseness of sexual mores, shrinking membership in established religious groups, and declining church attendance. As Lyon (1985) points out, however, there is no clear-cut evidence to support this claim. What is clear is that religion and religious practice have changed and are continuing to change. There will be additional references to this topic later in this chapter. At this point, we will consider briefly Thomas Luckmann's (1967) thoughts on the rise of "invisible" or individualized religion to illustrate further this institution's distinctive history and changing religious practice.

Luckmann says that organized religion is only one religious form and one that is currently ebbing in Canada and other Western societies. Taking its place is an individual form; this form is followed by individuals who construct their own systems of "ultimate significance" from ex-

The rising tide of secularization is expressed in many different ways.

isting principles, symbols, and practices of the religious institutions of their society. These individuals may not show up in church, but, privately, they express a faith of their own. This invisible religion receives little support from the social institutions. Instead, support comes from people, especially the family, but also neighbors, workmates, and leisure companions. Among the underlying themes of this new religiosity are individual autonomy, self-expression, self-realization, and familism.

ORGANIZED RELIGION

Organized religions are identifiable groups of religious practitioners. In the preceding paragraph, organized religions were contrasted with autonomous individual religions. Both are part of the contemporary institution of religion in North America. The organized varieties vary widely in their degree of bureaucratization; they vary in the extent to which they meet the criteria of being small groups or large-scale organizations. Over the years, sociologists and theologians have constructed several typologies of organized religions.

Troeltsch's Typology

Ernest Troeltsch (1931; published in German in 1911), a theologian and one of Max Weber's students, undertook the first sociological attempt to impose some theoretical order on the numerous Christian religious organizations. Inspired by Weber's thoughts about priests (who help to maintain the status quo) and prophets (who generate new religious ideas), Troeltsch decided to develop ideal types of, among others, the groups which are led by the priests and prophets. These groups, as Troeltsch explained, are the church and the sects.

A *church* is a large-scale religious organization. It is integrated with the secular community of which it is a part. A church is part of the power and value structures of the surrounding society; it is founded on an accommodation of its differences with the society, an accommodation worked out over decades or even centuries. Members are born into a church-type religious organization (as defined by Troeltsch) and most, if not all, people in a geographic area are members of the organization. The example on which Troeltsch based his writings was the thirteenth century Roman Catholic Church. No equivalent form exists today.

For Troeltsch, *sects* are the antithesis of the church. They are conceived in protest over the comfortable religious compromise struck between the national church and the secular world. Modern sociology often treats the sect as a small group, although Troeltsch stressed its qualities as a social movement undertaken by dissatisfied church members. Thus, in Canada, where religious freedom is legally protected, a sectarian rebellion is an act of legitimate deviance (see Chapter 17) against one of society's institutions. Accordingly, sects are frequently studied from two perspectives: the *sociology of religion* and the *sociology of deviance*. Among the many sects in North America are the Doukhobors, Pentecostalists, Scientologists, Hutterites, Old Order Amish, Jehovah's Witnesses, Seventh Day Adventists, and Salvation Army (Wilson, 1970). Quakers and Christian Scientists also are looked upon as sects.

Yinger's Typology

Troeltsch's church-sect dichotomy was tied to the historical circumstances of his native Germany. This tie seriously weakened the application of his ideas to North America. In his thinking about Troeltsch's dichotomy, Richard Niebuhr (1929), a theologian, proposed several modifications. For one thing, he identified the two types (church and sect) as poles on a continuum. Niebuhr also suggested the notion of *denomination*. Niebuhr said that religious groups move along this continuum as they gain respectability, becoming more like churches and integrating themselves into the community. At about the time of Niebuhr's proposals, Howard

Established sect: The Mormon Temple, Cardston, Alberta.

P. Becker (1932) added *cults* to the list, bringing the number of types to four.

Some sociologists analyze organized religion according to a sixfold typology arrayed along a continuum (Yinger, 1970: 256–280). This is Yinger's typology. It begins with the cult, which may transform itself into a sect and then possibly into an established sect. Also on the continuum are *denominations, ecclesia,* and a *universal church.* Among the criteria used to differentiate these types are the degree to which they include all members of a society. The types are sketched here in reverse order.

The Universal Church The universal church is much the same as Troeltsch's church. His church and the universal church both find their purest example in the thirteenth century Roman Catholic Church. That no equivalent exists today should not lead to the conclusion that the universal church is irrelevant. First, the universal church is useful as an analytic research tool in religious history. It facilitates comparisons of certain historical cases with contemporary types of organized religion and other historical types. Second, some present-day ecclesiae (explained in the next paragraph) have a tendency to push toward the status of a universal church. For instance, Roman Catholicism and Islam would likely be universal churches today were their growing dominance not checked by other religions and by secularism.

The Ecclesia The *ecclesia* is a firmly established religious organization which seeks to include all the members of a particular society within its fold, although it may fall short of this goal. An ecclesia often is a state church; those born in the country are born into the church. As a state church, the ecclesia exists harmoniously with the state and with the dominant social groups and classes of the society. The members of the ecclesia are not converted as members but are socialized as children or adults into the accepted practices and beliefs. Ecclesiae have an elaborate bureaucracy; at the top of the hierarchy are specially trained clergy, who may be the only individuals empowered to administer sacraments, teach the religion, and interpret and change doctrine. The present-day Catholic churches of Italy and Spain and the Anglican Church of England are ecclesiae. There is no ecclesia, or state church, in North America.

The Denomination A *denomination* is a firmly established religious organization with a significant membership. Denominations are paramount among the religious organizations in Canada and the United States; it can be said that the societies in Canada and the United States are "denominational societies" (Greeley, 1972: 1). The denomination accommodates to the secular world and to the polity of the larger society. The members of a denomination are born and socialized into denominations in much the same way that members are socialized into ecclesiae, although there is no attempt to establish any denomination as a national religion.

Some denominations recruit by means of conversion. Denominations are also likely to follow doctrines less closely than ecclesiae and to adhere to less formalized worship services.

As in ecclesiae, the clergy in denominations are professionally trained and certified by church authorities. Since denominations have no interest in becoming state churches, they typically have more friendly relations with other religious bodies, usually other denominations. One denomination may even enter into joint ventures with another denomination.

Sociologists (e.g., Fallding, 1978) and laymen occasionally distinguish between *mainline* churches and *fundamentalist* churches in Protestant denominations. Fundamentalists insist that their literal interpretations of the Scriptures are without error. They stress salvation by faith in the atoning death of Jesus as an event actually having occurred; an individual gains this faith through conversion. Among fundamentalist denominations are Southern Baptists, the Church of Christ, and Pentecostalists.

The mainline denominations tend to be more liberal and modernist in their religious views. In their view, the Bible, to some extent, is mythological; they do not believe in the literalness of miracles. They seek to integrate religion and science. The mainline denominations see God as omnipresent in everyday human affairs rather than as a purely supernatural force. Among the mainline denominations are Episcopalians, Anglicans, and the United Church of Canada. The liberal wings of the Baptist, Presbyterian, Lutheran, and Methodist denominations are considered mainline.[1] A minority of individuals in fundamentalist denominations hold mainline beliefs. The opposite is also true; a minority of those in mainline churches are fundamentalist in their views.

Sects A sect can be an *established sect* or a *pure sect.* Yinger (1970: 266) says of the established sect that it "is somewhat more inclusive, less alienated, and more structured than the sect, and therefore closer to the denomination." Established sects have developed ways of perpetuating themselves. In becoming established, they shut out the rest of the world by adhering to physical or doctrinal boundaries. The Amish, Mormons, and Hutterites are established sects.

Modern theory has added to Troeltsch's conception of *pure sects* that they are typically small in size when compared with denominations and ecclesiae. Leadership is usually informal, being carried out by lay members rather than by trained specialists. Sects, unlike denominations, gain adherents through conversion, although many members are born into them. A sect's doctrine is the basis for its rejection of established religion; sects reject mainline denominations as being too liberal in practice and principle. There is little of the spirit of compromise and tolerance among sectarians, for they are convinced that they alone have the right answers.

Cults Bromley and Shupe (1981: 23–24) describe *cults* as small, short-lived, religiously iconoclastic groups. A cult may succeed and eventually go on to become a sect, denomination, and even world religion (e.g., Buddhism, Islam, Christianity). Or, more commonly, the cult fails and disappears. Bromley and Shupe hold that:

> a cult is the starting point of every religion. Its organization is extremely simple. There is no bureaucracy or priesthood. In fact, there is barely any structure at all except for the single charismatic leader and his or her small band of devoted followers. Jesus and his twelve disciples offer a classic example of a cult. Nor are there scriptures, not only because the cult rejects all or part of society's dominant religious traditions but also because it is simultaneously engaged in the act of creating its own traditions out of which later generations will record "gospel" truths. The cult is thus nonconformist for two reasons. First, it struggles to start a radically new religious tradition, and, second, it exists in tension and conflict with what it regards as a corrupt, troubled world.

[1]The United Church of Canada is an amalgam, created in 1925, of Presbyterians, Congregationalists, and Methodists.

Among the cults which are active in North America today are the Unification Church ("Moonies"), Children of God, Hare Krishna Movement, Church of Scientology, and Divine Light Mission. The People's Temple (of the Jonestown suicides) was a cult.

As we have noted, Yinger's six types of organized religion are arrayed along a continuum. A given religion may transform itself over time into the next type on the continuum. For these reasons, the classification of a religion can be equivocal. This uncertainty has led some scholars to question the usefulness of the entire scheme, even in its ideal-typical form. Nonetheless, the typology has stimulated a great deal of research through the years. The research itself is of value to sociologists.

CHURCH AND STATE

Religious freedom exists in both Canada and the United States, although each traveled a different route in search of the freedom. In the United States, religious freedom is guaranteed by several amendments to the Constitution, particularly the First. But the amendments had little to do with establishing religious freedom; the colonies had insisted on freedom of religion long before the adoption of the Constitution. Several different religions existed in the thirteen colonies; the sects and denominations fought against any one of them gaining privileges at the expense of the others (e.g., the Church of England). As Moberg (1962: 369–370) notes, many factors encouraged the establishment of religious freedom.

The colonies favored religious individualism and Protestant tolerance. Needing settlers, the colonies expressed little concern about an individual's faith or religious preference. Out of this background of tolerance and acceptance came the First Amendment. The First Amendment decrees that there can be (1) no laws pertaining to the establishment of religion, (2) no laws prohibiting access to religion, and (3) no laws interfering with free speech and a free press, religious or otherwise.

According to Fallding (1978: 146–148), Canada's resolution of the church-state problem was more piecemeal and ad hoc. Yet factors similar to those in the United States pushed Canada toward institutional separation. Initially, however, Anglicanism was established in Canada as the state church (ecclesia), as it was in England. But the Anglican status gradually dwindled as two main groups, the French Catholics in Quebec and elsewhere and the expatriate American Methodists in Ontario (not those from Britain), resisted Anglican privilege. Thus, in time, Anglican influence became insignificant.

There are instances of Canadian and American social life where church and state are anything but separated. Clark (1962: Part II) writes that the general tendency of Canadian Christianity has been to seek social integration by supporting political authority, particularly at the provincial level. Historically, church and state, although neither legally joined nor legally separated, have developed compatible orientations on many issues potentially threatening to the status quo (e.g., totalitarian groups, sexual deviance). In the United States, the Constitution forbids official endorsement of any religion. Yet it is possible for the American federal government to declare a religious group illegal when its beliefs and practices threaten the established order (Wilson, *Religion,* 1978: 196–200). On these grounds, the U.S. government is empowered to decide which groups are religious and which are not. It can also control religious activities by limiting the ways in which members of a religious group may educate children (e.g., mandating a standard curriculum).

RELIGIOUS COMMITMENT

Sociologists have examined three types of commitment. Of the three types (see Chapters 16 and 17), it is *value commitment* that concerns those who specialize in religion. Stebbins (1970b: 526–527) defines value commitment as an attitude toward an identity, an attitude that develops because a person gains exceptional rewards from being in that identity. *Value commitment* is the attachment to gains or rewards from a church or religious group; it is a general idea of what is good or bad, right or wrong, for an individual and his or her identity. The critical problem in the study of value commitment is determining the factors that attract people to an identity and that hold them to the identity.

In the religious sense, value commitment is expressed in the gaining, maintaining, or renouncing of a faith and in switching from one faith to another. For example, an individual expresses a value commitment when he or she leaves a fundamentalist church and joins a church of a more liberal view. Religious value commitment often has an exceptional degree of emotion associated with it. It therefore is different from value commitments associated with other identities in life. For one thing, value commitment in religion takes in *religious sentiment:* the affective orientation toward sacred practices and beliefs.

Himmelfarb (1975) notes that religious commitment is directed at four types of sociocultural objects defined by religious people as important in their routine lives. First, there is the *supernatural.* Next is the *communal,* or group affiliations with coreligionists. Third, there are the *cultural* objects such as religious periodicals, books, art, and music. *Interpersonal* objects make up the fourth type. An individual's friends and acquaintances are interpersonal objects. The individual tries to treat friends and acquaintances in accordance with the moral principles of his or her religion.

In Everyday Life

The evidence to date suggests that religious commitment is multidimensional (Roof, 1979: 40). Glock (1962) proposes five dimensions along which this form of commitment varies. They were subsequently conceptualized for empirical study by Faulkner and DeJong (1966). The first is *ideological.* It has to do with doctrines; for example, is the Bible the work of God, does God forgive only after repentance, and are we ultimately accountable to God for our deeds on earth? The second dimension is *intellectual.* This dimension refers to religious knowledge and personal stance on the interpretation of sacred teachings. Is the story of creation true? Are the Biblical miracles real? Can you name three of the Gospels?

The *ritualistic* dimension focuses on religious practices. Respondents are asked about the amount of time they spend in prayer, reading the Bible, and attending church or synagogue. The *experiential* dimension includes the sentimental and personal interpretations of everyday religious events and activities. Are there particular moments when you feel close to the divine? Does religion offer a sense of security in the face of death? In what way does religion provide the individual with an interpretation of his or her existence? Finally, the *consequential* dimension centers on an expression in the secular world of one's religious commitment. The committed individual gives thought to behavior such as working on Sunday, cheating on an income tax return, and indulging in sexual intercourse before marriage.

Religious Conversion

Students of religious commitment have turned to sects and cults for much of their data. Anyone who joins a sect or cult must embrace a new religious commitment. The act is deliberate. John Lofland (1977: 31–62) points to a model of conversion composed of three predisposing conditions (tension, problem-solving perspective, religious seeking) and four situational contingencies (turning point, cult-affective bonds, extracult-affective bonds, intensive interaction).

Predisposing Conditions Before they get in touch with a religious group, preconverts must experience the predisposing conditions. Without a contact with the religious group, no conversion can occur. (1) Acute and enduring *tension* in the form of strain, frustration, or deprivation develops in response to an imagined ideal state of affairs in life and its contrast with current circumstances. Tension could arise in almost any segment of a person's life. The individual might be lonely and fearful somewhere in a large city or be drained by the oppressiveness of his or her job. (2) Preconverts have a special *problem-solving* perspective with which they handle this tension; it is a religious, rather than a political or psychiatric, perspective. Religious meaning is therefore imposed on the events of everyday life. For preconverts, conventional religious solutions failed to solve the tension. Accordingly, (3) they become seekers, or people in search of solutions to their problems, solutions which are more radical than institutionalized religion can offer.

Situational Contingencies Before direct contact with the cult or sect can lead to successful conversion of individuals predisposed toward it, they must pass through the four situational contingencies. (1) When they make contact with the group, preconverts are at or close to a major *turning point* in their lives; examples of such turning points are having lost or quit a job, having graduated from college, or having moved to another part of the country. Individuals at a turning point are aware of the need to do something with their lives and of the relevant opportunities which make one action or another possible. (2) Contact with the sect or cult also leads to the development of *cult-affective bonds;* such bonds imbue the contact with a personal touch. Positive emotional relationships with existing members help swing the preconvert's allegiance toward the group. Meanwhile, (3) there are either no influential *extracult-affective bonds* (say, because the preconvert recently migrated), or bonds of this sort are with persons who have a similar religious interest. Eventually, (4) total conversion occurs following a period of *intensive interaction* between preconverts and core members of the sect or cult. Through this process, the preconverts acquire the ideological, intellectual, ritualistic, and experiential components of commitment, transforming them into true converts to that religion.

RELIGIOUS CHANGE

All institutions change, albeit slowly. Like the slow speed at the center of a merry-go-round, change is slower near an institution's core than near the periphery. On the periphery lie the quasi-institutional forms and processes. Beyond the periphery are forces and influences that are deviant and potentially threatening.

We have already considered one instance of change near the core of the institution of religion. This change is the emergence of invisible religion. Another change, much different, has been observed by Samuel Heilman (1981). Heilman observed the ways in which American Orthodox Jews reconstruct their religious doctrines to bring them in line with modern circumstances. Two processes are involved. The processes are *contemporization* and *traditioning.*

In contemporization, the past frames and explains the present. Among Orthodox Jews this is accomplished by making Torah, the Jewish scripture, part of and relevant to the modern world. In traditioning, new elements in the present, where they intrude into the past, are reconsidered in the light of old forms. For example, the Torah, with its traditional meanings, is not

Religious change: TV religion is now a major mode of religious teaching.

Becoming a Lubavitcher

In the beginning the recruit's attachment to orthodox Judaism and to Lubavitch are tenuous. If he feels inclined to observe a precept he does; if he does not feel so inclined, he does not. Although during this time he becomes increasingly preoccupied with orthodox Judaism and Lubavitch, he still meets with his nonreligious friends who do not necessarily share his new found interests. In time, however, he begins losing contact with many of them. For instance, he will no longer meet with them on a Saturday afternoon to drive to a non-kosher restaurant. What further separates him from them is his feelings that he shares little in common with them. As one Lubavitcher expressed it:

> You know, you do lose contact . . . if I'm visiting X (name of city) having contact with [previous non-orthodox friends] or trying to renew contact with them is sort of futile because we have so little in common. You know, so little interests in common other than our family and home and furniture. I did go to see one of my old friends when I was back last spring and we had a very enjoyable afternoon. But I don't think we could ever establish a close friendship together because there is so little to go on.

The alternative is to choose new friends with whom common interests are shared:

> I enjoy the friends that I do have and I have quite a few friends whom I'm quite close to here in Montreal and I enjoy their friendship and I depend on that very much. But it's meaningful to me. There is a definite exchange of interests and I think that there are things that we share, and these are very important to me, that I would be reluctant to do without.

The majority of new friends are likely to be from Lubavitch and it is with these people that the recruit finds most in common. It is they who teach him what he wants and is expected to know. Since they spend a considerable amount of their time in the Yeshiva, he is likely to do the same. His social life begins to centre around the Yeshiva and he begins to spend much of his time in the presence of Lubavitcher.

The female recruit also experiences a dissociation from her previous circle of friends. For her, increasing involvement in the Lubavitch community comes by way of attending meetings of one of the women's groups, getting involved in one of the Lubavitch women's telephone circles, or participating in the various other women's activities. Along with this, certain changes are expected and come about in her appearance. She may resist these changes initially but she is made to recognize the importance of conforming to certain standards of dress. She notices that Lubavitch women do not consider it necessary to keep abreast with the latest styles and fashions. Instead she is informed of the *Rebbe's* emphasis on *tzneeus*—modesty—in appearance. By seeing others she learns that one's hair is to be always covered in public, preferably with a *shytl,* that dresses are to be long-sleeved, high-necked, and of approximately knee length. Though it may be difficult to conform to these expectations with one's old wardrobe, the change gradually occurs. In the privacy of her home she may not be meticulous about the length of her dress or sleeves, yet when before others she tries to present herself appropriately. Conversations with two *baal tshuvess* help illustrate this:

> Well, it came about gradually. At first I didn't think anything about it. No one told me anything, but I gradually heard and learned that they wear their sleeves three quarter length. At first I didn't know. Even when I knew, somehow I don't feel it would be wrong if I came in short sleeves. Up until last year I would sometimes go. I have a lot of short sleeved dresses and I don't feel undressed if I wear them, although lately . . . all of a sudden . . . it just comes over you and you feel in their presence at least . . . this is how I should be dressed and I would feel uncomfortable if I did otherwise . . . Now, I try it. If I know somebody is coming over I'll probably wear long sleeves. If I do housework I have to wear a sleeveless dress and I'm often embarrassed if the bell rings and you have these men collecting. So I feel I'm not dressed properly.

and:

> Well, if I go out and forget my hat, I go back and get it. Or if I go out and realize that I'm wearing a dress that might be bothersome to someone, I will go back and get a sweater. I don't want to be disrespectful.

Male recruits also change their style of dress. The most important features that identify them and commit them to behave like orthodox Jews include wearing a hat and/or *yarmlke* at all times, a dark-coloured suit or appropriate substitute, a *talless kotn* (fringed undershirt), and in most cases a beard.

SOURCE: William Shaffir. *Life in a Religious Community: The Lubavitcher Chassidim in Montreal,* pp. 209–211. Toronto: Holt, Rinehart & Winston of Canada, 1975.

readapted to the present. Rather, the reverse occurs: the present is held up against the Torah, revealing, in this fashion, new important truths for today.

> Thus . . . the ancient and sacred menstrual prohibitions and injunctions are reinterpreted as a period of psychological and physical regeneration. What, without such reinterpretation, might seem as a restrictive period, defined by archaic demands becomes—once traditioned—a symbol of the human effort to reestablish equilibrium. (Heilman, 1981: 145)

A Dilemma

In fact, institutions carry the very seeds for their own change, whether core or peripheral. O'Dea (1961) explains that religious experience tends to be incompatible with the process of institutionalization. Herein lies a key dilemma: institutionalization in religion transforms individual religious experience and makes it routinely available for large numbers of people. But will this transformed experience appeal to them? The horns of this dilemma are more concretely expressed in five subdilemmas.

The dilemma of (1) *mixed motivation* is evident in the way some officials in established religious organizations serve selflessly, while others serve so as to facilitate their careers. This dilemma is also evident among the members in general, some of whom are more solidly attached to existing principles and practices than others.

The symbolic dilemma (2) *objectification versus alienation* centers on the problem of the estrangement of individual religious response from collective worship. Some individual response is expected and encouraged here. Yet, individual response must be patterned if it is to become part of a continuous group response such as a ritual. But, then, a point is reached where ritual becomes routine, with the resulting loss of symbolic impact. Saying grace at the dinner table each day or reciting the same responsive reading in church each Sunday can become so routine that the ideas expressed in these passages lose their impact, if not their meaning. As such, the passages become little more than mechanical repetitions of words. In a sense, the ritual becomes secularized, being pursued chiefly for extrinsic reasons.

The dilemma of (3) *administrative order* comes from the problem of elaboration versus effectiveness. Elaboration refers to the emergence of statuses and roles and standardized procedures and to the transformation of leadership from charismatic to bureaucratic, all of which occurs during the course of religious institutionalization. Or, as we can see, a large-scale organization begins to take shape. But the effectiveness of the organization is lost if elaboration proceeds too far. Overbureaucratization divides labor unnecessarily, complicates communications, and obscures goals.

The dilemma of (4) *delimitation* is phrased as concrete definition versus substitution of letter for spirit. To have the desired impact on the laity, religious messages must be expressed in terms related to their everyday lives. Making them concrete in this fashion may, however, drain them of their philosophical profundity by turning them into a superficial set of rules to be followed for their own sake.

The dilemma of (5) *power* centers on the choice of conversion versus coercion. Few people are converted to a religion. Without conversion, they lack the strong commitment engendered by the unforgettable experience of having made a conscious, serious choice. Rather, individuals are born into their religion, and, because their commitment is weaker, they must be encouraged somehow to retain their faith. Being aware of this problem, religious leaders try to increase the appeal of their faith by aligning it with the general values of their society and its other institutions. But this ploy may weaken "the bonds of . . . religious community by weakening voluntary adherence and therefore diluting the religious ethos and substituting external pressures for interior conviction" (O'Dea, 1961: 37).

Core and Peripheral Change

The impact of these dilemmas helps explain changes at the core and periphery of our religious institution. At the periphery, we find the religious protest movements and their group manifestations as cults and sects. Many cults and sects wither and die. Intense, organized, and sometimes violent opposition to them has grown in many countries since the 1960s (Beckford, 1985). Those that survive gradually move along the scale to denominational status and into the circle of institutionalized religion. This advancement signals still further change in the religious establishment. Pentecostalism, Quakerism, or Mormonism could be among the next sects to become denominations in our lifetime. Indeed, Mormonism appears to be developing into a worldwide faith with enough acceptance to thrive in many countries (Stark, 1984).

Moreover, in pluralist, albeit generally Christian North America, where relative religious freedom prevails, the institution of religion includes non-Christian faiths. Judaism is the prime example. Several non-Christian sects are presently striving for acceptance. Perhaps Transcendental Meditation or the Hare Kirshna Movement will be the next such group to achieve a degree of respectability, with ultimate institutionalization.

RELIGION IN NORTH AMERICA

What is the nature of religion in North America? The answer to this question can perhaps be found in a consideration of two cultural values. One, we tend to hold religion in general to be good (unlike the view in Communist societies). Two, we tend to support the principle of religious freedom (unlike, say, Islamic societies). Religion in Canada is compared with religion in the United States in the sections which follow. Three topics—civil religion, religious pluralism, and religious correlates of socioeconomic status—enter into the comparison.

Civil Religion

Although the idea can be traced to Durkheim and still earlier thinkers, it was Robert Bellah (1967) who coined the term "civil religion." He describes civil religion as the public side of religion; the public side takes in national beliefs, symbols, and rituals.[2] Wilson (*Religion* 1978: 177) offers one of the clearest definitions:

> Civil religion is a faith not confined to the denominations, but one which emerges from the life of the folk and is manifested in loyalties, values, and ideas expressed in everyday life concerning the national purpose, society's values, its morals, and its traditions.

Civil religion is closely aligned with the polity and other secular institutions. In general, this religion dignifies existing practices, goals, and social arrangements. It is a system of attitudes and beliefs associated with one's love of country and respect for the government. How does civil religion in Canada differ from civil religion in the United States? The comparison which follows answers this question.

Harold Fallding (1978: 143–144) is one of a handful of scholars who have made the comparison. As he explains, civil religion in the United States is an expression of all that is held sacred in the collective lives of Americans, including their national goals. It enters into presidential inaugurations, where the noun "God" is frequently uttered; it is seen in national shrines such as Gettysburg and Arlington National Cemetary; it is honored on Thanksgiving Day and in Fourth of July celebrations; it is sung in the "Star Spangled Banner"; and it is recited in the Pledge of Allegiance to the American flag. Such acts and customs are sacred. They have religionlike meanings, even though familiar religious symbols are not always apparent. These elements and others in the American civil religion, though once Protestant, are now Judeo-Christian; they are expressions of the pursuit of the will of God in public and cultural affairs.

Civil religion in Canada legitimates and sanctifies established political authority. It is much more directly connected with the churches, especially Anglican, Presbyterian, United, and Roman Catholic (especially in Newfoundland and Quebec), than in the United States, where it "it is mainly a matter of supporting government and offering prayers for its success in securing order and justice" (Fallding, 1978: 143). Fallding points out that, under the monarchy, Canadian government was officially committed to defending the Christian religion. It was Christianity in general that was to be defended. But it was the mainline churches that helped unify the country and that became the dominant churches in the early years. Over the past hundred years they have left their imprint on national culture and the polity. Thus, the model of Christianity recognized today by the Canadian government bears a strong resemblance to these four faiths. And, like other industrialized nations, Canada has its sacred symbols, practices, and events. Among such traditions and symbols are Remembrance Day and Canada Day holidays, Morrisburg and Plains of Abraham battlefields, Fathers of Confederation, and the Queen (Michalos, 1982: 139).

Canadian civil religion is in need of further study. Despite the foregoing examples, Bellah and Hammond (1980: xiii) question whether civil religion actually exists in Canada.

[2]Durkheim stressed the moral nature of social solidarity.

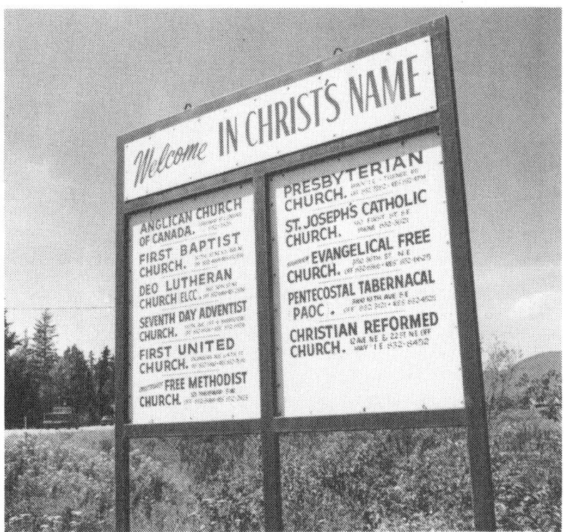

Religious pluralism is a distinctive part of life in many places in Canada.

Religious Pluralism

The pluralistic character of North American religion is made amply clear by Tables 15.1 and 15.2. Still, there are some noteworthy differences between Canada and the United States in the composition of their religious pluralism. Baptists are more numerous in the United States than in Canada. Canada has more Roman Catholics and somewhat fewer Protestants than the United States. The major denominations have churches in both countries. There are Episcopalians but no Anglicans in the United States. Table 15.1 lists the twelve denominations in the two countries.[3]

One should read carefully the figures in Table 15.1. Religious groups vary in the way they report the number of members on their rolls. Questions such as how active members are defined and how long a member must be inactive before being declared a nonmember are variously answered. In addition, this table gives no indication of the religion of the unchurched. They are included in Canadian census enumerations of the population's religious identification, but no such data are gathered in the United States.[4] Nor should these data be interpreted as evidence of religiosity. Membership is easier to acquire than devoutness. Those who practice the invisible religion, although religious, go unrecognized in Table 15.1.

Religious pluralism also has a different composition within sects in Canada and the United States. Numerous small religious groups, or sects, are currently pursuing alternative forms of religion (Christian and non-Christian) in an era when membership in the mainline Protestant denominations is declining. The sects constitute what has come to be known as *the third force* (Hiller, 1978). This challenge to established religion comes mainly from the Pentecostalists, Jehovah's Witnesses, Christian Scientists, Mormons, Quakers, and Seventh Day Adventists.

As Hiller points out, the United States has fostered many more sects and cults than Canada. The goal of religious freedom was paramount during the founding of America, while in Canada, under greater British influence, there was a concern for harmonious church-state relations. There was a desire for a strong central religious organization (although it failed to materialize) with, at the same time, a reluctance to innovate religiously. From the very beginning in the United States, sects and cults have from time to time grown out of the established churches. Canadians seeking similar spiritual involvement gained support from their more numerous like-minded American brethren.

Historically, Protestant pluralism has been higher in western Canada than in other parts of the country. Being far from British influence is partly responsible for the western pluralism.

[3]Both the Protestant Episcopal Church in the United States and the Anglican Church of Canada belong to the worldwide Anglican Communion, which is made up of those churches holding essentially the same faith, same form of organization, and same order of worship. Thus, Episcopalians in the United States and Anglicans in Canada are of the same religion, even though they go by different names. The Church of England is also part of the Anglican Communion.

[4]This is one of the areas in which the Constitutional separation of church and state is effective.

Table 15.1 U.S. AND CANADIAN RELIGIOUS BODIES, 1979–1980

United States		Canada	
Religion	**Members**	**Religion**	**Members**
Roman Catholic Church	49,602,035	Roman Catholic Church	10,123,329
Baptist Churches	26,693,709	United Church of Canada	907,222
Methodist Churches	12,826,827	Anglican Church	594,296
Lutheran Churches	8,595,934	Judaism	305,000
Latter-Day Saints (Mormons)	4,800,652	Lutheran Council in Canada	216,416
Eastern Orthodox Churches	4,788,000	Presbyterian Church	166,190
Presbyterian Churches	3,615,742	Baptist Federation of Canada	127,698
Episcopal Church	2,841,350	Pentecostal Assemblies	117,362
Judaism	2,706,000	Latter-Day Saints (Mormons)	66,000
Church of Christ	2,500,000	Jehovah's Witnesses	63,995
Pentecostal Churches	2,376,350	Plymouth Brethren	52,000
Islam	2,000,000	Christian Reformed Church	41,806

Source: Yearbook of American and Canadian churches, 1981 and 1982. Nashville, Tenn.: Abingdon.

Western Canada was settled in part by Americans espousing third force religious faiths. There are also fewer Roman Catholics in the western provinces.

Sects and cults have also flourished in the West in the United States. Additionally, there is a racial dimension to sect and cult formation and membership in the United States that is absent in Canada. American blacks have developed several third force religions of their own (e.g., Father Divine's Peace Mission, Black Muslims, Black Jews, Shrine of the Black Madonna). Blacks have also joined racially mixed sects such as the Pentecostalists.

Table 15.2 RELIGIOUS PREFERENCES IN CANADA AND THE UNITED STATES

Percent answering	Canada (1963)	United States (1974)
Protestant	55	60
Roman Catholic	40	27
Jewish	1	2
All others	4	5
No religious preference	NA	6

Source: A. C. Michalos. *North American social report,* vol. 5, p. 151. Dordrecht, Netherlands: Reidel, 1982.

Socioeconomic Status

There are at least two generalizations to be made about the religions of North America and the socioeconomic status (SES) of those who espouse them. One, the social classes are unequally represented in all religions. Two, all social classes are represented to some extent in all religions, although this pattern is weakest in Anglicanism and Episcopalianism. Table 15.3 contains data gathered between 1974 and 1978 on American religious preferences and SES.

Although, in the strictest sense of the word, there is no class church in North America, it is clear that American Episcopalians, Presbyterians, and Jews are disproportionately from the upper and middle classes. Membership in the Methodist church, the Catholic church, and the Baptist church is somewhat skewed in the opposite direction. In Canada, no analyses covering all major religions cross-tabulated by SES exist. What evidence there is suggests, however, that the pattern is much the same as in the United States (see Porter, 1965: 101–103; Crysdale, 1965: 4–6).

Church attendance and socioeconomic status in Canada differ in several ways from church attendance and socioeconomic status in the

Table 15.3 RELIGIOUS PREFERENCE AND SOCIOECONOMIC STATUS OF AMERICANS

	Socioeconomic status (percent)				
Affiliation	Upper class	Middle class	Working class	Lower class	*N*
Episcopalian	40.5	27.0	27.0	5.4	37
Presbyterian	30.8	29.2	20.0	20.0	65
Jewish	30.3	30.3	24.2	15.2	33
Methodist	25.9	20.6	30.2	23.3	189
Catholic	25.8	22.4	28.3	23.5	361
Lutheran	18.7	32.1	38.1	11.2	134
Baptists	16.2	17.8	34.3	31.7	309
Sects	15.6	30.0	28.9	25.6	90
					1218

Source: H. P. Chalfont, R. E. Beckley, and C. E. Palmer. *Religion in contemporary society,* p. 386. Palo Alto, Calif.: Mayfield, 1981.

United States (see Tables 15.4 and 15.5). For example, a higher percentage of Canadian Catholics regularly attend church than American Catholics, although attendance patterns by social class are parallel. A comparison of Anglican and Episcopalian attendance patterns on the social-class dimension reveals opposite tendencies. Although less apparent, a similar picture emerges among American Presbyterians and Methodists, on the one hand, and Canadian United Church members on the other. Overall, Canadians of high SES are more likely to attend church frequently than Americans of high SES. Church attendance in general has been declining for at least two decades in the United States and since World War II in Canada (Roozen and Carroll, 1979; Bibby, 1982a: 5). A downward trend in synagogue attendance and ritual observance has also been recorded for Jews in both Canada and the United States (Schoenfeld, 1978).

ECUMENISM

We live in an era of ecumenism, says Samuel Cavert (1968: 7). *Ecumenism* is the movement toward the worldwide unity of Christian faiths. In actuality, ecumenism may amount to little more than brief cooperation between two churches or denominations, or it may be an event of great moment such as the union of two denominations. For example, three large denominations joined and formed a single church in 1925 with the establishment of the United Church of Canada. In 1960, Norwegian, Danish, and German congregations formed the American Lutheran Church in the United States. Unitarians and Universalists in the United States merged in 1961. Wilson (*Religion,* 1978: 424–426) examines three theories which explain the present-day enthusiasm in some quarters for ecumenism.

First is the "melting pot" theory. This theory states that, as ethnic and social differences disappear, people become more willing to mingle with one another on religious grounds. Although there may be some truth to this assertion, it still fails to account for the facts that denominations try to retain their distinctiveness and independence and that the melting pot process, or ethnic assimilation, has been partially effective only in the United States, not to mention officially pluralist Canada (see Chapter 19).

Opposite to the melting pot theory is the "pluralist" model. The central tenet of the pluralist theory is that, in a pluralist society, reli-

Table 15.4 SOCIAL CLASS AND CHURCH ATTENDANCE BY RELIGION OF AMERICANS

	Attendance (percent)			
	Rarely	Some	Often	Regularly
Catholic				
Upper	13.1	22.6	10.7	53.6
Middle	17.1	17.1	13.2	52.6
Working	20.0	21.1	10.5	48.4
Lower	21.3	21.3	10.7	46.7
Jewish				
Upper	60.0	30.0		10.0
Middle	28.6	71.4		
Working	57.1	14.3	14.3	14.3
Lower	33.3	33.3		33.3
Baptist				
Upper	20.4	22.4	18.4	38.8
Middle	15.7	27.5	19.6	37.3
Working	31.1	20.0	24.4	24.4
Lower	17.5	26.3	27.5	28.8
Methodist				
Upper	33.3	31.3	13.3	22.2
Middle	23.7	18.4	36.8	21.1
Working	30.6	18.4	18.4	32.7
Lower	26.3	13.2	28.9	21.6
Lutheran				
Upper	12.5	37.5	29.2	20.8
Middle	28.2	41.0	15.4	15.4
Working	14.6	27.1	29.2	29.2
Lower	45.5	36.4	9.1	9.1
Presbyterian				
Upper	16.7	38.9	33.3	11.1
Middle	40.0	26.7	13.3	20.0
Working	50.0	16.7	8.3	25.0
Lower	55.6	22.2	11.1	11.1
Episcopal				
Upper	33.5	40.0	20.0	6.7
Middle	11.1	22.2	11.1	55.6
Working	44.4	22.2	11.1	22.2
Lower		100.0		

Source: taken with modification from H. P. Chalfont, R. E. Beckley, and C. E. Palmer. *Religion in contemporary society,* p. 391. Palo Alto, Calif.: Mayfield, 1981.

gions must compete for adherents. To guarantee themselves an adequate share of the populace, those in the competition tend toward similarity and ecumenism; this tendency is based on the presumption that the members of one church must be like the members of another church if the churches are to attract new members. Put otherwise, churches become standardized.

One problem with the pluralist model is that other pluralistic eras, at least in American history, have failed to spawn anything like ecumenism. Another is that it is unclear why religions should win the competition by standardizing the churches any more than by varying them, or by striving to be different.

The third theory—the "secularization" model—is based on the perception of a rising tide of secularism in everyday affairs. Given that

Table 15.5 CHURCH ATTENDANCE IN CANADA PERCENTAGE BY DENOMINATION AND OCCUPATION[a,b]

Occupation	United	Anglican	English Catholic	French Catholic	Others
Professionals, managers, farmers	30.1	25.4	76.0	93.9	34.7
White-collar, clerical, and sales	19.8	23.1	74.3	91.9	25.6
Blue-collar, skilled, unskilled, service	12.4	9.7	60.5	86.3	28.0

Source: Taken with modification from H. Mol. Major correlates of churchgoing in Canada. In *Religion in Canadian society,* eds. S. Crysdale and L. Wheatcroft, p. 248. Toronto: Macmillan of Canada, 1976.

[a]Attendance refers to those who went to church at least twice a month.

[b]The percentages in Table 15.5 refer to the proportion in each cell of regular as opposed to irregular churchgoers. Hence the figures are not addable either horizontally or vertically.

some people are dropping religion altogether while others are joining sects and cults, perhaps it is wise, many religionist conclude, to close ranks against the common enemies. Yet, what they see as most threatening is the irreligion, atheism, and agnosticism of the day, not the competition among themselves for members. The National Council of Churches (U.S.), Canadian Council of Churches, and the World Council of Churches are, to some extent, products of this line of reasoning. They are federated organizations. As we have seen, there have been several mergers of religious bodies in North America and abroad, although it is by no means clear, at least in the United States (Wilson, *Religion,* 1978: 434), that the unions were conceived of as strategies to combat secular trends.

OUTLINE AND SUMMARY

I. Introduction
Religious differentiation is a fact of social life. The sociological study of religion is as old as the discipline itself.

II. Durkheim, Marx, Weber
Durkheim, Marx, and Weber founded the sociology of religion.

III. Religion as an Institution
The institution of religion has helped to solve problems of collective living. These problems are hinted at in Milton Yinger's definition of religion: A system of beliefs and practices by means of which a group of people struggles with the ultimate problems of human life.

A. Patterns of Behavior
There are countless patterns of religious behavior. Among these patterns are religious rituals. *Rituals* are symbolic gestures of faith and conformity.

B. Religious Roles
As a member of a religious group, an individual has a role to play. Religious roles vary, as do rituals. The role of a clergyman is specialized.

C. Relationships
Roles are undertaken and carried out in a complicated structure of religious relationships. There is a relationship between clergy and laity. Some relationships go unnoticed by the laity. For example, the laity is largely unaware of the relationships between divinity students and professors of religion.

D. Religious Values
Religions place values on human beings with respect to their place and function in the universe and in relation to the supernatural entities.

E. History
Two events in the history of religion are the growth of secularism and the rise of individual religions.

IV. Organized Religion
Organized religion is an identifiable group of religious practitioners. Denominations are organized religions. Organized religion contrasts with Luckmann's notion of an individual "invisible" religion.

A. Troeltsch's Typology

A *church* is a large-scale religious organization. *Sects* are the antithesis of the church. Sects are studied from two perspectives: the *sociology of religion* and the *sociology of deviance.*

B. Yinger's Typology
Yinger's typology is a sixfold ideal typology arranged along a continuum consisting of *cult, sect, established sect, denomination, ecclesia,* and *universal church.*

1. The Universal Church
The universal church is the most inclusive religious organization, typically encompassing all people in a geographic area.

2. The Ecclesia
The ecclesia is a large-scale organization that is integrated with the secular community of which it is a part. It tries to include everyone in the community within its fold. An ecclesia often is a state church.

3. The Denomination
A *denomination* is a firmly established religious organization with a significant membership. Societies in Canada and the United States are "denominational societies." The denomination accommodates itself to the secular world, particularly to the polity of the larger society.

4. Sects
A sect can be a *pure sect* or an *established sect.* Each is small in size. Established sects are somewhat more inclusive, less alienated, and more structured than pure sects.

5. Cults
A *cult* is relatively short-lived, small, and religiously iconoclastic. The cult rejects established religion at the denominational level and beyond.

V. Church and State
Religious freedom existed in the United States prior to its guarantee in several Constitutional amendments. In Canada religious freedom gradually emerged as Anglicanism became less dominant.

VI. Religious Commitment
Religious commitment is expressed in the gaining, maintaining, and renouncing of a faith and in the switch from one faith to another.

A. In Everyday Life
The dimensions for empirical study are ideological, intellectual, ritualistic, experiential, and consequential.

B. Religious Conversion
Sects and cults have been a prime source of data for students of religious conversion.

1. Predisposing Conditions
Three predisposing conditions for religious conversion are *tension, problem-solving perspective,* and *seeking of religion.*

2. Situational Contingencies
Four situational contingencies for religious conversion are *turning point, cult-affective bonds, extracult-affective bonds,* and *intense interaction.*

VII. Religious Change
Like other institutions, religion changes more slowly at the core and more rapidly at the periphery. Change occurs in the institution of religion because religious experience tends to be incompatible with the process of institutionalization.

A. A Dilemma
Institutionalization in religion transforms individual religious experience and makes it routinely available to large numbers of people. But will this transformed experience appeal to them? Five subdilemmas are *mixed motivation, objectification, administrative order, delimitation,* and *power.*

B. Core and Peripheral Change
At the periphery are religious protest movements and their group manifestations as cults and sects. Many cults and sects are disbanded, but others achieve denominational status. This advancement signals

further change in the religious establishment.

VIII. Religion in North America
The cultural values define the nature of religion in North America. One, we tend to hold religion in general to be good. Two, we tend to support the principle of religious freedom.
  A. Civil Religion
  Civil religion is closely aligned with the polity and other secular institutions.
  B. Religious Pluralism
  Religious pluralism is extensive in both Canada and the United States.
  C. Socioeconomic Status
  The social classes are unequally represented in all religions in North America.

IX. Ecumenism
Ecumenism is the movement toward the worldwide unity of the Christian faiths. We live in an ecumenical age.

FOR FURTHER READING AND STUDY

Bellah, R.N. and Hammond, P. E., 1980. *Varieties of civil religion.* New York: Harper & Row. This is a collection of eight papers written over the years by either Bellah or Hammond. The papers focus on civil religion in modern societies.

Berger, P. L. 1967. *The sacred canopy: Elements of a sociological theory of religion.* Garden City, N.Y.: Doubleday. In a concise and lucid style, Berger applies a sociology of knowledge perspective to the phenomenon of religion. Specifically, he looks at religion from the standpoint of history and the social construction of reality.

Bromley, D. D. and Shupe, A. D., Jr. 1981. *Strange gods.* Boston: Beacon. The authors examine the cult scare in the United States, looking at the "big six" cults and the anticultists who oppose such groups.

Hoge, D. R. and Roozen, D. A. 1979. *Understanding church growth and decline: 1950–1978.* New York: Pilgrim. This anthology attempts to uncover the reasons for disrupted growth in American Protestant churches after the 1960s. Local, national, contextual, and institutional factors contribute to church growth and decline.

Lofland, J. 1977. *Doomsday cult,* enlarged ed. Englewood Cliffs, N.J.: Prentice-Hall. A participant observer study of conversion, proselytization, and maintenance of faith among members of the American branch of an international millenarian cult.

Luckmann, T. 1967. *The invisible religion.* New York: Macmillan. Luckmann argues that an invisible, individualized religion has arisen in modern times and that it is replacing the older organized religion. People are constructing their own systems of "ultimate significance."

McGuire, M. B. 1981. *Religion.* Belmont, Calif.: Wadsworth. A textbook surveying the sociology of religion. Although it contains some comparisons with other societies, its chief focus is on the United States.

O'Toole, R. 1983. *Religion.* Toronto: McGraw-Hill Ryerson. A textbook on the sociology of religion with a Canadian concentration. O'Toole also makes comparisons with other societies.

Shaffir, W. 1974. *Life in a religious community: The Lubavitcher Chassidim in Montreal.* Toronto: Holt, Rinehart & Winston of Canada. Shaffir did fieldwork among the Lubavitcher Chassidim, a devout community of Jews, to learn how they create a distinctive identity for themselves and develop a workable life-style.

KEY WORDS

church A large-scale religious organization.

cult A small, short-lived religiously iconoclastic group.

denomination A firmly established religious organization with a significant membership.

ecclesia A firmly established religious organization which seeks to include all the members of a particular society within its fold; it is often a state church.

ecumenism The movement toward the worldwide unity of Christian faiths.

fundamentalist church A church of a denomination which emphasizes literal interpretations of the Scriptures.

mainline church A church of a denomination which is liberal and modernist in its religious views.

organized religion An identifiable group of religious practitioners.

religion A system of beliefs and practices by means of which a group of people struggles with the ultimate problems of human life.

ritual A symbolic gesture of faith and conformity.

sect A small group which is the antithesis of the church; social movement undertaken by dissatisfied church members.

secularization The declining significance of religion accompanied by increasing worldly concerns.

universal church A large-scale religious organization; an example is the thirteenth century Roman Catholic Church.

value commitment The attachment to gains or rewards from a church or religious group.

chapter 16

Social Control

CHAPTER OUTLINE

INTRODUCTION

Many sociologists conceive of *social control* as a far-reaching set of processes. The interpersonal processes discussed in Chapter 5 (e.g., social interaction, definition of the situation) are part of this set, to the extent that they function according to Martindale's (1978: 56) definition of *social control* as "all processes that implement the legitimate order of a given community [or society]." In other words, social control is a system of behavioral regulation within society—a set of interrelated processes, the purpose of which is to discourage people from deviating from the established institutions in society.

With social control, almost everyone behaves in expected ways. People live up to what is expected of them. Literally every societal institution contributes to this overarching process, since each attempts to instill, through socialization, its own special values and norms in the members of the society; that is, each social institution tries to control those human actions that bear on its collective problems. Thus, Martindale continues, "The scope of social control ranges from the management of deviants to social planning, which can be viewed as the negative and positive management of power, respectively."

Although this chapter is included in Part 4, it should not be assumed that social control is an institution. Rather, social control is an aspect of all institutions; it is a process found in all walks of institutional social life. Its pervasiveness and its relationship to social order tie together much of what has been said so far about our major institutions. We can now dispense with the familiar litany of the six defining criteria of institutions. Social control imparts meaning to all the institutions.

On occasion, sociologists will refer to the military and police as institutions of social control. Occasionally, they also see prisons and hospitals for the mentally ill as social control institutions. Consistent with the approach of this book, however, the military, courts, police, and prisons are defined as polity-related, large-scale organizations. Hospitals for the mentally ill are among society's health care organizations. As will become evident later, police and the courts implement the means of social control, thereby helping to establish and to maintain the legitimate order.

As will soon become apparent, social control is by no means always successful. People sometimes violate the norms of the established institutions. Individuals who do not abide by the established rules make up the broad category of *norm violators.* Some norm violators have no regard for norms that the majority of society considers important and essential. These violators are referred to here and in Chapter 17 as *deviants* (e.g., criminals, cultists, swingers, homosexuals). Other norm violators violate less seriously held norms such as traffic laws or everyday customs (e.g., rules of etiquette). The various types of norm violators are further distinguished in Chapter 17. For the moment, it is important to remember that social control is concerned with all types of norm violations: deviance, civil violations, and nonconformity with customs.

SOCIAL CONTROL PERSPECTIVES

Robert Meier (1982) identifies two perspectives on the institutional problem of social control. The two perspectives have dominated sociological thinking since the 1950s. As a convenience, Meier labels these perspectives "functionalist" and "conflict," while recognizing that the work of some scholars is more typical of the labels than the work of others. In this chapter, then, the two perspectives have broader meanings than in other parts of this book. Noting that, in the 1950s, sociologists became aware that crises in a society change the society but rarely dis-

SOCIOLOGY OR COMMON SENSE

What do you think?

Which of the following statements do you agree with? Which statements do you disagree with? Make a note of your answers. Check your answers when you have completed your study of this chapter. Are your answers to the statements the same as those a sociologist would give?

1. Prisons teach prisoners to stay out of trouble once they return to the outside world.
2. People conform to social norms because they are threatened with unpleasant consequences for not doing so.
3. A juvenile delinquent who steals is just as hardened a criminal as a professional thief.
4. Canadians rely more heavily than Americans on imprisonment as a means of controlling crime.
5. Laws are established and enforced through the influence of certain groups to serve the interests of those groups.

solve the society, Meier (1982: 4) distinguishes the perspectives:

> Functionalists viewed the change as beneficial and progressive, and conceived social control as a set of independent variables, as mechanisms that reduce social strain and help maintain system stability. Those inclined toward a conflict perspective viewed the change with alarm, noted increased alienation and political repression, and conceived social control as a set of dependent variables.

What are the consequences of the existing mechanisms, or means of social control? What are their consequences for individual members of society? The answers to these questions are of interest to conflict-oriented sociologists.

It should be noted in passing that there are other perspectives on social control in sociology. The ethnomethodologists and the exchange theorists have also taken an interest in social control, which they view as a process leading to the creation and maintenance of social order. But, in this chapter, we have space only for the functionalist perspective and the conflict perspective.

FUNCTIONALIST PERSPECTIVE

The central tenets of the functionalist perspective on social control are found in the writing of several thinkers, including Parsons (1951: Chapter 7) and LaPiere (1954). Running through the work of these men and their colleagues is the theme that social control is sometimes inadequate and ineffective. This inadequacy leads to deviance, or the violation of norms (Meier, 1982: 46). Stebbins (1983) summarizes the functionalist perspective under three headings: phases, approaches, and types.

Phases: Values and Sanctions

The functionalist perspective conceives of social control as occurring in two phases, discussed here as *values* and *sanctions.* First, the society as a whole or an influential segment of it values a certain pattern of action or thought; for example, Canadian society looks with favor on individual enterprise and achievement. Moreover, Canadian society values the harmonious fit of one pattern with other patterns (individual achievement with prestige in the community, for example).

Second, the valued pattern, which is the first phase of the two-phase sequence, encourages the use of particular *sanctions,* or *mechanisms,* as they are variously called. *Sanctions* are the reinforcements of a person's behavior produced by other people (Scott, 1971: 65); praise and acclaim for a person's achievement are sanctions. In other words, sanctions (second phase) are the means for achieving the value pattern (first phase). As noted in the following section, sanctions are either negative or positive. The valued pattern is inherently conservative, inasmuch as its proponents want either no change or smooth, gradual change.

Table 16.1 contains a partial list of the sanctions used in many parts of the world to establish or preserve valued patterns. Some of these sanctions are more characteristic of industrial societies than of nonindustrial societies. One of them—imprisonment—has received considerable attention from sociologists. It will be examined in greater detail later in this chapter. An additional example from the research literature demonstrates the operation of some of the other negative sanctions. For example, Whitehurst (1975: 433) argues that nearly all Canadians value the sexual intimacy of the marital dyad so much that they consider alternatives such as swinging and communal family living intolerable. Gossip, ridicule, and ostracism are among the sanctions which are used to discourage such behavior.

Approaches: Positive and Negative

When people are offended or threatened by the violation of a norm, they turn to one or both of

Table 16.1 APPROACHES TO SOCIAL CONTROL BY PHASES

Phases	Approaches	
	Positive	Negative
Value	Internalization	Compliance
Sanctions	Praise Ritual Acclaim Privilege Money Gifts Promotion	Death Torture Fines Imprisonment Demotion Scolding Gossip Ridicule Satire Ostracism Firing

two approaches: They use *positive sanctions* or *negative sanctions.* The aim of sanctioning is to encourage people to conform to the norm. Positive control is usually achieved through internalization of a value, whereas negative control is usually achieved through compliance with that value. We turn first to positive control through internalization.

Internalization Internalization is "the propensity to conform to the norm—to behave in the way the norm reinforces—at a spatial or temporal remove from the sanctions" (Scott, 1971: 88). With internalization, people identify so strongly with the values and their associated norms that their actions become largely, though never entirely, self-regulating. Put otherwise, people experience the values as if they were their own. The opposition to cannibalism and incest in North America illustrates the internalization of particular norms. An individual who conforms to the norms is rewarded by being looked on as a man or woman of character with a good reputation. The positive sanctions, Scott (1971: 92) says, have to be experienced from time to time. For example, we are more inclined to work diligently and do a good job when the boss is occasionally complimentary than when he or she is indifferent. The internalized values and norms motivate those in society to behave in ways acceptable to their friends and associates (Parsons, 1951: 206–207). When conforming individuals encounter an opportunity to deviate, their firm "moral commitment" (in Scott's terms) to the established order prompts them to ignore the temptation.[1]

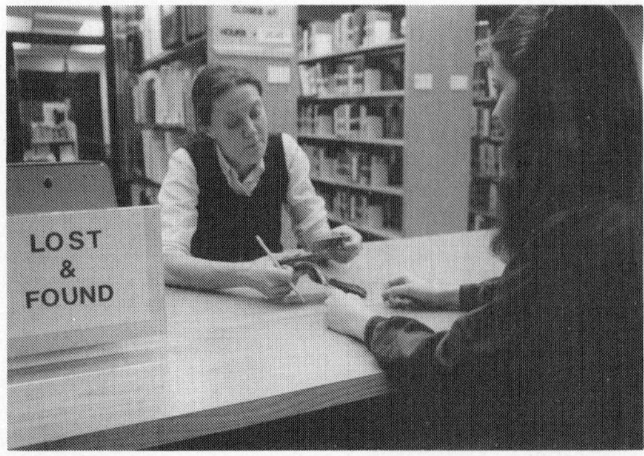

Internalization of the value of honesty is functional for society.

In the sanctions phase, positive social control is brought about through various rewards, some of which are listed in Table 16.1. Given the self-interested orientation of almost everyone nearly all the time, sociologists believe individuals try to achieve the best possible ratio of rewards to costs. The use of these sanctions is guided by sets of institutionalized norms composed of all or a combination of the following: laws, rules, regulations, and customs. The act of receiving rewards or even of abiding by established norms engenders society's approbation. This approbation is rewarding in itself and therefore is likely to reinforce the individual's pattern of acceptable behavior. Thus, the "good corporate employee" who has internalized the commandment "thou shalt not steal," when faced with a chance to embezzle company funds, not only rejects the opportunity but even shrinks from the thought of committing such an act. For conforming to a standard of honesty and dependability, the individual can take pride

[1]Moral commitment is similar in meaning to the idea of religious value commitment, which is discussed in the preceding chapter.

(a reward) in being a trustworthy, responsible, dependable worker.

Compliance There are individuals and groups who fall into unacceptable ways instead of abiding by the ways of the established, conforming majority. For these individuals, social control is negative; coercive methods must be used to force their *compliance* with or superficial conformity to the values of the dominant segment. The would-be norm violators are compelled to live by moral standards they would reject were it not for the high cost of rejection. With a desire to avoid negative sanctions, they are motivated to conform to the social rules.

To keep potential norm violators in line, those who accept the status quo or their agents (e.g., police, clergy, schoolteachers) threaten negative sanctions, or, in some instances, they may actually apply negative sanctions as a means of bringing violators into line. Among the negative sanctions are fines, imprisonment, torture, and death. Other negative sanctions are scolding, gossip, ridicule, satire, and ostracism. An employer's sanctions sometimes are demotion and firing. Potential norm violators are said to be in need of external control. For them, self-regulation is apparently lacking. The relationship between the phases of the social control and the approaches to social control are set forth in Table 16.1.

Compliance is sometimes the most reasonable response to the social control efforts of others.

Types: Formal and Informal

It may be evident by now that the approaches to social control can be broken down into two types: *formal* and *informal.* The formal type is codified, scheduled, organized, or regulated in some way, as in ritual, firing, promotion, demotion, satire, monetary payment, and mass media acclaim. The informal type of control has opposite conditions. It is casual and unwritten; it lacks regulation, scheduling, and organization. The informal type consists of casual praise, ridicule, gossip, and ostracism. A miscreant or deviant may be scolded or even tortured. A gift is a positive sanction.

A society usually attempts to manage deviant actions by using both formal and informal types of social control. For instance, ostracism and ridicule may torment a man fired from a sensitive civil service position because of homosexual activities. Table 16.2 contains a cross-tabulation of the means of social control by approach and type.

Table 16.2 SOCIAL CONTROL SANCTIONS BY APPROACH AND TYPE

	Type	
Approach	**Formal**	**Informal**
Positive	Ritual Money Privilege Promotion Mass media acclaim	Casual praise Gifts
Negative	Imprisonment Fines Public execution Demotion Satire Firing	Ridicule Ostracism Gossip Torture Scolding

It is doubtful if there is a society that fails to use all four kinds of sanctions. The four are *positive-formal, positive-informal, negative-formal,* and *negative-informal.* No society benefits from total acceptance of its social order by its members, nor does it experience total rejection of that order. Still, the ratio of formal to informal and positive to negative sanctions varies considerably from one culture to the next. It appears, for instance, that totalitarian countries rely more heavily on negative sanctions than do democratic countries. Canada falls closer to the positive pole of the approach dimension than, say, present-day Iran or El Salvador. But negative sanctions are used in Canada to achieve and maintain an order defined as desirable by those in control. The existence of courts and prisons alone attests to the fact that some members of Canadian society have rejected the established institutions.

The Failure of Social Control

It is clear from the preceding paragraph that social control occasionally fails, despite the use of sanctions to gain compliance from the community's would-be norm violators. Mainstream functionalism offers little insight into the reasons for a rejection of the norms. This is understandable, because a theory of the failure of social control is also part of the broader theory of the causes of norm violation.

There is presently no complete theory of the failure of social control. Efforts at constructing such a theory have centered narrowly on the *deviance* of adolescents and young adults who, for reasons as yet only partly understood, fail to develop a moral commitment to the conventional norms and identities. At the same time, very few of these young people are committed on a value basis solely to deviant norms and identities. Instead, they drift between the world of respectability and the world of deviance. They are

> neither compelled to deeds nor freely choosing them; neither different in any simple or fundamental sense from the law abiding, nor the same; conforming to certain traditions in American life while partially unreceptive to other more conventional traditions. (Matza, 1964: 28)

Matza was writing about American males who were juvenile delinquents. He found the youths firmly attached to certain marginal, masculine, "subterranean" traditions, or ways of life. They found satisfaction in drinking, smoking, renouncing work, being tough, and pursuing the hedonistic pleasures of "real" men. Matza's subjects looked on themselves as grown and mature, but their behavior was hardly a true picture of adult life in general in the United States (and Canada). Lemert (1972: 79–80) explains how this peculiar orientation can set one adrift toward the specific form of norm violation known as *deviance:*

> While some fortunate individuals by insightful endowment or by virtue of the stabilizing nature of their situations can foresee more distant social consequences of their actions and behave accordingly, not so most people. Much human behavior is situationally oriented and geared to meeting the many and shifting claims which others make upon them. The loose structuring and swiftly changing facade and content of modern social situations frequently make it difficult to decide which means will insure ends sought. Often choice is a compromise between what is sought and what can be sought. . . . All this makes me believe that most people drift into deviance by specific actions rather than by informed choices of social roles and statuses.

Social control fails for groups of delinquent adolescents and young adults. This failure occurs because it is important for each delinquent individual to be in good standing with his or her friends in the group. He or she attains good standing by honoring and practicing the marginal, or subterranean, traditions which Matza mentions. The quest for honor among peers thus helps explain how entire groups of juveniles can drift toward deviance (Hirschi, 1969: 230).

Social Control in the Institution of Religion

The ACM's [Anti-Cult Movement] gradually emergent ideology was intended to confer a specific deviant status on those individuals who joined new religions and thereby legitimated the exercise of specific forms of social control over them. Because members were defined as "brainwashed" and therefore considered completely unable to manage their own lives and decisions, a correspondingly extreme form of social control termed deprogramming that treated individuals as dehumanized automatons whose apparent volitions and actions were not really their own emerged to aid in restoring earlier-valued social relationships. However, the anti-cult associations, as we have shown, were largely incapable of undertaking individual recovery attempts. These associations were essentially interest groups; hence, their members' participation in terms of time, energy, and resources was limited. Indeed, the structures of anti-cult associations rarely provided role definitions or opportunities for more intense involvement by constituents. Thus, despite the fact that the major objective of the ACM was always the "recovery" of individual family members who had become involved in "cults," the members of these ACM groups were frequently in a poor position to carry out coercive deprogrammings.

Such direct action became by and large reserved for the ACM's deprogramming component, a group at its small nucleus composed of full-time ACM proponents who were to struggle throughout the 1970s with mixed fortunes to gain public and legal acceptance for their assumptions and techniques and to have deprogramming recognized as a new, alternative profession. As we shall show, deprogrammers performed several vital functions for the entire ACM. The "cult" members whom they abducted and persuaded to recant their faiths seemingly reinforced the validity of the brainwashing ideology and reaffirmed the "cults' " presumed perniciousness. Perhaps just as important for frustrated, distraught parents, the deprogrammers provided dramatic evidence of hope, should the right circumstances arise, that something severe but effective could be done to "recover" offspring. They even began to assume a somewhat heroic, even romantic image within the ACM. . . .

There were numerous options available to parents who were unable to accept their offsprings' participation in deviant religions. Undoubtedly, achieving a formal definition of them as mentally ill, for example, which some parents tried . . . would have yielded the same degree of social control over rebellious offspring as believing them brainwashed and then having them deprogrammed. However, deprogramming offered a number of advantages. One obvious advantage was expedience: Deprogrammers often were willing to "cut corners" and violate the law by outright kidnapping and forcibly detaining young adults. . . .

A second major advantage was the relative lack of stigma which accrued to the deprogrammee. Once applied, a label of mental illness could prove exceedingly difficult to remove and would likely confront both the young adults and the parents with a semipermanent stigma that could prove detrimental to a number of later careers. By contrast, once deprogrammed, an individual . . . returned . . . with little stigma.

SOURCE: Anson D. Shupe, Jr., and David G. Bromley. *The new vigilantes: Deprogrammers, anti-cultists, and the new religions,* pp. 125–127. Beverly Hills, Calif.: Sage Publications, 1980.

Those who drift toward deviance are ambivalent about conventional adult ways and unconventional deviant ways. Delinquent drift, Matza points out, is significantly different from participating in a compact, organized deviant subculture rooted in a strong commitment to unconventional values and norms. In fact, Hirschi believes there are no large groups in the United States, even at the older adult level, directly promoting and engaging in crime. Such groups do come into being around the more tolerable forms of deviance (see the references to homosexuality, mental disorders, and the use of marijuana in Chapter 17).

It appears that much, if not all, of this is applicable to Canada. For instance, a comparative study conducted in California and Alberta indicates that ties to peers are important considerations among the sample delinquent youth, while being in touch with home and school are valued much less (Linden and Fillmore, 1981).

This attention to drift is not to deny that strong commitments to deviant norms and values do develop among tolerable, often noncriminal, deviants and among small groups of older adult criminals and isolates of that age. Such people, however, pass through a stage of drift earlier in their deviant careers (Stebbins, 1971a).

What sociological concept does this scene exemplify?

RESOCIALIZATION

As defined in Chapter 5 *socialization* is a process by means of which members of society learn the values, norms, knowledge, beliefs, and skills facilitating role performance and collective goal attainment. In short, socialization is learning how to take part in the social life of a group, whatever its size. *Internalization,* as defined, is the propensity of individuals to conform independently to the norms and values they have learned through socialization; it is the individual's moral commitment to the components of culture and its institutions. Internalization is thus an important product or outcome of the process of socialization, or social learning.[2]

Every society faces the problem of having a minority of its members fail, for various reasons, to become socialized. The minority fails to learn the norms and values of society, or, if they are learned, fails to internalize the norms and values. As we have suggested, some individuals may even become committed to a deviant lifestyle. This is the problem of inadequate social control. From the standpoint of functionalist theory, there is a need for *resocialization:*

> That process wherein an individual, defined as inadequate according to the norms of a dominant institution(s), is subjected to a dynamic program of behavior intervention aimed at instilling and/or rejuvenating these values, attitudes, and abilities which would allow him to function according to the norms of said domi-

[2]When internalization is referred to as a process in, for example, internalizing norms, it is synonymous with the active dimension of socialization (see Chapter 5, "Socialization").

nant institution(s). (Kennedy and Kerber, 1973: 39)

This concept implies that something is awry with individual learning and that the faulty learning must be "corrected," "rehabilitated," or "treated." It also implies that the agents of socialization (e.g., family, school, and church institutions) usually perform their jobs effectively and that the agents' norms and values are appropriate to present-day circumstances. That institutions might be old-fashioned or that improvements might be needed in the conduct of earlier socialization are alien thoughts to the resocialization perspective.

Resocialization is, for the most part, a special form of adult socialization. It differs from *developmental or secondary socialization* discussed in Chapter 5: the further training of people beyond their primary socialization. Developmental adult socialization builds on a foundation of earlier learning. It is this earlier learning that is assumed to be deficient or absent among those subjected to adult resocialization.

Total Institutions

Considerable scientific attention has been directed toward the resocialization of deviant norm violators, with most attention being given to criminals and the mentally disordered. To the extent that it succeeds, resocialization of criminals and the mentally ill is possibly more drastic than anyone else's, since it is frequently conducted within the confines of what Goffman (1961: xiii) refers to as a *total institution:*

Total institution: an oil exploration camp, Melville Island, Northwest Territories.

> A total institution may be defined as a place of residence and work where a large number of like-situated individuals, cut off from the wider society for an appreciable period of time, together lead an enclosed, formally administered round of life.

Total institutions differ from social institutions such as the family and the school. A total institution is a social establishment, usually an organization, located in "rooms, suites of rooms, buildings, or plants in which activity of a particular kind regularly goes on" (Goffman, 1961: 3). The "total" nature of these institutions is evident in the way they prevent most or all interaction between their inmates and the outside world; interaction is blocked by walls or locked doors or by water, forests, and cliffs. Some total institutions, however, have little to do with resocialization. These include tuberculosis sanitariums, monasteries, isolated work camps, ships, and military installations. Some forms of resocialization are carried out in establishments that are not total institutions. Training the hard-core unemployed (e.g., Kennedy and Kerber, 1973: Chapter 20) and converting the religious (e.g., Gecas, 1981: 192–194) are examples.

Criminals

Despite official rhetoric about "correcting" and "rehabilitating"—i.e., resocializing—incarcerated criminals, the recidivism rates in Canada and the United States continue to range from 60 to 70 percent (see Waller, 1974: xiii–xiv, 152–153; Reid, 1985: 559). The *recidivism rate* is the number of ex-offenders returning to prison in proportion to the number of ex-offenders released in a specified period of time. The rate should be accepted with caution, however, since it is only an estimate. The practice of estimating is fraught with procedural difficulties.

Given that many ex-offenders return to prison on new charges (whatever the actual proportion), it may be concluded that prisons seldom achieve resocialization. Prisons are a means of protecting the public from criminals (a custodial function) and of punishing criminals for their deeds (a penal function). In view of all this, North American prisons in general have been portrayed as chiefly custodial and penal rather than as places for resocialization (Thomas and Peterson, 1977: 26–33; Ekstedt and Griffiths, 1984: 223–226). Indeed, prisons may abolish certain aspects of earlier primary, conventional socialization when inmates are incarcerated for many years and thereby prevented from practicing their social skills in the wider society. To the extent that prisons do succeed in controlling deviant behavior (i.e., by keeping ex-offenders from recidivism), they do so through compliance, not by means of internalization.

Working against whatever effort there is toward rehabilitation is the developmental socialization process known as *prisonization.* With prisonization, prisoners are assimilated or absorbed into the inmate culture. That is, they learn inmate norms and values. The norms and values encourage deviance such as homosexuality and drug use and engender hostile attitudes toward guards and prison officials. As inmates become prisonized, efforts to resocialize them falter. Akers et al. (1977) found, in a study of prisonization in the United States and four other countries, that prisonization is greater in de facto custodial institutions than in those with a genuine treatment or resocialization orientation. They concluded that findings of this nature in the United States hold for other countries as well.

Perhaps it is for this reason that the use of prisons in North America, whatever their goals, declined for many years during a period up to 1972 to 1973 (see Figure 16.1). But in an era of law-and-order thinking, the tendency to rely on

The custodial function of prisons is evident in their walls, bars, and barbed wire.

imprisonment became the general practice in both Canada and the United States from the early 1970s to 1982 (U.S. Bureau of the Census, 1984: 194; Statistics Canada, 1982–1983: 156–157, 171). Nevertheless, Canada appears to continue to rely more heavily than the United States on imprisonment. That is, Canada has a much lower overall crime rate than the United States (see Chapter 17), but only a moderately lower rate of imprisonment (Michalos, 1980c: 51).

Community-based corrections constitute a category of alternatives to incarceration. There are several of these, including probation, parole, and community residential centers. *Probation* is the act of suspending a convicted offender's sentence with the proviso that he or she promises good behavior, agrees to a specified level of

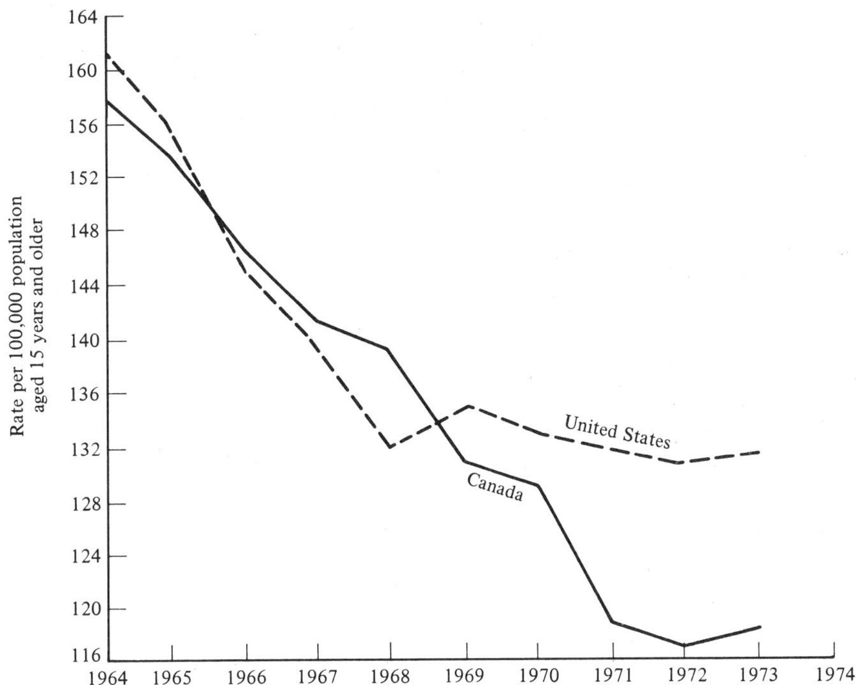

Figure 16.1 Prison Population: Federal, State, Provincial. (*Source:* A. C. Michalos. *North American Social Report,* Vol. 2. Dordrecht, Holland: D. Reidel, 1980, p. 140.)

supervision (usually by a probation official), and accepts other possible requirements and conditions. By contrast, *parole* is a conditional and revocable release from prison; the convict who is granted a parole is serving an indeterminate or unexpired sentence. Supervision, often by a parole officer, is imposed. *Community residential center* is the modern term for the halfway house. It is a prerelease residence designed to help inmates adjust to community life just prior to completing a lengthy sentence.

Do actions such as parole and probation help resocialize a criminal? Researchers have evaluated these efforts, and some have concluded that the effectiveness of community-based corrections remains unproved. Martinson (1974: 25) concluded from one extensive review of American programs that "with few and isolated exceptions, the rehabilitative efforts that have been reported so far have had no appreciable effect on recidivism." Some scholars have challenged Martinson's conclusions (for example, see Reid, 1985: 555–558), while others have accepted them (e.g., Sullivan, 1980: 54). Griffiths, et al, (1980: Chapter 8) and Hagan (1984: 221–223) find few grounds for optimism about the effectiveness of Canadian community-based corrections. In Canada and the United States, as well as abroad, methodological problems plague researchers attempting to measure the effectiveness of any effort to resocialize criminals.

Mental Patients

The rehospitalization rates for discharged mental patients, although sometimes lower than the recidivism rate for ex-offenders, are still far from negligible. Goldstein (1979: 403) reports that in 1974 in the United States two-thirds of all patients receiving extended care were readmitted, whereas the readmission rate in 1978 in Canada was 49 percent (Statistics Canada,

1981a: 16–19). As Gallagher (1980: 340) notes, there is disagreement here, too, about the accuracy of rehospitalization rates as a measure of failure to adjust to community social life. One reason for this inaccuracy is that fewer and fewer people are being treated for mental disorders in hospitals. This trend is most evident in the psychiatric hospitals, where the number of patients in the 1970s in Canadian and American hospitals was about half of what it was in the 1960s (Michalos, 1980a: 234). It will also be pointed out in this section that defining mental illness is still more art than science.

Still, the implication is that resocialization also fails for a substantial proportion of the mentally disordered. But the nature of acceptable (i.e., conforming) behavior vis-à-vis mentally ill behavior is subject to considerable interpretation even by professional practitioners (see Chapter 17). Hence, resocializing mental disorder, when compared with resocializing criminality, is a much more nebulous undertaking. How does a psychiatrist deal with a person who claims that he or she is Jesus Christ? Paranoid schizophrenia is a common psychosis. Many disturbed individuals have paranoid feelings about persons in authority; as they see it, the authority figure is "out to get me." A person may harbor delusions of someday becoming company president. Paranoid and delusional thoughts may have a degree of objective possibility, even if the probability of a thought becoming true is regarded as unlikely by the associates of the disturbed person.

Analogous to prisonization among incarcerated criminals, in the sense that it militates against resocialization, is the *continuance commitment* of mental patients; the mentally ill person is committed to a psychotic identity. Like the value commitment mentioned in the preceding chapter, continuance commitment helps explain a person's involvement with a status, or social identity. But, unlike value commitment, which explains this involvement by stressing the rewards of the identity, continuance commitment explains the involvement by stressing the penalties that accrue from renouncing the identity and trying to adopt another (Kanter, 1968; Stebbins, 1970b). To remain in an identity to which one is committed on a continuance basis is, in the case of the mentally disordered person, to accept the least evil choice; in the eyes of the deranged individual, it is better to remain as one is than to change. The individual feels that penalties are greater in other (nondeviant) identities than in the deviant one. An explanation of how this works is found in the next chapter.

There has been a decline in the number of individuals admitted to psychiatric hospitals. The statistics, however, mask what some observers believe is an increase in mental illness in North America. The widespread reliance on psychotropic drugs and the contemporary emphasis on patient-community relations have combined to encourage patients to avail themselves of services other than hospital treatment. Compilations in the United States show that the number of people using the inpatient facilities of hospitals (general hospitals, private hospitals, Veterans Administration hospitals) is increasing moderately, while the number turning to inpatient and outpatient facilities of community health centers and seeking the help of private counselors is increasing dramatically (U.S. Bureau of the Census, 1985: 112, Table 177).

Canada has no central agency for gathering data on patient services. It is therefore difficult to make comprehensive estimates of the number of individuals who are treated for mental illness in Canada. Still, Statistics Canada (1981b) reports a 25 percent increase between 1965 and 1978 in psychiatric admissions in all inpatient facilities. Since admissions in psychiatric hospitals in Canada are declining, it may be concluded that this increase is in inpatient treatment at other facilities. Instead of seeking care at psychiatric hospitals, mental patients in Canada appear to be turning to general hospitals, private hospitals, and community health centers for help.

Does all this mean that more people now need resocialization of their outlook on reality?

Bruce Dohrenwend (1975) says it does, because of the burdensome strain of modern life. But others disagree (e.g., Hagan, 1977: 63; Gallagher, 1980: 193–194). Modern psychiatry, they say, has broadened its definition of mental illness, thereby redefining as psychotic individuals previously looked on only as eccentric or criminal. Moreover, at least in the United States, blacks and the poor are more likely to receive treatment today than in the past.

Whether or not mental illness is more prevalent today than yesterday, the current interest in outpatient and brief inpatient treatment in community-health centers is still unproved as a resocialization mechanism (Kirk and Therrien, 1975). Successful resocialization of the mentally disturbed may hinge as much on changing public attitudes as on changing those who are afflicted.

CONFLICT PERSPECTIVE

In Meier's (1982: 47–49) review of the sociological literature on social control, the conflict perspective is conceptualized as a perspective in which social control itself is the subject of the study, not a problem or consideration of which social control is a part. Functionalists are concerned with the consequences of social control and how the consequences bear on the maintenance of the social system. As Meier puts it, the functionalists are concerned with "system interests." This contrasts with the conflict theorists, who are concerned with the consequences of social control with regard to the individual and with the "self-interested" use of social control by certain groups. This perspective relies heavily on the concept of power, for those who can use the means of social control to their advantage have power, an invaluable resource. Accordingly, the focus of the conflict perspective is chiefly on deviant norm violation, as opposed to civil violations and nonconformity. Meier uses the label "conflict theorist" in broader than usual fashion to refer to adherents of both the labeling perspective and the Marxist perspective.[3] In the area of social control, these two perspectives do share some important common ground.

The Labeling Perspective

The labeling perspective centers on the way society creates deviance by developing norms (some of which are laws) and by applying the norms selectively to particular categories of people who do not abide by the norms and are therefore labeled deviant (Becker, 1963: 9). Previously, Lemert (1951: Chapter 3) had noted that the discovery of deviants in our midst provokes a "social reaction," which takes the form of imprisonment, fines, ostracism, ridicule, supervision, or other sanctions that are intended to induce compliance. The labeling theorists diverge from the functionalists' concern for the consequences of being labeled a deviant.

These ideas steered Lemert (1972: Chapter 3) to the notions of "primary deviation" and "secondary deviation." *Primary deviation* is enacted with little change in the individual's everyday routine or life-style. In general, there is little change because the individual engages infrequently in the deviance, has few compunctions about the action, and encounters few practical problems in indulging in the behavior. The person who occasionally smokes marijuana supplied by someone else exemplifies primary deviation.

This deviation becomes *secondary* if the deviant sees it as substantially modifying his or her way of life. A need to deviate or a feeling of extreme guilt can foster a redefinition of one's deviant activities, but being accused of deviance is typically the most influential factor behind the redefinition. Being labeled by the authorities as gay, criminal, alcoholic, or mentally disordered and sanctioned for such behavior force the deviant to change drastically his or her life-style. As Lemert (1972: 63) puts it, "This sec-

[3]Both perspectives are covered in somewhat greater detail in Chapter 17, "Deviance."

ondary deviant . . . is a person whose life and identity are organized around the facts of deviance."

The study of secondary deviation is one of two directions taken by labeling theorists in the field of social control. The other, Meier points out, is the study of moral entrepreneurs:

> Rules are the products of someone's initiative and we can think of the people who exhibit such enterprise as *moral entrepreneurs.* Two related species—rule creators and rule enforcers—will occupy our attention. (Becker, 1963: 147)

The prototype of the rule creator, Becker observes, is the "crusading reformer," whose dissatisfaction with existing rules is acute and who therefore campaigns for legal change (adding new laws or procedures, rescinding old laws or procedures) and, sometimes, for a change in attitude designed to produce what he or she considers proper behavior. Canadian society is replete with crusades, both past and present. One group or another has thought to eliminate drug abuse, discourage the overuse of alcohol, reduce environmental pollution, and stop the exploitation of women in the workplace. Organizations have been formed to stress the need for mental health and physical fitness.

The crusading reformers are numerous. They have organized themselves and have generated social movements effectively (see also Chapter 21). In the case of physical fitness, the crusaders' goal appears to be primarily one of a change in attitude, not a change in law or public policy. It should be clear, then, that the scope of moral enterprise is considerably broader than simply the control of deviant behavior or even norm violation. Moral enterprise may be undertaken with reference to any treasured value and not just values with moral implications.

Some crusades fail. A crusade may fail because of the power and influence of opposing interest groups, some of whom are themselves crusaders. Lo (1982: 108) refers to such interest groups as "right-wing movements," which he defines as "social movements whose stated goals are to maintain structures of order, status, honor, or traditional social differences or values." Right-wing movements are generally interested in perpetuating or increasing existing economic or political inequalities. By contrast, left-wing movements usually seek to eliminate such inequality. The struggle over abortion practices in North America exemplifies the conflict between left-wing movements and right-wing movements.

When crusaders succeed in getting new laws on the books, it may become necessary to retrain the authorities who enforce the laws. Alternatively, new enforcers may be hired. With the retraining of existing enforcers or the hiring of new enforcers, the movement can be said to have become institutionalized; it has become institutionalized as part of the social control function of the polity, economy, religion, education, or other relevant institution of the society. Becker wrote about legal enforcers, to wit, judges, detectives, and police officers. A relatively new addition to this coterie are the security personnel at airports in North America. Attendants at airport check-in points run air travelers through electronic baggage checks as a means of preventing the highjacking of airplanes; anyone with a gun or other weapon in his or her baggage is arrested and prevented from boarding the airplane. The entrepreneurs' campaign to prevent the highjacking of airplanes was swift and popular.

Entrepreneurs also enforce rules. The rules make it possible to apply norms to those who misbehave or step out of line. The entrepreneurs' newly legislated rules provide the enforcers (police, security personnel) with jobs and justification for their jobs. Since the enforcers usually want to keep their jobs, they are eager to demonstrate that enforcement is being properly carried out. Yet, they also realize that there are more infractions than they can possibly prevent and guard against; they must establish priorities. Thus:

> whether a person who commits a deviant act is in fact labeled a deviant depends on many things extraneous to his actual behavior: whether the enforcement official feels that at this time he must make some show of doing his job in order to justify his position, whether the misbehaver shows proper deference to the enforcer, whether the "fix" has been put in, and where the kind of act he has committed stands on the enforcer's list of priorities. (Becker, 1963: 161).[4]

It is no accident, then, that the least influential members of society (i.e., the poor, certain ethnic groups) are often disproportionately caught in the web of social control and labeled deviant.

The Marxist Perspective

Moral enterprise is the jumping-off point for today's Marxists. They argue that the labeling theorists take too soft a line toward the controlling elites in society. According to the Marxists, it is naive to call on the elite to be more tolerant and more humane; it is presumptive to expect the elite to become less sensitive to what labeling theorists say are really actions of minor consequence. As Ian Taylor (1982: 131) phrases it, "The politics of the literature on moral enterprise are really of a Romantic variety." There are powerful, self-interested people in society, he says, who want others in society to think and act in certain ways and who care little about how the others regard their control tactics. The only way to change this "injustice" is to redistribute power in the society:

> There is an ultimate conflict of interest between those who earn their livelihood through the sale of mental or manual labor and the owners of capital. . . . To hold a theory that links social interest to social structure is to recognize that minds are changed not by persuasion (or even by majority democratic votes) but by force of circumstances (specifically, by changes in the social structure internal to a society). (Taylor, 1982: 132)

[4]A *fix* is an arrangement designed to obtain legal immunity by applying some form of influence, usually political or monetary, to the enforcers.

Expanding on the recent ideas of British sociologist Stanley Cohen and the earlier ideas of Emile Durkheim, Taylor describes how the moral outrages of the day serve an important social function. Influential members of the community look on some deeds as objectionable or reprehensible. For example, they are appalled by a rapist's criminal assault and by the apparent brainwashing of the Moonies. Rape and brainwashing offend the individuals' sense of right and wrong and stimulate their desire to control such actions. Such events make us aware of our collective sentiments, which may have been dormant. They also help crystallize social types of undesirable behavior, which, in Francis's (1963) words, then serve as "antimodels."

Morality and its definition by society's elites is constantly changing. A study of how moral outrages activate the collective conscience and engender antimodels leads to an explanation of moral crusades. This explanation is missing in the labeling perspective on social control.

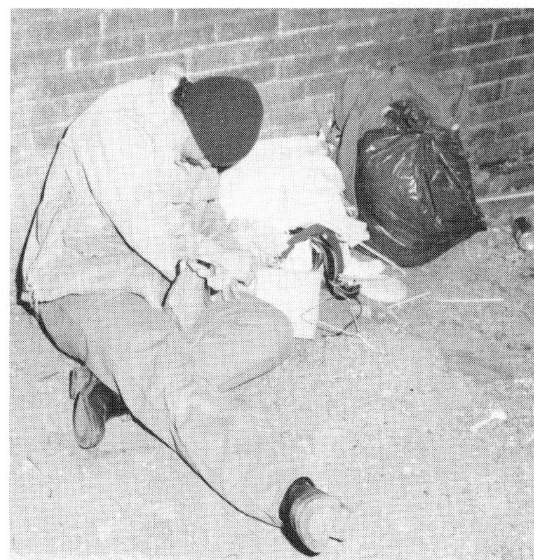

An antimodel: Even the habitués of skid row serve a purpose in society.

The Marxists of today who study deviance and social control refer to themselves as *radical criminologists.* What do they propose? Antony (1980), in a recent review, summarized their program, to the extent that it is formed. She says these writers, among them Ian Taylor and Richard Quinny (see Chapter 17), urge a humanistic definition of crime in place of the prevailing legalistic one. In their view, laws should be humanistically defined as just or unjust; they should be based on egalitarian standards. Such a definition would highlight the true workings of the legal system by making visible its clusters of power and privilege.

With this approach, the individual is given priority over society's institutions. Radical criminologists say that, since modern criminal law is politically motivated, it should be abolished to make way for the widest possible tolerance of diversity. Finally, radical criminologists are instructed to avoid being put into advisory roles (as happened to labeling theorists) which are designed to patch up the present criminal justice system; instead, they are urged to join the ongoing political struggle. Ian Taylor (1981: 125), who is now writing about *socialist criminology* rather than radical criminology, says the socialist kind

> must be formed in the practical context, responding to problems that arise in popular experience of the existing penal and welfare systems and, in particular, to popular demands for policing and a sense of social order. There are currently only five potential agencies in which to begin the task of constructing a practical socialist criminology. These are the prison movements, the police critics, the socialist lawyers and civil liberties groups, and the various organizations that have arisen within the woman's movement.

One theme found in both the functionalist and the conflict perspectives on social control is a concern with social norms (especially laws). For the functionalist, the problem is to explain how people come to adhere to the social norms. For the labeling theorist, the problem is to discover how moral enterprise works and what the consequences of moral enterprise are for deviants. For the Marxist-radical criminologist, the problem is to describe the injustices of such norms and to propose more humanistic norms to replace them.

SOCIAL CONTROL AND THE MASS MEDIA

We began this chapter by pointing out that social control is not an institution but a process of managing individual behavior and a process that is inherent in all institutions of a society. Socialization, resocialization, internalization, compliance, and sanctioning are the five processes operating in each institution to implement social control. In preindustrial societies, these processes are carried out through face-to-face communication such as gossip and ridicule. In industrial societies, direct interaction among all individuals in the society is impossible. Consequently, social control is frequently effected through public opinion and the mass media.

Public Opinion

A *public* is defined by Lauer and Handel (1977: 400) as an aggregate of people who see themselves as affected by an event of such interest that they seek further information about the event with the intention of better understanding it and controlling it. This shared interest is, however, the only thing the people have in common, since, on the whole, they are structurally unrelated. Canadians and people in other industrial societies are members of many publics. An individual's friends, relatives, and acquaintances may be members of the same public, but, in other publics, the members may be unacquainted with or unrelated to each other. We have already considered a number of publics;

the members of a social movement that develops around a moral enterprise constitute a public (e.g., feminists, environmentalists, antiabortionists).

Following Hill's advice (1981: 376, n.2), we shall regard attitude and opinion as synonymous. This avoids a tortured distinction that has plagued social psychology for decades with no perceptible benefit. One common definition of *attitude* (opinion) is that it is learned disposition to treat or define an object or set of objects in a particular and consistent way. Obviously, publics can have opinions about their objects of shared interest, whether the objects be political candidates, sports heroes, clothing fashions, food preferences, television programs, or the actions of other people.

The actions of people are of particular interest in this chapter. The actions raise questions such as, How does public opinion control behavior and how might it be used to control behavior? The first question is more easily answered than the second. Were we able to ask Durkheim for the answer, he would say that public opinion is an element in the collective conscience of a society or its subgroups. Thus, it has a constraining influence on the actions of the members of publics. For example, if we know many of our friends are opposed to marijuana smoking, we are apt to reject it too. If we know those same friends favor a special university program, we may likewise favor it.

Manipulating public opinion in one's own interest is difficult. In industrial societies, the evidence tends to support the hypothesis that anyone who dictates public opinion is limited to one topic, which narrows the individual's sphere of influence (Rogers and Shoemaker, 1971: 223–224). Martin (1978: 293–294) points out that the mass media mold public opinion by directing attention to issues around which publics may subsequently come into being. Some opinion leaders, of course, may be able to have their views circulated to their publics via the media.

The Media's Influence

The mass media (books, newspapers, magazines, radio, television, motion pictures) help control behavior by supplying the ideas and information on which members of society construct images of people, groups, and events in the institutionalized areas of social life. As we have noted, leaders of public opinion sometimes use the media to circulate their views. As suppliers of ideas and information, the mass media have been charged with bias; it is said, for example, that radio, television, and motion pictures have portrayed women in a slanted way and as sex objects (Reul, 1978). Consider the influence of Hollywood films in fostering the dreams of many young women who hope to become beautiful, celebrated movie stars, famous and rich.

Holz and Wright (1979: 208–210) review a number of studies bearing on the ways in which the mass media affect people. There is evidence that people in general are dependent on the various media for information about current events and public opinion; news stories guide people in forming their own opinions on the focal subjects and in deciding when and where to express their opinions, once the opinions are formed. Moreover, the citizenry's sense of the importance of an issue or event is frequently based on the amount of coverage it receives in the newspapers and on television. The implication here is that the media confer status on what they cover.

But the North American media, being mainly business enterprises, have goals in addition to the one of trying to cover the important issues and events. According to the media, anything which is "important" is an issue or an event which the people should know about. Information is important, but it should be recognized that another aim of today's media is to entertain people (Altheide and Snow, 1979: Chapter 2). Being entertaining and at the same time providing information about significant issues and events can be contradictory goals.

Holz and Wright also discuss research conducted in Great Britain which shows that the mass media help shape the people's understanding of the world around them. The media may be the only source of information from which people can construct images of issues and events. For instance, it would be difficult for those in North America to know about the activities of Chinese communists without the news stories in newspapers and on television. Different media express different views, but the facts and actualities which they reveal are the only information available to most people.

OUTLINE AND SUMMARY

I. Introduction
   Social control is all the processes that implement the legitimate order of a given community or society; it is not an institution but a process found in all institutions.

II. Social Control Perspectives
   Two sets of perspectives on the institutional problem of social control have dominated the field since the 1950s: the *functionalist perspective* and the *conflict perspective.*

III. Functionalist Perspective
   The mainstream functionalists hold that social control is sometimes inadequate. As they see it, this inadequacy leads to norm violation. The functionalist perspective is summarized under three headings: phases, approaches, and types.

   A. Phases: Values and Sanctions
      Society as a whole or an influential segment of it *values* a certain pattern of thought or action and the harmonious fit of the pattern with other patterns. The value encourages the use of particular sanctions. *Sanctions* are reinforcements of a person's behavior; other people exercise the reinforcement. Ridicule and ostracism are sanctions.

   B. Approaches: Positive and Negative
      When people are threatened by a form of deviance, they turn to *positive sanctions* or *negative sanctions.* Positive sanction is usually achieved through internalization of a value. Negative sanction is usually achieved through compliance with the value.

      1. Internalization
         Internalization is the propensity to conform to the norm; with internalization, people identify so strongly with the values and their associated norms that their actions become largely, though never entirely, self-regulating.

      2. Compliance
         Social control is negative for some of the individuals and groups who violate norms; coercive methods must be used to force their *compliance* with the values of the dominant segment of society. The would-be norm violators are compelled to live by moral standards they would reject were it not for the high cost of rejection. With a desire to avoid negative sanctions, they are motivated to conform to the social rules.

   C. Types: Formal and Informal
      The *formal* type of social control is codified, scheduled, organized, or regulated. The *informal* type is casual and unwritten, without regulation, scheduling, or organization.

   D. The Failure of Social Control
      Delinquent drift: Some adolescent and young adult males and females fail to develop a strong moral commitment either to conventional norms and identities or to deviant norms and identities. They drift between these two worlds. Being in good standing with friends in the delinquent group is important to each member of the group.

IV. Resocialization
   According to functionalism, members of society who fail to become socialized are deemed to be in the need of resocialization. *Resocialization* is a program of behavior intervention aimed at instilling or rejuvenating acceptable values, attitudes, and abilities into the thinking of the norm violator.

   A. Total Institutions

A *total institution* is a place of residence and work where a large number of like-situated individuals lead a sequestered life for long periods of time. A prison is a total institution.

B. Criminals
Resocialization of criminals in prisons has been rather unsuccessful, as a result, in good part, of prisonization or assimilation into inmate culture.

C. Mental Patients
The rehospitalization rates for mental patients, although somewhat lower than the recidivism rates of ex-offenders, are still far from negligible.

V. Conflict Perspective
The conflict perspective is concerned with the consequences of social control in regard to the individual; it is concerned with the "self-interested" use of social control by certain groups. This perspective relies heavily on the concept of power.

A. The Labeling Perspective
The labeling perspective centers on the way society gives rise to deviance. Society creates deviance by developing norms and by applying the norms selectively to particular categories of people. These people do not abide by the norms and hence they are labeled *deviant.* There are *primary deviance* and *secondary deviance.*

B. The Marxist Perspective
Marxists concern themselves with moral enterprise. As they see it, "injustice" can be abolished with the redistribution of power in society. Marxists who study deviance and social control refer to themselves as *radical criminologists.* Radical criminologists say that modern criminal law is politically motivated and that it should be abolished to make way for the widest possible tolerance of diversity.

VI. Social Control and the Mass Media
The mass media have an effect on social control.

A. Public Opinion
The *public* is an aggregate of people who see themselves affected by an event; they seek to understand the event and to control it.

B. The Media's Influence
People are dependent on the mass media for information about current events and public opinion. The media inform and entertain. Being entertaining and at the same time providing information can be contradictory goals.

FOR FURTHER READING AND STUDY

Brannigan, A. 1984. *Crimes, courts, and corrections: Law and social control in Canada.* Toronto: Holt, Rinehart & Winston of Canada. This lucid text examines social control in Canada, starting with the making of laws and moving from there to policing, court action, and correction efforts.

Gibbs, J. P. 1981. *Norms, deviance, and social control.* New York: Elsevier. Gibbs analyzes the many definitions of the terms "norm," "deviance," and "social control." After clarifying the meanings of these concepts, he develops his own theory of deviance and social control.

Goffman, E. *Asylums.* 1961. Garden City, N.Y.: Doubleday. A poignant field-research account of life in a mental hospital. Goffman introduces the idea of "moral career" in this book.

Roucek, J. S., ed. 1978. *Social control for the 1980s.* Westport, Conn.: Greenwood. This is an anthology of original papers on various aspects of social control theory and research.

Schur, E. H. 1971. *Labeling deviant behavior.* New York: Harper & Row. A short introduction to labeling theory by a man who helped shape this perspective.

Scott, J. F. 1971. *Internalization of norms: A sociological theory of moral commitment.* Englewood Cliffs, N.J.: Prentice-Hall. The main proposition underlying this book is that even when norms are well learned, moral commitment is strong, and obligations to conform are felt intensely, the maintenance of conscience and conformity depends on the existence of sanctions.

Sullivan, D. 1980. *The mask of love: Corrections in America.* Port Washington, N.Y.: Kennikat. This book examines the nature of modern corrections, the impossibility of rehabilitation, the question of safety from criminal threat, and the role of mutual aid in healing the severance of deviants from the rest of society.

Taylor, I. 1981. *Law and order: Arguments for socialism.* London: Macmillan. Taylor, a British-Canadian criminologist, develops a socialist criminology centered on the police, prisons, enforcement of law, and law and women.

KEY WORDS

compliance Conformity to a society's values.

continuous commitment Entrapment in an identity because of the penalties that accrue from trying to renounce that identity.

deviance Behavior which violates a society's seriously regarded norms.

internalization The propensity to conform to a norm or to behave in a way which the norm suggests.

parole A conditional and revocable release from prison of someone serving an indeterminate or unexpired sentence.

primary deviation A deviation which brings about little change in the individual's everyday routine and life-style.

prisonization The assimilation of prisoners into inmate culture.

probation The act of suspending a convicted offender's sentence with the proviso that he or she agree to supervision.

public An aggregate of people who seek to know more about an event which has an effect on them; they seek to understand and to control the event.

recidivism rate The number of ex-offenders who return to prison in proportion to the number of ex-offenders released in a specific period of time.

resocialization Behavior intervention which changes a norm violator and instills within him or her a respect for society's accepted values and norms.

sanction A reinforcement of behavior produced by other people; praise and acclaim for a person's achievement are examples of sanctions.

secondary deviance Deviant behavior which substantially modifies an individual's way of life.

social control The processes that implement the legitimate order of a community or society; the mechanisms which compel members of a society to behave in an acceptable way.

total institution A place of residence and work where like-situated individuals together lead an enclosed, formally administered life; a prison is a total institution.

five

DIFFERENTIATION

In Part Five we return to the society-as-process perspective introduced in Part Two. *Differentiation* is a process of spontaneous innovation. Through it, something new emerges from something old. A single unit becomes many units, a simple unit becomes a complex unit, and a homogeneous unit becomes a heterogeneous unit. Social differentiation, as opposed to biological, psychological, and geological differentiation, occurs through the proliferation of roles (and associated statuses) in a society. There is role development within and across institutions. The development proceeds from simplicity and homogeneity to complexity and heterogeneity.

chapter 17

Deviance

CHAPTER OUTLINE

INTRODUCTION

If, as William Cowper insisted, "Variety's the very spice of life," then we should be thankful for humankind's tendency to differentiate itself and for sociology's efforts to make us aware of the differentiation. The discipline's founding fathers wrote about it, particularly Spencer and Durkheim. They were influenced by Charles Darwin's theory of evolution and the idea of natural selection. The eighteenth and nineteenth century biologists were themselves indebted to a long line of philosophers stretching back to Plato, who recognized the process we now call *social differentiation.*

The human variety that adds spice to our

lives is psychological, biological, and social. Psychological and biological factors account for variations in characteristics such as personality, physique, weight, height, intelligence, temperament, face, skin color, and hair color. The examination of these characteristics is the province of psychologists and biologists. They leave to sociologists the study of social differentiation. *Social differentiation* is defined by Eisenstadt (1971: 4–5) as:

> (1) the situation that exists in every social unit, large or small, by virtue of the fact that people with different characteristics perform different tasks and occupy different roles, and (2) the fact that these tasks and roles are closely interrelated in several ways.

Before moving on to an explanation of differentiation resulting from deviant acts and non-deviant behavior, we must first look at the general idea of social differentiation. How is the process of social differentiation distinguished from related processes? What, in particular, is differentiated among human beings?

SOCIAL DIFFERENTIATION

In the view of sociologists, social differentiation is in many ways the same kind of process as *social control.* Social differentiation is vast and pervasive, as is social control. There the similarity ends. One outcome of social differentiation is the complex of roles (and associated statuses) comprising a society's institutions. A second outcome, as this part of the book makes clear, is the complex of roles intersecting the institutions. Among these roles are the roles of deviance, social stratification (wealth, prestige, power), sex, gender, age, and ethnicity. The differentiation of deviants further demonstrates that this process operates at the periphery of the institutionalized world, as well as at its core. It is in these ways, then, that differentiation is a vast and pervasive process.

Some of the socially differentiated roles we play are *ascribed* while other are *achieved.* The ascribed roles are gained perforce at birth or at a certain age. Among the ascribed roles are the roles of sex, race, nationality, majority, and age. The achieved roles are roles which are se-

The differentiated role: The shoe-shine boy at work on a city street.

SOCIOLOGY OR COMMON SENSE

What do you think?

Which of the following statements do you agree with? Which statements do you disagree with? Make a note of your answers. Check your answers when you have completed your study of this chapter. Are your answers to the statements the same as those a sociologist would give?

1. A deviant is not necessarily criminal.
2. Some deviance is legitimated by the law.
3. You can tell how much crime there is in your community by examining the crime rates published by the police.
4. The number of prostitutes and the number of acts of prostitution in North America have stabilized in the past two decades.
5. Types of mental illness can be diagnosed and treated like any other disease.

---

lected or somehow earned by a person. Among the achieved roles are the roles of deviance, power, gender, and social class. For example, individuals usually or always earn the role of a feminist, a prime minister, or a self-made rich man or woman. Even deviants such as alcoholics and compulsive gamblers earn their roles, although they are likely to regret their own initiative in causing their downfall. As this chapter makes clear, however, there are times when some people achieve the roles that are ascribed to others.

How does social differentiation differ from the division of labor? Social differentiation is a broader process than the division of labor, as the latter term is conventionally used in modern sociology. The division of labor was defined in Chapter 7 as the development and integration of the group's specialized roles into an effectively functioning unit. Analyses of a society's division of labor commonly center on the group and organizational functions of the society. These analyses seldom include cross-institutional roles such as deviance, age, and community status. The division of labor, in other words, is a social differentiation within institutions, with the differentiated roles consisting of relatively clear-cut tasks contributing to the functioning of some institutional group.

Persons in gender, deviant, and stratification roles perform tasks, too, but their tasks have no particular institutional locus. For example, when a woman handles food at home, she does so in her family role of mother or wife. When she serves the coffee and doughnuts at work (a duty some women now reject), she does so in her occupational role as secretary. The preparing and serving of food by women at different places and under different circumstances (at home, on a picnic, for the boss, at an office party, at a club meeting) is, at this level of generality, a traditional female gender-role task in our society (and one many feminists would like to change). Lifting heavy objects is a generalized male gender-role task, which also has its specific institutional counterparts.

DIFFERENTIATING DEVIANTS

Deviance is convincing evidence that social control efforts have failed. In commonsense terms, *deviance* is a breach of society's moral rules. Almost every day Canadians see evidence of the failure of social control in one or another breach of their society's moral code. Some miscreants worship the devil or keep idols in their homes, streetwise dealers push cocaine or sell bootleg whisky, affluent executives embezzle company funds or cheat on their income taxes, exhibitionists streak across a stage or cavort naked at a nudist camp, daring thieves steal cars or burglarize homes, and needy women engage in shoplifting or soliciting for prostitution. The list of moral infractions in our society is endless.

Until the early 1950s, most sociologists, psychiatrists, and psychologists never questioned this "absolutist" definition of deviance (Clinard and Meier, 1985: 5)—the definition of deviance as a breach of society's moral rules. It had the merits of simplicity and objectivity. Sociologists and psychologists accepted as valid the social scientist's labeling of an act such as theft or gambling as deviant, since it usually squared with what "everybody" knows about morality. Whether in the realm of social science or that of common sense, it seldom occurred to anyone that defining deviance would be problematic.

So far as common sense is concerned nothing has changed; the absolutist definition dominates the outlook. But it is different with social science. Sociologists in particular now realize that, contrary to common sense, the identification of and reaction to deviance in everyday life are essentially no different from our identifications and reactions to other kinds of behavior: all identifications and reactions hinge on one person's *interpretation* of another person's deeds. The chief difference between the interpretation of deviance and the interpretation of nondeviant behavior lies in the use of a moral yardstick in the interpretation of deviance. For example, a man is a murderer when he kills a bank teller in a holdup and a good soldier when he kills an enemy in wartime. To be sure, what is seen as deviant is part of everyday knowledge or commonsense reality (see Chapter 1). But it is also a socially constructed reality (Rock, 1973: 19).

Furthermore, as this reality is being constructed in the community, some people (the deviants) become differentiated, or set apart from the rest (the nondeviants):

> "Deviance matters" deal with the process of differentiation, how people become differentiated, and what moral significance is attached to their differences. The center of concern is moral ideas, their rise and fall, their invocation and application either as informal social designations or as administrative categories by agencies of social control. (Lemert, 1982: 238)

Lemert goes on to point out that deviant differentiation takes place through processes such as stigmatization, rejection, isolation, punishment, treatment, and rehabilitation.

Today, when it comes to defining deviants, most sociologists are *relativists* rather than absolutists. It is evident to them that deviance exists only with reference to particular circumstances; it is not an absolute trait or condition of the individual. "Beauty in things," said philosopher David Hume, "exists in the mind which contemplates them." The same may be said for deviance. It follows that human action is neither inherently deviant nor inherently nondeviant.

NORM VIOLATIONS

The strongest case for an absolutist definition of deviance can be made in the area of crime. *Crime* is a special subclass of deviance; it is a violation of the criminal law. If there is ever to be any precision in defining deviance, we should expect to find it here within the sweep of a carefully written legal code, which helps us differentiate a deviant act from a nondeviant act. Because they are usually painstakingly worked out and repeatedly tested through application, legal, or formal, norms certainly add a degree of simplicity, clarity, and objectivity to the handling of social delicts. Yet, even these norms are susceptible to relativistic interpretations. Indeed, the study of deviance concentrated on, among other things, how relativistic interpretations sneak into the formal social-control process to the chagrin of those who claim impartiality and absolutism in their processing of deviants (e.g., Rubington and Weinberg, 1981: Sections 7 and 8).

Numerically, most deviants are not criminal, for they have violated no criminal laws. Nevertheless, they are cast in a "deviant role" (Rock, 1973: 19–21) because they have acted in a morally reprehensible way as defined by an influential segment of the community. The following are generally considered criminal acts in North America: murder, rape, theft, burglary, forgery, assault, embezzlement, fraud, prostitution (except in certain Nevada counties), and being drunk in public. Some forms of drug use and gambling are also illegal, although several North American jurisdictions have legalized or decriminalized other forms.

There are other deviant roles into which people may be cast that sometimes (depending on jurisdiction) fall beyond the purview of the law or may even be legitimated by it. Here we find nudists, compulsive gamblers, alcoholics and heavy drinkers, homosexuals, swingers (mate swappers), striptease dancers, transvestites, occultists, transsexuals, drug addicts, mentally disordered persons, and political and religious deviants. It is noteworthy that addiction to alcohol, drugs, and gambling is not itself unlawful, even though some drug use and gambling are.

As if to confuse matters, Americans and Canadians scorn certain legitimate forms and noncriminal forms of deviance more than certain criminal forms. For instance, alcoholism, compulsive gambling, and severe mental disorder are commonly regarded as more serious breaches of our moral and social standards than casual marijuana use, illicit off-track betting, or perhaps even prostitution. Hence, no facile claim can be made that crime, as a category of deviance, is always more serious and therefore always more intolerable than noncriminal deviance.

Discussion at this point hints at the existence of a rough scale of seriousness of norm violation in North America. At the top as most serious and threatening are the violations of highly moral and emotionally significant norms, or mores, as they are referred to in Chapter 9. Cannibalism and incest are examples. Our mores are often formalized in the criminal law. Of somewhat less seriousness are the violations of other criminal laws and of noncriminal moral norms. Violations of the mores, criminal laws, and noncriminal moral norms are acts of deviance. By contrast, violations of ordinances and regulations are regarded less seriously, as mere civil infractions. Still lower on the seriousness scale are the violations of customs and folkways, which are seen as instances of nonconformity or eccentricity (see Table 17.1).

We are now in a position to present a sociological definition of deviance, which contrasts somewhat with the commonsense definition given earlier. *Deviance* is an act judged as in violation of the moral norms by the members of a community who are powerful enough to make this judgment stick. With this definition in mind, we move to the next section, which examines selected forms of criminal and noncriminal deviance in the United States and Canada. It is followed by a discussion of four standard sociological explanations of deviance. The final section takes up the question of the inevitability of deviance. An example of legitimate deviance is considered in Chapter 15, "Religion."

DEVIANT BEHAVIOR

We turn first to criminal deviance, where we look at representative property offenses (theft and burglary) and violent crimes (robbery and murder). Drug offenses and prostitution are considered subsequently. Since the rates and

A civilian violation: Is it deviant? Is a moral norm being violated?

Eccentricity is nonconformity from one standpoint while it is a form of distinctiveness from another.

Table 17-1 SERIOUSNESS OF NORM VIOLATION

Threat scale	Norms	Category of violations
Great	Mores	Deviance
	Criminal Laws	
Mild	Other Moral Norms	
Marginal	Ordinaces Regulations	Not deviance
None	Customs Folkways	Not deviance

trends of deviance tend to vary from country to country, this section presents comparisons of this sort for the United States and Canada. Following the discussion of criminal deviance is a discussion of noncriminal deviance and three of its representative forms, homosexuality, alcoholism, and mental disorder.

Criminal Deviance

Official crime rates are compiled monthly from the "Uniform Crime Reports" submitted by Canadian police departments to Statistics Canada and by American police departments to the Federal Bureau of Investigation. A *crime rate* is the number of offenses of a particular kind recorded by the police. It is wanting as an accurate measure of criminality because some crimes are never reported or some police officers fail to record reported crime, or both. Criminologists in Canada and the United States estimate that only 20 to 30 percent of all crimes are reported to the authorities, although the reporting rate varies considerably by type of crime (Statistics Canada, 1980a; 151: Skogan, 1977). Black and Reiss (1970) calculate that 35 percent of all crimes reported to American police go unrecorded. Some crime, of course, is never detected and hence impossible even to record. Donald Black (1970: 733) writes that "It has long been taken for granted that official statistics are not an accurate measure of all legally defined crime in the community."[1]

Property Offenses The Uniform Crime Reports say that *theft* is essentially an act of stealing. It is the unlawful taking and removing of personal property with the intent of depriving the rightful owner of the belongings. In the United States, theft is sometimes officially referred to as *larceny*. Throughout North America theft is distinguished from forgery (falsely making or altering something, e.g., forging a check, fraud (acquiring goods and services by deceit), and embezzlement (fraudulent acquisition of entrusted money). It is also distinguished from *break and enter,* or burglarizing the dwelling of another person to steal or attempt to steal something or to engage in some felonious act. Both theft and break and enter are "property offenses." They are unlawful acquisitions of property.

Despite the aforementioned reservations about the accuracy of official crime data, such data do communicate a general summary of the rates of theft and burglary in North America (see Table 17.2). But the level of error in these data prevents us from concluding that Americans are more inclined than Canadians to steal or burglarize. It is reasonable to conclude, however, that these two forms of deviance, theft and burglary, are increasing in both countries.

Violent Crimes Using robbery and murder as indicators, what picture emerges from violent crimes in North America? *Robbery* is the act of

[1]Surveys of victims produce a more accurate estimate of actual crime rates than official statistics such as the Uniform Crime Reports. Nationwide surveys of victims are available in the United States. But results from the 1981 Canadian Urban Victimization Survey were unavailable at the time this book went to press. Consequently, comparisons in this chapter, to the extent that they are on criminal deviance, have been made from the Uniform Crime Reports of both countries.

Table 17.2 THEFT AND BREAK AND ENTER IN THE UNITED STATES AND CANADA

	Rate per 100,000 population			
	United States		Canada	
Year	Theft	Break and enter	Theft	Break and enter
1966	—	—	1331	510
1967	1576	827	—	—
1970	2079	1085	2013	834
1974	2490	1438	2401	1040
1978	2744	1424	2672	1186
1981	3122	1632	3423	1518

Sources: U.S. Bureau of the Census. 1967–1982–83, *Statistical abstract of the United States* (various editions), Washington, D.C.; *Crime and traffic enforcement statistics,* 1962–1981, Cat. No. 85-205, Ottawa: Statistics Canada.

Table 17.3 ROBBERY AND MURDER IN THE UNITED STATES AND CANADA

	Rate per 100,000 population			
	United States		Canada	
Year	Robbery	Murder	Robbery	Murder
1966	—	—	28.5	1.1
1967	103.0	6.2	—	—
1970	172.0	7.9	54.6	2.0
1974	209.0	9.8	75.5	2.4
1978	191.0	9.0	83.7	2.6
1981	250.6	9.8	108.6	2.6

Sources: U.S. Bureau of the Census, 1967–1982–83, *Statistical abstract of the United States* (various editions), Washington, D.C.: Statistics Canada, 1967–1981, *Crime and traffic enforcement statistics,* Cat. No. 85-205, Ottawa.

taking or attempting to take something of value from a person by force or threat of force. People are robbed; dwellings and other buildings are broken into, or burglarized. The instrument of violence in robbery may be a knife, a club, or a handgun. Some robbers use brute strength alone.

Murder is willful felonious homicide; it is the taking of the life of another human being. There are several categories and degrees of murder, depending on the criminal's level of premeditation and intent. Thomas and Hepburn (1983: 267) and Jayewardene (1980) note that males are more likely than females to be murdered and that, in the United States, blacks are disproportionately numbered as both victims and offenders in homicide cases. Indeed, most homicide is intraracial; blacks kill blacks, and whites kill whites. Furthermore, murderers and victims tend to be in the same age category.

Since there are wide differences between Canadian and American rates (see Table 17.2), it may be concluded that, when it comes to robbery and murder, the United States is more prone to violence than Canada (for further evidence, see Hagan, 1984: 48–55). Although there was a dip in the U.S. rates in the mid-1970s, the general trend in robbery and murder rates in North America, as measured by police records, is upward. Canada's murder rate, since 1978, is the only exception to this trend (see Table 17.3).

Ferracuti and Newman's (1974: 194–195) analysis of international crime statistics indicates that even the United States is less violence-prone than some other societies. Out of sixty-nine countries it ranked twentieth and nineteenth from the top in murder and robbery rates, respectively.[2] Burma, the Congo, and Ethiopia had the highest murder rates, while Bermuda, Burma, and Israel had the highest rates of robbery.

Drug Offenses Nonmedical drug use takes a multitude of forms. The most celebrated or infamous drug, depending on one's point of view, is *cannabis* (marijuana, ganga, hashish, bhang). It is by far the most widely consumed illegal drug in North America. When taken for recreational purposes, *cocaine* and *opium,* including its derivatives morphine, heroin, and codeine, are the most socially disdained drugs. Unlike the use of cannabis, the continual use of cocaine and opium eventually results in severe addiction.

A comparison of the entries in Table 17.4 reveals a higher prevalence of marijuana use in Canada than in the United States. But illegal use of opium, its derivatives, and cocaine is noticeably greater in the United States than in Can-

[2]Ferracuti and Newman also present Canadian rates, but they differ from those available in the sources from which Tables 17.1 and 17.2 were constructed.

ada. The ratio of the number of opiate addicts in the United States to the number in Canada approximates the ratio of its use; the ratio is about four to one (Ball, 1979: 368).

Smoking cannabis exemplifies especially well the social side of illegal drug consumption. Howard S. Becker (1963: 41–58) points out that the technique of smoking a marijuana cigarette is learned from experienced users. These people tell the novice how to inhale the "joint's" smoke, what effects to look for, and what is pleasurable about the effects. Cannabis is typically smoked in small groups of friends, much as other people drink cocktails with associates (Goode: 1969; Sorfleet, 1976).

Novices somehow meet people who have cannabis and who will persuade them to try it. In the days when possession of cannabis was limited to jazz musicians, jazz buffs, writers, and painters, one needed special connections to acquire marijuana and to learn how to use it. Now, however, marijuana is widely available. It grows wild in fields and is efficiently trafficked by "pushers," who are in touch with the users. Almost anyone, regardless of age, sex, social class, or geographic location, can acquire the drug and find someone who knows how to use it. Correspondingly, the penalties meted out for simple possession have tended to be lighter in recent years than earlier (note the relative nature of what is deviant). Yet, in 1982, only ten states had actually decriminalized (punish with fines only) simple possession, while in all of Canada this offense is punishable by at least six months in prison. Thus, consuming cannabis is largely an illegal deviant activity and therefore one to be pursued cautiously:

> Most regular users, however, particularly those who live with their parents or have conventional jobs, are probably anxious about being publicly identified as cannabis users. Concealment of their use, not only from the police but from anyone else who may censure them, is a matter of continual concern. The risk of such disclosure is most often controlled through the compartmentalization of the user's daily activities so that cannabis use is reserved for those settings where potentially disapproving nonusers are unlikely to intrude. (Commission of Inquiry into the Nonmedical Use of Drugs, 1972: 192)

Prostitution There perhaps is a good case for identifying prostitution as the world's oldest occupation. The selling of sexual relations out of wedlock dates from the beginning of the human race. The act of prostitution is not itself illegal in Canada, although keeping a common bawdy house (being a madam), procuring or pandering or soliciting trade for a prostitute, and pimping or providing prostitutes for those who request their services are all federal crimes in Canada. The legal picture in the United States is more complicated, since much of the routine regulation of prostitution is left to the state legislatures.

In the states, except for fifteen of Nevada's seventeen counties, the very act of prostitution is illegal. Likewise, procuring, operating a brothel, and pimping are often proscribed (Rich, 1979: 94). Gagnon (1974: 259) reports that these laws apply only to the female in a liaison, with the exception of eight states where the customer, or "john," is also liable to arrest. Male prostitution (homosexual and heterosex-

Table 17.4 ARRESTS FOR USE OF DRUGS IN CANADA AND THE UNITED STATES

	United States (1980)		Canada (1981)	
	Number of arrests	Rate per 100,000 population	Number of arrests	Rate per 100,000 population
Opiates and cocaine	68,100	30.9	11,773	11.4
Marijuana	405,600	183.9	51,818	271.8

Sources: Crime in the United States, 1980, Washington, D.C.: U.S. Federal Bureau of Investigation; *Crime and traffic enforcement statistics,* Cat. No. 85-205, 1981, Ottawa: Statistics Canada.

Getting Connected and Surviving as a Street Transient

Recruiting Networks: "Getting Connected"

To the outsider, the street community appears to involve an increasing isolation and deviation from societal values. To the "street kid," however, getting connected and staying connected are fundamental processes of "survival." As we learn from their accounts (file S9; file S10), the most basic communal characteristic is invariably expressed in terms of survival activities—"making it on the street scene" (field notes, 24 June 1981).

Clearly, life on the streets is trouble laden. Were it not for the many difficulties on the street, it would not be necessary to immediately seek the aid of others. Young migrants to large urban centres quickly discover what help is available in and out of trouble. Given their limited work experience, even in unskilled jobs, and their limited education, street kids must find quick ways to feed, house, and clothe themselves while at the same time avoiding official detection. They have available to them various indispensable structures for attaching themselves to the street. From the outset, the newcomer is typically supplied with a set of interpersonal linkages usually with similarly circumstanced others who help manage the transition. These networks serve as mediating structures in facilitating the "adjustment" to new conditions. . . .

Staying Connected

As with many other adolescent friendship patterns, recruitment to street life occurs from a variety of social categories. Homophily remains relatively unimportant as a basis for interaction. Although street networks tend to be differentiated, specialized and segregated, there are numerous overlapping activities with considerable cross-cutting links. One such activity on which the street places a high premium —hustling—involves a multiplicity of ties. Briefly, hustling is a comprehensive term denoting many methods of securing a meagre subsistence for some; and a measure of financial independence for others. These activities may include gambling, theft, burglary or robbery. But on the street, hustling refers usually to public order offences, notably sexual procurement—solicitation, the purveying of light drugs, or simply panhandling. According to Carmichael, these informal income opportunities are based on a criminal's

> loosely structured sub rosa network comprised of local and migrant criminals flanked on one side by professionals and more organized criminals, and on the other side by essentially pre-criminal youths who are only minimally involved in crime.

Many of these lightweight street hustlers drift into and identify with illicit activities for the express purpose of acquiring money or favours. They remain fairly marginal not only to conventional life-styles but also to criminal careers. Basic to hustling are the processes of locating targets, promoting investments and developing contacts. Although the life-style appears individualistic in orientation, involvements with the support from certain links are crucial. Within this "shadow system of values", ties are essential in learning the ropes, "taking the edge" and in developing a repertoire of manipulative techniques.

Many young transients have few assets to exploit. It is not surprising that one of them is catering to the sexual tastes of others. In return, they are provided with food, a place to sleep, drugs, money and even love. As one hustler described

> They'd hustle for anything, maybe just some sniff—like a bottle of glue or nail polish . . . maybe money or drugs. In the winter they'd go with guys just so they'd let them sleep in the cars.

The most common forms of street prostitution involve females to males, and males to males. Within these sexual marketplaces the granting of sexual access on a realtively indiscriminate basis for repayment is made without obligation or commitment. Many of these activities lack a cohesive organization and do not have direct connections with organized crime. Young gay hustlers usually connect with older men, especially those from another community, who do not have time to establish contacts. These hustlers are chosen, among other reasons, for their youthfulness and for the fact that they protect the identity of their clients. Gay hustlers, however, enjoy a low status in the gay community and are often deprecated even by those who use them.

Violence, robbery, extortion and blackmail are associated with a few hustlers, known generally as rough trade. Those in this trade are defiantly straight and deny vehemently any enjoyment of these acts. Instead they may brag about luring a "trick" into some alley or his residence and then turn on him with a couple of buddies lying in wait to help assault him and relieve him of his wallet and watch.

Interestingly, hustling whether in the form of panhandling, prostitution, or drug dealing provides a source of revenue for a network of persons involved in the hustler's role set. Successful hustlers frequently share their earnings with those with whom they happen to "hang together." As one sixteen year old, Lee, reported (S9):

> The things I do are trying to help my street friends—other kids I go out at night with. My friends, in my head, are first all the time. I help them—they help me especially when I'm in a jam with the cops. I support about two or three, maybe four.

This network of friends is involved in exchanging skills and capital. Despite the absence of gangs or structured groups, drugs, accommodation, clothing, etc., will often be shared.

SOURCE: Livy A. Visano. Tramps, tricks, and troubles: Street transients and their controls. In *Deviant designations: Crime, law, and deviance in Canada,* Thomas Fleming and L. A. Visano, eds., pp. 215–256. Toronto: Butterworth, 1983.

ual) is presently illegal in forty-five states (Rich, 1979: 94–95), while in Canada the law applies only to females. Bell (1976: 230) holds that the homosexual variant of male prostitution (by far the most common) is more prevalent in the United States today than ever before.

In general, however, the number of prostitutes and the number of acts of prostitution in North America have stabilized in the past two decades (Esselstyn, 1968: 127; Statistics Canada, 1980a: 158). Local public "scares" and occasional police "crackdowns" do little to alter this pattern in a permanent way. Likewise, the rising rate of arrest, which increased from 1971 to 1980 in the United States by 79.9 percent (Federal Bureau of Investigation, 1980: 193) has had negligible impact on the rate of prostitution.[3]

Today, there are six types of prostitutes: the streetwalker, the bar prostitute, the massage parlor worker, the brothel prostitute, the call girl, and the escort girl. Their life-styles vary, in good part in relation to their likelihood of being arrested by the police. Streetwalkers especially, but also bar prostitutes, ply their trade publicly and therefore are always faced with the possibility that they are being observed by an officer from the local morals squad. The prostitute in the massage parlor has the advantage of working in a legitimate establishment where she can screen customers who ask for services such as masturbation, fellatio, and sexual intercourse. Those who work in bawdy houses, who are available as call girls, or who serve as escorts also can check out their customers. Bawdy houses, or houses of prostitution, are now rare in North America. They are found mostly in the southern United States and Nevada.

Using exploratory methods, a number of sociologists have studied the everyday life of the North American prostitute (e.g., Symanski, 1981; Davis, 1971; Copeland and MacDonald, 1971; Prus and Irini, 1980). These studies suggest that prostitutes in general, and the streetwalker in particular, must deal with the constant threat of public censure, possible arrest, venereal disease, and customer exploitation (including violence). The streetwalker and the bar prostitute are partly protected from exploitation by pimps, who, in return, demand the woman's loyalty and a share of her earnings.

Of the various types of prostitutes, the streetwalker is the most vulnerable to violence and harrassment.

Call girls and escorts are the most sophisticated and comely of the six types. Consequently, they serve a higher class of customer. These women mingle in the crowds at business and professional conventions; they frequent the lobbies and bars of respectable hotels and restaurants. They also have an answering service.

[3]By contrast, the number of Canadians "charged" with prostitution fell between 1971 and 1981 by 10.2 percent (Information Canada, 1971: 13; Statistics Canada, 1981f. cat. no. 85–205, Table 2.

Men desiring their company can obtain the number of the answering service from intermediaries such as bellhops, desk clerks, bartenders, taxi drivers, and former customers. Call girls and escorts operate out of public view, but they are not immune to occasional violence, requests for distasteful sexual services, and venereal disease. A call girl's "bouncer" protects her from violence and distasteful requests when she works at a customer's residence or in his hotel room (Rich, 1979: 102).

Noncriminal Deviance

The three examples of deviance considered in this section are treated as noncriminal. They are outside the law; there is neither legal prohibition nor legal assent. In actuality, legal control of North American homosexuality and alcoholism and drunkenness is more complicated than this. Mental disorder can also lead to legal entanglements, although it is clearly no violation of the law to be afflicted with mental illness. We turn first to homosexuality.

Homosexuality The laws pertaining to homosexuality are comparatively clear-cut in Canada. Present Canadian laws follow the recommendations of Britain's Wolfenden Committee (Committee on Homosexual Offenses and Prostitution, 1957), which declared that the law should stay out of the private lives of individuals and refrain from enforcing any particular pattern of behavior. In 1968, sexual activities conducted in private between husband and wife or between two consenting adults twenty-one years of age or older were excepted from the Criminal Code of Canada.

According to Pursley (1977: 115), thirteen American states have taken a similar route since 1961. Despite a National Institute of Mental Health task force report (Livingood, 1972) which agreed with the Wolfenden Committee, homosexual acts between willing partners are still illegal in most jurisdictions in the United States.

Male and female homosexuality increased in the 1920s when the general level of sexual freedom rose in North America (Tripp, 1975: 254). A number of surveys plus the sophisticated research of Alfred Kinsey and his associates (1948; 1953) have led to the estimate that roughly one in twenty men and women are homosexual, a ratio that has persisted since the changes of the 1920s (Tripp, 1975: 254).

Whatever their standing in law, homosexuals must still face an unfavorable public sentiment toward their sexual proclivities. Notwithstanding this opposition, they have, in the past fifteen years or so, begun to organize themselves into interest groups (e.g., the Mattachine Society, Daughters of Bilitis), political lobbies (e.g., North American Conference of Homosexual Organizations), churches (Metropolitan Community Churches), and counseling agencies to constitute what Laud Humphreys (1972) says is a social movement (see Chapter 21).

All this activity has encouraged many homosexuals to "come out of the closet" and make public their deviant sexual orientation. Others, however, are unable to bear the tension of such a disclosure and therefore choose to hide their homosexuality. They usually succeed at "passing" (Goffman, 1963: 73–91); Sawchuk, 1974: 237–239) in everyday life as heterosexual, while searching for clandestine homosexual liaisons in parks, gay bars, "tearooms" (public rest rooms), public baths, and city streets. Homosexual prostitutes frequent these locations to provide services for those unable to find them on their own (Reiss, 1961).

How secretive and cautious a person must be to satisfy homosexual desires depends to some extent on where the individual lives. Certain cities are known for their tolerance of homosexuals. In North America, the most celebrated of these is San Francisco and its "culture of civility" (Becker and Horowitz, 1970). New York has a similar reputation. Canadian homosexuals gravitate to their Mecca in Toronto (Johnson, 1971; Foster and Murray, 1972). In cities such as Toronto and San Francisco, homosexuality can be a way of life for those who want to spend their waking (and sleeping) hours in the company of like-minded men or women. In these cities, homosexuals form exclusive subcultures (see Chapter 8) consisting of associates in leisure, work, religion, politics, business, marriage (gay marriages), and personal service.

Alcoholism and Drunkenness Henry Black (1968: 587) defines a drunk as an individual whose judgment and control are substantially impaired because he or she is so thoroughly under the influence of alcohol. Drunkenness is a temporary state, whereas *alcoholism* is an addiction, a continuous dependence on drink. The alcoholic uses alcohol to excess. Drunkenness per se is not a crime in Canada or in twenty-five of the states (Rich, 1979: 194). In these jurisdictions, however, drunks who create a disturbance are sometimes charged with disorderly conduct. Police in some of the twenty-five states can also arrest drunken individuals for vagrancy or for loitering.

The American Uniform Alcoholism and Intoxication Treatment Act (1971) indicates that the United States is heading in the same direction as Canada. Like Canada, the United States is decriminalizing drunkenness and emphasizing treatment in place of punishment. As of 1976, 50 percent of the states have adopted this act, while twelve others have adopted parts of it (Rich, 1979: 193–194). The realization is growing in Canada, the United States, and Great Britain that alcoholism is a major social problem in need of enlightened government action (see *First Special Report to the U.S. Congress on Alcohol and Health,* 1972; Health Care and Welfare Canada, 1976; Special Committee of the Royal College of Psychiatrists, 1979). These official reports reflect the trend in society toward universal approval of social drinking and sympathy for those unable to handle alcohol on a social level (Linsky, 1970).

According to data gathered in 1976, a typical American drinks nearly 8 liters of absolute alcohol annually compared with the 8.5 liters drunk annually by a typical Canadian. The consumption of alcohol is greater in France than in any other country—16 liters per person annually. Norwegians have the lowest rate, with an annual consumption rate of about 4.3 liters per person (Statistics Canada, 1980a: 53). Rates of consumption in both Canada and the United States have been rising since 1960. Still, there are differences between the two countries, for the rates of death caused by cirrhosis of the liver in Canada and the United States diverge somewhat; cirrhosis is the usual measure of alcoholism. The rates were 13.5 deaths per 100,000 population in the United States (1980) and 12.1 deaths per 100,000 population in Canada (1978) (U.S. Bureau of the Census, 1984: 78; United Nations, 1983: 396). The difference is minor.

The life-styles of individual alcoholics can be vastly different. There are the habitués of our many urban skid rows, for many of whom drinking is a way of life and a chosen form of leisure. Skid-row drunks cycle in and out of local jails in what is known as the *revolving-door* pattern of developing alcoholic dependence; the skid-row drunk "dries out" during thirty to ninety days of incarceration and then returns to the street to start the cycle again (Giffen, 1966; Spradley, 1970). Other alcoholics must somehow try to conceal their habit while holding a

The revolving door is a way of life for some urban dwellers.

job and interacting with their families, ultimately an impossible goal. Until the problem obtrudes on the lives of others, these people feed their addiction by furtive nips from hidden supplies and by heavy drinking at public functions.

Sociologists have examined the effects of alcoholics on family roles. Joan Jackson (1954), after interviewing the wives of the members of an Alcoholic Anonymous group in Seattle, concluded that the typical family goes through seven stages of adjustment to the father's alcoholism. First (1), drinking becomes excessive. Then (2) the father's family becomes increasingly isolated from him in its attempts to alter his habit. To relieve tension, (3) the family eventually abandons its goal of controlling the father's drinking and (4) shifts family responsibility from him to the mother. This may result in (5) separation from the father and (6) subsequent reorganization of the family. In the final stage (7), the family reorganizes again, this time around the father, who has achieved sobriety (in Jackson's sample through Alcoholics Anonymous).

Margaret Cork's (1969) study in metropolitan Toronto shows how children suffer during the struggle with a father's alcoholism. The children say that everyone is perpetually angry at home, that those in the family never do things as a family in the way that their peers do, that they are frightened when one of their parents is drunk, and that, in the case of an alcoholic mother, they have to be their own mother.

Mental Disorder Defining mental disorder in theory and applying this definition to actual cases is still more an art than a science. Defining mental disorder is one of the best examples of the relativist approach to defining a form of deviance. Psychiatrists assume that mental patients have symptoms, as other medical patients do, and that these symptoms enable the trained professional to diagnose individuals as suffering from certain psychological disorders, such as acute schizophrenic episode, involutional melancholia, or anxiety neurosis. Several sociologists and psychologists have evidence suggesting the identification of mental disorder is more complicated than many psychiatrists are willing to admit.

In a field experiment, Rosenhan (1973: 251) demonstrated that the symptoms of mental disease when incorporated into psychiatric diagnoses "are in the minds of the observers and not valid summaries of characteristics displayed by the observed." After reviewing several studies, Scheff (1975) concludes that psychiatrists responsible for admitting patients to mental hospitals rely heavily on family and community definitions of an individual as psychologically unsound. Thomas Szasz, who is a psychiatrist, has gone a step further and suggested that "to understand institutional psychiatry (or the mental health movement), we must study psychiatrists, not mental patients" (Szasz, 1970: 98n).[4]

Scheff, however, goes even beyond Szasz. If psychiatrists take family and community definitions into account when diagnosing mental disorder, then perhaps we should be studying how patients' friends, relatives, and workmates see their curious actions. As Scheff (1975: 7) points out, identifying mental disorder is also problematic for friends and relatives:

> If people reacting to an offense exhaust the conventional categories that might define it (e.g., theft, prostitution, and drunkenness), yet are certain that an offense has been committed, they may resort to this residual category. In earlier societies, the residual category was witchcraft, spirit possession, or possession by the devil; today, it is mental illness. The symptoms of mental illness are, therefore, violations of residual rules.

Mental disorder as a violation of residual rules is a commonsense definition of this kind of deviance. People judge their behavior and that

[4]Institutional psychiatry refers to psychiatric intervention imposed on people by others to the point where clients or "patients" lose control over their relationship with the professional expert.

of others by these rules. Thus, it is reasonable, when estimating the prevalence of mental disorder, to ask people how they define their own actions. By means of such self-report surveys, researchers have concluded that about one-fourth of the North American population is impaired by psychological disorders (Hagan, 1984: 53).

The afflicted individual's close friends and relatives and the sympathetic professional practitioners who work with him or her usually prefer to describe and treat that person as "sick" or "ill" rather than as "crazy" (i.e., deviant). The important finding coming out of sociological research is that, however the individual is subsequently defined (defined sympathetically as "ill" or pejoratively as "crazy"), certain of his or her thoughts and actions are defined early on as so strikingly different and unsettling that they constitute a problem needing immediate attention. It is the way the problem is discovered and defined initially that justifies the sociological classification of mental disorder as a type of deviance.

The Mental Patient's Career The deviant career and life-style of the mental patient have also attracted considerable sociological attention. Goffman (1961), Cameron (1974), and others who have studied the careers of mental patients note that in the "prepatient phase" of this career, their closest friends or relatives or both collude with psychiatrists and legal authorities to persuade them to submit to a psychological examination. This is the first step in the process of committing these people to a hospital for the mentally ill or other treatment facility. This benign pressure ("it's for his own good") is necessary because few people voluntarily seek such treatment.

Once institutionalized, mental patients are given various amounts of medication and psychotherapy. Moreover, they soon discover that they are expected to act as if they belong in the hospital (Rosenhan, 1973). The patients are expected to manifest the stereotyped symptoms of their deviance such as strange movements, incoherent talk, irrational thoughts and actions, or delusions about identity ("I'm Jesus Christ"). Unfortunately, for all concerned, which behaviors and thoughts are truly symptomatic and which are not is open to considerable interpretation.

Once released from the mental hospital, former inmates quickly learn, in many subtle ways, that their associates are unwilling to forget that they were once treated for psychological problems. Indeed, the ex-patients' friends and relatives relate to them as if they were still sick (Scheff, 1984: 66–67; D'Arcy and Brockman, 1977). For example, when an ex-patient does something a member of the family thinks is strange (however reasonable the act might be when explained by the ex-patient), the tendency is to view it as a manifestation of the *remittent* mental illness. Carlton Brown (1974) describes how the stigma of being a mental patient contributes to the deterioration of some of his social and professional relationships in the community.

EXPLANATIONS OF DEVIANCE

We have considered six representative forms of criminal and noncriminal deviance. Neither sociology nor the other social sciences has a theory fully explaining these life-styles and patterns of action. But sociology does offer several explanations of aspects of these and other forms of deviance. Four such explanations are outlined here: differential association, anomie and opportunity, labeling and societal reaction, and conflict.

Differential Association

Edwin H. Sutherland first set forth his differential association theory of crime in the 1939 edition of *Principles of Criminology.* That statement differs little from the contemporary version written by Sutherland and Cressey (1978: 80–82). The theory consists of nine propositions, which describe the complicated pattern of interaction Sutherland called *differential association.* (1) People learn how to engage in crime. (2) This learning comes about through interaction with others who have already learned criminal ways. (3) The learning occurs in small, face-to-face groups. (4) What is learned is criminal technique (e.g., how to open a safe), motives, attitudes, and rationalizations. (5) Among criminals one important learned attitude is a disregard for the community's legal code. (6) One acquires this attitude by differentially associating with those who hold it and failing to associate with those who do not. (7) Differential associations with criminals and noncriminals vary in frequency, duration, priority, and intensity. (8) Learning criminal behavior through differential association rests on the same principles as learning any other kind of behavior. (9) Criminal behavior is a response to the same cultural needs and values as noncriminal behavior. For instance, one man steals to acquire money for a new suit of clothes, while another works as a carpenter to reach the same goal. Consequently, tying societal needs and values to crime fails to explain it.

Based on what we know about the etiology of crime, Sutherland's theory offers a valuable, albeit partial, explanation of theft, burglary, prostitution, and use of marijuana. And differential association is often a major antecedent in the use of addictive drugs, in the pursuit of homosexual relations, and in succumbing to alcoholism. It may even play a casual role in some mental disorders. But many other factors are also needed to explain these latter four forms, which dilute the importance of differential associations.

Anomie and Opportunity

The common English translation of the French word *anomie* is normlessness. Emile Durkheim gave fullest expression to this idea in his landmark study of suicide (Durkheim, 1951). Anomie suicide, which is one of three types examined by Durkheim, "results from man's activity's lacking regulation and his consequent sufferings" (1951: 258). This lack of regulation —i.e., normlessness—is a condition of society to which some of its members respond in the extreme by taking their lives.

Durkheim's theory was designed to explain one form of deviance. It was originally published in 1897. More than fifty years later, in the first edition of *Social Theory and Social Structure,* Robert K. Merton recast his ideas in a general theory of deviance. Revisions to the theory were made in a later edition; the discussion here is based on the later edition (Merton, 1957b: Chapters 4 and 5).

Merton's theory of anomie is a functionalist approach to deviance. According to his theory, people become deviant when the means for meeting their goals (success) are unavailable to them. That is, there is a malintegration of the goals and means. In some instances, training and educational opportunities are unavailable to individuals, who then resort to deviance. These people are not always from the lower class. Rather, they are people who feel that the jobs they hold do little to help them reach their goals in life. Thus, they turn to crime, to alcohol, or to radical politics or religion.

The malintegration of the goals and means—in Merton's terms, of culture and social structure—is called *anomie* (a meaning somewhat different from Durkheim's). Members of anomic society try to adapt to this unsettling condition. Merton developed a typology of five adaptive modes, arguing that four of them are deviant because they reject either the standard success goals or the standard institutionalized means or both. Modes II through V in Table 17.5 are deviant adaptations.

Deviant Adaptations Innovation (mode II) occurs when people accept society's success goals but reject the means for reaching them. The preceding illustration of Sutherland's ninth proposition also exemplifies innovation. In ritu-

Table 17.5 MODES OF INDIVIDUAL ADAPTATION[a]

Modes of adaptation	Cultural goals	Institutionalized means
I. Conformity	+	+
II. Innovation	+	−
III. Ritualism	−	+
IV. Retreatism	−	−
V. Rebellion	±	±

Source: Adapted from R.K. Merton. *Social theory and social structure,* rev. ed., p. 140. Glencoe, Ill: Free Press, 1957.

[a] +, Acceptance; −, rejection; ±, rejection followed by acceptance of new goals and means.

alism (mode III) individuals scale down their personal success goals, thereby rejecting those normally pursued by people like themselves. Meanwhile, they continue to strive for their reduced goals via socially acceptable means. The middle-aged bureaucrat who discards all thought of advancement (a goal many middle-aged bureaucrats have) because he anticipates a demotion may seek only to obviate the feared eventuality.

Retreatist deviants (mode IV) reject both goals and means by turning to alcohol, drugs, life on skid row, or devotion to a deviant religion (e.g., the Hare Krishna Movement, the "Moonies"). Finally, one may adapt to anomie by rebelling (mode V); new goals and means supplant the rejected ones. Communalists who wander off to the wilderness to form a new society exemplify this mode, as do revolutionaries whose intention is to replace the existing government with a "better" one of their own.

Opportunity Merton's theory sparked a tremendous amount of research and theorizing on deviant behavior (see Clinard, 1964), which helped extend, revise, and define the original statement. Richard Cloward (1959) made one of the extensions; he noticed that Merton wrote only about legitimate institutionalized means. But, to engage in deviance, one needs access to illegitimate means, which Cloward said are of two types: *learning structures* and *opportunity structures.* Building on differential association theory, he pointed out that tomorrow's deviants must first make contact with practicing deviants, from whom they learn antisocial techniques. Moreover, they must find opportunities to express what they have learned.

Returning, for a moment, to our earlier example of the use of marijuana, we can observe how novices must have the opportunity to learn how to smoke the weed. Novices must find experienced users to learn from; from them they learn how to inhale the smoke from the "joint." Experienced users advise them to be on the lookout for informers and "narcs." To share "pot" with others, novices meet in secluded places where it is unlikely they will be detected. Smoking cannabis is a furtive, secretive practice in which one learns how to get "high."

Labeling and Societal Reaction

Though others have also contributed much to the development of the labeling perspective, Edwin Lemert and Howard S. Becker are the men most frequently associated with it. The theories of differential association and anomie assumed that deviance can be explained by factors associated with the deviants themselves; among such factors are learning, motivation, attitude, adaptation, and rejection of standard goals and means. Lemert and Becker departed dramatically from this line of thought when they asserted that deviance is created by society:

> Social groups create deviance by making the rules whose infraction constitutes deviance, and by applying those rules to particular people and *labeling* them as outsiders. . . . The deviant is one to whom that label has successfully been applied; deviant behavior is behavior that people so label. (Becker, 1963: 9).[5]

Since the rules (norms) are applied to some people and not others and since the application process is sometimes biased, some people re-

[5] Italics added.

main at large as "secret" deviants, while others go through life "falsely accused" of unsavory acts they never committed. To discover why only certain groups of people are labeled deviant, we must study those who make the rules they have violated and learn how those rules are unequally applied.

Those publicly labeled deviants are typically subjected to some sort of community or societal reaction to their misdeeds (Lemert, 1951: Chapter 3). Depending on the nature of the deviance, one or more of the following is the deviant's fate: imprisonment, ostracism, a fine, torture, surveillance, ridicule. All labeled deviants soon discover that they must cope with stigma as well.

Partly because of the effect of societal reactions, deviants have careers in the role they play. The stigma of the deviance itself plus the unpleasant experiences associated with some of the other reactions, or sanctions (e.g., imprisonment), engender further problems of interaction with agents of social control and with nondeviant members of the community. For example, some employers are unwilling to hire a known homosexual or ex-convict. Some people are reluctant to continue their friendship with a person discovered to be mentally disordered or alcoholic. Some deviants have difficulty finding a spouse or, if they already have one, avoiding divorce or separation. In short, there is a deviant career, which intersects with conventional careers in family, work, and leisure. This intersection may eventuate in commitment to or entrapment in the deviant career, for there is nowhere else to turn—the deviant is socially excluded from the conventional careers (Stebbins, 1971a).

Conflict

The analytic problem of power, order, and interest discussed in Chapter 1 reaches a welcome level of concreteness in the study of deviance. Over the years a number of criminologists have tried to adapt parts of the general conflict perspective to the particular area of crime. One of the most successful of these theoretical efforts is that of Vold and Bernard (1979: 288):

> The whole political process of law making, law breaking, and law enforcement directly reflects deep-seated and fundamental conflicts between interest groups and their more general struggles for the control of the police power of the state. Those who produce legislative majorities win control over the police power and dominate the policies that decide who is likely to be involved in violation of the law.

This statement is obviously compatible with labeling and societal reaction. Both explanations direct attention to those who make the rules rather than to the deviants. And, while the conflict model expresses the idea more succinctly, both labeling and conflict underscore the arbitrariness inherent in making rules and identifying the violators of the rules.

Building on the works of Vold and others, Richard Quinney (1970: 15–24) has fashioned a conflict theory of crime resting on the principle of social reality. The theory has six propositions: (1) Certain human actions are defined as crimes by societal agents authorized to make such judgments. (2) The definitions of the agents describe behavior conflicting with the interests of groups who have the power to make laws. (3) These groups are also powerful enough to apply the laws which protect their interests; the groups protect themselves by means of law enforcement and the administration of justice. (4) The various segments of complex industrial societies develop distinctive patterns of behavior. Some segments have patterns of behavior which are poorly represented or wholly unrepresented. The actions of these segments are more likely to be defined as crime than are the actions of the segments which enact the laws and enforce them. (5) The definitions of crime are communicated in many ways to the different segments of society. In other words, cultural conceptions of crime emerge from the images of crime in the mass media and interpersonal relations. (6) The definitions of crime, their applications, the criminal behavior patterns, and the communicated concepts of crime, together constitute the *social reality of crime.* This reality is fluid; it is subject to constant change. It "is constantly being constructed in society."

IS DEVIANCE NECESSARY?

One of the defining criteria of a social institution is its provision of a solution to a major problem of collective living (see Chapter 9). An important component of this solution is the establishing of norms requiring some kinds of behavior and prohibiting other kinds. In the terminology of this chapter, rules (i.e., norms) either emerge or are enacted to guide human activities and interpersonal relations in the problematic sphere.

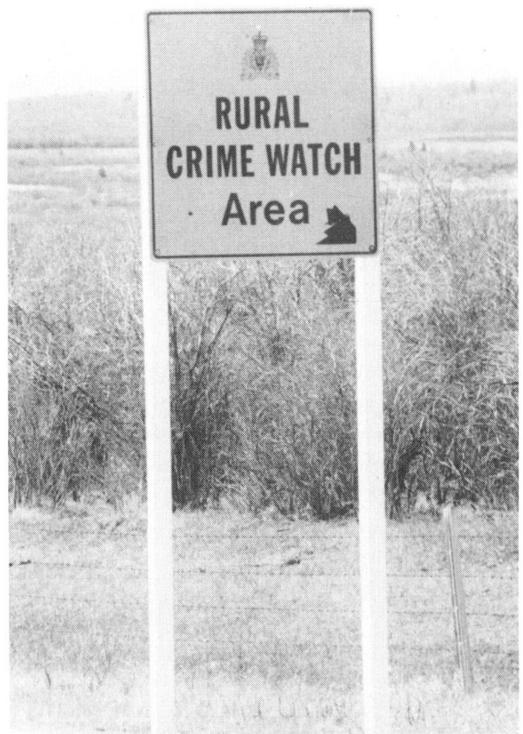

Crime is a social reality in this rural neighborhood.

Different Solutions

What was said in this chapter about rules can also be said about these solutions—they are arbitrary. Objectively speaking, other strategies are possible. That different solutions to the same problem are found in societies outside Canada, and occasionally in more than one community within Canada, substantiates this observation. The possibility of adopting a different solution is soon recognized by those in the community who are least committed to the prevailing one. The next logical step for them is to seize the initiative and to explore new options more compatible with their interests. Thus, there is always a sociological side to morality: exploration or straying from the accepted ways of meeting a particular recurrent problem is said to be "deviant" or "wrong," whereas abiding by those ways is "conforming" or "right."

It follows that since the moral, institutional solutions to the problems of community survival are arbitrary, some deviance from them is *inevitable:*

> Now there is no society known where a more or less developed criminality is not found under different forms. No people exists whose morality is not daily infringed upon. We must therefore call crime necessary and declare that it cannot be nonexistent, that the fundamental

A different solution to the institutional problem of knowledge.

conditions of social organization, as they are understood, logically imply it. Consequently, it is normal. (Durkheim, 1951: 362; original French edition published in 1897)

Deviance is stimulated further by the biological and psychological variation in people, since some of them fit more comfortably within the dominant normative structure than others. And today another force fans the flames of deviant behavior; as more communities in North America are undergoing rapid social change, institutionalized survival strategies quickly become obsolete.

In the end, if human deviance is inevitable, it is also *irradicable.* Conforming community members must learn to live with what is for many of them a cruel reality of omnipresent aberrant behavior, which necessarily contains the possibility of destroying their way of life. It should be clear from this chapter and the preceding one that such behavior is more than merely disgusting or annoying. Swearing in polite company, spitting on the sidewalk, or playing loud music in an apartment building are "improprieties" or eccentric norm violations rather than immoral acts; the first two have few, if any, of the long-range consequences the third is thought to have. And even immoral acts have been shown to have positive consequences under certain conditions (see page 28). Deviance is a more seriously regarded form of norm violation. It is behavior formally or informally labeled (i.e., interpreted) by members of the community as a violation of its norms of *morality.*

OUTLINE AND SUMMARY

I. Introduction
Until the early 1950s, most sociologists never questioned the absolutist definition of deviance, which is simply that deviance is a violation of society's moral rules. This commonsense meaning is still generally accepted. But sociologists now favor the relativist definition: the identification of and reaction to deviance requires interpretation by one person of another person's deed.

II. Social Differentation
In the view of sociologists, social differentiation is in many ways the same kind of process as *social control.* One outcome of social differentiation is the complex of roles (and associated statuses) comprising a society's institutions. Another outcome is the complex of roles intersecting the institutions. Social differentiation is a broader process than the division of labor.

III. Differentiating Deviants
Deviance is evidence that social-control efforts have failed. In commonsense terms, *deviance* is a breach of society's moral rules. A definition of deviance hinges on one person's interpretation of another person's deeds. When it comes to defining deviants, sociologists are relativists rather than absolutists.

IV. Norm Violations
Crime is a special subclass of deviance. A criminal code helps us differentiate a deviant act from a nondeviant act. Norms add a degree of simplicity and objectivity to the handling of social delicts. Yet, even the norms are susceptible to relativistic interpretations. Most deviants are not criminal. There are deviant roles that fall beyond the purview of the law (nudism, gambling, homosexualism). The sociological definition of deviance contrasts somewhat with the commonsense definition. To the sociologist, *deviance* is an act judged as in violation of the moral norms of a community by those who are powerful enough to make this judgment stick.

V. Deviant Behavior
Examples of criminal deviance are theft, burglary, robbery, murder, drug offenses, and prostitution. The rates of criminal deviance tend to vary from country to country. Examples of noncriminal deviance are homosexuality, alcoholism, and mental illness.

A. Criminal Deviance
Official crime rates are compiled

monthly in Canada and the United States. A *crime rate* is the number of offenses of a particular kind recorded by the police. The crime rate is not an accurate measure of criminality because some crimes are never reported. Some crimes are never detected.

1. Property Offenses
   Theft and *break and enter* are property offenses. *Theft* is an act of stealing. It is distinguished from *break and enter*, or burglarizing the dwelling of another person to steal or attempt to steal something or to engage in some felonious act.
2. Violent Crimes
   Robbery and *murder* are violent crimes. *Robbery* is the act of taking or attempting to take something of value from a person by force or threat of force. *Murder* is willful felonious *homicide,* or the taking of the life of another human being.
3. Drug Offenses
   Nonmedical drug use comes in a multitude of forms. The most infamous drug, depending on one's point of view, is *cannabis* (marijuana, ganga, hashish, bhang). Among other drugs are *amphetamines* and *hallucinogens.* There is a greater use of marijuana in Canada than in the United States. The illegal use of opium, its derivatives, and cocaine is greater in the United States than in Canada.
4. Prostitution
   The act of prostitution is not itself illegal in Canada, although keeping a common bawdy house, procuring or pandering, and pimping are all federal crimes. The act of prostitution is illegal in the United States, except for fifteen of Nevada's seventeen counties. In general, the number of prostitutes and the number of acts of prostitution in North America have stabilized in the past two decades. There are six types of prostitutes: the streetwalker, the bar prostitute, the massage parlor worker, the brothel prostitute, the call girl, and the escort girl.

B. Noncriminal Deviance
Three examples of noncriminal deviance are homosexuality, alcoholism, and mental illness.

1. Homosexuality
   Homosexuality is a noncriminal form of deviance in Canada and thirteen states. Since the 1920s, the ratio of homosexuals to heterosexuals in North America has been estimated to be holding steady at about one to twenty. Homosexuals face a hostile public. The gay movement of the past fifteen years has encouraged many homosexuals "to come out of the closet." Homosexuals have found some acceptance in cities such as Toronto, New York, and San Francisco.
2. Alcoholism and Drunkenness
   There is a strong trend in North America toward decriminalizing drunkenness as a crime in itself. This is undoubtedly a response to the increasing rate of consumption and approval of social drinking. Alcoholics are found in somewhat greater number in the United States than in Canada. Alcoholics vary in life-style from that of the skid-row denizen, who drinks openly, to that of the middle-class white-collar employee, who nips furtively until the habit is beyond concealment.
3. Mental Disorder
   Psychiatrists assume that mental patients have symptoms, as other medical patients do, and that these symptoms enable the trained professional to diagnose individuals as suffering from psychological disorders such as acute schizophrenic episode, involutional melancholia, or anxiety neurosis. Mental disorder as a violation of residual rules is a commonsense definition of this kind of deviance. People judge their

own behavior and that of others by these rules.

4. The Mental Patient's Career
Close friends or relatives or both collude with psychiatrists and legal authorities to persuade the mentally disturbed person to submit to a psychological examination. This is the first step in the process of committing the mental patient to a hospital. Once institutionalized, mental patients are given various amounts of medication and psychotherapy. Upon their release from the hospital, former patients quickly learn that their associates are unwilling to forget that they were once treated for mental illness. The ex-patients' friends and relatives relate to them as if they were still ill.

VI. Explanation of Deviance
Neither sociology nor the other social sciences have a theory fully explaining the deviant life-style and patterns of action. But sociology does offer four explanations: *differential association, anomie and opportunity, labeling and societal reaction,* and *conflict.*

A. Differential Association
Deviance is learned through selective interaction with other deviants.

B. Anomie and Opportunity
Deviance results from the malintegration of cultural success goals and institutionalized means of reaching the goals.

1. Deviant Adaptations
The adaptation which the deviant uses depends on the learning and opportunity structures available to him or her as an anomic person.

2. Opportunity
To engage in deviance, the wayward individual needs access to illegitimate means, which are of two types: *learning structures* and *opportunity structures.* Deviants must find opportunities to express what they have learned.

C. Labeling and Societal Reaction
The labeling perspective shifts attention to those who make and enforce the rules, thereby labeling some people as outstanding, and, by means of the strength of the subsequent societal reaction, forcing them into a deviant career.

D. Conflict
Conflict theory centers on the social reality of crime as it develops from the label of deviance and from criminal behavior patterns and communicated concepts of crime.

VII. Is Deviance Necessary?
The arbitrariness of moral rules noted by the labeling theorists and conflict theorists leads to the conclusion that other institutional solutions to major problems of collective living are objectively possible. It follows that deviance is then both inevitable and irradicable.

A. Different Solutions
Different solutions to a particular form of deviance are found in societies outside Canada and occasionally in more than one community within Canada. Given that the solutions are arbitrary, some deviance from them is inevitable.

FOR FURTHER READING AND STUDY

Bahr, H. M. 1973. *Skid row: An introduction to disaffiliation.* New York: Oxford University Press. A somewhat dated, but still excellent, review of the theories of and research about skid row. Though largely concerned with American skid rows, there are occasional references to those in Canada.

Conrad, P. and Schneider, J. W. 1980. *Deviance and medicalization: From badness to sickness.* St. Louis: Mosby. The authors explore the transformation in American society of the designations of certain forms of deviance from the earlier religious and criminal designations to the modern medical designations. Deviants are now often looked on as sick rather than immoral or bad.

Foster, M. and Murray, K. 1972. *A not so gay world.* Toronto: McClelland & Stewart. Two journalists travel from Vancouver to St. John's to gain, through observation and personal interviews, a sense of the life-styles of Canadian homosexuals.

Hagan, J. 1984. *The disreputable pleasures,* 2nd ed. Toronto: McGraw-Hill Ryerson. This is a textbook on the types of crime and other deviance and how they may be explained. Hagan compares Canada with the United States and other countries for which there are relevant data.

Platt, T. and Takagi, T., eds. 1982. *Crime and social justice.* Totowa, N.J.: Rowman & Littlefield. A collection of papers on the mainstream of new thinking in radical criminology.

Prus, R. and Sharper, C. R. D. 1977. *Road hustler: The career contingencies of professional card and dice hustlers.* Lexington, Mass.: Lexington Books. A participant observer and personal interview study of Canadian and American gamblers by a sociologist and a full-time hustler.

Rubington, E. and Weinberg, M. S., eds. 1981. *Deviance: An interactionist perspective,* 4th ed. New York: Macmillan. A collection of articles on the social aspects of deviance, the formal regulation of deviance, the various deviant subcultures, and the nature of the deviant identity.

Symanski, R. 1981. *The immoral landscape: Female prostitution in Western societies.* Toronto: Butterworths. Symanski synthesizes several different kinds of data including his own participant observation into a wide-ranging analysis of the many kinds of female prostitution.

Tripp, C. A. 1975. *The homosexual matrix.* New York: New American Library. At once a very readable, thorough, and scientifically impeccable account of the nature, origin, and consequences of homosexuality in modern industrial society.

KEY WORDS

anomie State of normlessness in a society; malintegration of cultural success goals and institutionalized means of reaching them.

break and entry Act of entering the dwelling of another person to steal or attempt to steal something.

burglary See break and entry.

crime Subclass of deviance in which a criminal law has been said to have been violated.

crime rate Number of offenses of a particular kind recorded by the police.

deviance Behavior judged as in violation of the moral norms of a community by those who are powerful enough to make this judgment stick.

deviant career Passage of an individual who has been labeled deviant through the period of time in which he or she is in the deviant role.

differential association Process by which individuals learn criminal behavior through interaction with others who define such behavior favorably and in isolation from those who define it unfavorably.

labeling Process by which some people are identified as deviant by other members of the community.

opportunity structures Opportunities to use illegitimate means to obtain cultural goals.

primary deviation Deviation which brings about little change in the individual's everyday routine and life-style.

robbery Act of taking or attempting to take something of value from a person by force or threat of force.

secondary deviance Deviant behavior which substantially modifies an individual's way of life.

social differentiation Broad social process in which people are distinguished from one another according to age, sex, deviant, ethnic, and social stratification roles.

theft Act of stealing.

chapter 18

Social Stratification

CHAPTER OUTLINE

INTRODUCTION

The idea of stratification appears to have made its way into sociology from geology. The geologist defines the term "stratification" as the arrangement of sedimentary rock in layers, or geological strata. The analogy is apt. *Social stratification* is the layering, or stratifying, of people along three dimensions: *wealth, prestige,* and *power.* People are ranked according to their statuses and roles in the community and the larger society. Over time individuals find themselves in a more or less homogeneous aggregate, or *stratum.* There are three types of homogeneous strata. The three types are known as *social classes, estates,* and *castes* (to be considered later).

Social stratification is the process of differen-

What dimension of social stratification is expressed by this picture?

tiation by which these three types of strata develop and maintain themselves. The hierarchic order of the strata is relatively stable. That is, it is *institutionalized,* or woven into the social structures of each institution of the society. Put otherwise, the hierarchic order is the society's *stratification system.*

Social stratification is broader than sex stratification and age stratification (Chapter 19). It also has greater scope than ethnic stratification (Chapter 20). In fact, the generic process of stratification is one of the most pervasive forms of social differentiation. This chapter concentrates almost exclusively on differentiation by wealth, prestige, and power; it also takes account of *social mobility,* or upward and downward movement within a system of stratification. All stratification systems give rise to inequality. But accompanying the inequality and differences in wealth, prestige, and power is the possibility of social mobility. How much social mobility comes into play, however, depends on the type of system being considered. We shall return to this topic in a subsequent section.

The system of stratification considered throughout most of this chapter is the one at the national level rather than those at the local level or the international level. Admittedly, this simplifies an extremely complex and as yet only partly understood interrelationship among these three levels—the national, local, international. The Canadian's image—and also the influence—of corporation executives, labor leaders, sports heroes, television personalities, motion picture stars, and arts celebrities hints at the ways these three levels are intertwined. Jet-set celebrities have local, national, and international ties.

Owners of multinational corporations (see Chapter 13) provide an example. They are powerful individuals whose decisions have something to say about the lives of workers and consumers across the world. Moreover, these owners are often able to influence relevant government policies in their own country (e.g., protective tariffs on competitive imports). The company presidents and other executives live as members of the wealthy elite in their local communities; they enjoy security and luxury. These industrial magnates are differentiated along the three dimensions of stratification—wealth, prestige, power.

WEALTH, PRESTIGE, POWER

Sociological interest in social stratification is commonly traced to Max Weber and Karl Marx. Weber's definitions of the three dimensions—wealth, prestige, power—continue to be among the most frequently cited in sociology (Weber, 1958: 180–187). Only when we understand these dimensions of stratification can we understand the strata that form along them.

Wealth

According to Max Weber, *wealth* (he actually used the term "class") is the opportunity an individual has for a supply of goods, satisfactory living conditions, and rewarding personal life experiences as determined by the marketplace.[1] In general, wealth is measured by the amount of property and income one has, by those things

[1]Wealth is used to avoid the confusion, often emerging in discussions of social stratification, between "class" as Weber used it and "social class" as modern sociologists use it.

having a monetary or exchangeable value. The individual's occupational income is the primary measure of wealth which enters into sociological studies of stratification.

But income is not the only measure, for wealth can also come from investments, inheritance, and other forms of property having a monetary or exchangeable value. This is evident in the variety of indicators which point to wealth. Researchers have looked at indicators such as residential accommodation (e.g., an expensive suburban house vs. a cheap inner-city apartment), the price of consumer goods (e.g., a console color television set vs. a 12-inch black-and-white set), the type of hired services (e.g., going to the hairdresser once a week vs. giving oneself a permanent), and the nature of vacations (e.g., two weeks in a condominium in Hawaii vs. two weeks in a camper at a public campground). In industrial societies such as Canada, wealth usually is equivalent to the goods and services money can buy. It should be noted, however, that people may acquire goods and services through nonmonetary exchange (e.g., neighbors helping each other with large-scale domestic projects).

Prestige

Sociologists often look upon *prestige* as being interchangeable with *status* (when not conceived of as a position in social structure). Both terms refer to the positive and negative estimation of an individual's public standing on one or more dimensions which society values. There are several such dimensions in North America; among them are religion, income, residence, family standing, leisure pursuits, and level of education. Weber, for example, wrote extensively about family standing. But many contemporary sociologists have been especially interested in occupation as an indicator of honor.

Sociologists have tried to gauge the public's estimate of occupational prestige by means of national surveys. Haug (1977: 53) notes that it is still unclear what these estimates mean to those making them. For example, is a respondent's ranking of an occupation based on its perceived utility, remuneration, qualifications, danger, or scarcity of people to fill it? Within these limitations, however, studies of occupational prestige estimates have been conducted in the United States and Canada. There are also several international comparisons of such rankings.

For instance, Pineo and Porter (1967: 30) found a correlation of .98 between their study of occupational prestige ranking in Canada and Hodge et al.'s (1964) study of these rankings in the United States (a perfect correlation is 1.00). The estimates by French and English Canadians are also similar (a correlation of .95). Indeed, there is a "substantial uniformity in occupational prestige evaluations throughout the world" (Treiman, 1977: 80). Table 18.1 shows the prestige levels of fifty common occupations

---

SOCIOLOGY OR COMMON SENSE

What do you think?

Which of the following statements do you agree with? Which statements do you disagree with? Make a note of your answers. Check your answers when you have completed your study of this chapter. Are your answers to the statements the same as those a sociologist would give?

1. In North America, the affairs of government, business, and the military are run by a few exceedingly powerful people.
2. There will be a revolution by the working class against the capitalist class, which will result in the establishment of a classless, communist state.
3. Canada and the United States are lands of milk and honey; no really poor people live here.
4. North Americans live in the midst of unlimited opportunity; with a little pluck, one can advance from a low position to a high position in life.
5. A physician is more important for the society in which he or she works than a trash collector is.

Table 18.1 OCCUPATIONAL PRESTIGE RANKING IN 27 COUNTRIES

Standard scale code	Standard occupational title	Standard scale score[a]
00610	Physician	77.9
01310	University professor	77.6
01210	Lawyer, trial lawyer	70.6
02111	Head of large firm	70.4
00220	Engineer, civil engineer	70.3
02114	Banker	67.0
00410	Airline pilot	66.5
01320	High school teacher	64.2
00670	Pharmacist	64.1
10001	Armed forces officer	63.2
01410	Clergyman	59.7
01610	Artist	57.2
01330	Teacher, primary teacher	57.0
01510	Journalist	54.9
01100	Accountant	54.6
03102	Civil servant, minor	53.6
00710	Nurse	53.6
02116	Building contractor	53.4
01730	Actor	51.5
03310	Bookkeeper	49.0
04321	Traveling salesman	46.9
06110	Farmer	46.8
08550	Electrician	44.5
04410	Insurance agent	44.5
03930	Office clerk	43.3
08430	Garage mechanic	42.9
08490	Mechanic, repairman	42.8
04100	Shopkeeper	42.4
09210	Printer	42.3
03210	Typist, stenographer	41.6
05820	Policeman	39.8
07910	Tailor	39.5
07000	Foreman	39.3
10003	Soldier	38.7
09540	Carpenter	37.2
09510	Mason	34.1
08710	Plumber	33.9
04510	Sales clerk	33.6
03700	Mail carrier	32.8
09853	Driver, truck driver	32.6
09852	Bus, tram driver	32.4
07110	Miner	31.5
05700	Barber	30.4
08010	Shoemaker, repairer	28.1
05320	Waiter	23.2
06210	Farm hand	22.9
04521	Street vendor, peddler	21.9
05510	Janitor	21.0
05400	Servant	17.2
09995	Street sweeper	13.4

Source: D. J. Treiman. *Occupational prestige in comparative perspective.* pp. 155–56. New York: Academic Press, 1977. Adapted from Table 7.2.

[a] Based on 55 countries.

as estimated in twenty-seven countries (including Canada and the United States). The higher the standard-scale score of an occupation, the higher is its estimated prestige.

There are ways of ranking the prestige of occupations other than by surveying random samples of the population. Edwards (1943) combined theoretically weighted levels of income and education to develop a hierarchical occupational classification for use in reporting census data in the United States.[2] There have since been several modifications of his pioneer

Prestige is one way by which members of modern societies are ranked.

[2] While occupations are also classified in the census of Canada, the occupational categories are not ranked by prestige.

scheme in both Canada and the United States (e.g., Erbe, 1975; Blishen and McRoberts, 1976). The following is a typical occupational classification used by North American sociologists (Hall, 1969: 68–69):

Professionals
Managers, proprietors, officials
Clerks and kindred workers
Skilled workers and foremen
Semiskilled workers
Unskilled workers (including farm and nonfarm workers)

Other classifications may have more or less detail.

Power

Power is a major dimension of social stratification. Empirically, we have seen that people with power occupy leadership positions in both small groups and large-scale organizations, although only the positions in large-scale organizations are ordinarily visible enough to be ranked in the society's stratification system. A person's membership in influential organizations is a measure of power, as are the offices he or she holds in such organizations. How often does the individual attend the meetings of voluntary associations? This, too, is a measure of power. Power is associated with political participation (see Chapter 14) and with personal contact with political leaders. Other sources of power are money, knowledge, verbal facility, intellectual skills, and instruments of violence.

Weber's theory of social class formation—that classes form along the dimensions of wealth, prestige, and power—is frequently contrasted with Marx's theory of how social classes form. For Marx, power and wealth are determined by the individual's relationship to the means of production. As noted in Chapter 2, Marx predicted that there would be a growing tendency for people to fall into one of two great classes: a class consisting of those who own and operate the means of production (i.e., business enterprises such as factories) and a class consisting of those who work for the owners and operators. These classes are the *bourgeoisie* (the owners) and the *proletariat* (the workers). To the extent that prestige was a factor in Marx's theory of stratification, it was related to the conditions of ownership and nonownership of the means of production.

Weber's framework is more widely accepted by present-day sociologists who study stratification than Marx's framework, although the latter has recently been gaining prominence in North American social-science circles. Bendix (1974: 153) describes the differences between these two thinkers:

> Marx thought that in the long run ownership of the means of production would prove the decisive determinant (of rank in society), and Weber did not. . . . For analytic purposes Weber thought it convenient to define classes [wealth] and status-groups [prestige] in terms that are mutually exclusive. Where market mechanisms predominate, personal and family distinctions are discounted. Where considerations of prestige predominate, economically advantageous activities are often stigmatized. . . . By assuming that class or status-oriented behavior prevails only for a time, Weber suggests a model of alternating tendencies without predicting a final outcome.

Note the contrast with Marx, who considered economic determinants decisive in the long run and on that basis predicted the overthrow of capitalism.

STRATIFICATION SYSTEMS

When hierarchically arranged, social strata show up in distinct stratification systems. Three such systems are *caste, estate,* and *social class.* These three systems are explained in this section. By looking first at castes and then at estates, we learn much about the social-class system that predominates in North America. That is, we learn about our stratification system by discovering what it is not.

The Caste System

A caste system is made up of several strata. In the ideal type, each stratum, or caste, has its own level of prestige and privilege. Membership in a caste system is an ascribed status; individuals are born into a caste and are highly likely to remain there for life. Thus, movement between castes occurs infrequently. There is little upward mobility within a caste system.

Caste systems are typically rooted in the familial and religious institutions of the society. Caste membership is an extension of family *endogamy;* that is, members are usually forced to marry someone from the same caste. The religious order of the society justifies the entire arrangement, including the roles ascribed to members of the caste and the ways they ought to behave with reference to people in other castes.

The Hindus of India still maintain the vestiges of what was once one of the purest instances ever of the caste system. Although officially outlawed, the system in India has been in existence in pure or diluted form for more than three thousand years. The ancient system was composed of, in order of dominance, the Brahmans (the religious priests), Kshatriyas (the warriors and rulers), Vaisyas (the merchants, traders, manufacturers, and farmers), and Sudras (the peasants and laborers). The major role of the Sudras was to serve the first three. Outside these four strata lies still another stratum, variously known as the outcasts, untouchables, or pariahs. They were part of the system, since they filled menial occupational roles important to the rest of Hindu society (e.g., tanner). In addition, the four main castes had literally hundred of subdivisions, constituting together, then and now, one of the world's most complicated systems of stratification.

Some sociologists see parallels between the Hindu caste system and the stratification of blacks and whites in the American South, particularly prior to World War II. Berreman (1960) holds that there is more movement between castes in the Indian system than the ideal type portrays (i.e., in actuality, statuses are less ascribed) and that there is considerable resentment among the pariah and Sudra castes over their place in the system. As Berreman points out, blacks, too, object to the status ascribed to them. Many distinctions, norms, and definitions of intercaste situations persist in everyday life, among both the Hindus and the American blacks.

The Estate System

An *estate* is an aggregate of people in a community or a society who are distinguished by their special, legally prescribed, social and political rights and obligations. The purest instance of the estate system existed in medieval Europe. Like castes, estates were hereditary and generally endogamous strata. Unlike castes, they were part of a feudal society, where the civil and political rights and duties and interestate relations of members were legally framed. Religion also played a role, for it was used to justify, as divinely inspired, the status quo.

There were typically three or four estates in the European system. Since there were no outcasts, the serfs occupied the lowest stratum. Other strata included the nobility at the top, the clergy on the next level, and below them the commons, a miscellaneous collection of urban craftsmen, bourgeoisie (traders, entrepreneurs), and other townspeople of substance. Poland had only two estates: nobility and priests. Sweden had four, the nobility, priests, burghers (i.e., townspeople), and peasants (Bloch, 1961).

Although limited, there was some mobility between estates. One might, for example, move up within the hierarchy of the Roman Catholic Church to priesthood. Each estate had a separate voice in the limited popular government permitted by the sovereign (i.e., king, feudal lord).

The estate system was a product of a preindustrial society. Industrialization and the rise of capitalism, with their voracious appetites for efficient, specially trained workers, eventually made the system obsolete. It was gradually replaced by the social-class system we know today. The Indian caste system, which thrived in an agrarian milieu, has been withering away for similar reasons.

The Social-Class System

John Porter (1965: 7–8) compares the concept of *social class* with caste and estate:

> A class system of stratification is distinguished from the other two mainly by the fact that all members of the society share a common legal status of citizenship. All are equal before the law; all are entitled to hold property; and all, theoretically, can choose their occupations because there are no legal barriers to taking on particular kinds of work as there are in the other systems of stratification. In other words, although the rank order exists, it is not legally recognized. Nor are there rank symbols appropriated by one class and forbidden to another.

The upshot of this is that the lines separating social classes are fuzzier than those separating castes and estates. Moreover, we shall see later that social-class systems offer the possibility of mobility from one class to another, of the achievement of at least some statuses rather than ascription to them.

There is an inconsistent and occasionally ambiguous usage of terms. It should be recognized that terms have a public appeal. Modern industrial societies have experienced rapid social change. There is a complicated and still only partly understood interrelationship of wealth, prestige, and power. All this has conspired to wreak definitional havoc on the sociological study of social stratification. The labels "class" and "social class" are used interchangeably by some scientists; others distinguish the terms rigorously. Sometimes either or both terms denote strata ranked solely on the wealth dimension, while in other instances the terms denote a combination of wealth and prestige or wealth, prestige, and power.

It is necessary to be clear about what is being considered here. In this book, the terms "class" and "social class" are used as synonyms, each denoting the composite rank of a stratum on all three dimensions—wealth, prestige, and power. The term frequently used to refer to the combination of wealth and prestige alone is "socioeconomic status" (SES).

What with the indistinctness of social classes, it is hardly surprising that sociologists should encounter difficulties discerning adjacent classes clearly enough to study them as separate entities. When compared with castes and estates,

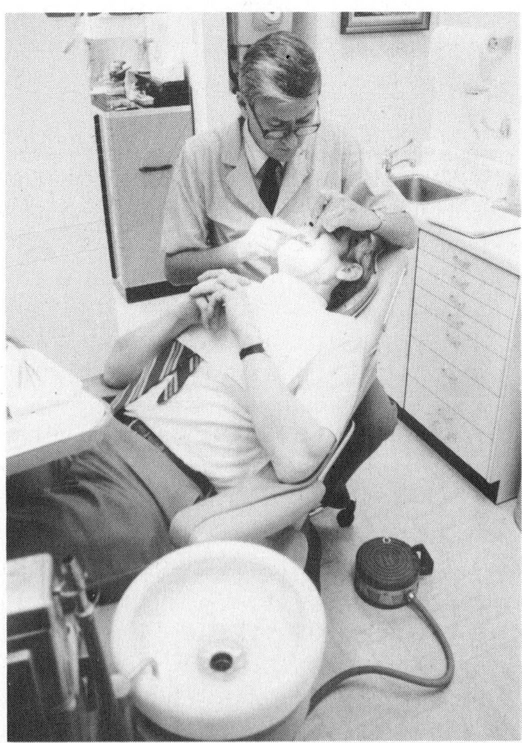

Most professions are accompanied by high socioeconomic status.

The University Degree and Social Mobility

The analyses presented in this paper reveal a marked deterioration in intergenerational upward occupational mobility prospects for both male and female university graduates. This decline in mobility prospects . . . sets in after 1964. In the later years of the 1960s, the general unemployment rate in Ontario rose and the labour market for many types of university-trained workers, including B.A. and B.Sc. graduates, started to weaken. Although mobility prospects have declined for both males and females, males still experience more upward mobility than females in all of the time periods for which data are available. The difference between the sexes, however, shows some evidence of diminishing over time, a consequence of males experiencing a sharper decline in mobility prospects rather than any improvement in the prospects for females.

Public investment in university education in Canada was greatly expanded during the decade of the 1960s. Various policy objectives were attached to this expansion including the development of human capital, a contribution to general social and cultural development, and the provision of greater equality of opportunity. One way in which university education might be viewed as contributing to equality of opportunity is by providing a route, via educational attainment, to higher level occupations and, by implication, improved prospects for upward social mobility. The findings reported in this paper have numerous implications for this issue.

The findings show that a university education no longer yields the same opportunities for upward social mobility that obtained in 1960 and, in particular, in 1964. This decline in mobility occurred during a period when a larger proportion of university graduates came from lower socioeconomic backgrounds and, hence, there was a larger proportion of graduates who could in theory be upwardly mobile. In the data used in the present analyses 18.8 per cent of male graduates came from low socioeconomic backgrounds in 1960, a number which had risen to 24.4 per cent in 1976. The corresponding percentages for females are 10.2 per cent in 1960 and 22.2 per cent in 1976.

Although a university degree has become a less effective path to upward intergenerational occupational mobility, one cannot infer from these findings that it is less important to socioeconomic achievement. A recent study has revealed that university graduates still experience socioeconomic advantage through higher income returns to education than persons with other types of educational qualifications. Our findings suggest that while a university degree has declined as a path to upward mobility, it would still appear to be important for persons from low occupational status backgrounds and, for persons from higher occupational status backgrounds, it may serve as a hedge against downward mobility.

Finally, regional analyses point to differences in the distribution of father's occupational prestige in Canada which serve to establish, most notably in Québec, different structural conditions for intergenerational occupational mobility.

SOURCE: Edward B. Harvey. The changing relationship between university education and intergenerational social mobility. *Canadian Review of Sociology and Anthropology* 21: 275–286, August 1984.

social classes are unorganized. Still, members of the same class share similar interests, life-styles, and living conditions, stemming from their common position on the dimensions of wealth, prestige, and power. And sociologists, looking for a facile method for identifying and analyzing these aggregated similarities, have developed scales to measure two or three of the dimensions. Alternatively, they have tried various indirect approaches, such as recording a person's place of residence in a metropolitan area (e.g., Forcese, 1980: 35–36; Matras, 1984: 117).

One of the best known social-class scales in North America is Hollingshead's (1957) *index of social position* (ISP). It combines the weighted ranks of occupation and education to form a scale ranging in value from 11 to 77. The procedure for weighting occupation is too complicated to explain here. For our purposes, it is important to know only that the ISP identifies five categories of occupation-education; the five categories correspond to five social classes. The ISP is similar to Edwards' scale (discussed earlier), except that Edwards and the U.S. Census stop short of identifying classes.[3] Given the prominence of occupation as a status locator in urban society and an indicator of one's education and income, it is to be expected that occupational prestige rankings have also been used to identify social classes.

These various attempts to measure class with scales are often complicated by the fact that there is sometimes a lack of correspondence between education, income, and occupation. For example, many social welfare workers and musicians in a symphony orchestra, though they have more education and prestige than, say, electricians and truck drivers, have a lower income than electricians and truck drivers. Some professional athletes, with annual incomes of up to $1,000,000 or more, have more wealth than many physicians and lawyers, but less formal education. The athletes also may have more prestige than doctors and attorneys. This lack of correspondence has led Barber (1968: 294) to identify the *problem of status inconsistency:* the task of explaining why a lack of correspondence occurs.

The number and kinds of social classes identified by these methods depend, in part, on the community studied and the detail needed for the analysis. Although some prefer other classifications, most contemporary sociologists hold that industrial societies are composed of the following social classes

Upper class
Upper-middle class }
Lower-middle class } Middle class
Working class }
Lower class } Working or lower class

Marxists combine the upper and upper-middle classes in the category of bourgeoisie and the lower-middle, working, and lower classes in the category of proletariat. According to Marx, with the approach of the revolution, the lower-middle class and a segment of the upper-middle class will join the proletariat in their struggle against the capitalists, or bourgeoisie.

[3]In fact, for researchers interested only in the objective classification of occupations by level of prestige, the U.S. census categories are preferred, since the ISP is becoming dated (Haug, 1977: 59).

SOCIAL CLASS IN NORTH AMERICA

The measuring scales of Hollingshead and Edwards are objective instruments, since those who are surveyed are never asked to place themselves in a particular social class. This is done for them by the researcher, who bases his or her conclusion on the information which the respondents provide (information pertaining to income, education, occupation, residence). Studies using these instruments have produced a broad picture of the stratification system in North America.

That picture is sketched here within the frame of Matras's three main groupings of classes in the United States (1984: Chapter 9): the privileged upper stratum, the middle stratum, and the underprivileged lower stratum. The following portrayal of the first class also draws on Hunter's analysis of Canada's bourgeoisie (1981: Chapter 11) and the portrayal of the second class on Hunter's analysis of its petite bourgeoisie and working class. And, like any picture, all that can be depicted is a static view of North American stratification, which, in fact, is a changeable phenomenon. In other words, a different picture would have been painted, say, fifty years ago and certainly a different one will emerge fifty years hence.

The Upper Strata

The *bourgeoisie* are a major part of the privileged upper strata. Since they own or control the production and allocation of goods and services, their wealth comes from profits gained in commercial and industrial enterprise. As defined here, the bourgeoisie comprise the corporate elite of North America; they own a substantial proportion of stock in the multinational empires and the large national conglomerate enterprises discussed in Chapter 13. Members of the bourgeoisie sit on one or more boards of directors of these firms, or they serve as top managers in one of them (Useem, 1980: 41–42).

The question has been raised in Canada, but not in the United States, about the existence within its upper strata of a *parasite* elite. Within this elite, we find the heads of multinational corporations who control certain Canadian enterprises from outside the country (Porter, 1965: 266–273; Clement, 1975: 36, 117–122). If such an elite exists, it is made possible by processes such as corporate concentration and foreign direct investment (see Chapter 13).

Overlapping the bourgeoisie is the *leisure class.* The leisure class is made up of people whose income from investments, rent, or inheritance enables them to spend much of their time away from work, away from the relatively unappealing activity of earning a living. Some members of the leisure class entered this stratum on the day they were born, having been born into families of considerable wealth. Others moved upward into the leisure class much later in life through personal achievement and the accumulation of wealth.

The privileged upper strata also include the *power elite;* the men and the few women who fill the top positions in government, business (i.e., the bourgeoisie), and the military are the power elite (Mills, 1959; Porter, 1965). Those who control our major labor, religious, educational, and mass media organizations are also at this level. Arts, sports, and entertainment celebrities round out the membership of this social class. Except for those in arts, sports, and entertainment, the privileged upper strata are primarily constituted of whites.

Members of the privileged upper strata are unequal even among themselves; some have more wealth, prestige, and power than others. The owners of Canadian Pacific Limited are more powerful than football stars or concert pianists. Pianists still have to work for an income, as do the American president and the Canadian prime minister, while members of old and wealthy families may spend most, if not all, of their days at leisure. Moreover, backgrounds vary within this social class. For example, while a significant proportion of the current economic, political, and educational elites in the

United States and Canada have graduated from prestigious universities (e.g., Harvard, Princeton, Yale, Toronto, and McGill), this educational homogeneity is absent among the elites of labor, entertainment, and the fine arts. Moreover, there may be less educational homogeneity than we realize. Olsen (1980: 74) found that nearly two-thirds of the governmental elite in Canada had attended neither of the two high-prestige universities, McGill University and the University of Toronto.

How much power do these elites actually have? There are three schools of thought on this question. The *power-elite* theorists hold that those running the government, business, and military affairs of the country are an exceedingly powerful and more or less permanent group. The *plural-elite* theorists are unconvinced by their arguments and data. Among them are scholars such as Ralf Dahrendorf (see later), who believed that coalitions of various interest groups achieve power for a limited period of time, only to be replaced by an opposing coalition. Their elite status is frequently temporary.

Some American scientists (e.g., Rose, 1967) reject the idea of an elite in any sphere of their society; they note the presence of *veto groups.* The interests of one veto group are incompatible with the interests of other veto groups; on balance, the veto groups keep each other from gaining significant power for long. Even Porter (1965: 27) offers this interpretation at some points in his otherwise power-elite interpretation of Canadian social stratification (Heap, 1974: 135–137). The veto group position is that many pressure groups in North America have some power (e.g., organizations of consumers, environmentalists, manufacturers, professionals, retailers, and religionists), but none has enough power to establish hegemony and to become either a power elite or a plural elite.

Methodological and theoretical problems presently stand in the way of a resolution of the competing claims of these three schools of thought (Mintz et al., 1976).

The Middle Strata

It is almost an understatement to point out that the middle strata are a diverse lot. There are four main strata: the petite bourgeoisie, the salariat, the blue-collar entrepreneurs, and the unionized blue-collar employees. The rank order of these four is by no means always clear, for there is considerable variation in class, prestige, and power even within them. Moreover embourgeoisement may be further blurring their differences.

The Four Strata We turn first to the *petite bourgeoisie.* Hunter divides his discussion of the petite bourgeoisie into the old and the new. The *old* portion, which is composed of independent commodity producers and small-business people, has been declining for many decades relative to the total population (Johnson, 1972: 147–148; Mills, 1956: 22–23). Numbering among the independent commodity producers are farmers, fishermen, and craftworkers who run their own enterprises. In the small-business category one finds retailers, landlords, small manufacturers, and free-lance salespeople.

Meanwhile, the *new* petite bourgeoisie has been growing and prospering. It consists of the various types of independent or fee-for-service professionals, the most prominent of whom are the physicians, lawyers, and dentists. Indeed,

The petite bourgeoisie is still an economic force in North America.

Parkin (1979: 54–58) sees these people as being powerful and prestigious enough to include them in the privileged upper strata. After all, they have, through their credentials, a legal monopoly on their valuable services.

Outside the petite bourgeoisie but very much within the middle strata in American and Canadian society are the *salariat,* or salaried personnel of large-scale organizations. They constitute the amorphous category of white-collar workers, at the top of which is the salaried professional. Some in this class have university and postgraduate degrees, whereas others, usually in the clerical and sales fields, have lower credentials. Toward the bottom of this set of strata lie what Matras (1984: 142) calls the *blue-collar entrepreneurs*—the tradesmen and shop proprietors. At the same level is the larger working class of *unionized blue-collar employees* in industry, service, craftwork, and skilled jobs.

Embourgeoisement One question puzzling sociologists these days is whether members of the petite bourgeoisie are becoming more homogeneous in certain ways. There are sociologists in both the United States and Canada who believe *embourgeoisement* is occurring; that is, the working class is acquiring middle-class ways, values, life-styles, and relationships (Westley and Westley, 1971; DeFronzo, 1974). Others, however, accept the Marxian hypothesis, namely that much of the new middle class of salaried workers will eventually become "proletarianized," at which point they will join the working class in their revolt against the capitalists (e.g., Mills, 1956: 295–298). This requires sufficient inner-class unity for collective action (Poulantzas, 1975). A factor in embourgeoisement, if it actually is occurring, is the development of periodic economic recessions. Since blue-collar workers and members of the lower strata suffer most from hard times (through layoffs, wage cuts, reduced work hours), they could be prevented from acquiring a middle-class life-style.

Which stratum in Canadian society works here?

A number of differences still separate the various middle strata. Professionals are generally more satisfied with their occupational role than blue-collar workers are. Handel and Rainwater (1964) write that blue-collar workers are more likely to repair their automobiles, refrigerators, washers, and dryers than are professionals and small-business people, who tend to pay someone for these services. Matras (1984: 148) describes some of the differences in leisure life-style between white-collar workers and blue-collar workers:

> The blue-collar strata tend to spend their vacations and weekends at home, with relatives, in outdoor recreation such as camping, fishing, and hunting, or in travel in the family automobile. The white-collar strata are more likely to patronize hotels and resorts, to travel by air to distant vacation areas, to go abroad, or to take winter vacations in warm climates or in winter sports resorts. The various resorts, vacation spots, and recreation centers tend to have specialized, stratum-specific clientele. Thus, the local, state and national parks cater largely to families of blue-collar workers and lower white-collar employees; Miami Beach caters to Jewish and French Canadian proprietors and fee professionals.

The Lower Strata

The "hard core," chronically unemployed, poor people who inhabit the slums, skid rows, and subsistence farming areas of North America fall into the lower strata. Work for them is typically intermittent, low-paying, nonunion, without fringe benefits, and, for the most part, unskilled. Some of the able-bodied eke out a living on a day labor basis. Others become fully employed only during a particular season (e.g., trapping, fishing, fruit picking). All draw unemployment insurance benefits to the limits of their eligibility and whatever additional forms of government relief they qualify for. Many members of the lower strata are women with dependent children.

The causes of underprivilege are far too numerous to list here in their entirety. Ethnic discrimination is a factor, since Mexican-Americans, Puerto Ricans, blacks, and Indians in the United States and Indians, Métis, and Inuit in Canada are disproportionately represented at the bottom of society.[4] Other factors include disability and poor health, often in conjunction with old age. Lack of a job skill, lack of a high school education, and, possibly, lack of the ability to read also contribute to becoming and remaining poor. And, according to Marx, capitalism creates a surplus pool of alienated, degraded labor that eventually winds up in poverty due to no fault of the laborers.

The lower strata may be urban or rural.

[4]Black poverty is not completely absent in Canada, only less prevalent than in the United States (see Institute of Public Affairs, 1970).

Being considered here, then, are those described in Canada as "low income families and unattached individuals" and in the United States as "families and unrelated individuals below the poverty level." Tables 18.2 and 18.3 show the levels of income received by people in this social class. These two tables afford no comparison between the United States and Canada on levels of poverty. Definitions and data collection methods are sometimes different, and Table 18.3 presents average poverty levels, whereas Table 18.2 presents cutoffs separating the categories of poverty and nonpoverty. For the same reasons, no comparisons should be attempted with the figures in Table 18.4. They indicate, for each country, the proportion of all families and individuals living in underprivileged conditions.

The information in the three tables paints a statistical picture of the amount and level of underprivilege in North America. The facts give us no sense of what it is like to live in such circumstances. To start, the underprivileged are almost completely powerless even to defend their basic rights of free speech, equal justice, property ownership, and the like. Needless to say, their prestige is negative. Some of them are counted among society's deviants (e.g., tramps, prostitutes); many are regarded as social problems (e.g., the indigent aged, the slum dwellers, the hard-core unemployed).

Poverty is not necessarily a long-term condition, though it can become so for the disabled and chronically ill. Single-parent, low-income families, many through marriage or remarriage, become two-parent families and double their income. Unemployed youths may eventually find steady work. But the situation is precarious for families and individuals who are poverty-stricken. Poverty is a way of life; the poverty-

Table 18.2 LOW-INCOME CUTOFFS OF FAMILY UNITS IN CANADA, 1982

Size of family unit	Low-income cutoff (dollars)				
	Urban areas 500,000 and over	100,000 to 499,999	30,000 to 99,999	Less than 30,000[a]	Rural areas
	1969 base				
1 person	7,257	6,794	6,597	6,068	5,273
2 persons	10,518	9,850	9,565	8,796	7,653
3 persons	13,421	12,570	12,200	11,228	9,763
4 persons	15,963	14,948	14,508	13,351	11,607
5 persons	17,844	16,705	16,221	14,928	12,979
6 persons	19,589	18,341	17,808	16,385	14,244
7 or more persons	21,479	20,105	19,524	17,959	15,618
	1978 base				
1 person	8,914	8,466	7,941	7,342	6,592
2 persons	11,761	11,162	10,414	9,663	8,615
3 persons	15,732	14,909	13,934	12,961	11,537
4 persons	18,129	17,229	16,107	14,982	13,336
5 persons	21,126	20,002	18,654	17,379	15,507
6 persons	23,073	21,800	20,377	18,953	16,930
7 or more persons	25,396	24,047	22,475	20,901	18,654

Source: Statistics Canada. *Income distribution by size in Canada, 1982,* p. 31. Cat. No. 13-207. Ottawa, 1982.

[a]Includes cities with a population between 15,000 and 30,000 and small urban areas (under 15,000).

Table 18.3 POVERTY LEVELS IN THE UNITED STATES: NONFARM FAMILIES AND INDIVIDUALS, WEIGHTED AVERAGES, 1970–1982

Size of Unit	1970[a]	1975[a]	1979[a]	1980[a]	1981	1982
1 person (unrelated individual)	$1,954	$2,724	$3,689	$4,190	$4,620	$4,901
Under 65 years	2,010	2,797	3,779	4,290	4,729	5,019
65 years and over	1,861	2,581	3,479	3,949	4,359	4,626
2 persons	2,525	3,506	4,725	5,363	5,917	6,281
Householder under 65 years	2,604	3,617	4,878	5,537	6,111	6,487
Householder 65 years and over	2,348	3,257	4,390	4,983	5,498	5,836
3 persons	3,099	4,293	5,784	6,565	7,250	7,693
4 persons	3,968	5,500	7,412	8,414	9,287	9,862
5 persons	4,680	6,499	8,775	9,966	11,007	11,684
6 persons	5,260	7,316	9,914	11,269	12,449	13,207
7 or more persons	6,468	9,022	12,280	13,955	(NA)[b]	(NA)
7 persons	(NA)	(NA)	(NA)	(NA)	14,110	15,036
8 persons	(NA)	(NA)	(NA)	(NA)	15,655	16,719
9 or more persons	(NA)	(NA)	(NA)	(NA)	18,572	19,698

Source: U.S. Bureau of the Census. *Statistical abstract of the United States: 1984,* 104th ed., p. 447. Washington, D.C., 1984.

[a]Poverty levels for nonfarm families.

[b]NA, not available.

Table 18.4 PERSONS IN THE LOW INCOME-POVERTY CATEGORY: PERCENTAGE IN THE UNITED STATES AND CANADA

Persons	Canada (1982)	United States (1981)
In families	10.1	12.5
Individuals		
Unattached	27.1	
Unrelated		23.4

Sources: Statistics Canada, *Income distributions by size in Canada, 1982,* Cat. No. 13-207, p. 162, Ottawa, 1982; U.S. Bureau of the Census, *Statistical abstract of the United States, 1984,* 104th ed., p. 473, Washington, D.C., 1984.

stricken lack the resources to secure adequate nourishment, shelter, clothing, and health care. Inadequate health care may come as a surprise to Canadians, who are guaranteed medical treatment under provincially administered programs. Medical and hospital facilities, dental treatment, and good nutrition are far from equally distributed in Canada (*Financial Post,* 1984: 25–26).

Social Class: A Subjective View

Given what was just said about the three main social classes in North America, it is easy to see why a subjective or personal view of class identification might lead to results strikingly different from those produced by objective measures such as those of Hollingshead and Edwards. Goyder and Pineo (1979: 443–444), after studying the sizable American and Canadian literature on this topic, conclude that subjective social class identification is highly similar in the two countries. When respondents in a national survey are asked to choose among the alternatives of upper class, middle class, working class, and lower class, between 30 and 50 percent place themselves in the working class and, except for 4 to 6 percent who say they are either upper or lower class, the remaining individuals view themselves as middle class (i.e., 44 to 66 percent). Measurement difffculties still to be ironed out, including the names of the classes (e.g., lower vs. working class), preclude at present a statement any more precise than this. Comparing these findings with the proportions in Table 18.4 suggests that some people, probably for reasons of self-esteem, understandably prefer to avoid the implication that they belong with the poor.

The subjective view of class and class consciousness (discussed later) are distinct, albeit related, orientations. The difference can be easily summarized as the difference between *identification of* people, by themselves or others, as being members of a certain category (here a social class) and *identification with* a status or role as an aspect of value commitment (see Chapter 15) (Stone, 1962). The subjective view of class is a form of identification *of* oneself (by oneself), whereas class consciousness is a form of identification *with* one's social class. The discussion later of social mobility will show why this distinction is important.

STRATIFICATION THEORIES

How does modern sociology account for the phenomenon of social class in industrial societies? Three theories have been in the academic limelight off and on over the years since the initial conceptualizations of Marx and Weber. They are *functional theory, conflict theory,* and *functional-conflict synthesis.* The third, which was originally proposed by Gerhard Lenski, is built on the common ground shared by the functional theory and conflict theory. Even today the ideas of Weber and Marx, but especially those of Weber (Blumberg, 1978: 69), pervade the three frameworks.

The Functional Theory

Consonant with the functionalism of other areas of sociology, functionalism in social stratification is often said to be conservative. That is, it expresses conservatism in its explanation of why social classes form and persist. Briefly put, functionalists hold that society produces classes without a conscious intent on the part of anyone in the society. That is, classes result from the broad process of differentiation. According to functionalism, the most important positions in society are filled by those most capable of enacting them. Davis and Moore's (1945: 243) early statement of the functional theory of stratification is still considered basic, albeit controversial:

> If the rights and perquisites of different positions in a society must be unequal, then the society must be stratified, because that is precisely what stratification means. Social inequality is thus an unconsciously evolved device by which societies insure that the most important positions are conscientiously filled by the most qualified persons. Hence every society, no matter how simple or complex, must differentiate persons in terms of both prestige and esteem, and must therefore possess a certain amount of institutionalized inequality.

Stratification systems differ from one society to the next, which the functionalists explain by noting that each society has its special ways of rewarding its various positions. The level of reward (e.g., amount, kind) is determined by two factors: functional importance and scarcity of personnel. A role is *functionally important* when it is central to maintaining the society as an ongoing social system. Rewards of sufficient magnitude must exist to encourage people to fill such roles competently. *Scarcity of personnel* refers to two conditions: a situation which exists when there is a shortage of people competent enough to fill an important role and a situation which exists when the training of personnel is costly or lengthy or both. The more important the role and the harder it is to find someone to fill it, the higher are the rewards (e.g., pay, prestige, perquisites) available to those who do fill it and, consequently, the higher is their rank or social-class position. The degree of functional importance, say Davis and Moore, is difficult to judge. In part, it depends on how functionally unusual a particular position is and how dependent on it other positions are.

The Davis and Moore paper provoked a rash of criticisms, perhaps the most famous of which are contained in several papers written by Melvin Tumin.[5] He and others (e.g., Simpson, 1956) were concerned with the lack of objectivity with which functional importance was assigned to roles. Who is to say, Simpson argued, that the garbage collector is any less important than many higher-status roles? In fact, an objective measure of functional importance is still to be developed (Abramson et al., 1980: 101).

Tumin also challenged the Davis-Moore assertion that role stratification and the inequality it enforces are both functional and inevitable. He observed that class stratification systems encourage us to search only in specific strata for the talent needed to fill certain positions, thus overlooking talent available elsewhere in the society. Furthermore, such systems distribute loyalty across a society unequally; those with the greatest stake in their positions (i.e., power, prestige, high salary) are more likely to be loyal than those with the least stake. In sum, Davis and Moore failed to incorporate in their theory some of the major dysfunctions of the social-class system of stratification.

The functionalist theory also overlooks one of the main findings of social mobility research (see later in this chapter), namely that educational attainment and subsequent occupational status are heavily affected by the socioeconomic status of the individual's family of orientation. As many sociologists point out, because some people are born into families of low SES, they have an unequal opportunity from the start to acquire the education that would qualify them for high-prestige, functionally important jobs. The sociologists say that these individuals' low status as adults is accounted for by family back-

[5]Tumin wrote nearly a dozen articles on the Davis-Moore position and social stratification theory. Several are reprinted in Tumin (1970). Only a short summary of these is presented in this chapter.

ground and not by the functionalist theory of stratification.

Conflict Theory

Both the conflict ideologists and the conflict theorists have developed theories of stratification. Since we have covered the essential aspects of both in Chapter 2 and several subsequent chapters, the aim in this section is to illustrate the present-day conflict explanations of social stratification that build on either the Marx-Engels thesis or the general conflict theory. We turn first to a contemporary expression of the Marx and Engels thesis.

Nicos Poulantzas (1975) distinguishes three dimensions: productive and unproductive labor, supervisory and nonsupervisory personnel, and mental and manual labor. *Productive labor* contributes directly to the creation of surplus value. *Surplus value* is defined as the difference between the value of the work done or the commodities produced and the wages received by the workers. For instance, women making dresses in a factory are engaged in productive labor, which generates a surplus value calculated as the difference between the price of the dresses and their wages. This surplus value, when transmuted into money, becomes the factory owner's profit.

Poulantzas says the modern proletariat is composed of productive, nonsupervisory, manual laborers. Since they fall outside the ranks of the supervisors, they lack knowledge about the production process. This knowledge is supplied by managers, engineers, efficiency experts, and similar personnel. The supervisors and other white-collar workers (the managers, engineers) have more knowledge about the production process than the proletariat, which means that the interests of the supervisors are different from the interests of the proletariat. To some extent, the supervisors' interests are harmful to the proletariat.

Ralf Dahrendorf (1959: Chapters 7 and 8), whose ideas were first encountered in Chapter 9, is representative of the broad sociological conflict-theory approach to class formation and maintenance. His theory contains both Weberian and Marxian elements. In it he argues that no single person or group rules permanently. But, while in power, the ruling class has four components: the bureaucracy, governmental elite, majority political party, and veto groups in its favor. With these components, the ruling class temporarily dominates the society. Those in power, whether at the society or the organizational level, have the specific rights of legitimate authority, while those whom they rule have only the general rights of citizenship. Citizens in a democratic state share a "basic power common to all" (Dahrendorf, 1959: 293). But their level of dominance is minimal compared with the level of dominance of the political and organizational decision makers.

The proletariat plays an indispensable role in our society.

Incompatible goals and values spawn conflict between the rulers and the ruled. That is, the ruling class cherishes its legitimate authority and the subordinate classes cherish their basic rights (e.g., a plant manager wants the stockroom employees to work extra hours, but the workers believe they have a right to a certain amount of free time). To pursue their interests more effectively, the subordinate classes organize themselves into labor unions, political parties, and professional associations. The power potential of these organizations is considerable. But any one of the organizations gains ascendancy only to lose it to another at some point in the future. Thus, the social-class structure of their society is continuously in flux.

Functional-Conflict Synthesis

Lenski (1966: Chapters 2, 3, and 4) notes that survival is the first interest of the individual human being. Though ranked differently in different societies, the interests of wealth, prestige, and creature comfort are next to survival in importance and need. Societal interests are "those ends toward which the more or less coordinated efforts of the whole are directed—without regard to the harm they may do to many individual members, even the majority" (Lenski, 1966: 41). When it comes to interests, both societies and individuals are fundamentally self-seeking entities.

From this view of human nature, Lenski proceeds to his two laws of distribution. The first law is that people will share the fruits of their labor to the extent necessary for their own survival and for the survival of others whose actions benefit them. The second law is that the power of individuals will determine how the surplus production of goods and services (i.e., that production not needed for survival) is distributed in society. Prestige is chiefly a function of power and privilege in those societies where there is a substantial surplus to distribute (e.g., Canada and the United States).

The struggle for power in a society goes on not only between individuals and social classes but also between class systems. A *class system* is "a hierarchy of classes ranked in terms of some single criterion" (Lenski, 1966: 80), such as ethnicity, education, sex, or age. Struggles between class systems—let us say the income system, education system, and sex system—are struggles for the dominance of different principles of distribution. For example, should we distribute income by the level of education of the worker or by his or her sex? We have seen that, historically, sex has sometimes been the dominant distributive principle. Feminists and others argue that this principle should be replaced by education, experience, and other principles stressing merit (see Chapter 19).

SOCIAL MOBILITY

The recent research interests of sociologists in social stratification have centered primarily on changes in stratification systems and on movement or social mobility within them. New occupations are continually emerging, while some of the old ones are disappearing. The power, prestige, and remuneration of existing occupations may rise or fall over the years. In the meantime, individuals move to new positions, which may be more or less prestigious or powerful than the ones they left. The static conception of Davis and Moore has been put aside in order to study the dynamics of this social stratification.

Social mobility was defined earlier as upward or downward movement within a stratification system. People who move upward and downward experience a change in their societal rank. For better or worse, they acquire more or less wealth, honor, or power and, consequently, membership in a new social class. Social mobility is distinguished from physical or geographic mobility, which is covered in Chapter 22 under the headings of internal migration and immigration.

Although some social mobility has been observed in all three systems of stratification, it is minimal in those built on castes and estates.[6] Only the social-class system qualifies as an *open system*. It is conventionally contrasted with the other two as *closed systems*. The difference between the two types is a matter of degree, for open systems do contain some barriers to mobil-

[6]In the traditional Indian caste system, for example, a small group would pass for a higher-status group by adopting the customs and life-style of the latter. Soon the originally lower-status group was regarded as equivalent in prestige to the higher group (Srinivas, 1966).

ity. Several types of mobility have been identified in the open system.

Types of Mobility

First, mobility may be *inter*generational or *intra*generational. Its prefix indicates that intergenerational mobility is movement between generations. The comparison is between offspring and parents, as in the example of a schoolteacher whose father was a bricklayer. In intragenerational mobility (also known as *career mobility*), the comparison is with oneself; it is movement within a generation. That is, one might start one's occupational career as a bricklayer, go back to school to get a university education, and wind up teaching high school.

Both examples in the preceding paragraph are of *upward* mobility. People do occasionally move in the opposite direction, either within a generation or between generations. This is *downward* mobility. Note that the basis of comparison for intergenerational mobility is the individual's father. Although this practice may be changing, North Americans have traditionally identified a family's social status by the social-class rank of its male breadwinner.

There are two subtypes of intergenerational mobility: *structural,* or forced, and *circulation,* or exchange. *Structural mobility* is sometimes called *forced mobility* because sons may find it impossible to enter their father's occupation. Daughters wishing to enter his line of work could encounter the same problem. Because of changes in the supply of goods and services and the demand for them and, consequently, because of changes in the labor force, some occupations become saturated, or fully staffed. In time, there may even be fewer jobholders within a particular occupation. In either case, there are no openings for a father's children who wish to continue in his occupational footsteps. Teaching jobs for the children of elementary and secondary teachers in the past ten years or so are a good illustration of this situation. The children, in the meantime, must look elsewhere for work, which may move them laterally, up, or down in their society's stratification system.

Circulation mobility is alternatively called *exchange mobility.* In circulation mobility, a job is exchanged between individuals; one person displaces another in a given job. Someone must leave a position before someone else can move into it; this can occur under conditions of no change in the labor market and especially when there is no expansion in the number of jobs. People leave jobs through death, promotion, demotion, or retirement. Circulation mobility occurs even when the economy is stagnant. Structural mobility occurs in times of economic growth. Circulation mobility and structural mobility are mutually exclusive processes operating at the societal level of social life. By way of illustration, one can move into the profession of teaching in a stagnate economy when a teacher leaves a vacancy to be filled. Unlike the structural variety, circulation mobility may also occur on an intragenerational basis.

North American Patterns

What are the patterns of social mobility in North America? Let us turn first to Canada. Findings from the Canadian Mobility Study, conducted in 1973 (the first national study of this process in Canada), indicate that there is a moderate amount of mobility within the white-collar stratum of the population and also within the blue-collar stratum, but there is very little mobility between white-collar workers and blue-collar workers (McRoberts, 1982).

Consistent with studies done in other nations, upward mobility is more prevalent in Canada than downward mobility. Upward mobility also tends to be short in distance; an individual moves up an occupational level or two rather than up several levels. This suggests that the level of occupational status is frequently inherited (same as one's family of orientation). Farming is the main exception to this inheritance tendency; many youths migrate from the farm to the cities, where they look for jobs.

Those who do become farmers almost invariably have fathers who farmed.

The patterns of Canadian mobility closely resemble those of the United States. The U.S. pattern is explained in the report *Occupational changes in a generation study of 1962 and 1973* (OCG I and OCG II) (see Blau and Duncan, 1967; Featherman and Hauser, 1978). One cannot conclude from this likeness, however, that mobility rates are the same throughout North America. No standardized measure exists with which to make cross-national comparisons of this sort (Matras, 1984: 411–412).

Still, the rates of circulation mobility in the two countries (calculated after removing the effects of structural mobility) are also similar. Those rates were virtually identical from 1925 through 1953 (McRoberts and Selbee, 1981; Hauser et al., 1975). The same may be said for status attainment.

Status, or occupational attainment (see Chapter 11) is the achievement of social rank in society. After surveying a large random sample of Americans, Blau and Duncan (1967: Chapter 5) proposed the following status attainment model, which is also applicable to Canada (McRoberts, 1982). It has three stages: (1) the socioeconomic status of one's family of orientation has the greatest effect on one's educational attainment; (2) educational attainment has the greatest effect on the level of one's first full-time job (entry into the labor force); (3) current occupational status (several years after entry into the labor force) is affected significantly by earlier educational attainment and level of first full-time job. The importance of education in status attainment throughout an individual's lifetime cannot be overestimated: "Overall, the model shows that the single most important factor in the determination of current (i.e., later) occupational status is educational attainment" (McRoberts, 1982: 391). Still, this generalization cannot be applied to occupations in the arts, sports, and entertainment fields, where training is often informal (e.g., Stebbins, 1984). In addition, Guppy et al. (1984) found that the limitations imposed on one's educational attainment at the high school level by the socioeconomic status of the family of orientation have weakened somewhat in this century.

Nevertheless, educational attainment remains the single most important factor in upward social mobility, especially when ethnicity of the would-be climber is considered. We draw here on the Boyd et al. (1980) study of status attainment among immigrants in Israel, Canada, and the United States. Focusing on the immigrants to Canada and the United States, their research reveals that, in general, educational level rather than ethnic background accounts for the immigrants' social mobility or for a failure to move upward. When compared with the first and the third generations, the second generation was found to benefit most from education, inasmuch as those in the second generation reported the greatest occupational achievement. In other words, immigrants arrive in North America with various levels of education; their education qualifies them for certain occupational positions. Their children, aided by significantly more education than they had, tend to climb the occupational prestige ladder (i.e., upward intergenerational mobility). Their grandchildren usually have the ability to climb even further in occupational status, but not as far as their children did. By the third generation, there is presumably somewhat less to attain.

Boyd and her colleagues also report exceptions to their generalizations. Even after considering factors such as parental occupation and education, the following still acquired a higher level of education than other immigrants: native-born Americans of Russian, Chinese, and Japanese parentage, native-born Canadians of Polish and Ukrainian parentage, and foreign-born Canadians of American and German parentage. Foreign-born Mexicans in the United States and foreign-born Italians in Canada had significantly lower educational attainment levels than the others, even after controlling for the aforementioned factors plus broken homes.

A number of scholars on both sides of the

Canadian-American border are convinced that elites lurk in our midst. Most Americans, however, regard the elites as penetrable, to some extent, by qualified upwardly mobile outsiders. Scientific opinion on this issue in Canada is currently divided. Porter's (1965: 558) study and Clement's (1975) follow-up, for instance, suggest the presence of closed elites in Canada. But more recent research (e.g., Ornstein, 1981), a review by Ogmundson (1982), and parts of this chapter contradict their findings.

CLASS CONSCIOUSNESS

The notion of class consciousness originated in Marx's writings. Marx referred to the proletariat's recognition of their exploitation by the bourgeoisie. *Class consciousness* is the awareness and acceptance of the similar attitudes, beliefs, and life-styles of others in one's social class (Giddens, 1980: 111). Marx saw it as a crucial precondition to the proletariat's determination to organize themselves for a revolutionary fight against inequality.

The question asked these days by some students of North American stratification is, given the presence of institutionalized inequality, certain routes of upward mobility, embourgeoisement, and other patterns, does class consciousness exist? Marx said little about the possible effects of social mobility on class consciousness. What is more, he was inclined to use the term with a good deal of imprecision and inconsistency (Giddens, 1980: 80, 93).

One view of the matter comes from Mary Jackman and Robert Jackman (1983), whose research demonstrates the presence of class consciousness in the United States. This consciousness, however, has not led to a polarized population such as owners versus workers or manual employees versus white-collar employees. Rather, social classes in the United States are actually a graded series of subcultures (see Chapter 8), referred to by the Jackmans as "status groups." That is, each class is a community of people loosely bound together by certain shared interests and socioeconomic rewards. The Jackmans found that these communities are recognized at the grass-roots level through perceived similarities and differences in everyday life-style and social contacts. This awareness does not extend to the broader sphere of politics. Within the ranking of status groups, the lower groups, or classes, have a stronger sense of uniqueness than the upper groups, or classes. J. H. Westergaard (1972: 97–98), a British social scientist, sums it up by noting that social class in capitalist society and its attendant inequality are alive and well, but that it in no way follows that *revolutionary* class consciousness, as opposed to Dahrendorf's *conflict* class consciousness, is enjoying a similar vitality:

> Point for point the evidence underlines the same broad conclusion: the structural inequalities of capitalist society remain marked. Disparities of economic condition, opportunity, and power persist—modified, if at all, only within fairly narrow limits. There is no built-in automatic trend toward diminishing class differentials. But it does not necessarily follow that the persistent, objective lines of class division will also be, or continue to be, the lines within which consciousness of class takes shape or across which conflict occurs. That there need be no such neat correspondence is very clear from the example of the United States. It is the claim of many contemporary commentators that Britain, and Western Europe generally, are now going the way of North America in this respect. Among arguments in support of this claim are those which stress a lessened significance or visibility of inequality—as the old insecurities of working class life are reduced or eliminated; as overall levels of living increase; as opportunities for individual social mobility, while not increased, become institutionalized through the system of formal education. . . .
>
> Though the evidence is far from adequate, there is no reason to doubt that in a number of respects working class "patterns of culture" are changing, and becoming less distinctive in the process. It seems reasonable to assume that those features of working class life will be

weakening which, in the past, were conditioned primarily by low absolute levels of living, extreme insecurity, and marked local or social isolation. There are indications in that direction. . . .

There is as yet no certainty about the extent and pace of all such changes in working class culture and environment. The main dispute, however, is not about the facts, but about their implications.

OUTLINE AND SUMMARY

I. Introduction
Social stratification is the process of differentiation by which the three types of strata (castes, estates, social classes) develop and maintain themselves along the dimensions of wealth, prestige, and power. *Stratification system* is the stable and institutionalized hierarchical order of the various strata.

II. Wealth, Prestige, Power
Only when we understand the dimensions of stratification—wealth, prestige, power—can we understand the strata that form along them.

A. Wealth
Wealth is the opportunity an individual has for a supply of goods, living conditions, and personal life experiences as determined by the marketplace. It is property with an exchangeable or monetary value. Income is a primary measure of wealth in industrial societies.

B. Prestige
Prestige is the positive and negative estimation of an individual's public standing on one or more dimensions which society values. Occupation is an indicator of prestige. Another indicator is education. Scales for measuring prestige are based on occupation and education.

C. Power
Power is measured by indicators such as political participation, membership in organizations, offices held in organizations, and attendance at meetings of voluntary associations.

III. Stratification Systems
Three stratification systems are *caste, estate,* and *social class.*

A. The Caste System
Individuals are born into a caste and are likely to live out their lives in the caste. Membership in a caste is endogamous. The Hindus of India still maintain the vestiges of what was once a firmly established caste system. Some sociologists see similarities between the Hindu caste and the stratification system of blacks and whites in the Old South.

B. The Estate System
Estates are also hereditary and endogamous, but they are founded on the legal prescription of civil and political rights, rather than on religious prescriptions as in caste systems. An estate system existed in medieval Europe.

C. The Social-Class System
The terms "class" and "social class," as used in this book, refer to the composite rank of a stratum on the three dimensions of wealth, prestige, and power.
Socioeconomic status (SES) denotes the combination of wealth and prestige alone. The lines separating classes are fuzzier than those separating castes and estates. The members of a particular class share similar interests, life-styles, and living conditions.
Sociologists commonly speak of two to five classes in industrial societies: *upper class, upper-middle class, lower-middle class, working class,* and *lower class.* Marx saw only two: the *bourgeoisie,* or capitalists, and the *proletariat.*

IV. Social Class in North America
The three main groupings of classes in the United States are the privileged upper stratum, the middle stratum, and the underprivileged lower stratum.

A. The Upper Strata
Among the upper strata are the bourgeoisie (own or control the production and allocation of goods and services), leisure class, power elite in government, business, and the military, leaders in religion, education, labor, and the mass media, and top figures in the arts, sports, and entertainment fields. The power-elite theorists hold that those running the country's government, business, and military affairs are an exceedingly powerful, permanent group. Plural-elite theorists disagree, stating that coalitions of various interests gain power, though only momentarily. Veto group theorists maintain that the sundry pressure groups prevent the emergence of either a plural elite or a power elite.

B. The Middle Strata
Within the middle strata are the petty bourgeoisie, the salariat, the blue-collar entrepreneurs, and the unionized blue-collar workers.

1. The Four Strata
The *petite bourgeoisie* are divided into the old and the new. The old petite bourgeoisie are independent commodity producers and small-business people. The new petite bourgeoisie are the fee-for-service professionals (physicians, lawyers, dentists). The *salariat* are salaried personnel of large-scale organizations. At the bottom of the strata are the blue-collar entrepreneurs (tradesmen and shop proprietors) and the unionized blue-collar workers in industry, service, craftwork, and skilled jobs.

2. Embourgeoisement
Embourgeoisement is the acquisition by the working class of middle-class ways, values, life-styles, and relationships. Marxists say proletarianization is taking place instead: middle-class workers are becoming alienated and powerless as are the proletariat.

C. The Lower Strata
Within the lower strata are the hard-core, chronically unemployed poor people in North America. Among these people are blacks, Indians, Métis, Inuit, Puerto Ricans, and Mexican-Americans. People in the lower strata are powerless.

D. Social Class: A Subjective View
Subjective class identification (of *oneself*) is similar in Canada and the United States: 30 to 50 percent of respondents place themselves in the working class. Nearly all others say they belong to the middle class.

V. Stratification Theories
Three theories are referred to as explanations of social stratification: the *functional theory,* the *conflict theory,* and the *functional-conflict synthesis.*

A. The Functional Theory
The functionalists hold that the most important positions in society are filled by those most capable of enacting them. Critics argue that this theory is inaccurate and fails to incorporate some of the major dysfunctions of our stratification systems.

B. The Conflict Theory
The Marxian wing: The modern proletariat is composed of productive, nonsupervisory, manual laborers who lack knowledge about the production process. They therefore have interests which are fundamentally different from the interests and goals of white-collar workers. The broad conflict theory wing: Class conflict occurs between the ruling class with its legitimate authority and the subordinate classes with their basic rights. No elite holds power for long.

C. Functionalist-Conflict Synthesis
Both societies and individuals are self-seeking entities. People will share the fruits of their labor to the extent necessary for their own survival. The power of individuals will determine how surplus production is distributed in society. The struggle for power goes on

not only between individuals and between social classes but also between class systems.

VI. Social Mobility

Social mobility is an upward or downward movement within a stratification system.

A. Types of Mobility

Mobility may be intergenerational or intragenerational. *Intergenerational mobility* is upward or downward movement in status between generations. *Intragenerational mobility* is upward or downward movement in status within a generation. Subtypes are *structural mobility* and *circulation mobility.* Structural mobility, or *forced mobility,* demands that sons and daughters seek occupations other than their father's occupation; the sons or daughters move upward, downward, or laterally in status. *Circulation mobility* occurs when someone moves into a job which another person has left.

B. North American Patterns

There is moderate mobility within white-collar strata and also within blue-collar strata of the population, but very little mobility across the white-collar, blue-collar division. Occupational status is frequently inherited. Educational achievement is the single most important factor affecting the level and status of one's first job. With certain exceptions, education even overrides ethnic background.

VII. Class Consciousness

Class consciousness is the awareness and acceptance of the similar attitudes, beliefs, and life-styles of others in one's social class. That is, one identifies with that class. The Jackmans' research demonstrates the presence of class consciousness in the United States, which is, however, expressed in status groups in similarities and differences in everyday life-style and social contacts. Despite the inequality in capitalist society, revolutionary class consciousness appears to be relatively weak.

FOR FURTHER READING AND STUDY

Coffield, F., Robinson, P., and Sarsby, J. 1980. *A cycle of deprivation? A case study of four families.* Exeter, N.H.: Heinemann Educational Books. Three British sociologists explore the question of whether a cycle of deprivation exists. They conclude there is no such thing; that the fates of those raised in deprived families vary significantly.

Hunter, A. A. 1981. *Class tells: On social inequality in Canada.* Toronto: Butterworths. A textbook on social stratification, which stresses the social inequality in present-day Canadian society.

Jackman, M. R. and Jackman, R. W. 1983. *Class awareness in the United States.* Berkeley, Calif.: University of California Press. A national survey demonstrates that Americans have a pervasive class awareness when asked to identify with one of five classes ranging from poor to upper class.

Matras, J. 1975. *Social inequality, stratification, and mobility.* Englewood Cliffs, N.J.: Prentice-Hall. A textbook on social stratification and social mobility pertaining to the United States.

Mills, C. W. 1956. *The power elite.* New York: Oxford University Press. The classic statement of power concentration in the United States. Mills's book has become the benchmark for North American research and theory in this area since its publication.

Olsen, D. 1980. *The state elite.* Toronto: McClelland & Stewart. Olsen examines the backgrounds and careers of the members of Canada's "state elite," which consists of politicians, judges, and federal civil servants.

Porter, J. 1965. *The vertical mosaic.* Toronto: University of Toronto Press. The classic study of power, status, and social class in Canada, which was stimulated by C. W. Mills's *Power Elite* and which, in turn, has stimulated several subsequent studies both inside and outside Canada.

Silk, L. and Silk, M. 1980. *The American establishment.* New York: Basic Books. This is a study of the elite in American society who lie outside the realm of formal politics, but who nonetheless exert considerable influence on the political process. That elite consists of the network of people who run the foundations, independent councils, and upper-class voluntary associations.

KEY WORDS

capitalist Entrepreneur who owns the means of production; one of the bourgeoisie.

circulation mobility Movement that occurs when someone moves into a job that another person has left.

class consciousness Awareness and acceptance of the similar attitudes, beliefs, and life-styles of others in one's social class.

embourgeoisement acquisition of middle-class ways, values, life-styles and relationships by the proletariat.

estate Hereditary stratum founded on the legal prescription of civil and political rights.

intergenerational mobility Upward or downward movement in status between generations.

internal migration Migration within a country.

international migration Migration consisting of emigration and immigration.

intragenerational mobility Upward or downward movement in status within a generation.

migration Process of changing residence by moving from one location to another within a country or between two countries.

petite bourgeoisie Those who run small businesses or fee-for-service professional offices.

prestige Positive and negative estimation of an individual's public standing on one or more dimensions that society values.

proletarian A worker; one who labors for a capitalist.

proletariat Lower-class workers, some of whom are unemployed and many of whom are alienated from their labor.

social class Composite rank of a stratum on the dimensions of wealth, prestige, and power.

social mobility Upward or downward movement in status within a stratification system.

social stratification Process of differentiation by which the three types of strata (castes, estates, social classes) develop and maintain themselves along the dimensions of wealth, prestige, and power.

socioeconomic status Combination of wealth and prestige.

structural mobility Forced mobility to another occupation from that of one's father.

subjective class Social class one identifies oneself as belonging to.

wealth Supply of goods, living conditions, and personal life experiences of an individual as determined by the market place.

chapter 19

Gender and Age

CHAPTER OUTLINE

INTRODUCTION

Sit back in your chair for a moment and try out the following experiment: Imagine what it would be like if all the age and sex roles you could think of were reversed—males would do what females do, females would do what males do, the young would do what the old do, and the old would do what the young do. From such fantasies, you might picture a world in which men stay at home to do housework, women generals command the armed forces, men attend baby showers, and women only (a female clergy) preach sermons in the churches.

Try the experiment with age. What if all people did not go to work and pursue careers until they were thirty-five years old? What if they continued to work until they died? What if all clothing fashions were set by the elderly? What if the fashions were modeled only by men and women in their sixties and seventies? What if professional baseball players were men in their sixties? What if all Members of Parliament were men and women in their twenties?

Your imaginary world would be different and strange, but, bear in mind, it is a possible world. All the role reversals which you have imagined are physically possible, although they are unlikely to occur in Canadian society as we presently know it. Yet, today, we live in an age in which many people are questioning the practice of limiting roles to one sex or age category. They are also questioning the practice of treating people in the same role differently based on their sex or age.

Although often considered separately in social-science research and in university classrooms, sex and age are frequently paired with one another in everyday life. Phrases such as "act like a lady" (when said to a little girl), "he's a dirty old man," "boys will be boys," and "she's the grandmotherly type" suggest that age often is associated with sex. We are expected to behave differently as men and women and, at the same time, behave in a way appropriate for our age. Sex and age are closely intertwined in everyday life. Therefore, a discussion of age is combined with a discussion of sex in this chapter. The first section opens with an explanation of gender and sex terminology. It concludes with an examination of the sociological differences between gender and age.

GENDER AND SEX TERMINOLOGY

We draw here on the definitional efforts of Gould and Kern-Daniels (1977) and Lipman-Blumen and Tickamyer (1975: 302–303). Their articles have contributed greatly to clarification of the main concepts of gender-role theory. Lipman-Blumen and Tickamyer note that:

> the topic of gender roles is of relatively recent interest and has a somewhat confusing status. Different writers use the term differently, and it is necessary to distinguish among sex, sex identity, sex role, gender, gender identity, and gender role. These distinctions cannot always be made clearly.

Gender is a social determination of one's sex. The term is commonly defined as one's awareness of one's self as a sexual being and as thinking and behaving in a masculine or feminine way. It is often distinguished from the biological fact of one's *sex*. A person's sex depends on whether one's society classifies one at birth as male or female; *sex* is a biological determination. The sex classification is related to his or her sex identity and sex role. *Sex identity* is the identification by others and by oneself as male or female. *Sex role* is the expected behavior and attitude associated with the biological condition of male or female. For example, a female sex role is the role of childbearer, which corresponds to the male sex role as sperm donor.

Likewise, a person's gender is related to his

SOCIOLOGY OR COMMON SENSE

What do you think?

Which of the following statements do you agree with? Which statements do you disagree with? Make a note of your answers. Check your answers when you have completed your study of this chapter. Are your answers to the statements the same as those a sociologist would give?

1. Many older people are pleasantly surprised with their life-style.
2. Women are healthier than men.
3. The discrepancies in occupational income between men and women are accounted for by differences in levels of training and length of experience.
4. Many young women who plan to work also intend to get married and have a family.
5. Men and women are equal before the law.

---

or her *gender role* and *gender identity.* When considering gender, one identifies oneself as feminine or masculine and is identified by others as feminine or masculine. In recognition of gender, one plays the expected role and has the personality expected of a masculine or feminine person. For instance, being a mother is the gender role of a woman, and being a father is the gender role of a man. Gender, when compared with sex, is a distinctly social definition. Occasionally, a psychological or a biological disorder (e.g., transsexualism) proves that a person's sex and gender identities and sex and gender roles are imperfectly matched.

Gender Images

Gender and age roles are social patterns superimposed on fundamental anatomical, psychological, and hormonal differences. A great deal of fact and fiction mingles in this area of science and common sense. Concerning sex-gender differences, Lipman-Blumen and Tickamyer (1975:300–301) conclude that "almost any given result may be contradicted by other studies and models," suggesting that all findings here are to be treated cautiously.

Still, a few generalizations command wide scholarly agreement. For one thing, women, when compared with men, are generally smaller and weaker, but healthier. That is, they live longer and are less often seriously ill. Life expectancy tables show that, in North America, women born in 1971 will live an average of 6.5 to 7.5 years longer than men born in the same year. Physical exercise by women does little to change the size and strength differential between the sexes.

Other generalizations—for instance, that women are conventionally more emotional (i.e., quicker to change moods), expressive, dependent, and passive than men—have been accepted by some specialists and rejected by others (Maccoby and Jacklin, 1974: Chapter 5). Those who reject that proposition see these qualities as parts of a false image. Ambert (1976: 18–27) explores a variety of alternative cultural and situational explanations of these observed differences, suggesting that they can be accounted for, in large measure, by the ways we are socialized and are expected to act as boys and girls and, later, as men and women. In other words, we meet up here (Chapter 5) with the age-old *nature-nurture* question. Which aspects of personality and behavior are explained by genetic inheritance and which by cultural learning?

What is true and what is believed to be true are sometimes two different versions of reality. Although the world's societies vary in many ways, every society has its images of the sexes (Ambert, 1976: 38–39). Williams and Best (1982) surveyed university students in 25 countries, including the United States and Canada, on their stereotyped views of male and female traits. Fifty male-associated traits and 50 female-associated traits were found to be common in the countries studied (taken from Williams and Best, 1982: 81, Table 3.7). A list of the traits is given in the table at the top of page 384.

Monica Boyd (1984: 49) analyzed data gathered in 1982 by the Canadian Institute of Public Opinion (the Gallup poll) on the question: "Do you think that married women should take a job outside the home if they have young children?" Fifty-two percent of all the women interviewed still hold traditional views on this issue; they answered "no." Forty-one percent answered "yes," while 7 percent answered "don't know." University-educated respondents are somewhat more liberal; 43 percent said "no" and 48 percent said "yes." Roughly half of these respondents were male.

Age Images

There are also age images. The Louis Harris polling firm (Harris, 1981) was commissioned in 1974 and again in 1981 by the National Council on the Aging to survey the attitudes of Americans toward aging and, specifically, to measure the differences between the public's expectations for the elderly and the elderly's actual ex-

Male-Associated		Female-Associated	
Active	Loud	Affected	Modest
Adventurous	Obnoxious	Affectionate	Nervous
Aggressive	Opinionated	Appreciative	Patient
Arrogant	Opportunistic	Cautious	Pleasant
Autocratic	Pleasure-seeking	Changeable	Prudish
Bossy	Precise	Charming	Self-pitying
Capable	Progressive	Complaining	Sensitive
Coarse	Quick	Complicated	Sentimental
Conceited	Rational	Confused	Sexy
Confident	Realistic	Curious	Shy
Courageous	Reckless	Dependent	Softhearted
Cruel	Resourceful	Dreamy	Sophisticated
Cynical	Rigid	Emotional	Submissive
Determined	Robust	Excitable	Suggestible
Disorderly	Serious	Fault-finding	Talkative
Enterprising	Sharp-witted	Fearful	Timid
Greedy	Show-off	Fickle	Touchy
Hardheaded	Steady	Foolish	Unambitious
Humorous	Stern	Forgiving	Unintelligent
Indifferent	Stingy	Frivolous	Unstable
Individualistic	Stolid	Fussy	Warm
Initiative	Tough	Gentle	Weak
Interests wide	Unfriendly	Imaginative	Worrying
Inventive	Unscrupulous	Kind	Understanding
Lazy	Witty	Mild	Superstitious

pectations. Some of the results of this study are shown in Table 19.1. Clearly, the public expects the elderly to encounter many more serious problems than they actually do. In fact, the surveys revealed that three of every four elderly persons are pleasantly surprised with their lifestyle, particularly those who are more affluent. Roadburg's (1985: 140–164) interviews of a Canadian sample of elderly persons revealed that two-thirds considered themselves happy and satisfied in their later years.

It is impossible, in the limited space of this chapter, even to begin covering the multitude of psychological and anatomic changes which occur as we age. A summary of what happens is provided by Hendricks and Hendricks (1981: 87):

> We carry with us not only the accumulated results of our genetic heritage but also the affects of a lifetime of stress, trauma, and disease. Together these factors serve to lessen the body's ability to cope with displacing stimuli or disruption of homeostatic conditions. This inability to repair is a process called *senescence;* it leaves people increasingly vulnerable over time. In fact, declining physiological adaptability is one of the most recognizable hallmarks of aging.[1]

One significant conclusion arising from the recognition of senescence is that a person's chronological and physiological ages may be discrepant. That is, a person might be fifty years old chronologically but fifty-five physiologically. This hiatus could, for instance, reduce significantly his or her ability to compete successfully against physiologically younger colleagues at work.

GENDER AND LIFE CYCLE

The family life-cycle framework consists of four imprecisely bounded phases (see Chapters 10 and 12). The first phase begins at birth and ends

[1]Italics in the original.

Table 19.1 PROBLEMS OF THE ELDERLY AND PUBLIC EXPECTATIONS

Q: Now I'm going to read you some problems that other people have mentioned to us. For each, would you tell me whether it is a very serious problem, a somewhat serious problem, or hardly a problem at all for *you personally.*

Q: And how serious a problem would you say (READ EACH ITEM) is for most people over 65 these days —a very serious problem, a somewhat serious problem, or hardly a problem at all for most people over 65?

		1981			1974		
		Personal experience: "Very serious" problems felt personally by public 65 and over	Public expectation: "Very serious" problems attributed to most people over 65		Personal experience: "Very serious" problems felt personally by public 65 and over	Public expectation: "Very serious" problems attributed to most people over 65	
Rank as actual very serious problem for 65 and over (No.)		**(%)**	**By public 18–64 (%)**	**By public 65 and over (%)**	**(%)**	**By public 18–64 (%)**	**By public 65 and over (%)**
4	Not having enough money to live on	17	68	50	15	63	59
3	Poor health	21	47	40	21	50	53
6	Loneliness	13	65	45	12	61	56
10	Poor housing	5	43	30	4	35	34
2	Fear of crime	25	74	58	23	50	51
8	Not enough education	6	21	17	8	19	25
8	Not enough job opportunities	6	51	24	5	47	32
7	Not enough medical care	9	45	34	10	45	36
1	High cost of energy such as heating oil, gas, and electricity	42	81	72	x[a]	x	x
5	Getting transportation to stores, to doctors, to places of recreation, and so forth	14	58	43	x	x	x

Source: L. Harris and Associates. *Aging in the eighties: America in transition,* p. 10. Washington, D.C.: The National Council on the Aging, 1981.

[a] x, Not asked.

with adolescence (roughly age sixteen to eighteen). One then enters young adulthood, a period lasting to approximately age twenty-five. The establishment phase runs from age twenty-five to roughly age fifty-five. People live out the remainder of their lives in the later-years period.[2]

Much of the discussion in this section centers on comparisons of male and female gender roles. These comparisons are a contemporary response to the historical tendency in sociological research to treat males and females as if they were the same. These comparisons show that there are many significant differences between men and women. Also, because of lack of space, scant attention is given in this chapter to North American ethnic gender and age roles. Nevertheless, a modest literature on these topics exists (see Stephenson, 1977: Part 4; Hacker, 1975; Hendricks and Hendricks, 1981: Chapter 13).

Adolescence

Chapter 5 covered, among other things, the topic of gender-role socialization in the family, school, and peer contexts. It was noted that parents are theorized to be influential models of femininity and masculinity for their children, although this has yet to be established empirically (Maccoby and Jacklin, 1974: 300). In addition, the parents and other members of the family treat children according to their understanding of how young males and females ought to be differentially dressed, fed, played with, loved, and taught. For example, girls are more often cuddled, while boys are more often roughly handled and discouraged from clinging (Lewis, 1972). Boys are given toys suggesting implements typically used by men (e.g., tools, trucks, trains), whereas girls are handed playthings dealing with homemaking and nursing. A boy's toys stimulate activity and rough play. A girl's dolls and tea set encourage passivity and solitary play (Ball, 1967). Gender-role differentiation begins at this point. Agents of socialization in the school and peer contexts continue the characterological developments started in the family.

In the teenage years, self-concept and personal identity assume major importance. The boy or girl acquires the proper gender-related personality traits, goals, interests, and values. One issue here is the hypothesis that, compared with boys, girls are reared to be underachievers and to fear success.

Fear of Success Studies conducted in Canada (Kimball, 1977) and the United States (Horner, 1970) even suggest that, as adolescence progresses, girls experience a growing fear of success. From adolescence onward, significant numbers of women may be avoiding competition with men. This situation is believed to promote further divergence of male and female roles. Many young women, it is hypothesized, willingly accept the subtle and, at times, not so subtle directions from parents, teachers, and even peers to be markedly less active, independent, and achievement-oriented than young men. Men, in the meantime, are pushed toward independence and achievement, with a high regard for success.

Researchers have been forced to deal with thorny methodological problems in studies designed to test the fear of success hypothesis. To some extent, the problems have undermined the confidence of many researchers in these studies. Moreover, recent investigations have indicated that, at least for those in higher education, fear of success is experienced by both men and women (see Brooks-Gunn and Matthews, 1977: 259–260). Finally, fear of success may be declining at the university level among American men and women (Tresemer, 1977). Table 19.2 provides partial evidence of this potential trend for North America as a whole. At the graduate

[2]The terms "adolescence" and "retirement" used to identify the first and last phases of the family life cycle are those of Robert Rapoport and Rhona Rapoport. The physiological period of adolescence and the date of occupational retirement occur within these larger phases (see Chapter 10).

level, Canada appears to be making slower progress in this regard than the United States. Brooks-Gunn and Matthews (1977: 260) conclude:

> Although fear of success research has been criticized, often justifiably, the concept of achievement avoidance is a useful one, one that is particularly relevant to women who are seeking careers in traditionally male fields. The belief that certain careers and forms of success are unfeminine contributes to women's reluctance to enter such fields.

This brings us to the question of the nature of masculinity and femininity. Walum (1977: 5) says that "when a male is acting in culturally condoned gender-appropriate ways, he is viewed as *masculine,* and when a female is acting in gender-appropriate ways, she is seen as *feminine.*" The research assumption made in regard to these two sets of personality traits is that people possess either one set or the other and that they should be thankful if the set they possess corresponds to their sex.

Androgyny Sandra Bem (1974) rejects the idea that individuals are either feminine or masculine. She has constructed a scale for measuring androgyny. *Androgyny* is the degree to which people are both masculine and feminine. To the extent that a person is both, he or she is said to be *androgynous* (Greek for male and female), rather than masculine or feminine. In Bem's studies, masculinity and feminity are treated as two separate dimensions, not as poles of a single dimension.

Even the same activity has gender-appropriate ways for its conduct.

One proposition to spring from this research is that androgynous individuals have flexible personalities which enable them to adapt better than either masculine or feminine individuals. Androgynous persons are never forced into narrow, stereotyped gender roles. Jones et al.'s (1978) findings suggest, however, that androgyny may be more adaptive for women than for men. No androgynous male subject was found to be more adaptive or competent than the masculine subjects. Females with some masculine traits were more adaptive and competent, and hence more secure, than more feminine subjects.

Whatever the outcome of research in this area, a new line of inquiry has been initiated. A

Table 19.2 UNIVERSITY DEGREES AWARDED BY SEX IN CANADA AND THE UNITED STATES, 1969–70 AND 1980 (PERCENT)

	Canada				United States			
	1969		1980		1970		1980	
Degree	M	F	M	F	M	F	M	F
Bachelor's	81.8	18.2	50.5	49.5	58.5	41.5	52.7	47.3
Master's	78.6	21.4	62.6	37.4	60.3	39.7	50.7	49.3
Doctorate	89.3	10.7	77.0	23.0	86.7	13.3	70.2	29.8

Sources: Statistics Canada, *Education in Canada,* Cat. No. 81-229, pp. 150–155, Ottawa, 1982; U.S. Bureau of the Census, *Statistical abstract of the United States, 1984,* 104th ed., p. 168, Washington, D.C., 1984.

number of thinkers believe the new approach reveals a trend toward gender-role transcendance in our society. For some of them, androgyny is the final stage in this process; for others, the final stage is a unisex society (Rebecca et al., 1976; Kaplan and Bean, 1976). Data supporting these predictions, however, appear to be lacking (Heilbrun, 1981: 64–66).

Young Adulthood

A good deal of what has been said about adolescents applies to men and women in young adulthood and to individuals in later phases of the life cycle. New gender-role issues appear for the first time as youth leave high school. The issues arise when young men and women get married, get a job, or seek further education.

Some of the gender-role related issues in young adulthood have been considered elsewhere in this book. Table 19.2 shows that, during the 1970s, more North American women than previously received university degrees. Furthermore, men and women marrying for the first time have recently been doing so at an increasingly later median age (Table 10.3). Besides the general rise in the participation of women in the labor force, there is a tendency in the United States and Canada for more women to continue working after marriage, whether or not they have children; many women reenter the labor force soon after the birth of a child (Stockard and Johnson, 1980: 260; Eichler, 1983: 246–248).

Working Women Paid employment is a major status locator in modern industrial societies. Regardless of the intrinsically satisfying or dissatisfying character of work, it does give the employee a sense of contributing directly to the functioning of his or her society—a feeling of being "somebody" in the community—and a monetary return for the effort. These motives help explain the dramatic increase in the participation of females in the labor force and in the inclination of young women to continue working after marriage and childbirth.

This in no way means that women always work for self-actualizing and self-expressive reasons. Apart from their limited involvement in certain professions (e.g., medicine and law), most women fill rather humdrum clerical, semiskilled, and unskilled jobs (see Table 19.3), although they are now represented in some measure in all occupations. That many working women find their jobs dull and unchallenging (Ferree, 1976) is not a unique quality of their occupational lives, however, for many men have similar complaints about their work. As Table 19.3 indicates, there are differences between the

Table 19.3 PERCENT OF FEMALE EMPLOYMENT, 1982

Industry	Canada	United States
Agriculture, forestry, fisheries	23.1	19.4
Mining	13.1	16.0
Manufacturing	28.0	32.3
Trade	43.9	47.1
Wholesale	NA	27.4
Retail	NA	51.9
Finance, insurance, real estate	62.0	57.2
Banking, other finance	NA	64.3
Insurance, real estate	NA	51.6
Services	50.0	60.9
Automotive	NA	11.7
Private household	NA	84.9
Hotels, lodging places	NA	65.8
Entertainment, recreation, arts	39.9	40.9
Medicine	81.7	NA
Hospitals	NA	76.2
Health services	NA	75.8
Teaching	59.1	65.0
Elementary, secondary	55.6 (1981)	70.0
College, university	23.4 (1981)	50.8
Welfare, religious agencies	NA	59.4
Religion	14.3	NA
Clerical	79.0	NA

Sources: Statistics Canada, *The labour force, Annual averages, 1975–83,* Cat. No. 71-529 Ottawa, 1984; U.S. Bureau of the Census, *Statistical abstract of the United States: 1984,* 104th ed., p. 421, Washington, D.C., 1984; Statistics Canada, *Education in Canada,* Cat. No. 81-229, Ottawa, 1981.

employment of females in Canada and their employment in the United States. The employment differences in the service, educational, religious, and manufacturing industries are presently without explanation.

As we have seen, there is an increased number of recent female university graduates, but there still is evidence that many women who plan to work also intend to get married and have a family (Lopata, 1971: 48; Ambert, 1976: 98–99; *Calgary Herald,* 1983: B7). These goals are realistic when we consider the socialized outlook of many young women toward men's and women's work, women's place in the home, male power, and male influence on the job. Marriage and children, however, could be a barrier for women striving to succeed in the workplace, whatever their degree of fear of success.

Sex Discrimination Greenglass (1982: 194–197) and Hitchman (1976: 137–144) have documented discriminatory sex-related practices and attitudes in North American higher education. For example, some male professors, accepting the stereotype, believe that a woman's place is in the home. Correspondingly, these professors do all they can to persuade female students to accept this point of view. That these students may have had their commitment to their academic programs weakened by the factors mentioned in the preceding paragraph is naively interpreted by the professors as support for their beliefs. In addition, less counseling is sometimes given to women than to men, and fewer informal meetings are held with female students than with male graduates and undergraduates. Hitchman adds that the required full-time residency for graduate students in some Canadian universities discriminates against women who are forced by family obligations to pursue a degree on a part-time basis.

A subculture of sex discrimination develops in universities where the stereotype is prevalent. This subculture is passed along to new female students by senior students and by women on the faculty. Symons (1978) hypothesizes that it weakens the female students' determination to complete their university work, ultimately confirming the prophecy (albeit a self-fulfilling one) of cynical male professors and administrators.

Establishment

Establishment is the stage during which the children in the family have grown up and have left the nest. For many mothers, especially those employed solely at home, this is a painful transition. Particularly among working-class women and less well educated women, the absence of children often means a drop in status and a threat to the women's self-conceptions (Lopata, 1971: 41). To the extent that gainfully employed parents identify with and are committed to their occupational careers, this domestic transition is less traumatic. Lowenthal et al., (1975: 18–20, Chapter 5) found that middle-aged men, when compared with their working wives, were both more committed to their jobs and more likely to consider their work a central life interest. As Lowenthal and her colleagues see it, it is no wonder men are happier than women at this stage of life.

Sex Stratification The social standing of North American men and women in the establishment phase of life has led several scholars to the concept of sex stratification. *Sex stratification* is the institutionalized, differential ranking of the sexes along dimensions such as occupation, education, income, and power. Sex stratification is to some degree an expression of *sexism:* prejudice and discrimination against one or the other sex. The result wherever stratification occurs is inequality.

In both Canada and the United States, women continue to be employed, for the most part, in the occupations in which they have traditionally worked for many years (U.S. Bureau of the Census, 1985: 402, Table 676; Statistics Canada, 1984f: Charts 10[a], 10[b]). Thus, with the exceptions of nursing, social work, library

Sex stratification is a built-in facet of many parts of our society.

work, and elementary and secondary teaching, women remain substantially underrepresented in the professions (Greenglass, 1982: 180–181). Even in professions where they are now accounting for an increasingly large proportion of the work force, as in medicine and law, they still meet with opposition from males. The men, it has been observed, try to keep the women in subordinate positions; some men find it unsettling to have a woman as their immediate superior. Greenglass also points out that occupational segregation is a two-way street, cutting into the employment flexibility of males as well as women. For example, men who take jobs as nurses or kindergarten teachers are under social pressure to move into "men's jobs."

Income sex stratification parallels the stratification in occupations (see Table 19.4). To some extent one might expect a lower average income for women, since they fill proportionately lower level positions. One might expect some fields to pay better than others, a difference inadequately reflected in figures such as those in Table 19.4. Finally, one might expect the discrepancies in this table to result from the different amounts of experience of men and women in the same occupations. For instance, in medicine and law, where significant increases in the number of female practitioners have occurred recently, there are many female beginners whose salaries are commensurate with their limited experience.[3]

Table 19.4 ANNUAL MEAN INCOME, AGES 35–44 (1982)

Sex	Canada (Canadian dollars)	United States (U.S. dollars)
Male	26,958	24,376
Female	12,999	10,970

Source: Statistics Canada, *Income distribution by size in Canada, 1982,* Cat. No. 13-207, Ottawa, 1982; U.S. Bureau of the Census, *Statistical abstract of the United States, 1984,* 104th ed., p. 460, Washington, D.C., 1984.

Yet, even when the type of occupation and level of education are held constant, the average incomes of men and women with full-time jobs vary greatly (see Tables 19.5 and 19.6).[4] Moreover, Suter and Miller (1973) and Marchak (1977) have found that, when experience differentials are taken into account, there is still an income gap of a third or more between men and women in the same occupation. The gap may be widening over the long haul throughout North America (Gunderson, 1976), although this is a difficult trend to measure. In short, the evidence leads to the ineluctable conclusion that discrimination by sex accounts for a significant portion of the difference in income between men and women in the same occupation who have equal experience and equal training.

Religious Doctrine Put otherwise, sex stratification is an institutionalized imbalance of power in society. We have just seen its manifestations in regard to work and occupations. Sex stratification also occurs in religion and law. Here sex stratification has become engrained over several centuries of male dominance. This has led to many entrenched practices that have

[3]Ages 35–44 are used in Table 19.4 because it is in this range that average income reaches its maximum.

[4]Only general comparisons of Canada and the United States are possible with the data in these two tables, since some of the occupational and educational categories are differently defined in the two countries.

Table 19.5 AVERAGE INCOME, 1982

Occupational category	Canada (mean income Canadian dollars)		United States (median income U.S. dollars)	
	Men	Women	Men	Women
Professional	29,566	18,503		
Professional speciality			27,940	18,423
Managerial	36,272	19,998		
Executives, administrators, and managerial			28,820	17,326
Clerical	20,175	13,223		
Administrative support, including clerical			20,508	12,693
Sales workers	20,949	10,152	21,901	11,002
Farming	15,813	7,980		
Farming, forestry, fishing			9,093	5,348
Processing and machining	21,984	12,487		
Machine operators, assemblers, and inspectors			17,826	10,876
Product fabrication	21,204	11,503		
Precision production, craft, and repair			20,913	13,591
Construction	20,563	Nil	—	—
Transport	20,266	11,277	18,508	12,990
Service workers, including household workers	16,790	8,351	14,459	8,565

Sources: Statistics Canada, *Income distributions by size in Canada, 1982,* Cat. No. 13-207, Ottawa, 1982; U.S. Bureau of the Census, *Money income and poverty status of families and persons in the U.S., 1982,* Current Population Reports, Series P-60, No. 140, pp. 13–14, Washington, D.C., 1983.

Table 19.6 INCOME AND EDUCATION, 1982

Educational category	Canada (mean income Canadian dollars)		United States (median income U.S. dollars)	
	Men	Women	Men	Women
Elementary (grades 0–8)	15,705	7,596	14,220	9,192
Some high school or high school degree	18,191	9,587	20,642	12,637
Some university	18,224	10,268	23,633	15,594
University degree or four years university	33,898	19,427	28,030	17,405

Sources: Statistics Canada, *Income distribution by size in Canada, 1982,* Cat. No. 13-207, Ottawa, 1982; U.S. Bureau of the Census, *Money income and poverty status of families and persons in the U.S., 1982,* Current Population Reports, Series P-60, No. 140, pp. 13–14, Washington, D.C., 1983.

only recently been recognized as unequal and in need of change. Marlene Mackie (1983: 199–200) describes the discriminatory practices and prejudicial beliefs leading to sex stratification in religion:

> Church organization has traditionally assigned different roles to women and to men. The hierarchy of church structure is consistent with both religious teaching and the fact that most of the major prophets and leaders of Western religions have been men. With few exceptions, men are the authority figures—deacons, priests, clergymen, bishops, cardinals, popes. . . . Ceremonial ties with the deities are maintained by men.

One consequence of this situation, Ambert notes, is that women have a less than equal say in matters significantly affecting their lives. She cites the current official Roman Catholic position on abortion as illustrative of man-made decisions in the church. To be sure, the decisions are based on religious doctrine, but, nevertheless, they ignore the woman's point of view. Men have ruled on abortion even though it is the women who bear children and who are more directly involved in the rearing of children than men.

Religious doctrine is often the ultimate source of authority justifying policies such as the Catholic Church's view on abortion. Walum (1977: 126–130) examines our Judeo-Christian heritage from this perspective. She reminds us that two accounts of the creation of humankind are found in Genesis. The one which the faithful tend to ignore suggests that God is not a male or a female or any combination of the two. Also, this account clearly states that God created man and woman simultaneously. By contrast, the familiar creation story proclaims that God first created Adam and later created Eve from one of Adam's ribs. Woman in general was considered a "helpmeet" for man. Walum (1977: 126–127) refers to other doctrinal passages which, together, form a cultural frame within which daily decisions about religious matters are made by both the clergy and the laity (including many women):

> *Leviticus* 12: 2, 5—If a woman conceives and bears a male child, then she shall be unclean for seven days. . . . But if she bears a female child, then she shall be unclean for two weeks.
>
> *Job* 4: 4—How can he be clean that was born of a woman?
>
> *Daily Orthodox Jewish Prayer* (for men)—I thank Thee, O Lord, that thou has not made me a woman.
>
> *St. Paul*—Let the woman learn to silence with all subjection. . . . I suffer not a woman to usurp authority over men, but to be in silence.
>
> *Ephesians* 5:23–24—Wives, submit yourself unto your husbands. . . . for the husband is the head of the wife, even as Christ is the head of the church.

Legal Status The constitutions of Canada and the United States have established the legal status of women in the two countries. In their original form, neither the U.S. constitution nor the Canadian constitution guaranteed equal legal rights for both men and women. The proposed Equal Rights Amendment to the Constitution of the United States failed to be ratified by the minimum thirty-eight states before the deadline of June 30, 1982. The failure to ratify leaves American women with no firmer legal protection than they have had for more than two hundred years. With a new constitution, the women in Canada have only recently escaped an identical plight. In 1985, women in Canada were guaranteed equality "before and under the law . . . and the right to the equal protection and equal benefit of the law without discrimination" under Section 15, Part I, Charter of Rights and Freedoms, Constitution Act, 1982.

Hence, American women will continue to suffer the subtle inequities inherent in North America's legal heritage, British common law. Walum (1977: 108) supplies some thought-provoking examples from the United States: Some states require a wife to take her husband's surname. In some states, wife beating for the first time is considered a legal act. A husband, in some states, can sue for divorce on the grounds that his wife acted with "gross neglect of duty," such as by failing to keep a clean house and kempt children or by refusing to grant him sexual intercourse. As a whole, divorce laws accord unequal treatment to the sexes. Meanwhile, Canadian men and women will be faced with painstaking adjustments of such legal biases, to bring them in line with the principles of their new Charter of Rights and Freedoms.

THEORETICAL PERSPECTIVES

Sex stratification in industrial societies has been the explanatory target of two major theoretical perspectives: *functionalism* and *conflict theory.* We now turn to the first of these.

Functionalism

Gerald Marwell (1975) provides an example of functionalist theorizing in the field of gender roles. His propositions rest on two assumptions: that (1) many societies, Canada included, are organized around the conjugal family, which functions as the basic economic unit, and (2) there are skills members of a family must acquire if their group is to function successfully. Marwell then hypothesizes that a man and a woman come together in a marriage based on complementary characteristics learned in earlier socializations. From this functionalist perspective, there are four areas where this complementarity is crucial: (a) procreation, (b) socialization of the young, (c) emotional support and the release of tension between husband and wife, and (d) productivity in the family economy along with the management of the family economy. There are many household specializations for which either the husband or the wife is responsible. By working together, the man and woman make the household a going concern. Among the specializations are skills such as cooking, sewing, laundering, cleaning, repairing, painting, gardening, and budgeting. The couple's cooperative undertaking is motivated by appropriate values and attitudes. Marwell (1975: 449) concludes that:

Household specialization by sex has long been a part of family life in North America.

> it may be difficult for the society to pay the price of training everyone to all of these, or for anyone to spend the time and effort to acquire them all. It may also be necessary for all or most of them to appear in a family for the family to work.

This is why our family institution includes gender and sex roles for males and females.

Marwell's theory starts us down the road toward a theory of sex stratification by explaining how the sexes are differentiated. But, before we can reach this destination, we must also be able to account for the differentiation of males and females along the lines of income, occupation, education, and prestige. This is where we meet up with the Marxist and the conflict theorists.

Conflict Theory

Following the footsteps of Friedrich Engels, Peggy Sanday (1974) offers a "theory of female status in the public domain" centering on the woman's role in solving the institutional problems of subsistence. All societies must solve the problems of reproducing and socializing their young, mastering nature (subsistence), and controlling deviant behavior. The reproduction and socialization are undertaken chiefly by women, while mastering nature and controlling deviance, in most instances, are dealt with entirely or predominantly by men. In general, and to the extent that women can gain public recognition by working in the subsistence domain, they can achieve power and hence equality with men.

But, if they are to attain power and equality, women must deal with other problems. For one thing, they must be able to control the goods they produce for profitable trade or sale. They must have something to say about distribution. According to Sanday, when males occupy the distributional role, female producers are relegated to a subservient role. (This sometimes comes about through religious doctrine, which has women serving in slavelike roles.) Under the conditions of war, natural disasters, or accident,

Women gain public recognition by working in the subsistence domain.

women may find themselves temporarily in control of production because their society is short of men, a troublesome situation. But, as Sanday sees it, only when men and women share equally and permanently in production will women ever be equal in status.

Complementing Sanday's theory is Eichler's (1977) theory of the married woman as a "personal dependent" who is economically, socially, and possibly even legally tied to a man who has authority over her. As a dependent, the woman derives her status from her "personal master." Women who are unable to circulate publicly because they are tied down by family-related tasks are socially invisible, notwithstanding the importance of the women's tasks to the maintenance of the society. Moreover, women depend on others for their daily needs (which are more immediate and urgent than the long-term society needs of producing and rearing young). Thus, over the course of history, women have lost power, slipping into an inferior position vis-à-vis men.

Still, sex stratification along the power dimension may not be as extreme as some thinkers claim. Applicable here as well is Emerson's power-dependence hypothesis, which states that the weaker of two individuals in a relationship becomes stronger to the extent that the stronger person becomes dependent on the weaker (Chapter 4). The desire to preserve the dyad as a unit also limits the use of power by either of its members. With this desire, one or the other acquires veto power under certain conditions (Chapter 6).

LATER YEARS

There are at least two related facts helping to distinguish the later years of the life cycle from preceding phases. One is the general loss of status experienced by all elderly people in North America. Berg and Boguslaw (1985: 247–250) describe how the status of the elderly in the United States has more or less deteriorated from colonial times, when the few elderly were respected, to the 1960s, when youth was celebrated. Out of sight in retirement homes or in nursing centers and suffering from reduced income and sometimes poor health, the aged have come to be seen as strange and useless in the youth-oriented society swirling about them. While research may turn up different historical details, Canadian gerontologists note that the elderly in Canada are similarly regarded (Marshall, 1980: 61).

Role and Status

In both Canada and the United States, the decline of status accompanying old age is greater for men than women, since the men usually have higher status in their earlier years. But women suffer in a number of ways, too. Abu-Laban (1980: 201), in summarizing the literature, notes that, when compared with elderly men, elderly women are more likely to be poor, widowed, living alone, denied the opportunity to remarry, seen as physically unattractive, institutionalized, and excluded from the traditional avenues of prestige and power. As if it were a fateful punishment from on high, women tend to live longer in these circumstances than their husbands (and some even longer than their sons).

The second fact is that husbands and wives in their retirement years tend to become more alike; their personalities become similar. This results, in part, from relinquishing some of the roles that previously differentiated the pair (e.g., husband's work role, wife's mother role). But, as McGee and Wells (cited in Stockard and Johnson, 1980: 268) point out, some distinctive roles remain, as exemplified in the continuation of domestic duties (sewing, cooking, cleaning the house) for many wives and the continuation of household maintenance and repairs for many husbands.

The study of the four stages of the life cycle by Lowenthal and her colleagues (1975) shows that characterological changes can occur during the later years. For example, women who are no longer responsible for rearing children acquire a new sense of freedom. Being able to pursue their own interests on a grand scale, perhaps for the first time in thirty years, they also gain self-confidence and self-assurance. Thus, they move closer, characterologically, to their husbands. It was found that husbands in retirement demand more physical comfort and attention than in earlier years. In response to their husbands' demands, the wives impart concern and attention. They develop a degree of assertiveness through the exchange.

On the whole, however, men retain their status superiority, even in the later years. Joyce Nielson (1978: 70) summarizes the changing levels of prestige between men and women over the life course:

> To summarize, we can make several generalizations about the relation between age and sex and their combined effect on status. As people get older, their status increases, reaching a peak in young adulthood for women and ending abruptly at retirement for men. Status differences between the sexes are greatest during middle age, when men are at the height of their earning power and women are experiencing losses in two of their major social roles—motherhood and sexual attractiveness. A comparison of women and men at the same age shows that men outrank women in status at each stage in the life-cycle.

As you may have noted, this chapter has as its focus the many different engagements or involvements of North Americans in regard to their age and sex. In the late 1950s and early 1960s, social gerontologists began to ask how old age is related to these various engagements. They developed two frameworks for answering this question. The frameworks are known as *disengagement* and *activity.*

Disengagement

The framework known as *disengagement* is a variant of functionalism. Cumming and Henry (1961: 14), the original proponents of disengagement theory, held that the aging process is an "inevitable mutual withdrawal or disengagement, resulting in decreased interaction between the aging person and others in the social system he belongs to." This process may be initiated by the individual or by others. In either case, withdrawal is double-edged; aging persons withdraw from the society, and it withdraws from them.

The process of disengagement was said to be universal; it was seen as a fact of life in every society. It is looked on by the elderly as an inevitable, but mutually satisfying, process occurring before death; the process, once under way, is irreversible. It is also a happy arrangement for all concerned. The aging gradually and gracefully bow out of public and semipublic involvements, while the roles they leave are filled by younger members of the society. Individual

The Loneliness of Old Age

Mr Blandford is a fifty-nine year old widower living off Social Security in a privately-rented flat in South London. I walked down a long row of Edwardian villas looking at the bay windows with foliate carving, cracked tessellated courtyards, privet hedges and fragments of ironwork railings. Many of the houses have been turned into flats, not for multi-occupation, but into two apartments, with only the vestibule shared, a ghostly neutral space of dusty cornices and thistle-carvings speaking of ceremonial arrivals and departures that the present occupants know nothing of.

Mr Blandford lives in the upstairs flat. The stairs spiral upwards to a spacious landing, dark and windowless, where the breath condenses and there is a faint smell of mildew—perhaps from behind the corrugating wallpaper in pale Regency stripes. The living room is what was originally the master bedroom of the house. It is neat and orderly: there are many pictures and ornaments but they do not manage to abolish the oppressive sense of space. The objects in the room date chiefly from the 'fifties—maroon moquette chairs with wooden arms and timidly abstract designs, upright dining chairs, a china cabinet. A china model of two Mabel Lucie Attwell lovers on a rustic bench stands on top of the gas-fire.

Mr Blandford lives alone and sees virtually no one. He gets a disability pension for his emphysema, and receives just under £10 a week. When I visited it was 28 December. He had spoken to no one since 23 December, and then it had been to the counter-clerk at the Post Office where he collects his pension. For Christmas dinner he had eaten a tin of Irish stew.

Mr Blandford is thin, and possibly undernourished: a nervous, methodical man, who likes everything in its place. He was a driver on London Transport underground for most of his working life, but then became a rat-catcher for a South London borough until he was forced to retire after a long illness. His wife died eleven years ago. He has tried, unsuccessfully to find someone to share the flat. He showed me the whole flat, kitchen, bathroom and the one bedroom, in which there was a huge bed covered with a pink candlewick bedspread. Pointing to the bed, he said: That's why I can't find anybody to share, that's the reason. They see the bed and they think I just want somebody for sex. I went to the borough Social Services. I said I'd got plenty of room. They sent somebody down to look at the flat and I never heard another word from them. I went to the drug place down Camberwell—same thing. They came to look at it and said wouldn't it be better if I had two single beds? How can I afford to buy single beds on £10 a week?

What I'd really like is a young woman, an unmarried mother with a child, somebody who'd be grateful, be thankful to have somewhere to lay her head. If sex came along I wouldn't mind, but if she didn't want it, I'd just turn my back and go to sleep, I wouldn't bother. . . .

I was happy with my wife. Well, we had our ups and downs. She died of pneumonia; they took her into hospital at one o'clock in the morning. By three o'clock she was dead. I just don't remember how I got back here from the hospital that night; it's a blank in my memory.

I've got three children, all boys. None of them want to know. Two of them live near here, the other one lives in Kent. They've all got good jobs, but I never see them. Never any help. They wouldn't ask me over to spend Christmas, any of them. . . .

I don't get any help. How am I supposed to pay the TV licence, out of ten pounds a week? I pay a quid a week off my gas-bill, it's never clear. If I had somebody to stay with me, I wouldn't charge her, just for food that's all. You can live much cheaper if there's two of you. I wouldn't mind who she was: I'm not prejudiced on colour or anything like that. I want somebody to look after. I'm not bothered about sex. But I don't want to live like this, do I?

SOURCE: Jeremy Seabrook. *Loneliness,* pp. 23–26. London: Maurice Temple Smith, 1973.

physiology, personality, life-style, and role complexes help determine when and how people embark on their courses of disengagement.

Needless to say, the theory provoked a rash of studies to test its validity. For ten years or so, numerous critiques and revisions made their way into the literature. In 1975, Hochschild (1975: 562) wrote that the original question posed by Cumming and Henry is still vital, "but as it now stands, the theory will not do." There has been too little empirical support for the theory in general and too little for its claim of universality in particular. In fact, several investigations employing the data Cumming and Henry used (from the Kansas City Study of Late Life) found that the data fit better the second of the two frameworks, activity (Blau, 1981: 3).

Activity

The disengagement furor in academic and practitioner circles stirred dormant ideas about the importance of being engaged or active in old age. Soon the *activity hypothesis* (a symbolic interactionist hypothesis) was circulating as an alternative to Cumming and Henry's ideas. The activity hypothesis states that, like other people, old people have self-images. Their self-images are sustained through continuous participation in the roles comprised by the images. When these roles end, such as by occupational retirement, others must be found; without the new roles, individuals hardly can avoid feeling unimportant and estranged from their social worlds. Put otherwise, activity contributes to life satisfaction at all ages.

In short, instead of accepting disengagement, activity theory urges older people to pursue a moderately active life-style. But little direct research has been conducted on the activity thesis. The scant indirect evidence offers only slight support for it (Lemon et al., 1972; Longino and Kart, 1982). One problem facing theorists in regard to activity is that bodily changes eventually force all people to modify their physical

An active senior. How inevitable is disengagement for the elderly?

behavior. The elderly, who are acutely aware of this process, regret it, although they accept it as a natural part of life. Thus, as a basis for social policy, activity theory can lead to some rather insensitive advice:

> Indeed, by suggesting that the aged "ought" to remain active to age "successfully" it places people who are not, or cannot remain, active in an awkward position, implying that they are failures. (Ward, 1984: 83)

Ward's review (1984: 82–85) of the research on the activity and disengagement theories indicates that the two theories are still being tested. (For a Canadian test of a Marxist version of disengagement, see Myles, 1979.) As the two theories stand now, however, they are too simple. People adjust to old age by disengaging at some points in their remaining years and not at others, by seeking activity at some points and not at others. Research efforts are complicated by the ideological overtones of both theories, which proclaim that the elderly *should* be active or *should* disengage.

Age Stratification

Precisely how a society's elderly are disengaged depends, to some extent, on its system of age stratification. Riley (1976) observes that societies partition the continuous variable of age into categories associated with socially significant aspects of people and roles. Two processes are at work in the formation of age strata in industrial societies: (1) People are members of a birth cohort. A *birth cohort* is a group of individuals who were born in the same year. As the individuals move through life, the birth cohort adapts to new roles, relinquishes old ones, has experiences, acquires knowledge, and changes biologically and psychologically. (2) But because the society is constantly changing, each cohort encounters along the way a pattern of roles and experiences which differs from the pattern of the cohorts preceding it and following it. For example, the age of mandatory occupational retirement in the United States was raised from sixty-five to seventy years of age in 1978. In Newfoundland, high school students, to be graduated, now must complete twelve grades instead of eleven grades. The twelve-grade requirement was enacted in 1982.

The stratificational or ranking aspect enters the picture in the following manner: Each birth cohort, because of physical, social, or psychological factors, differs from the others in the society in the kinds of contributions the cohort can make to that society's overall functioning. Correspondingly, roles come to be allocated to people at the optimum age range for fulfilling them. Each cohort passes through the age range of the age-graded roles (e.g., parent, athlete, executive, trainee, retiree, grandparent), with some of its members assuming the roles.

Riley and her associates call this a "flow" process, which they liken to riding an escalator. Proximal birth cohorts, each on its own step, pass through space and sights which are much the same; they see and experience many of the same events and circumstances. But the spaces, sights, and experiences change over the long run, with distant cohorts leading significantly different lives. Among the experiences one passes through on the escalator are the aforementioned age-graded roles.

Society values some of these roles more than others. Consequently, we have age stratification, which rests on *ageism;* with ageism, there is prejudice and discrimination against particular age groups. Ageism has its counterparts in sexism and racism. There is also inequality in age stratification. A frequent outcome of inequality is conflict. The level of present-day ageism in North America indicates that the retirement cohorts rank near the bottom of the age stratification continuum, while the youth cohorts rank near the top. In time, of course, youth will age and will become the retirement cohort. Will ageism be as strong then as now? The answer to this question depends on the effectiveness of the gray-power movement.

An age-graded sex role. Do you think it is likely to change in the future?

PROTEST MOVEMENTS

Ageism and its gender counterpart, sexism, are under attack by activists who are determined to achieve equality of treatment for the elderly and women. Such a goal demands organization. Aging-based organizations (Hudson and Binstock, 1976: 381) may be composed of elderly people (e.g., American Association of Retired Persons, the National Pensioners and Senior Citizens Federation [Canada]). Or they may offer goods and services to the elderly (e.g., American Nursing Home Association, Associated Homes for Special Care [Canada]). Some aging-based organizations are composed of practitioners who serve the elderly (e.g., Canadian Association on Gerontology [CAG], Gerontological Society of America [GSA]). The latter two organizations also do research on the aging.

It is clear, however, that the majority of the aged have yet to develop a politically effective voice. Hendricks and Hendricks (1981: 377) suggest that the elderly are politically powerless because there is no generalized age-group consciousness. Active interest groups, they note, organize around several points of concern, not a single point, such as aging. When age awareness among the elderly is pronounced, the old people have been found to seek political participation, desire interaction with others of their age, and favor the establishment of age-based organizations (Rose, 1965). Although political activism is generally weak among the aged, the National Council of Senior Citizens (a U.S. organization) was apparently enough of a threat to the Nixon administration to win a place on its "enemies list" (Butler, 1975: 327).

The fight against sexism is carried on by activists in the women's movement. The women's effort has been considerably more successful than the fight against ageism carried on by the elderly. According to Lucile Duberman (1975: 17–29), the revival of organized feminism in the United States was stimulated by President Kennedy's Commission on the Status of Women (established in 1961) and subsequently by the founding in 1966 of the National Organization for Women (NOW) by Betty Friedan (author of *The Feminine Mystique*) and members of the commission.

Duberman describes the American women's movement in the mid-1970s as having two distinct branches. One is represented by NOW. It is composed primarily of white, middle-class, middle-aged professional women (some men belong, too). This "bureaucratic" branch uses existing channels to press for changes important to women in the legal, political, and economic segments of their lives. The second branch, which has no main organizational locus such as NOW, appeals to a younger, more heterogeneous, more radical set who are more informally organized. One of their aims is to make women aware of their collective plight, thereby encouraging them to fight the problem of sexism. The younger women argue that there is a tendency for women to mistake their gender-role problems for individual difficulties.

Writing on sexism, Strong-Boag (1977: 271) suggests that "Canada does not generally evidence the same degree of misogynic and conservative reaction as the United States." In other words, the need for organized opposition in Canada may be less since Canadians are more open to changes in sex relations than Americans. Nevertheless, Morris (1980) was able to trace the start of a "new feminist movement" in Canada to the Royal Commission on the Status of Women in Canada (Information Canada, 1970). Canadian women at that time were clearly influenced by the agitation of their sisters in the United States, who had just founded NOW. The Voice of Women, which came into being in Canada in 1960 as an antinuclear body, became a crucial link in the 1970s between leftist groups and mainstream, upper-middle-class feminist organizations. It appears that the women's movement in Canada can also be described as having a more formal, moderate branch composed largely of middle-aged women and a less formal, radical branch composed largely of younger women. Each has goals similar to those of the corresponding branches in the United States.

OUTLINE AND SUMMARY

I. Introduction
Your world would be strange if all the age and sex roles were reversed.

II. Gender and Sex Terminology
Gender is one's awareness of one's self as a sexual being and as thinking of oneself as behaving in a masculine or feminine way. *Sex* classifies one at birth as male or female. It is a biological classification.

A. Gender Stereotypes
Gender and age roles are social patterns superimposed on fundamental anatomical, psychological, and hormonal differences. As a group, women are smaller and weaker than men, but they are healthier. Every society has its stereotypes of differences between the sexes.

B. Age Stereotypes
As we age, we carry with us the accumulated results of our genetic heritage, plus the effects of a lifetime of stress, trauma, and disease. These factors contribute to *senescence.*

III. Gender and Life Cycle
The family life-cycle framework consists of four imprecisely bounded phases: adolescence, young adulthood, establishment, later years.

A. Adolescence
Parents are influential models of femininity and masculinity. The socialization of boys differs from the socialization of girls. In the teenage years, self-concept and personal identity assume major importance.

1. Fear of Success
Girls may experience a growing fear of success. From adolescence onward, many women avoid competition with men. Women tend to be less active and achievement-oriented than men.

2. Androgyny
A person can have both masculine traits and feminine traits. *Androgyny* is the degree to which people are both masculine and feminine. To the extent that a person is both, he or she is said to be *androgynous* rather than masculine or feminine.

B. Young Adulthood
There has been an increase in the number of women who have joined the labor force and who are working. Still, getting married and having a family are important goals for many young women who plan to work.

1. Working Women
Women do not always work for self-actualizing and self-expressive reasons. Women usually fill humdrum clerical, semiskilled, and un-

skilled jobs. They are paid less than men.

2. Sex Discrimination
   There are sex-related practices and attitudes in North American higher education. Some professors feel that a woman's place is in the home. They do all they can to persuade female students to accept this point of view.

C. Establishment
   Establishment is the stage during which the children in the family have grown up and have left the nest. This is a painful transition for many mothers. When compared with their working wives, men in the establishment phase are more committed to their jobs and more likely to consider their work a central life interest.
   1. Sex Stratification
      Sex stratification is the institutionalized, differential ranking of the sexes along dimensions such as occupation, education, income, and power.
   2. Religious Doctrine
      Sex stratification also occurs in religion. Religions in the modern world are male-dominated. Women have a less than equal say in matters significantly affecting their lives. An example is the attitude of the Roman Catholic Church toward abortion.
   3. Legal Status
      American women now have no firmer legal protection than they have had for more than two hundred years. With a new constitution, the women in Canada have only recently escaped an identical plight.

IV. Theoretical Perspectives
   A. Functionalism
      Sex stratification in industrial societies has been the exploratory target of two major theoretical perspectives: *functionalism* and *conflict theory.* Many societies are organized around the conjugal family, which functions as the basic economic unit. There are skills members of a family must acquire if their group is to function successfully.
   B. Conflict Theory
      All societies must solve the problems of reproducing and socializing their young, mastering nature (subsistence), and controlling deviant behavior.

V. Later Years
   The later years are the final phase of the life cycle. The elderly generally lose status in North America.
   A. Role and Status
      In both Canada and the United States, the decline of status accompanying old age is greater for men than for women.
   B. Disengagement
      In retirement, the aging process is a mutual withdrawal or disengagement, resulting in decreased interaction between the aging person and others in the social system to which he or she belongs.
   C. Activity
      Old people, like others, have self-images, which are sustained through continuous participation in the roles comprising the images. If one role is lost, say through occupational retirement, another must be found. This hypothesis lacks empirical support.
   D. Age Stratification
      Two processes are at work in the formation of age strata: (1) people are members of a birth cohort; (2) each cohort encounters a somewhat different pattern of roles and experience as it moves through life. Society values some age-graded roles more than others. With ageism, retirement cohorts rank near the bottom on the age stratification continuum, while youth rank near the top.

VI. Protest Movements
   The majority of the aged have yet to develop a politically effective voice to fight ageism. The women's movement in both Canada and the United States has a middle-aged, liberal, bureaucratically oriented branch and a young, leftist, informally oriented branch.

FOR FURTHER READING AND STUDY

Eichler, M. 1980. *The double standard: A feminist critique of feminist social science.* New York: St. Martins. Eichler explores the use of the double standard in everyday life and in social science theory and research. Sex-role socialization is, among other things, systematic training in the double standard.

Greenglass, E. R. 1982. *A world of difference: Gender roles in perspective.* Toronto: Wiley. A textbook on sex and gender relations with a North American focus.

Illich, I. *Gender.* 1983. New York: Pantheon. One of the most provocative social critics of our time examines the changing roles of the sexes and the work that each performs. Illich is anything but optimistic about the chances of women obtaining equality.

Lopata, H. Z. 1971. *Occupation: Housewife.* New York: Oxford University Press. The author tells of in-depth personal interviews with urban housewives. The women were married and each was the mother of at least one preschool child. Lopata asked them about their daily routines and about their attitudes toward their homemaker role.

McPherson, B. D. 1983. *Aging as a social process.* Toronto: Butterworths. A textbook on aging and the elderly concentrating chiefly on the Canadian and American scenes.

Perun, P. J., ed. 1982. *The undergraduate woman: Issues in educational equity.* Lexington, Mass.: Lexington Books, 1982. A collection of original papers on the historical trends in women's university experience. Among the topics covered are women's access to universities and the outcomes of their undergraduate careers. There are references to personal experiences.

Tresemer, D. W. 1977. *Fear of success.* New York: Plenum. A synthesis of research into the fear of success hypothesis.

Tamir, L. M. 1982. *Men in their forties: The transition to middle age.* New York: Springer. Tamir uses survey data to develop indices and other measures of satisfaction, happiness, well-being, psychological symptoms, time perspective, value orientations, and alcohol and drug use.

Williamson, J. B., Evans, L., Powell, L. A., Hesse-Biber, S. 1982. *The politics of aging: Power and policy.* Springfield, Ill. Thomas. The authors explore the themes of the social control, power, and political participation of the elderly in American society and in preindustrial and modernizing societies.

KEY WORDS

activity theory The elderly have self-images, which are sustained through continuous participation in social roles.

age stratification Social ranking by age category.

disengagement Process of estrangement from society by the elderly that results in decreased interaction between them and other people.

gender One's awareness of one's self as a sexual being and one's thinking of oneself as behaving in a masculine or feminine way.

life course Experiences and changes which occur from day to day in an individual's life.

senescence Accumulated effects of our genetic heritage plus the effects of a lifetime of stress, trauma, and disease.

sex One's biological classification at birth as male or female.

sex stratification Institutionalized differential ranking of the sexes along such dimensions as occupation, education, income and power.

chapter 20

Race and Ethnicity

CHAPTER OUTLINE

Introduction
Race and Races
Immigration to North America
- **The United States**
- **Canada**

Ethnic Relations
- **Ethnic Conflict: Attitudes**
  - *Prejudice*
  - *Ethnocentrism*
- **Ethnic Conflict: Behavior**
  - *Discrimination*
  - *Segregation*
  - *Inequality*
  - *Expulsion*
- **Ethnic Conflict: Resistance**
- **Ethnic Harmony**
  - *Assimilation*
  - *Amalgamation*
  - *Accommodation*
  - *North American Pluralism*
  - *Canadian Multiculturalism*
- **Submission and Acceptance**
- **Avoidance**
- **North American Minorities**
- **Ethnic Revival**

INTRODUCTION

In 1983, the resident population of the United States was 234.2 million. Canada is roughly one-tenth the size; the Canadian census, in 1983, recorded a population of 25 million people. People of different races and ethnic groups live together in these two countries, sometimes in harmony, sometimes in conflict. There are racial intermarriages, racially mixed clubs, ethnically mixed associations, and face-to-face interchanges between the members of different racial and national groups. Many exchanges between individuals of different races and different ethnic groups are warm and harmonious. But there is also discrimination. People have been killed and injured in race riots and disturbances. There are ideologists who promote the doctrine of racial purity. There are, in North America, troublesome instances of racial and ethnic conflict.

Strictly speaking, from the standpoint of biological science, "races" do not exist. As we shall see, there is no biological basis for the concept of race. Still, anthropologists have recognized that humankind has divided itself into identifiable physical categories. One such category is *race;* the commonsense idea of race is based on inherited physical similarities among the individuals who make up a "race." There are similarities in skin color, hair texture, lip size, eye contour, and bone structure. Whites, blacks, Orientals, and Indians are among the racial categories inhabiting North America.

People in a society are differentiated not only by their race but also by their ethnicity. *Ethnicity* is an ethnic quality or affiliation. The word "ethnic" is an English language oddity, for it still has much the same meaning its Greek predecessor had more than two thousand years ago. In ancient Greek, the word "ethnos" referred to a nation and the word "ethnikos" to a foreign or national group within society. By the time Christianity gained acceptance toward the end of the Roman era, the Latin "ethnicus" had acquired the added meaning of "heathen" as a qualifier of the earlier Greek idea of foreigner.

Although the sense of *ethnic* as heathen or pagan has remained to the present, the word "ethnic" is now commonly defined as: of or relating to racially or culturally distinct categories of people. Ethnic categories are rarely groups in the sense communicated in Part 3 of this book; still, sociologists refer to these categories as *ethnic groups.* The ethnic group is a category in society distinguished by its unique racial, cultural, and behavioral traditions and by the sense of identity resulting from this visibility.

We have said that ethnicity is an ethnic quality or affiliation. The word refers to an ethnic group's identifying traditions, usually a combination of religion, nationality, race, language, and perhaps other cultural traits. An ethnic group that endures prejudice and discrimination at the hands of the dominant group is called a *minority.* Among the ethnic groups in North America are the blacks, Irish, Italians, Germans, Chinese, Mexicans, French Canadians, Amerindians, and East Asians. At times these groups, and others, are treated as minorities.

RACE AND RACES

The relationship between race, on the one hand, and ethnic group, on the other, is complex. Biologically, a *race* is a subdivision of the species *Homo sapiens.* Race is a form of physical differentiation. Physical anthropologist Ashley Montagu (1960: 409–419) describes three major racial groups: Negroid, Caucasoid, and Mongoloid. The three groups correspond roughly to our everyday terms "black," "white," and "yellow" (Oriental). As a result of centuries of inter-

---

SOCIOLOGY OR COMMON SENSE

What do you think?

Which of the following statements do you agree with? Which statements do you disagree with? Make a note of your answers. Check your answers when you have completed your study of this chapter. Are your answers to the statements the same as those a sociologist would give?

1. We live in an age more tolerant than any other of ethnic and moral differences.
2. Some stereotypes are flattering.
3. The United States is now and always has been the great ethnic melting pot of the world.
4. The law in North America is fair and equal; it does not discriminate against minority group members.
5. Members of ethnic groups have the same opportunities for occupational success as the members of the dominant majority have.

Ethnic group: A traditional Ukranian wedding (1970).

breeding, however, there is considerable overlapping of racial traits among individual members of these three classes. Thus, some Negroids have lanky hair, and some Caucasoids have thick lips. There are Caucasoids with dark skin (e.g., those in India and Sri Lanka) and Mongoloids with pointed noses. These anomalies indicate that any racial categorization must be based on the exceptional presence of certain traits rather than on their exclusive presence. Even this distribution is empirically difficult to determine. Furthermore, racial traits, and hence any abstract racial classifications, are of minor biological significance; they contribute little to the physical survival of the species.

What *is* of great significance is the social meaning of racial traits. Notwithstanding the scientifically proved inadequacy of traits as discriminators of a race, certain visible traits have gained prominence in the lay circles as identifiers of racial membership (e.g., skin color, hair texture, hair color). Based on such presumptions, racially differentiated ethnic groups the world over have been subordinated by members of other races more powerful than they.

The social meaning of racial traits is of far greater interest to sociologists than the scientific classification of people as belonging to one race or another. Such classification is the province of physical anthropology. By contrast, sociology is inclined to treat racial traits (as socially defined) as simply one of several indicators of ethnicity. At least as important as indicators of ethnicity are the religion, nationality, language, and customs of the group being investigated. In this technical sense, then, the sociology of race and ethnicity is more a study of ethnicity than it is of race. Ethnicity is a form of *social differentiation,* although one criterion used to differentiate people by ethnicity is certain clusters of racial traits and their meaning to us.

IMMIGRATION TO NORTH AMERICA

The United States and Canada were founded by several distinct racial and ethnic groups. They took the land from the native inhabitants. These founding groups, or charter groups, sometimes rejected and sometimes accepted the immigrants who followed them. This has resulted in both conflict and harmony in North American ethnic relations over a period of roughly two hundred years. In broad perspective, the historical patterns of ethnic arrivals and immigration policies are similar for both Canada and the United States. A close look at these patterns, however, reveals some important dissimilarities. The dissimilarities exist because Americans and Canadians have sometimes responded differently to the immigrants who landed on their shores.

The United States

From colonial days to approximately 1880, people from northern and western Europe settled in the United States, making up its population. These immigrants came primarily from Ireland, Scandinavia, Germany, France, Switzerland, the Netherlands, and the United Kingdom. The British and the Irish, during this period, exerted the dominant social, cultural, political, and economic influence. Partly in response to deterioration of living conditions at home, a new and different wave of immigrants began to arrive after 1880. They came from southern and eastern Europe, from Greece, Italy, Austria, Hungary, Russia, and Poland. By 1896, they were landing on American shores in greater numbers than the old-wave immigrants.

The old- and new-wave immigrants tell only the Atlantic side of the American immigration saga. The discovery of gold on the Pacific Coast in the 1850s created a demand for inexpensive labor to perform menial tasks such as cooking and laundering for the miners. The Chinese filled these jobs. But the completion of the first transcontinental railroad in 1869 eliminated the need for their services, leaving them in precarious economic circumstances. Soon they began competing with white Americans for jobs in what the Americans felt was their labor market. The result was America's first restrictive immigration legislation: In 1882 Congress passed the Chinese Exclusion Act, which eliminated all inmigration from China for ten years. The act was renewed several times after the initial ten-year period; eventually, the time was removed, making exclusion permanent. The Japanese, who started arriving later and in smaller numbers than the Chinese, were quickly subjected to similar discriminatory practices. For example, the federal Antialien Land Act of 1913 barred the Japanese from purchasing land in the United States.

By the end of the second decade of this century, the new-wave immigrants were entering the country in large numbers. This trend, plus the new immigrants' cultural differences, stirred anxiety among the old wave. There was a clear and present danger of the old-wave immigrants destroying the newcomers' hard-earned way of life. Antialien sentiments mounted, leading to the introduction of legislation in 1917 that culminated in the Immigration Act of 1924. This act set out a quota system biased toward northern and western Europeans and against most groups outside this geographical area. No controls were placed on immigrants from the Americas and the West Indies. Immigrants from Cuba, Jamaica, Haiti, and Puerto Rico continued to arrive at a brisk pace.

Although the immigration system was tinkered with from time to time, it remained basically intact until its termination in 1965. Amid charges of blatant racism, it was replaced by a system of quotas for the Eastern and Western Hemispheres, which gave preference to relatives of citizens and also to people with needed occupational skills. Canadians and Latin Americans still have a slight advantage under this legislation, although nothing like their advantages prior to its introduction. Special acts are occasionally passed to permit entry of refugees from countries in political turmoil, such as Vietnam, Uganda, and Cuba.

Canada

Although it has followed the same general pattern as the United States, Canadian immigration has also had its peculiarities. There were two distinct phases in the early flow of Europeans to Canada. The first was dominated by the French. They were followed in the second phase by the British, in what is referred to by historians as the "British conquest." During both phases, northern and western European migrants predominated, as they did in early American immigration.

The French started immigrating to New France, parts of which are now in Canada and other parts of which are in the United States, around 1667. It was primarily a time for French empire building in which explorers from France penetrated as far west as the Mississippi valley and as far south as New Orleans. It was also a time for spreading Roman Catholicism and other aspects of French culture such as cooking and philosophy. This phase ended at approximately 1765.

The British conquest constituted the second phase. It ended earlier in the United States (with the Declaration of Independence in 1776) than in Canada, where it ended with confederation in 1867, the federal union of the first five provinces of Canada. Among those involved in the British conquest in Canada were the United Empire Loyalists, who fled to Canada from the United

States shortly before and after the signing of the Declaration of Independence.

The British North American Act (1867) was a benchmark in relations between the English in Canada and the country's largest minority, the French. The act was intended to guarantee a place in Canada for the French and their culture. This guarantee, however, was most effective at the provincial level and then only for Quebec, since that was where nearly all the French lived in 1867. The act provided little guidance, nevertheless, on many important issues. For example, would the bilingualism of Quebec be extended to the new provinces in the west? Would there be denominational schools for all in their mother tongue (Bell and Tepperman, 1979: Chapter 4)? The struggles with these questions and others have given ethnic relations in Canada a distinct character when compared with those in the United States.

The years between 1867 and 1895 were ones of relatively unrestricted entry, as Canada strove to populate its vast hinterland and counteract substantial emigration to the United States (Information Canada, 1974: 3–4). One major exception to this laissez-faire policy was the passage of the federal Chinese Immigration Act (1885), which limited but never banned the in-migration of the Chinese. By this time Orientals were being looked upon in British Columbia, as in California, Oregon, and Washington state, as an acute problem. Of note is the fact that no such law was passed concerning American ex-slaves who continued to flee to eastern Canada until the Civil War.

Immigration from 1896 to 1914 reflected the ideas of Clifford Sifton, Minister of the Interior, who pursued an aggressive policy of agricultural development in the western provinces. Nearly 200,000 people migrated annually to Canada from Europe and elsewhere in one of the largest population movements in world history (Anderson and Frideres, 1981: 134). The migration consisted of English-speaking groups from the United Kingdom, German-speaking groups (e.g., Mennonites, Hutterites), French-speaking groups from France and Belgium, Slavic groups (e.g., Ukrainians, Poles, and Russian Doukhobors), and Scandinavian groups. Throughout this period, a selective immigration policy was taking shape via the addition of special regulations to the Immigration Act of 1869. This policy put impediments (usually financial) in the way of would-be migrants from Asia and eastern southern Europe.

World War I and the Great Depression reduced immigration to a trickle. Those who immigrated to Canada in the 1920s were chiefly Britons and Americans. Although Canadians stopped short of the sort of quota system in use at this time in the United States, they were as apprehensive as their southern neighbors about admitting people whose cultures meshed poorly with their own. But the persistent need for land settlement seemed to stimulate a somewhat more open policy in Canada than in the United States:

> Immigration was still regarded primarily as a matter of land settlement, with the immigration service organized to serve that objective. British and American immigrants were the most favored. Northern Europeans were relatively well received. Nonwhites were not welcome. Immigration policy and law had hardly developed at all. The main policy contributions of the 1914–1945 period were the introduction of the concept of sponsored immigration, and the use of the visa to control immigration at source. (Information Canada, 1974: 17)

The Russian immigrants to Canada brought many of their old ways with them.

Table 20.1 CANADA-UNITED STATES IMMIGRATION BY PERCENT OF TOTAL POPULATION AT END OF PERIOD

	Period			
Country	**1951–60**	**1961–70**	**1971–75**	**1951–75**
Canada	8.8	6.6	3.7	16.7
United States	1.4	1.6	0.9	3.6

Source: Adapted from Statistics Canada. *Perspectives Canada III,* p. 298, Table 15.3. Ottawa, 1980.

The system of preferences continued during the period from the end of World War II to 1960. Britons and Americans retained their preferred status, although, in actuality, continental Europeans, especially those from Germany, Italy, and the Netherlands, supplied the larger numbers. As in the United States, humanitarian considerations led to special arrangements for refugees from Hungary, Suez, Uganda, Greece, and elsewhere. In 1967, Canada followed in the same steps as the United States to remove all racial and national criteria from its immigration policy. For unsponsored immigrants, other criteria such as personal qualities, occupational demand, age, education, skill, and prearranged employment are given weights in a going system to determine qualifications for admission to the country.

Immigration to both Canada and the United States has generally been in decline since World War II (See Table 20.1). Nevertheless, the proportion of immigrants to total population has been many times higher in Canada than in the United States, partly as a result of Canada's need for skilled and professional workers and for people to settle and work in its remote areas. Consonant with this picture is the trend toward declining migration between the two countries, although it began only in 1974 for Americans migrating to Canada, ten years after it began for Canadians going in the other direction, often to enroll in American colleges and universities (see Figure 20.1). Since 1977, however, the number of Canadians migrating to the United States has once again become greater than the number of Americans moving to Canada (Bagnall, 1982). In 1980, roughly two Canadians were moving to the United States for every American moving to Canada (Statistics Canada, 1980 –1981b).

Today, ethnic composition of both countries is highly varied, although far from identical. This is evident in Table 20.2, which contains the percentage of total population contributed by the ten largest national groups in each.[1] If any single factor were singled out to account for these differences in ethnic composition, it would be Canada's much closer cultural ties with Great Britain and France than America's.

ETHNIC RELATIONS

Sociology's interest in ethnicity is conveniently and effectively summed up in the phrase "ethnic relations." Ethnic relations is a complex, sweeping social process encompassing several smaller processes. Among these processes are the nearly countless social interactions among individuals of different ethnic backgrounds (e.g., a Chinese waiter serving Caucasian diners). There are also a variety of interchanges between ethnic groups (e.g., native Indians contesting the government over land claims), and the history of such interchanges between various minority groups and the dominant group in the society is of great interest to sociologists. In this section, we consider three main group processes in the field of ethnic studies: *conflict, harmony,* and *avoidance.* Their historical manifestation is then examined within the framework of ethnic relations cycles. The chapter ends with a discussion

[1]Neither Canada nor the United States is listed in Table 20.2. Information on each as an *ethnic group* in the other country is incomplete.

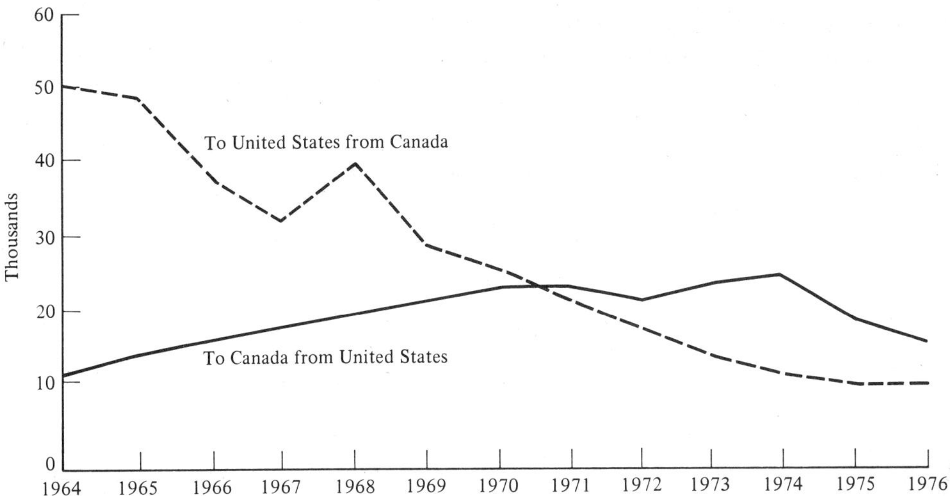

Figure 20.1 Migration Between Canada and the United States, 1964–1975. (*Source: International and Interprovincial Migration in Canada,* Cat. 91-208. Immigration Statistics, Department of Manpower and Immigration, Ottawa, 1964–1976.)

of minorities in North America and the current ethnic revival.

Ethnic Conflict: Attitudes

It is well established that we live in an age more tolerant than any other of ethnic and moral differences (Davis, 1975; Nunn et al., 1978). Yet, ethnic relations in North America have sometimes been brittle. Despite the comparative calm of today, ethnic conflict is by no means a problem of the past. It remains a problem in contemporary society.

Any aspect of ethnicity has the potential for provoking interpersonal and intergroup tension. Religious, national, racial, cultural, and linguistic differences, alone or together, have been grounds for hostile attitudes or behavior or both. It has been the practice in sociology to examine attitudes and behavior separately, since behavior has sometimes been found to correspond poorly to attitudes. The classic study of this inconsistency was conducted by Richard LaPiere (1934). He solicited written statements from several California hotel proprietors, many of whom said they would graciously receive a Chinese couple. When the couple actually turned up, they were refused the usual services. A recent extensive review of the search and theory on attitude-behavior consistency is more optimistic, however: moderate consistency between the two has been found under a variety of research and methodological conditions (Hill, 1981).

Prejudice The attitude side of ethnic conflict is expressed as prejudice, stereotype, ethnocentrism, and racism. The word "prejudice," when used by sociologists, refers to an unfavorable, often emotional, orientation toward a category of people.[2] Many sociologists add the criterion that, consonant with its etymological roots, prejudice is essentially a "previous judgment" based on faulty and inflexible generalizations. That is, qualities of the ethnic group that are objectively absent are imputed by other members of the society, or qualities that are objectively missing are held to be present. Prejudice rests on key beliefs, such as the view, found in Canadian social studies textbooks, that Indians

[2]Some sociologists hold that prejudice is synonymous with bias, that it can be favorable or unfavorable (e.g., Secord and Backman, 1974: 165).

Table 20.2 NATIONAL ORIGIN BY PERCENT OF TOTAL POPULATION[a]

National origin	United States (1980)	Canada (1981)	National origin
United Kingdom (including Ireland)	43.9	44.9	United Kingdom (including Ireland)
Germany	21.3	28.4	France
France	5.6	4.7	Germany
Italy	5.3	3.1	Italy
Poland	3.6	2.4	USSR (including Ukraine)
Mexico	3.3	1.7	Netherlands
Netherlands	2.7	1.2	China
Sweden	1.9	1.1	Poland
Norway	1.5	0.8	India-Pakistan
USSR (including Ukraine)	1.5	0.8	Portugal
Czechoslovakia	0.8	0.6	Greece

Sources: U.S. Bureau of the Census, *1980 Census of population: Ancestry of the population by state,* Supplementary Report, Washington, D.C., 1980; Statistics Canada, *Census of Canada,* Cat. No. 92-911, Table 1, Ottawa, 1981.

[a]These percentages are based on multiple and single national origins.

are primitive, unskilled, aggressive, and hostile (McDiarmid and Pratt, 1971) or the occasionally heard view that they are lazy and untrustworthy (Stymeist, 1975). Prejudicial images also change with time. Maykovich (1972) found, after interviewing a sample of white California college students, that they saw blacks as musical, impulsive, and aggressive. The traditional white image portrayed blacks as superstitious and lazy.

The images found in prejudice are called *stereotypes.* A *stereotype* is a biased set of beliefs one category of people has about another category of people. These beliefs are untested by evidence; as such, they may be distortions, exaggerations, or gross simplifications. They are folk beliefs, not scientific generalizations.[3] When beliefs about the target group are derogatory, stereotype is usually synonymous with prejudice. Sociologists also write about stereotypes of occupations, of the sexes, and of groups and categories organized or identified on bases other than ethnicity. Some of these are flattering. But this is seldom true of ethnic stereotypes, as Hughes' (1965: 12–13) description of the traditional Eskimo stereotypes demonstrates. It depicts:

> a people living (presumably year round) in snow houses (sometimes called "ice houses"), eating fish, swallowing raw meat, rubbing noses, swapping wives, leaving old people out on the ice to die, being childishly delighted with white man's tools, having no "government" (and hence according to some no social order), always wandering. These traits compose the image often stimulated by the word "Eskimo."[4]

The derogatory, unflattering stereotype is the usual focus of ethnic research.

Ethnocentrism Unlike prejudice, which is aimed at other groups and individuals, ethnocentrism is a special orientation toward one's own group. It promotes ethnic conflict based on cultural criteria, for the ethnocentric person defines his or her culture or way of life as superior to that of another ethnic group. The other group's different language, religion, customs, and moral practices are judged from the standard of one's own language, religion, and customs. These differences are seen by the ethnocentric person as evidence of the other group's inferiority.

Ethnocentrism, and hence the sort of prejudice to which it is linked, is at the root of *nation-*

[3]Mackie (1973) says that social scientists frequently assume the stereotype to be factually erroneous. Yet they seldom provide evidence for this assumption.

[4]As noted in Chapter 8, *Inuit* is the name North American Eskimos use for themselves.

alism when it refers to the exaltation of one's own nation over others. In its most virulent form, it is called *chauvinism.* But ethnocentrism finds its extreme expression in *racism:* the doctrine that some races are inherently superior to others. If this idea of race were strictly biological, as in the definition given earlier in this chapter, then it would fail to qualify as a kind of ethnocentrism, since ethnocentrism is a cultural phenomenon. Racists know no such scientific bounds. While their conception of race may contain some biological or physical elements, it also includes many cultural ones, such as language, religion, and beliefs, which are viewed as inferior and threatening.

Although the recent large-scale development of racism typically cited by sociologists is the Aryanism of Nazi Germany, racism has by no means disappeared from the contemporary North American scene. Even Nazism is still an attractive political program for a small but vociferous number of Americans (Bell, 1973). The Ku Klux Klan continues its activities in parts of the United States and in Ontario, Alberta, and British Columbia (Clairmont and Wien, 1976: 187; Sher, 1983). Canada has its own brand of white supremacy, as evidenced by the 31 percent of a national sample who would support an all-white society (*Globe and Mail,* 1982: 6). Nevertheless, it is important to ponder the thoughts of Simpson and Yinger (1972: 721, n.65):

> Racism tends to be a "swearword," not an analytic term; as such, in most of its present uses, it freezes the mind and perpetuates a vocabulary of praise and blame that we think reduces our ability to understand—and therefore reduce—intergroup hostilities and injustices.

Simpson and Yinger note that social scientists sometimes try to use racism to explain ethnic conflict. But a group's racist view is only part of the conflict situation, which itself requires explanation.

Ethnic Conflict: Behavior

The hostile attitudes and categorizations just described have various behavioral and, ultimately, structural consequences. These include discrimination, segregation, expulsion, and inequality. A man who hates Jews has antisemitic attitudes. At the opportune moment, he is likely to express his feelings by means of discriminatory actions such as refusing to hire a Jew or patronize a Jewish business.

Discrimination This term refers to the unequal treatment of a less powerful individual or group by a more powerful individual or group. Sociologists tend to use the term to denote unequal and unfavorable treatment and, hence, to denote a particular expression of prejudice. Nevertheless, discrimination can be favorable (for the target group). This is evident in the affirmative action programs in higher education and employment, which legislate equal opportunities for and equal handling of certain ethnic minorities and women.

Unfavorable discrimination in ethnic rela-

Ethnic stratification is still evident in many places in North America.

tions is often institutionalized in custom or law or both. Customary discrimination once forced American blacks to sit at the back of buses in the South. Such discrimination still forces many nonwhite Canadians to accept unemployment because, among other perceived drawbacks, they are said to lack "Canadian experience" (House of Commons, 1984: 32). In the nineteenth century, the police in some eastern cities in the United States jailed drunken Irishmen but helped native Americans in the same condition to get home safely (Stivers, 1976: 141). This is another example of customary discrimination.

Legal discrimination stems from laws that block an ethnic group's efforts to attain social goals. The group may be denied advantages, values, and services by laws that regulate the activities of ethnic groups. Historically, in North America laws have been enacted to obstruct a group's enrollment in a school, its residence in a neighborhood, its employment in a particular job, and even its entry into the country. For instance, the so-called Black Codes were enacted in the postbellum South to restrict the elective franchise to whites. In British Columbia, the Chinese were disenfranchised from 1872 to 1947, while they were unable to vote in Saskatchewan from 1908 to 1944 (Roy, 1981).

More often than not, legal discrimination simply formalizes customary practice. Therefore, at least initially, abolition of legal discrimination may fail to end customary practice, because custom continues to stimulate biased behavior. It may be necessary to pass and enforce laws making it illegal to discriminate in the areas of social life in question.

Segregation When applied to the sociology of ethnic relations, the term "segregation" often means the separation of a category of people by forcing them to reside in a certain part of the city or countryside separated from the dominant group. School segregation is the enrollment of only one racial or ethnic group in a school. The segregated children have no contact in the classroom with children from other racial or ethnic categories. When it is forced, ethnic segregation differs from the ecological process of voluntary, or self-selective, segregation considered in Chapter 8.

In ethnic relations forced residential segregation is usually customary, sometimes legal, and inevitably a factor in the development of stigmatized ghettos, Chinatowns, ethnic districts, and other subcommunities formed around the distinctive traits of the outcast group. Perhaps the two most blatant cases of North American ethnic segregation are the sequestering of Indians on "reservations" in the United States and on "reserves" in Canada and the relocation of Japanese Americans and Canadians during World War II (see O'Neil, 1981). Given the unfriendly social world outside their community, it is hardly surprising that minority group members also practice a certain amount of self-segregation.

The patterns of discrimination and segregation examined here have recently been given the bitter conceptual label of *institutional racism,* because they are woven into the very fabric of society. They have become established as interconnected laws, structural relationships, and stable interaction sequences and hence as parts of the social institutions of Canadian and American society. Baron (1969: 144) says of American blacks, for example, that:

> the school system uses the neighborhood-school policy, which, combined with residential segregation, operates as a surrogate for direct segregation; suburbs in creating very restrictive zoning regulations, or urban-renewal developments in setting universally high rents, can eliminate all but a very few black families on the basis of income; given the racial differentials produced by the school system, an employer, by using his regular personnel tests and criteria, can screen out most blacks from desirable jobs.

Institutional racism is to be distinguished from individual racism as practiced by people expressing (sometimes with great publicity) their personal views of particular ethnic groups.

Inequality Discrimination and segregation culminate in *inequality* among members of a society. That is, supposedly universally available opportunities and rewards are, in fact, unequally distributed to people whose ethnicity is the only de facto barrier to gaining these values. This situation prevails in spite of our democratic ideology, which asserts (erroneously) that universally available opportunities exist for all individuals, regardless of ethnicity.

Ethnic inequality is apparent in our system of stratification. Individual members of an ethnic group usually occupy several social classes, with their ethnicity acting as a ceiling on their mobility through the class structure. Ethnic stratification exists in both the United States and Canada (David, 1978: 71–72; Anderson and Frideres, 1981: 292–293). For example, James Blackwell's (1975: 88) study of American blacks indicates that disproportionately more blacks than whites are found in the lower classes (roughly half of all blacks). In Canada, an unpublished research report indicates that 60 percent of the income differential between Montreal anglophone and francophone employees is the result of a clear preference of anglophone employers for anglophone workers (McRoberts and Posgate, 1980: 127).

Expulsion When dominant group prejudice grows to the extreme of overriding all other values which an ethnic group might provide its hosts (e.g., labor, land development), then *expulsion* looms as a realistic alternative in the conflict. Although this is no longer practiced in Canada and the United States, both countries once expelled groups defined momentarily as undesirable (e.g., blacks, Asians, Acadians, Orientals). One of the more recent cases of ethnic expulsion occurred in 1972, when Uganda's president at the time, Idi Amin, expelled 45,000 Asians from his country.

The expulsion of the Acadians offers another example. Acadia was the name given by France to its seventeenth century possessions along the northeast Atlantic coast of North America. When the British gained control of these possessions after numerous battles, they had reason to believe that the French Acadians would be unloyal subjects. Accordingly, the Acadians were expelled in 1775. In "Evangeline" Henry Wadsworth Longfellow described the ordeal of one group who, after the British burned their village, migrated southward, eventually settling in the New Orleans area:

Many a weary year had passed since the burning of Grand-Pre,
When on the falling tide the freighted vessels departed,
Bearing a nation, with all its household gods, into exile,
Exile without an end, and without an example in story.
Far asunder, on separate coasts, the Acadians landed;
Scattered were they, like flakes of snow, when the wind from the northeast
Strikes aslant through the fogs that darken the Banks of Newfoundland.
Friendless, homeless, hopeless, they wandered from city to city,
From the cold lakes of the North to sultry Southern savannas,
From the bleak shores of the sea to the lands where the Father of Waters
Seizes the hills in his hands, and drags them down to the ocean,
Deep in their sands to bury the scattered bones of the mammoth.
Friends they sought and homes; and many, despairing, heart-broken,
Asked of the earth but a grave, and no longer a friend nor a fireside.
Written their history stands on tablets of stone in the churchyards.

Ethnic Conflict: Resistance

So far we have been treating the subject of ethnic conflict mostly as a one-way action; we have suggested that only the dominant group perpetrates hostile actions. Sometimes this is true, for subordinate people may passively accept their unequal treatment, as blacks, Chicanos, and French Canadians once did. But today is a time of protest and activism, spearheaded, in part, by several prominent ethnic minorities who are no longer inclined to put up with discrimination against them. This has resulted in riots, sit-ins, and other kinds of civil disturbances, on the one hand, and organized political activities, on the other.

The 1960s and 1970s spawned political pressure groups intent on serving all sorts of ethnic interests; among these groups are the Mexican-American Political Association (in California), American Indian Movement, Congress of Racial Equality (CORE), National Black Coalition (in Canada), National Indian Brotherhood (in Canada), and Inuit Tapirisat of Canada. Older groups such as the National Association for the Advancement of Colored People (NAACP) and the Anti-Defamation League of B'nai B'rith suddenly found new allies in their struggle against inequality.

These resistance strategies are born of prejudice and discrimination. Following an extensive review of the literature in this area, Williams (1975: 149) notes that deprivation is one important precondition of these strategies. This deprivation is seen by the subordinated ethnic groups as directed at them, as a denial of something they can obtain and have a right to. Therefore, they define their singular treatment as arbitrary and unjust. Resistance then occurs, engendering a genuine conflict, with both parties contending against one another.

Ethnic Harmony

There are also several social processes underlying ethnic harmony. Actions leading to ethnic harmony may gain their impetus from official government policy or, informally, from evolving cultural trends. In North America, government policy and cultural trends have combined to engender, at least so far, warm ethnic relations in some areas of life. Ethnic harmony has been accomplished chiefly through the subprocesses of assimilation and accommodation.

Which expression of ethnic harmony do you see here?

Assimilation *Assimilation* has two meanings in sociology. One is the mutual absorption of two or more initially distinct cultural groups to the point where they lose their distinctiveness, becoming one culturally homogeneous unit. In this version of assimilation, the cultures blend into one. Ultimately, those who share the culture identify solely with the new hybrid culture and its related group structures, usually several generations after the process begins. The "melting pot" ideology associated with immigration to the United States prior to World War I exemplifies this two-way assimilation. In William Jennings Bryan's words:

> Great has been the Greek, the Latin, the Celt, the Teuton, and the Saxon; but greater than any of these is the American, who combines the virtues of them all. (Quoted by Park and Burgess, 1924: 734)

This melting pot, incidentally, rarely, if ever, contained nonwhites; while it existed, it cooked up a national rather than a racial mixture.

By the end of the nineteenth century, the melting pot ideology was being challenged by the emerging Americanization movement, the principal aim of which was to ensure what sociologists refer to as "Anglo-conformity." Alarmed by the "strange" ways of the many Asians and eastern and southern Europeans arriving in the country, the Anglo-Saxon majority cast aside social values and official policy favoring two-way assimilation and took up the position that the newcomers should adopt American cultural traits and American behavioral patterns. The school had a major part in this dramatic transformation. Though it engendered many painful conflicts between immigrant parents and their offspring, the school became the main instrument for Americanizing the children.

Still, one-way assimilation, whether in the United States or elsewhere, is never entirely unilateral. The host society always absorbs from the migrants something (and usually many things) it finds attractive. The foods of the Greeks, Italians, and Chinese constitute one obvious example. The extent of the American (and Canadian) cultural exchange with the Indians is evident in the adoption of snowshoes, tobacco, maize, canoes, moccasins, maple sugar, and other items (Driver, 1961: Chapter 26).

Amalgamation When widespread and accompanied by assimilation, amalgamation is another potential source of harmony in ethnic relations. *Amalgamation* is the blending of racial types through interbreeding. It is brought about by *miscegenation,* or racial intermarriage. This physical blend may be accompanied by a cultural blend. Racial intermarriage is increasing in the United States among blacks, Filipinos, Chinese, Japanese, Indians, Mexicans, and whites (e.g., Gordon, 1964: 5). American interracial marriages increased by nearly 13 percent between 1970 and 1982 (U.S. Bureau of the Census, 1984: 45). The present-day Hawaiians are an amalgam of whites, Asians, and the original inhabitants of the Hawaiian Islands.

Miscegenation and racial intermarriage are common in pluralistic societies.

Canadians are more approving of racial and ethnic intermarriage than ever before (Bibby, 1982b). Nevertheless, actual trends in intermarriage in Canada are presently unknown except for Indian-white unions, which, on the whole, are rising (Ponting and Gibbins, 1980: 64). Here the prime example has been the Métis, who are mostly the progeny of Indian women and Scots or French fur traders and settlers. In this instance, amalgamation has so far failed to culminate in assimilation. Hence, today's Métis are caught in the middle as "marginal men." They lie between white and Indian societies, where they suffer the stigma of "half-breed" (Harrison, 1985: Chapter 5).

Accommodation *Accommodation* is a form of limited desegregation, lying near the total segregation end of a continuum and running from there to total assimilation. In general terms, this process is seen as a way to reduce or avert conflict. It is the combined effect of subprocesses such as cooperation, compromise, tolerance, and trust. In ethnic accommodation, groups that are actually or potentially antagonistic maintain their cultural distinctiveness, although it usually happens that one group compromises, tolerates, and accepts more than the other. The conflict between ethnic groups and between other types of groups (e.g., labor and management, juvenile gangs, rival businesses), whether potential or ongoing, is never resolved. But, as long as the accommodation lasts, it remains sufficiently in the background in everyday life to allow affairs to proceed largely without incident.

There are numerous examples of ethnic accommodation throughout the world. The Swiss Confederation is composed of Protestants, Roman Catholics, French, Germans, and Italians. In Belgium, the Dutch-speaking Flemings and the French-speaking Walloons have maintained a somewhat shaky coexistence for more than 150 years. Fifteen major linguistic groups and at least as many religions accommodate one another in modern India.

North American Pluralism When ethnic groups accommodate one another, *pluralism* can be said to have become established. In Canada, official efforts to achieve accommodation and pluralism have sprung up under the catchword of "multiculturalism." This is the name given the federal government policy of "multiculturalism within a bilingual framework," which was established in October 1971 on the basis of recommendations contained in the *Report of the Royal Commission on Bilingualism and Biculturalism.*[5] Canadian multiculturalism was known as "pluralism" before the 1971 change in policy. It began to develop in earnest in the early 1960s, when a clamor arose from various ethnic groups over their unequal social and political treatment in Canadian society.

As Jean Elliott (1983) points out, however, Anglo-conformity has also been the dominant orientation in Canada since the founding of the country. This situation has prevailed historically, despite the role of the French as a charter group (Porter, 1965: 60–61). In other words, multiculturalism, or accommodation, represents a marked shift, at least in official policy, away from the largely one-sided assimilation characteristic of the first one hundred years since Confederation.

The goal of the Canadian government's multiculturalism policy is to foster the distinctiveness of the country's ethnic minorities through financial assistance, public recognition, and establishment of national agencies designed to promote their unique cultures. Its ultimate aim is ethnic equality (Burnet, 1978: 108). All this is to be achieved within the bilingual framework of French and English.

Canadian Multiculturalism The equality ideal in Canadian multiculturalism has so far led to only a slight increase in accommodation (Bibby, 1982b). Ethnic stratification continues; in John Porter's (1965: 90) words, there is a "vertical mosaic"; It has brought about a hierarchy of distinct ethnic groups stratified along the dimensions of class, status, and power. Some of these groups are concentrated near the top (e.g., British, Germans, Scandinavians, Dutch) and others near the bottom (e.g., Italians, Ukrainians, Poles). One of the two charter groups, the French, is found largely between the two extremes.[6]

[5]This commission was established to examine the claims of the Quebec nationalists. But its mission eventually came to include an examination of similar claims being made by many other ethnic groups in the country.

[6]The British North America Act of 1867 gave the French and English legal rights to such privileges as perpetuation of their separate languages and cultures. Notwithstanding the new government multiculturalism policy, these rights have never been extended to other ethnic groups. In 1981 the Canadian population consisted of 40.1 percent English, 26.7 percent French, and 33.2 percent all other ethnic groups.

Gypsy Culture

Gypsy occupations certainly deviated from the norm of dominant European society. Their involvement in certain occupations cannot be separated from the social system in which they found themselves. By filling the few occupational niches available to them, they automatically violated acceptable norms. Such professions as fortune telling by palmistry or tarot cards and the selling of secret herbal remedies and recipes for elixirs and drugs linked the Gypsies with witchcraft and black magic.

The Gypsy religion was viewed as a deviation from Christendom. Their religion or, as they prefer to call it, the Gypsy Tradition, is an accumulation of formal beliefs and ancestor worship. This Gypsy lore includes tales about demons and certain saints unknown to the Christian world.

Gypsies have their own system of justice called the *Kris,* which is headed by a council of elders who have the responsibility of applying the law. *Romania,* or Gypsy law, is a set of moral codes that govern the behavior of the Rom. The *Romania* provides a guideline for the traditions, customs, beliefs, rituals, and attitudes of the group. Differences among the Gypsies are deliberated at a *diwano* (discussion-meeting) and settled by the *Romano Kris* (Gypsy tribunal).

Gypsies have always lived in extended families or *kumpania,* which is a group of families living and working together as a unit. Gypsy clans consist of numerous *kumpania.* Each clan recognizes the authority of a male chief who is elected for life. The chief is usually an older man who is chosen because of his intelligence, strength, and feeling for justice. He has the right to preside over the council of elders, pronounces measures of exclusion, and decides about migrations. The female counterpart to the chief is the *Phuri dai,* or old wise woman. She is the authority in matters concerning women and children.

The Gypsy tribe is composed of a greater or lesser number of clans. There are many different Gypsy tribes in Europe, such as the Kalderash or Coppersmiths of the Balkans, the Gitanos of Spain, or the Manouches of France.

Marriage and divorce practices among the Gypsies involve a complex set of laws and traditions. Marriage between the Rom assumes several forms: abduction (by force or consent), purchase, or mutual consent. In all these forms a bride price is involved. The most common form of marriage is that of purchase. The wedding ceremony is usually officiated by the chief of the clan. Intermarriage between a Gypsy and *Gajo* has resulted in exclusion from the tribe. Divorce is often a case of simple mutual consent or arbitration before the *Romano Kris.*

Even in the areas of illness and medicine, the Rom have preferred to deal with problems themselves. The Rom attribute sickness and disease to the Supernatural. They have an elaborate classification of disease-producing demons and spirits. A highly complex belief system has been developed which includes thousands of rules and rituals for Gypsies to follow in order to avoid illness.

The Gypsy healer and herbalist is almost always a woman. Her knowledge of medical remedies is passed on from generation to generation to her female offspring. Through centuries of living outdoors, the Gypsies have gathered a tremendous inventory of medical remedies derived from plants and minerals.

SOURCE: Marlene Sway. Gypsies as a perpetual minority: A case study. *Humboldt Journal of Social Relations* 3: 48–55, 1975.

Yet, in reality, just how different is the accomplishment of ethnic harmony in Canada from the achievement in the United States? A recent appraisal of Canadian multiculturalism (Anderson and Frideres, 1981: 327–328) indicates that the official aims are far from met. In other words, Anglo-conformity assimilation persists, though now in somewhat diluted form. Among ways in which this is manifested are a continued loss of ethnic language (Reitz, 1974) and a diminishing sense of ethnic community (Breton, 1964). Meanwhile, in the United States, certain ethnic groups are promoting their individuality, arguing, in effect, for a multicultural existence (see the final section of this chapter). Simpson and Yinger (1972: 20) note that, despite the general assimilationist orientation in the United States, pluralism today is both a fact and an ideal, and the assertiveness of blacks, Chicanos, Orientals, Indians, and others is gaining public acceptance.

Current writings view the pluralism-multiculturalism trend as evidence of a new American value on ethnicity (e.g., De Vos, 1977; A.F. Gordon: 1981). Palmer (1976: 515–523) sees the United States and Canada as strikingly similar in their levels of an orientation toward the "new ethnicity" and "multiculturalism," respectively.

Whether it is called "multiculturalism" or "cultural pluralism," its ideal form rests on the attitude of *cultural relativism.* Cultural relativism is the antithesis of ethnocentrism. People who are culturally relativistic act toward the behavior patterns, belief systems, and associated material items of another ethnic group on the basis of the role these considerations play in the group's social world. With cultural relativism, the outsider recognizes the importance of the traits and practices which a foreign culture has developed and used through the years. A relativistic attitude precludes judgments of inferiority and superiority. Whatever one might say about the increasingly pluralistic nature of North American society, cultural relativism is still far from becoming a universal outlook within it.

Submission and Acceptance

Avoidance through minimized contact with the majority shades into *submission,* or the passive endurance of a resignation to the daily injustices of minority living. The noun "submission" in no way implies that members of the ethnic group necessarily identify with the image of themselves communicated through the stereotypes and discrimination of the majority. Submission occurs when ethnic groups lack the power to change the situation to their advantage. As a stopgap, they outwardly comply with the re-

Integration brings the minority into the activities and objectives of the dominant group.

sented patterns forced on them, such as by lackadaisical job performance or derisive humor directed at the majority.

Submission has been a common type of ethnic harmony in North America. Until recently, blacks, Orientals, and Indians, in particular, have tended to adjust in this way. It won for those blacks who used it the appellation of "Uncle Tom" and, at least in Canada, those Indians who used it that of "Uncle Tomahawk" (Cardinal, 1969: 22).

Submission, in turn, may shade into *acceptance.* Here compliance is not only expedient, but also morally right. In acceptance, members identify little with their ethnic group and, for the most part, identify with the majority. They may view themselves as inferior and the majority as superior. Some degree of acceptance by national and religious minorities is necessary if they are to assimilate (on a one-way basis) with the dominant group and its ways. Name changes, disowning ethnic background, cultivation of neutral linguistic accents, and the like, all of which may lead to passing as a member of the majority, are strategies of assimilation following on the acceptance of oneself as part of an undesirable, or at least unappealing, minority group.

In the end, ethnic harmony is achieved through *integration:* "a process whereby units or elements of a society are brought into an active and coordinated compliance with the ongoing activities and objectives of the dominant group" (Schermerhorn, 1970: 66). The integration of white and black students in schools is a familiar American example. In Canada, it was federal government policy in the 1950s and 1960s to "integrate" Indian students into provincial public schools by removing them from religious schools (King, 1983: 188). The noun "compliance" in the definition hints at the problem of the legitimacy of integration, whether at school or elsewhere. Schermerhorn (1970: 70) notes that both dominant and subordinate groups may have differential views of their status as legitimate, partly legitimate, or wholly illegitimate.

Avoidance

Avoidance is the third group process in ethnic relations. Here the ethnic minority either shuns contact, as much as possible, with the majority or escapes to a friendlier location. History is replete with examples of the second alternative. American Indians fled westward to avoid the encroaching white culture. Some Southern slaves sought help through the Underground Railroad to reach Canada, where they hoped to avoid discriminatory practices. The Zionist movement is motivated, in part, by the desire of many Jews to escape persecution (Berry and Tischler, 1978: 390). Sometimes avoidance is largely political, as in the current separatist movement in Quebec.

But others stay in the same country and even the same locale, where they adjust to routine discrimination and prejudice. Under these circumstances, they minimize contact with the threatening majority group by staying close to their segregated subcommunity (e.g., the ghetto, the Indian reservation, the religious enclave). Or they "keep their place" by taking traditional jobs, behaving in ways acceptable to the majority, and stoically suffering discriminatory treatment. In this fashion they avoid extended contact and further trouble with those who dominate them.

North American Minorities

The terms *minority* and *minority group,* while part of sociology's technical vocabulary, are vaguer than its concept of ethnic group. Often all three are used synonymously. When separate meaning is intended, the principal referent of minority is to the number of ethnic group members; the group in question is usually small compared with the majority or dominant group in the society. Minorities endure unfavorable discrimination of some sort stemming from the majority's pejorative view of them. In this sense, the concept of minority clearly excludes certain small North American ethnic groups, such as the Scandinavians and Germans, who are held in high regard and who therefore experience no unfavorable discrimination. Occasionally, minorities are numerically larger than the dominant group. Blacks in South Africa are a case in point. The word "minority" may even be applied to categories who suffer unfavorable discrimination, but who are not an ethnic group, for example, women and the disabled.

Certain North American ethnic groups have a minority status, inasmuch as they are numerically smaller than the white, largely Anglo-Saxon majority and suffer significant unfavorable discrimination. Blacks, Orientals (Chinese, Japanese, Koreans, Vietnamese), and North American Indians are considered minorities in both Canada and the United States. In Canada the French are the largest and most important minority, while blacks hold this position in the United States. The Hispanic minorities, which include Mexicans, Puerto Ricans, and Cubans, are prevalent only in the United States. They constitute a very small group in Canada. By contrast, Asian Indians and Pakistanis have been more visible in Canada over the years than in the United States. Table 20.3 lists the four largest minorities in both countries by percent of total population.

Ethnic Revival

Both Canada and the United States are in the midst of an ethnic revival, said by Smith (1981) to be a worldwide movement today. Several ethnic groups have more or less consciously begun to stress and promote their unique identities, the effect of which has been the renunciation of older assimilationist goals (e.g., TeSelle, 1973; Anderson and Frideres, 1981: 307–309; Novak, 1971; Isawij, 1978). Some of these groups, such as blacks, Chicanos, French Canadians, and North American Indians, are also minorities. Others, including Germans, Italians, and Scandinavians, have begun to emphasize an ethnicity that is no longer problematic, if it ever was.

The term "ethnic revival" suggests an "intensification of ethnic attachments and allegiance in recent years" (Reitz, 1980: 2). Among the groups where this process is evident, the intent appears to be one of preserving ethnic identity through accentuation of a combination of national, religious, racial, and linguistic differences. For some groups this amounts to little more than replacing a vague self-hatred with pride in ancestry. This, in turn, tends to increase member interaction and, subsequently, their sense of togetherness (Reitz, 1980: 100).

There are several theories of ethnic revival, the common theme of which is that the upsurge of ethnicity in the 1960s and 1970s was a response to the specific cultural needs (Reitz, 1980: 43–50). For instance, middle-class bureaucratic culture is highly rational and therefore lacking in emotion and imagination. A return to one's ethnic roots is part of the middle-class way of balancing the expressive and ra-

Table 20.3 FOUR LARGEST MINORITIES BY PERCENT OF TOTAL POPULATION

Minority (by rank)	Canada (1981)	United States (1980)
1. French Canadians	25.7	
Blacks		11.7
2. North American Indians and Inuit	1.7	
People of Spanish origin		6.5
3. Orientals	1.4	0.9
4. Other Asians	1.3	
North American Indians, Inuit, and Aleuts		0.6

Source: 1981 Census of Canada and U.S. Census of Population, 1980.

Ethnic revival: These Ukranian women display their artistry at a craft sale.

tional sides of life. Thus, ethnicity provides an identity for those who have become lost in the faceless mass of large-scale organizations. In addition, the white segment of the American middle class is suffering from political alienation, stemming from the loss of control it once traditionally enjoyed in many areas. Ethnicity seems to offer enduring values formerly available in these areas.

Among lower-class and lower-middle-class whites the ethnic revival is believed to be a reaction to equal opportunity advances recently made by blacks, and perhaps it is a strategy to gain the advantages of ethnic emphasis that presumably worked for blacks. In Canada, some ethnic revivals are regional and linguistic. Nationally, ethnicity is an occasional barrier to upward social mobility, which can be corrected only by improving the group's public image. The current multiculturalism policy jibes nicely with these aims.

OUTLINE AND SUMMARY

I. Introduction
There is no biological basis for the concept of race. Still, anthropologists have recognized that humankind can be divided into identifiable categories. People in a society are also differentiated by their ethnicity.

II. Race and Races
The relationship between race, on the one hand, and ethnic group, on the other is complex. Biologically, a *race* is a subdivision of the species, *Homo sapiens.* Race is based on physical traits.

III. Immigration to North America
The United States and Canada were founded by several distinct racial and ethnic groups.

A. The United States
Old-wave immigrants and new-wave immigrants settled in the United States. They came from northern and western Europe. With the discovery of gold on the Pacific Coast in the 1850s, Chinese arrived; they took menial jobs. Changes were made in the immigration system in 1965.

B. Canada
Although it has followed the same general pattern as the United States, Canadian immigration has also had its peculiarities. There were two distinct phases in the early flow of Europeans to Canada. The first was dominated by the French. The British conquest constituted the second phase. The system of preferences continued during the period from the end of World War II to 1960.

IV. Ethnic Relations
The term *ethnic relations* refers to a sweeping social process encompassing several smaller processes.

A. Ethnic Conflict: Attitudes
Ethnic relations in North America have sometimes been brittle. Ethnic conflict remains a problem in contemporary society.

1. Prejudice
Prejudice is an unfavorable, often emotional, orientation toward a category of people.

2. Ethnocentrism
Ethnocentrism is a special orientation toward one's own group. The ethnocentric person defines his or

her culture or way of life as superior to that of another ethnic group.

B. Ethnic Conflict: Behavior
Hostile attitudes and categorizations have various behavioral and, ultimately, structural consequences. These include discrimination, segregation, expulsion, and inequality.
   1. Discrimination
   Discrimination is the unequal treatment of a less powerful individual or group by a more powerful individual or group.
   2. Segregation
   When applied to the sociology of ethnic relations, the term "segregation" often means forcing a category of people to reside in a certain part of the city or countryside separated from the dominant group. School segregation is the enrollment of only one racial or ethnic group in a school.
   3. Inequality
   Discrimination and segregation culminate in *inequality* among members of a society.
   4. Expulsion
   When dominant group prejudice grows to the extreme of overriding all other values which an ethnic group might provide its hosts (e.g., labor, land development), then *expulsion* looms as a realistic alternative in the conflict. In the past, both Canada and the United States have expelled groups defined momentarily as undesirable.

C. Ethnic Conflict: Resistance
Today is a time of protest and activism. There have been riots, sit-ins, and other kinds of civil disturbances. Minorities have entered into political activities.

D. Ethnic Harmony
Several processes underlie ethnic harmony.
   1. Assimilation
   Assimilation is the mutual absorption of two or more distinct cultural groups into one culturally homogeneous unit. The pressure toward Anglo-conformity gave rise to another kind of assimilation. North Americans insisted that newcomers should adopt Canadian and American cultural traits.
   2. Amalgamation
   Amalgamation is the blending of racial types through interbreeding.
   3. Accommodation
   Accommodation is a form of limited desegregation. It is a way to avert or reduce conflict. In ethnic accommodation, groups that are actually or potentially antagonistic maintain their cultural distinctiveness, although it usually happens that one group compromises, tolerates, and accepts more than the other group. The Swiss Confederation is an example of accommodation.
   4. North American Pluralism
   Pluralism is established when ethnic groups accommodate one another.
      a. Pluralism under the name of multiculturalism is official policy in Canada. There is evidence of a growing public sentiment favoring pluralism in the United States.
      b. Pluralism rests on cultural relativism: acceptance of the behavior patterns, belief systems, and associated material items of another ethnic group because of the importance of these traits and practices to that group.
   5. Canadian Multiculturalism
   Canadian multiculturalism has brought about a hierarchy of distinct ethnic groups stratified along the dimensions of class, status, and power.

E. Submission and Acceptance
Avoidance through minimized contact with the majority shades into *submission,* or the passive endurance of resig-

nation to the daily injustices of minority living.

F. Avoidance
The ethnic minority either shuns contact with the majority or escapes to a friendlier location. It avoids the majority. American Indians fled westward to avoid the encroaching white culture.

G. North American Minorities
Minority groups endure unfavorable discrimination, which stems from the majority's pejorative view of them. French Canadians and blacks are the largest ethnic minority groups in Canada and the United States, respectively.

H. Ethnic Revival
Both Canada and the United States are said to be in the midst of an ethnic revival. Several minority groups have more or less consciously begun to stress and promote their unique identities, the effect of which has been the renunciation of older assimilationist goals. There are several theories of ethnic revival.

FOR FURTHER READING AND STUDY

Anderson, A. B. and Frideres, J. S. 1981. *Ethnicity in Canada.* Toronto: Butterworths. A textbook on the sociology of race and ethnicity in Canada.

Berry, B. and Tischler, H. L. 1978. *Race and ethnic relations,* 4th ed. Boston: Houghton Mifflin. A textbook on the sociology of race and ethnicity, with special reference to the United States.

Bethel, E. R. 1981. *Promiseland: A century of life in a Negro community.* Philadelphia: Temple University Press. This is a social history of an all-black community in the Piedmont area of South Carolina. Bethel's study brings out the importance of kinship structures and tradition in the experience of rural blacks.

Helmreich, W. B. 1982. *The things they say behind your back: Stereotypes and the myths behind them.* Garden City, N.Y.: Doubleday. Helmreich explores the origins of contemporary stereotypes of Jews, Italians, blacks, Japanese, Chinese, Poles, Irish, and Hispanic Americans. About half the stereotypes studied originally had a degree of factualness.

Reitz, J. G. 1980. *The survival of ethnic groups.* Toronto: McGraw-Hill Ryerson. This is largely a Canadian study (with some reference to American ethnic groups) of the cultural and economic factors bearing on the formation and maintenance of ethnic groups. Reitz's empirical research leads to the development of a theory of ethnic survival.

Smith, A. D. 1981. *The ethnic revival.* Cambridge, England: Cambridge University Press. Today there is an ethnic revival throughout the world. Smith explores the causes, origins, and significance of ethnic movements in the modern world. He finds that existing interpretations of these movements are inadequate.

Stymeist, D. H. 1975. *Ethnics and Indians: Social relations in a Northwest Ontario town.* Toronto: Peter Martin Associates. A participant observer study of the relations among "white ethnics" (e.g., Poles, Italians, Ukrainians) and the North American Indians in a small, isolated community where one's ethnicity is an important identifier.

Sutherland, A. 1975. *Gypsies: The hidden Americans.* London: Tavistock. This is a moving participant observer study of a community of California Gypsies by an anthropologist.

KEY WORDS

accommodation Form of limited desegregation in which each ethnic group maintains its cultural distinctiveness while tolerating the distinctiveness of the other groups.

amalgamation Blending of racial types through interbreeding.

assimilation Mutual absorption of two or more distinct cultural groups into one culturally homogeneous unit.

avoidance Process by which an ethnic minority shuns contact with the majority or escapes to a friendlier location.

caste Usually religiously based stratum into which one is born and likely to live out one's life.

discrimination Unequal treatment of a less powerful individual or group by a more powerful individual or group.

ethnic relations Sweeping social process that encompasses the narrower processes of ethnic conflict, harmony, avoidance, submission, acceptance, and revival.

ethnic revival Process by which ethnic groups stress and promote their unique identities.

ethnic segregation Forced physical separation of an ethnic group from other groups.

ethnocentrism Special positive orientation towards one's own group.

prejudice Unfavorable, often emotional, orientation toward a category of people.

race Subdivision of the species *homo sapiens.*

submission Passive endurance of the daily injustices of minority living.

six

SOCIAL DYNAMICS

The idea that sociology is founded on both a dynamic view of society and a static view of society was discussed in the Introduction to Part Five, "Differentiation." These two perspectives, which are referred to as *social dynamics* and *social statics,* are as old as the discipline itself. From Auguste Comte to the present, sociologists have contrasted the dynamic aspects of social life, or the patterns of sociocultural growth and change, with its static aspects, or the laws of social order and the forces of equilibrium operating in a stable society. A complete sociological examination of society encompasses both, even though some theories emphasize one or the other (i.e., functionalism deals mostly with statics, whereas symbolic interactionism deals mostly with dynamics).

Florian Znaniecki in his *Method of Sociology* (published in 1934) made a strong appeal for the need to avoid regarding the static and dynamic aspects of society as mutually exclusive perspectives. "Order versus change," he argued, is a false scientific problem. Rather, order and change are continuous features of social life; in actuality, society is a "dynamic system." At any single point in time, sociologists should be examining both order and change, since societal systems contain both structure and organization that are undergoing change and changes that are in the course of stabilizing as identifiable structure and organization. Social dynamics and social statics are useful perspectives that call attention to the simultaneous operation of two major processes constantly at work in society, namely change and institutionalization.

chapter 21

Collective Behavior

CHAPTER OUTLINE

INTRODUCTION

This chapter is one of perhaps two chapters in this book having a title that gives few clues about what the chapter contains. (The other chapter with such a title is Chapter 5, "Human Interaction.") Having read through twenty chapters, you may find it evident that sociology pertains to behavior that is collective, in that two or more people act in concert to reach a goal, as in a small group or a large-scale organization. Still, we already have a name for this kind of behavior; it is "joint action" (see Chapter 5). This terminological convention leaves the term "collective behavior" in the sociologist's lexicon as the label for

> that form of group behavior which emerges and develops in undefined and emotional situations; it is marked by a process of interaction in which impulses and moods are aroused, spread, organized, and mobilized on specific objects of action. It should be distinguished from that form of group behavior which, while collective, is organized in terms of established cultural norms and lines of social structure. (Blumer, 1964: 100)

In other words, this study of collective behavior (also known as *crowd behavior*) is the study of panics, mobs, riots, crowds, crazes, fads, fashions, publics, and social movements. In short, *collective behavior* is the spontaneous, noninstitutionalized, often emotional action of an aggregate of people whose thinking, feeling, and behavior are more or less unstructured and, in some instances, impulsive.

Gustave Le Bon (1841–1931), a French physician and sociologist, is often credited with founding the modern study of collective behavior. His book *The Crowd* (Le Bon, 1960) is still considered a classic in the field. It was Robert Park and Ernest Burgess (1921: 865), however, who coined the term "collective behavior" and who established it as an important branch of sociology. These two men, joined later by Herbert Blumer, argued that collective behavior is the basis for certain new social forms. Referring back to Figure 4.2, "The social causation cycle," we can see that collective behavior takes its place in the social causation cycle as an expression of definitions of particular situations. These definitions of the situation and their associated patterns of behavior, when they persist, eventually crystallize as new social realities (in this instance, as new social forms).

The underlying theme here, as elsewhere in this part of the book, is *process;* specifically, the theme takes in the rise and change of new social forms and behavior patterns from definitions of situations and from some sort of interaction. In other words, the human actions of interest at this point lie *initially* outside society's institutions. Some of these actions, however, eventually become institutionalized as recognizable social forms.

THE ELEMENTARY FORMS

The two main elementary forms of collective behavior are the *crowd* and the *mass.* The crowd and the mass and their subforms are the basis for the advanced forms of collective behavior. The advanced forms are the various types of social movements. The subforms of the crowd and the mass include panics, terrors, disasters, riots, mobs, revivals, revelries, crazes, and fashions. These and other subforms are discussed in this section.

Lofland's Typology

John Lofland (1981: 413) notes that an elementary form of collective behavior, such as a crowd

---

SOCIOLOGY OR COMMON SENSE

What do you think?

Which of the following statements do you agree with? Which statements do you disagree with? Make a note of your answers. Check your answers when you have completed your study of this chapter. Are your answers to the statements the same as those a sociologist would give?

1. People participating in a riot or mob are uncontrolled; they do anything that comes to mind.
2. People who converge on the scene of a natural disaster are either sightseers or looters.
3. Many social movements neither succeed nor fail.
4. A religious revival meeting and a crowd celebrating their hockey team's Stanley Cup championship are alike.
5. A popular song is a form of collective behavior.

Crowds are a common and sometimes annoying aspect of daily living.

or mass, typically consists of five components: (1) The collective behavior begins with the situation as defined by those present. In some crucial way, their taken-for-granted world (or frame, as it is referred to in Chapters 1 and 3) is consciously defined as problematic. (2) This feeling about the problematic nature of everyday life is shared by a relatively large number of people, enough to constitute a crowd or mass. (3) Furthermore, the feeling arouses a significant level of emotion among those present. (4) The emerging definition of the situation, especially its emotional qualities, spawns a behavioral reaction to the immediate circumstances. (5) This definition and its high degree of emotional arousal are sustained over time.

Three Dimensions

An instance of collective behavior which consists of these five components can be examined along three dimensions. The collective behavior in one dimension varies from the collective behavior in other dimensions. The first dimension is referred to as the *dominant emotion.* The dominant emotion is defined as "the publicly expressed feeling perceived by participants and observers as most prominent in an episode of collective behavior" (Lofland, 1981: 414). The emotions most often investigated by social scientists are the emotions of fear, hostility, and joy. But other emotions, such as grief, disgust, surprise, and shame, can also become dominant.

The second dimension is the *organizational form* of collective behavior. The four principal organizational forms isolated over several decades of research are the *crowd, mass, public,* and *social movement.* Publics were considered in Chapter 14, and the other organizational forms are taken up in this chapter. Although the term has other meanings, many scholars define the *crowd* as a sizable aggregate of people in close proximity to one another for a transitory period of time. The *mass* has been defined as a set of heterogeneous, anonymous individuals who interact little with one another (i.e., who are distant) and who lack a definite leadership (Blumer, 1975: 35). This definition is consonant with the use of the word "mass" in such phrases as "mass culture," "mass media," and "mass society."

The third dimension is the *emotional level* of collective behavior. Lofland lists fear, hostility, and joy, in descending order of intensity, as the three most intense dominant emotions. Assuming that crowds hold a greater potential for emotional arousal than masses, six rank-ordered subforms emerge from a cross-classification of the two organizational forms, crowds and masses, and from the three dominant emotions (see Table 21.1).

CROWDS

An elementary form of collective behavior is fear. A crowd experiences fear, just as do individuals. Among other elementary forms which have a bearing on the behavior of crowds are *joy* and *hostility.* Each of the forms has at least two subforms. The spontaneity of human

Table 21.1 ELEMENTARY FORMS OF COLLECTIVE BEHAVIOR BY LEVEL OF EMOTIONAL INTENSITY

Emotional intensity	Collective behavior form	Dominant emotion: Fear	Dominant emotion: Hostility	Dominant emotion: Joy
Greater ↓	Crowds	(1) Crowd fears	(3) Crowd hostilities	(5) Crowd joys
Lesser	Masses	(2) Mass fears	(4) Mass hostilities	(6) Mass joys
	Emotional intensity	Greater ⟶		Lesser

behavior and the inventiveness of the human mind give rise to these subforms.

Crowd Fears

Fear is the anticipation or actual experience of pain or severe distress. In crowds, the purest expression of fear is panic. *Panic* is a sudden, overpowering fright. Among the subforms of fear are *terror, dread,* and *horror* (Lofland, 1981: 417–421).

Lang and Lang (1961: 85) conceive of panic as the collective retreat from group goals to a "privatized" orientation in which individuals are concerned only with their personal safety and security. Panic is the form of collective behavior observed when fire breaks out in a theater, night club, or dance hall.

A memorable instance of panic occurred in 1938 when a radio network broadcast the H. G. Wells play *The War of the Worlds.* The dramatic broadcast aroused fear in living rooms across the United States (Cantril et al., 1940). The hour-long program consisted of a series of "news bulletins" concerning an invasion from Mars. There was no truth to the "news," but many listeners thought otherwise. As they listened to the realistic broadcast, many individuals panicked, some rushing from their homes into the street, others seeking refuge in their basements, and still others jamming the hospitals in a state of shock. The fearful reaction to the broadcast became a news story in itself, but there is evidence that the level of panic may have been overstated in the press and by Cantril and his colleagues.

Crowd fear: A terrifying dust storm (1942).

Although, with a commonsense understanding, we might associate panic with terror, Lofland uses the term "terror" in reference to frightened aggregates of people. For example, individuals held hostage in banks, in private homes, or on hijacked airplanes experience terror. *Terror* is the enduring fear that arises from being trapped in a dangerous situation for a period of time. Compared with panic, episodes of terror are apt to last longer, sometimes much longer (e.g., the taking of hostages at the American Embassy in Iran in 1979; the Americans were captured in November 1979 and were not released until January 1981). An episode of terror is one thing. An act of terrorism such as the bombing of a building or the poisoning of a community water supply is something else. Terrorists' acts can lead to panic.

A lower intensity of fear is dread. *Dread* is "a

persistent and chronic apprehension of a more diffuse danger" (Lofland, 1981: 420). One common example is the apprehension of individuals trapped by a physical force (e.g., shipwreck, mine cave-in, urban power failure). The immediate well-being of the hapless individuals is unproblematic, but their long-term survival is in doubt. When dread is prolonged, a partially new social order may emerge; the realignment arises along with the individuals' concern about rescue, escape, and possibly death. There is an acceptance of codes by which to live until one eventuality or another occurs.

Rex Lucas (1968) describes some of the social patterns emerging among those buried in the 1958 Springhill, Nova Scotia, mine disaster. For example, although many of the buried miners remained alive, they were regarded as dead by other trapped miners. Men who were silent (and badly injured) but still breathing were thought to be dead. Norms of emotional restraint developed with reference to dead colleagues and the dangerous plight of those still alive. Certain topics recurred in conversation; the survivors spoke of the nature of death, the consequences of unfilled roles at home, and their accomplishments in life.

Bystanders in a crowd who become unwilling witnesses to an event which is frightful and upsetting experience *horror.* For example, individuals who observe someone jumping to his or her death from the top of a tall building are horrified. A drowning at a public beach sometimes generates the same social reaction. For such events to be classified as collective behavior, however, the individually felt horror would have to spread among the observers and be mobilized by them in some way (see earlier definition).

Crowd Hostilities

Lofland (1981: 427) distinguishes three levels of collective hostility. The lowest level is *symbolic.* Displeasure is expressed at this level by means of signs, speeches, rallies, and protest marches. On the intermediate level, hostility is directed toward *real and personal property.* Looting, boycotting, destroying property, occupying an office or other space, and going on strike (labor) all are collective hostility at the intermediate level. The third level is a *direct attack on individuals.* Victims are captured, assaulted, or murdered.

There are four types of crowd hostilities: *political, leisure, street,* and *captive.* The aim of a *hostile political crowd* is to get other people to do what it wants them to do. There are several varieties of political crowd. In one, citizens are pitted against an individual. A mob that attacks a public speaker whose affiliation or ideology it detests is a hostile crowd of this type. The attack occurs on one of the three levels (hostility against symbols, property, or individuals). Another type is the hostility of citizens against other citizens. Here aggregates clash (again on one of the three levels) over ideological differences, as in the street fighting between Protestants and Catholics in Northern Ireland. A third type emerges when citizens contend against establishments. The protest march and rally express hostility against the establishment. For example, women have picketed at the national capital to call attention to the government's sexist policies.

Hostile leisure crowds spring up among spectators at sporting events, rock concerts, and other scenes of pleasure. Citizen-against-citizen crowds develop as fans of rival sports teams square off in a display of mutual dislike. British soccer is rich in examples. Gladys Lang (1981) reviews some of the incidents of crowd behavior at the British soccer matches along with such incidents in Canadian and American sport. Crowd hostilities at matches and games are not always of the citizen-citizen variety, as her typology of "sports riots" suggests:

1. A *fanatic public* "extends" its support of a player or team through some form of *collective protest* against a decision or act it views as damaging to the reputation (or chance for victory) of the player or team;

2. An *acquisition crowd* acts spontaneously in a form of *anomic protest* against a decision or act it defines as "against the rules of fair play" and/or incurring some kind of personal damage or loss of self;
3. The *licentious* (or *exuberant*) crowd seizes an opportunity to indulge individual whims and appetites, resulting—whether willfully or accidentally—in *destructive behavior* or *public disturbance;*
4. The *polarized audience* seizes the occasion to *continue a conflict that has its primary roots outside the sports arena.* (Lang, 1981: 418)

There are also citizen-establishment hostilities expressed by leisure crowds. Some of Lang's types can be reinterpreted in these terms.

The spontaneous eruption constituting the *hostile street crowd* comes about in three ways: (1) One way is citizens against an individual. A poignant historical example of this variant is the angry lynch mob practicing its own version of justice on a reputed community villain. (2) Citizen-citizen street crowd hostilities occur specifically as race riots and generally as "communal riots" (Janowitz, 1968) where neighborhoods clash in competition over scarce resources of housing, employment, or recreation. (3) Ghetto riots that include looting and burning are of the citizen-establishment variety of crowd hostility, often having been touched off by an act of the police (e.g., shooting a black youth) which onlookers consider highly unjust.

The angry inmates in total institutions (the captives) join together in *hostile captive crowds.* Prison riots are now a fact of life in North America. Some of the riots are prisoner-prisoner encounters. The celebrated disturbances, however, involve a portion of the total prison population in a struggle against guards and prison officials over some festering issue.

Crowd Joys

Lofland (1981: 435) defines *collective joys* as "the emotion evoked by well-being, success or good fortune or by the prospect of possessing what one desires." It is a state of happiness. It may be the dominant emotion of a face-to-face aggregate or of a dispersed set of people who are more or less simultaneously attending to the same event or circumstance and who are aware of others doing the same.

There are five dimensions along which joyous crowds vary: (1) They vary by the amount of combined emotional and motor activity they display. (2) They vary by the proportion of members of the crowd who act in this way. (3) The nature and meaning of the collective joy vary. (4) These crowds differ in the amount of preplanning of their expressive actions and the degree of the regularity of those actions. (5) Collective joys vary in their length at a single occasion of arousal and by whether they are linked in a rapid series of such occasions.

Variations on these dimensions are evident in six kinds of crowds. All five dimensions apply to crowds known as *ecstatic upheavals. Ecstasy* is a mental and bodily state that is substantially beyond the control of the individual. Hence, people in ecstasy lose their inhibitions, doing and saying things they would never do and say otherwise.

Goodman's (1974) description of a "trance-based upheaval" in a Yucatan village is an excellent example. The upheaval started with a small Apostolic church. The leader of the church encouraged *glossolalia* (ecstatic, usually unintelligible, speech). His fervent religious messages about the Second Coming of Christ plus the heavy, rhythmic glossolalia engendered ecstatic upheavals among the congregation. These episodes went on for nearly a month, ultimately involving most of the village populace and temporarily halting many of the everyday routines. These outbursts were eventually terminated by regional church officials who felt their church's interests were being undermined by the glossolalia and zealous preaching. Social movements may begin with ecstatic upheavals.

The *ecstatic convention* differs from the upheaval primarily in its tendency to be regularized (preplanned) and sufficiently controlled by group leaders. It poses no threat to the established order (unlike the upheaval). But, for the most part, the behavior in ecstatic convention is more or less the same as that in ecstatic upheaval. Glossolalia, religious hallucinations, shrieking and barking, bodily agitations of great variety (rolling on the ground, peculiar gestures, dancing, shaking)—all are a part of the ecstatic convention. Revivalist sects define these actions as evidence of the presence of a power external to the actor's body. That power is God.

Ecstatic congregations engage in similar actions, except that the conduct lasts only from a few hours to the larger part of a day, but no longer. The behavior occurs among people who know one another and who have a leader. These people participate in a religious "service," a portion of which is reserved for collective joy. Faith healing is frequently an aim of these routines. Recreation is another.

Revivalist crowds are a more restrained and carefully preplanned version of the congregation. They also involve a considerably larger number of people. Evangelists such as Billy Graham and Oral Roberts conduct "revival meetings." In closing, the revivalist preachers call on individuals to express a faith and become members of a church.

Among the remaining types of crowd joys are those of the revelrous crowd and the excited crowd. The *revelrous crowd* gathers at wild parties and celebrations. People caught in the grip of the crowd's intense, exuberant interhuman feelings sing, dance, shout, and carry on almost out of control; the crowd occasionally destroys property and effaces the surroundings. Listiak (1974: 21) reports on the events of the 1972 Grey Cup Week in Hamilton, Ontario, where people from across Canada gathered to watch the championship game between the Hamilton Tiger-Cats and the Saskatchewan Roughriders professional football teams:

> Indeed the week's activities certainly lived up to the finest Grey Cup tradition. Legitimate deviant behaviour abounded as social control was relaxed and tensions were released. King Street, Hamilton's main street, was filled to overflowing by thousands of people who danced, drank, cheered, sang, rang cowbells, and fought their way up and down the main business section of the street until at least 4:00 a.m. on each of the last three nights of the festivities. While people flowed in all directions on both sides of the street, the hard-core revellers moved continuously up and down King Street within a six-block limit, moving west up King on the north side, crossing over and returning east down King on the south side, crossing over and starting the trip again. Just as the throngs of people on foot moved up and down King Street whooping it up, so the traffic, jammed up for over half a mile, circled the downtown area to contribute its share to the intensity of the merriment already taking place in the main business section. As the jam moved along, honking all the way, drivers and passengers would jump out of their cars to dance, shout, pass drinks among each other, etc. Several pedestrians were moving in and out of the traffic passing out drinks to the motorists. Cars were painted in Tiger-Cat and Roughrider colours; people were hanging over the outside of the vehicles, and also on the hood, roof, and trunk. Convertibles had their tops down and were filled with people; pick-up trucks were similarly loaded up with celebrants. When traffic moved ahead a few feet, the revellers would hang their heads out of the windows and renew their shouting and cheering.

Compared with a revelrous crowd, *excited crowds* restrain their vivacity, keeping within the bounds of good taste and public order. Their numbers simply respond excitedly to staged events, showing an exceptional degree of spontaneous involvement in the concert, stage show, or sports contest unfolding before them.

MASSES

Of lesser emotional intensity than crowds (and their various forms) are the various elementary

An excited, joyful crowd, at least until the opposing team scores.

forms of the mass. In this section, we examine the forms identified in (2) and (6) of Table 21.1. The limitations of space preclude a consideration of (4), mass hostilities.

Mass Fears

Lofland (1981: 421–427) classifies *mass fears* according to whether the events causing the fears are *true* or *false,* a distinction that will be clarified in the paragraphs which follow. The events in question are of two kinds: *environmental* and *social disasters* and *environmental* and *social trends.* Mass fears are more common than crowd fears. The mass fears also grip many more people and spring from events affecting a much larger physical area than do crowd fears.

Found among the *true environmental disasters* are earthquakes, tornadoes, hurricanes, blizzards, floods, and typhoons; such events are more or less suddenly occurring catastrophes. Fritz and Matheson (1957) have observed that various individuals of differing traits tend to "converge" on the scene of a disaster (once it is over). Some of these people are sightseers. Others are "returnees" who have come to inspect property damage and guard against theft and looting. The "anxious" who were away during the disaster itself are looking for close friends or members of their family; the catastrophe has separated friends and close kin. Those who come with sincere intentions of lending a hand are labeled "helpers" by Matheson and Fritz. There are also the "exploiters"; they are there to loot. Their numbers tend to be exaggerated in newspaper accounts.

A recent instance of *true social disaster* is the Tylenol scare in Chicago of late 1982. Someone contaminated with cyanide some of the extra-strength Tylenol capsules being sold in the Chicago suburbs. As a result, seven people who took the poisoned medicine died. The manufacturers of this popular pain reliever quickly recalled their product following the deaths. Although the deaths occurred only in the Chicago area, collective fear caused sales to drop sharply throughout the United States and Canada for a while.

True environmental trends and *social trends* have in common the fact that they are less urgent and sudden but, in the long run, possibly just as threatening as disasters. Here Lofland discusses the behavior of activists in response to the sundry forms of environmental pollution and damage; activists stage rallies, marches, sit-ins, and various sensational acts. For roughly fifteen years, pollution has been a consistent tar-

What kind of crowd behavior is suggested by this picture?

get of the activists in North America. The threat of nuclear war has aroused a fluctuating mass response. Of course, none of these trends arouses the entire population. Only a small proportion (but still large enough to constitute a mass) respond to the trends with fear. Moreover, why certain trends cause fear at one point in history rather than at another time is one of the fascinating research questions in this area of sociology. The "Red scare" of 1919 and 1920 in the United States exemplifies mass fear stimulated by a social trend. The belief that America was about to be taken over by Communists became an exceptional fear during this time.

False environmental and social disasters rest on the popular belief that there is an alarmingly large number of occurrences of a real and frightening physical or human phenomenon. Still, these occurrences, as defined by common sense, are scientifically unverifiable. Nevertheless, they result in *mass hysteria:* an outbreak of conduct characterized by unmanageable fear or emotional excess among sets of people.

Klapp (1972: 115–120) reviews several examples of hysteria, including the Seattle windshield-pitting epidemic of 1954. The collective belief that some mysterious force was causing the sudden appearance of pits in the windshields of automobiles in Seattle gave rise to hysteria. The mass media reported on the speculation concerning the pitting. Some individuals believed the pits were caused by meteoric dust. Others theorized that sandfleas had laid eggs on the glass and that hatching from the eggs caused the pits. Those who saw the pits as a normal outcome of city traffic experienced neither alarm nor hysteria. Kerckhoff (1970: 88) summarizes the typical sequence leading to this kind of collective behavior:

> A number of people are exposed to common sources of strain from which no very attractive means of escape are present, although it may be known that acts which have negative consequences might serve to reduce the tension. The combination of the original strain and the impossibility of using any known solution brings about a general state of tension whose intensity is probably increased by interstimulation among the people so situated. The state of unresolved tension leads to the experience of physiological symptoms. These symptoms become associated in the minds of the distressed people with some credible (though factually incorrect) "cause" in the situation, the connection deriving from what are probably random events that become interpreted in the context of the experienced discomfort. This external cause both objectifies the source of the discomfort and adds a further source of strain to the situation: fear of a threatening agent. The belief in the threatening agent, the rising number of victims, and the legitimating actions of outside experts will increase the sense of tension and the probability of experiencing symptoms which may be defined as relevant to the presumed source of the spreading sickness.

Metaphorically speaking, hysterical feelings spread among a population by *contagion.*

Crime waves exemplify well the *false environmental and social trends.* Such trends are actually illusory. Fishman (1978) points to the role of the mass media in spreading the "news" that a certain type of crime has recently reached dangerous proportions in the community.

Mass Joys

Like crowd joys, the three principal mass joys—crazes, fashions, and fads—vary in their degree of emotional intensity, their degree of seriousness, and their scope, duration, and regularity of participant involvement. "Put differently, the degree of obtrusiveness into participants' lives differs from the craze to the fashion to the fad" (Lofland, 1981: 441).

A *craze,* or *mania,* is excessive and unreasonable enthusiasm for a special object or prize. At the height of a craze, people lose control over their emotional and mental processes; they remain in this state for long periods of time. The

California and Yukon gold rushes of the last century and the Florida land boom of this century are examples. The Florida land boom occurred in 1925–1926, when a man proposed to build a community on soil dredged from Tampa Bay. After $3 million were made on land sales before the project even began, word spread across the nation that immense profits were to be had by buying this real estate for subsequent resale at a higher price. People who never intended to live in Florida bought and sold lots at a frenetic pace, trying to take advantage of existing prices before they escalated. Diminishing confidence in the scheme and a hurricane in 1926 ended the fanaticism.

Both crazes and fashions are transitory, but fashions are less emotionally intense. A *fashion* is a prevailing, short-lived custom, usage, or style. Blumer (1968) points out that fashions are often introduced by the highest strata of society, from whom they diffuse to those below (to the extent that the less privileged can afford them). Katz and Lazarsfeld (1955: 263–268) found, however, that women in the middle strata are also leaders in clothing, cosmetics, and the like. As Simmel (1956: 541) observes:

> Fashion is a form of imitation and so of social equalization, but, paradoxically, in changing incessantly it differentiates one time from another and one social stratum from another. It unites those of a social class and segregates them from others. The elite initiates a fashion and, when the mass imitates it in an effort to obliterate the external distinctions of class, abandons it for a new mode.

There are fashions in, among other things, clothing, automobiles, housing, objects of scientific research, humor, medical treatment, diets, and exercise. Some of these are anything but frivolous.

Ray L. Gold (1964: 256) defines a *fad* as: "markedly novel, trivial, and ephemeral behaviour which spreads rapidly through whatever portions of society choose to adopt it." Imitation is also a basic process underlying the adoption of a fad. Moreover, fads are usually brief. Often they are circumventions of the norms and mores of the society and consequently forms of minor deviance or breaches of etiquette. Lofland (1981: 445) classifies fads as *objects* (e.g., popular songs, smiling faces, bumper stickers), *ideas* (e.g., astrology), *activities* (e.g., miniature golf, video games, water slides), and *people* (e.g., Michael Jackson, Farrah Fawcett-Majors).

THEORIES OF COLLECTIVE BEHAVIOR

The different elementary forms of collective behavior give substance to the several theories of collective behavior, which have helped organize research in this area. The elementary forms illustrate the broader principles of the theories, as do social movements, which are discussed in the next section. The theories are not always named the same way in the sociological literature. Furthermore, there is some overlap in their propositions. They are covered here under the titles of *symbolic interactionist theory, convergence theory, emergent-norm theory,* and *value-added theory.*

Symbolic Interactionist Theory

Blumer (1975) is one of the principal architects of the symbolic interactionist explanation of collective behavior.[1] He theorized that collective behavior emerges when there is "social unrest," or a breakdown of some sort in the social order. During social unrest, people behave erratically and aimlessly as they search for something or for a way to avoid something; they are not sure what. These times are characterized by exaggerated opinions, rumor, and distorted perceptions. Consequently, individuals tend to be especially irritable and suggestible.

Blumer listed five types of social unrest: (1) In one, there is *anxiety* about vague but "dire

[1]Blumer initially published his theory of collective behavior in 1939 (Blumer, 1939).

possibilities" in the future. (2) Another type is founded in *frustration* or *protest* over an existing social arrangement. Social unrest here often leads to the formation of hostile crowds. (3) A third type is characterized by a desire to flee the world, which commonly manifests itself in Utopian movements and certain kinds of ecstatic crowds. (4) In the fourth type, people are keen to do something, but they lack direction. (5) Finally, there are those who despair of something or are grievous over it (e.g., environmental and social trends), which spreads unrest among them.

Three forms of interaction occur among crowds reacting to social unrest. First, there is *milling.* Milling is fostered by the process of "circular reaction": the process by which one person's behavior stimulates a response in another person whose response then stimulates the first person. Milling may lead to *collective excitement,* in which people imitate the agitated and emotional behavior of those nearby. It is difficult to ignore such conspicuous behavior. This leads to *contagious interaction,* which entails a loss of self-consciousness, a lowered resistance to group influence, and a heightened tendency to do what others are doing in the immediate situation. According to this theory, social contagion is powerful enough to affect many of the bystanders looking at the milling crowd from the periphery. They are soon pulled into its vortex and commence to behave like the other participants.

Convergence Theory

Contrasting to some extent with Blumer's scheme, convergence theory is a conceptual product of mainstream psychology and psychoanalysis. The convergence theory proceeds from the assumption that human beings share a number of latent predispositions, which are socially controlled (i.e., by the superego; see Chapter 5). These predispositions include sexual desire, aggressiveness, defensive reactions against danger, and frustration. Frustration has been said to lead to aggression, although most specialists no longer accept this hypothesis in this simplified form (Penner, 1978: 108). Crowd behavior is the overt expression of these collective predispositions under conditions fostering contagious reactions to an effective stimulus. Hostile crowds exemplify well the convergence thesis.

Other psychologists have a somewhat different model of crowd behavior. They argue that crowd behavior is the sum of individual reactions to a common stimulus (Milgram and Toch, 1969: 551–552). Because the members of a crowd share similar past experiences, they are inclined to react similarly to immediate stimuli. The other people on the scene help intensify an individual's reaction; that is, he or she sees other individuals reacting and follows suit.

Convergence theory calls attention to the importance of group influence on individuals and to enduring predispositions (the latter was overlooked by Blumer). It cannot be assumed, however, as this theory does, that every latent disposition of the participants is activated by the object or event which gives rise to the stimulus. One question left unanswered by the theory is why some predispositions are activated while others, though potentially relevant, are not.

Emergent-Norm Theory

Emergent-norm theory is closely associated with Ralph H. Turner and Lewis M. Killian (1972: 21–25), some of whose ideas come from experimental social psychology. Turner and Killian hold that crowds are not initially characterized by unanimity of motives, goals, and values. Rather, a norm emerges in the situation, as each person observes what the others are doing there and defines their actions as appropriate. Instead of conceiving of collective behavior as a response to the breakdown in normative control, Turner and Killian see it as a response to an emergent norm. This expectation or set of expectations sets limits on the behavior of those in the crowd. The notion of emergent norms originated with Sherif's study of the autokinetic effect (see Chapter 6).

Indeed, the emergent norm may make it possible for collective behavior to occur in the first place, since it shows would-be participants that their involvement in the crowd will remain within their moral bounds. For instance, the norm in the Grey Cup celebration referred to earlier was dancing, cheering, drinking, and horn honking. It was not breaking windows, overturning cars, or raping women. Turner and Killian bring us back to that insufficiently examined aspect of collective behavior, namely that crowd members seldom express all relevant latent predispositions. Certain behaviors are appropriate, whereas others are inappropriate, whether in hostile, ecstatic, or fearful crowds. This suggests a reexamination of the significance of anonymity, which previous theories have singled out as one characteristic of crowds. Control via an emergent norm may be most effective where anonymity is lowest and vice versa. Norms also emerge in nonepisodic forms of collective behavior (e.g., public opinion, social movements).

Value-Added Theory

Neil J. Smelser's (1962; 1964) value-added theory, which is a variant of sociological functionalism, is regarded by many students of collective behavior as the most systematic conceptual statement in the field. Smelser stated that an episode of collective behavior evolves through a sequence of five determinants.[2] At each stage in this sequence the number of alternative possibilities for subsequent action is reduced. That is, toward the end of the sequence collective behavior becomes more and more likely. Each determinant operates within the scope of the preceding one, moving thus from a broad to a narrow focus. The "value-added" metaphor is taken from the economics of manufacturing, where the value of the raw materials (e.g., water, flour, yeast) is increased when they are combined into a finished product (e.g., bread). Accordingly, Smelser's illustration of his scheme is that of financial panic.

The first determinant is *structural conduciveness:* to what degree does any social arrangement permit a particular type of collective behavior (i.e., crowd or mass fear, hostility, joy)? In the case of financial panic, people must be able to dispose of their resources rapidly and freely. For example, property tied up by family restrictions, such as being available to the would-be seller only on the death of his or her father, fails to meet this condition.

Strain is the second determinant, which, in Smelser's illustration, is the threat of financial loss. Strain, however, can lead to reactions other than panic (e.g., scapegoating, reform movements). For strain to lead to the third determinant, it must operate within the context of conduciveness.

The third determinant is the development of a *generalized belief* exaggerating the threat and stressing its imminence. In the example of financial panic, collective behavior begins to emerge as this belief reaches the proportions of hysteria, stimulated by various "precipitating factors" (e.g., a bank closure) that are interpreted as commonsense evidence of the threat.

The fourth determinant is the *mobilization* of those who accept the generalized belief. The believers are mobilized for some kind of action. This could be a single act, such as panic selling, or an action more enduring, such as the start of a social movement. In the enduring action, a leader emerges. The leader directs the participants toward their common goals.

Fifth is the *social control,* which is actually a counterdeterminant. Some counterdeterminants act to prevent the initial occurrence of one or more of the earlier determinants. Thus,

[2] In a later revision of his theory, Smelser (1972: 101) lists six determinants. "Precipitating factors" is the addition to the original five. He then proceeds to throw it out on the grounds that "it is a way of saying that one of the other determinants comes to be established in a particularly sudden and dramatic way." Precipitating factors, he says, are not separate determinants of collective behavior.

Crowd social control is a major function of the modern police force.

spiking scare rumors or closing the stock market to preclude panic selling nips in the bud any collective behavior. Other counterdeterminants limit existing collective behavior (e.g., closing the stock market to prevent *further* panic selling).

Smelser's theory has its critics, too. One of the more widespread criticisms centers on the third determinant. Some scholars contend that Smelser overlooked the heterogeneity of beliefs among leaders and followers; there is often no "common culture" on which to base mobilization, action, and leadership. Unfortunately, there have been but a few attempts to test this theory (Marx and Wood, 1975: 407).

SOCIAL MOVEMENTS

Late twentieth century North America is virtually awash with *social movements.* Roland Warren (1977: 89) defines social movements as:

> widespread networks of activities and supporting beliefs taken by individuals and organizations in connection with a salient and value charged issue, directed toward bringing about social change in various parts of the society in relation to the issue, and in the direction of the asserted values.

Several points suggested by this definition warrant further consideration. One, social movements are not social groups, but rather networks (defined later) of groups, organizations, and individuals. For an individual participant, interaction is possible only with a small portion of the totality of these three components. Two, social movements are fired by an *ideology:* a somewhat loosely integrated set of beliefs, theories, values, and goals constituting a sociopolitical program for change or maintenance of the status quo. One of the functions of a social movement's ideology is to justify the pursuit of particular interests shared by participants in the movement. In general, the interests are to initiate or prevent social change. Three, social movements usually encompass many more people than a typical elementary form of collective behavior such as a riot or a lynching.

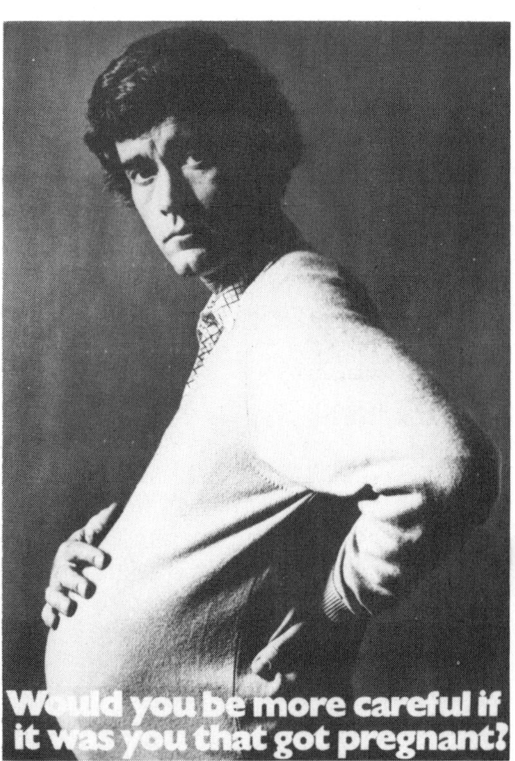

Would you be more careful if
it was you that got pregnant?

The Planned Parenthood social movement has specific changes it would like to see take place.

Movements are likely to be regional, national, and even international in scope.

Types of Movements

In an area rife with typologies, David Aberle's (1966) fourfold classification of social movements is considered one of the most useful and comprehensive. It is constructed along two dimensions: *locus* and *amount* of desired change. Concerning the first, some movements strive to change individuals while others strive to change the social structure. The amount of change sought may be partial or total. The cross-classification of these two dimensions reveals four types of movements: transformative, reformative, redemptive, and alternative.

Transformative Movements A transformative movement seeks a total change in the social structure. One colorful example is the millennial or chiliastic movement, which holds that for one thousand years (a millennium) holiness will triumph and Christ will reign on earth. This period is said to start with Christ's appearance in visible form in this world. Evangelist David Berg organized a group of teenagers in California in 1968 that became the nucleus of the Children of God movement. Intense public hostility in the United States has since driven the adherents to the Children of God movement to Europe, Africa, and South America. From these locations they espouse the following timetable for the second coming of Christ along with a total transformation of present-day society as we know it (Bromley and Shupe, 1981: 29–30):

1. In 1968, Berg revealed, the "End of Time of the Gentiles" and the beginning of the "Restoration of the Remnant of Israel in the Children of God" occurred. COG's special function since then has been to spread this message, cut members' ties to the Whore of Babylon (i.e., larger society), and gather the faithful, who will survive the coming troubles.
2. The "Time of the Great Confusion" will occur in the late 1970s or early 1980s. Sociologist Roy Wallis (1976: 819), who has made one of the best analyses of COG doctrines, describes the Time in this way:

   > . . . the Children of God expect a progressive worsening of the world situation, rampaging inflation, increased pollution, civil strife, political chaos, and economic disaster. Berg believes that the United States, being the nation most objectionable to God, will suffer particularly. He believed that Nixon would establish a dictatorship of the radical right, leading in turn to revolution by the left. The time-scale here is not altogether clear, but more or less simultaneously Berg believed that the Arab-Israeli War would intensify, drawing invasion of Israel by Russia, World War III, and the virtual destruction of America.

   During this time the Anti-Christ is supposed to emerge as an important world leader who wins support of the masses by pledges of peace and international stability.

3. By 1985–1986, when the Anti-Christ has assumed supreme international power, the preparations for the battle of Armageddon foretold in the Book of Revelations will take place. During the first three and one-half years of the final seven-year period, international communism will spread in relatively conflict-free fashion. The latter three and one-half years, however, will be known as the Great Tribulation. The masses will be required to worship the Anti-Christ as God, and all who resist will be persecuted.
4. Around 1993 "The Rapture of the Saints" will occur. The returning Christ and his defenders will do battle with the followers of Anti-Christ, achieve victory, and establish a throne in Jerusalem with COG members serving as important rulers and officials during Christ's 1000-year reign.

Reformative Movements Reformative movements aim for partial change of the social structure. Many of them work toward some sort of social reform. The women's movement and the environmentalist movement are examples. The campaign for nuclear disarmament is reformative in nature. In fact, the list of contemporary reformative movements is long.

Redemptive Movements The *redemptive movements* seek to bring about a total change in individuals. Here the inner condition of people is felt to be in need of modification; the proposed modification is looked on as a way of solving some personal or social problem. The Jesus Movement provides an illustration. Richardson et al. (1972) write that members of this movement recruit new members by pointing out the potential members' guilt, usually found to be associated with a personal history of drinking, using drugs, engaging in premarital sex, or advocating radical politics. The goal of the movement is to change and control the individual's mind through religious conversion (defined in the next section) in accordance with the aims of the movement. One must be a committed Christian, "accept Christ," and do so within a rather inflexible timetable set by the leaders of the movement. The Salvation Army is a less extreme instance of this type of collective behavior.

What kind of social movement does this picture depict?

Alternative Movements The alternative movements seek a partial change in people. The current striving for weight loss, physical fitness, and quitting smoking, which appear to have reached movementlike emphasis, are examples. The antismoking movement has at least two components. One component is made up of people who are trying to quit smoking. They avail themselves of various kinds of assistance, such as medical advice, self-help groups, personal programs, and pharmaceutical aids. The other component is composed of people who oppose smoking in the presence of nonsmokers. They lobby for restrictions on smoking in public places, forbid it in their homes and offices, and even campaign for higher tobacco taxes, which they believe will help curb smoking.

Participation in Movements

People are an essential resource for social movements (Wilson, 1973: 169), for it is through people that movements advance their causes. Recognizing the importance of individual support, movements put a great deal of effort into recruiting new members. Recruitment is a routine but major activity. As Zurcher and Snow (1981: 449–464) point out, an individual's decision to participate in a movement initially and over time is affected by several interrelated factors: movement ideology, social network contacts, value commitment to the movement, and conversion to its ideology.

Psychologists and sociologists have identified a variety of motives for joining social movements: (1) Some people join in the hope of adding meaning to their lives (see Chapter 15). (2) Several studies indicate that authoritarian personalities—i.e., highly prejudiced, insecure, dogmatic individuals—are attracted to movements at the poles of the political left or right (Zurcher and Snow, 1981: 450). (3) A variant of the search for meaning is the search for an attractive, personal identity or for some kind of social anchorage in mass society (Klapp, 1969). (4) Involvement in a movement may help counteract social isolation or (5) enhance one's sense

The Decriminalization of Marijuana Use as a Social Movement

Voice was given to the millions of marijuana users in 1970 when a young Washington lawyer established NORML, the National Organization for the Reform of Marijuana Law, with a grant from the Playboy Foundation. As the founder of NORML put it: "The only people working for reform then were freaks who wanted to turn on the world, an approach that was obviously doomed to failure. I wanted an effective, middle-class approach, not pro-grass but antijail. . . ."

Things moved in fits and starts in the early years, and NORML had an important impact on the move to decriminalize marijuana possession—done in 10 states—and to reduce marijuana possession from a felony to a misdemeanor—done in all but two of the remaining states. In 1979 NORML changed its tune and is now calling for the legalization of the use and sale of marijuana. The action of NORML that had brought the most joy to college students is their distribution of the 1936 movie *Reefer Madness.* The film "depicts a group of high-school students trying marijuana, with murder, rape, prostitution and madness as the swift result of their folly. It is so bad, it is really good and should help young people understand some of the factors that shaped attitudes about marijuana in the 1930s. NORML has grown in membership and influence since the early seventies and has been *the* national organization urging the decriminalization of marijuana use and possession for personal use.

The year 1972 was a turning point in the fight to decriminalize marijuana. There are many variations on the theme, but the basic concept of decriminalization is that there should be no prison sentences for the possession of a small amount of marijuana for personal use. Usually any amount less than an ounce is considered to be for personal use and not for sale or resale. Possession for personal use may still be illegal, as is exceeding the speed limit on the highway, but the penalty is a fine, not prison, and the individual who is fined does not have a police record.

If you remember, the Comprehensive Drug Abuse Prevention and Control Act of 1970 established a Commission on Marijuana and Drug Abuse. . . . It was to study the issues comprehensively and make "recommendations for legislative and administrative actions" within 2 years. The commission members were known to be very conservative on questions of drug use, so not much was expected. And even if the report was balanced or liberal on various drug issues, what would happen? The 1962 President's Ad Hoc Panel on Drug Abuse had concluded "that the hazards of marijuana per se have been exaggerated and that long criminal sentences imposed on an occasional user or possessor of the drug are in poor social perspective." Nothing happened.

The wheel turns. Time marches on. Things look different when you change your position. Both the interim and the first reports of the Marijuana Commission not only agreed with the 1962 panel, but recommended legislative changes.

> The Commission recommended that federal and state laws be changed so that private possession of small amounts of marihuana for personal use, and casual

> distribution of small amounts without monetary profit, would no longer be offenses, though marihuana possessed in public would remain contraband. Cultivation, distribution for profit, and possession with intent to sell would remain felonies. Criminal penalties would be retained for disorderly conduct associated with marihuana intoxication and driving under the influence of marihuana, and a plea of marihuana intoxication would not be a defense to any criminal act committed under its influence.

The 184-page report was excellent. It provided a social and historical perspective and an honest evaluation of the status of marijuana research at that time. The sluice gates were lifted a little, and some of the pressure behind the dam was released. In May 1972, the Canadian government commission issued its report, the LeDain report, and recommended that possession of marijuana be *legalized.* It seems that every month in that year some action was taken that either actually or symbolically expressed a different attitude toward marijuana and its users. Throughout the year, states began releasing some of the 2000 individuals previously jailed for marijuana possession. Not only was amnesty for those in prison catching on, but so was leniency for those arrested (but sometimes not even charged) with small amounts of marijuana. In September, Ann Arbor, Michigan, changed its city laws so that possession of marijuana was only a $5 fine, and smoking in public increased.

Because most people had concerns about the effects of marijuana on health, it was of special significance that in June 1972 the AMA came out in favor of dropping criminal penalties for possession of "insignificant amounts" of marijuana and noted that "there is no evidence supporting the idea that marijuana leads to violence, aggressive behavior or crime." This was a very significant change from the 1968 AMA position that declared, "Cannabis is a dangerous drug and as such is a public health concern."

In August 1972 the American Bar Association (ABA) called for the reduction of criminal penalties for possession but did not recommend decriminalization, although it did a year later.

In November 1977, the AMA and the ABA issued a joint (!) statement endorsing the decriminalization of marijuana for personal use.

A week before Christmas in 1972 it came to pass that the best-known and most literate of American conservatives proclaimed in favor of the decriminalization of marijuana, saying:

> It isn't silly to say that the user should not be molested, even though the pusher should be put in jail. It was so, mostly, under prohibition, when the speakeasy operators were prosecuted, not so the patrons. Thus it is, by and large, in the case of prostitution; and even with gambling; and most explicitly with pornography, the Supreme Court having ruled that you can't molest the owner, even though you can go after the peddler.

SOURCE: Oakley Ray. *Drugs, Society, and Human Behavior,* 3rd ed., pp. 442–443. St. Louis: Mosby, 1983.

of belonging. (6) There are individuals whose need for power is met by joining a social movement. (7) People whose social status is threatened may try to eliminate the threat by starting a crusade that develops into a movement.

The problem with explaining participation in social movements on the basis of motivation is that some people who are predisposed to join a social movement fail to do so (Zurcher and Snow, 1981: 453). A complete theory of participation requires additional propositions. Two of these are fashioned from the concepts of social network and ideology. A *social network* is the web of relationships and acquaintanceships in which an individual is embedded; it is the netlike set of people to whom the individual is linked by the dint of the contacts he or she has.

Zurcher and Snow review a number of studies which reveal that people who join a social movement learn of it through their network contacts with participants in the movement. Directly or indirectly, many recruits know someone who is already active and involved in the movement. Moreover, the network serves as an information pipeline through which outsiders learn of the movement's ideology and its goals. In terms of Smelser's theory, *ideology* (the third determinant of belief) mobilizes individuals and their actions for the good of the movement. *Mobilization,* then, refers to recruitment as well as to the planning of strategies.

Still other concepts are needed to account for an individual's continued participation in a movement once recruited to it (Snow and Machalek, 1984: 171). The notions of value commitment and conversion introduced elsewhere in this book (particularly in Chapter 15) are germane here as well. Strength of commitment has been found to vary from member to member, although a high level of commitment is a factor in faithful participation among those who are so oriented. *Conversion* is the process through which a new or formerly peripheral set of symbols, beliefs, and outlooks comes to function as a person's primary authority (Snow and Machalek, 1984: 170). As indicated in Chapter 15, conversion helps bolster one's value commitment to a religion or, in more general terms, to a social movement.[3]

Social Movement Organizations

Sociologists have also shown considerable interest in the history of social movements. They are interested in how social movements take root, grow and thrive, wither and die. One of the most succinct statements on this process comes from Zald and Ash (1966). They examine the large-scale organizations within social movements.

Zald and Ash note that movement organizations differ from other kinds in two important ways: First, as noted earlier, the goal of movement organizations is to change a society or its members. Second, their incentive structure is composed primarily of "purposive incentives," or those encouraging members to work for the values of the movement. Other types of organization offer different incentives to their members; for instance, work organizations offer the material incentive of money, and Greek-letter societies offer the solidary incentives of friendship and prestige.

Origin of Movements How do social movements start? Sometimes they start as crowds—as elementary collective behavior—which develop "a more enduring sense of group identity and pursue a plan of action requiring more sustained activity than can be maintained through crowd conditions" (Turner and Killian, 1972: 245). The theories of collective behavior help explain these social movements, developing as they do through combinations of contagion, convergence, emergent norms, generalized beliefs, and mobilizations. Crowd movements have a *spontaneous beginning,* which contrasts with the *planned beginning* of other social movements. Wilson (1973: 332–333) described

[3]Conversion as defined and used here can be other than religious. There are secular movement ideologies of various kinds (e.g., political, moral) to which one might be converted.

the typical "career," or history of the planned type. Here large-scale organizations begin early on to play a major role:

> The typical career begins with a small band or coterie of like-minded people, gathered together to agitate for social change, who are extremely optimistic about the likelihood of attaining their goals swiftly and with facility. The air is full of the promise of rapid and significant gains. The band has a leader who is surrounded by helpers or disciples who are his personal devotees. These disciples relate to one another on an informal and personal basis and recognize no differences of status among themselves. The extreme optimism of the group and its intense enthusiasm for the cause stimulate little thought for the morrow. Accordingly, scant attention is paid to the problem of setting up an organization. Indeed this is probably not seen as a problem at all. However, this phase rarely lasts long, for there comes the time when enthusiasm begins to wane as the continued frustrations experienced by the movement take their toll and when the movement grows so much that the original communitas is lost. Under these circumstances, the disciples begin to find living uncertainly from day to day irksome, and the leader begins to find relying on ad hoc decision making unmanageable. Members then experience a need for some order, some predictability in the conduct of their affairs, while the leader desires to extend his hold over a growing number of followers. The typical response is to establish procedures which regulate the affairs of the movement and equip it for an indefinite future. These procedures concern the most pressing interactional concerns of the movement, such as the admission and control of new members, the continued instruction of members in the teachings of the movement, the setting of times and places for meetings, the purchase or rent of property, the raising of funds and distribution of resources, and so on. To the extent to which activities such as these become set and consistent, the group has undergone a process of routinization. This is meant not so much in the sense of behavior becoming habitual or regular but in the sense that relations become governed by norms pertaining to the mundane world of expedience and custom rather than the sacred world of ideology.

Of course, crowd behavior may accompany even the planned emergence of social movement organizations, as evidenced in the race riots during the racial equality movement in the United States and in the prison riots during the prison reform movement throughout North America. Moreover, it is necessary that there be mass media coverage of the movement, its aims, and (it is hoped) its progress if the movement is to come to the attention of the public (Cohn and Gallagher, 1984)

Routinization As the history of a social movement and its organizations unfolds, its early, often charismatic leaders are replaced by a more bureaucratic type. *Charismatic leaders* rule by dint of their commanding personal qualities, which attract devoted followers over whom the leaders have exceptional influence and control. The departure of such figures, as by retirement or death, commonly sparks major changes in the movement. No one can fill the shoes of these leaders. Charisma must now be *routinized:* leadership must be transformed into a bureaucratic or institutionalized role.

Zald and Ash note that, during this transition, there is often a decline in membership, as those who were more attached to the leader than to the movement drift away. Moreover, the power vacuum left by that person's departure may engender factionalism and power struggles among his or her lieutenants. Finally, there is, at the organizational level, a trend toward bureaucratization (i.e., proliferation of formal positions, roles, and rules) and toward professionalism among the executive core.

Problems One of the problems movement organizations face is their inability to reach their goals or to come sufficiently close to doing so and thus satisfy the majority of members. Many of these organizations, say Zald and Ash, are neither successes nor failures. Rather, they have succeeded to the point of making a place for themselves in their society. Still, their growth has slowed or possibly even ceased. The old esprit de corps is gone. Members expect the goals to be attained only in the distant future. Organizational leaders in these circumstances, because they have a personal stake in the continuation of their group, tend to become conservative; that is, they grow reluctant to pursue radical goals for fear of endangering their organization. They are also inclined toward *oligarchy* (see Chapter 7), for this prevents new leaders from taking over and implementing threatening changes.

Successful movement organizations have a different problem. What do they do when they succeed in eradicating the disease (as in the case of poliomyelitis) or getting the law on the books (as in the case of women's suffrage)? One alternative is to cease operation. Another is to *transform* the organization's goals into something appropriate for the times and of interest to the members of the organization. This is precisely what the War Amputations of Canada are planning to do when there are no longer any war amputees. They will become the Canadian Amputees Foundation, which will offer assistance to child amputees through a program now under way in the War Amputations organization.

Zurcher and Ash note that the transformation of goals is most likely to occur when the organization enjoys the unquestionable support of its members and when it has its own fund-raising base. In addition, the short-term material benefits bind members to each other and to the group.

Failure A number of reasons account for the failure of movement organizations. Members may lose confidence in their group's ability to reach its goals. Or leaders may attempt to transform the goals, discovering too late the rank and file's opposition to a change. Occasionally, the government (or more specifically the police) takes an active role in bringing about the demise of a movement (e.g., the Solidarity Trade Union Movement in Poland in 1982). And, some of these organizations fail because their legitimacy in the community and among their supporters becomes suspect. This was the predicament in which Social Credit, a conservative, rural, political protest movement in Quebec, found itself in the early 1970s:

> Social Credit with its right-wing protest ideology and its rural and semiurban base is a movement which responds in an appropriate way to that segment of Quebec's population which feels itself seriously threatened by these tendencies. These fears are justified in that, in the long run, the rural and semiurban traditions of Quebec are destined to give way to the inexorable forces of modernization. In these regions there will be marked economic decline and diminution of population as well as a transformation of the value structure of the young. Social Credit itself is destined to decline as a political force unless it changes into a fundamentally different phenomenon such as a moderate conservative party capable of attracting voters from the growing urban and industrial sectors of the population.
>
> To sum up, Social Credit has two choices; to radicalize its right-wing protest and thus separate itself from the Quebec of today; or modernize its ideology, recruit a new urban elite, and become a moderate right-of-centre party. (Stein, 1975: 361)

By the end of the decade, Quebec Social Credit had faded from the scene, having failed to implement either of these two choices.

RECENT DEVELOPMENTS

Sociology and psychology have traditionally stressed the distinctive, emergent, noninstitutionalized, nonstandard nature of collective behavior. Recently, however, at least in sociology, it has become fashionable to analyze collective behavior with the same sets of categories used to analyze conventional behavior (Marx and Wood, 1975: 368). Weller and Quarantelli (1973), for example, study collective behavior from an organizational standpoint, examining its norms and social relationships. This approach is evident in this chapter with reference to the emergent-norm theory and in the section on movement organizations.

Using emerging and enduring norms and relationships to differentiate them, Weller and Quarantelli discern four types of collective behavior: (1) Collective behavior manifesting emerging norms and emerging relationships is found in search and rescue groups, among people trying to survive a disaster, and in the formation of religious cults. (2) Emerging norms and enduring relationships are evident in individuals' acceptance of fads and fashions and—this is an example of a specific instance—in the efforts of a hospital to take care of people injured in a disaster. (3) Lynchings and coups d'etat exemplify relationships emerging around enduring norms. (4) The fourth type, which is different from the other three, involves a collectivity "acting out of character," so to speak, as in a normally passive professional teachers' association making an about-face by ordering its members to strike. Such groups dissociate themselves from certain norms and relationships that have been a part of their past culture. This approach, then, represents a swing of the pendulum away from the narrow view of collective behavior as something bizarre to one which is more balanced and which takes note of the conventional aspects.

OUTLINE AND SUMMARY

I. Introduction

Collective behavior is that form of group behavior emerging and developing in undefined and emotional situations. It is marked by a process of interaction in which impulses and moods are aroused, spread, organized, and mobilized on specific objects of action.

II. The Elementary Forms

The two main elementary forms of collective behavior are the *crowd* and the *mass.* There are subforms and advanced forms.

A. Lofland's Typology

Lofland notes that an elementary form of collective behavior such as a crowd or mass typically consists of five components: (1) a situation; (2) many people share feelings about the situation; (3) the feelings arouse a significant level of emotion; (4) the definition of the situation spawns a behavioral reaction to the immediate circumstances; (5) the definition and its high degree of emotional arousal are sustained over time.

B. Three Dimensions

Three dimensions for comparing collective behavior are (1) dominant emotion (fear, hostility, joy), (2) organizational form (crowd, mass), (3) emotional level (fear, hostility, joy in descending order of intensity).

III. Crowds

Fear is an elementary form of collective behavior. A crowd experiences fear, just as do individuals. Other elementary forms which crowds experience are *joy* and *hostility.*

A. Crowd Fears

Fear is the anticipation of pain or the actual experience of pain or severe distress. In crowds, the purest expression of fear is panic. *Panic* is a sudden, overpowering fright. Among other subforms of fear are *terror, dread,* and *horror.*

B. Crowd Hostilities

There are three levels of collective hostility: (1) symbolic (signs, speeches, rallies), (2) that which is directed toward real and personal property, (3) that which is a direct attack on individuals. There are four types of crowd hostility: (1) political, (2) leisure, (3) street, (4) captive.

C. Crowd Joys

Collective joys are the emotions evoked by well-being, success, good fortune, or the prospect of possessing what one desires. It is a state of happiness. Joyous crowds vary. Variations are evident in six kinds of crowds. The six kinds are (1) ecstatic upheavals, (2) ecstatic convention, (3) ecstatic congregation, (4) revivalist, (5) revelrous, and (6) excited.

IV. Masses
Like crowds, masses experience fear and joy, but with an intensity which is less than the intensity of crowds.

A. Mass Fears
Mass fears are classified according to whether the events causing the fears are true or false. The events are of two kinds: (1) environmental and social disasters and (2) environmental and social trends. Among true environmental disasters are earthquakes, tornadoes, hurricanes, blizzards, and floods. The Tylenol scare in Chicago in late 1982 is an example of a true social disaster. The behavior of activists against environmental pollution is an example of a true environmental and social trend. False environmental and social disasters are scientifically unverifiable; they result from popular beliefs giving rise to mass hysteria.

B. Mass Joys
Three mass joys—crazes, fashions, and fads—vary in their degree of emotional intensity, their degree of seriousness, and their scope, duration, and regularity of participant involvement.

V. Theories of Collective Behavior
Theories of collective behavior are the symbolic interactionist theory, convergence theory, emergent-norm theory, and value-added theory.

A. Symbolic Interactionist Theory
Collective behavior emerges when there is social unrest or a breakdown of some sort in the social order. There are various forms of social unrest. Three forms of interaction occur among crowds reacting to social unrest: (1) milling, (2) collective excitement, (3) contagious interaction.

B. Convergence Theory
The convergence theory proceeds from the assumption that human beings share a number of latent predispositions, which are socially controlled. These predispositions include sexual desire, aggressiveness, defensive reactions against danger, and frustration. Crowd behavior is the overt expression of these collective predispositions under conditions fostering contagious reactions to an effective stimulus.

C. Emergent-Norm Theory
Collective behavior is a response to an emergent norm; a norm emerges in the situation. Norms also emerge in nonepisodic forms of collective behavior.

D. Value-Added Theory
Collective behavior evolves through a sequence of five determinants: (1) structural conduciveness, (2) strain, (3) generalized belief, (4) mobilization, (5) social control.

VI. Social Movements
Social movements are activities supporting beliefs taken by individuals and organizations in connection with a salient and value-charged issue.

A. Types of Movements
There are four types of social movements: (1) transformative, (2) reformative, (3) redemptive, (4) alternatives.

1. Transformative Movements
A *transformative movement* seeks a total change in the social structure. An example is the millennial or chiliastic movement, which holds that for one thousand years holiness will triumph and Christ will reign on earth. The Children of God movement anticipates the second coming of Christ and calls for a total transformation of present-day society.

2. Reformative Movements
Reformative movements aim for partial change of the social structure. The women's movement and the environmental movement are examples.

3. Redemptive Movements
   The *redemptive movements* seek to bring about a total change in individuals. The Jesus Movement is an example. The goal of the Jesus Movement is to change and control the minds of individuals.
4. Alternative Movements
   The *alternative movements* seek a partial change in people. The striving for weight loss and physical fitness is an example.

B. Participation in Movements
Movements advance their causes through people. Recognizing the importance of individual support, movements put a great deal of effort into recruiting new members. Recruitment is a routine but major activity. People have a variety of motives for joining movements.

C. Social Movement Organizations
Movement organizations differ from other kinds of organizations in two important ways: (1) in their goal and (2) in their incentive structure.

1. Origin of Movements
   Movements sometimes start as crowds which develop an enduring sense of group identity and which pursue a plan of action. The movements develop through combinations of contagion, convergence, emergent norms, generalized beliefs, and mobilizations. Crowd movements have a spontaneous beginning. Other social movements have a planned beginning.
2. Routinization
   A social movement's charismatic leaders are replaced by a more bureaucratic type. Charisma must then be routinized. That is, the leadership of the movement must be transformed into a bureaucratic, or institutionalized, role.
3. Problems
   One of the problems movement organizations face is their inability to reach their goals. Successful movement organizations have a different problem. They must decide what to do once they have reached their goals.
4. Failure
   A number of reasons account for the failure of movement organizations. A movement may fail because members lose confidence in the movement's ability to reach its goal Or leaders may attempt to transform the goals, thereby bringing about the movement's end.

VII. Recent Developments
Recently, in sociology, it has become fashionable to analyze collective behavior with the same sets of categories used to analyze conventional behavior. Collective behavior is studied from an organizational standpoint. Norms and social relationships are examined.

FOR FURTHER READING AND STUDY

Clark, S. D., Grayson, J. P., and Grayson, L. M., eds. 1975. *Prophecy and protest: Social movements in twentieth-century Canada.* Toronto: Gage. A collection of articles on Canadian social movements in the areas of religion, politics, nationalism, and trade unionism.

Evans, R. R., ed. 1975. *Readings in collective behavior.* Chicago: Rand McNally. An anthology of articles on various forms of collective behavior in the United States.

Goodman, F. D., Henny, J. H., and Pressel, E., eds. 1974. *Trance, healing, and hallucination.* New York: Wiley. Three anthropological field studies of religious experience in Brazil, Yucatan, and the Caribbean. The studies exemplify joyous crowd behavior.

Liebman, R. and Wuthnow, R., eds. 1983. *The new Christian right.* Hawthorne, N.Y.: Aldine. A book of original essays on the emerging and changing forms of the new Christian right. The contributors raise questions concerning the nature of religion, the role of status groups, and the directions of American culture.

Lofland, J. and Fink, M. 1982. *Symbolic sit-ins: Protest occupations at the California capital.* Washington, D.C.: University Press of America. The authors describe fifteen episodes of protest by various groups at the California capital between 1975 and 1980. Using exploratory methodology, they develop numerous generalizations about the origins, forms, and effects of sit-ins.

Pinard, M. 1971. *The rise of a third party.* Englewood, Cliffs, N.J.: Prentice-Hall. A study of the rise of a third party, the Social Credit Party in Quebec, in the late 1950s and early 1960s. Social Credit in Quebec found support among the young and among poor but employed segments of the population.

Turner, R. H. and Killian, L. M. 1972. *Collective behavior,* 2nd ed. Englewood Cliffs, N.J.: Prentice-Hall. A widely used textbook on collective behavior, covering both elementary forms and social movements.

Wood, J. L. and Jackson, M. 1982. *Social movements.* Belmont, Calif.: Wadsworth. This text approaches the subject of social movements from various theoretical perspectives. Several articles reporting empirical work illustrate the different kinds of movements and the insights available from the perspectives.

KEY WORDS

alternative movement A social movement which seeks a partial change in people.

collective behavior The spontaneous, emotional action of an aggregate of people whose thinking and behavior are more or less unstructured and, in some instances, impulsive.

collective excitement A behavior in which people imitate the agitated and emotional behavior of those nearby.

collective joy The emotion evoked by well-being, success, or good fortune or by the prospect of possessing what one desires.

contagious interaction A behavior which entails a loss of self-consciousness, a lowered resistance to group influence, and a heightened tendency to do what others are doing in the immediate situation.

conversion An act or process which helps to bolster one's value commitment to a religion or a social movement.

craze An excessive and unreasonable enthusiasm for a special object or prize.

crowd A sizable aggregate of people in close proximity to one another for a transitory period of time.

dread A persistent and chronic apprehension of a more diffuse danger.

ecstasy A mental and bodily state that is substantially beyond the control of the individual.

fashion A prevailing, short-lived custom, usage, or style.

fear The anticipation or actual experience of pain or severe distress.

horror Experiencing an event which is frightful and upsetting.

mass A set of heterogeneous, anonymous individuals who interact little with one another and who lack a definite leadership.

milling The process by which one person's behavior stimulates a response in another person, whose response then stimulates the first person.

mobilization The recruitment of individuals and the planning of strategy.

panic A sudden, overpowering fright.

redemptive movement A social movement which seeks to bring about a total change in individuals.

reformative movement A social movement which seeks a partial change in the social structure.

routinization A process in which charismatic leadership is transformed into a bureaucratic or institutional role.

social movement A network of activities and supporting beliefs of individuals and organizations in connection with a salient and value-charged issue.

social network The web of relationships and acquaintanceships in which an individual is embedded; the set of people to whom an individual is linked by the contacts he or she has.

terror An enduring fear that arises from being trapped in a dangerous situation for a period of time.

transformative movement A social movement which seeks a total change in the social structure.

chapter 22

Population Dynamics

CHAPTER OUTLINE

INTRODUCTION

Sociologists are much concerned with the dynamics of population—its changes, growth, shrinkage, transitions, and variables. The study of population is known as *demography,* a specialty or subdiscipline of sociology. Social factors affect the way populations change and the overall dynamics of population.

The poet T. S. Eliot came remarkably close to explaining demography with his reference to "birth, and copulation, and death. That's all the facts when you come to brass tacks." Hauser and Duncan's definition (1959: 31) is more complete and informative, even if it lacks the poetic ring and appeal of Eliot's observation:

> Demography is the study of the size, territorial distribution, and composition of population, changes therein, and components of such changes, which may be identified as natality, mortality, territorial movement, and social mobility.

Certain terms in Hauser and Duncan's definition require further elucidation. "Composition of population" refers to the attributes of the unit (e.g., community, region, nation, world) under investigation. These include age, sex, marital status, race, and ethnicity. Other factors are health, mental capacity, acquired skills, education, labor force status, family status, religious affiliation, and genetic makeup. Indeed, any measurable characteristic of the human race capable of being summarized in a frequency distribution may be incorporated in an analysis of population composition.

Hauser and Duncan also identify the four main components of population change. These are *natality, mortality, migration,* and *social mobility.* The term "natality" is more likely to be called "fertility" today. Both terms denote the rate of reproduction, or the *birthrate* of a population. *Mortality* is the population's rate of deaths. Territorial movement now is usually referred to as "migration," the process of changing residences by moving from one geographic location to another within a country or between two countries. The fourth component is *social mobility,* or the movement that changes an individual's status in a society (see Chapter 18). The four components plus many related factors account for the changes in the composition of a population.

THREE MODELS

The study of population is by no means the exclusive domain of sociology. William Peterson (1975: 2–3) describes the intellectual division of labor in this multidisciplinary field. Population trends, he says, are analyzed from three separate models:

> 1. [Population change] is a self-contained process; for example, a high (or low) fertility tends to generate an age structure with a large (or small) proportion of potential parents in the following generation.
> 2. Such self-propelled population processes, however, are controlled in their rate and especially in their ultimate limit by other factors such as natural resources, economic growth, social mobility, and family norms, all of which can be taken as independent variables that together determine the population.
> 3. On the other hand, population growth acts

SOCIOLOGY OR COMMON SENSE

What do you think?

Which of the following statements do you agree with? Which statements do you disagree with? Make a note of your answers. Check your answers when you have completed your study of this chapter. Are your answers to the statements the same as those a sociologist would give?

1. The poor and the uneducated have large families, whereas the rich and the well educated have small families.
2. Those who are widowed, divorced, and single have higher death rates than those who are married.
3. The elderly migrate little. They like the familiar surroundings where they have lived for many years.
4. The world overpopulation problem is caused by the birth of too many babies.
5. People live longer today than formerly because of the elimination and control of infectious disease rather than because of its treatment.

Migration from one geographic location to another is a common experience for Canadians.

> also as an independent variable, as a cause of change in the economy or in society—for instance, as a stimulus to business activity or as an impediment to development.

Formal demography is the name given to the statistical branch of the discipline. It addresses questions raised by the first model, which are mostly about the composition of population. Included here are the "vital statistics" collected by national governments (i.e., data about births and deaths, family status, and health status). What is variously called *population analysis, population studies,* or *social demography* falls within the ambit of the second and third models. Here the social setting affecting and being affected by a population's composition and its changes is the object of study. The latter two models are most attractive for social scientists, among them sociologists, economists, geographers, and historians, while the first appeals chiefly to mathematicians and biologists.

Population is a topic which fits well in this part of the book dealing with trends. For we shall see that the three variables of fertility, mortality, and migration have a definite and complicated impact on the social dynamics of a society or community and on the society's or community's sociocultural growth and change. As you may recall, we were concerned with the fourth variable (social mobility) in Chapter 18; for the most part, this chapter deals with the first three variables within the framework of the three models.

BIRTHS AND FERTILITY

At some point in its history every country experiences high fertility (see later on demographic transition). Since some countries have passed beyond this state while others are still there, it is possible to classify all countries as having either high or low fertility. *High-fertility* nations predominate in Africa, Asia, Central America, and South America. Among the countries with *low fertility* are Japan, Israel, Canada, Australia, New Zealand, the United States, and most nations in northern, western, and central Europe.

The level of fertility is most commonly expressed as the *crude birthrate:* the number of live births per one thousand population during a particular year or some other time period. Figure 22.1 shows the wide gap between high-fertility and low-fertility countries as measured by this ratio. Although beyond the scope of this book, it should be noted that demographers have developed several age-specific measures of fertility, which are called "specified birthrates" or "fertility rates." The age-specific measures are more precise than the crude birthrate. An example of the specific birthrate appears later in this section.

Why do demographers use crude birthrates when more accurate rates can be calculated? The chief weakness of crude birthrates is that they include irrelevant segments of the population in the calculation of the rates; people who do not or cannot influence the birthrate are in-

A Glimpse into the Demographic Future

The second [problem] I would suggest is the beginning of doubts about the economics of growth. . . . In the first place, with the flow of aid reduced to a pitiful 0.3 percent of gross national product and trade barriers maintained on every side, there are no instruments of redistributive justice. And now we are faced with a new possibility. No quick bonanza awaits the ex-colonial countries. On the contrary, the assumption that we made until the day before yesterday—that the resources of the planet were virtually unlimited and could provide so much wealth at the top that in the end, the very last sharecropper could get a square meal—that assumption is beginning to be questioned. Ultimately our planet is a finite system. Ultimately its resources run out. Nobody has decided precisely what the limits may be. We know that we can put any number of figures into a computer—of population, of demand, of available resources, of pollution—and come up with the answers that match the figure put in in the first place. This leaves large areas of uncertainty. Shall we collapse by 2010 or 2050, or, by a longer reach of the imagination, the year 3000, or by further centuries still?

What is certain is that if we take an annual 2.5 percent increase in population roughly on to the tercentenary of Thomas Malthus's birth, the world's population could be increasing by a billion a year. And that is clearly impossible. I cite this as simply one of the ultimate limits. There are others—of resource use, of the biosphere's carrying capacity—which tell us unmistakably that we have to learn to achieve a more modest use of resources with a redefinition of living standards toward less consumptive joys. All these are true limits. But I am not sure that the most pressing limit of all may not prove to be the patience with which two-thirds of humanity are prepared to accept the present consequences of trickle-down economics—which is that they stay poor now while we grow richer and may be asked to stay poor forever so that the world's carrying capacity may remain equal to providing incomes of $10,000 a year for developed peoples without precipitating ecological disaster. In a limited biosphere with unlimited material ambitions built into the life style of the developed peoples, this is where we are tending, unless the poor stay very poor indeed. And frankly I doubt if they will accept a world society which is so hopelessly lopsided. Their patience will blow up in anarchy before the biosphere reaches the point of no return.

Barbara Ward. Speech for Stockholm. In *Who speaks for Earth?,* Maurce F. Strong, ed., pp. 19–31. New York: Norton, 1973.

cluded. For example, a crude birthrate is calculated on the general population, but not everyone in the population is capable of producing babies. Demographers use crude birthrates because in many instances greater precision is unnecessary. Crude birthrates give a quick but sufficiently accurate comparison of populations.

Social Factors

A variety of social factors account for high fertility. High fertility is common in agrarian, preindustrial societies, where people are said to be *pronatalist;* they hold attitudes favoring reproduction. In preindustrial societies, children

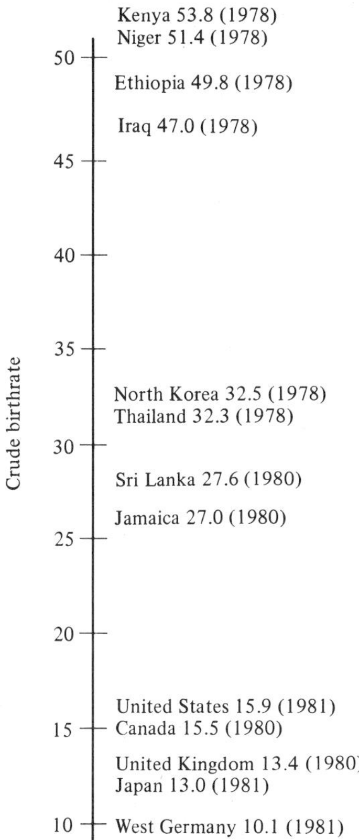

Figure 22.1 Crude Birthrates for Selected Countries. (*Source:* United Nations, *Demographic Yearbook: 1981.* New York: United Nations Publishing Service, 1981, pp. 518–539.)

are consciously wanted and often looked on as laborers who can help their families master nature (e.g., work the fields). In some societies, young adults are expected to support their aging parents, which gives the latter an incentive to propagate and raise children. Furthermore, many societies practice patrilineal descent and inheritance. Because these matters are traced through the father and the male side of the family, sons are needed to perpetuate the kin group. Finally, societies threatened by a high death rate define children as replacements, as a means of ensuring the continuation of these social systems.

Cultural A society's birthrate is influenced greatly by cultural values related to fertility and having children. Kingsley Davis (1948: 557–561) writes that all societies develop norms regulating the intimate association of males and females (e.g., celibacy, seclusion of women, status restrictions). These norms bear especially on copulation. They express such values as virginity, refraining from adultery, and marrying at the proper age. In Canada, children are valued for many reasons (Hoffman and Hoffman, 1973). They confirm their parents' adult status ("old enough to have kids"). Children are viewed as enjoyable and stimulating. Boys and girls are also individuals, perhaps the only individuals whom their parents can dominate. They may figure prominently in the family's drive for prestige, too (e.g., child as outstanding athlete, musician, equestrian, student).

Cultural factors correlate with low fertility. For example, low fertility is characteristic of industrial societies. After examining nineteenth and twentieth century industrial societies, Benedict (1972) concluded that personal wealth and prestige are two important conditions underlying low fertility. But subsequent research casts doubt on this proposition. Only five years later Matras (1977: 183–184) had this to say about the effects of prestige and wealth on fertility rates in North America, Europe, and Oceania:

> More recently, however, considerable evidence has pointed to a growing convergence of fertility rates, or at least to substantially diminishing differentials, among the different socioeconomic categories (especially when certain other characteristics, like religion, rural-urban migration status, and socioeconomic background, have been held constant). At the same time, in the upper socioeconomic groups, there has been growing evidence of a direct relationship between fertility and income, educational level, and occupational status.

The growing convergence of birthrates is explained, in part, by the tendency for women of all levels of socioeconomic status (SES) to marry later than previously and, while married, to have children later. In the past, women of higher SES were inclined to marry and have children later than women of lower SES.

Urban and Rural There are also differences in urban and rural birthrates. In some of the high-fertility nations of Asia, Africa, and South America, birthrates are higher in the countryside than in the cities (United Nations, 1980: 253–261, Table 9). Numerous factors bear on this pattern. There is less room for a large family in the congestion of the city. Children are more expensive to rear in cities since, for example, food must be purchased indirectly rather than harvested directly from the land. In cities, there are more work and leisure alternatives for women, which may tempt them to forego having as many children as they might otherwise. Scant labor advantages accrue from having children in an urban setting, inasmuch as many city people are employed by others rather than being self-employed or forced to eke out a living as subsistence farmers.

Religion Religion is another factor in the variation of fertility. Throughout much of the Western world, Jews and those with no religious affiliation have the smallest families, Protestants the next smallest, and Roman Catholics the largest. Crosscutting this pattern of affiliation is that of commitment to a religion (level of religiosity). The higher the commitment, the higher is the rate of fertility. For instance, Catholics who are weakly committed to the Church would likely have smaller families (similar in size perhaps to those of highly committed Protestants) than highly committed Catholics.

Whatever the reason, Catholic birthrates have been dropping in Western countries as younger church members increasingly ignore official rules on contraception (Overbeek, 1980: 79; Westoff and Bumpass, 1973). There is evidence that Catholic women are slower to adopt birth control methods than non-Catholic women. With respect to contraceptive pills, their rates of use in the United States and Canada are now similar (Allingham et al., 1969).

Race Last, but not least, are the differences in fertility rates among the races. These differences are substantial in North America. In 1980 a crude birthrate of 14.9 for whites and 22.5 for blacks and other races was reported for the United States (U.S. Bureau of the Census, 1984: 64). In Canada this ratio is reported as a specific birthrate: the number of live births per thousand ever married women aged 15 to 44.[1] In 1981 in Canada women of British background (as representative of whites) had a specific birthrate of 1793, whereas Indian and Inuit women had a specific birthrate of 2995 (Statistics Canada, 1981c: p. 10-1, Table 10). Race, however, is generally considered a correlate of fertility differences rather than a cause of them. For instance, the fact that a greater proportion of blacks, Indians, and Inuit than of whites live in rural areas helps account for these differences.

The social factors considered here have a complicated interactive effect on fertility, which is only beginning to be understood. The facts set forth here allow the following hypothesis, which illustrates what social demographers are up against when they try to develop theory in this area: Some North American blacks are Jewish and live in large cities. We should therefore hypothesize that they would have birthrates lower than the average for their race (as calculated in the United States).

Physical Factors

There are also many physical factors affecting birthrates. One of these is *fecundity,* defined as the physiological capacity to reproduce. For women this capacity is usually expressed as being present between ages 15 and 44 or 15 and 49. People incapable of reproducing are said to be *sterile.* Sterility may be an inherited deficiency, a correlate of age (too old, too young), a consequence of ill-health (malnutrition, vene-

[1]This is an example of the specific birthrate or fertility rate mentioned earlier. It compares the number of infants born with those capable of bearing them, rather than with the overall population.

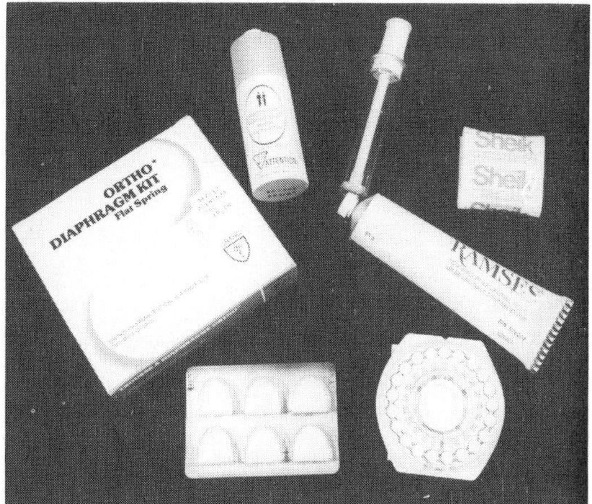

Widespread birth control can affect the population of a country.

real disease), or a result of some other condition. *Birth control* (contraception) is the intention to reduce the possibility of conception during copulation. Its effect on the society's fertility level obviously depends on the effectiveness of the method chosen. The methods range from condoms, coitus interruptus, and the rhythm method to intrauterine devices (IUDs), sterilization, and birth control pills.[2] When birth control fails, an increasing number of North American women are resorting to *abortions* as a means of avoiding unwanted children.

Of course, stong social influences bear on the last two physical factors. Apart from the issue of differential effectiveness, the choice of a particular contraceptive is affected by availability, personal preference, religious doctrine, and ease of use. The same holds for abortion. An abortion may be out of reach financially, distasteful to some women, forbidden by their religious values, or impossible to acquire locally.

MORTALITY

A marked decline in world death rates, or mortality, has been evident since 1915 (Population Reference Bureau, 1976: 19). As we shall see later, this happy fact, when coupled with the continuing high birthrates in many parts of the globe, has had the sobering consequence of triggering the present-day overpopulation crisis. Mortality is frequently discussed in terms of the *crude mortality rate,* or *crude death rate:* the number of deaths per thousand people in a population during a given year or other time period. As with fertility, demographers also calculate "specific death rates" which are more precise than the crude rates. Figure 22.2 shows the

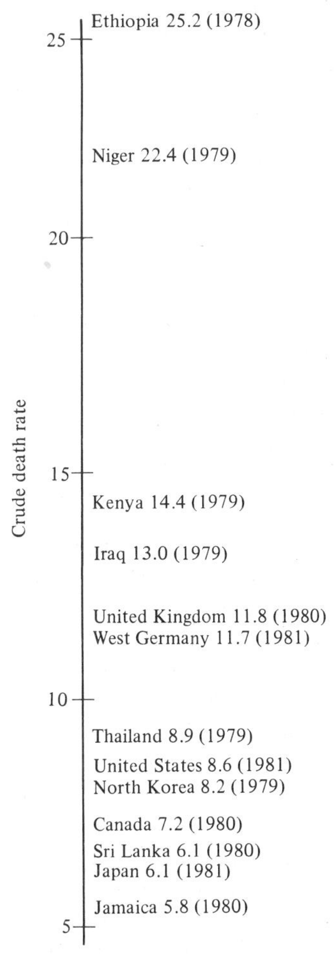

Figure 22.2 Crude Death Rates for Selected Countries. (*Source:* United Nations, *Demographic Yearbook: 1981.* New York: United Nations Publishing Service, 1981, pp. 322–326.)

[2]Coitus interruptus is ejaculation of the sperm outside the vagina.

crude death rates of the countries listed in Fig. 22.1. The intention here is to demonstrate the discrepancies between high fertility and low mortality now existing in many African, Asian, and Middle and South American societies.

Various conditions have made possible the decrease in world mortality. Within the past hundred years or so advances in preventive medicine have made possible the control of communicable or infectious diseases, which are often fatal (e.g., diphtheria, smallpox). Elimination and control of infectious disease have contributed more to the reduction of mortality than the treatment of such disease. Today, the major causes of death by disease in advanced societies are from noncommunicable or degenerative ailments; among these afflictions are cancer, stroke, and heart disease. Thus, for more than a century, people less than five years of age and more than forty years of age have enjoyed the greatest reduction in mortality, because they are the most susceptible to infectious disease. *Morbidity* is the demographer's term for the incidence of disease (fatal or otherwise) in a population.

Many of the other factors contributing to the decline of death rates throughout the world have been operating for two centuries or more. Among them are improved sanitation and diet. Both prevent disease. More remote is the set of factors leading to higher standards of living (e.g., improved working conditions, minimum wage laws, available health services) and to political stability and harmony. Increases in the level of general education of a population are associated with the reduction of its mortality. Education instills an understanding of sanitation, nutrition, political systems, health care, and the like.

Life Expectancy

Declining mortality in a population tends to raise the life expectancy of individuals in the population. *Life expectancy* is the number of years the typical person born in a particular year can expect to live. This number of years is a statistical average. Life expectancy differs from the concept of life span. *Life span* is the biological age limit of human beings; it is estimated under ideal conditions, with death occurring from degenerative disease rather than accident or infectious disease. The present human life span is thought to be about 120 years.

In his summary of the literature on the historical growth of life expectancy at birth, Preston (1977: 163–165) reports that it is estimated to have been approximately eighteen to twenty-five years in prehistoric times. It rose to between twenty and thirty years in the Roman era. By 1780, European aristocracy had a life expectancy of thirty-seven years; the British aristocracy, by 1780, could anticipate a life expectancy of forty-six years. Gradual improvement continued until the late nineteenth century, when the wonders of dietetics, sanitation, and preventive medicine began to be felt. The gains from roughly 1880 to the present have been greater than the combined gains made prior to 1880. Until recently, infant mortality rates had a significant influence on life expectancy. Life expectancy rose considerably among those who survived the first year of life. Between 1977 and 1979, the life expectancy at birth for North American females was approximately seventy-seven and one-half years. For males, the life expectancy between 1977 and 1979 was seventy years (see Table 22.1).

Despite these overall gains in life expectancy, it still varies according to the level of development of a society (see Table 22.1). In every country female life expectancy outstrips that of males, a gap that is wider today than ever. Preston (1977: 166–167) discusses two factors responsible for this difference. First, while males and females are equally vulnerable to infectious disease, males die more quickly from degenerative afflictions, particularly those affecting the cardiovascular system (heart disease, for example). Retherford (1975: Chapter 2), after examining a range of studies on various animal species, concluded that, on the average, all female animals outlive the males. Perhaps males have

Table 22.1 LIFE EXPECTANCY AT BIRTH OF MALES AND FEMALES IN SELECTED LESS AND MORE DEVELOPED COUNTRIES

* Canada + US similar

Countries	Males	Females
Less developed		
Iraq (1975–1980)	53.60	56.70
Kenya (1975–1980)	53.90	57.50
Niger (1975–1980)	40.60	43.80
More developed		
Canada (1975–1977)	70.19	77.48
Japan (1980)	73.32	78.83
United States (1979)	69.90	77.80

Source: United Nations. *Demographic Yearbook: 1981,* pp. 414–441. New York: United Nations Publishing Service, 1981.

a congenitally lower resistance to degenerative disease than females.

Second, the male life-style in more developed nations accelerates the rate at which men contract degenerative disease. Preston lists six health-related practices contributing to the widening gap between male and female life expectancy. The six factors are cigarette smoking, lack of exercise, high amounts of animal fat in the diet, obesity, excessive alcohol consumption, and hard-driving, time-oriented personalities.

Social Factors

Mortality and life expectancy are affected by many of the same factors that affect fertility. These factors include race and urban and rural life-style. The cultural factors of marriage, prestige, and SES also affect mortality rates. Age, however, plays a more important role in explaining mortality than in explaining fertility.

Racial Differences In the United States in 1978 life expectancy at birth for white males and white females was approximately four years longer than for black males and black females (U.S. Bureau of the Census, 1984: 73).[3] The life expectancy of white males and females was also higher than that of other minority groups. Overbeek (1980: 51), noting the lack of equivalent data for Canada, believes nevertheless that a similar pattern holds there between whites and other races, including Indians and Inuit. Demographers trace these differences not to inherited deficiencies but to nutrition, education, and medical care. Whites eat more nutritious food than blacks; in general, they eat balanced diets. Whites also have educational opportunities unavailable to blacks and have better medical care than blacks and other minorities.

Rural-Urban Differences There is no easy way to summarize the rural-urban differences in mortality. There are more deaths per capita in cities than in rural areas. Cities are congested and filth-ridden; environmental pollution now adds to the filth. Urban centers provide better medical care for a larger number of people than do rural areas. Yet the sundry occupational, ethnic, racial, and age groups in the city have unequal access to medical facilities. The inequality suggests that a single demographic ratio describing urban mortality masks a great deal of significant variation.

Cultural Differences The relationship between SES and mortality is by no means clearcut. For example, the rich have less dangerous occupations and can afford better health care and nutrition than the poor. But the rich also have more stressful jobs, get less exercise while at work, and possibly drink more (the rich have the money with which to buy liquor). Antonovsky (1967) concluded, after reviewing the research in this area, that there are now few class differences in mortality in the United States, if there ever were any of significance. Overbeek (1980: 50) reached a similar conclusion for Canada, Sweden, and the Netherlands.

[3]Curiously, the crude mortality rate for blacks and other races in the Unied States in 1980 was slightly *lower* (8.8) than for whites (8.9) (U.S. Bureau of the Census, 1984: 75). This seeming anomaly is partly explained by the fact that the median age of blacks about that time was roughly 6 years lower than that of whites (U.S. Bureau of the Census, 1984: 32).

Marital Status What about marital status and mortality? As far as North America is concerned, being married is an advantage in this respect (Statistics Canada, 1980c: xvi, Chart 4; Gove, 1973). Those who are widowed, divorced, and single have higher death rates than those who are married. Marriage tends to routinize one's life, enforcing regular eating and sleeping habits. When one is sick or disabled, one's spouse is usually a source of nurturance and care. Gove (1973: 65) found that differences between married and unmarried Americans "are particularly marked among those types of mortality where one's psychological state would appear to affect one's life chances."

Age Last, age is a factor in mortality, even beyond the obvious fact that the elderly have high death rates. Indeed, one of humankind's most fatal years is the first year of life. In North America, it is not until men reach their late fifties and women their early to middle sixties that their rates of mortality surpass the *infant mortality rate,* or the number of deaths per unit of population below age one. Even then a major portion of the historical decline in world mortality has been accounted for by the increasingly effective prevention of infant deaths.

NATURAL INCREASE

One measure of a population's growth or shrinkage is its rate of natural increase. The *natural increase* is determined by subtracting the death rate from the birthrate. Recent natural increases for the thirteen representative countries listed in Figs. 22.1 and 22.2 are presented in Table 22.2.[4]

From 1970 to 1976, the rate of natural increase in North America dropped significantly. The rate in 1970 in the United States was 8.8 per 1000 population. It dropped to 7.4 per 1000 population in 1984 (U.S. Bureau of the Census, 1984: 9). Meanwhile, in Canada the rate of natural increase was 10.0 per 1000 population in 1970. By 1984 it had dropped to 7.9 per 1000 population (Statistics Canada, 1985a).

The rate of natural increase affords a vivid demonstration of the overpopulation problem facing Third World countries today. That problem is brought on by dramatic reductions in infant mortality without equivalent reductions in fertility. The mortality rates of these countries would be higher were not the majority of their populations in the low-mortality age categories. Their rates contrast with those of the more developed countries, whose populations are older. High birthrates produce a population age structure sharply skewed toward youth. The size of a population is also affected by another important process, namely migration. This is the third demographic variable.

MIGRATION

There are two types of migration: *international migration* and *internal migration.* International migration consists of *emigration* (departure from a country) and *immigration* (arrival in a country). With immigration, the population of a country increases. The population decreases when individuals leave a country, or emigrate.

Demographers studying population increase and decrease are interested in *net international migration,* or the difference between the number of immigrants and emigrants in a given time period. The estimated annual net international migration rates for 1970 through 1974 were 4.4 and 1.7 per 1000 population for Canada and the United States, respectively (United Nations, 1979). Many Communist bloc countries lost population during this period, while Australia and New Zealand had higher rates of gain than Canada.

Migration is change of residence, a special

[4]Some of the component birth and death rates in the rates of natural increase in Table 22.2 are based (unavoidably) on different years (never more than two years apart). This poses no problem when done, as it is here, for instructional purposes. Researchers would want their natural increase rates to be based on a country's fertility and mortality of the same year.

Table 22.2 NATURAL INCREASE FOR SELECTED COUNTRIES PER 1000 POPULATION

Less developed countries	Natural increase	More developed countries	Natural increase
Kenya	39.4	Canada	8.3
Iraq	34.2	United States	7.3
Niger	29.0	Japan	6.9
Ethiopia	24.6	United Kingdom	1.6
North Korea	24.3	West Germany	–1.6
Thailand	23.4		
Sri Lanka	21.5		
Jamaica	21.2		

Source: Figures 22.1 and 22.2.

kind of geographic mobility to a new habitation where the migrant will stay for a substantial length of time. Since large numbers of people typically migrate from one place (country, city, region) to another, demographers refer to *streams of migration* and to *counterstreams* of migrants returning from the new area. Lee (1966) hypothesizes that every stream spawns a counterstream. There are several reasons for this: (1) Communication between the old and new areas improves (as between friends and relatives). (2) For some migrants the appeal of the new area wears off. (3) Other migrants never intended to remain there permanently.

Selective Migration

The migration that takes place when part of a population decides to migrate is called *selective migration,* because only certain people in the population make this decision. Selective migration is related to a variety of social characteristics of the migrants and to crucial arrangements and events beyond their control. Among the social characteristics are age, sex, family status, and occupation.

Age Both types of migration (international and internal) are composed primarily of late adolescents and young adults. These people are commonly at the beginning, that is, at the "initial" or "trial" stages, of their occupational careers (see Chapter 12). By moving, they can take advantage of opportunities. But older people are also on the move. In 1980, 4.5 percent of all movers in the United States were 65 years or older (U.S. Bureau of the Census, 1984: 17). Likewise, in Canada in 1983 and 1984 those who were 60 and over and who migrated between provinces constituted 4.9 percent of all interprovincial movers (Statistics Canada, 1985b: 78).

Sex Bogue (1969: 167) states, with reference to the sex of migrants, that men tend to migrate long distances and across national borders, while women tend to migrate short distances within their homelands. This pattern is partly shaped by conditions at the end of the move (e.g., insecurity, hardship). For instance, rough-and-tumble frontier areas (e.g., parts of Alaska, the Northwest Territories) are populated largely by men. Both Canada and the United States may be exceptions to this generalization, however. At least their *sex ratio* of immigrants, defined as the number of men per hundred women, is currently about even, that is, near one hundred (Tomlinson, 1976: 297; Kalbach and McVey, 1979: 180). Still, rural-to-urban migration in North America is consistent with the generalization, since more females than males move from the country to the city.

Former patterns of migration consisted mostly of single males (e.g., as pioneers) and single females (e.g., as domestic servants). This is much less true today; entire families now move within and across international borders. A quest for new occupational opportunities, relief from political tension, and better standards of living are among the motives for family relocation. Within this trend married couples without children are more likely to move than families with children. Families with preschool children tend to move more frequently than families with children in the elementary grades or in high school (Ritchey, 1976: 380).

Occupation There is also a complicated occupational dimension to migration. Understandably, the unemployed are more migratory than the employed. Generally speaking, professional and semiprofessional workers are internal migrants, while laborers and service workers are external migrants. But there are many exceptions to this rule. For instance, professionals sometimes migrate from one country to another for specific job-related reasons, thus contributing to the international problem of the *brain drain:* emigration of large numbers of highly trained workers.

Peterson (1978: 540) summarizes several studies of why British chemists and physicists migrated to the United States. One of their reasons was the dearth of critical research equipment at home. Both Canada and the United States have recruited large numbers of physicians from the United Kingdom. The British doctors were interested in working on a fee-for-service basis; their own state medical programs denied them this option (Overbeek, 1980: 116). The vacant medical posts in Britain were filled by Pakistani and East Indian physicians. The drain to the United States from Canada (including some of the British physicians) has begun to rise again (see Chapter 20). It has always been offset, however, by a *brain gain* from other countries (Parai, 1965).

Peterson's Types

Some selective migration is shaped by forces coercing migrants to relocate. Peterson (1975: 321–326) distinguishes six types of migration. Only in the *free* type is the migrant's decision the main factor in his or her emigration. *Primitive* migration occurs when the environment can no longer sustain a human community. Drought, soil depletion, changes in animal migration patterns, and similar conditions leave people who are dependent on these aspects of nature with little choice but to try to find a more hospitable place to live.

People who have, objectively speaking, a choice to remain in their country, but leave because of foreboding political changes, embark on *impelled* migration. They differ from *forced* migrants, who are officially expelled from a country, as were hundreds of thousands of Ghanaians from Nigeria in 1983 amid charges of being illegal aliens. Forced migrants may also be driven from their homeland by conditions too appalling to endure. The historical exodus of Jews from different societies exemplifies this situation.

Group migration, which is a variant of free migration, refers to the movement of collectivities larger than a family, for instance, a clan, tribe, or community. The westward trek of the Mormons in North America is a case in point. When migration to a distant point develops into a social movement, it is called *mass* migration. This type is illustrated by the influx of Swedes to the United States between 1861 and 1870. Ninety-three hundred people left Sweden annually during that period.

The mass migration of Chinese to Canada occurred in the late nineteenth century.

Migration in North America

Internal migration in the United States and Canada is considerable. Between 1975 and 1980, more than 45 percent of Americans age five and older moved from one housing unit to another (U.S. Bureau of the Census, 1981: 15, Table 18). The percentage for Canada between 1976 and 1981 was close to 48 percent (Statistics Canada, 1983: 4). Canada and the United States are alike in their configurations of internal migration to the extent that (1) there has been, historically, a generally westward movement of population, (2) there has been a substantial movement from the countryside to the city, and (3) there have been patterns of movement within metropolitan areas. As we shall see shortly, factor 2 works to blur factor 1 in Canada.

A popular method of revealing the degree of westward expansion in the United States is to trace the historical movement of the country's "center of population." In 1790, the center of population was located twenty-three miles east of Baltimore. By 1980, it had moved to one mile west of the Desota city hall in Jefferson County, Missouri. In Canada, westward expansion is illustrated by comparisons such as the following: In 1901, 88 percent of Canadians lived in the Maritime Provinces, Quebec and Ontario. By 1981, only 71.1 percent lived in these regions. Some of the population growth in the Canadian west, however, resulted from government policy, which channeled immigrants to remote areas of the country to reduce labor shortages and to settle the land (see Chapter 20).

The westward movement of population in North America.

Strict attention to westward expansion of population on this continent would lead us to overlook the migration streams flowing in other directions and to overlook the patterns of geographic distribution. The idea of a center of population, which is a weighted distribution of all people in the United States, hints only at the historical tendency in the United States for people to concentrate in its northeast quarter. Changes in values are now modifying this tendency to concentrate in the Northeast; there is now an extensive movement to California from the Northeast, upper Midwest, Southeast, and Southwest (Tomlinson, 1976: 313). There is also a flow of people from the Northeast to the Southeast (Morrison and Wheeler, 1976). While these streams are manifestations of an interest in the warmth and climate of the "Sun Belt," it is noteworthy that other values (e.g., high-paying jobs) made Alaska the second fastest growing state during the years 1980 to 1982.

The geographic distribution of Canadians is decidedly different from that of Americans. Richmond (1976: 129) describes the Canadian pattern:

> Canada is the largest country in the Western Hemisphere and the second largest in the world. The population, however, is concentrated in a comparatively small area. There is no permanent settlement in approximately 89 percent of the country, much of which consists of mountains, rocks, lakes, wilderness, and arctic tundra. More than half the population of Canada lives in the area between the American border and a line from Quebec City to Sault Ste. Marie. The most densely settled areas make up only 2.2 percent of the total area of Canada.

Indeed, most of Canada's population has settled within two hundred miles or so of the U.S. border.

The westerly flow of migrants is less clear-cut in Canada than in the United States. Historically, the Atlantic area has lost population to Ontario (with Quebec being largely bypassed). Ontario and Quebec have lost population to each other. Migrants from Manitoba have tended to go east to Ontario. From the early 1970s through the early 1980s Alberta and British Columbia gained population from the rest of the country, particularly Ontario and Quebec (Kubat and Thornton, 1974: 64; Statistics Canada, 1982b: 10). However, the economic recession in the West in the 1980s stopped and actually reversed this stream.

As the pace of urbanization quickened in North America through the late nineteenth and early twentieth centuries, much of this directional migration could increasingly be interpreted as rural to urban. As time went on, more and more of the migrants who were heading west journeyed to cities with job opportunities and with good schools, adequate health care, and attractive leisure activities. Even immigration between Canada and the United States in the past one hundred years or so can be partly understood in these terms. Since rural to urban, urban to rural, and metropolitan migration were covered in Chapter 8, no further consideration of these subjects is undertaken here.

AGE AND SEX IN THE POPULATION

The age and sex composition of a population is often portrayed with a *population pyramid,* which is a graphic representation approximating the form of a two-dimensional triangle. Figures 22.3 and 22.4 compare early and recent population pyramids for the United States and Canada. The bulges at the lower ends of the 1974 and 1976 pyramids are projected to work their way toward the middle of these figures (25 to 50 years of age) as the two populations grow older over the next three to five decades. The aging of the North American population is the result of the low birth rate and increasing life expectancy.

The data in Figs. 22.3 and 22.4 serve as a springboard for a brief discussion of model 1 presented earlier in this chapter. That model treats population composition as an independent variable. For example, sex structures vary from one population to the next. Although the sex ratio at birth the world over averages between 104 and 107 males to 100 females (Visaria, 1967), the sex ratio for the entire population drops to 98.3 males to 100 females in Canada (1981) and to 94.5 males to 100 females in the United States (1982). These ratios are typical for industrial nations. The sex structure of a society, if substantially skewed toward males or females, has a bearing on the number of families that can be formed; it figures in the sex-related medical services offered, goods sold in stores, leisure services, and special events.

Age is also an important independent variable. A society with a young population has a greater interest in schools and elementary education than a society with an old population. An older population is more concerned with recreation for the middle-aged, health care for the elderly, and the problems of loneliness and financial need which the elderly face. A population with a preponderance of middle-aged people would center its interests on occupational careers and work-related interests.

WORLD POPULATION IN THE FUTURE

It must be stressed that the gathering and reading of information on births, deaths, and migration are to be undertaken with caution. Definitions of these variables (including even death) are by no means uniform. Furthermore, accuracy and consistency in noting their occurrence vary widely. Peterson (1975: 45–49) distinguishes four types of errors in demographic data. Errors of *coverage* occur when a person or population characteristic is missed or counted twice. Another error emerges during *classification.* For example, respondents sometimes lie to a census-taker about their ages. Or the latter might mark the wrong box on the survey form

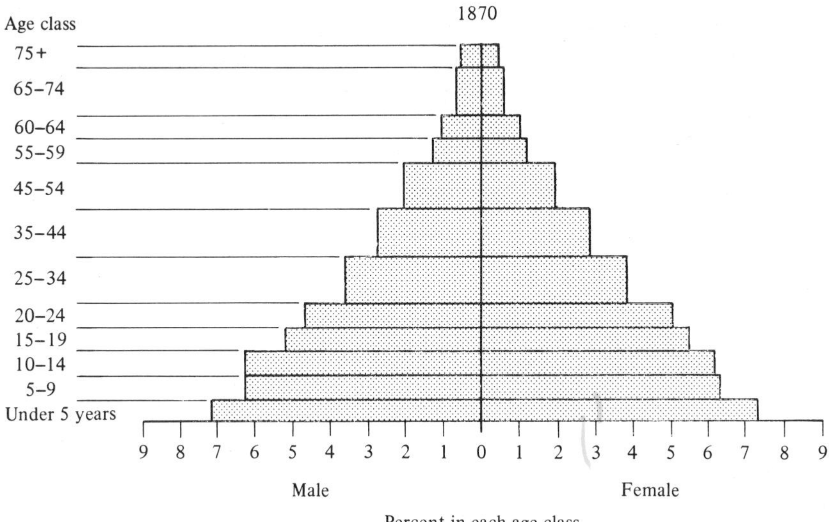

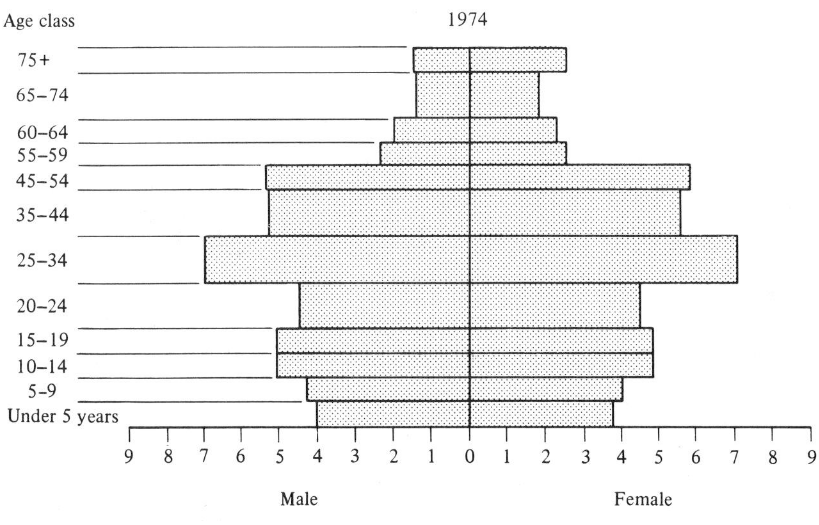

Figure 22.3 Population Pyramids for the United States, 1870–1974. (*Source:* J. Matras. *Introduction to Population.* Englewood Cliffs, NJ: Prentice-Hall, 1977, pp. 60–61.)

after hearing the response. This is an error in *recording. Processing* errors happen when, for instance, some of the completed census forms are lost or certain items of information are inconsistently classified by an analyst.

Notwithstanding the errors in demographic data, it is clear that there is a momentous consequence of the interplay of fertility and mortality. That consequence is the ominous increase in world population of today. As will soon become apparent, not every country is being rocked by a population explosion, but the international

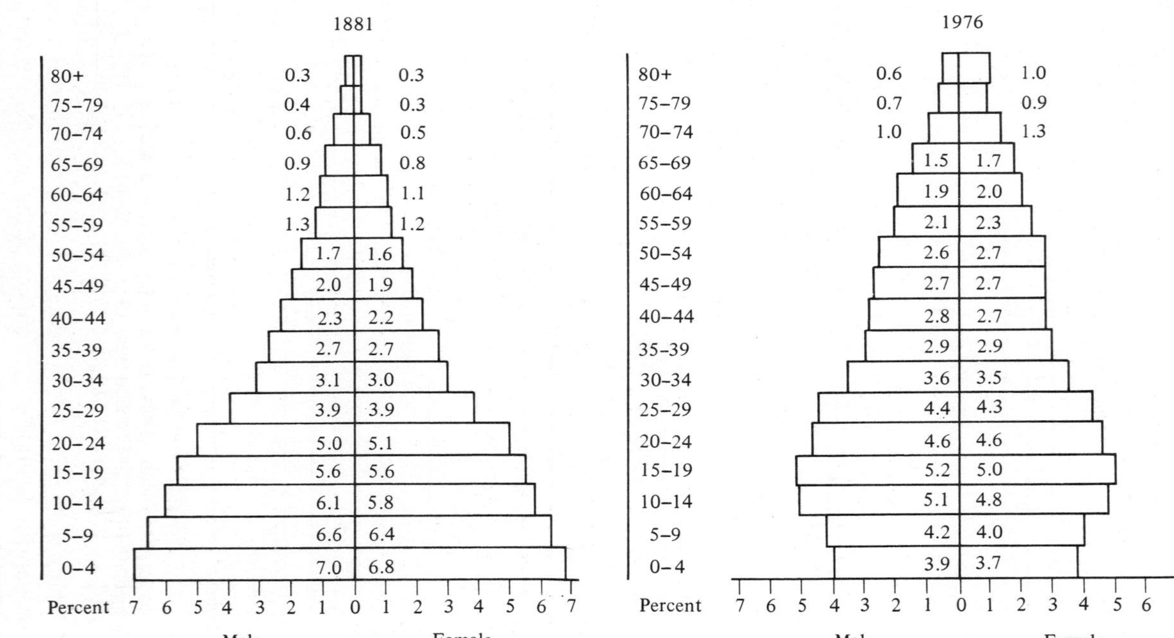

Figure 22.4 Population Pyramids for Canada, 1871 and 1976. (*Source:* Dominion Bureau of Statistics, *Census of Canada,* Vol 2., Ottawa, 1921, Table 4; Statistics Canada, *Five Year Age Groups,* Cat. 92-823. Ottawa, 1976, Table 11.)

fallout from those that are cannot be ignored. World overpopulation is hardly a new issue.

Malthus's Theory

Thomas Robert Malthus (1766–1834), a clergyman and professor of history and political economy in England, sounded the alarm in his famous work, "An essay on the principle of population as it affects the future improvement of society," published in 1798.[5] The central point in Malthus's (1798: 13–14) essay was that

> population, when unchecked increases in a geometrical ratio. Subsistence increases only in an arithmetical ratio. A slight acquaintance with numbers will show the immensity of the first power in comparison of the second.

Malthus was writing about world population rather than national populations and therefore could ignore the process of internal migration. He was concerned strictly with natural increase, which was said to occur geometrically, or as 1, 2, 4, 8, 16, 32, 64, 128, 256, while subsistence was said to increase arithmeticaly, or as 1, 2, 3, 4, 5, 6, 7, 8, 9. Malthus predicted that in two centuries the ratio of population to means of subsistence would be 256 to 9 and, in three centuries, 4096 to 13. The agricultural technology of the day would be unable to keep pace with the demand for food.

Population Checks The only way to head off this insidious disaster, Malthus believed, was to abstain from having children. This was a "preventive check." It would operate effectively only on the best elements of the society, however, while the worst elements would propagate freely. This would have the inevitable consequence of corrupting the society's sex morals and ultimately of weakening its family bonds and expressions of parental affection. Why? Because only the best elements, who are small in number, would practice "moral restraint," that is, would abstain from having children. Vice was another preventive check, freighted with the same consequences. There were, in addition, "positive checks." Malthus branded hindrances and troubles such as dangerous occupations, extreme poverty, and strenuous, hazardous labor as positive checks; disease, war, famine, and seasonal events (a killing frost, for example), in Malthus's view, are also positive checks (a *positive check* is an event or condition which causes deaths and reduces the population). By causing death, the positive checks would help keep down the size of a population.

Malthus was convinced that nothing could be gained by implementing social reforms as long as population growth went uncontrolled. Still, a growth in population would lead to intense competition for jobs, which would be needed for survival. The competition for jobs, it was believed, would depress wages to the point where workers would earn barely enough money to live and reproduce themselves. It is no wonder that Thomas Carlyle, writing some fifty years later, referred to economics as "the dismal science," a sobriquet that has stuck with economics to this day.

Reactions to Malthus's Theory

Malthus's theory stirred considerable debate in the Western world, both during his lifetime and for a while afterward. That debate centered partly on its major weaknesses. There are three obvious weaknesses: First, Malthus underestimated the improvements in store for agriculture such as new fertilizers, improved cultivation, and gains in the breeding of plants and animals. Second, he never foresaw the rise in the standard of living. Third, he overlooked the possibility that contraceptives would become more effective and more widely used and accepted.

As the shortsightedness of Malthus's theory became apparent, scientists turned to other statements more in step with the times. It was

[5] Malthus published six revisions of his original statement. This discussion draws, in part, on these as well.

not until the end of World War I that Malthus's geometric ratio was rediscovered and its implications pondered again (Spengler, 1978: 46). Despite a temporary drop in birthrates in North America and Europe during the 1930s, Malthus has remained more or less in the academic limelight since. No one really believes that his predictions have come true, but present conditions suggest that they might unless something is done to ameliorate those conditions. Mönckeberg (1979: 125) states the problem:

> One hundred and eighty years have passed since then. What has happened during this time? Has what Malthus predicted come true? At least until today, we must recognize that it has not. On the one hand, the population's growth has exceeded the most pessimistic expectations. From the 800 million inhabitants the world had at that time, population has increased to four billion. On the other hand, however, food production during this period has exceeded the growth of the population. Thus, for example, the rate of the production of cereal, which represents 70 percent of the calories consumed by the world, has remained above the growth of the population, allowing an annual improvement of per capita consumption of about one percent. This has also meant an improvement in nutrition. It could be said that the best levels of nutrition in the whole history of humanity have been reached.
>
> Malthus's prophecy has not yet come to pass, but the food crisis of 1972 once again raised the problem. It is true that on the average, the nutritional situation has improved, but never before have there been so many undernourished people in the world. Approximately 500 million individuals are undernourished and two billion are underfed. The situation is uneven and seems to have deteriorated during recent decades. Rich countries have increased their cereal production at a rate of 3 percent per year, and their population by 1 percent per year. This has left a surplus 2 percent per year available in cereal supplies. In poor countries, the population growth rate has reached 2.5 percent per year, and cereal production has increased by 3 percent per year, leaving only one-half of 1 percent cereal surplus available. As a consequence, the populations of rich countries have improved the quality and quantity of their diets, because their surplus in cereal production has been used to feed animals and thus increase the availability of animal protein. On the other hand, in the poor countries, the increase in cereal production has been used directly for human consumption.

In Paul Ehrlich's (1971) words, this situation has created "the population bomb." That is, there is serious overpopulation. On the most general level, Ehrlich says that overpopulation occurs when there are too many people in relation to the necessities and amenities of life. Overpopulation becomes a problem for us when it threatens our values (e.g., when deprived people overthrow their government, which was supplying cheap raw materials to our manufacturers). The population bomb has been produced because the demographic transition is still incomplete in many parts of the world.

The Demographic Transition

The theory of the demographic transition was developed over a sixteen-year span by Warren Thompson (1929) and Frank Notestein (1945). The transition takes place in three stages: (1) It starts in preindustrial societies, which have high fertility and mortality rates and hence low rates of natural increase. (2) As these countries industrialize—move from a preindustrial to an industrial economic base—they effect a reduction in their mortality rates (see earlier in this chapter). Nonetheless, birthrates remain high, forcing up the rate of natural increase. (3) Once industrialization is achieved, the fertility rate drops (as a result of factors discussed earlier) and so does the rate of natural increase.

These three stages have distinctive economic characteristics. In the first the economy is one of low productivity, little sophisticated use of energy resources, and primitive standards of living (see Chapter 9). In the intermediate stage, the society is mechanizing, agricultural output is increasing, and people are anticipating a boost in their standard of living. Still, the supplies of food and consumer goods lag far behind the demands for them made by rapidly multiplying numbers of people. The society is simply not productive and efficient enough to meet the demands. In the third stage, the economy becomes productive and efficient, thereby engendering a high standard of living such as we have in North America.

Stolnitz (1964: 20) comments that while transition theory has its faults, "demographic transitions rank among the most sweeping and best-documented trends of modern times . . . based upon hundreds of investigations, covering a host of specific places, periods, and events." One of the theory's faults is its lack of power to predict the levels of fertility and mortality of societies about to enter the transition stage and to predict the point at which fertility declines as a sign that they are moving to the third stage.

The Nature of the Problem

The Population Reference Bureau in Washington, D.C., made a study of the world's overpopulation problem as it existed during the decade 1965 to 1975. The scope of the problem is alarming: "World population is now the largest in history and is rising at a pace that if not reduced could double human numbers in the next four decades" (Population Reference Bureau, 1976: 1). Figure 22.5 explains this predicament. (In 1983, there were an estimated 4,722,000,000 people on earth.) In the decade under study birthrates did drop significantly, and at a rate greater than the decline of death rates. This means that the percentage increase is slowing down, a significant advance for those hoping to control population growth. Indeed, some experts say it is possible that the world's crude birthrate may drop from thirty in 1974 to twenty in 1984.

A lower percentage increase (in the birthrate) means, however, that there is still a numerical increase of some magnitude. In this case that increase is fueled by a *population momentum:* In developing countries, young people are marrying and having babies at a higher rate than their fellow citizens are dying. Momentum is expected to continue until the proportions of younger and older people become equal. This will result in a more or less rectangular population pyramid.

Although the world birthrate declined by an average of 4 infants per 1000 population between 1965 and 1975, this decline was unevenly distributed. The already low rates of the industrialized nations (including the United States and Canada) generally declined even further. There were also substantial declines in Asia and the Near East. But in Central and South America the rate fell by only 1 per 1000 people. A similar decline was recorded for most of Africa. In the majority of Caribbean countries, the decrease was more than the world average.

ZERO POPULATION GROWTH

In 1970 the idea of *zero population growth* (ZPG) was conceived in the United States following a startling report to the Club of Rome (Meadows et al., 1972). The report was filled with pessimism about the possibility of controlling world population growth of the sort we have been discussing. That year the ZPG movement quickly got under way, and as quickly spread from the United States to other countries.

Meadows and her associates delineated three interrelated threats. One is the rapid increase of world population. The ghost of Malthus has returned to haunt the world with the facts of limited arable land and with the production of only limited amounts of food for ever increasing numbers of people. The second threat is the depletion of nonrenewable mineral resources (e.g., oil, potassium, iron, copper). Third is the threat of environmental deterioration; there is

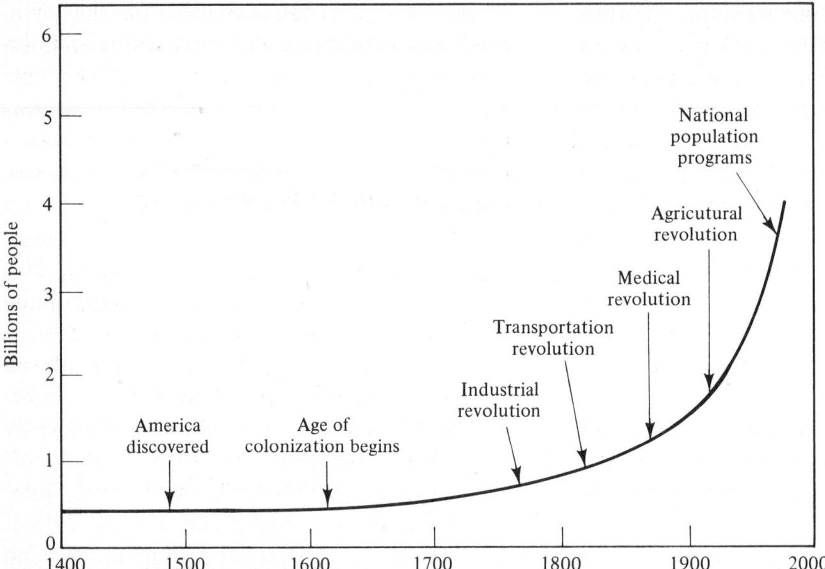

Figure 22.5 World Population Growth, 1400–1975. (*Source:* Population Reference Bureau, *World Population Growth and Response: 1965–1975—A Decade of Global Action.* Washington, D.C., 1976, p. 4.)

pollution of the air we breathe, the water we drink, the soil we grow our food in (deterioration by erosion), and the agricultural products we purchase (deterioration through use of antiparasitic chemicals).

The remedy for these world ills advocated by the proponents of ZPG is twofold. The first part, of course, is to stop population growth. The second is to stop, or at least substantially reduce, increasing economic consumption. Zero economic growth (ZEG) is as important as ZPG, since our drive for economic growth is largely responsible for the second two threats, which, when allowed to go unchecked, weaken our resources for dealing with the first.

Depleting a nonrenewable mineral resource. What will we do when the resource is gone?

The actions required to implement these goals must be tailored to the special circumstances of each country and then only encouraged, never forced:

> To curb exuberant growth, the specific remedy, as in so many other circumstances, is neither to impose nor to dictate, but to provoke, as it were, a spontaneous decision; it is vital that
>
> (1) Each government of a country at risk discover for itself the overriding necessity of limiting its population growth.
>
> (2) Each family in that country feel strongly the need to limit its progeny. (Sauvy, 1975: 180)

The ideal of ZPG has few opponents. Where the movement encounters resistance is in the demand by some of the proponents, gripped as they are with a sense of urgency, that the no-growth state be achieved at once. Many demographers believe that sudden changes of the sort proposed would bring too many unwanted repercussions. There might be major abrupt changes in the supply of and demand for consumer goods and labor. For example, an unanticipated large decrease in the number of infants and children would precipitate economic chaos as the society struggled with an oversupply of baby food, diapers, toys, schools, and teachers along with an undersupply of leisure, consumer goods, and consumer services for its adults, who, with fewer offspring, would have more time and money to spend on leisure and consumer goods than was forecast.

These fears are real and imminent. Austria, Luxembourg, West Germany, and East Germany have already gone beyond ZPG, while several other European nations are fast approaching it. Westoff (1978) predicts that the United States will reach zero population growth by 2015.[6]

POPULATION AND SOCIAL CHANGE

As we now can see, the components of population change—fertility, mortality, migration, and mobility—are important factors in the broad process of social change. We have discussed fertility, mortality, and migration in this chapter; mobility was considered in Chapter 18.

It is evident that an increase in socioeconomic status for a set of people (a form of upward mobility) affects both fertility and mortality rates in the community where they live. Moreover, the desire to move upward in the social stratification system is often a stimulus for people to migrate; by migrating, they hope to obtain better jobs. In these and many other ways, the study of population is a study of social dynamics. Put in the context of the next and final chapter of this book, population dynamics constitute a set of factors in *historical change.*

[6]For a discussion of several projections of when ZPG might be reached in more developed and less developed countries, see Tapinos and Piotrow (1978: 74–79).

OUTLINE AND SUMMARY

I. Introduction
Demography is the study of the size, territorial distribution, and composition of a population. The study takes in the changes of a population. It considers demographic variables associated with the changes. Among the variables are *fertility, mortality, migration,* and *social mobility.*

II. Three Models
Population trends are analyzed in terms of three separate models: (1) A population process is self-contained; (2) the processes are controlled in their rate and in their ultimate limit; (3) population growth acts as an independent variable. *Formal demography* is concerned with the statistical aspect of population studies. *Social demography* concentrates on the social setting affecting and being affected by a population's composition and its changes.

III. Births and Fertility
There are high-fertility countries and low-fertility countries. The level of fertility is most commonly expressed as the *crude birthrate,* that is, the number of live births per thousand population during a particular year or some other time period. High fertility is accounted for by pronatalist attitudes (e.g., children viewed as a source of labor). Among the influences on fertility are cultural values, wealth, environment (urban or rural), religion, and race.

A. Social Factors
Industrial societies usually have low fertility. Research indicates that wealth and prestige have little bearing on fertility. But there is some evidence of a direct relationship between

fertility and income, educational level, and occupational status.

1. Cultural
   Cultural values and norms regulate the intimate association of the sexes. The influence of wealth and prestige on fertility appears to be dwindling.
2. Urban and Rural
   Birthrates tend to be higher in rural areas than in urban centers. Work and leisure activities in cities may tempt women to forego having as many children as they might otherwise. City people gain scarcely no labor advantage from having children.
3. Religion
   Religion is a factor in the variation of fertility. Jews and those with no religious affiliation have the smallest families. Protestants have the next smallest, and Roman Catholics have the largest families.
4. Race
   There are differences in fertility rates among the races. Blacks have a higher crude birthrate than whites. But race is generally considered a correlate of fertility differences rather than the cause of them. Social factors such as environment (rural or urban) explain the differences.

B. Physical Factors
   Physical factors also affect birthrate. One of the physical factors is *fecundity,* that is, the physiological capacity to reproduce. *Birth control* (contraception) is the effort to reduce the possibility of conception during copulation. Its effect on the society's fertility level depends on the effectiveness of the method chosen.

IV. Mortality
   The *crude death rate* is the number of deaths per thousand population. High birthrates and low death rates have triggered the present-day overpopulation crisis. The prevention of infectious disease has been a major factor in reducing the world death rate. *Morbidity* is the incidence of disease in a population.

A. Life Expectancy
   Declining mortality in a population tends to raise the life expectancy of individuals in the population. *Life expectancy* is the number of years the typical person born in a particular year can expect to live. Life expectancy differs from *life span,* which is the biological age limit of human beings. The present human life span is thought to be about 120 years.

B. Social Factors
1. Racial Differences
   In the United States, life expectancy for whites is longer than life expectancy for blacks.
2. Rural-Urban Differences
   There are more deaths per capita in cities than in rural areas.
3. Cultural Differences
   Today there are few class differences in mortality in the United States and Canada.
4. Marital Status
   Those who are widowed, divorced, and single have higher death rates than those who are married.
5. Age
   Age is a factor in mortality. One of humankind's most fatal years is the first year of life. It is not until men reach their late fifties and women their early to middle sixties that their rates of mortality surpass the infant mortality rate.

V. Natural Increase
   One measure of a population's growth or shrinkage is its rate of natural increase. *Natural increase* is determined by subtracting the death rate from the birthrate. From 1970 to 1976 the rate of natural increase in North America dropped significantly.

VI. Migration
   There are two types of migration: *international migration* and *internal migration.*

A. Selective Migration
Only certain people in a population decide to migrate. The decision to migrate is related to the variables of age, sex, and occupation.
1. Age
Both types of migration are composed primarily of late adolescents and young adults.
2. Sex
Though there are exceptions, internal (short-distance) migrants are predominantly female and international (long-distance) migrants predominantly male.
3. Occupation
Professionals migrate internationally for specific job-related reasons. They often cause a "brain drain" in the countries from which they leave.

B. Peterson's Types
Peterson distinguished six types of migration: free, primitive, impelled, forced, group, and mass.

C. Migration in North America
There has generally been a westward movement of population in North America. There has also been a substantial rural-urban movement, some of which has been westward. Finally, there are patterns of movement within metropolitan areas.

VII. Age and Sex in the Population
The age and sex composition of a population is often portrayed with a population pyramid. A population pyramid is a graphic picture of the age and sex population, approximating the form of a two-dimensional triangle. This composition of age and sex has far-reaching consequences for a society.

VIII. World Population in the Future
Gathering and reading information on births, deaths, and migration must be done with caution. There are four types of error in demographic data: coverage, classification, recording, and processing.

A. Malthus's Theory
Malthus said that population, when unchecked, increases in a geometric ratio while subsistence increases only in an arithmetic ratio.
1. Population Checks
The only way to head off a disaster, Malthus believed, was to abstain from having children. Malthus also identified *positive checks,* or events which cause deaths and reduce the population. Among positive checks which Malthus identified are dangerous occupations, extreme poverty, disease, war, and famine.

B. Reactions to Malthus's Theory
There are three obvious weaknesses in Malthus's theory. (1) He underestimated improvements in agriculture; (2) he never foresaw the rise in the standard of living; (3) he overlooked the possibility that contraceptives would become effective.
1. Malthus's predictions have not yet come true, but present conditions suggest that they might unless something is done to ameliorate those conditions.
2. Thus, we are said to be sitting on a population bomb, so called because it threatens our values through an explosion of people too numerous to support.

C. The Demographic Transition
The demographic transition takes place in three stages. (1) It starts in preindustrial societies, which have low rates of natural increase. (2) In industrializing societies there is a high rate of natural increase, owing to lowered death rates. (3) Fully industrialized societies are characterized by low rates of natural increase, achieved through reduced birthrates.

D. The Nature of the Problem
The world population problem is alarming. But the amount of increase in world population is slowing down. A *population momentum* adds to the numerical increase in population. In developing countries, young people

are marrying and having children at a higher rate than their fellow citizens are dying.

IX. Zero Population Growth
The proponents of zero population growth (ZPG) advocate (1) an end to population growth and (2) an end to increasing economic consumption. The idea of ZPG has few opponents.

X. Population and Social Change
The components of population change—fertility, mortality, migration, and mobility—are important factors in the broad process of social change. An increase in socioeconomic status for a set of people affects both fertility and mortality rates. The desire to move upward in the social stratification system is often a stimulus for people to migrate. The study of population is a study of social dynamics.

FOR FURTHER READING AND STUDY

Beaujot, E. and McQuillan, K. 1982. *Growth and dualism: The demographic development of Canadian society.* Toronto: Gage. A textbook about the population issues facing Canadians. The influences of regionalism and language are also taken into account.

Bouma, G. D. and Bouma, W. J., 1975. *Fertility control: Canada's lively social problem.* Don Mills, Ontario: Longmans. The Boumas examine the controversy over birth control as it is developing in Canada.

Fligstein, N. 1981. *Going north: Migration of blacks and whites from the south.* New York: Academic Press. The author studies, by means of a careful quantitative analysis, the forces stimulating and shaping the large-scale migration from the American South to the northern cities.

Kalbach, W. E. and McVey, W. W. 1979. *The demographic bases of Canadian society,* 2nd ed. Toronto: McGraw-Hill Ryerson. This is a compendium of the major demographic characteristics of Canadian society. In addition to those on the demographic variables, there are chapters on ethnicity, religion, education, employment, family, and housing.

Kleinmann, D. S. 1980. *Human adaptation and population growth: A non-Malthusian perspective.* Montclair, N.J.: Allanheld, Osmun. The author effectively challenges the proposition that population growth is at the root of all social evils and that fertility control has been and will be based on modernization.

Peterson, W. 1975. *Population,* 3rd ed. New York: Macmillan. A widely read textbook written by one of the most respected sociologists in this field. Peterson addresses population issues across the world, but he also pays particular attention to problems and concerns in the United States.

Spengler, J. J. 1978. *Facing zero population growth.* Durham, N.C.: Duke University Press. Spengler is concerned with how scholars have interpreted the consequences of the cessation of population growth in some countries and how the economics in those countries can best adjust to zero population growth.

Tapinos, C. and Piotrow, F. T. 1978. *Six billion people: Demographic dilemmas and world politics.* New York: McGraw-Hill. This book addresses the pros and cons of the various options available for world population policy in the 1980s and 1990s.

Warwick, D. P., ed. 1982. *Bitter pills: Population policies and their implementation in eight developing countries.* New York: Cambridge University Press. An extensive examination of what happens when national governments and international donors try to promote birth control in developing countries.

KEY WORDS

birthrate The rate of production, or natality.

crude birthrate The level of fertility; the number of births per one thousand population during a particular year or some other time period.

demography The study of population.

emigration Departure from a country.

fecundity The physiological capacity to reproduce.

formal demography The statistical branch of demography.

immigration Arrival in a country.

infant mortality rate The number of deaths per unit of population below age one.

internal migration Migration within a country.

international migration Migration consisting of emigration and immigration.

life expectancy The number of years the typical person born in a typical year can expect to live.

life span The biological age limit of human beings; the present human life span is thought to be about 120 years.

migration The process of changing residence by moving from one location to another within a country or between two countries.

mortality A population's rate of death.

natality The rate of production, or fertility.

natural increase A measure of a population's growth or shrinkage; it is determined by subtracting the death rate from the birthrate.

population check An event or condition which causes death and reduces the population.

social demography A population analysis or a population study.

chapter 23

Social Change

CHAPTER OUTLINE

INTRODUCTION

Moving as it has from social organization and structure to institutions, to differentiation, and to trends, this book has taken you from social statics to change and social dynamics. This concluding chapter is an end to the progression; we now explore social dynamics in its broadest sense. The following definition expresses the meaning and scope of *social change:* It is

> the process by which alteration occurs in the structure and function of a social system.

> Change is seen as a process, not as a state. Because of its process nature, social change is without beginning or end, continuous, and flowing through time. (Rogers, 1973: 76)

Social change as a process takes its place beside those other two vast and pervasive processes, *social differentiation* and *social control.* Social change (unlike most organizational change) spans social institutions and affects the entire society. Social change consists of localized, finite processes, including social interaction, definition of the situation, and institutionalization.

The key word in Rogers's definition of social change is "alteration." Alteration enters into the social dynamics of a society; it occurs in a society's patterns of differentiation and social control and in its institutions and groups. The rate of alteration or change is markedly faster in Canada and other industrial societies than in preindustrial societies.

THE SOCIAL CAUSATION CYCLE

Thus we turned to the social causation cycle explained in Chapter 4. So far we have examined the role of collective behavior in promoting new social forms and in changing existing social forms. In addition, we have looked at the main population variables, noting the changes their fluctuation brings about. This chapter rounds out the discussion of social dynamics in presenting the holistic view of change, as it flows from individuals' definitions of situations and other acts of innovation through an institutionalization that leads to constructed forms of reality (see left side of Fig. 4.2, "The social causation cycle"). This is *innovational change.* Innovational change is then contrasted in this chapter with *historical change.*

The study of social change shows more promise than accomplishment. Many of the intricate details have yet to be worked out scientifically. Sociologists are still trying to explain fully how and why social forms rise and change and how and why reality is socially constructed. Martindale (1976: x) laments the current state of the art:

> [The] *theory of social change is the weakest branch of sociological theory.* . . . To confess that sociology—which was born as a science of interhuman behavior—can account for structure but not for change is like saying that one can account for a bird at rest, but not for a bird in flight.[1]

This chapter provides a sense of just how far we have come toward eliminating this weakness.

To be clear about what this chapter covers, we will be looking at change on the societal level (such as change in institutions and their social structures) and on the civilizational level. Change on the societal level takes in institutional and structural change, but excludes organizational and personal change. One approach to societal-civilizational change, nevertheless, holds that such change starts in the minds of individuals, whence come innovations.

INNOVATIONAL CHANGE

Lin and Zaltman (1973: 96–97) refer to three usages of the term "innovation." In one usage, the term is synonymous with the invention of an idea, thing, relationship, or behavior pattern. Reference here is to some kind of *creativity.* The second usage of the term is related to *adoption,* or internalization of an already created idea, thing, relationship, or pattern. It follows that, in the first usage, one can be innovative without adopting an (other) innovation. In the second usage, one can be innovative without being inventive or creative. The third usage treats innovation as something that is *described* according to its novel characteristics. For this usage little attention is paid to the creative circumstances leading up to the innovation or to the process of adoption.

[1]Italics in the original.

Innovation as Creativity

Portions of the works of Everett E. Hagen (1962: Chapter 5) and Sigmund Freud (see McLeish, 1969: Chapter 3) fall within this tradition. Like Freud, Hagen stresses the personality side of creativity.

Hagen's Theories Hagen, a professor of economics, is interested in explaining economic growth. He traces changes in growth to the "innovational personalities" of individual members of society. *Innovation* occurs when people organize reality into new relationships based on new concepts, thereby producing something of greater use to them than an existing idea (thing, behavior pattern). An innovation is often, though not necessarily, hatched in two steps. First, there is the birth of the new idea. Second, it is transformed into some form of action such as a new mechanical contrivance, a unique form of social organization, an original piece of music, a scientific hypothesis, a new dance step, or a way of solving a problem. In other words, innovation is a creative act.

Hagen points to seven important concomitants of creativity. (1) There is *openness to experience*—the capacity to see phenomena that steer one toward new analyses. There is a tendency to see these phenomena as parts of novel forces or ideas interacting with each other. (2) There is *creative imagining,* or giving free rein to one's unconscious processes (in Freud's terms the id is temporarily liberated from the superego; see Chapter 5). (3) The innovator has *confidence* in his or her creations. (4) He or she also gains *satisfaction* from solving the problem, from eliminating the nettlesome confusion that stimulated the invention. (5) Innovational personalities are motivated by a sense of *duty,* or responsibility to achieve. (6) They have the energy, or *perseverance,* to complete their innovation. (7) Some creative people are *threatened* by something; consequently, they are driven to try to eliminate the threat. The innovational personality contrasts sharply with the authoritarian personality mentioned briefly in Chapter 21.

Some writers prefer to analyze only one or two of these concomitants, as Meadows (1971: Chapter 9) does, for example, with respect to the role of *analogies* in scientific innovation. Analogous phenomena or objects existed in the scientist's imagination, suddenly enabling him or her to see new correspondences between the analogies and the phenomena or objects being studied. We previously discussed some of the ways certain biological analogies aroused new ideas in the thinking of early sociologists. Their use of the analogy of society as an organism led to the search for those social arrangements capable of sustaining the life of organism and of society, causing the organism or society to become "enfeebled," fostering its evolution, and so on.

Freud's Thinking Freud's patients recounted their dreams to him. His patients' dreams aroused Freud's interest in the creative process.

SOCIOLOGY OR COMMON SENSE

What do you think?

Which of the following statements do you agree with? Which statements do you disagree with? Make a note of your answers. Check your answers when you have completed your study of this chapter. Are your answers to the statements the same as those a sociologist would give?

1. The ancient Romans said that necessity is the mother of invention.
2. People determine history. History does not determine people.
3. We are now entering the third industrial revolution. It is based on microelectronics and capable of wider and deeper penetration into social life than either of the first two revolutions.
4. History never repeats itself.
5. To people in the Third World, the Western economy and the Soviet economy are merely two varieties of the same species.

Freud's mode of theorizing led him to the more inclusive level of unconscious conflicts, which arise early in personality formation. Among the most famous are the Oedipus conflict in males and the Electra conflict in females, which are named for figures in Greek legend. Freud argued that children of ages three to six, approximately, develop strong libidinal (vaguely sexual) feelings for their parent of the opposite sex. Sensing rivalry and hence possible retaliation from the parent of the same sex for having such sentiments, children tend to repress these feelings. The conflict is thus left unresolved.

Freud believed these unresolved Oedipal and Electra conflicts in the unconscious personalities of certain men and women are the basis for creative expressions, which are actually over-resolutions of these conflicts. The superego is caught off guard, releasing the captive energy of the Oedipus or Electra conflict to manifest itself in the disguised and usually respectable form of a creative or innovational act.

As Adoption

Rogers and Shoemaker (1971: Chapter 6) developed a model of the process of innovation as adoption. According to their model, as more and more members of a local group adopt an innovation, the accumulation of adopters over time approximates the shape of an S when plotted on a graph. First, a handful of people try out the new thing, idea, or behavior pattern and accept it. They are the *innovators.* They are marginal, adventuresome individuals who look beyond their social circles for new ideas, objects, and solutions to problems.

Next come the *early adopters,* who are more integrated in the local group than innovators. Constituting a somewhat larger segment of it, they also function as respected opinion leaders; their adoption of the innovation constitutes an endorsement of it. The opinion leaders' adoption encourages a still larger number of people in the group to accept the innovation. These people deliberate at length over their decision,

Innovation as adoption of an invention. The first automobile in town (1905).

but in time the innovation is theirs. This more cautious segment is the *early majority.*

Another segment is the *late majority.* This faction is about the same size as the early majority. Its adoption of the innovation may arise from economic necessity, or it may be a response to social pressure "to get with it" and to be like everyone else. This segment is more cautious about and skeptical of the innovation than the early majority. Much smaller in number than the two majority segments are the *lag-*

What kind of adopter is portrayed here?

gards. They are isolates who are the last to adopt the innovation because they are the last to hear of it.

Watson (1973) lists a number of factors promoting resistance to change among potential adopters. One of these is *habit,* to the extent that it satisfactorily serves the habituated person, as habits usually do. *Selective perception and retention* may prevent people from recognizing the shortcomings of their old ways and the advantages of new ones. Some members of the community are more inclined to *conform to its norms* than others. Early adoption of an innovation may be considered eccentric, different, perhaps even deviant. The level of resistance depends, too, on where in the social structure the innovation originates. The diffusion of fashions downward from the upper classes, but rarely upward from the lower classes, illustrates how this factor works (see Chapter 21).

Rogers and Shoemaker offer several generalizations about the socioeconomic characteristics of the different categories of adopters. For example, while early adopters are roughly the same age as other types, they have more education and higher social status. They are also more upwardly mobile. And consistent with their adventurous nature is their exceptional willingness to borrow money.

Characterologically, early adopters are less dogmatic than late adopters. They are also more rational people whose superior intelligence and ability to reason abstractly enhance their ability to grasp the significance of innovations. Consistent with this generalization is the one that early adopters are more achievement-oriented and less fatalistic than other types.

Socially, early adopters are more cosmopolitan than late adopters. They have greater exposure to the agents of change (e.g., scientists, salespeople, community development experts). They also seek from these sources additional information about the innovation. In the long run, early adopters acquire more knowledge about innovations than do their fellows. With knowledge, the early adopters acquire leadership in forming opinions within their social circles.

Innovations rarely diffuse upward from the lower social classes.

As Object or Idea

According to Lin and Zaltman (1973: 99–105) the characteristics of innovation vary along seven dimensions. (1) One dimension is *cost.* It is more expensive to make or adopt some objects than to make or adopt other objects. Some objects, ideas, and behavior patterns have greater social costs than others (e.g., industrial robots putting people out of work). (2) Related to the cost of an innovation is the *return on investment* that it is likely to produce or that it actually produces. A new furnace may reduce home heating costs, but not enough to offset its high purchase price with money saved on the cost of fuel over a period of years.

(3) Another dimension is *efficiency.* At issue here is the amount of time saved and discomfort avoided. The sodium-sulfur automobile battery presently on the drawing boards is attractive because it can be made from readily and cheaply

available materials, operates well at high and low temperatures, and is small and lightweight (Best, 1984: 2). (4) But what about another characteristic of innovations: their *risk and uncertainty?* The demand for the sodium-sulfur battery is tied to the development and adoption of the electric automobile. The fate of the electric automobile is tied, in part, to the price and availability of petroleum for running today's gasoline-powered vehicles.

(5) In addition, some innovations are more *communicable* than others. As a mass product, the sodium-sulfur battery would pose no problem in this regard. Nor would a recorded popular song. By contrast, an original oil painting, even if it manages to gain exposure in some major art galleries, is not very communicable.

(6) Turning to another dimension, we may ask: How *compatible* is the innovation with the values, beliefs, and needs of its potential adopters? How compatible is it with the established norms of their culture? Barnett, quoting an earlier work by W. I. Thomas, describes the friction that can develop between religious values and beliefs, on the one hand, and notable inventions, on the other:

> In Berlin, for example, street lighting was opposed because it was a "presumptuous thwarting of Providence, which had appointed darkness for the hours of the night." In other places iron plows were rejected because they were against the will of God and poisoned the soil; lightning rods were considered evil because they flew in the face of divine will; and there were protests against the use of chloroform in obstetrical cases because to alleviate childbirth pains was to "avoid one part of the primeval curse on woman." In 1848 the school board of Lancaster, Ohio, objected to the use of a schoolhouse for a debate on the use of railroads because "such things as railroads and telegraphs are impossibilities and rank infidelity." The school board went on to say that there was nothing in the Bible about them and that if God had intended that his creatures travel at the "frightful speed of fifteen miles an hour by steam He would clearly have foretold it through his holy prophets." (Barnett, 1953: 249)

(7) Finally, the *relative advantage* of an innovation is often important. One aspect of this characteristic is the ease with which advantages can be demonstrated. This has been a major stumbling block for some educational innovations. For instance, educational problems can be so complex that the theories and facts put forth by experts to solve them (an innovation) are next to impossible to explain to potential adopters. Being difficult to demonstrate, the innovation never gains acceptance (Fullan 1982: 84–85).

Innovation in North America

The level of innovation (as creativity) in Canada can be compared with the level in the United States by looking at the gross national product (GNP) of each country. How much of Canada's GNP is allocated to research and development (R&D) in comparison with the allocation in the United States? *Gross national product* is the total value of goods and services produced in a nation during a specified period, normally twelve months. Usually expressed in monetary terms, it is an index of the rate of flow of cash in the society. Figure 23.1 indicates that Canada lags far behind the United States and other industrialized countries in the proportion of GNP devoted to R&D. This gap is accounted for, to some extent, by the branch-plant nature of Canada's economy; much of the R&D of new products is conducted externally in the firms' home offices (Craib, 1981: 12–15). Nevertheless, it is the goal of the Canadian federal government to reach 1.5 percent of GNP for R&D by 1985 *(Financial Post,* 1983: 40).

Another index of innovation is the number of *patents* per thousand R&D personnel in a nation. There were only 57 patents issued in 1974 to every thousand R&D Canadians, compared with 96 issued to every thousand R&D Ameri-

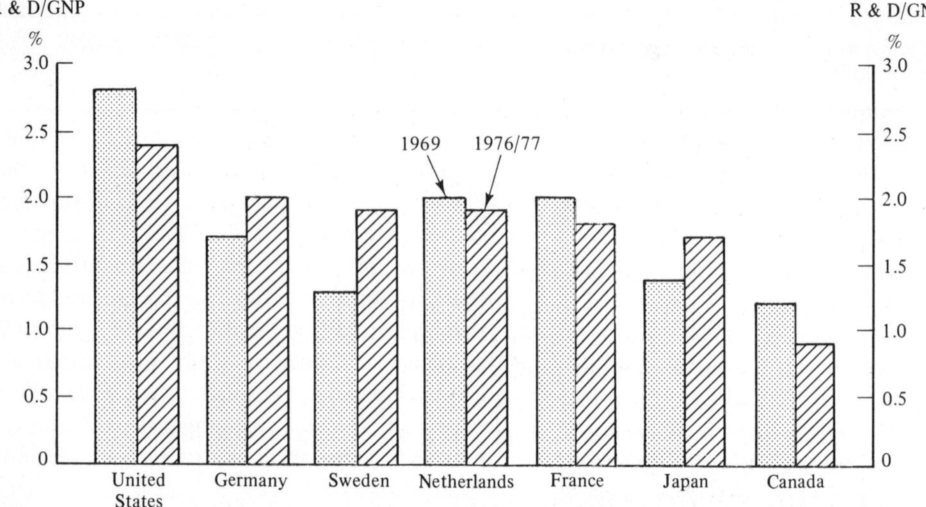

Figure 23.1 Research and Development Expenditures for Several OECD Countries. (*Source:* Statistics Canada, *Informat:* Weekly Bulletin, Cat. 11-002E. Ottawa (June, 6), 1980, p. 1.)

cans (Michalos, 1981: 30). This represents a dramatic decline for Canada, which only ten years earlier issued more than 55 percent *more* patents than the United States.

Governments issue patents for new and useful processes, machines, and manufactures and for new and useful improvements of these innovations. New ideas in the artistic, literary, and music fields (books, magazines, newspaper stories, musical compositions) are protected by *copyrights.* This third measure of innovation also shows a noticeable difference between Canada and the United States. Based on registrations per 100,000 population, there are typically three to four times as many copyrights issued in the United States as in Canada (Michalos, 1981: 173).

Diffusion of Innovations

From a social change perspective, adoption of an innovation is only part of the story. For social change to occur, members of the society must adopt the change in numbers sufficient to constitute a new pattern of culture or social structure. In other words, the innovation must *diffuse,* or spread throughout the social system to its eventual adopters. Although there is little detailed knowledge of how the diffusion of life's many innovations actually proceeds, its general outline is something like the following:

> While individuals are contemplating the implications of adopting an innovation, they are probably also discussing them with relatives and acquaintances, especially those directly concerned within it. In a finite number of encounters, an innovation is responded to and discussed. This allows group members, through the many processes of interaction (e.g., pressure to conform, development of working agreements, altercasting), to exchange their definitions of it. Hence, it is possible that new forms and modifications of old ones reach a degree of crystallization even with a limited circle of interactants. For a burgeoning form of modification to become widely accepted by societal members, definitions of the innovation must circulate beyond the border of the primary group. In this fashion still more time is added to the process of crystallization, as members of different groups associate through their social networks and large-scale organizations. It is likely that during this part of the crystallization process further shaping and abstrac-

Social Change as Marx Saw It

The premises from which we begin are not arbitrary ones, not dogmas, but real premises from which abstraction can be made only in the imagination. They are the real individuals, their activity and their material conditions of life, including those which they find already in existence and those produced by their activity. These premises can thus be established in a purely empirical way.

The first premise of all human history is, of course, the existence of living human individuals. The first fact to be established, therefore, is the physical constitution of these individuals and their consequent relation to the rest of Nature. Of course we cannot here investigate the actual physical nature of man or the natural conditions in which man finds himself—geological, oro-hydrographical, climatic and so on. All historiography must begin from these natural bases and their modification in the course of history by men's activity.

Men can be distinguished from animals by consciousness, by religion, or by anything one likes. They themselves begin to distinguish themselves from animals as soon as they begin to *produce* their means of subsistence, a step which is determined by their physical constitution. In producing their means of subsistence men indirectly produce their actual material life.

The way in which men produce their means of subsistence depends in the first place on the nature of the existing means which they have to reproduce. This mode of production should not be regarded simply as the reproduction of the physical existence of individuals. It is already a definite form of activity of these individuals, a definite way of expressing their life, a definite *mode of life.* As individuals express their life, so they are. What they are, therefore, coincides with their production, with *what* they produce and with *how* they produce it. What individuals are, therefore, depends on the material conditions of their production.

This conception of history . . . shows that history does not end by being resolved into "self-consciousness," as "spirit of the spirit," but that at each stage of history there is found a material result, a sum of productive forces, a historically created relation of individuals to Nature and to one another, which is handed down to each generation from its predecessors, a mass of productive forces, capital, and circumstances, which is indeed modified by the new generation but which also prescribes for it its conditions of life and gives it a definite development, a special character. It shows that circumstances make men just as much as men make circumstances.

SOURCE: *Karl Marx. Selected Writings in Sociology and Social Philosophy,* trans. T. B. Bottomore, pp. 53–55. New York: McGraw-Hill, 1964.

tion of the emerging form or modification takes place. Members of the different groups now have an opportunity to compare definitions of the same innovation constructed from other perspectives. Maturation of the form or modification is achieved when a widespread consensus finally develops around a *composite* definition of the innovation as worthy of widespread adoption. Legislation, special influence, and communication through the mass media may

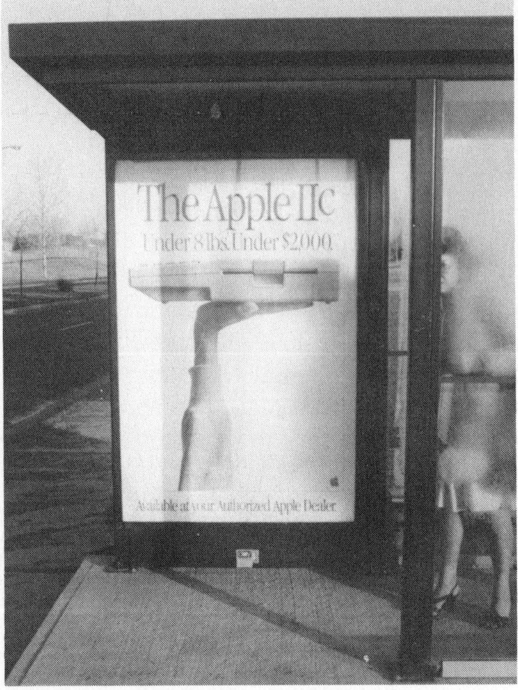

A modern communication channel for innovations.

> hasten, confound, clarify, and otherwise qualify the way societal members define and exchange their definitions of focal innovations.[2]

Computer simulation may be the most fruitful method yet devised for studying the processes of diffusion and crystallization (Rogers and Shoemaker, 1971: 194).

Mass Media Rogers and Shoemaker (1971: 18–38) examine several facets of the diffusion process. One of these is the nature of the communication channels over which information about an innovation travels. They note that *mass media* channels are the most efficient and rapid means of informing people of its existence. But, if they must be persuaded to adopt it, then *interpersonal channels* are more effective than those of the mass media. For this purpose, face-to-face contact is recommended.

[2]Taken with modifications from Stebbins (1974a: 115–116).

Time Another facet of the diffusion process is *time.* The effects of time are evident in three ways: (1) Once aware of an innovation, individuals take time to decide whether to adopt it. (2) It takes time for information about an innovation to reach the individuals in a society. (3) And, as we have just seen, the diffusion of innovation in a social system occurs over time.

The first effect of time—the innovation-decision process—has five stages (1) initial awareness; (2) interest (seeking further information about the innovation); (3) evaluation (forming a favorable or unfavorable attitude toward the innovation); (4) small-scale trial; and (5) adoption or rejection. The second effect (the innovation-adoption process) was considered in the reference to types of adopters.

Along with the third effect (time) is the rate of adoption of the innovation in a given social system. That rate depends on the various characteristics of the innovation (also mentioned earlier). For instance, an innovation that costs little and returns well on its investment and that is efficient, unrisky, advantageous, and compatible with local values and beliefs is apt to be adopted more quickly than an innovation lacking some or all of these desirable attributes.

Complexity Diffusion takes on a different hue when the innovation circulating through the populace is a complex process or complex solution to a problem, rather than a single idea, object, or behavior pattern. Zollschan and Perrucci (1964) note that, assuming enough people have an interest in the problem, there is a tendency to organize a *collective solution* to it. For social change to occur in these circumstances, this new set of relationships must diffuse through the social system; that is, it must become institutionalized (crystallized) as a new social form.

The garage sale, an innovation that broke into full swing in the 1970s (Herrmann and Soiffer, 1984), offers an excellent example of a collective solution to several problems. For one, it provides a way to get rid of unwanted possessions in the attic or the basement. The people whose possessions are sold make some extra money, while buyers pick up items they can use at a low price.

How is the collective, innovative solution to these problems implemented? Several neighbors usually get together to hold the sale. They display their discarded goods in a garage or backyard. The organizers set a date for the sale, advertise it locally, and work as salespeople on the day it is held. Once the sale is over, everyone helps clean up the premises. This activity, or some facsimile, has become common enough in North America to be regarded as a part, albeit a "subterranean" part, of the economic institution (Herrmann and Soiffer, 1984). Presumably, the idea spread through participation in this system of exchange as either a seller or a buyer.

HISTORICAL CHANGE

Karl Marx expressed the ultimate social implications of creative innovational change in his remark (see earlier) that "men make history, but not in circumstances of their choosing." All social change, innovational and historical, develops from individual definitions of the situation, innovations, and innovation diffusion. This is what historical sociologists are presently calling the "bottom-up" theory of history (Roy, 1984). But there are forms of change too broad in scope to be analyzed effectively within this framework alone. Over the years, decades, and even centuries communities, societies, and civilizations undergo substantial transformations that are most visible when the scientist looks beyond the everyday, situation-defining, innovational life of a people and their routine existence. That type of change is referred to here as *historical change.* Four sociological theories have been developed to explain historical change: *evolutionary, functionalist, conflict,* and *cyclical.* Unfortunately for simplicity, some theorists are difficult to identify as belonging exclusively to one or the other of these schools of thought. All theorists however, share, an interest in examining the entire forest of social change rather than its innovational trees.

There has been historical change in education: classroom in Neepawa, Manitoba.

Social Evolution Theory

The sociological examination of social change is as old as sociology itself. Comte's pioneering work in social dynamics affirms his interest in this subject, which he passed on to Durkheim, Spencer, and several other sociologists. All these men studied change from the evolutionary perspective, possibly the most widely applied theoretical framework of the day. Even now, evolution is one of the few concepts serving in both the biological and social sciences. Charles Darwin, who is generally acknowledged as the chief architect of this construct, was, in fact, strongly influenced by Malthus and Spencer. Darwin, in his turn, had a profound impact on Durkheim and Sumner, among others.

Principles of Evolution What with this diversity of thinkers, it is no wonder that the concept of social evolution is rather fuzzy. Theories of social evolution, some of which are more accurately called *doctrines,* are composed of one or more of the following principles: *change, order, direction, progress,* and *perfectibility.* Confining our discussion to social systems (as opposed to

There has clearly been evolutionary change in the record player industry. What will happen next?

biological systems), the principle of *change* is easily stated: the current system is the result of more or less continuous alteration from its original state. This is the simplest version of evolution, which nonetheless distinguishes it from static conceptions of social life or ones in which change is rare.

Some evolutionists add to the principle of change the idea that change must have an *order,* or be orderly. Otherwise, they say, there is no real change. By way of illustration, consider the properties of a deck of playing cards. Repeatedly shuffling the cards rearranges them, but the rearrangement is random; there is never any order. But the cards can be ordered by a means other than shuffling, such as by intentionally sorting them into the four suits and from there into descending numerical value. Ordered change has now occurred.

Other evolutionists combine the principles of change and order with *direction,* thereby suggesting the proposition that there is a natural *linear* order of change in a system. The evolutionary process is then described as passing through distinct and successive states of that system. The types of preindustrial societies explained in Chapter 9—hunting and gathering, horticultural, and agricultural—when followed by the modern industrial society constitute a directional evolutionary pattern of societal development recognized as valid by some sociologists. Durkheim's bifold classification of mechanical and organically solidary societies, discussed in Chapter 9, also suggests a directional evolutionary pattern. Comte also proposed a directional theory of society by suggesting that it evolves from a theological orientation, to a metaphysical orientation, to a positivistic orientation (see Chapter 2).

It is sometimes difficult in evolutionary theory to differentiate simple direction from *progress.* Progress carries with it moral implications suggesting or proclaiming that change is occurring in the way it ought to occur. There were flagrant judgments of this sort in Comte's sociology, but they were only hinted at in the sociology of Durkheim and many other late nineteenth century sociologists. The common theme in this literature is that societies progress over time to a point where they industrialize and develop in the way of Western nations. Extreme expressions of this stance are contained in the notion of *perfectibility:* societies continue to progress to some ideal advanced state of industrialization.

Ogburn's Answer A celebrated extension of this line of thought was worked out by William F. Ogburn (1886–1959). The twentieth century shift away from the excesses of evolutionary theory left many unanswered questions. One of them is, Why is our society so complex, while earlier societies were simpler? Ogburn found the answer in technology.

Inventions, Ogburn theorized, are evidence of social evolution. They are the products of the superior intelligence of inventors, the need in society for their creations ("necessity is the mother of invention"), and the presence of many items in the culture from which to develop new ideas. Inventions accumulate, thereby adding to that cultural base of items. Because their cultural soil is more enriched with previous inventions and other fertile developments, advanced societies produce more inventions than less advanced societies.

Once invented, the new items diffuse through the culture, forcing people to adjust to them. Many adjustments take a long time, a process Ogburn named *cultural lag.* A change occurs in the material culture (the invention of the cotton gin, for example), but there is a lag—a cultural lag—in a correlated change in values, ideas, and norms. Ogburn (1964: 29–30) offered the following example of cultural lag:

> Because of this interrelationship an invention occurring in one part and producing a change therein will also occasion a change in a part closely correlated. Thus the invention of the factory with machinery driven by steam produced a change in the family by taking occupations out of the home, especially those of women, and putting them in factories. Hence an invention in one part of a culture may produce many changes in other differing parts of a culture.

People must adjust to innovations.

Ogburn's theory ran into empirical difficulties when he added the claim that prostitution, crime, mental disorder, and the like are lagging *mal*adjustments to inventions. This hypothesis was never convincingly supported.

One of the problems with the older theories of evolution was that they too often contained untestable, sometimes ethnocentric propositions. We have no way of scientifically measuring the notion of progress or perfectibility. Not infrequently, societies were said to progress to a stage of development suspiciously resembling the home of the writer (usually France, Germany, England, or the United States). Value judgments had crept in. These and other weaknesses led to the theory's wholesale repudiation. Still, elements of it have been salvaged in the modern functionalist and conflict theories of historical change.

Functional Theory

It might appear at first to be a contradiction in terms to assert that a theory such as functionalism, which is largely about social statics, can enlighten us about social dynamics. Indeed, functionalists have encountered problems in incorporating the notion of change in their framework. That they have considered the process of change seems to have resulted, at least in part, from charges that their theorizing ignored the changes occurring in modern society (Smith, 1973: 2).

Notwithstanding this background, there is a functional theory of historical change. The theory significantly adds to our knowledge of historical change, a complex phenomenon. Van den Berghe (1963: 696), in evaluating this approach, also provides an excellent summary of it as put forward by its main proponents:

1. Societies must be looked at holistically as systems of interrelated parts.
2. Hence, causation is multiple and reciprocal.
3. Although integration is never perfect, social systems are fundamentally in a state of dynamic equilibrium, i.e., adjustive responses to outside changes tend to minimize the final amount of change within the system. The dominant tendency is thus toward stability and inertia, as maintained through built-in mechanisms of adjustment and social control.
4. As a corollary of No. 3, dysfunctions, tensions and "deviance" do exist and can persist for a long time, but they tend to resolve themselves or to be "institutionalized" in the long run. In other words, while perfect equilibrium or integration is never reached, it is the limit toward which social systems tend.
5. Change generally occurs in a gradual, adjustive fashion, and not in a sudden, revolutionary way. Changes which appear to be drastic in fact affect mostly the social superstructure [i.e., are superficial], while leaving the core elements of the social and cultural structure largely unchanged.
6. Change comes from basically three sources: adjustment of the system to exogenous (or extrasystemic) change; growth through structural and functional differentiation; and inventions or innovations by members of groups within society.
7. The most important and basic factor making for social integration is value consensus, i.e., underlying the whole social and cultural structure, there are broad aims or principles which most members of a given social system consider desirable and agree on. Not only is the value system (or ethos) the deepest and most important source of integration, but it is also the stablest element of sociocultural systems.

Limitations Van den Berghe lists several limitations to the amount and kinds of social change explainable by the functionalist concept of dynamic equilibrium. First, reaction to exogenous change is sometimes maladjustive for a significant part of the society, as exemplified in the reaction of the primitive Yir Yiront of Australia to the steel axes given them by missionaries (Sharp, 1952). The missionaries distributed the axes in the hope they would help improve living conditions in the tribe. However, the older stone axes had religious significance and served as status symbols for tribal elders. Hence, only the younger members of the tribe would use the new steel axes. Soon the younger members were more efficient than the elders. The elders, in turn, became dependent on the younger members, which reduced the social standing of the elders.

Second, social systems do occasionally go through long periods of malintegration, as events surrounding the economic recession of the early 1980s clearly demonstrate. High unemployment, governmental indecision, negligible economic growth, and personal and commercial bankruptcy were the stuff of which the malintegration of this period was made. Third, the functionalist model neglects revolutionary change, which is profound and sudden. A good example close to home is Fidel Castro's overthrow in 1959 of the conservative Cuban dictatorship of Fulgencio Batista, which he replaced with a variant of communism.

In their search for a solution to these and other problems plaguing functional analyses of social change, Van den Berghe and later Cole (1966) fall back on the old proposition that the social structure contains the seeds for its own change. Social structure contains internal contradictions. As Van den Berghe and Cole saw it, functionalism can become a more powerful theory of change by incorporating the process of the dialectic (see Chapter 9) Such a recommendation, of course, steers the generally conservative ship of functionalism tantalizingly close to the radical shores of Marxism, a prominent wing of the conflict theory of historical change.

Conflict Theory

By viewing the problem of social change from the vantage point of the dialectic, we discover that every pattern of behavior, belief, and social structure tends to generate an opposing reaction. Modern life is teeming with examples: the push for legalized abortion has provoked the antiabortion movement; the growth of computer crimes has spawned special crime control legislation and policing; the tendency toward more liberal sex attitudes has led to open denunciation of the trend itself; and the feminist movement has excited a moderate male rights backlash. Even institutionalized patterns of thought, behavior, and usage have their opponents. Among them are the deviants examined in Chapter 17.

The thesis-antithesis discords in these examples will eventually resolve themselves, it is predicted, in unique syntheses, which are part of the dynamic equilibrium of society described by the functionalists. Compromise, tolerance, assimilation, and accommodation—processes discussed in Chapter 20—are among the ways these syntheses are achieved. And that usually takes many years.

Marx, of course, recognized all this. "Force," he wrote, "is the midwife of every old society pregnant with a new one. It is itself an economic power" (1956: 227). But he was hardly interested in dynamic equilibrium. His prediction was that the contrast between the thesis (the "brute force" of capitalism) and the antithesis (the downtrodden proletariat) would be so glaring that the only synthesis possible was revolutionary historical change (i.e., communism and the classless state). Marx's theory of economic change conceived of change as occurring at the very heart of social life. Hence, much of the rest of social life must change as well.

Other conflict theories of change are less radical and hence more akin to functionalism. Dahrendorf's theory, reviewed in Chapters 9 and 18, is essentially a conflict model of historical change and perhaps the best known (outside Marx's) and most complete of these models (Lauer, 1982: 207). It exemplifies well the basic premise of this framework: one of the outcomes of conflict among groups is social change. So, too, does the work of French sociologist Raymond Aron (1968), whose reliance on the dialectic demonstrates further the small piece of common ground occupied by the change theorists espousing the functionalist and conflict approaches.

Aron identifies three basic themes in modern societies. (1) Modern societies are beset by the *dialectic of equality.* That is, they are egalitarian, since they encourage their members to aspire to higher social stations, but they are also hierarchical, since, whatever their members' aspirations, they are eventually stratified along the dimensions of wealth, power, and ethnicity. (2) There are also *contradictions of socialization.* Members strive for individuality in modern mass societies. But they are also forced to work for a living and to earn the money with which to pursue individuality in systems of production that alienate and depersonalize them. (3) The *dialectic of universality* refers to the global unification of humankind through new technology, transportation, and communication, on the one hand, and the internecine conflict among nations over unequal shares in the good life, on the other.

Running through these three dialectical themes is a contradiction between the real and the ideal. The result: group conflict followed by historical change. Of course, conflict theories of change, as this one makes clear, never predict outright a dynamic equilibrium as the denouement of these struggles. Still, many of the non-Marxist theories see conflict-based societies as persisting, with the conflict producing infinite shifting patterns of stability. Put otherwise, these theorists stress the dynamic side of this fluctuating stability, while the functionalists stress its static side. For the latter, the term "dynamic equilibrium" fits better the tenor of their theory than does the term "dialectic."

Cyclical Theory

The basic premise of the cyclical theories is straightforward: societies, cultures, and civilizations pass through stages of change, starting and ending with the same stage. This passing through stages is called a *cycle.* The cycle, when completed, repeats itself over and over again. Martindale (1962: 9) points out that evolutionary theories of change are unique to Western civilization. The ancient civilizations in Greece, China, and India, by contrast, saw change as occurring in cycles. In modern times, the primary sociological representative of this perspective was the American scholar Pitirim Sorokin (1889–1968). His theory actually departs somewhat from the basic premise.[3]

Sorokin's Theory Sorokin's (1957: Part 9) theory rests on the *principle of immanent sociocultural change:* any sociocultural system (i.e., society, civilization) changes by virtue of its own forces and properties. In this regard, it is evident that Sorokin and the proponents of the dialectic also share some common ground. At the same time, Sorokin appears to accept the functionalist principle of dynamic equilibrium, for he theorizes that complete equilibrium is never reached. Complete equilibrium would cause the sociocultural system ultimately to stagnate and die. Inasmuch as such systems contain "the seeds of their own destiny," they and their members have the power to chart their future. In short, we determine history, rather than the reverse. Still, this is done within the context of external forces and with respect to the general direction in which the system is heading (i.e., evolving). North American civilization is presently heading toward increased use of and reliance on microelectronic technology (see later). One external force, discussed in the preceding chapter, is overpopulation and its sobering ramifications.

The principle of immanent sociocultural change is linked to a second principle, namely the *principle of limited possibilities of change.* There is a limit to the number of changes that can develop in a system. For example, there is a limit to new forms of change, to the direction of change, and to new patterns of behavior. The system simply runs out of combinations. Consequently, unless it dies, it must eventually start running through the changes again.

There is thus "recurrence" or "rhythm" in the histories of sociocultural systems. That is, their histories are cyclical. In their detailed aspects, however, the new cycles are never identical because, as parts of the system, the people in them have changed, and for the same reason so has the external environment (other sociocultural systems). In spite of this special condition of unique cycles, Sorokin's theory is still normally classified as cyclical.

Sociocultural Supersystems Within every sociocultural system there are three supersystems of truth, three views of reality that change according to these two principles (Sorokin, 1957: Chapter 2). One of these is the *ideational supersystem.* It is marked by truth received from outside this world, as from God or some other deity or external source. It is spiritualistic, mystical, and indeterminate. By contrast, the *sensate supersystem* is based, so to speak, on a down-to-earth view of reality. It neither seeks ideational

Ideational supersystem: A Bella Coola Indian shaman at work (1885).

[3]Historians, notably Arnold Toynbee and Oswald Spengler, also share an interest in this theory of change.

truth nor believes in it. This is the realm of science and of direct sensory experience. It is an empirical system of truth; that is, it is a system of knowledge. Between these two, and having certain characteristics of both, lies the "intermediate" *idealistic supersystem.* In his book, Sorokin describes what this latter system consisted of at various times in recorded history.

For our purposes, it is important to know that one of the three systems rises to prominence at some point in the history of a society or civilization, dominates, and then declines as one of the other two is ascending. Sorokin (1957: 681) explains how and why this occurs:

> But because each of the three systems has also an invalid part—error and fallacy side by side with truth—each of these systems leads its human bearers away from the reality, gives them pseudoknowledge instead of real knowledge, and hinders their adaptation and the satisfaction of their physiological, social, and cultural needs. When such a system of truth and reality ascends, grows, and becomes more and more monopolistically dominant, its false part tends to grow, while its valid part tends to decrease. Becoming monopolistic or dominant, it tends to drive out all the other systems of truth and reality, and with them the valid parts they contain. At the same time, like dictatorial human beings, becoming dominant, the system is likely to lose increasingly its validities and develop its falsities. The net result of such a trend is that as the domination of the system increases, it becomes more and more inadequate. As such, it becomes less and less capable of serving as an instrument of adaptation, as an experience for real satisfaction of the needs of its bearers; and as a foundation for their social and cultural life. The society and culture built on such a premise become more and more empty, false, inexperienced, ignorant; therefore, powerless, disorderly, and base; nobody can build his or society's life and culture on error, ignorance, and pure illusion. The moment comes when the false part of the system begins to overweigh its valid part. Under such conditions, the society of its bearers is doomed either to perish, or it has to change its major premise—to "redefine the situation"—and with it, its system of culture. In this way the dominant system prepares its own downfall and paves the way for the ascendance and domination of one of the rival systems of truth and reality, which is, under the circumstances, more true and valid than the outworn and degenerated dominant system. The new dominant system undergoes again the same tragedy, and sooner or later is replaced by its rival.

Sorokin (1957: 699–704) sees Western civilization as struggling through the waning stages of its sensate supersystem. He wrote in the final section of his book, which he entitled "The end of the road," that:

> The central process for the last few decades has consisted in (a) the progressive decay of sensate culture, society, and man; and (b) the emergence and slow growth of the first components of the new—ideational or idealistic—socioculture order.

To the extent that change and order inhere in the conflict and cyclical theories of historical change, they are also evolutionary. But they clearly part company with the evolutionary approach when it comes to the principles of linear direction, progress, and perfectibility. In so doing, they make a unique contribution to the sociological explanation of social change.

DEVELOPMENT THEORY

In one way or another the four preceding theories of historical change are all represented in the hybrid model of historical change known as *development theory.* The two principal forms of development theory—*modernization theory* and *world-system theory*—are explained in this section. As background, we turn to Aron's (1967: Chapter 1) review of the three sources of development theory, which established what it is and what it focuses on.

The first source is the long-term, statistical study of economic growth. Research and theory in this tradition paint a quantitative and linear picture of a country's progress along a scale or set of scales; for instance, prosperity and per capita income are indicators. Every country is seen as progressing thus, with some (e.g., the United States, Canada) getting an earlier start toward development than others (e.g., Niger, Iraq). All countries, it is believed, eventually reach full development.

The second source springs from the contrast between rich countries and poor countries or, in the language of the preceding chapter, between countries that are more developed and those that are less developed. This source brings out the qualitative differences separating the two kinds of societies. For example, as countries develop, there is a transfer of labor from primary industrial functions to secondary and tertiary functions (see Chapter 13).

The third source of development theory comes from comparing the Soviet economy and social organization with the Western economy and social organization. Despite political ideology, Aron observes that there are many developmental phenomena shared by both. From the standpoint of the Third World, these systems are merely two varieties of the same species:

> . . . "socialist construction" or "economic development," they both involve industrialization, urbanization, generalized primary education, expansion of secondary and higher education, a trend toward the nuclear as opposed to the extended family, separation between family life and work, between home and place of work, the setting up of large-scale production units, rigorous differentiation of social function, and so on. (Aron, 1967: 12)

Modernization Theory

Aron (1967: 18) says that development theory "is an integral part of the scientific doctrines and ideologies in the countries of the Eastern Bloc, just as much as in the West." The doctrinal-ideological element is evident in modernization theory and its evolutionary-functionalist foundation (Portes, 1967: 61–68). Modernization theory, as constructed by the functionalist sociologists, replaces the old linear (directional) model, where societies are held to evolve through a set of stages, with a bipolar model consisting of two ideal types. In the modernization theory, societies are predicted to develop from an earlier stage (variously called traditional, less developed, underdeveloped) to a later state (modern, more developed, developed). Each society moves, gradually and irreversibly, from lesser to greater development, growing more specialized and functionally interdependent as time goes on (similar to Durkheim's progression from mechanical to organic solidarity). Other structural changes along the way include bureaucratization, urbanization, and industrialization. In sum, there is social, political, and economic evolution.

One of the most lucid and influential theories of modernization was proposed by economic historian W. W. Rostow (1960). His scheme of five stages of economic growth also illustrates Aron's first source of development theory. The beginning stage is the *traditional society,* an example of which was encountered in Chapter 9 in the form of the agricultural society. The second stage is composed of the *preconditions for take-off.* Societies at this point are in transition. They are developing ways "to exploit the fruits of science," starting to alter their value structures (e.g., economic progress becomes desirable), and drifting toward a money economy.

The third stage is *take-off,* "the great watershed in the life of modern societies." The old barriers to development are torn down by this point in time, allowing modernization to proceed unfettered. Major changes occur in agriculture, as it strives to meet the challenge of supporting a rapidly increasing population (i.e., the intermediate stage of the demographic transition; Chapter 22). Industry expands. Economic growth is evident everywhere. By the fourth stage, or the *drive to maturity,* a variety of new industries are fostering regular economic expansion. The country has now achieved a place in the world economy. According to Rostow, maturity is reached sixty years or so after take-off commences.

In the *age of high mass consumption,* the fifth stage, large numbers of affluent people in the society have money to spend on goods and services which can be used for doing more than satisfying the basic needs of food, shelter, and clothing. Technological and entrepreneurial skills are now used to produce whatever the society chooses. At this stage, dependence on raw materials from other countries is more a matter of choice than of necessity. Figure 23.2 indicates that the United States and Canada have been in this stage since just after 1920, but that approximately forty years separates their take-off. Obviously, the assumption of linear development is violated in the cases of Canada and Australia.

World-System Theory

Portes (1976: 65–67) makes several criticisms of modernization theory, two of which are covered here. First, the theory predicts that historical change is smooth, gradual, and irreversible, but, according to Portes, this proposition fails at

The age of high mass-consumption has its recognizable aspects.

times to agree with the facts. At least in the short run, societies do suffer setbacks, as in the recession of the early 1980s. And development can be anything but smooth, since different groups may battle one another over which route to the good life their society should travel.

Second, in Portes's view, modernization theory tends to ignore the external factors affecting societal development. Today, the economic and political affairs of nations are often intricately intertwined, rendering them vulnerable to unilateral changes in the policies of one of them. One need only contemplate the far-reaching effects of a major shift in the oil prices as set by producer nations to get an instant and vivid sense of how important external factors are in development.

The most penetrating critique of modernization theory, however, comes from world-system theory. *World-system* theory is a Western version of dependency theory, a theory that emerged from Third World, and particularly Latin American, intellectual circles in the late 1960s and early 1970s. Third World dependency theorists argue that underdevelopment is not a way station on the modernizationists' road to high mass consumption, but a position of economic weakness exploited by the capitalist superpowers. True development is the vehicle of escape from this predicament.

Several writers (e.g., O'Brien, 1975; Frank, 1969) observe that dependent nations are created by multinational corporations (MNCs), which, as noted briefly for Canada in Chapter 13, control to their advantage the prices of their products in those countries (whether imported or manufactured there). Internally, MNCs foster a parasite elite (Chapter 18) and other privileged groups, thereby furthering the inequality of each dependent country's stratification system. Moreover, underdeveloped nations become dependent on the technological skills and capital they get from developed countries to help them modernize. Meanwhile, substantial amounts of local money leave these countries via the MNCs, causing a financial drain on their

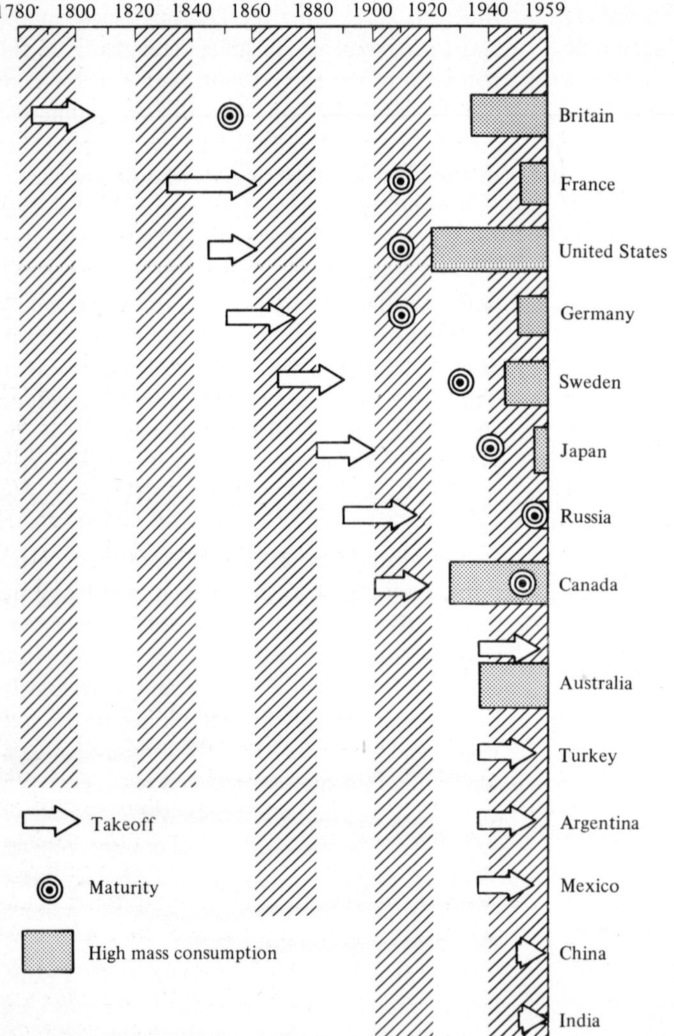

Figure 23.2 Stages of Economic Growth in Selected Countries. (*Source:* W. W. Rostow, *The Stages of Economic Growth: A Noncommunist Manifesto.* London: Cambridge University Press, 1960, p. xii.)

economies. From the Marxian standpoint of the dependency theorists, these conditions contribute to greater social inequality, rapid urbanization, and concurrent growth of a massive, impoverished labor force, much of which is exploitatively employed by the MNCs. This is hardly the kind of social change developing nations are seeking.

Chirot and Hall (1982: 90) view world-system theory as "in most ways merely a North American adaptation of dependency theory." American sociologist Immanuel Wallerstein (1979) coined the phrase "world-system" and, during the 1970s, published its attendant theory. Much of his work is historical, serving as background for his present-day program of a worldwide, Marxist-style revolution. His ideas are too voluminous even to summarize here.

Instead, only a brief sketch of certain parts of his theory of change are attempted.

Wallerstein (1979: 5) argues that the only kind of social system today is the *world-system,* "which we define quite simply as a unit with a single division of labor and multiple cultural systems." Multiple cultural systems are the nation-states of modern times, across which spreads an international stratification system based on the economic functions performed by workers. The contemporary world-system is primarily one of *world-economies,* or economically homogeneous geopolitical areas of the globe. These areas are of three types: core, periphery, and semiperiphery.

As the term implies, the *core* areas have a concentration of high profit, high technology, high wage, and high diversification in production. They contain mass market industries, native-born bourgeoisie, and advanced agricultural production. They engage in considerable international and internal commerce. The *periphery* is mostly the opposite. Its economy is based on low profit, low technology, low wage, and low diversification in production. If these types sound familiar, it is because they refer, respectively, to the more developed countries and the less developed countries discussed earlier in this book. The *semiperiphery* falls between the core and the periphery on the dimensions just listed. Wallerstein places Canada here. The United States is part of the core.

This world-system spawns international class conflict. Crosscutting the core, peripheral and, to some extent, semiperipheral areas are a global bourgeoisie and proletariat. Class cleavages in individual nation-states are merely adjuncts of this larger structure. Since the majority of the proletariat live in the periphery and, to a lesser extent, the semiperiphery, the socialist revolution must come primarily from there. Given the way the world-system works, even the Soviet Union cannot single-handedly carry out this form of social change.

The emotional and ideological penumbra of the dependency and world-system frameworks makes it difficult at times to separate fact from fiction. Countries such as Canada and Australia are said to be dependent. In Canada's case, it is chiefly dependent on the United States (see Chapter 13). Still, Canada, Australia, and similar countries lack the poverty and general misery found in many dependent Third World societies, which means that Third World dependency is substantially different from Canadian-Australian dependency (O'Brien, 1975). In this regard, Wallerstein's classification of Canada and Australia as semiperipheral is a helpful distinction. A further weakness in this research tradition is its largely exclusive emphasis on international forces to the neglect of internal ones, such as regional dependence (Portes, 1976: 78). A short treatment of these forces in the United States and Canada is also available in Chapter 13.

THE FUTURE

The theories of historical change leave us with a confused outlook on the future of North America. Sorokin's cyclical theory holds that we are about to embark on a shift toward an ideational or idealistic sociocultural system. World-system theory sees a global proletarian revolution in the offing. Functionalism predicts no major change, only minor change as needed to maintain dynamic equilibrium. Modernization theory, as a hybrid of functionalist and evolutionist thought, argues that less developed nations will continue to advance to the point of high mass consumption.

While on the subject of modernization theory, we should bring up the question being asked in some scholarly quarters these days of whether there is life after high mass consumption. Jenkins and Sherman (1979: Chapter 4), among others (see Stebbins, 1982), think there is. The "third industrial revolution" has just got under way (the first was in machinery, the second in transportation). This revolution, which is capable of wider and deeper penetration into social life than the first two, is based on the technology of microelectronics. Its effect on work, leisure, and many other areas of life is only beginning to be explored. Whether we know it or not, all of us are now experiencing its impact (e.g., television sets, hand-held calculators, home computers, telecommunications, word processors). What bearing microelectronics will have on the forecasts which are based on the theories of historical change remains to be seen.

OUTLINE AND SUMMARY

I. Introduction
Social change is the process by which alteration occurs in the structure and function of a social system. Social change is part of the social causation cycle. It flows from individuals' definitions of situations and other acts of innovation.

II. The Social Causation Cycle
Collective behavior promotes new social forms and changes in existing social forms. There are population variables. The cycle continues with innovational change and historical change.

III. Innovational Change
Innovation is an invention, an idea, an object, or pattern of behavior. It is a creative act. Innovation occurs when people organize reality into new relationships based on new ideas. Innovation can be an *adoption,* or internalization of an already created idea, thing, relationship, or pattern.

A. Innovation as Creativity
Hagen and Freud looked on innovation as creativity. They stressed the personality side of creativity.

1. Hagen's Theories
Hagen is interested in explaining economic growth. He traces changes in growth to the "innovational personalities of individual members of society." Hagen points to seven important concomitants of creativity.

2. Freud's Thinking
The dreams of Freud's patients stimulated his interest in the creative process. Freud learned of the Oedipus conflict in males and the Electra conflict in females. He believed that the Oedipus conflict and the Electra conflict were the basis for creative expressions.

B. As Adoption
Innovation as adoption is the internalization of an already created idea, thing, or behavior pattern. Five types of adopters are *innovators, early adopters, early majority, late majority,* and *laggards.* Factors promoting resistance to change are habit, selective perception and retention, conformity to community norms, and origin of innovation.

C. As Object or Idea
Characteristics of innovation vary along seven dimensions: *cost, return to investment, efficiency, risk and uncertainty, communicableness, compatibility, relative advantage.*

D. Innovation in North America
Canada lags far behind the United States and other industrialized countries in the proportion of gross national product allocated to research and development. Another index of innovation is the number of patents per thousand R&D personnel in a nation. Canada lags behind the United States in the issuance of patents. Copyrights are another measure. The United States issues more copyrights than Canada.

E. Diffusion of Innovations
For change to occur, innovations must diffuse, or spread, throughout the social system of their eventual adopters. The innovations then become crystallized as part of the system's institutional structure. Information about the innovation may be conveyed interpersonally or by the mass media.

1. Mass Media
Mass media are the most efficient and rapid means of informing people of an innovation. But if *interpersonal channels* must be persuaded to adopt the innovation, then interper-

sonal channels are more effective than those of the mass media. Face-to-face contact is an interpersonal channel.

2. Time

Time is a facet of the diffusion process. Once aware of an innovation, individuals take time to decide whether to adopt it. It takes time for information about an innovation to reach the individuals in a society. The diffusion of innovation in a social system occurs over time.

3. Complexity

An innovation can be a complex process or a complex solution to a problem. There is a tendency to organize a collective solution to a problem. For social change to occur, the collective solution must diffuse through the social system. A garage sale is an example of a collective solution to problems.

IV. Historical Change

Historical change consists of the substantial transformations occurring over long periods of time in communities, societies, and civilizations. Four sociological theories have been developed to explain historical change: *evolutionary, functionalist, conflict,* and *cyclical.*

A. Social Evolution Theory

The sociological examination of social change is as old as sociology itself. For many years, sociologists have studied change from the evolutionary perspective. Evolution is one of the few concepts serving in both the biological and social sciences.

1. Principles of Evolution

Theories or doctrines of social evolution are composed of one or more of the following five principles: *simple change, orderly change, change in a linear direction, change in a linear direction interpreted as progress, change in a linear direction interpreted as progress toward perfectibility.*

2. Ogburn's Answer

According to Ogburn, inventions accumulate. The accumulation enriches the cultural soil for further inventions. New innovations diffuse through the culture, forcing behavioral adjustments, some of which are delayed (i.e., cultural lag).

B. Functional Theory

Since societies are never perfectly integrated, they are in a state of dynamic equilibrium; that is, there are gradual adjustive responses to outside changes that tend to minimize the amount of change within the system. Dysfunctions, tensions, and deviance tend eventually to become institutionalized.

1. Limitations

The dialectic is one suggestion for resolving the theoretical difficulties associated with the functional theory. Social structure contains the seeds for its own change.

C. Conflict Theory

The conflict theory takes the dialectic (opposites) as central to social life. Aron's three basic conflicts of the real and ideal in modern societies: (1) dialectic of equality: egalitarianism vs. hierarchy; (b) contradictions of socialization: individuality vs. worker alienation and depersonalization; (c) dialectic of universality: international human unification vs. competitive struggles.

D. Cyclical Theory

Basic premise: societies, cultures, and civilizations pass through stages of change, starting and ending with the same stage. This cycle repeats itself indefinitely.

1. Sorokin's Theory

Sorokin's theory rests on the *principle of immanent sociocultural change:* any sociocultural system (i.e., society, civilization) changes by virtue of its own forces and properties. This principle is linked to the *principle of limited possibilities of change.*

2. Sociocultural Supersystems

Within every sociocultural system

there are three supersystems of truth, three views of reality that change. These are (1) the *ideational supersystem,* (2) the *sensate supersystem,* and (3) the *"intermediate" idealistic supersystem.*

V. Development Theory
The theories of historical change are represented in the hybrid model of historical change known as *development theory.* The two principal forms of development theory are *modernization theory* and *world-system theory.*

A. Modernization Theory
Societies are said to evolve from one ideal-typical (underdeveloped) society to a second ideal-typical (developed) society. Rostow's five stages of economic growth are *traditional society, preconditions for take-off, take-off, drive to maturity,* and *age of high mass consumption.*

B. World-System Theory
Criticisms of modernization theory: (a) It predicts smooth, gradual, irreversible change, which fails to agree with the facts, and (b) it ignores external factors affecting development. The dependency theory: underdevelopment is a position of economic weakness exploited by the capitalist superpowers. It is not a stage of development and can never become one as long as the present system of dependence on multinational corporations exists. World-system theory: A world-system is a unit with a single division of labor and multiple cultural systems. The world economies cluster into three homogeneous geopolitical areas: *core, periphery,* and *semiperiphery.* The present world-system spawns international class conflict between a global bourgeoisie and proletariat.

VI. The Future
The theories of historical change leave us in a confused outlook on the future of North America. Where do we go after the age of high mass consumption? We are entering the third industrial revolution, which is rooted in the technology of microelectronics.

FOR FURTHER READING AND STUDY

Bruyn, S. T. and Rayman, P. M., eds. 1979. *Nonviolent action and social change.* New York: Irvington. Fifteen original papers on the theory and strategy for nonviolent social change. The book contains sections on change theory, firsthand experiences in confronting authority, and community development in various countries.

Etzioni-Halevy, E. 1981. *Social change.* Boston: Routledge & Kegan Paul. Etzioni-Halevy critically reviews the theories of social change and their expression in theories of modernization and development. Both functionalist and Marxist viewpoints are considered.

McLuhan, H. M. 1968. *War and peace in the global village: An inventory of some of the current spastic situations that could be eliminated by more feedforward.* New York: McGraw-Hill. An examination of some of the effects of technological innovations on humankind, including various forms of violence. Every major new technology alters our sense of identity and provokes violence.

McRoberts, K. and Posgate, D. 1980. *Quebec, social change, and political crisis.* Toronto: McClelland & Stewart. The authors analyze the rise of the *Parti Québécois,* the first years in power, and the 1980 provincial referendum, which proposed "sovereignty association" (a quasiseparatist relationship) with the rest of Canada.

Ossenberg, R. J., ed. 1980. *Power and social change in Canada.* Toronto: McClelland & Stewart. This book contains seven articles on social change and the use of power written from the political economy and Marxian perspectives.

Rogers, E. M. and Shoemaker, F. F. 1971. *Communication and innovation: A cross-cultural approach.* New York: Free Press. A thorough and readable review of the theory and research on innovations and innovational change.

KEY WORDS

cultural lag A delay in a society's change in values, ideas, and norms in response to a change in the matrial culture.

diffusion The process by which an innovation spreads throughout a social system; there is no social change without diffusion.

Electra conflict A female child's libidinal feelings for her father.

gross national product The total value of goods and services produced in a nation during a specified period, normally twelve months.

historical change A substantial transformation of a community, society, or civilization over a period of decades or even centuries.

innovation The invention of an idea, thing, relationship, or behavior pattern; a creative act.

innovational change A change resulting from an innovation; it flows from individuals' definitions of situations through an institutionalization that leads to constructed forms of reality.

innovators Individuals who try out a new thing, idea, or behavior pattern and accept it.

social change The process by which alteration occurs in the structure and function of a social system.

References

Abelson, R. P. 1965. Lectures on computer simulation. In *Mathematics and social sciences,* ed. S. Sternberg, pp. 443–482. Paris: Mouton.

Aberle, D. F. 1966. *The peyote religion among the Navaho.* Chicago: Aldine.

Abramson, M., Mizruchi, E. H., and Hornung, C. A. 1980. *Stratification and mobility.* New York: Macmillan.

Abu-Laban, S. M. 1980. Social support in older age. *Essence* 4: 195–210.

Ad Hoc Committee Respecting Student Matters. 1972. *Perceptions of school and education: A comparative study of three surveys conducted at the secondary level.* Willowdale, Ont.: North York Board of Education.

Adams, B. N. 1968. *Kinship in an urban setting.* Chicago: Markham.

Adams, B. N. 1980. *The Family,* 3rd ed. Chicago: Rand McNally.

Akers, R. L., Hayner, N. S., and Gruninger, W. 1977. Prisonization in five countries. *Criminology* 14: 527–554.

Alberoni, F. 1966. Society, culture, and mass communication media. *Ikon* 19: 29–62.

Aldous, J. 1978. *Family careers.* New York: Wiley.

Alexander, W. E. and Farrell, J. P. 1975. *Student participation in decision-making.* Toronto: Ontario Institute for Studies in Education.

Alford, R. R. 1963. *Party and society.* Chicago: Rand McNally.

Alford, R. R. and Friedland, R. 1975. Political participation and public policy. In *Annual review of sociology,* vol. 1, eds. A. Inkeles, J. Coleman, and N. Smelser, pp. 429–479. Palo Alto, Calif.: Annual Reviews Inc.

Alinsky, S. D. 1971. *Rules for radicals.* New York: Random House.

Allingham, J. D., Balakrishnan, T. R., and Kantner, J. F. 1969. Time series of growth in use of oral contraception and the differential diffusion of oral anovulants. *Population Studies* 23: 43–51.

Allport, G. W. 1961. *Pattern and growth in personality.* New York: Holt, Rinehart & Winston.

Altheide, D. L. and Snow, R. P. 1979. *Media logic.* Beverly Hills, Calif.: Sage.

Ambert, A. M. 1976. *Sex structure,* 2nd ed. Don Mills, Ont.: Longmans Canada.

Anderson, A. B. and Frideres, J. S. 1981. *Ethnicity in Canada.* Toronto: Butterworths.

Anisef, P., Okihiro, N., and James, C. 1982. *Losers*

and winners: The pursuit of equality and social justice in higher education. Toronto: Butterworths.

Antonovsky, A. 1967. Social class, life expectancy, and overall mortality. *Milbank Memorial Fund Quarterly* 45: 31–73.

Antony, A. E. C. 1980. Radical criminology. In *Crime in Canadian society,* 2nd ed., eds. R. A. Silverman and J. J. Teevan, Jr., pp. 234–247. Toronto: Butterworths.

Armstrong, P. and Armstrong, H. 1984. *The double ghetto: Canadian women and their segregated work,* 2nd ed. Toronto: McClelland & Stewart.

Arnold, S. J. and Tigert, D. J. 1974. Canadians and Americans: A comparative analysis. *International Journal of Comparative Sociology* 15: 68–83.

Aron, R. 1967. *The industrial society.* New York: Praeger.

Aron, R. 1968. *Progress and illusion.* New York: Praeger.

Asch, S. E. 1958. Effects of group pressure upon the modification and distortion of judgments. In *Readings in social psychology,* 3rd ed., eds. E. E. Maccoby, T. M. Newcomb, and E. L. Hartley, pp. 174–183. New York: Holt, Rinehart & Winston.

Atchley, R. L. 1975. The life course, age grading and age-linked demands for decision making. In *Life-span developmental psychology: Normative life crises,* eds. N. Datan and L. H. Ginsberg, pp. 261–278. New York: Academic Press.

Axelrod, M. 1956. Urban structure and social participation. *American Sociological Review* 21: 13–18.

Axelson, L. J. 1960. Personal adjustment in the post-parental period. *Marriage and Family Living* 22: 66–68.

Babbie, E. 1983. *The practice of social research.* 3rd ed. Belmont, Calif.: Wadsworth.

Back, K. W. 1981. Small groups. In *Social psychology,* eds. M. Rosenberg and R. H. Turner, pp. 320–343. New York: Basic Books.

Backman, C. W. 1981. Attraction in interpersonal relationships. In *Social psychology,* eds. M. Rosenberg and R. H. Turner, pp. 235–268. New York: Basic Books.

Bagnall, J. 1982. U.S. threatens brain drain of our skills. *The Financial Post* (3 April): 1–2.

Bainbridge, W. S. and Stark, R. 1982. Church and cult in Canada. *Canadian Journal of Sociology* 7: 351–366.

Balakrishnan, T. R. and Jarvis, G. K. 1979. Changing patterns of spatial differentation in urban Canada, 1961–1971. *Canadian Review of Sociology and Anthropology* 16: 218–227.

Bales, R. F. 1950. *Interaction process analysis: A method for the study of small groups.* Reading, Mass.: Addison-Wesley.

Bales, R. F. and Borgatta, E. F. 1965. Size of group as a factor in the interaction profile. In *Small groups,* 2nd ed., eds. A. P. Hare, E. F. Borgatta, and R. F. Bales, pp. 495–512. New York: Knopf.

Bales, R. F. and Slater, P. E. 1955. Role differentiation in small decision-making groups. In *Family, socialization, and interaction process,* eds. T. Parsons and R. F. Bales, pp. 259–306. Glencoe, Ill.: Free Press.

Ball, D. W. 1967. Toward a sociology of toys. *Sociological Quarterly* 8: 447–458.

Ball, J. C. 1979. An international overview—the treatment of drug abusers. In *Handbook on drug abuse,* eds. R. I. Dupont, A. Goldstein, and J. O'Donnell, pp. 367–371. Washington, D.C.: National Institute on Drug Abuse.

Barber, B. 1968. Social stratification. In *International encyclopedia of the social sciences,* vol. 15, ed. D. L. Sills, pp. 288–296. New York: Crowell, Collier, Macmillan.

Barchas, P. R. 1976. Physiological sociology. In *Annual review of sociology,* vol. 2, eds. A. Inkeles, J. Coleman, and N. Smelser, pp. 299–334. Palo Alto, Calif.: Annual Reviews Inc.

Barnett, H. G. 1953. *Innovation: The basis of cultural change.* New York: McGraw-Hill.

Baron, H. M. 1969. The web of urban racism. In *Institutional racism in America,* eds. L. L. Knowles and K. Prewitt, pp. 134–176. Englewood Cliffs, N.J.: Prentice-Hall.

Baron, R. A. and Byrne, D. 1984. *Social psychology,* 4th ed. Boston: Allyn & Bacon.

Bartell, G. D. 1971. *Group sex.* New York: Wyden.

Batiuk, M. E. and Sacks, H. L. 1981. George Herbert Mead and Karl Marx. *Symbolic Interaction* 4: 207–224.

Bavelas, A. A., Hastorf, A. H., Gross, A. E., and Kite, R. W. 1965. Experiments on the alteration of group structure. *Journal of Experimental and Social Psychology* 1: 55–70.

Beal, E. W. 1980. Separation, divorce, and single-parent families. In *The family life cycle,* eds. E. A. Carter and M. McGoldrick, pp. 241–264. New York: Gardner.

Becker, H. P. 1932. *Systematic sociology.* New York: Wiley.

Becker, H. P. 1957. Current sacred-secular theory and its development. In *Modern sociological theory,* eds. H. Becker and A. Boskoff, pp. 133–185. New York: Holt, Rinehart & Winston.

Becker, H. S. 1963. *Outsiders.* New York: Free Press.

Becker, H.S. and Geer, B. 1958. The fate of idealism in medical school. *American Sociological Review* 23: 50–56.

Becker, H. S. and Horowitz, I. L. 1970. The culture of civility. *TRANS-action* 7 (April): 12–19.

Beckford, J. A. 1985. *Cult controversies.* London: Tavistock.

Bell, D. and Tepperman, L. 1979. *The roots of disunity.* Toronto: McClelland & Stewart.

Bell, L. V. 1973. *In Hitler's shadow, The anatomy of of American Nazism.* New York: Kennikat.

Bell, R. R. 1976. *Social deviance,* rev. ed. Homewood, Ill.: Dorsey.

Bell, R. R. 1979. *Marriage and family interaction,* 5th ed. Homewood, Ill.: Dorsey.

Bellah, R. N. 1967. Civil religion in America. *Daedalus* 96: 1–21.

Bellah, R. N. and Hammond, P. E. 1980. *Varieties of civil religion.* New York: Harper & Row.

Bem, S. L. 1974. The measurement of psychological androgyny. *Journal of Personality and Social Psychology* 42: 155–162.

Ben-David, J. 1984. *The scientist's role in society.* Chicago: University of Chicago Press.

Ben-David, J. and Sullivan, T. A. 1975. Sociology of science. In *Annual review of sociology,* vol. 1, eds. A. Inkeles, J. Coleman, and N. Smelser, pp. 203–222. Palo Alto, Calif.: Annual Reviews Inc.

Bendix, R. 1974. Inequality and social structure: A comparison of Marx and Weber. *American Sociological Review* 39: 149–161.

Benedict, B. 1972. Social regulation of fertility. In *The structure of human population,* eds. G. A. Harrison and A. J. Boyce, pp. 73–89. London: Oxford University Press.

Bennett, N. 1976. *Teaching styles and pupil progress.* Cambridge, Mass.: Harvard University Press.

Berg, W. M. and Boguslaw, R. 1985. *Communication and community.* Englewood Cliffs, N.J.: Prentice-Hall.

Berger, P. L. 1963. *Invitation to sociology.* Garden City, N.Y.: Doubleday.

Berger, P. L. 1967. *The sacred canopy: Elements of a sociological theory of religion.* Garden City, N.Y.: Doubleday.

Berger, P. L. and Kellner, H. 1970. Marriage and the construction of reality. In *Recent sociology No. 2,* ed. H. P. Dreitzel, pp. 49–72. New York: Macmillan.

Berger, P. L. and Luckmann, T. 1967. *The social construction of reality.* New York: Penguin.

Bernard, J. 1956. *Remarriage.* New York: Dryden.

Bernard, J. 1973. *The sociology of community.* Glenview, Ill.: Scott, Foresman.

Berreman, G. D. 1960. Caste in India and the United States. *American Journal of Sociology* 66: 120–127.

Berry, B. and Tischler, H. L. 1978. *Race and ethnic relations,* 4th ed. Boston: Houghton Mifflin.

Bertrand, A. L. 1972. *Social organization.* Philadelphia: Davis.

Best, F. 1973. Introduction. In *The future of work,* ed. F. Best, pp. 1–4. Englewood Cliffs, N.J.: Prentice-Hall.

Best, P. 1984. Deal on sodium-sulphur battery in the making. *Financial Post,* 19 May.

Bhatnagar, J. 1976. The education of immigrant children. *Canadian Ethnic Studies* 3: 52–70.

Bibby, R. W. 1982a. Religionless Christianity: A profile of religion in the Canadian 80s. Lethbridge, Alta.: Department of Sociology, University of Lethbridge.

Bibby, R. W. 1982b. The precarious mosaic: Intergroup relations in the Canadian 80s. Lethbridge, Alta.: Department of Sociology, University of Lethbridge.

Bibby, R. W. 1982c. The moral mosaic: Sexuality in the Canadian 80s. Lethbridge, Alta.: University of Lethbridge.

Bird, C. 1980. Deviant labeling in school: The pupils' perspective. In *Pupil strategies,* ed. P. Woods, pp. 94–107. London: Croom Helm.

Bjerstedt, A. 1965. The rotation phenomenon in small groups. *Educational and Psychological Interactions* 4: 1–7.

Black, D. J. 1970. Production of crime rates. *American Sociological Review* 35: 733–747.

Black, D. J. and Reiss, A. J. 1970. Police control of juveniles. *American Sociological Review* 35: 63–77.

Black, H. C. 1968. *Black's law dictionary,* 4th ed. St. Paul, Minn.: West.

Blackwell, J. E. 1975. *The black community.* New York: Dodd, Mead.

Blau, P. M. 1964. *Exchange and power in social life.* New York: Wiley.

Blau, P. M. 1968. Social exchange. In *International encyclopedia of the social sciences,* vol. 7, ed. D. L. Sills, pp. 452–457. New York: Crowell, Collier, Macmillan.

Blau, P. M. 1970. A format theory of differentiation in organization. *American Sociological Review* 35: 201–218.

Blau, P. M. and Duncan, O. D. 1967. *The American occupational social structure.* New York: Wiley.

Blau, P. M. and Meyer, M. M. 1971. *Bureaucracy in modern society,* 2nd ed. New York: Random House.

Blau, P. M. and Schoenherr, R. A. 1971. *The structure of organizations.* New York: Basic Books.

Blau, P. M. and Scott, W. R. 1962. *Formal organizations.* San Francisco: Chandler.

Blau, Z. S. 1981. *Aging in a changing society,* 2nd ed. New York: Watts.

Blauner, R. 1964. *Alienation and freedom.* Chicago: University of Chicago Press.

Blishen, B. R. and McRoberts, H. A. 1976. A revised socioeconomic index for occupations in Canada. *Canadian Review of Sociology and Anthropology* 13: 71–79.

Bloch, M. 1961. *Feudal Society.* London: Routledge & Kegan Paul.

Blumberg, R. L. 1978. *Stratification: Socioeconomic and sexual inequality.* Dubuque, Iowa: Brown.

Blumenfeld, H. 1949. On the concentric-circle theory of urban growth. *Land Economics* 25: 209–212.

Blumer, H. 1939. Collective behavior. In *An outline of the principles of sociology,* ed. R. E. Park, pp. 219–280. New York: Barnes & Noble.

Blumer, H. 1964. Collective behaviour. In *A dictionary of the social sciences,* eds. J. Gould and W. L. Kolb, pp. 100–101. New York: Free Press of Glencoe.

Blumer, H. 1968. Fashion. In *International encyclopedia of the social sciences,* vol. 5, ed. D. L. Sills, pp. 341–345. New York: Crowell, Collier, Macmillan.

Blumer, H. 1969. *Symbolic interactionism.* Englewood Cliffs, N.J.: Prentice-Hall.

Blumer, H. 1975. Outline of collective behavior. In *Readings in collective behavior,* ed. R. R. Evans, pp. 22–45. Chicago: Rand McNally.

Blyth, J. A. 1972. *The Canadian social inheritance.* Toronto: Copp Clark.

Bogardus, E. S. 1933. A social distance scale. *Sociology and Social Research* 17: 265–271.

Bogue, D. J. 1969. *Principles of demography.* New York: Wiley.

Bonjean, C. M., Hill, R. J., and McLemore, S. D. 1978. *Sociological measurement: An inventory of scales and indices.* San Francisco: Chandler.

Boocock, S. S. 1978. The social organization of the classroom. In *Annual review of sociology,* vol. 4, eds., R. H. Turner, J. Coleman, and R. C. Fox, pp. 1–28. Palo Alto, Calif.: Annual Reviews Inc.

Booth, A. 1977. Wife's employment and husband's stress: A replication and refutation. *Journal of Marriage and the Family* 39: 645–650.

Borgatta, E. F. 1981. The small groups movement. *American Behavioral Scientist* 24: 607–618.

Bosserman, P. and Gagan, R. 1972. Leisure behavior and voluntary action. In *Voluntary action research: 1972,* eds. D. H. Smith, R. D. Reddy, and B. R. Baldwin, pp. 109–126. Lexington, Mass.: D. C. Heath.

Bottomore, T., ed. 1973. *Karl Marx.* Englewood Cliffs, N.J.: Prentice-Hall.

Boutilier, R. G., Roed, J. C., and Svendsen, A. C. 1980. Crisis in the two social psychologies. *Social Psychology Quarterly* 43: 5–17.

Bowles, S. 1971. Unequal education and the reproduction of the social division of labor. *Review of Radical Political Economics* 3: 1–30.

Bowles, S. and Gintis, H. 1976. *Schooling in capitalist America.* New York: Basic Books.

Boyd, M. 1984. *Canadian attitudes toward women: Thirty years of change.* Ottawa: Labour Canada.

Boyd, M., Featherman, D. L., and Matras, J. 1980. Status attainment of immigrant and immigrant origin categories in the United States, Canada, and Israel. *Comparative social research,* vol. 3, ed. R. F. Tomasson, pp. 199–228. Greenwich, Conn.: JAI Press.

Braverman, H. 1975. *Labor and monopoly capital.* New York: Monthly Review Press.

Breton, R. 1964. Institutional completeness of ethnic communities and the personal relations of immigrants. *American Journal of Sociology* 70: 193–205.

Brettel, C. B. 1980. Ethnicity and entrepreneurs: Portuguese immigrants in a Canadian city. In *People, power, and process,* eds. A. Himmelfarb and C. J. Richardson, pp. 300–307. Toronto: McGraw-Hill Ryerson.

Bromley, D. G. and Shupe, A. D., Jr. 1981. *Strange gods: The great American cult scare.* Boston: Beacon.

Bronfenbrenner, U. 1970. *Two worlds of childhood: U.S. and U.S.S.R.* New York: Russell Sage Foundation.

Brookover, W. B. and Erickson, E. L. 1975. *Sociology of education.* Homewood, Ill.: Dorsey.

Brooks-Gunn, J. and Matthews, W. S. 1977. *He and she: How children develop their sex-role identity.* Englewood Cliffs, N.J.: Prentice-Hall.

Brown, C. 1974. Memoirs of an intermittent madman. In *Decency and deviance,* eds. J. Haas and B. Shaffir, pp. 179–195. Toronto: McClelland & Stewart.

Bryan, G. L. 1973. Introduction. In *Work and nonwork in the year 2001,* ed. M. D. Dunnette, pp. 1–11. Monterey, Calif.: Brooks/Cole.

Burgess, E. W. 1925. The growth of the city. In *The city,* eds. R. E. Park, E. W. Burgess, and R. D. McKenzie, pp. 47–62. Chicago: University of Chicago Press.

Burgess, E. W., Locke, H. J., and Thomas, M. M. 1971. *The Family,* 4th ed. New York: Van Nostrand.

Burke, P. J. 1971. Task and social-emotional leadership role performance. *Sociometry* 34: 22–40.

Burma, J. H. 1963. Interethnic marriage in Los Angeles, 1948–59. *Social Forces* 42: 156–165.

Burnet, J. 1978. The policy of multiculturalism within a bilingual framework: A stock-taking. *Canadian Ethnic Studies* 10: 107–113.

Burrell, G. and Morgan, G. 1979. *Sociological paradigms and organisational analysis.* London: Heinemann.

Bush, D. M. and Simmons, R. G. 1981. Socialization processes over the life course. In *Social psychology,* eds. M. Rosenberg and R. H. Turner, pp. 133–164. New York: Basic Books.

Butler, R. N. 1975. *Why survive? Being old in America.* New York: Harper & Row.

Calgary Herald. 1983 (Saturday, 12 February).

Canadian classification and dictionary of occupations, 4th ed. 1982. Ottawa: Employment and Immigration Canada.

Cameron, D. 1974. Tim Crawford meets the mind police. In *Decency and deviance,* eds. J. Haas and B. Shaffir, pp. 167–178. Toronto: McClelland & Stewart.

Campbell, D. T. 1963. Social attitudes and other acquired behavioral dispositions. In *Psychology: A study of a science,* vol. 6, ed. S. Koch, pp. 94–172. New York: McGraw-Hill.

Campbell, E. Q. 1969. Adolescent socialization. In *Handbook of socialization theory and research,* ed. D. A. Goslin, pp. 821–860. Chicago: Rand McNally.

Cantril, H., Gaudet, H., and Herzog, H. 1940. *Invasion from Mars.* Princeton, N.J.: Princeton University Press.

Caple, R. B. 1978. The sequential stages of group development. *Small Group Behavior* 9: 470–476.

Caporaso, J. A. 1973. Quasi-experimental approaches to social science. In *Quasi-experimental approaches,* eds. J. A. Caporaso and L. L. Roos, Jr., pp. 3–38. Evanston, Ill.: Northwestern University Press.

Cardinal, H. 1969. *The unjust society: The tragedy of Canada's Indians.* Edmonton: Hurtig.

Carisse, C. B. 1975. Family and leisure: A set of contradictions. *The Family Coordinator* 24: 191–197.

Carlton, R. A., Colley, L. A., and MacKinnon, N. J., eds. 1977. *Education, change, and society: A sociology of Canadian education.* Toronto: Gage Educational Publishing.

Carroll, G. R. 1984. Organization ecology. In *Annual Review of Sociology,* vol. 10, eds. R. H. Turner and J. F. Short, Jr., pp. 71–93. Palo Alto, Calif.: Annual Reviews Inc.

Cartwright, D. and Zander, A., eds. 1968. *Group dynamics,* 3rd ed. New York: Harper & Row.

Cavert, S. 1968. *The American churches and the ecumenical movement, 1900–1968.* New York: Association Press.

Champion, D. J. 1975. *The sociology of organizations.* New York: McGraw-Hill.

Chaplin, J. P. 1968. *Dictionary of psychology.* New York: Dell.

Charles, E. 1936. *The twilight of parenthood.* London: Watt's.

Charon, J. M. 1985. *Symbolic interactionism,* 2nd ed. Englewood Cliffs, N.J.: Prentice-Hall.

Chattopadhyay, P. 1974. Political economy: What's in a name? *Monthly Review* 25: 23–33.

Chesler, M. A. and Cave, W. M. 1981. *A sociology of education.* New York: Macmillan.

Chi, N. H. 1976. Class cleavage. In *Political parties in Canada,* eds. C. Winn and J. McMenemy, pp. 89–111. Toronto: McGraw-Hill Ryerson.

Chirot, D. and Hall, T. D. 1982. World-system theory. In *Annual review of sociology,* vol. 8, eds. R. H. Turner and J. F. Short, Jr., pp. 81–106. Palo Alto, Calif.: Annual Reviews Inc.

Chow, E. and Billings, C. 1972. An experimental study of the effects of style of supervision and group size on productivity. *Pacific Sociological Review* 15: 61–82.

Christaller, W. 1933. *Die zentralen Orte in Süddeutschland.* Jena, Germany: Gustav Fisher Verlag.

Citizen (Ottawa). 1982. Wednesday, 15 December.

Clairmont, D. H. and Wien, F. C. 1976. Race relations in Canada. *Sociological Focus* 9: 185–198.

Clark, B. R. 1960. The cooling-out function in higher education. *American Journal of Sociology* 65: 569–576.

Clark, S. D. 1962. *The developing Canadian community.* Toronto: University of Toronto Press.

Clark, S. D. 1966. *The suburban society.* Toronto: University of Toronto Press.

Clatworthy, N. M. 1975. Living together. In *Old family/new family,* ed. N. Glazer-Malbin, pp. 67–89. New York. Van Nostrand.

Clayton, R. R. 1979. *The family, marriage, and social change.* Lexington, Mass.: D. C. Heath.

Clayton, R. R. and Voss, H. L. 1977. Shacking up: Cohabitation in the 1970s. *Journal of Marriage and the Family* 39: 273–283.

Clement, W. 1975. *The Canadian corporate elite.* Toronto: McClelland & Stewart.

Clement, W. 1977. *Continental corporate power.* Toronto: McClelland & Stewart.

Clinard, M. B., ed. 1964. *Anomie and deviant behavior.* New York: Free Press.

Clinard, M. B. and Meier, R. F. 1985. *The sociology of deviant behavior,* 6th ed. New York: Holt, Rinehart & Winston.

Cloward, R. A. 1959. Illegitimate means, anomie, and deviant behavior. *American Sociological Review* 24: 164–176.

Cohen, A. M. and Brawer, F. B. 1982. *The American community college.* San Francisco: Jossey-Bass.

Cohen, E. G. 1972. Sociology and the classroom: Setting the conditions for teacher-student interaction. *Review of Educational Research* 42: 441–452.

Cohen, K. J. et al. 1960. The Carnegie Tech management game. *The Journal of Business* 33: 303–321.

Cohen, L. and Manion, L. 1981. *Perspectives on classrooms and schools.* New York: Holt, Rinehart & Winston.

Cohn, S. F. and Gallagher, J. E. 1984. Gay movements and legal change. *Social Problems* 32: 72–86.

Cole, C. L. 1977. Cohabitation in social context. In *Marriage and alternatives,* eds. R. W. Libby and R. N. Whitehurst, pp. 62–79. Glenview, Ill.: Scott, Foresman.

Cole, R. 1966. Structural-functional theory, the dialectic, and social change. *Sociological Quarterly* 7: 39–58.

Coleman, J. S. 1961. *The adolescent society.* New York: Free Press.

Coleman, J. S. 1974. *Power and the structure of society.* New York: Norton.

Commission of Inquiry into the Nonmedical Use of Drugs. 1972. *Cannabis.* Ottawa: Information Canada.

Committee on Homosexual Offenses and Prostitution. 1957. *Report of the Committee on Homosexual Offenses and Prostitution.* London: Her Majesty's Stationery Office.

Connell, R. W. 1971. *The child's construction of politics.* Melbourne, Aust.: Melbourne University Press.

Conway, J. F. 1978. Populism in the United States, Russia, and Canada: Explaining the roots of Canada's third parties. *Canadian Journal of Political Science* 11: 99–124.

Cooley, C. H. 1894. The theory of transportation. *Publications of the American Economic Association* 9: 312–322.

Cooley, C. H. 1922. *Human nature and the social order,* rev. ed. New York: Schocken.

Copeland, C. L. and McDonald, N. A. 1971. Prostitutes are human beings. In *Deviance, reality, and change,* ed. H. T. Buckner, pp. 261–268. New York: Random House.

Cork, R. M. 1969. *The forgotten children.* Toronto: Addiction Research Foundation.

Coser, L. A. 1956. *The functions of social conflict.* New York: Free Press.

Cottrell, W. F. 1951. Death by dieselization: A case study of reaction to technological change. *American Sociological Review* 16: 358–365.

Covington, M. V. and Berry, R. G. 1976. *Self-worth*

and school learning. New York: Holt, Rinehart & Winston.

Craib, P. W. 1981. Canadian-based research and development: Why so little? In *Work in the Canadian context,* eds. K. L. P. Lundy and B. D. Warme, pp. 7–22. Toronto: Butterworths.

Crosbie, P. V. 1975. *Interaction in small groups.* New York: Macmillan.

Crysdale, S. 1965. *The changing church in Canada: National survey of the United Church in Canadian society.* Toronto: United Church of Canada.

Crysdale, S. 1976. Some problematic aspects of religion in Canada. *Sociological Focus* 9: 137–148.

Crysdale, S. and Beattie, C. 1977. *Sociology Canada,* 2nd ed. Toronto: Butterworths.

Crysdale, S. and Wheatcroft, L., eds. 1976. *Religion in Canadian society.* Toronto: Macmillan of Canada.

Cumming, E. and Henry, W. E. 1961. *Growing old: The process of disengagement.* New York: Basic Books.

Curtis, J. 1971. Voluntary association joining: A cross-national comparative note. *American Sociological Review* 36: 872–880.

D'Arcy, C. and Brockman, J. 1977. Public rejection of the ex-mental patient. *Canadian Review of Sociology and Anthropology* 14: 68–80.

Dahrendorf, R. 1959. *Class and class conflict in industrial society.* Stanford, Calif.: Stanford University Press.

Dallas Times Herald. 1974. Monday, 23 December, p. A-10.

Danziger, K. 1974. The acculturation of Italian immigrant girls in Canada. In *Sociology Canada: Readings,* eds. S. Crysdale and C. Beattie, pp. 134–145. Toronto: Butterworths.

David, F. 1978. *Minority-dominant relations.* Arlington Heights, Ill.: AHM Publishing Co.

Davids, L. 1975. What will they be like, these Canadian parents? In *Marriage, family and society,* ed. S. P. Wakil, pp. 447–452. Toronto: Butterworths.

Davis, F. 1971. *On youth subcultures: The hippie variant.* New York: General Learning Press.

Davis, J. A. 1975. Communism, conformity, cohorts, and categories: American tolerance in 1954 and 1972–73. *American Journal of Sociology* 81: 491–513.

Davis, K. 1948. *Human society.* New York: Macmillan.

Davis, K. 1976. Sexual behavior. In *Contemporary social problems,* 4th ed., eds. R. K. Merton and R. Nisbet, pp. 219–261. New York: Harcourt, Brace & World.

Davis, K. 1977. *Human behavior at work,* 5th ed. New York: McGraw-Hill.

Davis, K. and Moore, W. E. 1945. Some principles of stratification. *American Sociological Review* 10: 242–249.

Davis, K. and Scott, W. G., eds. 1969. *Human relations and organizational behavior,* 3rd ed. New York: McGraw-Hill.

Davis, N. J. 1971. The prostitute. In *Studies in the sociology of sex,* ed. J. M. Henslin, pp. 297–322. New York: Appleton-Century-Crofts.

De Vos, G. A. 1977. The passing of passing: Ethnic pluralism and the new ideal in the American society. In *We the people,* ed. G. J. DiRenzo, pp. 110–154. Westport, Conn.: Greenwood.

deCharms, R. and Muir, M. S. 1978. Motivation: Social approaches. In *Annual review of psychology,* vol. 29, eds. M. R. Rosenzweig and L. W. Porter, pp. 91–113. Palo Alto, Calif.: Annual Reviews Inc.

DeFronzo, J. 1974. Embourgeoisement in Indianapolis. *Social Problems* 21: 269–283.

Delamont, S. 1976. *Interaction in the classroom.* London: Methuen.

Demerath, N. J., III and Roof, W. C. 1976. Religion—Recent strands in research. In *Annual review of sociology,* vol. 2, eds. A. Inkeles, J. Coleman, and N. Smelser, pp. 19–34. Palo Alto, Calif.: Annual Reviews Inc.

Denfield, D. 1974. Dropouts from swinging. *The Family Coordinator* 23: 45–49.

Denscomb, M. 1980. Pupils' strategies and the open classroom. In *Pupil strategies,* ed. P. Woods, pp. 50–73. London: Croom Helm.

Dewey, R. 1960. The rural-urban continuum. *American Journal of Sociology* 66: 60–66.

DiRenzo, G. J. 1977. Theoretical and methodological perspectives on the study of social character. In *We, the people: American character and social change,* ed. G. J. DiRenzo, pp. 285–310. Westport, Conn.: Greenwood.

Dickinson, G. E. 1975. Dating behavior of black and white adolescents before and after desegregation. *Journal of Marriage and the Family* 37: 602–608.

Dictionary of occupational titles, 4th ed. 1977. Washington, D.C.: Department of Labor.

Ditton, J. 1979. *Controlology: Beyond the new criminology.* London: Macmillan.

Dohrenwend, B. P. 1975. Sociocultural and social-psychological factors affecting personal responses to psychological disorder. *Journal of Health and Social Behavior* 16: 365–392.

Douglas, J. D. 1976. *Investigative social research.* Beverly Hills, Calif.: Sage.

Drache, D. 1978. Rediscovering Canadian political economy. In *A practical guide to Canadian political economy,* eds., W. Clement and D. Drache, pp. 1–53. Toronto: Lorimer.

Dreeben, R. 1968. *On what is learned in school.* Reading, Mass.: Addison-Wesley.

Driver, H. E. 1961. *Indians of North America.* Chicago: University of Chicago Press.

Duberman, L. 1975. *Gender and sex in society.* New York: Praeger.

Dubin, R. 1965. Supervision and productivity. In *Leadership and productivity,* eds. R. Dubin, G. C. Homans, F. C. Mann, and D. C. Miller, pp. 1–50. San Francisco: Chandler.

Dubin, R. 1976. Work in modern society. In *Handbook of work, organization, and society,* ed. R. Dubin, pp. 5–36. Chicago: Rand McNally.

Dubin, R. 1979. Central life interests. *Pacific Sociological Review* 22: 405–426.

Dumazedier, J. 1967. *Toward a society of leisure,* trans. S. E. McClure. New York: Free Press.

Dunn, L. M., ed. 1973. *Exceptional children in the schools,* 2nd ed. New York: Holt, Rinehart & Winston.

Durkheim, E. 1933. *The division of labor in society,* trans. G. Simpson. New York: Free Press.

Durkheim, E. 1938. *The rules of sociological method.* New York: Free Press.

Durkheim, E. 1947. *The division of labor in society,* trans. G. Simpson. Glencoe, Ill.: Free Press.

Durkheim, E. 1951. *Suicide.* New York: Free Press.

Durkheim, E. 1954. *Elementary forms of the religious life,* trans. J. W. Swain. New York: Free Press.

Easton, D. 1968. Political science. In *International Encyclopedia of the social sciences,* vol. 12, ed. D. L. Sills, pp. 282–297. New York: Crowell, Collier, Macmillan.

Easton, D. and Dennis, J. 1969. *Children in the political system: Origins of political legitimacy.* New York: McGraw-Hill.

Edmonston, B. 1975. *Population distribution in American cities.* Lexington, Mass.: D. C. Heath.

Edwards, A. M. 1943. *U.S. census of population, 1940: Comparative occupational statistics 1870–1940.* Washington, D.C.: Government Printing Office.

Effrat, M. P., ed. 1974. *The community.* New York: Free Press.

Ehrlich, P. R. 1971. *The population bomb,* rev. ed. New York: Ballantine.

Eichler, M. 1977. Woman as personal dependents. In *Women in Canada,* rev. ed., ed. M. Stephenson, pp. 49–69. Don Mills, Ont.: General Publishing.

Eichler, M. 1983. *Families in Canada today.* Toronto: Gage.

Eisenstadt, S. N. 1968. Social institutions: The concept. In *International encyclopedia of the social sciences,* vol. 14, ed. D. L. Sills, pp. 409–421. New York: Crowell, Collier, Macmillan.

Eisenstadt, S. N. 1971. *Social differentiation and stratification.* Glenview, Ill.: Scott, Foresman.

Eitzen, S. 1976. Sport and social status in American public secondary education. *Review of Sport and Leisure* 1: 139–155.

Ekstedt, J. W. and Griffiths, C. T. 1984. *Corrections in Canada.* Toronto: Butterworths.

Elder, G. H., Jr. 1974. *Children of the Great Depression.* Chicago: University of Chicago Press.

Elkin, F., Halpern, G., and Cooper, A. 1962. Leadership in a student mob. *Canadian Journal of Psychology* 16: 433–449.

Elkin, F. and Handel, G. 1984. *The child and society,* 4th ed. New York: Random House.

Elliott, J. L., ed. 1983. *Two nations, many cultures: Ethnic groups in Canada,* 2nd ed. Scarborough, Ont: Prentice-Hall.

Emerson, R. M. 1976. Social exchange theory. In *Annual review of sociology,* vol. 2, eds. A. Inkeles, J. Coleman, and N. Smelser, pp. 335–362. Palo Alto, Calif.: Annual Reviews Inc.

Emerson, R. M. 1981. Social exchange theory. In *Social psychology,* eds. M. Rosenberg and R. H. Turner, pp. 30–65. New York: Basic Books.

Encyclopedia Britannica. 1982. "Communes," vol. III, p. 44. Chicago: Encyclopedia Britannica Inc.

Erbe, B. M. 1975. Race and socioeconomic segregation. *American Sociological Review* 40: 801–812.

Erikson, E. H. 1963. *Childhood and society,* 2nd ed. New York: Norton.

Erikson, K. T. 1981. Notes on the sociology of deviance. In *Deviance,* 4th ed., eds. E. Rubington and

M. S. Weinberg, pp. 25–28. New York: Macmillan.

Esselstyn, T. C. 1968. Prostitution in the United States. *The Annals of the American Academy of Political and Social Science* 376: 123–135.

Fallding, H. 1978. Mainline Protestantism in Canada and the United States. *Canadian Journal of Sociology* 3: 141–160.

Faulkner, J. E. and DeJong, D. F. 1966. Religiosity in 5-D: An empirical analysis. *Social Forces* 45: 246–254.

Fearn, G. 1973. *Canadian social organization.* Toronto: Holt, Rinehart & Winston.

Featherman, D. L. and Hauser, P. M. 1978. *Opportunity and change.* New York: Academic Press.

Federal Bureau of Investigation. 1980. *Crime in the United States.* Washington, D.C.

Fein, M. 1976. Motivation for work. In *Handbook of work, organization, and society,* ed. R. Dubin, pp. 465–530. Chicago: Rand McNally.

Feltz, D. 1979. Athletics in the status system of female athletes. *Review of Sport and Leisure* 4: 110–118.

Ferracuti, F. and Newman, G. 1974. Assaultive offenses. In *Handbook of criminology,* ed. D. Glaser, pp. 175–208. Chicago: Rand McNally.

Ferree, M. M. 1976. Working-class jobs: Housework and paid work as sources of satisfaction. *Social Problems* 23: 431–441.

Fiedler, F. E. 1972. The effects of leadership training and experience: A contingency model explanation. *Administrative Science Quarterly* 17: 453–470.

Filley, A. C., House, R. J., and Kerr, S. 1976. *Managerial processes and organizational behavior,* 2nd ed. Glenview, Ill.: Scott, Foresman.

Financial Post. 1983. R & D lags. Saturday, 24 December.

Financial Post. 1984. 14 April.

Fine, G. A. 1981. Friends, impression management, and preadolescent behavior. In *The development of children's friendship,* eds. S. R. Asher and J. M. Gottman, pp. 29–52. Cambridge, England: Cambridge University Press.

First Special Report to the U.S. Congress on Alcohol and Health. 1972. Washington, D.C.: Government Printing Office.

Fischer, C. S. 1984. *The urban experience,* 2nd ed. New York: Harcourt Brace Jovanovich.

Fishman, M. 1978. Crime waves as ideology. *Social Problems* 25: 531–543.

Flacks, R. and Turkel, G. 1978. Radical sociology: The emergence of neo-Marxian perspectives in US sociology. In *Annual review of sociology,* vol. 4, eds. R. H. Turner, J. Coleman, and R. C. Fox, pp. 193–238. Palo Alto, Calif.: Annual Reviews Inc.

Foote, N. N. 1951. Identification as the basis for a theory of motivation. *American Sociological Review* 16: 14–21.

Forcese, D. 1980. *The Canadian class structure,* 2nd ed. Toronto: McGraw-Hill Ryerson.

Foster, M. and Murray, K. 1972. *A not so gay world.* Toronto: McClelland & Stewart.

Francis, R. G. 1963. The antimodel as a theoretical concept. *Sociological Quarterly* 4: 197–205.

Frank, A. G. 1969. *Latin America: Underdevelopment or revolution?* New York: Monthly Review Press.

Frank, A. W., III, 1979. Reality construction in interaction. In *Annual review of sociology,* vol. 5, eds., A. Inkeles, J. Coleman, and R. H. Turner, pp. 167–191. Palo Alto, Calif.: Annual Reviews Inc.

Freedman, M. B. and Lozoff, M. 1972. Some statistical background. *Archives of Sexual Behavior* 1: 30–32.

French, J. R. P., Jr. and Raven, B. 1959. *The bases of social power.* Ann Arbor, Mich.: Institute for Social Research.

Friesen, D. 1968. Academic-athletic-popularity syndrome in the Canadian high school society. *Adolescence* 3: 39–52.

Fritz, C. E. and Mathewson, J. H. 1957. *Convergence behavior in disasters.* Washington, D.C.: National Academy of Sciences, National Research Council, Publ. No. 476.

Frizell, A. and Zureik, E. 1974. Voluntary participation: The Canadian perspective. In *Voluntary action research: 1974,* ed. D. H. Smith, pp. 253–276. Lexington, Mass.: D. C. Heath.

Fullan, M. 1970. Industrial technology and worker integration in the organization. *American Sociological Review* 35: 1028–1039.

Fullan, M. 1982. *The meaning of educational changes.* Toronto: Oise Press (Ontario Institute for Studies in Education).

Fuller, F. F. and Brown, O. H. 1975. Becoming a teacher. In *Teacher education. Seventy-fourth yearbook of the National Society for the Study of*

Education, part II, ed. K. Ryan, pp. 25–52. Chicago: University of Chicago Press.

Gagnon, J. H. 1974. Sexual conduct and crime. In *Handbook of criminology,* ed. D. Glaser, pp. 233–272. Chicago: Rand McNally.

Gagnon, J. H. and Simon, W. 1973. *Sexual conduct.* Chicago: Aldine.

Galbraith, J. R. 1977. *Organizational design.* Reading, Mass.: Addison-Wesley.

Gallagher, B. J., III. 1980. *The sociology of mental illness.* Englewood Cliffs, N.J.: Prentice-Hall.

Gallup Poll of Canada. 1982. Toronto: Canadian Institute of Public Opinion, 15 December.

Gamson, W. A. 1961. An experimental test of a theory of coalition formation. *American Sociological Review* 26: 565–573.

Gans, H. J. 1974. *Popular culture and high culture.* New York: Basic Books.

Garfinkle, H. 1967. *Studies in ethnomethodology.* Englewood Cliffs, N.J.: Prentice-Hall.

Garigue, P. 1956. French Canadian kinship and urban life. *American Anthropologist* 58: 1090–1101.

Garigue, P. 1968. The French-Canadian family. In *Canadian society,* 3rd ed., eds. B. R. Blishen et al., pp. 151–166. Toronto: Macmillan of Canada.

Gaskell, J. S. 1975. The sex-role ideology of working-class girls. *Canadian Review of Sociology and Anthropology* 12: 453–461.

Gates, M. 1977. Homemakers into widows and divorcees: Can the law provide economic protection? In *Women into wives: The legal and economic impact of marriage,* eds. J. R. Chapman and M. Gates, pp. 215–232. Beverly Hills, Calif.: Sage.

Gecas, V. 1972. Parental behavior and contextual variations in adolescent self-esteem. *Sociometry* 35: 332–345.

Gecas, V. 1981. Contexts of socialization. In *Social psychology: Sociological perspectives,* eds. M. Rosenberg and R. H. Turner, pp. 165–199. New York: Basic Books.

Gibbs, J. P. and Browning, H. L. 1966. The division of labor, technology, and the organization of production in twelve countries. *American Sociological Review* 31: 81–92.

Giddens, A. 1980. *The class structure of the advanced societies,* 2nd ed. London: Hutchinson.

Giffen, P. J. 1966. The revolving door. *Canadian Review of Sociology and Anthropology* 3: 154–166.

Gilford, R. and Bengston, V. 1979. Measuring marital satisfaction in three generations. *Journal of Marriage and the Family* 41: 387–398.

Ginsberg, E., Ginsburg, S. W., Axelrod, S., and Herma, J. L. 1951. *Occupational choice: An approach to a general theory.* New York: Columbia University Press.

Glaser, B. G. 1978. *Theoretical sensitivity.* Mill Valley, Calif.: Sociology Press.

Glaser, B. G. and Strauss, A. L. 1967. *The discovery of grounded theory.* Chicago: Aldine.

Glick, P. C. 1975. A demographer looks at American families. *Journal of Marriage and the Family* 37: 15–26.

Globe and Mail. 1982. Tuesday, 9 March.

Globe and Mail. 1985. Friday, 29 March.

Glock, C. Y. 1962. On the study of religious commitment. *Research Supplement to Religious Education* 57: 98–110.

Goffman, E. 1959. *The presentation of self in everyday life.* Garden City, N.Y.: Doubleday.

Goffman, E. 1961. *Asylums.* Garden City, N.Y.: Doubleday.

Goffman, E. 1963. *Stigma.* Englewood Cliffs, N.J.: Prentice-Hall.

Goffman, E. 1974. *Frame analysis.* New York: Harper & Row.

Gold, G. L. 1975. *St. Pascal.* Toronto: Holt, Rinehart & Winston of Canada.

Gold, H. 1976. The dynamics of professionalization: The case of urban planning. In *Social change,* eds. G. K. Zollschan and W. Hirsch, pp. 835–863. New York: Wiley.

Gold, R. L. 1964. Fads. In *A dictionary of the social sciences,* eds. J. Gould and W. L. Kolb, pp. 256–257. New York: Free Press of Glencoe.

Goldman, N. 1973. The changing role of women in the armed forces. *American Journal of Sociology* 78: 892–911.

Goldman, S. 1971. School board control of the schools. In *The encyclopedia of education,* vol. 8, ed. L. C. Leighton, pp. 23–28. New York: Macmillan and Free Press.

Goldstein, M. S. 1979. Sociology of mental health and illness. In *Annual review of sociology,* vol. 5, eds. A. Inkeles, J. Coleman, and R. H. Turner, pp. 381–409. Palo Alto, Calif.: Annual Reviews Inc.

Golembiewski, R. T. 1962. *The small group: An analysis of research concepts and operations.* Chicago: University of Chicago Press.

Goode, E. 1969. Multiple drug use among marijuana smokers. *Social Problems* 17: 48–63.

Goode, W. J. 1959. The theoretical importance of love. *American Sociological Review* 24: 38–47.

Goodman, F. D. 1974. Disturbances in the Apostolic church: A trance based upheaval in Yucatan. In *Trance, healing, and hallucination,* eds. F. D. Goodman, J. H. Henny, and E. Pressel, pp. 227–364. New York: Wiley.

Goodwin, D. 1977. *Delivering educational service.* New York: Teachers College Press, Columbia University.

Gordon, A. I. 1964. *Intermarriage: Interfaith, interracial, interethnic.* Boston: Beacon.

Gordon, M. M. 1981. Models of pluralism: The new American dilemma. In *Annals of the American Academy of Political and Social Science,* vol. 454, ed. M. M. Gordon, pp. 178–188.

Gottman, J. 1961. *Megalopolis: The urbanized northeastern seaboard of the United States.* New York: Twentieth Century Fund.

Gould, M. and Kern-Daniels, R. 1977. Toward a sociological theory of gender and sex. *American Sociologist* 12: 182–189.

Gove, W. R. 1973. Sex, marital status, and mortality. *American Journal of Sociology* 79: 45–67.

Gowan, D. S., Ketrow, S. M., Spear, S., and Metzger, J. 1984. Social deviance and occupational status. *Small Group Behavior* 15: 63–86.

Goyder, J. C. and Pineo, P. C. 1979. Social class self-identification. In *Social stratification: Canada,* 2nd ed., eds. J. E. Curtis and W. G. Scott, pp. 431–447. Scarborough, Ont.: Prentice-Hall of Canada.

Grant, G. 1965. *Lament for a nation: The defeat of Canadian nationalism.* Toronto: McClelland & Stewart.

Graubard, A. 1972. The free school movement. *Harvard Educational Review* 42: 351–370.

Grayson, J. P., ed. 1980. *Class, state, ideology, and change: Marxist perspectives on Canada.* Toronto: Holt, Rinehart & Winston of Canada.

Greeley, A. M. 1972. *The denominational society.* Glenview, Ill.: Scott, Foresman.

Greenglass, E. R. 1982. *A world of difference: Gender roles in perspective.* Toronto: Wiley.

Greer, S. 1956. Urbanism reconsidered: A comparative study of local areas in a metropolis. *American Sociological Review* 21: 19–25.

Griffin, J. H. 1977. *Black like me,* 2nd ed. Boston: Houghton Mifflin.

Griffiths, C. T., Klein, J. F., and Verdun-Jones, S. N. 1980. *Criminal justice in Canada.* Toronto: Butterworths.

Gross, E. and Etzioni, A. 1985. *Organizations in society.* Englewood Cliffs, N.J.: Prentice-Hall.

Gross, N., Mason, W. S., and McEachern, A. W. 1958. *Explorations in role analysis: Studies of the school superintendency role.* New York: Wiley.

Gue, L. R. 1977. *An introduction to educational administration in Canada.* Toronto: McGraw-Hill Ryerson.

Guest, A. M. 1969. The applicability of the Burgess zonal hypothesis to urban Canada. *Demography* 6: 271–277.

Guetzkow, H. 1959. A use of simulation in the study of inter-nation relations. *Behavioral Science* 4: 183–191.

Gunderson, M. 1976. Time patterns of male-female wage differentials: Ontario 1946–71. *Industrial Relations* 31: 57–71.

Guppy, N., Mikicich, P. D., and Penakur, R. 1984. Changing patterns of educational inequality in Canada. *Canadian Journal of Sociology* 9: 319–331.

Haas, J. and Shaffir, W. 1977. The professionalization of medical students. *Symbolic Interaction* 1: 71–88.

Haavio-Mannila, E. 1971. Satisfaction with family, work, leisure, and life among men and women. *Human Relations* 24: 585–601.

Hacker, H. M. 1975. Class and race differences in gender roles. In *Gender and sex in society,* ed. L. Duberman, pp. 134–184. New York: Praeger.

Hagan, J. 1977. *The disreputable pleasures.* Toronto: McGraw-Hill Ryerson.

Hagan, J. 1984. *The disreputable pleasures,* 2nd ed. Toronto: McGraw-Hill Ryerson.

Hagen, B. J. H. and Burch, G. 1985. The relationship of group process and group task accomplishment to group member satisfaction. *Small Group Behavior* 16: 211–233.

Hagen, E. E. 1962. *On the theory of social change: How economic growth works.* Homewood, Ill.: Dorsey.

Hagstrom, W. O. and Selvin, H. C. 1965. Two dimensions of cohesiveness in small groups. *Sociometry* 28: 30–43.

Hall, P. M. 1981. Political sociology. In *Current per-*

spectives in social theory, ed. S. G. McNall, pp. 15–20. Greenwich, Conn.: JAI.

Hall, R. H. 1969. *Occupations and the social structure.* Englewood Cliffs, N.J.: Prentice-Hall.

Hall, R. H. 1977. *Organizations,* 2nd ed. Englewood Cliffs, N.J.: Prentice-Hall.

Hameed, S. M. A. 1974. 4 day, 32 hour work week. In *Three or four day work week,* eds. S. M. A. Hameed and G. S. Paul, pp. 5–30. Edmonton: Faculty of Business Administration, University of Alberta.

Handel, G. and Rainwater, L. 1964. Persistence and change in working-class life-style. *Sociology and Social Research* 48: 281–288.

Hare, A. P., ed. 1976. *Handbook of small group research,* 2nd ed. New York: Free Press.

Harris, C. 1985. How we stack up internationally. *Financial Post,* 15 June.

Harris, C. D. and Ullman, E. L. 1945. The nature of cities. *Annals of the American Academy of Political and Social Science* 242: 7–17.

Harris, L. and associates. 1981. *Aging in the eighties: America in transition.* Washington, D.C.: National Council on the Aging.

Harrison, J. D. 1985. *Metis: People between two worlds.* Vancouver, B.C.: Douglas & McIntyre.

Harvey, E. 1968. Technology and the structure of organizations. *American Sociological Review* 33: 247–258.

Haug, M. R. 1977. Measurement in social stratification. In *Annual review of sociology,* vol. 3, eds. A. Inkeles, J. Coleman, and N. Smelser, pp. 51–78. Palo Alto, Calif.: Annual Reviews Inc.

Hauser, P. M. and Duncan, O. D. 1959. Overview and conclusions. In *The study of population,* eds. P. M. Hauser and O. D. Duncan, pp. 1–26. Chicago: University of Chicago Press.

Hauser, P. M., Koffel, J. N., Travis, H. P., and Dickinson, P. J. 1975. Temporal change in occupational mobility: Evidence for men in the United States. *American Sociological Review* 40: 279–297.

Havighurst, R. J. and Levine, D. U. 1979. *Society and education,* 5th ed. Boston: Allyn & Bacon.

Health and Welfare Canada. 1976. *Alcohol problems in Canada* (Technical Report Ser. No. 2). Ottawa.

Heap, J. L., ed. 1974. *Everybody's Canada: The vertical mosaic reviewed and reexamined.* Toronto: Burns & MacEachern.

Heaton, T. B. and Fuguitt, G. V. 1980. Dimensions of population redistribution in the U.S. since 1950. *Social Science Quarterly* 61: 508–523.

Heilbrun, A. B., Jr. 1981. *Human sex-role behavior.* New York: Pergamon.

Heilman, S. C. 1981. Constructing orthodoxy. In *In Gods we trust: New patterns of religious pluralism in America,* eds. T. Robbins and D. Anthony, pp. 141–157. New Brunswick, N.J.: Transaction Books.

Hendricks, J. and Hendricks, C. D. 1981. *Aging in mass society.* Cambridge, Mass.: Winthrop.

Henshel, A. M. 1973. Swinging: A study of decision making in marriage. *American Journal of Sociology* 78: 885–891.

Herold, E. S. 1984. *Sexual behaviour of Canadian young people.* Markham, Ont.: Fitzhenry & Whiteside.

Herrmann, G. M. and Soiffer, S. M. 1984. For fun and profit: An analysis of the American garage sale. *Urban Life* 12: 397–422.

Hertzler, J. O. 1961. *American social institutions.* Boston: Allyn & Bacon.

Hickson, D. J., McMillan, C. J., Azumi, K., and Horvath, D., 1979. Grounds for comparative organization theory. In *Organizations alike and unlike: International and inter-institutional studies in the sociology of organizations,* eds. C. J. Lammers and D. J. Hickson, pp. 25–41. London: Routledge & Kegan Paul.

Hickson, D. J., Pugh, D. S., and Pheysey, D. C., 1969. Operations technology and organization structure: An empirical reappraisal. *Administrative Science Quarterly* 14: 378–397.

Higgins, D. 1976. The political Americanization of Canadian children. In *Foundations of political culture: Political socialization in Canada,* eds. J. H. Pammett and M. S. Whittington, pp. 251–264. Toronto: Macmillan of Canada.

Hill, R. 1955. Impediments to freedom of mate selection in Puerto Rico. *Journal of Home Economics* 47: 189–197.

Hill, R. J. 1981. Attitudes and behavior. In *Social psychology,* eds. M. Rosenberg and R. H. Turner, pp. 347–377. New York: Basic Books.

Hiller, E. T. 1941. The community as a social group. *American Sociological Review* 6: 189–202.

Hiller, H. H. 1978. Continentalism and the third force in religion. *Canadian Journal of Sociology* 3: 183–208.

Hiller, H. H. 1982. *Society and change: S. D. Clark*

and the development of Canadian sociology. Toronto: University of Toronto Press.

Hillery, G. A., Jr. 1955. Definitions of community: Areas of agreement. *Rural Sociology* 20: 111–123.

Himmelfarb, H. 1975. Measuring religious commitment. *Social Forces* 53: 606–617.

Hinkle, R. C., Jr. and Hinkle, G. J. 1954. *The development of modern sociology.* New York: Random House.

Hirschi, T. 1969. *Causes of delinquency.* Berkeley, Calif.: University of California Press.

Hitchman, G. S. 1976. The female graduate student. In *Sex structure,* 2nd ed., ed. A. M. Ambert, pp. 137–144. Don Mills, Ont.: Longman of Canada.

Hobart, C. W. 1975. Reactions to premarital intercourse. In *Marriage, family, and society,* ed. S. P. Wakil, pp. 29–42. Toronto: Butterworths.

Hobart, C. W. 1980. Courtship process: Premarital sex. In *Courtship, marriage, and the family,* ed. G. N. Ramu, pp. 37–58. Toronto: Gage.

Hochschild, A. R. 1975. Disengagement theory: A critique and proposal. *American Sociological Review* 40: 553–569.

Hodge, R. W., Siegel, P. M., and Rossi, P. H. 1964. Occupational prestige in the United States, 1925–63. *American Journal of Sociology* 70: 286–302.

Hoffman, L. W. and Hoffman, M. L. 1973. The value of children to parents. In *Psychological perspectives on population,* ed. J. T. Fawcett, pp. 46–61. New York: Basic Books.

Hollander, E. P. 1964. *Leaders, groups, and influence.* New York: Oxford University Press.

Hollander, E. P. and Julian, J. W. 1970. Studies in leader legitimacy, influence, and innovation. In *Advances in experimental social psychology,* vol. 5, ed. L. Berkowitz, pp. 34–70. New York: Academic Press.

Hollingshead, A. B. 1957. Two-factor index of social position. New Haven, Conn.: Yale University, mimeo.

Holz, J. R. and Wright, C. R. 1979. Sociology of mass communication. In *Annual review of sociology,* Vol. 5, eds. A. Inkeles, J. Coleman, and R. H. Turner, pp. 193–217. Palo Alto, Calif.: Annual Reviews Inc.

Homans, G. C. 1950. *The human group.* New York: Harcourt, Brace.

Homans, G. C. 1958. Social behavior as exchange. *American Journal of Sociology* 62: 597–606.

Homans, G. C. 1974. *Social behavior: Its elementary forms,* 2nd ed. New York: Harcourt, Brace, Jovanovich.

Horner, M. S. 1970. Femininity and successful achievement: A basic inconsistency. In *Feminine personality and conflict,* eds. J. M. Bardwick, E. Douvan, M. S. Horner, and D. Guterman, pp. 45–76. Belmont, Calif.: Brooks/Cole.

Horowitz, I. L. 1973. The hemispheric connection: A critique and corrective to the entrepreneurial thesis of development with special emphasis on the Canadian case. *Queen's Quarterly* 80: 327–359.

House of Commons. 1984. *Report of the special committee on the participation of visible minorities in Canadian society.* Ottawa: Canadian Government Publication Centre.

House, J. D. 1981. From farm boy to oil man: The human side of dependent development in Alberta. In *Work in the Canadian context,* eds. K. L. P. Lundy and B. D. Warme, pp. 43–58. Toronto: Butterworths.

Hoyt, H. 1939. *The structure and growth of residential neighborhoods in American cities.* Washington, D.C.: Federal Housing Administration.

Hudson, R. B. and Binstock, R. H. 1976. Political systems and aging. In *Handbook of aging and the social sciences,* eds. R. H. Binstock and E. Shanas, pp. 369–400. New York: Van Nostrand Reinhold.

Hughes, C. C. 1965. Under four flags: Recent culture change among the Eskimos. *Current Anthropology* 6: 3–54.

Humphreys, L. 1972. *Out of the closets.* Englewood Cliffs, N.J.: Prentice-Hall.

Hunter, A. A. 1981. *Class tells: On social inequality in Canada.* Toronto: Butterworths.

Hunter, A. A. and Denton, M. A. 1984. Do female candidates "lose votes"? *Canadian Review of Sociology and Anthropology* 21: 395–406.

Illich, I. 1971. *Deschooling society.* New York: Harper & Row.

Information Canada. 1970. *Report of the Royal Commission on the Status of Women.* Ottawa.

Information Canada. 1971. *Concentration in the manufacturing industries of Canada.* Ottawa.

Information Canada. 1974. *The immigration program.* Ottawa.

Inkeles, A. 1968. Society, social structure, and child socialization. In *Socialization and society,* ed. J. A. Clausen, pp. 73–129. Boston: Little, Brown.

Institute of Public Affairs. 1970. Socio-economic conditions of Negroes in Halifax. In *Poverty and so-*

cial policy in Canada, ed. W. E. Mann, pp. 336–343. Toronto: Copp Clark.

Irving, H. 1972. *The family myth: A study of the relationships between married couples and their parents.* Toronto: Copp Clark.

Isawij, W. W. 1978. Olga in wonderland: Ethnicity in a technological society. In *The Canadian ethnic mosaic,* ed. L. Driedger, pp. 29–39. Toronto: McClelland & Stewart.

Ishwaran, K., ed. 1976. *The Canadian family,* rev. ed. Toronto: Holt, Rinehart & Winston.

Jackman, M. R. and Jackman, R. W. 1983. *Class awareness in the United States.* Berkeley, Calif.: University of California Press.

Jackson, J. A., ed. 1968. *Social stratification.* London: Cambridge University Press.

Jackson, J. K. 1954. The adjustment of the family to the crisis of alcoholism. *Quarterly Journal of Studies on Alcohol* 15: 562–586.

Jackson, J. N. 1973. *The Canadian city.* Toronto: McGraw-Hill Ryerson.

James, J. L. 1974. *American political parties in transition.* New York: Harper & Row.

Janovitz, M. 1968. *Social control of escalated riots.* Chicago: University of Chicago Press.

Jayewardene, C. H. S. 1980. The nature of homicide: Canada 1961–1971. In *Crime in Canadian society,* 2nd ed., eds. R. A. Silverman and J. J. Teevan, Jr., pp. 267–289. Toronto: Butterworths.

Jenkins, C. and Sherman, B. 1979. *The collapse of work.* London: Eyre Methuen.

Jepson, H. 1976. The superintendent: The man in the middle. *ATA* (Alberta Teachers' Association) *Magazine* 56: 34–36.

Jerome, W. C. and Phillips, J. C. 1971. The relationship between academic achievement and interscholastic participation: A comparison of Canadian and American high schools. *Journal of the Canadian Association for Health, Physical Education, and Recreation* 37: 18–21.

Johnson, E. B., Goodchilds, J. D., and Raven, B. H. 1972. Male and female differences in response to status congruency-incongruency and status ambiguity in a restricted communication network. *Proceedings of the 80th Annual Convention of the American Psychological Association* 7 (Pt. 1): 215–216.

Johnson, L. A. 1972. The development of class in Canada in the twentieth century. In *Capitalism and the national question in Canada,* ed. G. Teeple, pp. 141–184. Toronto: University of Toronto Press.

Johnson, W. 1971. The gay world. In *Social deviance in Canada,* ed. W. E. Mann, pp. 380–389. Toronto: Copp Clark.

Jones, W. H., Chernovetz, M. E., and Hansson, R. O. 1978. The enigma of androgyny: Differential implications for males and females. *Journal of Consulting and Clinical Psychology* 46: 298–313.

Kalbach, W. E. and McVey, W. W. 1979. *The demographic bases of Canadian society,* 2nd ed. Toronto: McGraw-Hill Ryerson.

Kallen, E. and Kelner, M. 1976. Parents and peers: Who influences student values? In *The Canadian Family,* rev. ed., ed. K. Ishwaran, pp. 213–226. Toronto: Holt, Rinehart & Winston.

Kandel, D. B. and Lesser, G. S. 1972. *Youth in two worlds.* San Francisco: Jossey-Bass.

Kando, T. M. 1980. *Leisure and popular culture in transition,* 2nd ed. St. Louis: Mosby.

Kando, T. M. and Summers, W. C. 1971. The impact of work on leisure. *Pacific Sociological Review* 14: 310–327.

Kanter, R. M. 1968. Commitment and social organization. *American Sociological Review* 33: 499–517.

Kantner, J. F. and Zelnick. M. 1972. Sexual experience of young unmarried women in the United States. *Family Planning Perspectives* 4: 9–18.

Kaplan, A. G. and Bean, J. P., eds. 1976. *Beyond sex-role stereotypes.* Boston: Little, Brown.

Kaplan, M. 1960. *Leisure in America.* New York: Wiley.

Kaplan, M. 1975. *Leisure.* New York: Wiley.

Katz, A. M. and Hill, R. 1958. Residential propinquity and marital selection: A review of theory, method, and fact. *Marriage and Family Living* 20: 27–35.

Katz, E. and Lazarsfeld, P. F. 1955. *Personal influence.* Glencoe, Ill.: Free Press of Glencoe.

Katz, R. L. 1963. *Empathy: Its nature and uses.* New York: Free Press.

Kelly, J. R. 1974. Socialization toward leisure. *Journal of Leisure Research* 6: 181–193.

Kelly, J. R. 1982. *Leisure.* Englewood Cliffs, N.J.: Prentice-Hall.

Kennedy, D. B. and Kerber, A. 1973. *Resocialization: An American experiment.* New York: Behavioral Publications.

Kephart, W. M. 1976. *Extraordinary groups: The so-*

ciology of unconventional life-styles. New York: St. Martin's.

Kerckhoff, A. C. 1970. A theory of hysterical contagion. In *Human nature and collective behavior,* ed. T. Shibutani, pp. 81–93. Englewood Cliffs, N.J.: Prentice-Hall.

Kerckhoff, A. C. and Davis, K. E. 1972. Value consensus and need complementarity in mate selection. *American Sociological Review* 27: 295–303.

Kimball, M. M. 1977. Women and success: A basic conflict? In *Women in Canada,* rev. ed., ed. M. Stephenson, pp. 73–89. Don Mills, Ont.: General Publishing.

Kimberley, J. 1976. Organizational size and the structuralist perspective: A review, critique, and proposal. *Administrative Science Quarterly* 21: 571–597.

Kinch, J. W. 1963. A formalized theory of the self-concept. *American Journal of Sociology,* 68: 481–486.

Kinsey, A. C., Pomeroy, W. B., and Martin, C. E. 1948. *Sexual behavior in the human male.* Philadelphia: Saunders.

Kinsey, A. C., Pomeroy, W. B., Martin, C. E., and Gebhard, P. H. 1953. *Sexual behavior in the human female.* Philadelphia: Saunders.

Kirk, S. A. and Therrien, M. E. 1975. Community mental health myths and the fate of former hospitalized patients. *Psychiatry* 38: 209–217.

Kirkpatrick, C. 1963. *The family,* 2nd ed. New York: Ronald Press.

Klapp, O. E. 1969. *Collective search for identity.* New York: Holt, Rinehart & Winston.

Klapp, O. E. 1972. *Currents of unrest.* New York: Holt, Rinehart & Winston.

Kohn, M. L. 1959a. Social class and the exercise of parental authority. *American Sociological Review* 24: 352–366.

Kohn, M. L. 1959b. Social class and parental values. *American Journal of Sociology* 64: 337–351.

Kohn, M. L. 1963. Social class and parent-child relationships. *American Journal of Sociology* 68: 471–480.

Kohn, M. L. and Schooler, C. 1982. Job conditions and personality: A longitudinal assessment of their reciprocal effects. *American Journal of Sociology* 87: 1257–1286.

Komorita, S. S. and Chertkoff, J. M. 1973. A bargaining theory of coalition formation. *Psychological Review* 80: 149–162.

König, R. 1974. Sociological introduction. In *International encyclopedia of comparative law,* vol. IV, ed. A. Chloros, pp. 20–73. Tübingen, Germany: J. C. B. Mohr (Paul Siebeck).

Kourvetaris, G. A. and Dobratz, B. A. 1980. The state and development of political sociology. In *Political sociology,* eds. G. A. Kourvetaris and B. A. Dobratz, pp. 3–66. New Brunswick, N.J.: Transaction Books.

Krause, E. A. 1971. *The sociology of occupations.* Boston: Little, Brown.

Kreps, J. and Spengler, J. 1973. Future options for more free time. In *The future of work,* ed. F. Best, pp. 87–92. Englewood Cliffs, N.J.: Prentice-Hall.

Kresl, P. K. 1981. Canadian and American approaches to foreign direct investment and international trade policies. In *Comparative social research,* vol. 4, ed. R. F. Tomasson, pp. 135–158. Greenwich, Conn.: JAI Press.

Kroeber, A. L. and Kluckhohn, C. 1952. Culture: A critical review of concepts and definitions. *Papers of the Peabody Museum of American Archaeology and Ethnology,* vol. 47, no. 1.

Kubat, D. and Thornton, D. 1974. *A statistical profile of Canadian society.* Toronto: McGraw-Hill Ryerson.

Kuty, O. 1979. Kidney units. In *Organizations alike, and unlike: International and inter-institutional studies in the sociology of organizations,* eds. C. J. Lammers and D. J. Hickson, pp. 304–322. London: Routledge & Kegan Paul.

Kuvlesky, W. P. and Beals, R. C. 1972. A clarification of the concept "occupational choice." In *Sociological perspectives on occupations,* ed. R. M. Pavalko, pp. 105–116. Itasca, Ill.: Peacock.

Kuzel, P. and Krishnan, P. 1973. Changing patterns of remarriage in Canada, 1961–1966. *Journal of Comparative Family Studies* 4: 215–224.

Lancourt, J. E. 1979. *Confront or concede: The Alinsky citizen-action organizations.* Lexington, Mass.: D. C. Heath.

Landes, R. G. 1979. Political socialization among youth: A comparative study of English-Canadian and American school children. In *Childhood and adolescence in Canada,* ed. K. Ishwaran, pp. 366–386. Toronto: McGraw-Hill Ryerson.

Lang, G. E. 1981. Riotous outbursts in sport events. In *Handbook of social science of sport,* eds. G. R. F. Lüschen and G. H. Sage, pp. 415–436. Champaign, Ill.: Stipes.

Lang, K. and Lang, G. E. 1961. *Collective dynamics.* New York: Crowell.

LaPiere, R. T. 1934. Attitudes versus actions. *Social Forces* 13: 230–237.

LaPiere, R. T. 1946. *Sociology.* New York: McGraw-Hill.

LaPiere, R. T. 1954. *A theory of social control.* New York: McGraw-Hill.

Larson, L. E. 1971. The family and leisure in post-industrial society. In *Work and leisure in Canada,* eds. S. M. A. Hameed and D. Cullen, pp. 132–142. Edmonton: Faculty of Business Administration, University of Alberta.

Larson, L. E., ed. 1976. *The Canadian family in comparative perspective.* Scarborough, Ont.: Prentice-Hall of Canada.

Lauer, R. H. 1982. *Perspectives on social change,* 3rd ed. Boston: Allyn & Bacon.

Lauer, R. H. and Boardman, L. 1971. Role-taking: Theory, typology, and propositions. *Sociology and Social Research* 55: 137–148.

Lauer, R. H. and Handel, W. H. 1977. *Social psychology.* Boston: Houghton Mifflin.

Lauer, R. H. and Handel, W. H. 1983. *Social Psychology,* 2nd ed. Englewood Cliffs, N.J.: Prentice-Hall.

Lawrence, P. R. and Lorsch, J. W. 1967. *Organization and environment.* Boston: Graduate School of Business Administration, Harvard University.

Le Bon, G. 1960. *The crowd.* New York: Viking (originally published in 1895).

Lee, E. S. 1966. A theory of migration. *Demography* 1: 47–57.

Lefkowitz, B. 1979. *Breaktime.* New York: Penguin.

Leiter, K. 1980. *A primer on ethnomethodology.* New York: Oxford University Press.

Lemert, E. M. 1951. *Social pathology.* New York: McGraw-Hill.

Lemert, E. M. 1972. *Human deviance, social problems, and social control,* 2nd ed. Englewood Cliffs, N.J.: Prentice-Hall.

Lemert, E. M. 1982. What is deviance? In *The sociology of deviance,* eds. M. M. Rosenberg, R. A. Stebbins, and A. Turowetz, pp. 233–257. New York: St. Martin's.

Lemon, B. W., Bengston, V. L., and Peterson, J. A. 1972. An exploration of the activity theory of aging. *Journal of Gerontology* 27: 511–523.

Lenski, G. E. 1966. *Power and privilege: A theory of social stratification.* New York: McGraw-Hill.

Leslie, G. R. and Korman, S. K. 1985. *The family in social context,* 6th ed. New York: Oxford University Press.

Letkemann, P. 1973. *Crime as work.* Englewood Cliffs, N.J.: Prentice-Hall.

Levenger, G., Senn, D., and Jorgensen, B. 1970. Progress toward permanence in courtship: A test of the Kerckhoff-Davis hypothesis. *Sociometry* 33: 427–433.

Lever, J. 1976. Sex differences in the games children play. *Social Problems* 23: 478–487.

Levy, J. 1980. Leisure and the family: Towards some conceptual clarity. *Leisure Information Newsletter* 6: 6–7.

Levy, M. J., Jr. 1952. *The structure of society.* Princeton, N.J.: Princeton University Press.

Lewis, G. H. 1978. The sociology of popular culture. *Current Sociology* 26 (No. 3): 1–60.

Lewis, M. M. 1972. Culture and gender roles: There's no unisex in the nursery. *Psychology Today* 6: 54–57.

Lin, N. and Zaltman, G. 1973. Dimensions of innovations. In *Processes and phenomena of social change,* ed. G. Zaltman, pp 93–116. New York: Wiley.

Linden, R. and Fillmore, C. 1981. A comparative study of delinquency involvement. *Canadian Review of Sociology and Anthropology* 18: 343–361.

Linsky, A. S. 1970. The changing public views of alcoholism. *Quarterly Journal of Studies on Alcohol* 31: 692–704.

Lipman-Blumen, J. and Tickamyer, A. R. 1975. Sex roles in transition: A ten-year perspective. In *Annual Review of Sociology,* vol. 1, eds. A. Inkeles, J. Coleman, and N. Smelser, pp. 297–338. Palo Alto, Calif.: Annual Reviews Inc.

Lipset, S. M. 1964. Canada and the United States: A comparative view. *Canadian Review of Sociology and Anthropology* 1: 173–185.

Lipset, S. M. 1976. Radicalism in North America: A comparative view of the party systems in Canada and the United States. *Transactions of the Royal Society of Canada* (Series IV) 14: 19–55.

Lipset, S. M. 1979. *The first new nation.* New York: Norton.

Lipset, S. M., Trow, M. A., and Coleman, J. S. 1956. *Union democracy.* Glencoe, Ill.: Free Press.

Listiak, A. 1974, "Legitimate deviance" and social class: Bar behaviour during Grey Cup Week. *Sociological Focus* 7: 13–44.

Litwak, E. 1960. Geographic mobility and extended family cohesion. *American Sociological Review* 25: 385–394.

Livingood, J. M., ed. 1972. *National Institute of Mental Health Task Force on Homosexuality: Final report and background papers.* Rockville: Md.: National Institute of Mental Health.

Lo, C. Y. H. 1982. Countermovements and conservative movements in the contemporary U.S. In *Annual review of sociology,* vol. 8, eds. R. H. Turner and J. F. Short, Jr., pp. 107–134. Palo Alto, Calif.: Annual Reviews Inc.

Lofland, J. 1977. *Doomsday cult,* enlarged ed. Englewood Cliffs, N.J.: Prentice-Hall.

Lofland, J. F. 1981. Collective behavior: The elementary forms. In *Social psychology,* eds. M. Rosenberg and R. H. Turner, pp. 411–446. New York: Basic Books.

Lofland, L. H. 1973. *A world of strangers.* New York: Basic Books.

Lopata, H. Z. 1971. *Occupation housewife.* New York: Oxford University Press.

Lopreato, J. and Alston, L. 1970. Ideal types and the idealization strategy. *American Sociological Review* 35: 88–96.

Lortie, D. C. 1975. *Schoolteacher.* Chicago: University of Chicago Press.

Lowenthal, M. F., Thurnher, M., and Chiriboga, D. 1975. *Four stages of life.* San Francisco: Jossey-Bass.

Lowrie, S. 1956. Factors involved in the frequency of dating. *Marriage and Family Living* 18: 46–51.

Lucas, R. A. 1968. Social implications of the immediacy of death. *Canadian Review of Sociology and Anthropology* 5: 1–16.

Lucas, R. A. 1971. *Minetown, milltown, railtown.* Toronto: University of Toronto Press.

Luckmann, T. 1967. *The invisible religion.* New York: Macmillan.

Lupri, E. In press. *Reflections on marriage and the family in Canada.* Toronto: Holt, Rinehart & Winston of Canada.

Lupri, E. and Frideres, J. 1981. The quality of marriage and the passage of time: Marital satisfaction over the family life cycle. *Canadian Journal of Sociology* 6: 283–305.

Luxton, M. 1981. Taking on the double day. *Atlantis* 7: 12–22.

Lyman, S. M. and Scott, M. B. 1970. Territoriality. In *A sociology of the absurd,* eds. S. M. Lyman and M. B. Scott, pp. 89–110. New York: Appleton-Century-Crofts.

Lyon, D. L. 1985. Rethinking secularization. *Review of Religious Research* 26: 228–243.

Lyon, L., Felice, L. G., Perryman, M. R., and Parker, E. S. 1981. Community power and population increase: An empirical test of the growth machine model. *American Journal of Sociology* 86: 1387–1400.

Mabry, E. A. and Barnes, R. E. 1980. *The dynamics of small group communication.* Englewood Cliffs, N.J.: Prentice-Hall.

MacIver, R. M. 1964. *Social causation,* rev. ed. New York: Harper & Row.

MacKinnon, N. J. and Anisef, P. 1979. Self-assessment in the early educational attainment process. *Canadian Review of Sociology and Anthropology* 16: 305–319.

Maccoby, E. M. and Jacklin, C. N. 1974. *The psychology of sex differences.* Stanford, Calif.: Stanford University Press.

Mackie, M. M. 1973. Arriving at "truth" by definition: The case of stereotype inaccuracy. *Social Problems* 20: 431–447.

Mackie, M. M. 1977. On congenial truths: A perspective on women's studies. *Canadian Review of Sociology and Anthropology.* 14: 117–128.

Maddi, S. R. 1981. *Personality theories,* 4th ed. Homewood, Ill.: Dorsey.

Mahon, R. 1984. *The politics of industrial restructuring: Canadian textiles.* Toronto: University of Toronto Press.

Maines, D. R. 1977. Social organization and social structure in symbolic interactionist thought. In *Annual review of sociology,* vol. 3, pp. 235–260. Palo Alto, Calif.: Annual Reviews Inc.

Malthus, T. R. 1798. *An essay on the principle of population as it affects the future improvement of society.* New York: St. Martin's (reissued in 1966).

Mann, W. E. 1968. Sex behavior on campus. In *Canada: A sociological profile,* ed. W. E. Mann, pp. 115–126. Toronto: Copp Clark.

Marchak, M. P. 1977. The Canadian labour farce: Jobs for women. In *Women in Canada,* rev. ed., ed. M. Stephenson, pp. 148–159. Don Mills, Ont.: General Publishing.

Marchak, P. 1979. *In whose interests: An essay on multinational corporations in a Canadian context.* Toronto: McClelland & Stewart.

Marshall, V. W., ed., 1980. *Aging in Canada.* Don Mills, Ont.: Fitzhenry & Whiteside.

Martin, L. J. 1978. Public opinion. In *Social control for the 1980s,* ed. J. S. Roucek, pp. 286–296. Westport, Conn.: Greenwood.

Martin, W. B. W. 1970. Disparities in urban schools. In *The poor at school in Canada,* pp. 1–23. Ottawa: Canadian Teachers' Federation.

Martin, W. B. W. 1976. *The negotiated order of the school.* Toronto: Macmillan of Canada.

Martin, W. B. W. and Macdonell, A. J. 1982. *Canadian Education,* 2nd ed. Scarborough, Ont.: Prentice-Hall Canada.

Martindale, D. 1962. *Social life and cultural change.* New York: Van Nostrand.

Martindale, D. 1963. *Community, character, and civilization.* New York: Free Press.

Martindale, D. 1976. Introduction. In *Social Change,* eds. G. K. Zollschan and W. Hirsch, pp. ix–xxv. Cambridge, Mass.: Schenkman.

Martindale, D. 1978. The theory of social control. In *Social control for the 1980s,* ed. J. S. Roucek, pp. 46–58. Westport, Conn.: Greenwood.

Martindale, D. 1981. *The nature and types of sociological theory,* 2nd ed. Boston: Houghton Mifflin.

Martinson, R. 1974. What works? Questions and answers about prison reform. *Public Interest* 35: 22–54.

Marwell, G. 1975. Why ascription? Parts of a more or less formal theory of the functions and dysfunctions of sex roles. *American Sociological Review* 40: 445–455.

Marx, G. T. and Wood, J. L. 1975. Strands of theory and research in collective behavior. In *Annual Review of Sociology,* vol. 1, eds. A. Inkeles, J. Coleman, and N. Smelser, pp. 363–428. Palo Alto, Calif.: Annual Reviews Inc.

Marx, K. 1956. *Selected writings in sociology and social philosophy,* trans. T. B. Bottomore. New York: McGraw-Hill.

Matras, J. 1977. *Introduction to population.* Englewood Cliffs, N.J.: Prentice-Hall.

Matras, J. 1984. *Social inequality, stratification and mobility,* 2nd ed. Englewood Cliffs, N.J.: Prentice-Hall.

Matthews, B. 1983. Talk is not cheap. *Financial Post Magazine,* (1 September): 27–29.

Matza, D. 1964. *Delinquency and drift.* New York: Wiley.

Maxwell, M. P. and Maxwell, J. D. 1984. Women and the elite: Educational and occupational aspirations of private school females 1966/76. *Canadian Review of Sociology and Anthropology* 21: 371–394.

Mayhew, L. H. 1968. Society. In *International encyclopedia of the social sciences,* vol. 14, ed. D. L. Sills, pp. 577–586. New York: Crowell, Collier, Macmillan.

Maykovich, M. K. 1972. Reciprocity in racial stereotypes: White, black, and yellow. *American Journal of Sociology* 77: 876–897.

McCall, G. J. and Simmons, J. L. 1978. *Identities and interactions,* rev. ed. New York: Free Press.

McDiarmid, G. and Pratt, D. 1971. *Teaching prejudice.* Toronto: Ontario Institute for Studies in Education.

McGinnis, R. 1958. Campus values in mate selection: A repeat study. *Social Forces* 36: 368–373.

McGuire, J. W. 1963. *Business and society.* New York: McGraw-Hill.

McGuire, K. D. and Weisz, J. R. 1982. Social cognition and behavior correlates of preadolescent chumship. *Child Development* 82: 1478–1484.

McGuire, M. B. 1981. *Religion.* Belmont, Calif.: Wadsworth.

McHugh, P. 1968. *Defining the situation.* Indianapolis, Ind.: Bobbs-Merrill.

McIntyre, J. 1966. The structural-functional approach to family study. In *Emerging conceptual frameworks in family analysis,* eds. F. I. Nyes and F. M. Berardo, pp. 52–77. New York: Macmillan.

McKendry, T. and Wright, J. R. 1965. Home and school association activities in the Edmonton area. *Alberta Journal of Educational Research* 11: 90–95.

McKenzie, R. D. 1968. The scope of human ecology. In *Roderick D. McKenzie On human ecology,* ed. A. H. Hawley, pp. 19–32. Chicago: University of Chicago Press.

McLeish, J. 1969. *The theory of social change.* London: Routledge & Kegan Paul.

McMenemy, J. 1976. Parliamentary parties. In *Political parties in Canada,* eds. C. Winn and J. McMenemy, pp. 10–28. Toronto: McGraw-Hill Ryerson.

McMenemy, J. and Winn, C. 1976. Party personnel—Elites and activists. In *Political parties in Canada,* eds. C. Winn and J. McMenemy, pp. 152–166. Toronto: McGraw-Hill Ryerson.

McPherson, G. H. 1972. *Small town teacher.* Cambridge, Mass.: Harvard University Press.

McRoberts, H. A. 1982. Social mobility in Canada. In *Social issues: Sociological views of Canada,* eds. D. Forcese and S. Richer, pp. 375–394. Scarborough, Ont.: Prentice-Hall of Canada.

McRoberts, H. A. and Selbee, K. 1981. Trends in occupational mobility: Canada and the U.S. *American Sociological Review* 46: 406–421.

McRoberts, K. and Posgate, D. 1980. *Quebec: Social change and political crisis,* rev. ed. Toronto: McClelland & Stewart.

Mead, G. H. 1934. *Mind, self, and society.* Chicago: University of Chicago Press.

Mead, M. 1966. Marriage in two steps. *Redbook* (July): 48

Meadows, D. H., Meadows, D. L., Randers, J., and Behrens, W. W., III. 1972. *The limits of growth: A report for the Club of Rome's project on the predicament of mankind.* New York: Universe Books.

Meadows, P. 1971. *The many faces of change.* Cambridge, Mass.: Schenkman.

Mehan, H. 1978. Structuring school structure. *Harvard Educational Review* 48: 32–64.

Meier, G. S. 1979. *Job sharing.* Kalamazoo, Mich.: Upjohn Institute for Employment Research.

Meier, R.F. 1982. Perspectives on the concept of social control. In *Annual review of sociology,* vol. 8, eds. R. H. Turner and J. F. Short, Jr., pp. 34–55. Palo Alto, Calif.: Annual Reviews Inc.

Meighan, R. 1977. The pupil as client: The learner's experience of schooling. *Education Review* 29: 123–135.

Meighan, R. 1981. *A sociology of educating.* London: Holt, Rinehart & Winston.

Meissner, M. 1971. The long arm of the job. *Industrial Relations* 10: 239–260.

Meltzer, I. 1974. Longer daily hours: For how long? In *Three or four dsy work week,* eds. S. M. A. Hameed and G. S. Paul, pp. 31–40. Edmonton: Faculty of Business Administration, University of Alberta.

Mennell, S. 1980. *Sociological theory,* 2nd ed. London: Thomas Nelson.

Merton, R. K. 1957a. Role-set: Problems in sociological theory. *British Journal of Sociology* 8: 106–120.

Merton, R. K. 1957b. *Social theory and social structure,* rev. ed. New York: Free Press.

Merton, R. K. 1968. *Social theory and social structure,* rev. and enlarged ed. New York: Free Press.

Merton, R. K. and Kitt, A. S. 1950. Contributions to the theory of reference group behavior. In *Continuities in social research,* eds. R. K. Merton and P. F. Lazarsfeld, pp. 40–105. Glencoe, Ill.: Free Press.

Metz, M. H. 1978. *Classrooms and corridors: The crisis of authority in desegregated secondary schools.* Berkeley, Calif.: University of California Press.

Meyer, J. W. 1977. The effects of education as an institution. *American Journal of Sociology* 83: 55–77.

Meyer, J. W., Ramirez, F., Rubinson, R., and Boli-Bennett, J. 1977. The world education revolution, 1950–70. *Sociology of Education* 50: 242–258.

Meyer, J. W., Tuma, N. B., and Zagorski, K. 1979. Educational and occupational mobility: A comparison of Polish and American men. *American Journal of Sociology* 84: 978–986.

Michalos, A. C. 1980a. *North American social report,* vol. 1. Dordrecht, Netherlands: Reidel.

Michalos, A. C. 1980b. Vignettes of Canada and the United States. In *Perspectives Canada III,* pp. 295–306. Ottawa: Statistics Canada.

Michalos, A. C. 1980c. *North American social report,* vol. 2. Dordrecht, Netherlands: Reidel.

Michalos, A. C. 1981. *North American social report,* vol. 3. Dordrecht, Netherlands: Reidel.

Michalos, A. C. 1982. *North American social report,* vol. 5. Dordrecht, Netherlands: Reidel.

Michels, R. 1959. *Political parties,* trans. E. Paul and C. Paul. New York: Dover.

Michelson, W. 1977. Planning and amelioration of urban problems. In *Contemporary topics in urban sociology,* ed. K.P. Schwirian, pp. 562–633. Morristown, N.J.: General Learning Press.

Mifflen, F. J. and Mifflen, S. C. 1982. *The sociology of education.* Calgary, Alta.: Detselig Enterprises.

Milgram, S. and Toch, H. 1969. Collective behavior. In *Handbook of social psychology,* vol. 4, eds. G. Lindzey and E. Aronson, pp. 507–610. Reading, Mass.: Addison-Wesley.

Miller, D. C. and Form, W. H. 1980. *Industrial sociology,* 3rd ed. New York: Harper & Row.

Miller, G. 1978. *Odd jobs.* Englewood Cliffs, N.J.: Prentice-Hall.

Mills, C. W. 1940. Situated actions and vocabularies

of motives. *American Sociological Review* 5: 904–913.

Mills, C. W. 1956. *White collar.* New York: Oxford University Press.

Mills, C. W. 1959. *The power elite.* New York: Oxford University Press.

Mills, T. M. 1984. *The sociology of small groups.* Englewood Cliffs, N.J.: Prentice-Hall.

Mintz, B., Freitag, P., Hendricks, C., and Schwartz, M. 1976. Problems of proof in elite research. *Social problems* 23: 314–324.

Mitchell, W. C. 1968. Political systems. In *International encyclopedia of the social sciences,* vol. 15, ed. D. L. Sills, pp. 473–479. New York: Crowell, Collier, Macmillan.

Moberg, D. O. 1962. *The church as a social institution.* Englewood Cliffs, N.J.: Prentice-Hall.

Molotch, H. 1976. The city as a growth machine: Toward a political economy of place. *American Journal of Sociology* 82: 309–332.

Mönckeberg, F. 1979. Food and world population: Future perspectives. In *World population and development,* ed. P. M. Hauser, pp. 124–144. Syracuse, N.Y.: Syracuse University Press.

Montague, M.F.A. 1960. *Introduction to physical anthropology.* 3rd ed. Springfield, Ill.: Charles C. Thomas.

Moon, S. G. 1980. Courtship process: Dating and mate selection. In *Courtship, marriage, and the family,* ed. G. N. Ramu, pp. 26–36. Toronto: Gage.

Moore, W. E. 1966. Changes in occupational structures. In *Social structure and social mobility in economic development,* eds. N.J. Smelser and S.M. Lipset, pp. 194–212. Chicago: Aldine.

Morris, C. 1980. Determination and thoroughness: The movement for a royal commission on the status of women in Canada. *Atlantis* 5(2): 70–82.

Morrison P. A. and Wheeler, J. P. 1976. Rural renaissance in America? The revival of population growth in remote areas. *Population Bulletin* 31 (3).

Mortimer, J. T. and Simmons, R. G. 1978. Adult socialization. In *Annual Review of sociology,* vol. 4, eds. R. H. Turner, J. Coleman, and R. C. Fox, pp. 421–54. Palo Alto, Calif.: Annual Reviews Inc.

Mullins, L. S. and Kopelman, R. E. 1984. The best seller as an indication of societal narcissism. *Public Opinion Quarterly* 48: 720–730.

Mumford, L. 1968. City: Forms and functions. In *International encyclopedia of the social sciences,* vol. 2, ed. D. L. Sills, pp. 447–455. New York: Crowell, Collier, and Macmillan.

Murdock, G. P. 1949. *Social Structure.* New York: Macmillan.

Murstein, B. 1970. Stimulus-value-role: A theory of marital choice. *Journal of Marriage and the Family* 32: 465–482.

Mussen, P. H. 1969. Early sex-role development. In *Handbook of socialization theory and research,* ed. D. A. Goslin, pp. 707–732. Chicago: Rand McNally.

Myles, J. F. and Forcese, D. 1981. Voting and class politics in Canada and the United States. In *Comparative social research,* vol. 4, ed. R. F. Tomasson, pp. 3–32. Greenwich, Conn.: JAI Press.

Nader, G. A. 1975. *Cities of Canada,* vol. 1. Toronto: Macmillan of Canada.

Napier, R. W. and Gershenfeld, M.K. 1973. *Groups.* Boston: Houghton Mifflin.

Narr, J. L. 1974. Regional growth in the United States. *American Journal of Economics and Sociology* 33: 17–18.

Nett, E. M. 1976. The changing forms and functions of the Canadian family. In *The Canadian family,* rev. ed., ed. K. Ishwaran, pp. 46–76. Toronto: Holt, Rinehart & Winston.

Nett, E. M. 1980. Marriage and the family: Organization and interaction. In *Courtship, marriage, and the family,* ed. G. N. Ramu, pp. 59–77. Toronto: Gage.

Neugarten, B. L. and Hagestad, G. 1976. Age and the life course. In *Handbook of aging and the social sciences,* eds. R. Binstock and E. Shanas, pp. 35–52. New York: Van Nostrand.

Nie, N. H., Verba, S., and Petrocik, J. R. 1979. *The changing American voter,* enlarged ed. Cambridge, Mass.: Harvard University Press.

Niebuhr, H. R. 1929. *The social sources of denominationalism.* New York: Meridian.

Nielsen, J. M. 1978. *Sex in society.* Belmont, Calif.: Wadsworth.

Niemi, R. G. and Sobieszek, B. I. 1977. Political socialization. In *Annual review of sociology,* vol. 3, eds. A. Inkeles, J. Coleman, and N. Smelser, pp. 209–234. Palo Alto, Calif.: Annual Reviews Inc.

Nimkoff, M.F. 1965. *Comparative family systems.* Boston: Houghton Mifflin.

Nixon, H. L., III. 1979. *The small group.* Englewood Cliffs, N.J.: Prentice-Hall.

Norton, A. J. and Glick, P. C. 1976. Marital instability: Past, present, and future. *Journal of Social Issues* 35: 5–19.

Notestein, F. W. 1945. Population—the long view. In *Food for the world,* ed., T.W. Schultz, pp. 36–57. Chicago: University of Chicago Press.

Novak, M. 1971. *The rise of the unmeltable ethnics.* New York: Macmillan.

Novak, M. W. 1975. *Living and learning in the free school.* Toronto: McClelland and Stewart.

Nunn, C. Z., Crockett, H. J. and Williams, J. A., Jr. 1978. *Tolerance for nonconformity.* San Francisco: Jossey-Bass.

Nye, F. I. 1958. Employment status and recreational behavior of mothers. *Pacific Sociological Review* 1: 69–72.

Nye, F. I. 1974. Emerging and declining family roles. *Journal of Marriage and the Family* 36: 238–45.

Nye, F. I. and Berardo, F. M. 1973. *The family.* New York: Macmillan.

O'Brien, P. J. 1975. A critique of Latin American theories of dependency. In *Beyond the sociology of development, economy, and society in Latin America and Africa,* eds. I. Oxaal, T. Barnett, and D. Booth, pp 7–27. London: Routledge & Kegan Paul.

O'Dea, T. F. 1961. Five dilemmas in the institutionalization of religion. *Journal for the Scientific Study of Religion* 1: 30–39.

Ogburn, W. F. 1964. *On culture and social change,* ed. O. D. Duncan. Chicago: University of Chicago Press.

Ogmundson, R. 1982. Good news and Canadian sociology. *Canadian Journal of Sociology* 7: 73–78.

Ogmundson, R. and Ng, M. 1982. On the inference of voter motivation: A comparison of the subjective class vote in Canada and the United Kingdom. *Canadian Journal of Sociology* 7: 41–60.

Olmsted, M. S. and Hare, A. P. 1978. *The small group,* 2nd ed. New York: Random House.

Olsen, D. 1980. *The state elite.* Toronto: McClelland & Stewart.

O'Neil, D. J. 1981. American vs. Canadian policies toward their Japanese minorities during the Second World War. In *Comparative social research,* vol. 4, ed. R. F. Tomasson, pp. 111–134. Greenwich, Conn.: JAI Press.

Ornstein, M. D. 1981. The occupational mobility of men in Ontario. *Canadian Review of Sociology and Anthropology* 18: 183–215.

Orthner, D. K. 1975. Leisure activity patterns and marital satisfaction over the marital career. *Journal of Marriage and the Family* 37: 91–104.

Orum, A. M. 1983. *Introduction of political sociology,* 2nd ed. Englewood Cliffs, N.J.: Prentice-Hall.

Osterreich, H. 1965. Geographical mobility and kinship: A Canadian example. *International Journal of Comparative Sociology* 6: 131–145.

Overbeek, J. 1980. *Population and Canadian society.* Toronto: Butterworths.

Paisey, H. 1975. *The behavioural strategy of teachers.* Slough, Eng.: National Foundation for Educational Research (NFER).

Palmer, H. 1976. Mosaic versus melting pot?: Immigration and ethnicity in Canada and the United States. *International Journal* 31: 488–528.

Pammett, J. F. 1971. The development of political orientations in Canadian schoolchildren. *Canadian Journal of Political Science* 4: 132–141.

Pammett, J. F. and Whittington, M. S., eds. 1976. *Foundations of political culture: Political socialization in Canada.* Toronto: Macmillan of Canada.

Parai, L. 1965. *Immigration and emigration of professionals and skills during the post-war period,* Special Study No. 1. Ottawa: Economic Council of Canada.

Parelius, A. P. and Parelius, R. J. 1978. *The sociology of education.* Englewood Cliffs, N.J.: Prentice-Hall.

Park, R. E. and Burgess, E. W. 1921. *Introduction to the science of sociology.* Chicago: University of Chicago Press.

Parkin, F. 1979. *Marxism and class theory: A bourgeois critique.* New York: Columbia University Press.

Parsons, T. 1937. *The structure of social action.* New York: Free Press.

Parsons, T. 1951. *The social system.* New York: Free Press.

Parsons, T. 1960. *Structure and process in modern societies.* New York: Free Press.

Parsons, T. 1961. An outline of the social system. In *Theories of society,* eds. T. Parsons, E. Shils, K. D. Naegele, and J. R. Pitts, pp. 30–79. New York: Free Press.

Parsons, T. 1964. *Structure and process in modern societies.* New York: Free Press.

Parsons, T. and Bales, R. F. 1955. *Family socializa-*

tion and interaction process. Glencoe, Ill.: Free Press.

Pavalko, R. M. 1971. *Sociology of occupations and professions.* Itasca, Ill.: Peacock.

Paydarfar, A. A. 1967. Modernization process and demographic change. *Sociological Review* 15: 141–153.

Peers, F. 1970. Oh say, can you see? In *Close the 49th parallel etc.: The Americanization of Canada,* ed. I. Lumsden, pp. 135–156. Toronto: University of Toronto Press.

Penner, L. 1978. *Social psychology.* New York: Oxford University Press.

Perrow, C. 1970. *Organizational Analysis.* London: Tavistock.

Perrow, C. 1979. *Complex organizations: A critical essay,* 2nd ed. Glenview, Ill.: Scott, Foresman.

Perry, R. L. 1971. *Galt, U.S.A.: The American presence in a Canadian city.* Toronto: Maclean-Hunter.

Peter, K. 1976. The dialectic of family and community in the social history of the Hutterites. In *The Canadian family in comparative perspective,* ed. L. E. Larson, pp. 338–351. Scarborough, Ont.: Prentice-Hall of Canada.

Peters, R. S. 1958. *The concept of motivation.* London: Routledge & Kegan Paul.

Peterson, R. A. 1979. Revitalizing the culture concept. In *Annual review of sociology,* vol. 5, eds. A. Inkeles, J. Coleman, and R. H. Turner, pp. 137–166. Palo Alto, Calif.: Annual Reviews Inc.

Peterson, W. 1975. *Population,* 3rd ed. New York: Macmillan.

Peterson, W. 1978. International migration. In *Annual Review of Sociology,* vol. 4, eds. R. H. Turner, J. Coleman, and R. C. Fox, pp. 533–576. Palo Alto, Calif.: Annual Reviews Inc.

Pfeffer, J. and Salancik, G. R. 1975. Determinants of supervisory behavior: A role-set analysis. *Human Relations* 28: 139–154.

Piddington, R. 1973. The kinship network among French-Canadians. In *Communities and culture in French Canada,* eds. G. L. Gold and M. A. Trembley, pp. 123–141. Toronto: Holt, Rinehart & Winston.

Pincus, F. 1978. Tracking in community colleges. In *Reading, writing, and riches: Education and the socio-economic order in North American,* eds. R. W. Nelson and D. A. Nock, pp. 171–194. Scarborough, Ont.: Between the Lines.

Pineo, P. C. 1976. The extended family in a working-class area of Hamilton. In *The Canadian family,* rev. ed., ed. K. Ishwaran, pp. 545–554. Toronto: Holt, Rinehart & Winston.

Pineo, P. C. and Looker, E. D. 1983. Class conformity in the Canadian setting. *Canadian Journal of Sociology* 8: 293–317.

Pineo, P. C. and Porter, J. 1967. Occupational prestige in Canada. *Canadian Review of Sociology and Anthropology* 4: 24–40.

Pollard, A. 1980. Teacher interest and changing situations of survival threat in primary school classrooms. In *Teacher strategies,* ed. P. Woods, pp. 34–60. London: Croom Helm.

Ponting, J. R. and Gibbins, R. 1980. *Out of irrelevance.* Toronto: Butterworths.

Poor, R. and Steele, J. L. 1973. Work and leisure: The reactions of people at 4-day firms. In *4 days, 40 hours,* ed. R. Poor, pp. 69–92. New York: New American Library.

Poplin, D. E. 1979. *Communities,* 2nd ed. New York: Macmillan.

Population Reference Bureau. 1976. *World population growth and response, 1965–1975.* Washington, D.C.

Porter, J. 1965. *The vertical mosaic. An analysis of social class and power in Canada.* Toronto: University of Toronto Press.

Porter, J. 1967. Canadian character in the twentieth century. *Annals of the American Academy of Political and Social Science* 370: 48–56.

Porter, J. 1979. *The measure of Canadian society.* Toronto: Gage.

Porter, J., Porter, M., and Blishen, B. R. 1982. *Stations and callings.* Toronto: Methuen.

Portes, A. 1976. On the sociology of national development: Theories and issues. *American Journal of Sociology* 82: 55–85.

Poskocil, A. 1977. Encounters between blacks and white liberals: The collision of stereotypes. *Social Forces* 55: 715–727.

Poulantzas, N. 1975. *Class in contemporary capitalism.* London: New Left Books.

Presthus, R. 1978. *The organizational society,* rev. ed. New York: St. Martin's.

Preston, S. H. 1977. Mortality trends. In *Annual Review of Sociology,* vol. 3., eds. A. Inkeles, J. Coleman, and N. Smelser, pp. 163–178. Palo Alto, Calif.: Annual Reviews Inc.

Prus, R. C. 1975. Resisting designations: An extension of attribution theory in a negotiated context. *Sociological Inquiry* 45: 3–14.

Prus, R. C. and Irini, S. 1980. *Hookers, rounders, and desk clerks.* Toronto: Gage.

Prus, R. C. and Sharper, C. R. D. 1977. *Road hustler.* Lexington, Mass.: D. C. Heath.

Pugh, D. S., Hickson, D. J., Hinings, C. R., and Turner, C. 1969. Dimensions of organization structure. *Administrative Science Quarterly* 13: 65–91.

Pursley, R. 1977. *Introduction to criminal justice.* New York: Macmillan.

Quinney, R. 1970. *The social reality of crime.* Boston: Little, Brown.

Ramey, J. W. 1972. Communes, group marriage, and the upper middle class. *Journal of Marriage and the Family* 34: 647–655.

Ramirez, F. O. and Meyer, J. W. 1980. Comparative education. In *Annual review of sociology,* vol. 6, eds., A. Inkeles, N. J. Smelser, and R.H. Turner, pp. 369–399. Palo Alto, Calif.: Annual Reviews Inc.

Rapoport, R. and Rapoport, R. N. 1975. *Leisure and the family life cycle.* London: Routledge & Kegan Paul.

Raushenbush, W. 1979. *Robert E. Park: Biography of a sociologist.* Durham, N.C.: Duke University Press.

Rebecca, M., Hefner, R., and Oleshansky, B. 1976. A model of sex-role transcendence. *Journal of Social Issues* 32: 197–206.

Rees, A. 1968. Economics. In *International encyclopedia of the social sciences,* vol. 4, ed. D. L. Sills, pp. 472–485. New York: Crowell, Collier, Macmillan.

Rehberg, R. and Hotchkiss, L. 1972. Education decision-makers: The school guidance counselor and social mobility. *Sociology of Education* 45: 339–361.

Reid, S. T. 1985. *Crime and criminology,* 4th ed. New York: Holt, Rinehart & Winston.

Reiss, A. J., Jr. 1961. The social integration of queers and peers. *Social Problems* 9: 102–120.

Reiss, A. J., Jr. 1968. Sociology. In *International Encyclopedia of the social sciences,* vol. 15, ed. D. L. Sills, pp. 1–23. New York: Crowell, Collier, Macmillan.

Reiss, A. J., Jr. 1971. *The police and the public.* New Haven, Conn.: Yale University Press.

Reiss, I. L. 1965. The universality of the family: A conceptual analysis. *Journal of Marriage and the Family* 27: 443–453.

Reiss, I. L. 1976. *Family systems in America,* 2nd ed. New York: Dryden.

Reiss, P. J. 1976. The extended kinship system: Correlates of and attitudes on frequency of interaction. *Marriage and Family Living* 24: 333–339.

Reitz, J. 1974. Language and ethnic community survival. *Canadian Review of Sociology and Anthropology,* special issue: 104–122.

Reitz, J. 1980. *The survival of ethnic groups.* Toronto: McGraw-Hill.

Report of the Task Force on Sex-Role Stereotyping in the Broadcast Media. 1982. *Images of women.* Hull, Que.: Canadian Government Publishing Centre.

Retherford, R. D. 1975. *The changing sex differential in mortality.* Westport, Conn.: Greenwood.

Reul, M. R. 1978. Motion pictures, radio, and television. In *Social control for the 1980s,* ed. J. S. Roucek, pp. 310–320. Westport, Conn.: Greenwood.

Reynolds, L. T. and Henslin, J. M. 1973. *American society: A critical analysis.* New York: David McKay.

Rich, R. M. 1979. *The sociology of criminal law.* Toronto: Butterworths.

Richardson, J. T., Harder, M., and Simmonds, R. B. 1972. Thought reform and the Jesus Movement. *Youth and Society* 4: 185–202.

Richer, S. 1974. Middle-class bias of schools—fact or fancy? *Sociology of Education* 47: 523–534.

Richer, S. 1979. Sex-role socialization and early schooling. *Canadian Review of Sociology and Anthropology* 16: 195–205.

Richmond, A. H. 1973. *Migration and race relations in an English city.* London: Oxford University Press.

Richmond, A. H. 1976. Immigration, population, and the Canadian future. *Sociological Focus* 9: 125–136.

Ridgeway, C. L. 1983. *The dynamics of small groups.* New York: St. Martin's.

Riesman, D. 1961. *The lonely crowd,* abridged ed. New Haven, Conn.: Yale University Press.

Riley, M. W. 1976. Age strata in social systems. In *Handbook of aging and the social issues,* eds. R. H. Binstock and E. Shanas, pp. 189–217. New York: Van Nostrand Reinhold.

Rist, R. 1973. *The urban school: A factory for failure.* Boston: MIT Press.

Ritchey, P. N. 1976. Explanations of migration. In *Annual review of sociology,* vol. 2, eds. A. Inkeles, J. Coleman, and N. Smelser, pp. 363–404. Palo Alto, Calif.: Annual Reviews Inc.

Roadburg, A. 1985. *Aging: Retirement, leisure, and work in Canada.* Agincourt: Methuen.

Roberts, K. 1978. *Contemporary society and the growth of leisure.* London: Longman.

Robinson, J. P. 1977. *How Americans use time.* New York: Praeger.

Robinson, J. P. and Godbey, G. 1978. Work and leisure in America: How we spend our time. *Journal of Physical Education and Recreation, Leisure Today Supplement* 49: 6–7.

Rock, P. 1973. *Deviant Behavior.* London: Hutchinson.

Rogers, E. M. 1973. Social structure and social change. In *Processes and phenomena of social change,* ed. G. Zaltman, pp. 75–87. New York: Wiley.

Rogers, E. M. and Shoemaker, F. L. 1971. *Communication of innovations,* rev. ed. New York: Free Press.

Rogers, R. 1974. Normative aspects of leisure time behavior in the Soviet Union. *Sociology and Social Research* 58: 369–379.

Roof, W. C. 1979. Concepts and indicators of religious commitment. In *The religious dimension: New directions in quantitative research,* ed. R. Wuthnow, pp. 17–46. New York: Academic Press.

Roozen, D. A. and Carroll, J. W. 1979. Recent trends in church membership and participation. *Understanding church growth and decline: 1950–1978,* eds. D. R. Hoge and D. A. Roozen, pp. 21–41. New York: Pilgrim Press.

Rose, A. M., ed. 1962. *Human behavior and social processes.* Boston: Houghton Mifflin.

Rose, A. M. 1965. Group consciousness among the aging. In *Older people and their social world,* eds. A. M. Rose and W. A. Peterson, pp. 19–36. Philadelphia: Davis.

Rose, A. M. 1967. *The power structure: Political process in American society.* New York: Oxford University Press.

Rose, C. E. and Mirowsky, J. 1984. The social construction of reality in marriage. *Sociological Perspectives* 27: 281–300.

Roseborough, H. 1960. Some sociological dimensions of consumer spending. *Canadian Journal of Economics and Political Science* 26: 452–464.

Rosen, B. C. 1959. Race, ethnicity, and the achievement syndrome. *American Sociological Review* 24: 47–60.

Rosenbaum, J. 1976. *Making inequality: The hidden curriculum of high school tracking.* New York: Wiley.

Rosenhan, D. L. 1973. On being sane in insane places. *Science* 179: 250–258.

Ross, D. 1971. Leisure as a response to technological change in the economic system. In *Work and leisure in Canada,* eds. S. M. A. Hameed and D. Cullen, pp. 19–36. Edmonton: Faculty of Business Administration, University of Alberta.

Rossides, D. W. 1968. *Society as a functional process.* Toronto: McGraw-Hill of Canada.

Rostow, W. W. 1960. *The stages of economic growth.* London: Cambridge University Press.

Roth, J. A. 1963. *Timetables.* Indianapolis, Ind.: Bobbs-Merrill.

Roth, J. A. 1974. Professionalism: The sociologist's decoy. *Sociology of Work and Occupations* 1: 6–23.

Rothman, B. K. 1978. Childbirth as negotiated reality. *Symbolic Interaction* 1: 124–137.

Roy, P. E. 1981. Citizens without votes: East Asians in British Columbia. In *Ethnicity, power, and politics in Canada,* eds. J.. Dahlie and T. Fernando, pp. 151–171. Toronto: Methuen.

Roy, W. G. 1984. Class conflict and social change in historical perspective. In *Annual review of sociology,* vol. 10, eds. R. H. Turner and J. F. Short, Jr., pp. 483–506. Palo Alto, Calif.: Annual Reviews Inc.

Royal Commission on Corporate Concentration. 1978. *Report of the Royal Commission on Corporate Concentration.* Ottawa: Minister of Supply and Services.

Rubin, J. Z. and Lewicki, R. J. 1973. A three-factor experimental analysis of promises and threats. *Journal of Applied Social Psychology* 3: 240–257.

Rubington, E. and Weinberg, M. S., eds. 1981. *Deviance,* 4th ed. New York: Macmillan.

Sanday, P. R. 1974. Female status in the public domain. In *Woman, culture, and society,* eds. M. Z. Rosaldo and L. Lamphere, pp. 189–206. Stanford, Calif.: Stanford University Press.

Sanders, I. T. 1975. *The community,* 3rd ed. New York: Ronald.

Sanders, I. T. and Lewis, G. F. 1976. Rural community studies in the United States. In *Annual review of sociology,* vol. 2, eds. A. Inkeles, J. Coleman, and N. Smelser, pp. 35–54. Palo Alto, Calif.: Annual Reviews Inc.

Santee, R. T. and Jackson, S. E. 1982. Identity implications of conformity: Sex differences in normative and attributional judgments. *Social Psychology Quarterly* 45: 121–125.

Sarason, S. B. and Doris, J. 1979. *Educational handicap, public policy, and social history.* New York: Free Press.

Sauvy, A. 1975. *Zero growth?* trans. A. Maguire. Oxford, Eng.: Basil Blackwell (published in French in 1973).

Sawchuk, P. 1974. Becoming a homosexual. In *Decency and Deviance,* eds. J. Haas and B. Shaffir, pp. 233–245. Toronto: McClelland & Stewart.

Schafer, W. E. and Olexa, C. 1971. *Tracking and opportunity.* Scranton, Pa.: Chandler.

Scheff, T. J. ed. 1975. *Labeling madness.* Englewood Cliffs, N.J.: Prentice-Hall.

Scheff, T. J. 1984. *Being mentally ill,* 2nd ed. Chicago: Aldine.

Schermerhorn, R. A. 1970. *Comparative ethnic relations.* New York: Random House.

Schlesinger, B. 1976. Remarriage as family reorganization for divorced persons. In *The Canadian family,* rev. ed., ed. K. Ishwaran, pp. 460–478. Toronto: Holt, Rinehart & Winston of Canada.

Schlesinger, B. 1980. Remarriage. In *Courtship, marriage, and the family,* ed. G. N. Ramu, pp. 153–165. Toronto: Gage.

Schlesinger, J. A. 1968. Political parties: Party units. In *International Encyclopedia of the social sciences,* vol. 11, ed. D. L. Sills, pp. 428–436. New York: Crowell, Collier, Macmillan.

Schneider, D. J. 1981. Tactical self-presentations. In *Impression management theory and social, psychological research,* ed., J. T. Tedeschi, pp. 23–40. New York: Academic Press.

Schneider, L. and Dornbusch, S. M. 1958. *Popular religion.* Chicago: University of Chicago Press.

Schnore, L. F. and Jones, J. K. O. 1969. The evolution of city-suburban types in the course of a decade. *Urban Affairs Quarterly* 4: 421–442.

Schoenfeld, S. 1978. The Jewish religion in North America. *Canadian Journal of Sociology* 3: 209–232.

Schutz, W. C. 1961. The ego, FIRO theory, and the leader as a completer. In *Leadership and interpersonal behavior,* eds. L. Petrullo and B. M. Bass, pp. 48–65. New York: Holt, Rinehart & Winston.

Schwartz, M. A. 1981. Politics and moral causes in Canada and the United States. In *Comparative social research,* vol. 4, ed. R. F. Tomasson, pp. 65–90. Greenwich, Conn.: JAI Press.

Scimecca, J. A. 1980. *Education and society.* New York: Holt, Rinehart & Winston.

Scott, J. F. 1971. *Internalization of norms: A sociological theory of moral commitment.* Englewood Cliffs, N.J.: Prentice-Hall.

Scott, M. B. and Lyman, S. M. 1969. Accounts. *American Sociological Review* 33: 46–62.

Scott, W. G. and Hart, D. K. 1979. *Organizational America.* Boston: Houghton Mifflin.

Scott, W. R. 1975. Organizational structure. In *Annual review of sociology,* vol. 1, eds. A. Inkeles, J. Coleman, and N. Smelser, pp. 1–20. Palo Alto, Calif.: Annual Reviews Inc.

Scott, W. R. 1981. *Organizations.* Englewood Cliffs, N.J.: Prentice-Hall.

Secord, P. F. and Backman, C. W. 1974. *Social psychology,* 2nd ed. New York: McGraw-Hill.

Seeley, J. R., Sim, R. A., and Loosley, E. W. 1956. *Crestwood Heights.* Toronto: University of Toronto Press.

Seeman, M. 1972. Alienation and engagement. In *The human meaning of social change,* eds. A. Campbell and P. E. Converse, pp. 467–527. New York: Russell Sage Foundation.

Seeman, M. 1975. Alienation studies. In *Annual review of sociology,* vol. 1, eds. A. Inkeles, J. Coleman, and N. Smelser, pp. 91–124. Palo Alto, Calif.: Annual Reviews Inc.

Selznick, P. 1948. Foundations of the theory of organization. *American Sociological Review* 13: 25–35.

Sharp, L. 1952. Steel axes for stone age Australians. In *Human problems in technological changes,* ed. E. H. Spicer, pp. 69–92. New York: Russell Sage Foundation.

Shaw, M. E. 1981. *Group dynamics,* 3rd ed. New York: McGraw-Hill.

Shepard, H. A. 1949. Democratic control in a labor union. *American Journal of Sociology* 54: 311–316.

Sher, J. 1983. *White hoods: Canada's Ku Klux Klan.* Vancouver: New Star Books.

Sherif, M. and Sherif, C. W. 1956. *An outline of social psychology,* rev. ed. New York: Harper & Row.

Shivers, J. S. 1981. *Leisure and recreation concepts.* Boston: Allyn & Bacon.

Simmel, G. 1955. *Conflict,* trans. K. H. Wolff. New York: Free Press.

Simmel, G. 1956. Fashion. *American Journal of Sociology* 62: 541–558.

Simmons, J. and Simmons, R. 1969. *Urban Canada.* Toronto: Copp Clark.

Simmons, R. G., Rosenberg, F., and Rosenberg, M. 1973. Disturbance in the self-image at adolescence. *American Sociological Review* 38: 553–568.

Simpson, G. E. and Yinger, J. M. 1972. *Racial and cultural minorities,* 4th ed. New York: Harper & Row.

Simpson, R. L. 1956. A modification of the functional theory of stratification. *Social Forces* 35: 130–137.

Sjoberg, G. 1964. Community. In *A dictionary of the social sciences,* eds. J. Gould and W. L. Kolb, pp. 114–115. New York: Free Press.

Skeels, H. M. 1940. Some Iowa studies of the mental growth of children in relation to differentials of the environment: A summary. In *The thirty-ninth yearbook of the National Society for the Study of Education,* ed. G. M. Whipple, pp. 281–308. Bloomington, Ill.: Public School Publishing Co.

Skogan, W. G. 1977. Dimensions of the dark figure of unreported crime. *Crime and Delinquency* 23: 41–50.

Smelser, N. J. 1962. *Theory of collective behavior.* New York: Free Press.

Smelser, N. J. 1964. Theoretical issues of scope and problems. *Sociological Quarterly* 5: 116–122.

Smelser, N. J. 1972. Some additional thoughts on collective behavior. *Sociological Inquiry* 42: 97–103.

Smith, A. D. 1973. *The concept of social change: A critique of the functionalist theory of social change.* London: Routledge & Kegan Paul.

Smith, A. D. 1981. *The ethnic revival.* Cambridge, Eng.: Cambridge University Press.

Smith, D. H. and Baldwin, B. R. 1974. Voluntary associations and volunteering in the United States. In *Voluntary action research: 1974,* ed. D. H. Smith, pp. 277–306. Lexington, Mass.: D. C. Heath.

Smith, L. M. and Geoffrey, W. 1968. *The complexities of an urban classroom.* New York: Holt, Rinehart & Winston.

Smith, R. A. and Weller, R. H. 1977. Growth and structure of the metropolitan community. In *Contemporary topics in urban sociology,* ed. K. P. Schwirian, pp. 76–149. Morristown, N.J.: General Learning Press.

Smith, R. T. 1968. Family: Comparative structure. In *International encyclopedia of the social sciences,* vol. 5, ed. D. L. Sills, pp. 301–313. New York: Collier-Macmillan.

Smith, S. J. 1984. Crime in the news. *British Journal of Criminology* 14: 289–295.

Smith, V. H. 1974. *Alternative schools.* Lincoln, Neb.: Professional Educators Publications.

Snow, D. A. and Machalek, R. 1984. The sociology of conversion. In *Annual Review of Sociology,* vol. 10, eds. R. H. Turner and J. F. Short, Jr., pp. 167–190. Palo Alto, Calif.: Annual Reviews Inc.

Snyder, B. R. 1971. *The hidden curriculum.* New York: Knopf.

Social Psychology Quarterly. 1979. Editorial policy. 42: 4.

Sorfleet, P. 1976. Dealing hashish. *Canadian journal of Criminology and Corrections* 18: 123–151.

Sorokin, P. 1957. *Social and cultural dynamics,* rev. and abridged. Boston: Porter Sargent.

Special Committee of the Royal College of Psychiatrists. 1979. *Alcohol and Alcoholism.* London: Tavistock.

Spengler, J. J. 1978. *Facing zero population growth.* Durham, N.C.: Duke University Press.

Spradley, J. P. 1970. *You owe yourself a drunk.* Boston: Little, Brown.

Srinivas, M. N. 1966. A note on Sanskritization and Westernization. In *Class, status, and power,* 2nd ed., eds. R. Bendix and S. M. Lipset, pp. 552–560. New York: Free Press.

Stark, R. 1984. The rise of a new world faith. *Review of Religious Research* 26: 18–27.

Statistics Canada. 1971. *Crime Statistics, Police.* Ottawa: Information Canada.

Statistics Canada. 1972–73. *Salaries and qualifications of teachers in public elementary and secondary schools.* Cat. No. 81–202. Ottawa: Minister of Supply and Services.

Statistics Canada. 1976. *Fertility in Canada,* vol. 5, pt. 1, Cat. No. 99–706. Ottawa: Minister of Supply and Services.

Statisics Canada. 1976–79. *Correctional institution*

statistics, Cat. No. 85–207. Ottawa: Minister of Supply and Services.

Statistics Canada. 1978a. *Crime and Traffic Enforcement Statistics,* Cat. No. 85–205. Ottawa: Minister of Supply and Services.

Statistics Canada. 1978b. *Culture statistics, 1978.* Ottawa: Minister of Supply and Services.

Statistics Canada. 1978c. *Canada Yearbook, 1978–79.* Ottawa: Minister of Supply and Services.

Statistics Canada. 1980a. *Perspectives Canada III.* Ottawa.

Statistics Canada. 1980b. *Marriages and Divorces,* Cat. No. 84–205. Ottawa: Minister of Supply and Services.

Statistics Canada. 1980c. *Mortality,* Cat. No. 84–206. Ottawa: Minister of Supply and Services.

Statistics Canada. 1980d. *The Labour Force.* December.

Statistics Canada. 1980–81a. *Salaries and qualifications of teachers in public elementary and secondary schools,* Cat. No. 81–202. Ottawa: Minister of Supply and Services.

Statistics Canada. 1980–81b. *International and interprovincial migration in Canada, 1980–81,* Cat. No. 81–208. Ottawa: Minister of Supply and Services.

Statistics Canada. 1981a. *Mental health statistics, 1978,* vol. 1, Cat. No. 83–204. Ottawa: Minister of Supply and Services.

Statistics Canada. 1981b. One in eight. Mental illness in Canada. Ottawa (brochure).

Statistics Canada. 1981c. *1981 census of Canada,* vol. 1, Cat. No. 92–906. Ottawa: Minister of Supply and Services.

Statistics Canada. 1981e. *Canada yearbook, 1980–81.* Ottawa.

Statistics Canada. 1981f. *Crime and Traffic Enforcement Statistics,* Cat. No. 85–205. Ottawa: Minister of Supply and Services.

Statistics Canada. 1982a. *Population trends—1981 census* (Canada update from the 1981 census). Ottawa: Minister of Supply and Services.

Statistics Canada. 1982b. *International and interprovincial migration in Canada 1980–81,* Cat. No. 91–208. Ottawa: Minister of Supply and Services.

Statistics Canada. 1982c. *Education in Canada, 1982,* Cat. No. 81–229. Ottawa: Minister of Supply and Services.

Statistics Canada. 1982–83a. *Adult correctional services in Canada, 1982–83,* Cat. No. 85–211. Ottawa: Minister of Supply and Services.

Statistics Canada. 1982–83b. *Salaries and qualifications of teachers in public elementary and secondary schools,* Cat. No. 81–202. Ottawa: Minister of Supply and Services.

Statistics Canada. 1983. *Canada update from the 1981 census,* vol. 1, no. 5, p. 4. Ottawa: Minister of Supply and Services.

Statistics Canada. 1983–84. *Salaries and qualifications of teachers in public elementary and secondary schools,* Cat. No. 81–202. Ottawa: Minister of Supply and Services.

Statistics Canada. 1984a. *Culture statistics: Book publishing, 1979–1981,* Cat. No. 87–523. Ottawa: Minister of Supply and Services.

Statistics Canada. 1984b. *Culture statistics: Newspapers and periodicals, 1981,* Cat. No. 87–511. Ottawa: Minister of Supply and Services.

Statistics Canada. 1984c. *Urban growth in Canada,* Cat. No. 99–942. Ottawa: Minister of Supply and Services.

Statistics Canada. 1984d. *Canada's lone-parent families,* Cat. No. 99-933. Ottawa: Minister of Supply and Services.

Statistics Canada. 1984e. *The labour force,* June, Cat. No. 71-001. Ottawa: Minister of Supply and Services.

Statistics Canada. 1984f. *Women in the work world,* Cat. No. 99-940. Ottawa.

Statistics Canada. 1985a. *Quarterly estimates of population for Canada, the provinces, and the territories,* Cat. No. 91–001. Ottawa: Minister of Supply and Services.

Statistics Canada. 1985b. *Postcensal annual estimates of population by marital status, age, sex, and components of growth for Canada, provinces, and territories,* June 1, 1984, vol. 2, Cat. No. 91-210. Ottawa: Minister of Supply and Services.

Stebbins, R. A. 1969a. On linking Barth and Homans: A theoretical note. *Man* (n.s.) 4: 432–437.

Stebbins, R. A. 1969b. Social network as a subjective construct. *Canadian Review of Sociology and Anthropology* 6: 1–14.

Stebbins, R. A. 1970a. Career: The subjective approach. *Sociological Quarterly* 11: 32–49.

Stebbins, R. A. 1970b. On misunderstanding the concept of commitment: A theoretical clarification. *Social Forces* 48: 526–529.

Stebbins, R. A. 1971a. *Commitment to deviance: The*

nonprofessional criminal in the community. Westport, Conn.: Greenwood.

Stebbins, R. A. 1971b. The subjective career as a basis for reducing role conflict. *Pacific Sociological Review* 14: 383–402.

Stebbins, R. A. 1974a. Formalization: Notes on a theory of the rise and change of social forms. *International Journal of Contemporary Sociology* 11: 105–119.

Stebbins, R. A. 1974b. *The disorderly classroom: Its physical and temporal conditions.* St. John's, Nfld.: Faculty of Education, Memorial University of Newfoundland.

Stebbins, R. A. 1975. *Teachers and meaning: Definitions of classroom situations.* Leiden, Netherlands: Brill.

Stebbins, R. A. 1976. Conceited talk: A test of hypotheses. *Psychological Reports* 39: 1111–1116.

Stebbins, R. A. 1979. *Amateurs: On the margin between work and leisure.* Beverly Hills, Calif.: Sage Publications.

Stebbins, R. A. 1980a. Family, work, and amateur acting: The imperfect mesh. In *Social research and cultural policy,* ed. J. Zuzanek, pp. 245–255. Waterloo, Ont.: Otium.

Stebbins, R. A. 1980b. Avocational science: The amateur routine in archaeology and astronomy. *International Journal of Comparative Sociology* 21: 34–48.

Stebbins, R. A. 1981. Classroom ethnography and the definition of the situation. In *Schools, teachers, and teaching,* eds. L. Barton and S. Walker, pp. 243–264. Sussex, Eng.: Falmer.

Stebbins, R. A. 1982. Serious leisure: A conceptual statement. *Pacific Sociological Review* 25: 251–272.

Stebbins, R. A. 1983. Deviance and social control. In *An introduction to sociology,* eds. M. Weinfeld, M. Rosenberg, W. Shaffir, and A. Turowetz, pp. 403–431. Toronto: Methuen.

Stebbins, R. A. 1984. *Magician: Career, culture, and social psychology in a variety art.* Toronto: Irwin.

Stein, M. B. 1975. Social Credit in the province of Quebec. In *Prophecy and protest,* eds. S. D. Clark, J. P. Grayson, and L. M. Grayson, pp. 347–365. Toronto: Gage.

Stein, M. R. 1972. *The eclipse of community,* expanded ed. Princeton, N.J.: Princeton University Press.

Stephenson, M., ed. 1977. *Women in Canada,* rev. ed. Don Mills, Ont.: General Publishing.

Stinchcombe, A. L. 1983. *Economic sociology.* New York: Academic Press.

Stivers, R. 1976. *A hair of the dog: Irish drinking and American stereotype.* University Park, Pa.: Pennsylvania State University Press.

Stockard, J. and Johnson, M. M. 1980. *Sex roles.* Englewood Cliffs, N.J.: Prentice-Hall.

Stogdill, R. M. 1974. *Handbook of leadership.* New York: Free Press.

Stolnitz, G. J. 1964. The demographic transition: From high to low birthrates and death rates. In *Population: The vital revolution,* ed. R. Freedman, pp. 30–46. Garden City, N.Y.: Doubleday Anchor.

Stone, G. P. 1962. Appearance and the self. In *Human behavior and social processes,* ed. A. M. Rose, pp. 86-118. Boston: Houghton-Mifflin.

Stone, G. P. 1981. The play of little children. In *Social psychology through symbolic interaction,* 2nd ed., eds. G. P. Stone and H. A. Farberman, pp. 249–256. New York: Wiley.

Stone, G. P. and Farberman, H. A. 1967. On the edge of rapprochement: Was Durkheim moving toward the perspective of symbolic interaction? *Sociological Quarterly* 8: 149–164.

Stone, G. P. and Farberman, H. A., eds. 1981. *Social psychology through symbolic interaction,* 2nd ed. New York: Wiley.

Strauss, A. 1978. *Negotiations.* San Francisco: Jossey-Bass.

Strong-Boag, V. 1977. Cousin Cinderella: A guide to historical literature pertaining to Canadian women. In *Women in Canada,* rev. ed., ed. M. Stephenson, pp. 245–274. Don Mills, Ont.: General Publishing.

Stryker, S. 1962. Conditions of accurate role-taking. In *Human behavior and social processes,* ed. A. M. Rose, pp. 41–62. Boston: Houghton Mifflin.

Stryker, S. 1977. Developments in "two social psychologies." *Sociometry* 40: 145–160.

Stryker, S. 1980. *Symbolic interactionism.* Menlo Park, Calif.: Benjamin/Cummings.

Stub, H. R., ed. 1972. *Status communities in modern society.* Hinsdale, Ill.: Dryden.

Stymeist, D. H. 1975. *Ethnics and Indians: Social relations in a northwest Ontario town.* Toronto: Peter Martin Associates.

Suderman, M. 1979. Sex differences in high school

course choice and achievement (Research Report 79-08). Ottawa: Research Centre, Ottawa Board of Education.

Sudman, S. 1976. Sample surveys. *Annual review of sociology*, vol. 2, eds. A. Inkeles, J. Coleman, and N. Smelser, pp. 107–120. Palo Alto, Calif.: Annual Reviews Inc.

Sullivan, D. 1980. *The mask of love: Corrections in America.* Port Washington, NY: Kennikat.

Super, D. E. 1957. *The Psychology of careers.* New York: Harper.

Sussman, M. B. and Burchinal, L. 1962. Parental aid to married children. *Marriage and Family Living* 24: 320–332.

Suter, L. E. and Miller, H. P. 1973. Income differences between men and career women. *American Journal of Sociology* 78: 962–974.

Sutherland, E. H. and Cressey, D. R. 1978. *Principles of Criminology,* 10th ed. Philadelphia: Lippincott.

Suttles, G. D. 1972. *The social construction of communities.* Chicago: University of Chicago Press.

Sway, M. 1984. Economic adaptability: The case of the Gypsies. *Urban Life* 13: 83–98.

Symanski, R. 1981. *The immoral landscape: Female prostitution in Western societies.* Toronto: Butterworths.

Symons, G. L. 1978. Sex-status homophily, sponsorship, and professional socialization: Doctoral students. *Canadian Review of Sociology and Anthropology* 15: 385–393.

Szasz, T. S. 1970. *The manufacture of madness.* New York: Dell.

Tandan, N. K. 1974. Compressed work week and multiple job holdings. In *Three or four day work week,* eds. S. M. A. Hameed and G. S. Paul, pp. 51–61. Edmonton: Faculty of Business Administration, University of Alberta.

Tapinos, G. and Piotrow, P. T. 1978. *Six billion people: Demographic dilemmas and world politics.* New York: McGraw-Hill.

Task Force on Employment Opportunities for the 80s. 1982. *Work for tomorrow: Employment opportunities for the 80s,* Cat. No. XC2-321/4-01E. Ottawa: Speaker of the House of Commons.

Taylor, D. W. 1963. Thinking. In *Theories in contemporary psychology,* ed. M. M. Marx, pp. 475–493. New York: Macmillan.

Taylor, I. 1981. *Law and order: Arguments for socialism.* London, Eng.: Macmillan.

Taylor, I. 1982. Moral enterprise, moral panic, and law-and-order campaigns. In *The sociology of deviance,* eds. M. M. Rosenberg, R. A. Stebbins, and A. Turowetz, pp. 123–149. New York: St. Martin's.

TeSelle, S., ed. 1973. *The rediscovery of ethnicity.* New York: Harper & Row.

Tedeschi, J. T., ed. 1981. *Impression management theory and social psychological research.* New York: Academic Press.

Tedeschi, J. T., Schlenker, B. R., and Lindskold, S. 1972. The exercise of power and influence: The source of influence. In *The social influence processes,* ed. J. T. Tedeschi, pp. 287–345. Chicago: Aldine-Atherton.

Terkel, S. 1974. *Working.* New York: Pantheon.

Thomas, C. W. and Hepburn, J. R. 1983. *Crime, criminal law, and criminology.* Dubuque, Iowa: Wm. C. Brown.

Thomas, C. W. and Peterson, D. M. 1977. *Prison organization and inmate subcultures.* Indianapolis, Ind.: Bobbs-Merrill.

Thomas, D. L., Franks, D. D., and Calonico, J. M. 1972. Role-taking and power in social psychology. *American Sociological Review* 37: 605–614.

Thompson, J. D. 1967. *Organizations in action.* New York: McGraw-Hill.

Thompson, W. S. 1929. Recent trends in world population. *American Journal of Sociology* 34: 959–975.

Tomlinson, R. 1976. *Population dynamics,* 2nd ed. New York: Random House.

Travers, E. P. 1978. Eleven pressures that squeeze superintendents—and six ways to ease them. *American School Board Journal* 165: 43–44.

Treiman, D. J. 1977. *Occupational prestige in comparative perspective.* New York: Academic Press.

Treiman, D. J. and Terrell, K. 1975. The process of status attainment in the United States and Great Britain. *American Journal of Sociology* 81: 563–583.

Tremblay, M. A. 1966. Modèles d'autorité dans la famille Canadienne-Française. *Recherches Sociographiques* 7: 215–230.

Tresemer, D. W. 1977. *Fear of success.* New York: Plenum.

Tripp, C. A. 1975. *The homosexual matrix.* New York: New American Library.

Troeltsch, E. 1931. *The social teaching of the Christian churches,* trans. O. Wyon. New York: Macmillan.

Truzzi, M. 1978. Toward a general sociology of the folk, popular, and elite arts. In *Research in sociology of knowledge, science, and art,* ed. R. A. Jones, pp. 279–289. Greenwich, Conn.: JAT Press.

Tumin, M. M. 1970. *Readings in social stratification.* Englewood Cliffs, N.J.: Prentice-Hall.

Turner, R. H. 1962. Role-taking: Process versus conformity. In *Human behavior and social processes,* ed. A. M. Rose, pp. 20–40. Boston: Houghton Mifflin.

Turner, R. H. and Killian, L. M. 1972. *Collective behavior,* 2nd ed. Englewood Cliffs, N.J.: Prentice-Hall.

U.S. Bureau of the Census. 1980. *Statistical Abstract of the United States: 1980,* 101st ed. Washington, D.C.

U.S. Bureau of the Census. 1981. *Statistical abstract of the United States: 1981,* 102nd ed. Washington, D.C.

U.S. Bureau of the Census. 1982–83. *Statistical abstract of the United States: 1982–83,* 103rd ed. Washington, D.C.

U.S. Bureau of the Census. 1984. *Statistical abstract of the United States: 1984,* 104th ed. Washington, D.C.

U.S. Bureau of the Census. 1985. *Statistical abstract of the United States: 1985,* 105th ed. Washington, D.C.

United Nations. 1979. *World population trends and policies, 1977,* vol. 1. New York: United Nations Publishing Service.

United Nations. 1980. *Demographic yearbook: 1980.* New York: United Nations Publishing Service.

United Nations. 1983. *Demographic Yearbook,* 1981. New York.

Useem, M. 1980. Corporations and the corporate elite. In *Annual review of sociology,* vol. 6, eds. A. Inkeles, N. J. Smelser, and R. H. Turner, pp. 41–78. Palo Alto, Calif.: Annual Reviews Inc.

Valentine, C. 1968. *Culture and poverty.* Chicago: University of Chicago Press.

Vallee, F. G. and Whyte, D. R. 1968. Canadian society. In *Canadian society,* 3rd ed., eds. B. R. Blishen, F. E. Jones, K. D. Naegele, and J. Porter, pp. 833–852. Toronto: Macmillan of Canada.

Van Doorn, J. 1979. Organizations and the social order. In *Organizations alike and unlike: International and inter-institutional studies in the sociology of organizations,* eds. C. J. Lammers and D. J. Hickson, pp. 61–75. London: Routledge & Kegan Paul.

van den Berghe, P. L. 1963. Dialectic and functionalism: Toward a theoretical synthesis. *American Sociological Review* 28: 695–705.

Van Maanen, J. 1976. Breaking in: Socialization to work. In *Handbook of work, organization, and society,* ed. R. Dubin, pp. 67–130. Chicago: Rand McNally.

Vaz, E. W. 1976. *Aspects of deviance.* Scarborough, Ont.: Prentice-Hall of Canada.

Veblen, T. 1953. *The theory of the leisure class.* New York: New American Library.

Visaria, P. M. 1967. Sex ratio at birth in territories with a relatively complete registration. *Eugenics Quarterly* 14: 132–142.

Vold, G. B. and Bernard, T. J. 1979. *Theoretical criminology,* 2nd ed. New York: Oxford University Press.

Wakil, S. P. 1973. Campus mate selection preferences: A cross-national comparison. *Social Forces* 51: 471–476.

Wallace, R. A. and Wolf, A. 1980. *Contemporary sociological theory.* Englewood Cliffs, N.J.: Prentice-Hall.

Waller, I. 1974. *Men released from prison.* Toronto: University of Toronto Press.

Waller, W. 1932. *The sociology of teaching.* New York: Wiley.

Waller, W. 1937. The rating and dating complex. *American Sociological Review* 2: 727–734.

Wallerstein, I. 1979. *The capitalist world-economy.* London: Cambridge University Press.

Wallis, R. 1976. Observations on the Children of God. *The Sociological Review* 24: 807–829.

Walshok, M. L. 1971. The emergence of middle-class deviant subcultures: The case of swingers. *Social Problems* 18: 488–495.

Walton, J. 1976. Community power and the retreat from politics. *Social problems* 23: 292–303.

Walum, L. R. 1977. *The dynamics of sex and gender.* Chicago: Rand McNally.

Wamsley, G. L. 1970. Power and crisis in the universities. In *Power in organizations,* ed. M. N. Zald, pp. 50–58. Nashville, Tenn.: Vanderbilt University Press.

Ward, R. A. 1984. *The aging experience,* 2nd ed. New York: Harper & Row.

Ward, W. D. 1969. Process of sex-role development. *Developmental psychology* 1: 163–168.

Warren, D. I. 1981. *Helping networks.* Notre Dame, Ind.: University of Notre Dame Press.

Warren, R. L. 1973. The classroom as a sanctuary. *American Anthropologist* 75: 280–291.

Warren, R. L. 1977. *Social change and human purpose.* Chicago: Rand McNally.

Watson, G. 1973. Resistance to change. In *Processes and phenomena of social change,* ed. G. Zaltman, pp. 117–132. New York: Wiley.

Webb, E. J. et al. 1981. *Nonreactive measures in the social sciences,* 2nd ed. Boston: Houghton Mifflin.

Weber, M. 1946. *From Max Weber,* trans. H. H. Gerth and C. W. Mills. New York: Oxford University Press.

Weber, M. 1947. *The theory of social and economic organization,* trans. A. M. Henderson and T. Parsons. New York: Free Press.

Weber, M. 1958. *The Protestant ethic and the spirit of capitalism,* trans. T. Parsons. New York: Scribner.

Weber, M. 1968. *Max Weber on charisma and institution building.* Chicago: University of Chicago Press.

Weintraub, D. and Bernstein, F. 1966. Social structure and modernization: A comparative study of two villages. *American Journal of Sociology* 71: 509–521.

Weitz, S. 1977. *Sex roles.* New York: Oxford University Press.

Weller, J. M. and Quarantelli, E. L. 1973. Neglected characteristics of collective behavior. *American Journal of Sociology* 79: 665–685.

Westergaard, J. H. 1972. The withering away of class: A contemporary myth. In *The impact of social class,* ed. P. Blumberg, pp. 83–99. New York: Crowell.

Westley, M. A. and Westley, M. W. 1971. *The emerging worker.* Montreal: McGill-Queen's University Press.

Westoff, C. F. and Bumpass, L. 1973. The revolution in birth control practices of U.S. Roman Catholics. *Science* 179: 41–44.

Wheeler, S. 1966. The structure of formally organized socialization settings. In *Socialization after childhood,* eds. O. G. Brim, Jr. and S. Wheeler, pp. 51–106. New York: Wiley.

White, G. 1977. *Socialisation.* London, Eng.: Longman.

Whitehurst, R. N. 1975. Alternative life-styles and Canadian pluralism. In *Marriage, family, and society,* ed. S. P. Wakil, pp. 433–446. Toronto: Butterworths.

Whyte, W. F. 1981. *Street corner society,* 3rd ed. Chicago: University of Chicago Press.

Williams, J. E. and Best, D. L. 1982. *Measuring sex stereotypes.* Beverly Hills, Calif.: Sage.

Williams, R. 1976. *Key words: A vocabulary of culture and society.* Glasgow: Fontana/Croom Helm.

Williams, Jr., R. M. 1975. Race and ethnic relations. In *Annual review of sociology,* vol. 1., eds. A. Inkeles, J. Coleman, and N. Smelser, pp. 125–164. Palo Alto, Calif.: Annual Reviews Inc.

Wilson, B. 1970. *Religious sects.* New York: McGraw-Hill.

Wilson, F. D. 1984. Urban ecology. In *Annual Review of Sociology,* vol. 10, eds. R. H. Turner and J. F. Short, Jr., pp. 283–307. Palo Alto, Calif.: Annual Reviews Inc.

Wilson, J. 1973. *Introduction to social movements.* New York: Basic Books.

Wilson, J. 1978. *Religion in American society.* Englewood Cliffs, N.J.: Prentice-Hall.

Wilson, J. 1980. Sociology of leisure. In *Annual review of sociology,* vol. 6, eds. A. Inkeles, N. J. Smelser, and R. H. Turner, pp. 21–40. Palo Alto, Calif.: Annual Reviews Inc.

Wilson, S. 1978. *Informal groups.* Englewood Cliffs, N.J.: Prentice-Hall.

Winch, R. F., Ktsanes, T., and Ktsanes, V. 1954. The theory of complementary needs in mate selection. *American Sociological Review* 19: 241–249.

Wirth, L. 1938. Urbanism as a way of life. *American Journal of Sociology* 44: 1–24.

Wolfe, D. M. 1959. Power and authority in the family. In *Studies in social power,* ed. D. Cartwright, pp. 99–107. Ann Arbor, Mich.: Institute for Social Research, University of Michigan.

Woods, P. 1976. Having a laugh: An antidote to schooling. In *The process of schooling,* eds. M. Hammersley and P. Woods, pp. 178–187. London: Open University Press.

Woods, P. 1979. *The divided school.* London: Routledge & Kegan Paul.

Wright, R. G. 1977. *The nature of organizations.* Encino, Calif.: Dickenson.

Wrong, D. H. 1955. *American and Canadian viewpoints.* Washington, D.C.: American Council on Education, Canadian-United States Committee on Education.

Wylie, R. C. 1974. *The self-concept,* vol. 1, rev. ed. Lincoln, Neb.: University of Nebraska Press.

Yankelovich, D. 1979. Work, values, and the new breed. In *Work in America: The decade ahead,* eds. C. Kerr and J. M. Rosow, pp. 3–26. New York: Van Nostrand Reinhold.

Yankelovich, D. and Immerwahr, J. 1984. Putting the work ethic to work. *Society/Transaction* 21: 58–76.

Yeates, M. 1975. *Main street: Windsor to Quebec.* Toronto: Macmillan of Canada.

Yeates, M. and Garner, B. 1980. *The North American city,* 3rd ed. New York: Harper & Row.

Yinger, J. M. 1970. *The scientific study of religion.* New York: Macmillan.

Young, M. and Willmott, P. 1957. *Family and kinship in east London.* London: Penguin.

Zald, M. N. and Ash, R. 1966. Social movement organizations: Growth, decay, and change. *Social Forces* 44: 327–341.

Zelditch, M., Jr. and Evan, W. M. 1962. Simulated bureaucracies: A methodological analysis. In *Simulation in social science,* ed. H. Guetzkow, pp. 48–60. Englewood Cliffs, N.J.: Prentice-Hall.

Zelnick, J., Kantner, J. F., and Ford, K. 1981. *Sex and pregnancy in adolescence.* Beverly Hills, Calif.: Sage.

Zigler, E. and Child, I. L. 1969. Socialization. In *Handbook of social psychology,* vol. 3, 2nd ed., eds. G. Lindzey and E. Aronson, pp. 450–589. Reading, Mass.: Addison-Wesley.

Zollschan, G. K. and Perrucci, R. 1964. Social stability and social process: An initial presentation of relevant categories. In *Explorations in social change,* eds. G. K. Zollschan and W. Hirsch, pp. 99–124. Boston: Houghton Mifflin.

Zurcher, L. A. and Snow, D. A. 1981. Collective behavior: Social movements. In *Social psychology,* eds. M. Rosenberg and R. H. Turner, pp. 447–482. New York: Basic Books.

Zureik, E. 1971. Children and political socialization. In *The Canadian family,* ed. K. Ishwaran, pp. 186–203. Toronto: Holt, Rinehart & Winston of Canada.

Zureik, E. 1975. Introduction and overview. In *Socialization and values in Canadian society,* vol. 1, eds. E. Zureik and R. M. Pike, pp. 11–28. Toronto: McClelland & Stewart.

Glossary

accommodation Form of limited desegregation in which each ethnic group maintains its cultural distinctiveness while tolerating the distinctiveness of the other groups.

account Verbal defense of future behavior; two types are *excuses* and *justifications.*

action Act of will.

activity theory The elderly have self-images, which are sustained through continuous participation in social roles.

adolescence Period in life running from approximately age twelve to age twenty.

age stratification Social ranking by age category.

agenda Schedule of activities to be carried out over a period of time.

aggregate Gathering of people in temporary proximity who have no enduring ties or other marks of social organization.

agricultural society Society which grows and harvests plants by use of a plow and irrigation system.

alienation Social circumstances in which workers become estranged from the fruits of their labor.

allocation Process by which schools distribute pupils into different curricula, which lead to different types of post-high school education and work.

altercasting Placing of other people in particular identities and role types.

alternative movement Social movement which seeks a partial change in people.

alternative schools Free schools that have gained acceptance by a school board.

amalgamation Blending of racial types through interbreeding.

androgyny Degree to which people are both masculine and feminine.

anomie State of normlessness in a society; malintegration of cultural success goals and institutionalized means of reaching them.

anticipatory socialization Process by which aspirants to a particular role begin to discern what it would be like to function in that role.

archival research Research into audio recordings and visual media found in libraries, museums, government archives, business files, and private collections.

ascriptive motive Involuntary need to join a group; the joining is forced on one by circumstances or by someone else.

assimilation Mutual absorption of two or more distinct cultural groups into one culturally homogeneous unit.

attribute Inherent characteristic or quality.

avoidance Process by which an ethnic minority shuns contact with the majority or escapes to a friendlier location.

behavior Organism's reaction to a mental, physiological, or biological state without reference to conscious thought or interpretive reasoning.

birthrate Rate of reproduction, or natality.

bivariate analysis Analysis of two variables, which can be compared.

blue-collar entrepreneurs Those who work as tradesmen and shop proprietors.

body territory The human body itself and the space it encompasses.

bourgeoisie Those who own or control the production and allocation of goods and services.

break and entry Act of entering the dwelling of another person to steal or attempt to steal something.

bureaucracy Hierarchical authority structure designed to accomplish large-scale administrative tasks by systematically coordinating the work of many individuals.

burglary See break and entry.

capitalist Entrepreneur who owns the means of production; one of the bourgeoisie.

career A calling and a field of pursuit in professional or business life.

career pattern Different careers of an individual who has several occupations.

caste A usually religiously based stratum into which one is born and likely to live out one's life.

category Class of people who have something in common but who have no lasting relationship or intimate interaction.

central life interest Segment of an individual's life in which a substantial emotional investment is made.

church Large-scale religious organization.

circulation mobility Movement that occurs when someone moves into a job that another person has left.

class consciousness Awareness and acceptance of the similar attitudes, beliefs, and life-styles of others in one's social class.

classroom environment Surroundings of the school, peer group, and school administration within which classrooms operate.

coalition Joining of forces by individuals in a group; the individuals pool their resources of power to gain advantages for themselves.

cohabitation Association in which a man and a woman live together over an extended period of time without being legally married.

cohesiveness Sticking together of individuals in a group.

collective behavior Spontaneous, emotional action of an aggregate of people whose thinking and behavior are more or less unstructured and in some instances impulsive.

collective excitement Behavior in which people imitate the agitated and emotional behavior of those nearby.

collective joy Emotion evoked by well-being, success, or good fortune or by the prospect of possessing what one desires.

common sense Prudent but sometimes unsophisticated judgment derived from everyday thinking.

commune Type of community characterized by collective ownership and use of property by the members of the community.

community Social group with a common territorial base; those in the group share interests and have a sense of belonging to the group.

community elementary schools Schools controlled by community members.

compliance Conformity to a society's values.

concentric-zone theory Theory which holds that cities are an accretion of large rings, or zones, which radiate out from the downtown center; there is a different type of land use in each zone.

confirmation Demonstration of the validity of research findings by testing hypotheses.

conflict perspective View of society which looks on conflict as an element of social life and a cause of social change.

contagious interaction Behavior which entails a loss of self-consciousness, a lowered resistance to group influence, and a heightened tendency to do what others are doing in the immediate situation.

content analysis Analysis of written, audio, or visual materials to find out about ideas and social attitudes which are dominant in society.

context of socialization Condition in which the agents of socialization of organizations and institutions—the socializers—transmit culture.

continuity Uninterrupted progression.

continuance commitment Entrapment in an identity because of the penalties that accrue from trying to renounce that identity.

controlled observation Observation or experiment which makes use of controls.

conversion Act or process which helps to bolster one's value commitment to a religion or to a social movement.

coordinated leisure Leisure that is related to one's job in form or content but unrequired by the job.

corporate concentration Ownership of industrial and financial businesses by a few individuals.

courtship Intimate relationship between a male and a female which may become serious enough to lead to engagement and subsequent marriage.

craze Excessive and unreasonable enthusiasm for a special object or prize.

crime Subclass of deviance in which a criminal law has been said to have been violated.

crime rate Number of offenses of a particular kind recorded by the police.

crowd Sizable aggregate of people in close proximity to one another for a transitory period of time.

crude birthrate Level of fertility; number of births per thousand population during a particular year or some other time period.

cult Small, short-lived religiously iconoclastic group.

cultural lag Delay in a society's change in values, ideas, and norms in response to a change in material culture.

cultural production Process by which universities create new artistic, scientific, and humanistic knowledge and products.

culture Society's collective stock of knowledge, art, ideas, customs, values, norms, beliefs, laws, goals, outlooks, technologies, and patterns of behavior; society's way of life.

definition of the situation Meaning people ascribe to the immediate setting in which they find themselves in the course of everyday living.

demography Study of population.

denomination Firmly established religious organization with a significant membership.

dependent variable Variable which can be changed by an independent variable.

deschooling Program to develop the pupil's ability to deal critically and effectively with the world in which he or she lives.

deviance Behavior judged as in violation of the moral norms of a community by those who are powerful enough to make this judgment stick.

deviant career Passage of an individual who has been labeled deviant through the period of time in which he or she is in the deviant role.

differential association Process by which individuals learn criminal behavior through interaction with others who define such behavior favorably and in isolation from those who define it unfavorably.

diffusion Process by which an innovation spreads throughout a social system; there is no social change without diffusion.

discontinuity Lack of a smooth transition.

discrimination Unequal treatment of a less powerful individual or group by a more powerful individual or group.

disengagement Process of estrangement from society by the elderly that results in decreased interaction between them and other people.

division of labor Specialization of individuals' tasks in a group; development and integration of the group's specialized roles into an effectively functioning unit.

dread Persistent and chronic apprehension of a more diffuse danger.

dyad Group of two persons.

dysfunction Disruption in the social equilibrium; it lessens the adjustment of a system.

ecclesia Firmly established religious organization which seeks to include all the members of a particular society within its fold; it is often a state church.

economic institution Relatively stable set of relationships, patterns of behavior, norms, and values that emerge around the production, distribution, and consumption of goods and services.

economics Social science whose central concern is the production, distribution, and consumption of goods and services.

economy Social institution that develops around the production, distribution, and consumption of goods and services.

ecstasy Mental and bodily state substantially beyond the control of the individual.

ecumenism Movement toward the worldwide unity of Christian faiths.

education Process of educating others by fostering an expansion of knowledge, wisdom, and desirable qualities of mind and character.

ego Reactional, conscious part of personality.

Electra conflict Female child's libidinal feelings for her father.

embourgeoisement Acquisition of middle-class ways, values, life-styles, and relationships by the proletariat.

emigration Departure from a country.

empathy Participation in the feelings and emotions of another.

equilibrium Balance among the various elements in a social system; it is recognized by the functionalist theory.

estate Hereditary stratum founded on the legal prescription of civil and political rights.

ethnic relations Sweeping social process that encompasses the narrower processes of ethnic conflict, harmony, avoidance, submission, acceptance, and revival.

ethnic revival Process by which ethnic groups stress and promote their unique identities.

ethnic segregation Forced physical separation of an ethnic group from other groups.

ethnocentrism Special positive orientation towards one's own group.

ethnomethodology Study of the social construction of reality; study of how people define reality as they experience interactions from day to day.

exchange-distributive function Economic processes in a society by which its members distribute products from producer to consumer.

exchange theory Idea that people control one another's behavior by exchanging rewards and punishments; with this exchange, they express approval or disapproval of another's behavior.

excuse Socially approved mitigation which seeks to relieve responsibility for questionable actions.

exploration Means of acquiring an understanding of a phenomenon or event.

expressive motive Need to join a group because of a desire to interact with members of the group.

extended family Three-generational unit which includes a nuclear family, grandparents, aunts, uncles, and cousins.

extractive-transformative function Economic processes in a society by which its members obtain raw materials from the environment and transform them into usable products.

family Set of individuals related to each other by blood, marriage, or adoption, or, in rare instances, by another form of social ascription to a family.

fashion Prevailing, short-lived custom, usage, or style.

fear Anticipation or actual experience of pain or severe distress.

fecundity Physiological capacity to reproduce.

flexibility Flexible research design which brings about the discovery of new facts and ideas.

folk culture Cultural subsystem experienced directly through the senses (sight, hearing).

foreign direct investment An individual's investment of capital in assets or in ownership of a foreign enterprise.

formal demography Statistical branch of demography.

formal group Group with rules, roles, and goals that are more or less explicit.

frame Hidden set of social rules and categories that are a part of our cultural heritage.

free schools Schools that allow free choice and action for their pupils.

function Part of a social system that helps maintain the system.

functionalism Sociological perspective which explains social behavior on the basis of function; the functions of the interrelated parts of a society are examined.

functionalist perspective View of society which considers the relationships between the functions of a social system's various parts.

functional requisite Generalized condition necessary for the maintenance of the unit.

fundamentalist church Church of a denomination which emphasizes literal interpretations of the Scriptures.

Gemeinschaft Rural community characterized by close interpersonal relationships among kin and friends.

gender One's awareness of one's self as a sexual being and one's thinking of oneself as behaving in a masculine or feminine way.

Gesellschaft Community in which interpersonal relationships are more formal, specialized, and impersonal than in the Gemeinschaft community.

gesture Movement of an individual which acts as a stimulus calling for a response from another individual.

government Group made up of political parties and civil servants; its task is to order and adjust relations between individuals and the state and between groups and the state.

gross national product Total value of goods and services produced in a nation during a specified period, normally twelve months.

group Assembly of two or more persons who interact with each other while sharing common interests.

group development Progression which leads to the formation of a group; statuses, structures, and processes are established.

group formation Emergence of a collectivity.

high culture Products consumed by a special public dominated by creators and critics; it is the culture of writers, painters, composers, musicians, dramatists, and thespians.

historical change Substantial transformation of a community, society, or civilization over a period of decades or even centuries.

history Discipline that records and explains significant events of the past as they comprise a sequence of human activities.

holism Philosophical theory that entities in nature cannot be broken down to their component parts and cannot be analyzed as mere sums of the parts; emphasis is on the functional relation among parts and wholes.

home territory Area where regular participants have relative freedom of behavior accompanied by a sense of intimacy and control over the surroundings; a home, a homosexual bar, or a private club.

horror experience of an event as frightful and upsetting.

horticultural society Preindustrial society which subsists on its members' harvesting of plants and breeding of animals.

hunting and gathering society Preindustrial society which subsists on the food which its members hunt and gather.

id Instinctual, undisciplined side of personality.

ideology Loose system of ideas and values that are used to justify the use of power to achieve special interests.

immigration Arrival in a country.

impression management Attempt by an individual to influence another person's impression of him or her.

independent variable Variable which causes a change in another variable; variable which can be manipulated by the experimenter.

inductive reasoning Reasoning from the particular to the general.

infant mortality rate Number of deaths per unit of population below age one.

informal group Group which may not necessarily have clearly defined roles and goals.

innovation Invention of an idea, thing, relationship, or behavior pattern; a creative act.

innovational change Change resulting from an innovation; it flows from individuals' definitions of situations through an institutionalization that leads to constructed forms of reality.

innovators Individuals who try out a new thing, idea, or behavior pattern and accept it.

institution Relatively stable set of abstract relationships (social structure), patterns of behavior, roles, mores, and values that emerge as solutions to the problems of collective living; set of norms regulating human action for the purpose of achieving society goals.

instrumental motive Need to join a group because of an interest in the group's goals.

integration Meshing of parts.

interaction Reciprocal effect of the social actions of individuals on each other; behavior in which the action of one individual is a stimulus to the action of another.

interactional territory Place where social gatherings occur, for example, a ball park, a dance hall, a supper club.

interactionist perspective View of society which considers the interaction among people as they respond to symbols such as language, signs, and gestures.

intergenerational mobility Upward or downward movement in status between generations.

internalization Propensity to conform to a norm or to behave in a way which the norm suggests.

internal migration Migration within a country.

international migration Migration consisting of emigration and immigration.

interpersonal relationship Sustained orientation of one person toward another; reciprocal interaction between individuals.

intragenerational mobility Upward or downward movement in status within a generation.

justification Favorable light on an act in the face of someone's claim to the contrary.

labeling Process by which some people are identified as deviant by other members of the community.

language Verbal and nonverbal communication.

large-scale organization Massive social group formed for a specific purpose.

latent function Function not necessarily intended.

leadership Capacity to make important, binding decisions on all or nearly all members of a group.

learning structures Opportunities to learn illegitimate means to obtain cultural goals.

leisure Activity or part of an activity that is lacking in major obligation and responsibility and that is freely chosen for its own sake.

life course Experiences and changes which occur from day to day in an individual's life.

life expectancy Number of years the typical person born in a typical year can expect to live.

life span Biological age limit of human beings; the present human life span is thought to be about 120 years.

looking-glass self Reflection of the self cast by the behavior of others in reaction to one's own behavior.

macro-order Large-scale processes and structures in society.

mainline church Church of a denomination which is liberal and modernist in its religious views.

manifest function Intended function of a social element.

mass Set of heterogeneous, anonymous individuals who interact little with one another and who lack a definite leadership.

material culture Artifacts and things which human beings make (e.g., wheels, clothing, rockets, typewriters, books, skyscrapers, computers).

"me" Internal representation of an individual's many role identities.

mechanical solidarity Social cohesion in a society made up of members who share similar states of consciousness; the states of consciousness are beliefs and sentiments.

mechanism Mechanical operation.

micro-order The numerous day-to-day activities in society.

migration Process of changing residence by moving from one location to another within a country or between two countries.

milling Process by which one person's behavior stimulates a response in another person, whose response then stimulates the first person.

mobilization Recruitment of individuals and planning of strategy.

mortality Population's rate of death.

motivation State of mind that incites a person to action; process of inciting people to action.

multiple nuclei theory Theory which holds that a city is a composite of centers and subcenters called *nuclei.*

multivariate analysis Analysis in which several variables are examined simultaneously.

natality Rate of production, or fertility.

national character Relatively enduring personality characteristics and patterns that are modal among adult members of a society.

natural increase Measure of a population's growth or shrinkage; it is determined by subtracting the death rate from the birthrate.

nature Natural force such as heredity.

negotiation Process of bargaining or haggling over the terms of an exchange of social rewards.

nonreactive measure Indicator of human behavior that the alert researcher can observe without disturbing the behaving persons.

nuclear family Group consisting of one or both parents and dependent offspring.

nurture Training and general learning acquired while growing up; a synonym for socialization.

occupation Activity associated with a work role.

Oedipus conflict Male child's libidinal feelings for his mother.

open mind Orientation characterized by as few preconceived ideas as possible while being alert to new information.

opportunity structures Opportunities to use illegitimate means to obtain cultural goals.

organized religion Identifiable group of religious practitioners.

panic Sudden, overpowering fright.

parole Conditional and revocable release from

prison of someone serving an indeterminate or unexpired sentence.

participant observation Case study method in which the sociologist takes part in a group's activities.

pastoral society Society centered on the domestication and breeding of animals such as sheep, goats, cattle, reindeer, and horses.

peer One who belongs to the same group in society to which others belong; each member of the group is similar in age and status.

personalization Tendency of individuals to develop an image of political authority.

perspective Perceived interrelation which provides an overall view of a subject and its parts; a sociological perspective is a view of society.

petite bourgeoisie Those who run small businesses or fee-for-service professional offices.

political economy Study of the laws and relations of capitalist development, either critically from the Marxist perspective or more traditionally from the liberal view that affirms the legitimacy of capitalism.

political institution Relatively stable set of abstract relationships and patterns of behavior that develop around the collective problem of distributing political power and maintaining societal boundaries.

political participation Activities by private citizens that are more or less directly aimed at influencing the selection of governmental structures and personnel.

political party Political organization which actively and effectively engages in competition for elective office.

political socialization Political learning of children and adults.

political sociology Cross-fertilization of sociology and political science.

polity Specified form of political organization; it is a politically organized unit such as the federal government or a local government. It consists of the government and the state.

popular culture Mass culture transmitted indirectly by media and technology; it constitutes a culture of a social class or other large category.

population check Event or condition which causes death and reduces the population.

populism Political expression of a critique of capitalism calling for social reform in the interests of farmers and workers, the common people.

power Ability to control the behavior of others and to dominate a situation; potential of person A to obtain more favorable rewards at person B's expense than B is able to obtain at A's expense.

predisposition Enduring, acquired mental state; attitude, belief, or personal value.

prejudice Unfavorable, often emotional, orientation toward a category of people.

presentation of self Attempt to get someone else to impute to us the role we would like to play.

prestige Positive and negative estimation of an individual's public standing on one or more dimensions that society values.

primary deviation Deviation which brings about little change in the individual's everyday routine and life-style.

primary group Small number of people who interact with each other on a face-to-face basis over an extended period of time.

primary socialization First socialization by means of which children are trained to be satisfactory members of their society.

prisonization Assimilation of prisoners into inmate culture.

probation Act of suspending a convicted offender's sentence with the proviso that he or she agree to supervision.

proletarian A worker; one who labors for a capitalist.

proletariat Lower-class workers, some of whom are unemployed and many of whom are alienated from their labor.

public Aggregate of people who seek to know more about an event which has an effect on them; they seek to understand and to control the event.

public territory Area open to all who belong to the community or society; a park, sidewalk, street, or public conveyance.

questionnaire survey Means of collecting data through the mail or by telephone with the use of a questionnaire.

race Subdivision of the species *Homo sapiens.*

radical sociology New and provocative kind of sociology; an application of the earlier works of Marx and Engels.

reality construction Conceptualization of what one

is doing and the context in which the action is done.

recidivism rate Number of ex-offenders who return to prison in proportion to the number of ex-offenders released in specific period of time.

redemptive movement Social movement which seeks to bring about a total change in individuals.

reference groups Groups that provide us with a perspective from which to view parts of the social and physical world and the human behavior enacted therein.

reformative movement Social movement which seeks a partial change in the social structure.

religion System of beliefs and practices by means of which a group of people struggles with the ultimate problems of human life.

resocialization Behavior intervention which changes a norm violator and instills within him or her a respect for society's accepted values and norms.

ritual Symbolic gesture of faith and conformity.

robbery Act of taking or attempting to take something of value from a person by force or threat of force.

role Set of actions expected of an individual occupying a particular status.

role conflict Situation in which a role player within a group perceives that he or she is confronted with incompatible expectations.

role-identity Person's imaginative view of himself or herself in a particular status.

role-taking Putting oneself into the role of another individual.

romantic love Strong emotional attachment between adolescents or adults of opposing sexes, with at least the components of sex desire and tenderness.

routinization Process in which charismatic leadership is transformed into a bureaucratic or institutional role.

sanction Reinforcement of behavior produced by other people; praise and acclaim for a person's achievement are examples of sanctions.

science A *process* and a *product;* a way of finding out about things and also a body of knowledge.

secondary deviance Deviant behavior which substantially modifies an individual's way of life.

secondary group Organization of people who have little intimate contact but who work together for a specific purpose.

secondary socialization Socialization which adults experience.

sect Small group which is the antithesis of the church; social movement undertaken by dissatisfied church members.

sector theory Theory which holds that a city grows from its center in sectors, not in concentric zones.

secularization Declining significance of religion accompanied by increasing worldly concerns.

self The core of personality.

self-concept Social idea known to the individual.

senescence Accumulated effects of our genetic heritage plus the effects of a lifetime of stress, trauma, and disease.

sex One's biological classification at birth as male or female.

sex stratification Institutionalized differential ranking of the sexes along such dimensions as occupation, education, income, and power.

significant others Those whose judgments of our behavior are most likely to be incorporated within ourselves as guiding principles; they are parents, relatives, and close friends.

size Number of members in an organization.

social Of and relating to a sharing of language, beliefs, goals, and norms with other members of society.

social causation cycle Cycle which takes in the definition of the situation, interaction, social forms, and context.

social change Process by which alteration occurs in the structure and function of a social system.

social class Composite rank of a stratum on the dimensions of wealth, prestige, and power.

social control Processes that implement the legitimate order of a community or society; the mechanisms which compel members of a society to behave in an acceptable way.

social demography Population analysis or population study.

social differentiation Broad social process in which people are distinguished from one another according to age, sex, deviant, ethnic, and social stratification roles.

social identification Phase of young adulthood during which identification with key social institutions gets under way.

social identity Agreement or compromise about the status or social categories of each person which is honored by others.

social interaction Mutual effect of individuals on each other.

socialization Broad process of learning to be a member of society and of developing a personality that is more or less acceptable to others in the society.

socializees Those who are being socialized.

social mobility Upward or downward movement in status within a stratification system.

social movement Network of activities and supporting beliefs of individuals and organizations in connection with a salient and value-charged issue.

social network Web of relationships and acquaintanceships in which an individual is embedded; the set of people to whom an individual is linked by his or her contacts.

social organization Stable interrelationships of the society's groups, institutions, and networks of social relationships.

social stratification Process of differentiation by which the three types of strata (castes, estates, social classes) develop and maintain themselves along the dimensions of wealth, prestige, and power.

social structure Collectivity's stable pattern of abstract relationships.

social system Unit consisting of interdependent parts.

society Large, self-sufficient aggregation of people who maintain contact with each other through culture.

socioeconomic status Combination of wealth and prestige.

sociogram Two-dimensional picture of an individual's socioemotional preferences.

sociology Study of society.

sociometry Technique for describing socioemotional relations among members of a group.

state Cultural system which defines and guides the actions of the government.

statistical analysis Analysis that describes a sample or estimates how representative the sample is of a larger population.

status Position in a group.

structural mobility Forced mobility to another occupation from that of one's father.

structured interview Interview in which the interviewer records the respondents' answers to questions by filling in a form known as the *interview schedule.*

subculture Distinctive configuration of values, norms, beliefs, artifacts, and patterns of behavior which, together, constitute a special way of life for its members.

subjective class Social class one identifies oneself as belonging to.

submission Passive endurance of the daily injustices of minority living.

superego Control of the ego; it is conscience.

symbolic interactionism Theoretical perspective which considers the interaction among people as they respond to symbols such as language, signs, and gestures.

technology Technique or method used by organizations to reach their goals; application of scientific knowledge to the solution of practical problems; means of providing devices and advantages for human sustenance and convenience.

territoriality Organism's attachment to and control over space which it deems central for survival.

terror Enduring fear that arises from being trapped in a dangerous situation for a period of time.

theft Act of stealing.

theoretical perspective View of society and social behavior which provides for an assumption based on a theory.

theory Logically interrelated set of propositions; scientifically acceptable principle which explains a phenomenon or event.

total institution Place of residence and work where like-situated individuals together lead an enclosed, formally administered life; a prison is a total institution.

transformative movement Social movement which seeks a total change in the social structure.

triad Group of three persons.

unconditional leisure Activity chosen without reference to one's work.

universal church Large-scale religious organization; an example is the thirteenth century Roman Catholic Church.

universalism Application of uniform standards to our treatment and evaluation of other people.

unstructured interviewing Questioning of a subject with the use of an interview guide.

value commitment Attachment to gains or rewards from a church or religious group.

value consensus Agreement among individuals on the form integration should take.

variable Quantity that may assume any one of a set of specified values.

wealth Supply of goods, living conditions, and personal life experiences of an individual as determined by the marketplace.

work Goal-oriented activity leading to a personally desired accomplishment.

working agreement Understanding among interacting individuals as to who each person is and what he or she is to do.

Author Index

Subject Index